grant source

The most comprehensive and current resource on Minnesota grantmaking.

GUIDE TO MINNESOTA GRANTMAKERS
2007/2008 edition

Information on 1,400 foundations and corporate giving programs.

July 2007

Contents

Foreword
Principles for Grantmakers iv
Letter to Grantseekers v
About This Guide vi

Grantmaker Directory   1

Abbreviated Listings
Small Foundations/Foundations Not Accepting Unsolicited Proposals 227
Foundations Giving to Designated Recipients 261
Foundations Giving to Designated Scholarships 262
Foundations Giving Grants Only Outside Minnesota 263
Foundations Currently Inactive/No Recent Information 264
Foundations Recently Terminated 265

Information for Grantseekers
Grantmaking Basics 269
Grantseeking Basics 272
Grantseekers Toolbox 274
Writing a Successful Grant Proposal 276

Indexes
Geographic Focus 283
Areas of Interest 286
Types of Support 305
Intended Beneficiary 311
Officers and Trustees 316
Staff 333
Grantmaker Name 339

Addenda
Minnesota Common Grant Application Form 355
Minnesota Common Report Form 361

Principles for Grantmakers

Preamble

The desire to give is a defining human characteristic. As members of the Minnesota Council on Foundations, we honor diverse charitable expressions across the wide economic, racial, ethnic and social spectrum. We celebrate new and traditional forms of giving that respond to human needs, build community, increase knowledge and promote creative expression. We acknowledge the fundamental roles and responsibilities of engaged individuals and the public, private and nonprofit sectors in a just and equitable society.

As a community of grantmakers, we embrace philanthropy's role in a civil society. We are leading advocates for public policy to sustain robust philanthropy. We work strategically through grantmaking and other means to improve the vitality and health of our communities, to educate our members and the field, and to achieve our collective mission of strengthening and expanding philanthropy. We express a shared commitment to excellence by formally subscribing to the Principles for Grantmakers.

Principles

1. **ETHICS AND LAW PRINCIPLE**
   To sustain public trust by adhering to the highest ethical principles and practices and abiding by all state and federal laws that govern philanthropy.

2. **EFFECTIVE GOVERNANCE PRINCIPLE**
   To achieve effective governance by ensuring performance in the areas of stewardship of assets, donor intent, fiduciary responsibility and sound decision-making.

3. **MISSION AND GOALS PRINCIPLE**
   To be purposeful in our philanthropy by having a clearly stated mission and explicit goals.

4. **ENGAGED LEARNING PRINCIPLE**
   To foster continuous learning and reflection by engaging board members, staff, grantees and donors in thoughtful dialogue and education.

5. **RESPECTFUL RELATIONSHIPS PRINCIPLE**
   To build constructive relationships with applicants, grantees and donors by ensuring mutual respect, candor, confidentiality and understanding.

6. **TRANSPARENCY PRINCIPLE**
   To achieve transparency in our relationships with the public, applicants, grantees and donors by being clear, consistent and timely in our communications with them.

7. **DIVERSITY PRINCIPLE**
   To reflect and engage the diversity of the communities we serve in our varying roles as grantmakers, boards and employers, economic entities and civic participants.

8. **SELF-ASSESSMENT & COMMITMENT PRINCIPLE**
   To uphold the highest standards by regularly assessing ourselves against these principles and committing to implement them.

Adopted by the MCF Board of Directors in 2006; developed from the original 1996 version.

Letter to Grantseekers

July 2007

Welcome to the 2007/2008 edition of the Minnesota Council on Foundations *Guide to Minnesota Grantmakers*.

This 15th edition of the Guide continues the Council's tradition as the premier source of information on Minnesota's grantmaking field. It is more important than ever that the Council continues to provide comprehensive, accurate and timely information about the state's foundations and corporate giving programs, through the Guide and other information sources. The Guide demonstrates the commitment of the Council's members to be open and accessible about their work and to be effective partners with nonprofits to meet community needs.

The Guide can be a useful tool to help nonprofit organizations identify potential partners and financial supporters for the important work they do to help sustain and improve our communities. We remind grantseekers that this Guide should be considered only a first step in their research process. Grantmakers come in all shapes and sizes, with different interests and priorities.

- The profiles in this directory provide initial information about individual funders; further research is needed to determine whether a foundation or corporate giving program is an appropriate match for your organization's mission and needs.

- The Council also offers subscriptions to a searchable online database, Minnesota Grantmakers Online (MGO), the web's largest, most up-to-date database of Minnesota grantmakers and grants. For more information, www.mcf.org/mngrants.

We would like to express our thanks to the many grantmakers who answered our request for detailed information on their organizations and programs to supplement the information available from public records. We also thank Cyndi Nelson and her colleagues at the Minnesota Attorney General's Office for their support and generous assistance to our research staff.

Holly Sampson
MCF Board Chair
Duluth Superior Area Community Foundation

William R. King
President
Minnesota Council on Foundations

About This Guide

Information Sources

There are four principal sources of information for this *Guide to Minnesota Grantmakers*:

The most recent tax returns filed by foundations with the Internal Revenue Service (Forms 990-PF and 990). These documents are on file at the Minnesota Attorney General's Office. For this edition of the Guide, the fiscal year-end for most grantmakers falls between July 1, 2004, and June 30, 2007.

Annual reports and grant lists from individual grantmakers.

Other information provided by grantmakers. The Minnesota Council on Foundations invited Minnesota foundations, corporate giving programs and other grantmaking organizations to update their profiles on file in the Council's database; about 200 grantmakers responded.

Research by Council staff, using a variety of published sources.

Inside the Guide

The *Guide to Minnesota Grantmakers 2007/2008* lists more some 1,400 active Minnesota grantmakers and profiles 388 of these funding organizations.

GRANTMAKER PROFILES

A complete grantmaker profile in the Guide contains the following information (not all information may be available for every grantmaker):

Grantmaker name, address, county, telephone, fax, web and e-mail addresses.

Contact: Name of the grantmaker's contact person for inquiries regarding grant applications or other information.

Established: Date the foundation or giving program was created.

Donor: The person(s) who provided initial funding to establish the foundation.

Paid staff: A "yes" indicates that the grantmaker has one or more paid staff positions to support its work, which can be an indication that the funder has more resources available to handle proposal inquiries, provide assistance to grantees, etc.

Funder type: Specifies the grantmaker's legal status: private, corporate or community/public foundation; supporting organization; or corporate giving program (see "Types of Grantmakers" on page 269 for descriptions of each type).

PROGRAM DESCRIPTION

Program's purpose: The grantmaker's mission and goals for its funding program.

Funding priorities: The grantmaker's areas of specific interest or focus for its funding.

Program limitations/restrictions: What the grantmaker will not fund.

Geographic focus: Geographic areas the grantmaker serves. Twin Cities Metropolitan Area is Minneapolis, St Paul and their suburbs; Greater Minnesota is communities in the state of Minnesota excluding the metropolitan area; and Minnesota Statewide is the entire state. Areas outside Minnesota indicates that the grantmaker focuses on specific states, cities or other geographic regions outside Minnesota; and National Areas indicates that the grantmaker focuses on the nation as a whole. This section also indicates if the funder focuses its grantmaking just on the east metro or west metro regions of the Twin Cities, and if it gives outside of the United States.

Geographic limitations: Information about any geographic restrictions that a funder may have.

Areas of interest: Program areas the grantmaker will fund, using the 24 major field areas of the National Taxonomy of Exempt Entities (NTEE). Each major area of interest is listed in all capital letters, followed by NTEE subcategories and a funder's additional comments, if available. (see Areas of Interest Index on page 286 for a list of NTEE field areas).

Intended beneficiaries: Specific population groups served by the grantmaker, such as low-income people or migrant workers (see Intended Beneficiary Index on page 311 for a list of the population groups). Ethnic/racial populations indicates people of color; specific categories are Asians/Pacific Islanders, African Americans, Hispanics/Latinos and Native Americans/American Indians.

Types of support for organizations: The kinds of grants a funder will make. *Capital* means facilities or major equipment; *program development*, start-up or expansion of a program; and *in-kind*, donated products or services (see Types of Support Index on page 305 for a list of types of support).

Types of support for individuals: Indicates the type(s) of support, if any, a grantmaker provides to individuals.

Matching grants: If a corporate grantmaker matches employees' contributions to charities, this entry lists the types of charities that qualify for the match.

Dollars for Doers: A "yes" indicates that the grantmaker — usually a corporate grantmaker — operates a program that provides funding to nonprofit organizations where its employees volunteer. The details of such programs vary from funder to funder.

Exclusions: Specific types of recipients that are excluded from receiving funding from the grantmaker, per its guidelines and/or its legal charter.

Sample grants: Up to eight grants selected as representative of the funder's recent grant awards. The entry includes name of recipient organization, state where the recipient is located, purpose of grant (optional) and amount of grant.

FINANCIAL INFORMATION

Financial data for year ending: Shows fiscal year-end of the foundation or corporate giving program for the financial information provided in the Guide.

Foundation assets: The fair market value of a foundation's assets at the end of the fiscal year.

Grants paid: The total amount of all grants paid in the year indicated.

Program-related investments: If the funder makes loans for charitable purposes, the total number and amount of its annual PRIs are listed here (see page 271 for more information on PRIs).

Number of grants: The total number of grants paid in the year indicated.

Largest/smallest: The largest and smallest grants paid during the year.

Typical grant amount: The average size of a grant from the funder in the year indicated.

In-kind gifts: Estimated dollar value of the grantmaker's annual donations of in-kind products and/or services. This typically applies to corporate grantmakers.

Matching gifts: Total dollar value of the annual grants made by the funder to match donations from its employees. This typically applies to corporate grantmakers.

Largest multi-year grant approved: Grantmakers often approve multi-year grants that are not paid out entirely during one fiscal year and so are not reflected in the information above.

Purpose: (of the multi-year grant).

APPLICATION INFORMATION

Preferred form of initial contact: A letter of inquiry is a one- or two-page letter describing the nonprofit and why it is seeking funds. A complete proposal is more comprehensive (see "Applying for a Grant" on page 272 for a more detailed explanation).

Public information available by request: Indicates the type of information the funder will provide about its grantmaking program, including printed guidelines, annual reports, newsletters and website.

Accept common grant application: Indicates if the grantmaker accepts the Minnesota Common Grant Application Form (see "Applying for a Grant" on page 272 for more information).

Accept common report form: Indicates if the grantmaker accepts the Minnesota Common Report Form (see "Grant Decision & Follow-Up" on page 273 for more information).

Will view video: Indicates if the grantmaker will accept a video as part of the grant application.

Proposal deadlines: The date(s) by which the grantmaker wants to receive complete proposals and/or letters of inquiry. "Ongoing" indicates that the grantmaker accepts proposals throughout the year.

Preferred time for receiving proposals: Indicates if the grantmaker has any specific requirements, beyond deadline dates, regarding when it prefers to receive grant proposals.

Contribution decisions made by: Indicates who in the organization makes decisions about grants.

Frequency of contribution decisions: Indicates how often the funder makes decisions on grant awards.

Specific times board meets: Indicates the frequency of board meetings and/or their specific dates.

Typical time from application to notification of decision: Indicates how long the grant application process will typically take.

Special application procedures: Any special procedural information that is important for grant applicants to know before submitting a proposal.

STAFF/TRUSTEES

A list of board directors/trustees and selected staff members for the organization.

INDEXES

Grantmakers listed in the Guide are indexed by seven different categories:

Geographic focus: An alphabetical list of grantmakers, coded according to their geographic focus.

Areas of interest: Grantmakers listed under 24 broad categories of program areas, such as education or human service. Under each broad category, grantmakers are coded according to more specific areas of interest.

Types of support: Grantmakers listed under 10 broad categories of types of support, such as general purpose or program development. Under some categories, grantmakers are coded according to more specific types of support.

Intended beneficiaries: Grantmakers listed under five broad categories of the populations they intend to benefit with their grants. Under each category, grantmakers are coded according to more specific types of populations.

Officers and trustees: An index of the officers and trustees of grantmaking programs.

Staff: An index of the staff of grantmaking programs.

Grantmakers by name: An alphabetical listing of all grantmakers in the Guide, with the page number where you'll find more information about the organization.

ABBREVIATED LISTINGS

The Guide contains six listings of Minnesota grantmakers that do not have full profiles in the directory:

Small foundations/foundations not accepting unsolicited proposals. This section lists more than 700 Minnesota foundations that have assets of less than $500,000 or grants totaling less than $25,000 and/or that do not accept unsolicited grant applications. This appendix lists each funder's location, fiscal year, asset and grant size, and employer identification number (EIN).

Foundations giving only to designated recipients.

Foundations giving only to designated scholarship funds.

Foundations giving grants primarily outside Minnesota.

Foundations currently inactive or with no recent information available about the organization.

Foundations recently terminated.

Grantmaker Directory

3M/3M Foundation

3M Center
Building 225-1S-23
St Paul, MN 55144-1000
County: Ramsey
Phone: (651) 733-0144
Fax: (651) 737-3061
Website: www.3MGiving.com
Established: 01/01/1953
Funder type: Corporate foundation and corporate giving program

Program Description

Program's purpose: To positively impact 3M communities by preparing individuals and families for success.

Funding priorities: Education - focusing on math, science and economics/business; Health and Human Service - focusing on strengthening families and youth development through parenting, job training and prevention programs; Environment - focusing on biodiversity and climate change (by invitation only); Arts and Culture - focusing on organizations with strong education and community outreach programs. Board considers grant proposals for education and arts in December; for health and human services and environment in June.

Program limitations/restrictions: No applications considered from individuals; religious, individual K-12 schools, fraternal, social, veterans or military organizations; advocacy and lobbying efforts to influence legislation; travel for individuals or groups; purchase of equipment that has not been manufactured by 3M; for-profit organizations; endowment; diseases; film/video productions; nor scholarship funds.

Geographic focus: East Metropolitan Area/St Paul only, MN communities where 3M has facilities.

Geographic limitations: Primarily St Paul and East Metro area and over 60 communities nationally where 3M has a presence. In Minnesota, includes Fairmont, Staples, Alexandria, Park Rapids, Hutchinson, New Ulm, Eagan and Cottage Grove. No grants outside 3M communities.

Areas of interest:
ARTS, CULTURE, HUMANITIES: Arts/cultural multipurpose, Museums, Performing arts, Visual arts, Emphasis on education outreach.
COMMUNITY IMPROVEMENT: Nonprofit management, Volunteer bureaus.
EDUCATION: K-12: Math, science, economics education; college access; Higher Education/Graduate Education/Professional Schools: Technical, engineering and business colleges.
EMPLOYMENT/JOBS: Employment procurement/job training.
ENVIRONMENTAL QUALITY/PROTECTION/BEAUTIFICATION: Natural resources conservation/protection, Biodiversity and climate change programs that protect the earth's ecosystems.
HOUSING/SHELTER: Homeless, temporary housing, Housing support services.
HUMAN SERVICES: Children/youth services, Family services, Family services for adolescent parents, Family violence shelters and services, Multipurpose human service organizations.
PHILANTHROPY/VOLUNTARISM: Nonprofit sector assistance, Volunteerism promotion.
PUBLIC SAFETY/DISASTERS/RELIEF: Disaster preparedness and relief.
SCIENCE/TECHNOLOGY: Engineering/technology research.
YOUTH DEVELOPMENT: Adult/child matching programs, Multipurpose youth centers/clubs, Scouting organizations, Youth development programs.

Intended beneficiaries: Adults, Ethnic/racial populations - general, Poor/economically disadvantaged, Youth/adolescents - school age 5-18.

Types of support for organizations:
CAPITAL CAMPAIGNS: Building/renovation.
GENERAL PURPOSE/OPERATING SUPPORT.
PROGRAM DEVELOPMENT/PROJECT SUPPORT: Curriculum development, Faculty/staff development, Mentoring programs, Leadership programs.
STUDENT AID (GRANTS TO INSTITUTIONS): Fellowships.
IN-KIND PRODUCTS: Products manufactured by 3M.

Types of support for individuals: none.

Matching grants: employee matching, higher education, public broadcasting, volunteer matching.

Sample grants:
Boys & Girls Club - MN (Twin Cities)/MN/$90,000.
Comunidades Latinos Unidos en Servicio (CLUES)/MN/$7,500.
Merrick Community Services/MN/$50,000.
Metropolitan State University/MN/$300,000.
MN Independent School Forum/MN/$135,000.
MN Minority Education Partnership/MN/Minnesota College Access Network/$50,000.
Park Square Theatre Company/MN/$25,000.
Science Museum of MN, The/MN/$120,000.

Financial Information

Financial data for year ending: 12/31/2006
Foundation assets: $48,469,350
Grants paid: $23,831,000
Number of grants: 2200
Largest/smallest: $2,400,000/$200
In-kind gifts: $16,838,000

Application Information

Preferred form of initial contact: online application at www.3MGiving.com.

Public information available by request: proposal guidelines, application form, annual report, website, eligibility quiz.

Proposal deadlines: none.

Preferred time for receiving proposals: grants primarily by invitation; deadlines communicated to grantee.

Contribution decisions made by: staff, board of directors/trustees.

Frequency of contributions decisions: monthly.

Specific times board meets: June and December.

Typical time from application deadlines to notification: 12 weeks on average.

Special application procedures: All requests must be submitted online at www.3MGiving.com. Paper requests are no longer accepted.

Staff/Trustees

Staff: A. C. Cirillo Jr., staff vice president, community affairs, vice president, 3M Foundation; B. W. Kaufmann, manager, corporate contributions, community affairs; Cindy Kleven, manager, corporate contributions, secretary, 3M Foundation.

Directors/trustees: T. A. Boardman, staff vice president & deputy general counsel; G. W. Buckley, chairman of the board and CEO; J. L. Bushman, division vice president, occupational health and environmental safety division; A. C. Cirillo Jr., staff vice president, community affairs vice president, 3M Foundation; M. P. Delkoski, vice president, safety & security division; J. W. Ihlenfeld, senior vice president, research & development; B. W. Kaufmann, manager, corporate contributions, community affairs; Cindy Kleven, manager, corporate contributions, secretary, 3M Foundation; R. D. MacDonald, president, 3M Foundation; senior vice president, marketing & sales; R. M. Miller, vice president, Latin America; K. E. Reed, staff vice president, environmental health and safety operations; Donna Schorr, recording secretary; J. B. Stake, executive vice president, display and graphics business; S. K. Tokach, staff vice president, human resources; S. C. Webster, vice president, D & G Business; J. K. Woodworth, senior vice president, corporate supply chain operations; J. L. Yeomans, vice president and treasurer.

ACA International Foundation

PO Box 390106
Minneapolis, MN 55439-0106
County: Hennepin
Phone: (952) 928-8000
Fax: (952) 915-3922
E-mail: pr@ACAinternational.org
Website: www.ACAinternational.org
Contact: Jean Hayes Cottington
Paid Staff: Yes
Funder type: Community/public foundation

Program Description

Program's purpose: Providing educational outreach to the general public.

Funding priorities: The ACA Foundation strongly supports financial education and literacy programs, including creating and distributing Community Education Kits to help educate young adults, the economically disadvantaged and senior citizens, on financial issues affecting their everyday lives.

Areas of interest:
EDUCATION.
EMPLOYMENT/JOBS: Employment procurement/job training.

Financial Information

Financial data for year ending: 05/31/2005
Grants paid: $21,000

Staff/Trustees

Staff: Jean Hayes Cottington.

Acorn Foundation

PO Box 5178
Hopkins, MN 55343
County: Hennepin
Contact: Mark Hanson, vice president
Established: 08/21/1997
Funder type: Private foundation

Program Description

Program's purpose: The foundation has a primary interest in religious charitable organizations and social services that address the basic needs of people, including food, clothing, spiritual, housing and health needs, and that help alleviate or resolve problems faced by members of the community. Educational scholarship program.

Funding priorities: Education and religion are the primary focuses, along with health, human services and mental health areas.

Geographic focus: Twin Cities Metropolitan Area, Greater Minnesota, National Areas.

Areas of interest:
EDUCATION.
HEALTH - MENTAL HEALTH/CRISIS INTERVENTION.
HUMAN SERVICES.
RELIGION/SPIRITUAL DEVELOPMENT.

Intended beneficiaries: General public/unspecified.

Types of support for organizations:
STUDENT AID (GRANTS TO INSTITUTIONS).

Types of support for individuals: scholarships.

Sample grants:
Augsburg College/MN/tuition reduction/$5,000.
Belmont University/TN/tuition reduction/$2,500.
Central Baptist Seminary - MN/MN/tuition reduction/$5,000.
Concordia College - MN (Moorhead)/MN/tuition reduction/$20,000.
Concordia University - MN (St Paul)/MN/tuition reduction/$35,500.
Pillsbury Baptist Bible College/MN/tuition reduction/$25,000.
St Olaf College/MN/tuition reduction/$6,250.
St Thomas University/MN/tuition reduction/$7,500.

Financial Information

Financial data for year ending: 12/31/2005
Foundation assets: $7,387,489
Grants paid: $501,520
Number of grants: 40
Largest/smallest: $105,000/$2,500

Application Information

Preferred form of initial contact: complete proposal.
Proposal deadlines: None.
Special application procedures: Organization or individual should submit a detailed description of the organization or individual and the proposed activities and purposes of the organization or individual.

Staff/Trustees

Directors/trustees: Phil Fandrei, president; Mark Hanson, vice president; Shirly Hanson, secretary.

ADC Foundation

PO Box 1101
Minneapolis, MN 55440-1101
County: Hennepin
Fax: (952) 917-0965
E-mail: Bill.Linder-Scholer@adc.com
Website: www.adc.com/philanthropy
Established: 03/17/1999
Paid Staff: Yes
Funder type: Corporate foundation

Program Description

Program's purpose: To conduct broad-spectrum employee matching gifts programs balanced by highly focused strategic grants.

Funding priorities: 1) Science, mathematics and technology education; 2) technology for nonprofits.

Geographic focus: Twin Cities Metropolitan Area, Communities (including the Twin Cities) where ADC Telecommunications has facilities.

Geographic limitations: See ADC website for locations of giving communities outside the Twin Cities. No grants given in South America, Africa or Asia.

Areas of interest:

EDUCATION: K-12 math, science and technology education.

SCIENCE/TECHNOLOGY: Technology acquisition grants for smaller nonprofits.

Intended beneficiaries: see Areas of Interest.

Types of support for organizations:

PROGRAM DEVELOPMENT/ PROJECT SUPPORT.

IN-KIND SERVICES: Volunteer assistance.

Matching grants: employee matching, for 501(c)(3) organizations (except religious or political).

Dollars for Doers: yes.

Exclusions: Capital & endowment campaigns, Individuals, Non-501(c)(3), Political organizations, Religious organizations, Scholarships/loans, Tax-supported institutions.

Sample grants:

Community Technology Centers Network - DC/DC/To fund the CTC online volunteer resource center/$10,500.

Crisis Connection/MN/Call Center Software Upgrade/$10,000.

International Engineering Consortium - IL/IL/For sponsorship of the IEC's University Program whereby professors and their students receive tuition-free grants to attend the IEC's Forums/ $25,000.

ISD Minneapolis #282/MN/Girls in Engineering, Math, and Science Program/ $5,000.

La Oportunidad-Opportunity/St Paul, MN/To implement proposed technology upgrade project/$2,000.

MATHCOUNTS Foundation - VA/VA/To provide National Sponsor support for MATHCOUNTS, a nationwide program of middle school mathematics competitions and curriculum enrichment/$75,000.

MN Children's Museum/MN/Science Headstart program/$5,000.

St Paul Neighborhood Network/MN/To support CTEP AmeriCorps program/ $20,000.

Financial Information

Financial data for year ending: 10/31/2006
Foundation assets: $8,046,997
Grants paid: $1,625,983
Number of grants: 100
Largest/smallest: $50,000/$25
Typical grant amount: $5,000
Matching gifts: $323,328

Application Information

Preferred form of initial contact: letter of inquiry via web-based tool at www.adc.com/philanthropy.

Public information available by request: proposal guidelines, application form, annual report, website, online letter of inquiry, 990-PF.

Accept common report form: yes.

Proposal deadlines: accepted any time only through our web-based inquiry tool at www.adc.com/philanthropy.

Contribution decisions made by: employee committee, board of directors/trustees.

Frequency of contributions decisions: quarterly.

Specific times board meets: quarterly but variable.

Typical time from application deadlines to notification: 3 months.

Special application procedures: Proposals must fit into guidelines and must be submitted via ADC's online tool.

Staff/Trustees

Staff: Katy Friesz, volunteer coordinator and grants administrator; Bill Linder-Scholer, executive director.

Directors/trustees: Luis Mario Dena Torres, vice president, manufacturing, Mexico; Michael Hawtin, vice president, UK Operations; Gokul Hemmady, ADC CFO; Steve Mitchell, vice president, American sales; Jon Norton, director of engineering, Wireless; Pat O'Brien, vice president general manager Americas; Laura Owen, vice president, human resources; Richard Parran, president, APS professional services; Jeff Pflaum, vice president, general counsel and corporate secretary; Mary Quay, vice president, world wide operations; Robert E. Switz, foundation chair and CEO/president, ADC Telecommunications.

Affiliated Community Health Foundation

101 Willmar Avenue SW
Willmar, MN 56201
County: Kandiyohi
Phone: (320) 214-6821
Alt. Phone: (320) 214-6840
Fax: (320) 214-6826
E-mail: gregs@acmc.com
Website: www.acmcweb.com/acmc_link.cfm?acmcLinkID=6
Contact: Greg Spartz, foundation coordinator
Established: 01/01/1995
Paid Staff: Yes
Funder type: Community/public foundation

Program Description

Program's purpose: The goal of the foundation is to improve the overall population health for people living in the 13 counties of Affiliated Community Medical Center's service area in Southwest and West Central Minnesota.

Funding priorities: Promote good health practices, especially for children and adolescents; Reducing adult and youth tobacco use; Improving the health outcomes and management of chronic diseases; and reduce disparities in health care delivery related to barriers of age, culture, gender, poverty, rural location and language.

Geographic focus: Southwest and West Central Minnesota.

Geographic limitations: People living in the 13 counties of Affiliated Community Medical Center's service area in Southwest and West Central Minnesota.

Areas of interest:

HEALTH - DISEASES/MEDICAL DISCIPLINES.

HEALTH - GENERAL/ REHABILITATIVE: preventive.

Intended beneficiaries: General public/unspecified.

Types of support for individuals: aid to needy persons, research, specific projects that demonstrate improved health service, seeking grants with others and fiscal host for other organizations.

Exclusions: Capital and endowment campaigns, Political organizations, Non-501(c)(3) except Public Organizations.

Sample grants:

Kandiyohi County Tobacco Coalition/MN/Students Against Tobacco/$12,000.

Marshall ACTS/MN/Youth Tobacco Cessation program/$16,188.

Medical Interpreter Training - Southwest MN/$3,000.

Financial Information

Financial data for year ending: 06/30/2005
Foundation assets: $779,870
Grants paid: $45,143
Number of grants: 8
Largest/smallest: $16,188/$1,000

Application Information

Preferred form of initial contact: telephone inquiry, e-mail.

Public information available by request: website, brochures.

Proposal deadlines: See website for deadlines.

Preferred time for receiving proposals: deadlines to be announced - 2 per year.

Contribution decisions made by: Board of directors.

Special application procedures: contact Greg Spartz at (320) 214-6821 or via e-mail at gregs@acmc.com

Staff/Trustees

Staff: Greg Spartz, foundation coordinator.

Directors/trustees: Roger Deuth; Ronald L. Holmgren M.D., president; Robert Kaiser M.D.; Kathy Leedom; Burnell J. Mellema M.D.; Marvin Napgezek M.D.; David Ross M.D.; Gayne Stone; Roland Swenson; Terry Tone; Jay Trusty; Lyle Weismantel.

AgStar Fund for Rural America

PO Box 4249
Mankato, MN 56002
County: Blue Earth
Phone: (507) 345-5656
E-mail: jody.bloemke@agstar.com
Website: www.agstar.com/Default.aspx?pageid=58
Funder type: Corporate giving program

Program Description

Program's purpose: AgStar Fund for Rural America was created to extend the company's commitment to the agricultural community. AgStar has always been concerned with the issues facing rural America, and this fund underscores AgStar's dedication to agriculture and rural communities. Our mission: committed to enhancing the quality of life and future opportunities for rural residents and their communities.

Funding priorities: Education: Educating young, beginning or future farmers; Environment: Maintaining or improving the quality of the rural environment; Technology: Supporting the advancement and utilization of technology for the benefit of farmers and rural communities; Quality of Life: Programs or initiatives that enhance the quality of life for farmers and rural communities.

Program limitations/restrictions: Funds will generally not be approved for the following: Programs outside the four focus areas; Programs of religious groups except where they provide needed services to the community at large; Legislative or lobbying efforts; Political campaigns; Medical research or facilities; Fundraising; Sponsorship of organized sports teams or sporting activities; Construction or maintenance of recreational facilities; Arts-related facilities and activities; All or portions of public or private school teaching positions; Books and magazines, articles or advertising in professional journals; Fraternal societies and orders, or veteran organizations; Theatrical productions; Deficits already incurred, Loans or Debt Retirement; Programs or activities that directly benefit AgStar employees. Funding is limited to $10,000 per organization per year.

Geographic focus: Greater Minnesota, Areas outside Minnesota.

Geographic limitations: AgStar's local service area, including 69 counties in Minnesota and northwest Wisconsin.

Areas of interest:

COMMUNITY IMPROVEMENT: Rural economic development.

EDUCATION: For young, beginning or future farmers.

ENVIRONMENTAL QUALITY/PROTECTION/BEAUTIFICATION: Rural environment.

FOOD/NUTRITION/AGRICULTURE: Agricultural programs, Soil and water conservation/farm land preservation, Betterment of rural communities.

SCIENCE/TECHNOLOGY: For the benefit of rural communities.

Intended beneficiaries: Rural residents.

Types of support for organizations:

CAPITAL CAMPAIGNS: Computer systems/technology, Equipment.

GENERAL PURPOSE/OPERATING SUPPORT.

MANAGEMENT/TECHNICAL ASSISTANCE.

PROGRAM DEVELOPMENT/PROJECT SUPPORT.

Types of support for individuals: scholarships.

Exclusions: Capital & endowment campaigns, Individuals, Non-501(c)(3), Political organizations, Religious organizations.

Financial Information

Financial data for year ending: 12/31/2006
Grants paid: $300,000
Typical grant amount: $10,000

Application Information

Preferred form of initial contact: online application.

Public information available by request: proposal guidelines, website, online application.

Accept common report form: yes.

Proposal deadlines: grant applications accepted online October 1 to November 30.

Contribution decisions made by: board of directors/trustees; staff if under $2,500.

Frequency of contributions decisions: annually.

Typical time from application deadlines to notification: 3 months.

Staff/Trustees

Staff: Jody Bloemke, fund administrator.

AHS Foundation

c/o Lowry Hill
90 South Seventh Street
Suite 5300
Minneapolis, MN 55402
County: Hennepin
Phone: (612) 667-1784
Contact: Thomas Wright, secretary/treasurer
Established: 05/16/1968
Funder type: Private foundation

Program Description

Program's purpose: Relief of poverty, advancement of education, advancement of religion and community issues.

Geographic focus: Twin Cities Metropolitan Area, National Areas; the majority funded outside Minnesota.

Areas of interest:
ARTS, CULTURE, HUMANITIES.
COMMUNITY IMPROVEMENT.
EDUCATION.
HUMAN SERVICES.
RELIGION/SPIRITUAL DEVELOPMENT.

Intended beneficiaries: General public/unspecified.

Types of support for organizations:
GENERAL PURPOSE/OPERATING SUPPORT.
PROGRAM DEVELOPMENT/PROJECT SUPPORT.

Sample grants:
Bridge for Runaway Youth, The/MN/general support/$16,000.
Church Within a Church Movement/IL/general support/$30,000.
City Music Cleveland/OH/general support/$2,000.
Cleveland Public Theatre/OH/general support/$5,000.
Ebb&Flow Arts/HI/administrative support/$12,000.
Groundworks Dance Theater/OH/general support/$10,000.
Maui Arts & Cultural Center/HI/administrative support/$10,000.
Reconciling Congregation Program/Chicago, IL/general support/$30,000.

Financial Information

Financial data for year ending: 06/30/2006
Foundation assets: $10,022,386
Grants paid: $502,500
Number of grants: 42
Largest/smallest: $30,000/$2,000

Application Information

Preferred form of initial contact: letter of inquiry, letter with brief description of intended grant use.
Proposal deadlines: None.

Staff/Trustees

Directors/trustees: Gage A. Schubert, 2nd vice president; John D. Schubert, 1st vice president; Leland W. Schubert, president; Thomas Wright, secretary/treasurer.

Airport Foundation MSP

MSP International Airport
4300 Glumack Drive
D-2040
St Paul, MN 55111
County: Hennepin
Phone: (612) 726-5235
Fax: (612) 467-0420
E-mail: JVaughn@mspmac.org
Established: 12/08/1982
Paid Staff: Yes
Funder type: Community/public foundation

Program Description

Program's purpose: Enhance the experience of travelers at the Minneapolis/St Paul International Airport.

Funding priorities: Aviation-related causes specific to Minneapolis/St Paul International Airport and other airports governed by the Metropolitan Airports Commission.

Program limitations/restrictions: Grant to 501(c)(3) organizations.

Geographic focus: Twin Cities Metropolitan Area.

Geographic limitations: No grants to out-of-state organizations and agencies.

Areas of interest:
ARTS, CULTURE, HUMANITIES: Arts services, Other.
PHILANTHROPY/VOLUNTARISM: Philanthropy - general, Voluntarism promotion.
PUBLIC AFFAIRS/SOCIETY BENEFIT: Military/veterans' organizations, Public transportation services.

Intended beneficiaries: General public/unspecified.

Types of support for organizations:
GENERAL PURPOSE/OPERATING SUPPORT.
PROGRAM DEVELOPMENT/PROJECT SUPPORT.

Sample grants:
Armed Forces Service Center/MN/$6,000.
Lindbergh Fund, The Charles A/MN/$4,000.
MN Aviation Hall of Fame/MN/$3,000.
MSP Defibrillators/MN/$65,000.

Financial Information

Financial data for year ending: 12/31/2006
Foundation assets: $490,219
Grants paid: $47,525
Number of grants: 8
Largest/smallest: $27,000/$1,000

Application Information

Preferred form of initial contact: letter of inquiry.

Public information available by request: proposal guidelines, application form, annual report.

Proposal deadlines: none.

Contribution decisions made by: board of directors/trustees.

Specific times board meets: as needed.

Typical time from application deadlines to notification: 3 months.

Staff/Trustees

Staff: Jana Vaughn, executive director.

Allianz Life Insurance Company of North America

5701 Golden Hills Drive
Minneapolis, MN 55416-1297
County: Hennepin
Phone: (763) 582-6571
Fax: (763) 765-7229
E-mail: laura_juergens@allianzlife.com
Website: www.allianzlife.com
Paid Staff: Yes
Funder type: Corporate giving program

Program Description

Program's purpose: Allianz Life has a strong commitment to the community where employees live and work. Our corporate giving program is anchored by a philosophy of sharing financial resources, time, energy and expertise to build a stronger, more vibrant local community that improves quality of life for our customers, employees and the public.

Funding priorities: Employment Readiness and Financial Literacy; Arts and Community Involvement; Youth and Family Development.

Program limitations/restrictions: Allianz does not fund Individuals, Lobbying, political or fraternal activities, Program Endowments, Religious groups for religious purposes, Alumni drives, Labor unions and organizations whose chief purpose is to influence legislation or participate in political campaigns on behalf of or against any candidate for political office. Allianz does very little event sponsorship.

Geographic focus: Twin Cities Metropolitan Area.

Geographic limitations: Grants are primarily in the Twin Cities Metro Area.

Areas of interest:
ARTS, CULTURE, HUMANITIES: Arts/cultural multipurpose.
COMMUNITY IMPROVEMENT: Community coalitions, Community/neighborhood development/improvement.
EMPLOYMENT/JOBS: Employment procurement/job training, Financial literacy.
HUMAN SERVICES: Children/youth services, Family services, Family services for adolescent parents, Multipurpose human service organizations, Personal social services, Residential/custodial care, Senior centers and services.
PUBLIC AFFAIRS/SOCIETY BENEFIT: Citizen participation.
YOUTH DEVELOPMENT: Adult/child matching programs, Multipurpose youth centers/clubs, Scouting organizations, Youth development programs.

Intended beneficiaries: Adults, Aging/elderly/senior citizens, Children and youth (infants-19 years), Ethnic/racial populations - general, Females - all ages or age unspecified, Gay/lesbian/bisexual/transgender, Immigrants/newcomers/refugees, Males - all ages or age unspecified, Poor/economically disadvantaged.

Types of support for organizations:
CAPITAL CAMPAIGNS: Building/renovation, Computer systems/technology, Equipment.
PROGRAM DEVELOPMENT/PROJECT SUPPORT.

Types of support for individuals: none.

Exclusions: Non-501(c)(3), Political organizations, Religious organizations, Scholarships/loans, Endowments.

Sample grants:

AccessAbility Inc - MN/MN/to support their Project Connect Program/$5,000.

Achieve! Minneapolis/MN/to support their Achieve! Career and College Initiative program/$25,000.

African Assistance Program/MN/to support their Refugee Employment Project/$10,000.

BestPrep/MN/to support their Minnesota Business Venture Program and TECH Corps eMentor Program/$10,000.

Citizens League - MN (St Paul)/MN/to support their programs that address policy solutions engaging leaders and renewing policies, institutions and relationships in MN/$10,000.

Dunwoody Institute/MN/to support their The Youth Career Awareness Program/$10,000.

MN Children's Museum/MN/to support their Access Program/$5,000.

WomenVenture/MN/to support their Financial Literacy programming/$10,000.

Financial Information

Financial data for year ending: 12/31/2006
Grants paid: $1,250,000

Application Information

Preferred form of initial contact: e-mail request for Allianz guidelines.

Public information available by request: proposal guidelines, website, Allianz application form.

Proposal deadlines: February 1 - Employment Readiness and Financial Literacy; May 1 - Arts, Environment, & Community Involvement; September 1 - Youth and Family Development.

Preferred time for receiving proposals: Grant applications must be postmarked by the date for each deadline. We will not review grant requests outside of the stated deadline dates.

Contribution decisions made by: employee committee.

Frequency of contributions decisions: quarterly.

Specific times board meets: 6 times a year.

Typical time from application deadlines to notification: 2-3 months.

Staff/Trustees

Staff: Betty Carlson, executive administrative assistant; Laura Juergens, senior charitable giving specialist; Juli Wall, senior vice president.

Ameriprise Financial, Inc.

64 Ameriprise Financial Center
Minneapolis, MN 55474
County: Hennepin
Phone: (612) 671-3052
E-mail: ameriprise.financial.community.relations@ampf.com
Website: www.ameriprise.com
Contact: Tracy Hall, manager, grants management and gift matching programs
Established: 12/22/1987
Funder type: Corporate giving program

Program Description

Program's purpose: To serve the communities in which we live and work by supporting organizations whose shared goal is to improve the well-being of individuals from all walks of life.

Funding priorities: Giving platforms: 1. *Financial Well-Being for a Lifetime*℠; 2. Arts & Culture; 3. Employee- and Advisor-Driven Causes.

Program limitations/restrictions: No capital/endowment grants; no grants for travel, religious, political, fraternal or sports organizations; individuals; books and magazines; fundraising activities such as benefits, charitable dinners or sporting events; legislative or lobbying efforts; medical research or hospitals; loans; programs of religious groups except where they provide needed services to the community at large and do not include or promote a particular religious instruction or belief; programs that do not fall within one of our three focus areas.

Geographic focus: Twin Cities Metropolitan Area, Minnesota statewide, National Areas, Phoenix, AZ, Boston, MA, Albany and New York City, NY, Green Bay, WI.

Geographic limitations: Ameriprise Financial Community Relations program is a national giving program.

Areas of interest:

ANIMAL RELATED: Zoo/zoological societies; only requests for accredited zoos will be considered.

ARTS, CULTURE, HUMANITIES: Arts/cultural multipurpose, Premier arts organizations.

COMMUNITY IMPROVEMENT: Economic development.

EDUCATION: Adult/continuing education/literacy, Educational services, Higher education, Libraries/library science, Pre-school/elementary, Secondary, Vocational/technical.

EMPLOYMENT/JOBS: Employment procurement/job training.

ENVIRONMENTAL QUALITY/PROTECTION/BEAUTIFICATION: Accredited arboretums.

HUMAN SERVICES: Children/youth services, Emergency assistance (food/clothing/cash), Family services, Family violence shelters and services, Multipurpose human service organizations, Services to specific groups, Only nonprofits where our employees/advisors volunteer.

PUBLIC SAFETY/DISASTERS/RELIEF: Disaster preparedness and relief. No unsolicited requests will be considered.

YOUTH DEVELOPMENT: Youth development programs.

Intended beneficiaries: African Americans/Blacks, Aging/elderly/senior citizens, Asian/Pacific Islanders, Children and youth (infants-19 years), Disabled - general or unspecified disability, Ethnic/racial minorities - other specified group(s), Ethnic/racial populations - general, Females - all ages or age unspecified, Gay/lesbian/bisexual/transgender, General public/unspecified, Hispanics/Latinos, Immigrants/newcomers/refugees, Males - all ages or age unspecified, Native American/American Indians, Other minorities, Poor/economically disadvantaged, Single parents.

Types of support for organizations:
GENERAL PURPOSE/OPERATING SUPPORT.
PROGRAM DEVELOPMENT/PROJECT SUPPORT: preferred.

Types of support for individuals: none.

Matching grants: employee matching to any eligible 501(c)(3) nonprofit organization recognized and approved by the IRS.

Exclusions: Capital & endowment campaigns, Individuals, Non-501(c)(3), Political organizations, Religious organizations, Research, Scholarships/loans. Review our corporate giving guidelines at www.ameriprise.com.

Financial Information

Financial data for year ending: 12/31/2006
Grants paid: $7,300,000
Number of grants: 136
Largest/smallest: $250,000/$1,000

Application Information

Preferred form of initial contact: complete proposal. Visit www.ameriprise.com for eligibility requirements and instructions how to apply for a grant. Ameriprise Financial requires all requests to be submitted using our online application process. No paper applications will be accepted.

Public information available by request: proposal guidelines, application form, annual report, website, available at www.ameriprise.com.

Proposal deadlines: February 1, May 1 and September 1 - no exceptions. Check corporate website for deadlines. All proposals MUST be complete and submitted using the online application. No paper applications will be accepted.

Preferred time for receiving proposals: Do not submit a request sooner than six weeks prior to each deadline. Deadlines are firm; no exceptions will be made.

Contribution decisions made by: staff, board of directors/trustees, Ameriprise Financial Community Relations Governance Committee.

Frequency of contributions decisions: Three times per year (end of April, July, November) applicable to each cycle (*Financial Well-Being for a Lifetime*^{SM}), Arts & Culture, and Employee- and Advisor-Driven Causes).

Specific times board meets: three times per year.

Typical time from application deadlines to notification: 8-10 weeks.

Special application procedures: We strongly encourage all grantseekers to visit ameriprise.com regularly for any changes to our guidelines, eligibility requirements or application processes. Use the online application tool located at www.ameriprise.com. No paper applications will be considered. Requests for individual meetings are discouraged.

Staff/Trustees

Staff: Tracy Hall, manager, grants management and gift matching programs; Brad Pietsch, vice president, community relations and government affairs.

Lloyd and Barbara Amundson Charity Foundation, Inc.

100 East Main Street
Sleepy Eye, MN 56085
County: Brown
Phone: (605) 335-1508
Fax: (605) 535-1546
Established: 11/17/1995
Funder type: Private foundation

Program Description

Program's purpose: General charitable purposes.

Program limitations/restrictions: 501(c)(3) organizations.

Geographic focus: Twin Cities Metropolitan Area, Greater Minnesota, Minnesota statewide, Areas outside Minnesota.

Areas of interest:
ANIMAL RELATED.
ARTS, CULTURE, HUMANITIES.
COMMUNITY IMPROVEMENT.

EDUCATION.
HEALTH - DISEASES/MEDICAL DISCIPLINES.
HEALTH - GENERAL/REHABILITATIVE.
HUMAN SERVICES.
PHILANTHROPY/VOLUNTARISM.
PUBLIC AFFAIRS/SOCIETY BENEFIT.
PUBLIC SAFETY/DISASTERS/RELIEF.
RELIGION/SPIRITUAL DEVELOPMENT.
YOUTH DEVELOPMENT.

Intended beneficiaries: General public/unspecified.

Types of support for organizations:
GENERAL PURPOSE/OPERATING SUPPORT.
STUDENT AID (GRANTS TO INSTITUTIONS): Scholarship funds.

Types of support for individuals: none.

Sample grants:

American Swedish Institute - MN/MN/ $300.

Fire Department - Otter Tail, MN/MN/ $500.

Girl Scout Council - MN (River Trails)/MN/$1,000.

HEART (Help Enable Alcoholics Receive Treatment)/MN/$500.

Humane Society - HI (Maui)/HI/$300.

Kihei Lutheran Church/Kihei, HI/ $27,600.

Lupus Foundation - MN Chapter/MN/ $1,000.

United Way - MN (Detroit Lakes)/MN/ $200.

Financial Information

Financial data for year ending: 12/31/2005
Foundation assets: $605,348
Grants paid: $660,251
Number of grants: 28
Largest/smallest: $100,000/$25

Application Information

Accept common grant application: yes.
Proposal deadlines: none.
Contribution decisions made by: board of directors/trustees.

Staff/Trustees

Directors/trustees: Barbara Amundson; L. A. Amundson, president; Jane Harberts; Barbara Hegelund; A.R. Mixner.

Andersen Corporate Foundation (fka The Bayport Foundation of Andersen Corporation)

White Pine Building
342 Fifth Avenue North
Bayport, MN 55003-1201
County: Washington
Phone: (651) 439-1557
Fax: (651) 439-9480
E-mail: andersencorpfdn@srinc.biz
Website: www.srinc.biz/bp/
Contact: Sandra K. Fleitman, program officer
Established: 12/01/1941
Donor: Andersen Corporation
Paid Staff: Yes
Funder type: Corporate foundation

Program Description

Program's purpose: To better people's lives and strengthen communities, focusing primarily where Andersen employees live and work.

Funding priorities: Affordable housing, civic support, education, health and safety, human services.

Geographic focus: Twin Cities Metropolitan Area, Areas outside Minnesota, National Areas, International Areas, St Croix Valley including Washington County in Minnesota and six counties in western Wisconsin.

Geographic limitations: St Croix Valley - St Croix, Polk, Pierce, Dunn, Barron and Burnett counties in western Wisconsin; Washington County and portions of the east metro area in Minnesota; Des Moines, Iowa; Dubuque, Iowa; Huron/Perth Ontario Canada; London/Middlesex Ontario Canada; Luray, Virginia; and North Brunswick, New Jersey.

Areas of interest:
ARTS, CULTURE, HUMANITIES: Arts/cultural multipurpose, Museums, Performing arts, Visual arts.
COMMUNITY IMPROVEMENT: Build, support and preserve communities.
EDUCATION: Adult/continuing education/literacy, Pre-school/elementary, Secondary, Education focus on science, technology, engineering, and math, Intellectual and social opportunities with a focus primarily on young people, senior citizens and people with disabilities.
EMPLOYMENT/JOBS: Vocational rehabilitation.
HEALTH - DISEASES/MEDICAL DISCIPLINES: Disease prevention.
HEALTH - GENERAL/REHABILITATIVE: Health support services, Hospitals and related primary medical care facilities, Public health programs/wellness education, Recreational programs, Support organizations that promote safe and healthy environments, as well as organizations that seek to improve health through prevention and education programs primarily for young people, senior citizens and people in vulnerable situations.
HEALTH - MENTAL HEALTH/CRISIS INTERVENTION: Programs and services that promote mental health, wellness and safety.
HOUSING/SHELTER: Housing development/construction/management, Housing support services, Affordable housing for seniors, people with disabilities and people living in poverty.
HUMAN SERVICES: Children/youth services, Emergency assistance (food/clothing/cash), Family services, Family violence shelters and services, Multipurpose human service organizations, Personal social services, Senior centers and services, Enhance self-sufficiency for people living in poverty, senior citizens and people with disabilities.
PUBLIC PROTECTION - CRIME/COURTS/LEGAL SERVICES: Legal services, Protection/prevention - neglect/abuse/exploitation.
PUBLIC SAFETY/DISASTERS/RELIEF: Disaster preparedness and relief.
RECREATION: Physical fitness/recreational facilities, Recreational activities for individuals with specific disorders.
SCIENCE/TECHNOLOGY: Elementary and Secondary education in science, technology, engineering and math.
YOUTH DEVELOPMENT: Adult/child matching programs, Multipurpose youth centers/clubs, Scouting organizations.

Intended beneficiaries: Adults, Aging/elderly/senior citizens, Children and youth (infants-19 years), Disabled - general or unspecified disability, Ethnic/racial populations - general, Females - all ages or age unspecified, Homeless, Males - all ages or age unspecified, Mentally/emotionally disabled, Physically disabled, Poor/economically disadvantaged, Youth/adolescents (ages 14-19).

Types of support for organizations:
CAPITAL CAMPAIGNS: Building/renovation, Equipment, Land acquisitions.
GENERAL PURPOSE/OPERATING SUPPORT: Annual campaigns.
PROGRAM DEVELOPMENT/PROJECT SUPPORT.

Types of support for individuals: none.

Exclusions: Individuals, Non-501(c)(3), Political organizations.

Sample grants:
American Red Cross - MN (St Croix Valley Chapter)/MN/General operating and emergency services/$60,000.
Child Care Resource & Referral - MN/MN/Service expansion/$5,000.
Courage Center - MN (Golden Valley)/MN/General operating support for Courage St Croix/$35,000.
Family Pathways - MN/MN/Senior Services program/$7,500.
MN Public Radio - St Paul/MN/General operation support/$12,000.
Portico Healthnet/MN/Outreach and care management for the East Metro area/$15,000.
Science Museum of MN, The/MN/General operating/$20,000.

Financial Information

Financial data for year ending: 11/30/2006
Foundation assets: $55,530,087
Grants paid: $1,806,750
Number of grants: 128
Largest/smallest: $100,000/$1,000

Application Information

Preferred form of initial contact: telephone inquiry, request for guidelines, complete proposal.

Public information available by request: proposal guidelines, application form, website.

Accept common report form: yes.

Proposal deadlines: April 15, July 15, October 15, December 15.

Contribution decisions made by: board of directors/trustees.

Frequency of contributions decisions: quarterly.

Specific times board meets: January, May, July, November.

Typical time from application deadlines to notification: four months.

Staff/Trustees

Staff: Sandra K. Fleitman, program officer.

Directors/trustees: Phil Donaldson, treasurer; Jim Humphrey; Randy Iles; Jay Lund; Maureen McDonough, vice president, grants administration/secretary; Keith Olson, president; Julie Smith.

Andersen Corporation

100 Fourth Avenue North
Bayport, MN 55003
County: Washington
Phone: (651) 264-7432
Fax: (651) 351-3275
Website: www.andersenwindows.com
Contact: Susan Roeder, community relations manager
Funder type: Corporate giving program

Program Description

Program's purpose: Our grantmaking programs focus primarily on building strong communities; providing quality housing for people in need; and improving the built environment, particularly through programs relating to environmental stewardship, energy efficiency, safety, architecture and design, innovation and social responsibility.

Funding priorities: We make grants in four key areas. Shelter: To promote a better quality of life by funding residential housing for people in need through funding and in-kind donations. Architecture and Design: To promote the value of quality architecture and design in the built environment, through education, exhibitions and other special projects. We emphasize ideas relating to product aesthetics in form and function, energy efficiency, innovation, performance, safety and sustainability. Building Industry: This category emphasizes continuous improvement in the building industry relating to energy efficiency, safety, innovation, sustainability and product performance. Funding emphasis is on education and industry-related nonprofit organizations. Community: Our community emphasis is to improve the welfare of the people in our operating communities, headquarters region, and the communities where our employees live. Emphasis is on nurturing healthy, vital communities by supporting a wide variety of nonprofits, including health and human services, civic, education, safety, recreation, veterans, arts, shelter and environmental organizations.

Geographic focus: National Areas, East Metropolitan Area/St Paul only, St Croix Valley including western Wisconsin, other communities where Andersen Corporation operates.

Geographic limitations: Organizations must be located in communities where Andersen Corporation operates, or national organizations whose missions relate to shelter, architecture and design or the building industry.

Areas of interest:
ANIMAL RELATED.
EDUCATION.
ENVIRONMENTAL QUALITY/PROTECTION/BEAUTIFICATION.
HEALTH - GENERAL/REHABILITATIVE.
HOUSING/SHELTER: Housing development/construction/management, Architecture and Design.
HUMAN SERVICES.
PUBLIC SAFETY/DISASTERS/RELIEF.
RECREATION.

Intended beneficiaries: General public/unspecified.

Types of support for organizations:
IN-KIND PRODUCTS.

Types of support for individuals: none.

Matching grants: employee matching, United Way.

Exclusions: Individuals, Non-501(c)(3), Political organizations, Religious organizations.

Financial Information

Financial data for year ending: 12/31/2005
Grants paid: $2,570,815

Application Information

Preferred form of initial contact: letter of inquiry, complete proposal, submitted by U.S. Mail only.

Public information available by request: website.

Proposal deadlines: Proposals are reviewed throughout the year.

Typical time from application deadlines to notification: 30 days.

Staff/Trustees

Staff: Maureen McDonough; Susan Roeder, community relations manager; Lisa Wolff, community relations coordinator.

Elmer L. and Eleanor J. Andersen Foundation

2424 Territorial Road
St Paul, MN 55114-1506
County: Ramsey
Phone: (651) 642-0127
Fax: (651) 645-4684
E-mail: eandefdn@mtn.org
Contact: Mari Oyanagi Eggum, foundation administrator
Established: 11/30/1957
Funder type: Private foundation

Program Description

Program's purpose: To enhance the quality of the civic, cultural, educational, environmental and social aspects of life primarily in the metropolitan area of St Paul and Minneapolis.

Funding priorities: Arts and humanities, communications, education, libraries, environment and human services. The foundation will become involved in projects in other parts of Minnesota, outside the metro area, when the issues addressed by the project have a statewide impact. Environmental concerns are the major example of this broader involvement.

Program limitations/restrictions: The foundation awards no grants to individuals. In general, applications related to health will not be considered.

Geographic limitations: Primarily Twin Cities metro area of St Paul and Minneapolis, preference for St Paul area.

Areas of interest:

ARTS, CULTURE, HUMANITIES.
EDUCATION: Libraries/library science.
ENVIRONMENTAL QUALITY/PROTECTION/BEAUTIFICATION.
HUMAN SERVICES.

Exclusions: Individuals.

Sample grants:

Big Brothers/Big Sisters - MN (Greater Twin Cities)/MN/$1,000.
Coffee House Press/MN/$2,000.
Friends of the Library - Milaca/MN/Four year grant/$12,000.
Mixed Blood Theatre Company/MN/$1,000.
Parks & Trails Council of MN/MN/$1,000.
Ramsey County Historical Society/MN/$1,000.

Financial Information

Financial data for year ending: 11/30/2006
Foundation assets: $6,914,964
Grants paid: $269,000
Number of grants: 156
Largest/smallest: $10,000/$500
Typical grant amount: $1,000

Application Information

Preferred form of initial contact: request for guidelines.

Public information available by request: proposal guidelines, annual report.

Accept common grant application: yes.

Proposal deadlines: Please call office to confirm deadlines. Proposals must be postmarked by the first working day of February, May, August or November. A board meeting will be held in the month following a deadline date.

Contribution decisions made by: board of directors/trustees.

Specific times board meets: March, June, September, December.

Typical time from application deadlines to notification: 3 weeks after board meeting.

Special application procedures: Use of the Minnesota Common Grant Application is required.

Staff/Trustees

Staff: Mari Oyanagi Eggum, foundation administrator.

Directors/trustees: Amy Andersen, treasurer; Eleanor J. Andersen, vice president; Julian L. Andersen, president; Charles Dayton; Terry L. Slye, secretary.

Fred C. and Katherine B. Andersen Foundation

PO Box 80
Bayport, MN 55003-0080
County: Washington
Phone: (651) 264-7355
Contact: M. F. Gillstrom, director/assistant secretary
Established: 11/01/1959
Funder type: Private foundation

Program Description

Program's purpose: Primarily focus on higher education organizations that do not receive federal funding. The foundation also has an interest in nonprofits that provide youth, elderly and health services in St Croix, Pierce and Polk counties of Wisconsin and Washington county of Minnesota, as well as funds for capital projects.

Funding priorities: Higher education, youth, elderly and health programs.

Program limitations/restrictions: Grants are not awarded to colleges that receive federal aid. We do not support individual requests.

Geographic focus: Washington County, Minnesota; Pierce, Polk and St Croix counties, Wisconsin.

Geographic limitations: No international funding.

Areas of interest:

ANIMAL RELATED: Animal protection/welfare.

ARTS, CULTURE, HUMANITIES: Arts/cultural multipurpose.

EDUCATION: Higher education.

HEALTH - DISEASES/MEDICAL DISCIPLINES: Cancer.

HEALTH - GENERAL/REHABILITATIVE: Hospitals and related primary medical care facilities.

HEALTH - MENTAL HEALTH/CRISIS INTERVENTION: Alcohol/drug/substance, prevention and treatment.

HOUSING/SHELTER: Homeless, temporary housing.

HUMAN SERVICES: Children/youth services, Family violence shelters and services, Multipurpose human service organizations, Senior centers and services.

YOUTH DEVELOPMENT: Scouting organizations, Youth development programs.

Intended beneficiaries:
Aging/elderly/senior citizens, Blind/vision impaired, Children and youth (infants-19 years), Deaf/hearing impaired, General public/unspecified, Mentally/emotionally disabled, Physically disabled.

Types of support for organizations:
CAPITAL CAMPAIGNS: Building/renovation.
GENERAL PURPOSE/OPERATING SUPPORT: Annual campaigns.
PROGRAM DEVELOPMENT/PROJECT SUPPORT.

Sample grants:
American Red Cross - MN/MN/ $350,000.

Boy Scouts of America - MN (Indianhead - St Paul)/MN/$1,608,000.

Sharing & Caring Hands, Inc/MN/ $60,000.

St Paul Chamber Foundation/MN/ $450,000.

Financial Information

Financial data for year ending: 12/31/2005
Foundation assets: $711,986,497
Grants paid: $25,349,733
Number of grants: 196
Largest/smallest: $2,400,000/$2,000

Application Information

Preferred form of initial contact: letter of inquiry, request for guidelines.

Public information available by request: proposal guidelines.

Accept common grant application: yes.

Accept common report form: yes.

Proposal deadlines: March 18, July 22 and October 21. Must be received in the foundation's office, not postmarked, on or before the deadline date. If deadline falls on weekend, requests must be received the Friday before deadline.

Contribution decisions made by: board of directors/trustees.

Frequency of contributions decisions: 3 times a year.

Specific times board meets: May, September and December.

Staff/Trustees

Staff: M. F. Gillstrom, director/assistant secretary.

Directors/trustees: G. L. Benson, treasurer; D. L. Croft, director; M. F. Gillstrom, director/assistant secretary; G. O. Hoel, director; A. H. Johnson, vice president/secretary; J. D. Piepel, director; J. W. Wulf, president.

Hugh J. Andersen Foundation

White Pine Building
342 Fifth Avenue North
Bayport, MN 55003
County: Washington
Phone: (651) 439-1557
Fax: (651) 439-9480
E-mail: hjafdn@srinc.biz
Website: www.srinc.biz/hja
Contact: Bradley E. Kruse, program director
Established: 03/01/1962
Funder type: Private foundation

Program Description

Program's purpose: To give back to the foundation's community through focused efforts that foster inclusivity, promote equality, and lead to increased human independence, self-sufficiency and dignity.

Funding priorities: Human services; education, elementary/secondary in primary geographic area only; health and arts & humanities.

Program limitations/restrictions: No religious organizations for religious purposes, higher education, individuals.

Geographic focus: Twin Cities Metropolitan Area, Greater Minnesota, Areas outside Minnesota. The Foundation's primary geographic focus area is the St Croix Valley: Washington County in Minnesota and Pierce, Polk and St Croix Counties in Wisconsin.

Geographic limitations: Primary focus: St Croix Valley; Washington County in Minnesota; Pierce, Polk and St Croix counties in Wisconsin. Secondary focus: St Paul, Minnesota organizations serving St Croix Valley. No international funding or in states other than Minnesota and Wisconsin.

Areas of interest:

ANIMAL RELATED: Animal protection/welfare.

ARTS, CULTURE, HUMANITIES: Arts/cultural multipurpose, Humanities, Performing arts, Education and outreach; Artists and residencies.

COMMUNITY IMPROVEMENT: Community/neighborhood development/improvement, Nonprofit management.

EDUCATION: Adult/continuing education/literacy, Libraries/library science, Secondary, Elementary but not preschool.

EMPLOYMENT/JOBS: Employment procurement/job training.

ENVIRONMENTAL QUALITY/PROTECTION/BEAUTIFICATION: Environmental education for elementary/secondary students in St Croix Valley.

FOOD/NUTRITION/AGRICULTURE: Agricultural programs.

HEALTH - DISEASES/MEDICAL DISCIPLINES: AIDS/HIV, Breast cancer.

HEALTH - GENERAL/REHABILITATIVE: Health support services, Public health programs/wellness education, Reproductive health care.

HEALTH - MENTAL HEALTH/CRISIS INTERVENTION: Addiction disorders, Alcohol/drug/substance, prevention and treatment, Hotline/crisis intervention, Mental health associations, Mental health treatment and services.

HOUSING/SHELTER: Homeless, temporary housing, Housing development/construction/management, Housing support services, Affordable housing in St Croix Valley.

HUMAN SERVICES: Children/youth services, Emergency assistance (food/clothing/cash), Family services, Family services for adolescent parents, Family violence shelters and services, Multipurpose human service organizations, Personal social services, Senior centers and services, Victims services.

PHILANTHROPY/VOLUNTARISM: Nonprofit sector assistance, Philanthropy associations.

PUBLIC SAFETY/DISASTERS/RELIEF: Disaster preparedness and relief.

YOUTH DEVELOPMENT: Adult/child matching programs, Multipurpose youth centers/clubs, Scouting organizations, Youth development programs, Girl Scouts, YMCA camping, YWCA.

Intended beneficiaries: Adults, Aging/elderly/senior citizens, Children and youth (infants-19 years), Disabled - general or unspecified disability, Ethnic/racial populations - general, Females - all ages or age unspecified, Gay/lesbian/bisexual/transgender, Homeless, Immigrants/newcomers/refugees, Males - all ages or age unspecified, Mentally/emotionally disabled, People with HIV/AIDS, Physically disabled, Poor/economically disadvantaged, Youth/adolescents (ages 14-19).

Types of support for organizations:
CAPITAL CAMPAIGNS: Building/renovation, Equipment.
GENERAL PURPOSE/OPERATING SUPPORT: Annual campaigns.
PROGRAM DEVELOPMENT/PROJECT SUPPORT: Fundraising.

Types of support for individuals: none.

Exclusions: Individuals, Non-501(c)(3), Political organizations, Research, Scholarships/loans.

Sample grants:

Big Brothers/Big Sisters - MN (Greater Twin Cities)/MN/$6,000.

Girl Scout Council - MN (St Croix Valley)/MN/$43,000.

MN AIDS Project Inc/MN/Legal services program/$11,000.

Operation HELP - WI/WI/$8,500.

Southside Community Health Services - MN/MN/Support for the St Croix Valley Medical Center/$25,000.

St Croix Center for the Arts/Taylor Falls, MN/General operating support and ceramics studio improvements/$12,000.

St Croix Valley Community Foundation/WI/General operating support and Valley Arts Initiative/$30,000.

Store to Door/MN/General operating support and technology installation/$23,000.

Financial Information

Financial data for year ending: 02/28/2006
Foundation assets: $90,524,310
Grants paid: $3,689,480
Number of grants: 286
Largest/smallest: $250,000/$700
Largest multi-year grant approved: $35,000

Application Information

Preferred form of initial contact: letter of inquiry, telephone inquiry, request for guidelines, e-mail.

Public information available by request: proposal guidelines, application form, annual report, website, 990-PF.

Accept common report form: yes.

Proposal deadlines: March 15, June 15, August 15, November 15.

Contribution decisions made by: board of directors/trustees.

Frequency of contributions decisions: quarterly.

Specific times board meets: February, June, September, November.

Typical time from application deadlines to notification: 3 months.

Staff/Trustees

Staff: Bradley E. Kruse, program director.

Directors/trustees: Christine E. Andersen; Sarah J. Andersen, president; Lisa W. Copeland; William H. Rubenstein, secretary/treasurer; Stephen W. Wolfson, vice president.

The Antioch Company

2815 Clearwater Road
St Cloud, MN 56301
County: Stearns
Phone: (320) 526-5000
Website: www.antiochcompany.com
Contact: Andrea Lauer, charitable programs specialist
Paid Staff: Yes
Funder type: Corporate giving program

Program Description

Program's purpose: The Antioch Company is an organization that values people. It strives, in all of its endeavors, to be a good neighbor and contribute time, energy and resources to the communities in which we live and work.

Matching grants: employee matching.

Staff/Trustees

Staff: Andrea Lauer, charitable programs specialist.

Arsher Charitable Trust U/A

230 West Superior Street
Suite 400
Wells Fargo Trust
Duluth, MN 55801-0488
County: St Louis
Contact: Mark Danielson
Established: 10/05/1950
Funder type: Private foundation

Program Description

Program's purpose: General charitable purposes.

Geographic focus: Greater Minnesota.

Areas of interest:
HEALTH - DISEASES/MEDICAL DISCIPLINES: Cancer.
RELIGION/SPIRITUAL DEVELOPMENT.

Intended beneficiaries: Children and youth (infants-19 years), General public/unspecified.

Sample grants:

Boy Scouts of America - MN (Voyageurs Area)/MN/$10,000.

College of St Scholastica - Duluth/MN/$2,000.

Girl Scout Council - MN (Land of Lakes)/MN/$3,000.

Northwood Children's Home/Duluth, MN/$2,000.

Salvation Army - MN (Duluth)/MN/$10,000.

Sloan Kettering Cancer Center/New York, NY/$4,000.

Union Gospel Mission - MN (Duluth)/MN/$2,500.

Voyageurs Lutheran Ministry/MN/$1,000.

Financial Information

Financial data for year ending: 12/31/2005
Foundation assets: $5,602,841
Grants paid: $300,200
Number of grants: 24
Largest/smallest: $20,000/$1,000

Application Information

Preferred form of initial contact: request for guidelines.

Proposal deadlines: none.

Special application procedures: applications should be written requests only.

Staff/Trustees

Directors/trustees: Wells Fargo Bank; James E. Rhude.

Athwin Foundation

5200 Willson Road
Suite 307
Minneapolis, MN 55424-1332
County: Hennepin
Phone: (612) 379-3817
Fax: (952) 915-6148
E-mail: jstormcod1@aol.com
Website: www.catchcod.com/funding_athwin.php
Contact: Jim Storm, consultant
Established: 03/01/1956
Funder type: Private foundation

Program Description

Program's purpose: The Athwin Foundation, named for Atherton and Winifred Wollaeger Bean, seeks to provide support in the areas of human services, education, the arts and humanities, the natural environment, and organizational capacity building.

Funding priorities: Emphasis is placed on organizations that serve Minnesota or Western Montana or that have been important in the life of a family member.

Program limitations/restrictions: No grants to individuals. Only to applicants with 501(c)(3) status.

Geographic focus: Twin Cities Metropolitan Area, Minnesota statewide, Western Montana.

Geographic limitations: A small number of grants are made outside of of the target areas.

Areas of interest:

ANIMAL RELATED: Animal protection/welfare, Wildlife preservation/protection, Zoo/zoological societies.
ARTS, CULTURE, HUMANITIES: Arts services, Arts/cultural multipurpose, Historical societies, Humanities, Museums, Performing arts, Visual arts.
COMMUNITY IMPROVEMENT: Community coalitions, Community/neighborhood development/improvement, Nonprofit management.
EDUCATION.
EMPLOYMENT/JOBS.
ENVIRONMENTAL QUALITY/PROTECTION/BEAUTIFICATION.
HEALTH - MENTAL HEALTH/CRISIS INTERVENTION.
HOUSING/SHELTER.
HUMAN SERVICES: Children/youth services, Emergency assistance (food/clothing/cash), Family services, Family services for adolescent parents, Family violence shelters and services, Multipurpose human service organizations, Residential/custodial care, Victims services.
PHILANTHROPY/VOLUNTARISM: Nonprofit sector assistance.
RECREATION.
YOUTH DEVELOPMENT: Multipurpose youth centers/clubs, Youth development programs.

Intended beneficiaries: General public/unspecified.

Types of support for organizations:
CAPITAL CAMPAIGNS.
GENERAL PURPOSE/OPERATING SUPPORT.
PROGRAM DEVELOPMENT/PROJECT SUPPORT.

Types of support for individuals: none.

Exclusions: Individuals, Non-501(c)(3), Political organizations, Tax-supported institutions.

Sample grants:

American Composers Forum - St Paul/MN/$8,000.
Hartley Nature Center/MN/$7,000.
Kwanzaa Community Fellowship Presbyterian Church/Minneapolis, MN/$4,000.
Management Assistance Project/MN/$5,000.
Minneapolis College of Art & Design/MN/$17,000.
Northern Pines Mental Health Center/MN/$5,000.
Stevens Square Community Organization/MN/$1,000.

Financial Information

Financial data for year ending: 12/31/2005
Foundation assets: $10,213,515
Grants paid: $539,891
Number of grants: 90
Typical grant amount: $5,000

Application Information

Preferred form of initial contact: Review web page: www.catchcod.com/funding_athwin.php. Additional information via e-mail or telephone.

Public information available by request: proposal guidelines, application form, annual report, website. Guidelines for Letters of Inquiry at www.catchcod.com.

Accept common grant application: yes.

Proposal deadlines: All proposals due in office no later than date listed on invitation for proposal. If date falls on a weekend or holiday, materials are due the last working day prior to the weekend or holiday.

Preferred time for receiving proposals: Date for submission of invited proposals will be included in invitation for proposals.

Contribution decisions made by: board of directors/trustees.

Frequency of contributions decisions: Semiannual.

Specific times board meets: Twice per year.

Special application procedures: All requests require an initial Letter of Inquiry. See web page for dates and details.

Staff/Trustees

Staff: Candi Storm, grants administrator; Jim Storm, consultant.

Directors/trustees: Bruce W. Bean; Glen Atherton Bean; Mary F. Bean; Eleanor Nolan.

Bernard and Fern Badzin Foundation

2855 Eagandale Boulevard
St Paul, MN 55121-1202
County: Dakota
Phone: (651) 454-4100
Contact: Fern Badzin
Established: 12/01/1968
Funder type: Private foundation

Program Description

Geographic focus: West Metropolitan Area/Minneapolis only.

Areas of interest:
ARTS, CULTURE, HUMANITIES.
HUMAN SERVICES.
RELIGION/SPIRITUAL DEVELOPMENT.

Intended beneficiaries: General public/unspecified.

Sample grants:
Beth El Synagogue/MN/$29,535.
Minneapolis Institute of Arts/MN/$1,500.
Talmud Torah of Minneapolis/MN/$25,000.

Financial Information
Financial data for year ending: 12/31/2005
Foundation assets: $1,289,350
Grants paid: $82,034
Number of grants: 14
Largest/smallest: $25,000/$100

Application Information
Preferred form of initial contact: letter of inquiry, complete proposal. Letter should include name of organization, use of gift.
Proposal deadlines: none.

Staff/Trustees
Directors/trustees: Fern Badzin.

Bahl Foundation

PO Box 22094
St Paul, MN 55122
County: Ramsey
Phone: (952) 212-3204
Funder type: Private foundation

Program Description
Geographic focus: Twin Cities Metropolitan Area, Greater Minnesota, Areas outside Minnesota, National Areas, International Areas.
Areas of interest:
ARTS, CULTURE, HUMANITIES: Museums.
EDUCATION: Higher education.
YOUTH DEVELOPMENT.
Sample grants:
Metropolitan Museum of Art - NY/NY/$10,000.
MN Vikings Children's Fund Inc/MN/$1,000.
Rotary Club - MN/MN/Faribault Youth Service Strive scholarship program/$25,000.
University of California - Los Angeles Foundation/CA/$1,000.
Whitney Museum of American Art/NY/Support children's programming/$1,000.

Financial Information
Financial data for year ending: 10/31/2005
Foundation assets: $541,509
Grants paid: $68,300
Number of grants: 14
Largest/smallest: $25,000/$1,000

Application Information
Preferred form of initial contact: letter of inquiry.
Proposal deadlines: None.

Staff/Trustees
Staff: Penny Bailey, executive director.
Directors/trustees: Felicia V. Bahl; Tracy L. Bahl.

Marjorie and V.M. Baich Foundation

PO Box 198
Coleraine, MN 55722
County: Itasca
Phone: (218) 245-1484
Contact: Michael Baich, president/treasurer
Established: 01/01/1997
Funder type: Private foundation

Program Description
Program's purpose: Awards given for college/vocational education.
Funding priorities: Education.
Geographic focus: Greater Minnesota.
Geographic limitations: Residents and organizations within Itasca and southwest St Louis counties.
Areas of interest:
EDUCATION.
Intended beneficiaries: General public/unspecified, graduating high school students.
Types of support for organizations:
STUDENT AID (GRANTS TO INSTITUTIONS): Scholarship funds.
Types of support for individuals: scholarships.
Sample grants:
Bemidji State University/MN/scholarships/$2,000.
College of St Scholastica - Duluth/MN/scholarships/$4,000.
Hamline University/MN/scholarships/$5,000.
Hibbing Community College - MN/MN/scholarships/$1,000.
Itasca Community College/Grand Rapids, MN/scholarships/$13,000.
Lake Superior College/MN/scholarships/$2,000.
University of Minnesota - Minneapolis/MN/scholarships/$11,000.
Vermillion College/MN/scholarships/$2,000.

Financial Information
Financial data for year ending: 12/31/2005
Foundation assets: $710,707
Grants paid: $38,000
Number of grants: 17
Largest/smallest: $10,000/$1,000

Application Information
Preferred form of initial contact: letter of inquiry, request for guidelines.
Public information available by request: application form.
Proposal deadlines: applications received annually between February 1 and March 31.
Special application procedures: submit preprinted application with narrative.

Staff/Trustees
Directors/trustees: Gregory Baich; Michael Baich, president/treasurer; William Mager, secretary; Stephanie Smidt.

Gordon and Margaret Bailey Foundation

PO Box 25647
Woodbury, MN 55125
County: Washington
Phone: (651) 714-2992
Alt. Phone: (612) 978-8103
E-mail: gmbf@comcast.net
Contact: Joseph Bailey, president
Established: 06/20/1991
Donor: Gordon and Margaret Bailey
Funder type: Private foundation

Program Description

Funding priorities: 1) Healthcare w/ an emphasis on prevention of physical & mental disease. 2) K-12 education, public horticulture educational programs and scholarships for post secondary students in horticulture 3) Regional land preservation. 4) Programs that strengthen families (poverty, hospice, parent education).

Program limitations/restrictions: Programs sponsored by religious or civic organizations that address the foundation's priorities. Proposals for new ventures that address the foundation's priorities.

Geographic focus: Minnesota statewide, International Areas.

Geographic limitations: Local programs and programs that address global issues (where "local" is the Twin Cities of St Paul/Minneapolis).

Areas of interest:

ANIMAL RELATED: Zoo/zoological societies.
ARTS, CULTURE, HUMANITIES: Media/communications, Museums.
EDUCATION: Pre-school/elementary, Secondary, Horticulture education.
ENVIRONMENTAL QUALITY/PROTECTION/BEAUTIFICATION: Botanical/horticultural/landscape, Environmental beautification/open spaces, Natural resources conservation/protection.
FOOD/NUTRITION/AGRICULTURE: Food service/free food distribution.
HEALTH - MENTAL HEALTH/CRISIS INTERVENTION: Addiction disorders, Alcohol/drug/substance, prevention and treatment, Counseling/support groups, Mental health treatment and services, Prevention.
HOUSING/SHELTER: Homeless, temporary housing.
HUMAN SERVICES: Children/youth services, Emergency assistance (food/clothing/cash), Family services, Family violence shelters and services, Multipurpose human service organizations.

Intended beneficiaries: General public/unspecified.

Sample grants:

Dakota Communities/MN/Horticulture therapy program/$5,000.
Lincoln Elementary School - MN/MN/$1,000.
MN Landscape Arboretum/MN/$5,000.
Open Arms Orphanage/$5,000.
Second Harvest - MN (Heartland, St Paul)/MN/$10,000.
Twin Cities Public Television/St Paul, MN/Sponsorship/$10,000.

Financial Information

Financial data for year ending: 12/31/2006
Foundation assets: $4,500,000
Grants paid: $230,000
Number of grants: 50
Largest/smallest: $15,000/$500

Application Information

Preferred form of initial contact: letter of inquiry, complete proposal, using Minnesota Common Grant Application Form.
Public information available by request: proposal guidelines.
Accept common grant application: yes.
Accept common report form: yes.
Proposal deadlines: October 1.
Contribution decisions made by: board of directors/trustees.
Frequency of contributions decisions: annually.
Specific times board meets: November.
Typical time from application deadlines to notification: 2 months.

Staff/Trustees

Directors/trustees: Jerome Bailey; Joseph Bailey, president; Chris Bartch; Melissa Cullen; Lori Grant.

Baker Foundation

80 South Eighth Street
Suite 4900
Minneapolis, MN 55402
County: Hennepin
Phone: (612) 332-7479
Fax: (612) 332-2116
Contact: David C. Sherman, president
Established: 02/01/1954
Funder type: Private foundation

Program Description

Program limitations/restrictions: Subject to board discretion; concentrates on Minnesota organizations.

Geographic focus: Twin Cities Metropolitan Area.

Geographic limitations: Primarily Minneapolis/St Paul metropolitan area.

Areas of interest:

ARTS, CULTURE, HUMANITIES: Historical societies, Performing arts, Visual arts.
EDUCATION: Higher education.
ENVIRONMENTAL QUALITY/PROTECTION/BEAUTIFICATION: Environmental education/outdoor survival.
HEALTH - GENERAL/REHABILITATIVE: Hospitals and related primary medical care facilities.
HOUSING/SHELTER: Housing development/construction/management.
HUMAN SERVICES: Family services, Multipurpose human service organizations.
YOUTH DEVELOPMENT: Multipurpose youth centers/clubs, Scouting organizations.

Intended beneficiaries: General public/unspecified.

Types of support for organizations:
GENERAL PURPOSE/OPERATING SUPPORT: Annual campaigns.

Types of support for individuals: none.

Sample grants:

American Diabetes Association - MN (Minneapolis)/MN/general operating/$1,200.
Audubon Society - MN (Northwoods)/MN/general operating/$2,500.
Courage Center - MN (Golden Valley)/MN/general operating/$3,000.
Dale Warland Singers, The/MN/general operating/$2,000.

MN Orchestral Association/MN/general operating/$5,200.

Project for Pride in Living/MN/general operating/$3,000.

Ramsey County Historical Society/MN/general operating/$1,500.

Tubman Family Alliance - MN/MN/general operating/$2,000.

Financial Information

Financial data for year ending: 12/31/2005
Foundation assets: $4,638,602
Grants paid: $237,500
Number of grants: 75
Largest/smallest: $30,000/$100

Application Information

Preferred form of initial contact: complete proposal.

Accept common grant application: yes.

Proposal deadlines: none.

Contribution decisions made by: board of directors/trustees.

Frequency of contributions decisions: annually.

Staff/Trustees

Staff: David C. Sherman, president.

Directors/trustees: Doris Baker; Morris T. Baker; Mary Baker-Philbin; Laura Sherman Decker; Michael L. Decker; James W. Peter; Tobias R. Philbin; Charles C. Pineo III; Linda B. Pineo; David C. Sherman, president; Sandra B. Sherman, vice president & director; William J. Sherman.

Ann Bancroft Foundation

808 14th Avenue SE
Minneapolis, MN 55414
County: Hennepin
Phone: (612) 676-9410
Website: www.annbancroftfoundation.org
Contact: Anne Atwood
Paid Staff: Yes
Funder type: Community/public foundation

Program Description

Program's purpose: The Ann Bancroft Foundation supports girls and women to realize their highest dreams and potential. The foundation endeavors to live this mission by recognizing individual achievement and by promoting initiatives that inspire courage, risk-taking, integrity and individuality in girls and women.

Funding priorities: The foundation will: Provide mini-grants to girls age 10 through grade 10 to achieve a dream (grants paid to date: $210,000 to more than 570 girls); Provide inspiration and recognition to women and girls through awards; Shine a spotlight on outstanding programs; Encourage and support programs with girls' organizations; Form strategic partnerships with corporations to support programs implemented in other organizations; Be a convener in programs, special events and more.

Program limitations/restrictions: Dare to Dream Minigrants: Girls must be age 10 through grade 10 and have an adult mentor other than immediate family who will help guide her through the process. Grants go to the organization providing the activity, not individuals. We will not approve grants for activities already in progress or completed prior to written notification of approval by the foundation.

Geographic focus: Minnesota statewide.

Areas of interest:
PUBLIC AFFAIRS/SOCIETY BENEFIT: Leadership development/awards programs (other than youth), The Ann Bancroft Awards honor and encourage the achievements of girls and women. Each year we honor a girl and a woman for achievement and leadership, and an individual and an organization for support and encouragement. Each award winner receives $1,000.
YOUTH DEVELOPMENT: The Dare to Dream Minigrant Program provides small grants of $100 to $500 to girls age 10 through grade 10 who have a dream and need the financial and caring support of adults in order to achieve that dream.

Intended beneficiaries: Female adults, Female youth/adolescents (ages 10-16).

Sample grants:
Asian Media Access/MN/Support 4 girls and their project to help Hmong refugees/$2,000.

Cookie Cart/MN/Support girl's dream project/$500.

Wolf Ridge Environmental Learning Center/MN/Support 10 girls to attend/$2,000.

Financial Information

Financial data for year ending: 12/31/2005
Foundation assets: $112,187
Grants paid: $37,000

Application Information

Preferred form of initial contact: complete proposal, nomination form.

Public information available by request: application form, newsletter, website.

Proposal deadlines: Dare to Dream Minigrants: April 1 and November 15.

Contribution decisions made by: board of directors/trustees.

Frequency of contributions decisions: semiannually.

Typical time from application deadlines to notification: Dare to Dream Minigrants: 30 days.

Staff/Trustees

Staff: Anne Atwood.

Directors/trustees: Ann Bancroft, founder; Donna Biedron, secretary; Heather Faulkner; Carrie Gutierrez; Joan Higinbotham; Tami Jensen, treasurer; Sally Johnson, vice chair; Greg Lais; Jan Malcom; Marty Mumma, chair; Lisa Simer.

Baratz Family Foundation

2427 Presidential Way
Suite 903
West Palm Beach, FL 33401
Contact: Zollie Baratz, president
Established: 12/01/1976
Funder type: Private foundation

Program Description

Program's purpose: General charitable purposes.

Program limitations/restrictions: None.

Geographic focus: Twin Cities Metropolitan Area, Areas outside Minnesota.

Areas of interest:
ARTS, CULTURE, HUMANITIES.
COMMUNITY IMPROVEMENT.
EDUCATION.

HEALTH - DISEASES/MEDICAL DISCIPLINES: Cancer, Diabetes.

HEALTH - RESEARCH: Cancer research, Diabetes.

HUMAN SERVICES.

RELIGION/SPIRITUAL DEVELOPMENT.

YOUTH DEVELOPMENT.

Intended beneficiaries: General public/unspecified.

Sample grants:

Anti-Defamation League - NY/NY/$600.

Boys & Girls Club - MN (St Paul)/MN/$750.

Guthrie Theater, The/Minneapolis, MN/$100.

Jewish Community Action/MN/$700.

Jewish Federation - FL (Palm Beach)/FL/$15,471.

Juvenile Diabetes Foundation - MN/MN/$2,670.

Minneapolis Jewish Federation/MN/$104,918.

MN Teen Challenge/MN/$1,000.

Financial Information

Financial data for year ending: 12/31/2005
Foundation assets: $282,254
Grants paid: $207,838
Number of grants: 209
Largest/smallest: $40,000/$10
Typical grant amount: $250

Application Information

Preferred form of initial contact: letter of inquiry, request for guidelines, letter should set forth purpose of grant and amount needed.

Proposal deadlines: none.

Staff/Trustees

Directors/trustees: Stan Baratz, vice president; Zollie Baratz, president.

Beim Foundation

3109 West 50th Street
Suite 120
Minneapolis, MN 55410-2102
County: Hennepin
Phone: (612) 825-1401
E-mail: contact@beimfoundation.org
Website: www.beimfoundation.org
Contact: Carol Nulsen, president
Established: 02/14/1947
Funder type: Private foundation

Program Description

Program's purpose: The foundation supports proposals in human services, education, environment, the arts, and arts small capital & equipment grants for arts organizations with budgets of $300,000 or less. For further description within each funding area, see the website: www.beimfoundation.org.

Program limitations/restrictions: Only programs begun in the last 3 years will be considered for funding. General operating and capital requests for education, human services and environment will no longer be considered. At the spring meeting, ONLY Human Services and Education proposals will be considered. At the fall meeting, ONLY Arts, Arts Small Equipment & Capital, and Environment proposals will be considered.

Geographic focus: Twin Cities Metropolitan Area, Greater Minnesota, Minnesota statewide, Areas outside Minnesota.

Geographic limitations: Granting priority is given to organizations in the state of Minnesota; a limited number of proposals will be accepted from the county of Boulder, Colorado; Cumberland County, ME; Park & Gallatin Counties, MT; city of Seattle, WA.

Areas of interest:

ARTS, CULTURE, HUMANITIES: Arts services, Arts/cultural multipurpose, Humanities, Media/communications, Performing arts, Visual arts, small capital and equipment.

EDUCATION: Pre-school/elementary, Immigrants.

ENVIRONMENTAL QUALITY/PROTECTION/BEAUTIFICATION: Natural resources conservation/protection, Outdoor education.

HUMAN SERVICES: Children/youth services, Family services, Immigrants.

YOUTH DEVELOPMENT: Youth development programs.

Intended beneficiaries: General public/unspecified.

Types of support for individuals: none.

Exclusions: Individuals, Non-501(c)(3), Political organizations, Religious organizations, Private foundations, Memberships, Subscriptions, Tickets for events, Endowments, Multi-year commitments, International.

Sample grants:

Audubon Society - MN/MN/$10,000.

Fergus Falls Senior Citizens Program, Inc/MN/$1,500.

La Oportunidad, Inc./MN/$10,000.

Loft, The/MN/$4,000.

MN Environmental Partnership/MN/$10,000.

Northfield Union of Youth/MN/$1,000.

Resources for Child Caring/MN/$7,500.

Young Audiences - MN/MN/$9,500.

Financial Information

Financial data for year ending: 12/31/2006
Foundation assets: $13,543,000
Grants paid: $449,500
Number of grants: 66
Largest/smallest: $15,000/$1,000

Application Information

Preferred form of initial contact: complete proposal. No proposals will be accepted via e-mail.

Public information available by request: guidelines are on the website.

Accept common grant application: yes.

Proposal deadlines: Education & Human Services, Winter 2008. Arts (including small capital & equipment) & Environment, Summer 2008. See website for details.

Contribution decisions made by: board of directors/trustees.

Frequency of contributions decisions: semiannually.

Specific times board meets: Spring and fall.

Special application procedures: no more than one request per organization per calendar year.

Staff/Trustees

Staff: Kerrie Blevins, consultant; Mary Karen Lynn-Klimenko, consultant.

Directors/trustees: Patricia Arnold; Margo Conover, treasurer; Carol Nulsen, president; Julie Stephenson; Allison Villani.

The Bentson Foundation

3600 Minnesota Drive
Suite 700
Edina, MN 55435
County: Hennepin
Phone: (952) 844-2617
Contact: N. Lawrence Bentson, president
Established: 10/01/1956
Funder type: Private foundation

Program Description

Program's purpose: Provide for temporary or permanent relief and assistance for sick, needy, aged, disabled or distressed persons; to improve living conditions; to provide recreation for any or all classes; to further education and scientific research; to cooperate with and aid other corporations, societies or associations, organized and conducted for charitable, scientific, educational and cognate purposes, to the end of promoting the mental, moral, physical and social improvement of those who may be benefited thereby without discrimination as to age, sex, color or religious inclination; to foster and promote religious, charitable, scientific, literary or educational aims.

Geographic focus: Twin Cities Metropolitan Area, Areas outside Minnesota.

Areas of interest:
ANIMAL RELATED.
ARTS, CULTURE, HUMANITIES.
EDUCATION.
HEALTH - DISEASES/MEDICAL DISCIPLINES.
HEALTH - RESEARCH.
HUMAN SERVICES.
RECREATION.
RELIGION/SPIRITUAL DEVELOPMENT.

Intended beneficiaries: Disabled - general or unspecified disability, General public/unspecified, Poor/economically disadvantaged.

Sample grants:
Humane Society - DC/DC/$150.
Jewish Family & Children's Service - MN (Mpls)/MN/$250.
Minneapolis Institute of Arts/MN/$1,500.
MN Medical Foundation/MN/$5,000.
St Paul Chamber Orchestra/MN/$150.
St Paul Urban Tennis Program/MN/$500.
United Hospital Inc/MN/John Nasseff Heart Hospital/$60,000.
Variety Children's Association/MN/$5,240.

Financial Information

Financial data for year ending: 10/31/2006
Foundation assets: $1,338,143
Grants paid: $125,256
Number of grants: 72
Largest/smallest: $40,000/$10

Application Information

Preferred form of initial contact: letter of inquiry.
Proposal deadlines: none.

Staff/Trustees

Directors/trustees: N. Lawrence Bentson, president; Kimberly Kauth; Laurie Bentson Kauth; Mark S. Niblick, treasurer; George Reilly, secretary.

Lillian Wright and C. Emil Berglund Foundation, Inc.

Securian Trust Company
400 Robert Street North
St Paul, MN 55101-2098
County: Ramsey
Phone: (651) 665-4534
Fax: (651) 665-5414
Contact: Vicki M. Miller, grant administrator
Established: 11/01/1974
Funder type: Private foundation

Program Description

Program's purpose: Focus on children and youth in areas of health, education, leadership, culture, environment and recreation.

Funding priorities: Special attention will be given to requests in leadership, education, needs of handicapped children and children with special educational needs, and for special recreational and cultural opportunities.

Program limitations/restrictions: Grants not typically made for general operating expenses, capital fund drives or endowments. No grants to individual children or families.

Geographic focus: East Metropolitan Area/St Paul only.

Geographic limitations: Confines giving to the eastern half of the Twin Cities metropolitan area (Ramsey, Washington and Dakota counties).

Areas of interest:
ARTS, CULTURE, HUMANITIES: Arts services, Arts/cultural multipurpose, Historical societies, Museums, Performing arts, Visual arts.
EDUCATION: Educational services, Libraries/library science, Pre-school/elementary, Secondary, Student services/organizations of students, Vocational/technical.
ENVIRONMENTAL QUALITY/PROTECTION/BEAUTIFICATION: Botanical/horticultural/landscape, Environmental beautification/open spaces, Environmental education/outdoor survival.
HUMAN SERVICES: Children/youth services, Family services, Services to specific groups.
YOUTH DEVELOPMENT: Multipurpose youth centers/clubs, Youth development programs.

Intended beneficiaries: Children and youth (infants-19 years), Infants/children (ages 0-14), Youth/adolescents (ages 14-19).

Types of support for organizations:
PROGRAM DEVELOPMENT/PROJECT SUPPORT: Curriculum development, Mentoring programs, Performance/production costs, Leadership programs.

Types of support for individuals: none.

Sample grants:
Admission Possible/St Paul, MN/support cost of working with low-income students/$1,000.
COMPAS Inc - MN/MN/Lillian Wright Awards for Creative Writing/$1,600.
Frost Lake Magnet School/St Paul, MN/purchase of software and hardware/$500.

Hmong American Partnership - MN/ MN/ after-school program for youths age 5-8/ $1,000.

Public Library - St Paul/MN/program support/$1,500.

St Paul Chamber Orchestra/MN/general operating/$1,000.

Tree Trust - Twin Cities/MN/summer employment support/$1,000.

Twin Cities Public Television/St Paul, MN/support for Sesame Street programming/$1,000.

Financial Information

Financial data for year ending: 09/30/2005
Foundation assets: $1,391,907
Grants paid: $61,350
Number of grants: 27
Largest/smallest: $37,500/$100
Typical grant amount: $1,000

Application Information

Preferred form of initial contact: telephone inquiry, request for guidelines, e-mail.

Public information available by request: proposal guidelines.

Accept common grant application: yes.

Accept common report form: yes.

Proposal deadlines: March 15 for June grants; September 15 for December grants.

Contribution decisions made by: board of directors/trustees.

Frequency of contributions decisions: semiannually.

Typical time from application deadlines to notification: 6-8 weeks.

Staff/Trustees

Staff: Vicki M. Miller, grant administrator.

Directors/trustees: Mo Chang; Gregory Dewitt; Alice Hausman; Harold Kurtz, president; Paula Mielke; Vicki M. Miller, grant administrator; Jan Stafford; Sally A. Thompson.

Best Buy Children's Foundation

PO Box 9448
Minneapolis, MN 55440-9448
County: Hennepin
Phone: (612) 291-6108
Fax: (612) 292-4001
E-mail: communityrelations@bestbuy.com
Website: www.bestbuy.com/communityrelations
Established: 05/25/1994
Funder type: Corporate foundation

Program Description

Program's purpose: The Best Buy Children's Foundation supports nonprofit programs and organizations that make learning fun by combining kids, technology and learning.

Funding priorities: The foundation focuses on programs that develop and deliver innovative, interactive, technology-based programs for K-12 students in traditional and nontraditional learning environments. Best Buy Children's Foundation supports programs that reach national audiences and Twin Cities audiences.

Program limitations/restrictions: No fraternal organizations or social clubs; units of government or quasi-governmental agencies; labor organizations or political campaigns; organizations designed primarily for lobbying; for-profit organizations and travel programs; health, therapeutic or residential programs including camps; fundraising dinners, testimonials or other similar events; organizations for advertising purposes; individual requests for aid; religious organizations for religious purposes; third-party fundraising organizations; local affiliates of national organizations funded by BBCF.

Geographic focus: Twin Cities Metropolitan Area, Areas outside Minnesota, National Areas.

Geographic limitations: National programs must be accessible throughout the country; Twin Cities funding is available to qualifying organizations in the seven-county metro area.

Areas of interest:
EDUCATION: Elementary, Secondary, Programs that combine kids, technology and learning.
HUMAN SERVICES: Children/youth services, Emergency assistance (food/clothing/cash), Multipurpose human service organizations. We support United Way and the American Red Cross Disaster Relief.
PHILANTHROPY/VOLUNTARISM: TagTeam Awards are provided to organizations where employees volunteer for a minimum number of hours.
PUBLIC SAFETY/DISASTERS/RELIEF: Disaster preparedness and relief, American Red Cross.
SCIENCE/TECHNOLOGY: Programs that combine kids, technology and learning.
YOUTH DEVELOPMENT: Multipurpose youth centers/clubs, Youth development programs, Programs that combine kids, technology and learning.

Intended beneficiaries: Children in grades K-12 (generally ages 5-18).

Types of support for organizations:
PROGRAM DEVELOPMENT/PROJECT SUPPORT: Curriculum development.
STUDENT AID (GRANTS TO INSTITUTIONS): Scholarship funds.

Types of support for individuals: none.

Exclusions: Individuals, Non-501(c)(3), Political organizations, Religious organizations, Research, Tax-supported institutions, Health, therapeutic or residential programs, Fundraising dinners or other similar events.

Sample grants:
Ball State University/IN/Electronic field trips/$500,000.
Junior Achievement - MN (Upper Midwest, Maplewood)/MN/$25,000.
National Park Foundation - VA/VA/WebRangers/$250,000.
Sabathani Community Center Inc/MN/Horizons program/$15,000.
Toys For Tots Foundation, Marine - CA/CA/Toys for Teens/$250,000.
Youth Performance Company/MN/$12,000.

Financial Information

Financial data for year ending: 02/28/2007
Grants paid: $11,100,000
Number of grants: 791
Largest/smallest: $2,900,000/$350

Application Information

Preferred form of initial contact: Use website for guidelines.

Public information available by request: proposal guidelines, application form, website.

Proposal deadlines: Information is available at www.bestbuy.com/communityrelations. Twin Cities Fund applications need to be postmarked by February 1, May 1, August 1, November 1. Deadline for capital requests is February 1. Te@ch award deadline is September 30.

Contribution decisions made by: staff, board of directors/trustees, employee advisory committee.

Frequency of contributions decisions: quarterly.

Typical time from application deadlines to notification: approximately four months after the deadline.

Special application procedures: See website for general Best Buy Children's Foundation grant application and procedures.

Staff/Trustees

Staff: Jessica Haider, sr. community relations specialist; Stacy Hanley, sr. mgr community relations; Kris Kosek, sr. community relations specialist; Tola Oyewole, sr. community relations specialist; Jeffrey Peterson, director of community relations; Paula Prahl, VP public affairs; Rita Williams, community relations program lead.

Directors/trustees: Brad H. Anderson; Ruby K. Anik; David Berg, secretary; Marc Gordon, treasurer; Susan S. Hoff, president; Richard M. Schulze; Shawn Score; John R. Thompson.

The Beverly Foundation

5354 Parkdale Drive
Suite 310
St Louis Park, MN 55416-1603
County: Hennepin
Phone: (952) 545-3000
Contact: Beverly Deikel, president/treasurer
Established: 01/01/1999
Paid Staff: Yes
Funder type: Private foundation

Program Description

Program's purpose: The primary purpose of the organization is to administer funds for the purpose of providing monies to further charitable, religious, scientific or educational purposes to organizations that are exempt under Section 501(c)(3) of the Internal Revenue Code.

Geographic focus: Minnesota statewide, Areas outside Minnesota.

Areas of interest:
HUMAN SERVICES.

Intended beneficiaries: General public/unspecified, Poor/economically disadvantaged.

Types of support for organizations:
CAPITAL CAMPAIGNS.
GENERAL PURPOSE/OPERATING SUPPORT.
PROGRAM DEVELOPMENT/PROJECT SUPPORT.

Exclusions: Individuals, Non-501(c)(3), Political organizations, Scholarships/loans.

Sample grants:
Emergency Food Shelf Network/MN/$30,000.
I Love a Parade/MN/$7,500.
Israel Project - DC/DC/$100,000.
MN AIDS Project Inc/MN/$5,000.
People Serving People, Inc/MN/$5,000.
Pillsbury United Communities/MN/Elijah's Cup/$25,000.
Women's Candidate Development Coalition/MN/$1,500.

Financial Information

Financial data for year ending: 12/31/2006
Foundation assets: $32,000,000
Grants paid: $1,381,070
Largest/smallest: $250,000/$70

Application Information

Preferred form of initial contact: complete application.

Accept common grant application: yes.

Accept common report form: yes.

Proposal deadlines: none.

Contribution decisions made by: board of directors/trustees.

Special application procedures: Application must include most recent audit (or 990 if audits are not performed), actual income and expense statement for the current year, income and expense statement for the most recently completed fiscal year if the audit for that year is not available, current year's organizational budget showing projected income and expenses, and, if the application is for other than general operating, program/project budget showing projected income and expenses.

Staff/Trustees

Staff: Donna Sherlock, consultant.

Directors/trustees: Beverly Deikel, president/treasurer; Ronald Fingerhut, secretary.

F.R. Bigelow Foundation

55 East Fifth Street
Suite 600
St Paul, MN 55101-1797
County: Ramsey
Phone: (651) 224-5463
Fax: (651) 224-8123
E-mail: inbox@frbigelow.org
Website: www.frbigelow.org
Established: 01/01/1947
Funder type: Private foundation

Program Description

Program's purpose: The F.R. Bigelow Foundation was created in 1946 by Frederick Russell Bigelow, the fourth president of the St Paul Fire and Marine Co., in response to what he considered his family's civic responsibility to support charitable causes. It was established to promote the well-being of mankind and to support the civic, educational, religious and other needs of the community. It has helped shape and fund special projects that are strengthening neighborhoods in downtown St Paul, improving educational opportunities for youth and adults, and enhancing the quality of life in the St Paul area.

Funding priorities: The primary areas of interest are education, human services, humanities, the arts and community development. The foundation will consider grant applications from nonprofit corporations and public entities for capital projects, program expansion, or special projects of a time-limited nature; start-up costs for promising new programs that demonstrate sound management and clear goals relevant to community needs; support for established agencies that have temporary or transitional needs; funds to match contributions received from other sources or to provide a challenge to help raise new contributions.

Program limitations/restrictions: The foundation will not consider grant applications for annual operating expenses, sectarian religious programs, grants to individuals, or medical research.

Geographic focus: East Metropolitan Area/St Paul only, Dakota, Ramsey and Washington counties.

Geographic limitations: The primary geographic focus for grantmaking is the Greater St Paul metropolitan area, which includes Dakota, Ramsey and Washington counties, with a particular emphasis on serving people who live or work in the City of Saint Paul.

Areas of interest:
ARTS, CULTURE, HUMANITIES.
COMMUNITY IMPROVEMENT: Community/neighborhood development/improvement, Economic development.
EDUCATION.
HUMAN SERVICES.

Intended beneficiaries: General public/unspecified, General public/at-risk populations.

Types of support for organizations:
CAPITAL CAMPAIGNS.
PROGRAM DEVELOPMENT/PROJECT SUPPORT.

Types of support for individuals: none.

Exclusions: Individuals, Non-501(c)(3), Political organizations, Research, Scholarships/loans, 509(a)(3) Type III non-functionally integrated organizations.

Sample grants:

Amicus Inc/Minneapolis, MN/To help finance the budget of the Ramsey County Girls on Probation Program/$15,000.

City of St Paul - MN/MN/To help finance the budget for planning consultants and community engagement staff needed for the design and implementation of the Central Corridor Development Framework/$250,000.

Greater Frogtown Community Development Corporation/MN/To help finance the budget for organizing and coordinating the Dale Street Corridor Plan/$30,000.

Hmong American Partnership - MN/MN/To help finance the budget of the Hmong Refugee Language Program/$30,000.

Inver Hills Community College Foundation/MN/To help finance the budget of Project Breakthrough/$105,000.

MN Association for Children's Mental Health - St Paul/MN/To help finance the budget of the Parent-to-Parent Program for Cultural Communities in St Paul/$25,000.

Penumbra Theatre Company/MN/To help finance the budget of the Four-Year Restructuring Project/$50,000.

People Incorporated/MN/To help finance the budget of the integrated clinical charting and billing software system/$77,000.

Financial Information

Financial data for year ending: 12/31/2006
Foundation assets: $167,150,291
Grants paid: $6,140,534
Number of grants: 118
Largest/smallest: $750,000/$3,000

Application Information

Preferred form of initial contact: request for guidelines.

Public information available by request: proposal guidelines, application form, annual report, website.

Proposal deadlines: no specific deadline dates.

Preferred time for receiving proposals: 3 1/2 months prior to meeting dates in April, August and November.

Contribution decisions made by: board of directors/trustees.

Specific times board meets: April, August, November.

Typical time from application deadlines to notification: 4-5 months.

Staff/Trustees

Staff: John G. Couchman, assistant secretary; Jack H. Pohl, assistant treasurer; Carleen K. Rhodes, secretary.

Directors/trustees: James H. Bradshaw; Carolyn J. Brusseau, chair; Dr. Richard B. Heydinger; Terry D. Hoffman; Peter F. Jackson; Louise G. Jones; Judith Kishel; Constance B. Kunin, treasurer; Bert J. McKasy; Sally D. Patterson; Edward G. Pendergast, vice chair; John M. Scanlan.

Blandin Foundation

100 Pokegama Avenue North
Grand Rapids, MN 55744-3819
County: Itasca
Phone: (218) 326-0523
E-mail: bfinfo@blandinfoundation.org
Website: www.blandinfoundation.org
Established: 01/01/1941
Funder type: Private foundation

Program Description

Program's purpose: The mission of the Blandin Foundation is to strengthen rural communities in Minnesota. The foundation is based in Grand Rapids and is committed to the health and economic viability of its home area. Established in 1941 in Grand Rapids by pioneering newspaperman Charles K. Blandin, the foundation has a deep commitment in rural towns and cities of the state. While the foundation was once linked to the Blandin Paper Company, today the foundation is wholly distinct and independent. The Paper Company is owned by UPM Kymmene, based in Finland. The foundation has three district roles: provide leadership development programs designed to work with community leaders to create a better economy for the future; convene and develop initiatives to improve public policies affecting rural economic viability; and provide grants to strengthen the health of rural Minnesota communities.

Funding priorities: Since 1992, the Blandin Foundation's mission has been to strengthen rural communities in Minnesota. Today, the foundation remains firmly committed to working with rural communities across the state and in our home area of Grand Rapids/Itasca County. This commitment is imperative, given the growing challenges facing rural communities. The foundation focuses its grant making on supporting an asset-based approach that embraces economic opportunity, support educational attainment of rural Minnesotans who may not have had the same advantages as others, stimulate and promote fairness and opportunity, and priority for leadership development initiatives, support for rural residents to be their own voice through avenues to express rural perspectives in local and statewide policy issues and to promote greater inter-cultural competencies.

Program limitations/restrictions: No grants outside the state of Minnesota. No grants for religious activities, medical research, publications, films or videos, travel grants for individuals or groups, camping programs, ordinary governmental services, grants to individuals (except for the Grand Rapids/Itasca County area Educational Awards Program) or grants to influence legislation. Eligibility for a Blandin Foundation grant is restricted to nonprofit organizations that have a 501(c)(3) tax-exempt status from the Internal Revenue Service and are located in Minnesota. Units of government may apply for a grant, but only if the purpose of the grant goes beyond the usual, expected government services.

Geographic focus: Greater Minnesota.

Geographic limitations: The Blandin Foundation does not provide grants for organizations or programs that will impact the metropolitan areas of Minneapolis, St Paul, St Cloud, Duluth, Rochester or Moorhead.

Areas of interest:
ARTS, CULTURE, HUMANITIES: Provide annual support to Grand Rapids-area arts organizations, Strengthen intercultural competencies to generate positive interactions that bridge cultural differences.
COMMUNITY IMPROVEMENT: Support community and regional economic initiatives that capital on diverse assets.
EDUCATION: Operate a scholarship program for Itasca County high school graduates to attend college after high school, Provide grants to organizations to increase educational attainment for disadvantaged populations.
EMPLOYMENT/JOBS: Adult scholarship program for residents of Itasca County.
HUMAN SERVICES: Strive for fairness and opportunity in the Grand Rapids area through social justice and philanthropy.
PUBLIC AFFAIRS/SOCIETY BENEFIT: Public policy research and analysis.
YOUTH DEVELOPMENT: Youth development programs in the Grand Rapids area.

Intended beneficiaries: General public/unspecified.

Types of support for individuals: scholarships.

Sample grants:

African Development Center/MN/Support to transfer culturally competent business development and financial literacy practices to partners in rural Minnesota/$165,000.

Bridges Kinship Mentoring/MN/Support to provide mentoring opportunities for young people in the Itasca County area/$40,000.

Grand Rapids Area Community Foundation - MN/MN/For the Itasca County Sharing Fund, a crisis, emergency funding program/$100,000.

Itasca Development Corporation/MN/To promote economic development in the Itasca County area/$465,000.

MN Public Radio/MN/To provide news coverage to residents throughout rural Minnesota/$650,000.

Ready 4 K/StPaul, MN/To work with communities and individuals throughout the state to improve school readiness/$150,000.

Financial Information

Financial data for year ending: 12/31/2006
Foundation assets: $464,296,136
Grants paid: $13,026,423
Number of grants: 347
Largest/smallest: $2,150,000/$100
Matching gifts: $74,363
Largest multi-year grant approved: $465,000

Application Information

Preferred form of initial contact: letter of inquiry, online inquiries.

Public information available by request: application form, website, accept proposals online.

Accept common grant application: yes.

Proposal deadlines: March 15, September 15, December 15.

Contribution decisions made by: board of directors/trustees. Grants of $50,000 and under are reviewed by staff and ratified by the board of trustees.

Specific times board meets: March, June, December (planning retreat in September).

Typical time from application deadlines to notification: 3-4 months; less time for grant approvals of $50,000 and under.

Staff/Trustees

Staff: Janet Borth, director of human resources/board services; Terri Dufner, IT administrative assistant/receptionist; Wade Fauth, director of grants; Linda Gibeau, program officer; James Hoolihan, president & CEO; Bernadine Joselyn, director of public policy & engagement; Jim Krile, director of leadership; Becky LaPlant, program assistant; Melissa Ross, receptionist; Trisha Zimmerman, program assistant, leadership programs.

Directors/trustees: Marian Barcus; M. James Bensen; Timothy Bonner M.D.; Karen Diver; Kris Ferraro; Mike Johnson, vice-chair; Kenneth Lundgren; Brian R. Nicklason; Eugene Radecki, secretary; Bruce Stender; George Thompson, chair.

Blue Cross and Blue Shield of Minnesota Foundation/Blue Cross and Blue Shield of Minnesota

3535 Blue Cross Road
Route 459
Eagan, MN 55122-1154
County: Dakota
Phone: (651) 662-3950
Alt. Phone: (866) 812-1593
Fax: (651) 662-1361
E-mail: foundation@bluecrossmn.com
Website: www.bluecrossmn.com/foundation
Established: 03/25/1986
Funder type: Corporate foundation and corporate giving program

Program Description

Program's purpose: Looking beyond health care today for ideas that create healthier communities tomorrow.

Funding priorities: The Blue Cross Foundation has a new focus on key factors that determine health: early childhood development, housing, social connectedness and the environment. Our first grantmaking program under this new focus is Healthy Together, which aims to reduce health disparities for immigrants and improve the health of the entire community. Initial emphasis will be on the social adjustment and mental health of recent Hmong immigrants. A second grantmaking program, Growing Up

Healthy: Kids and Communities was launched in 2006 and is designed to work at the intersection of children's health and two or more of the following health determinants: early childhood development; stable, affordable housing; and the physical environment. Special emphasis is directed toward programs designed to address the needs of children of color and children living in poverty; and originate from and work with Native American communities.

Program limitations/restrictions: We generally do not make loans or provide grants for individuals; lobbying, political or fraternal activities; sports events or athletic groups; religious purposes; clinical quality improvement; biomedical research; capital purposes (building, purchasing, remodeling or furnishing of facilities); equipment or travel, except as related to requests for program support; retiring debt or covering deficits; payment of services or benefits reimbursable from other sources; supplanting funds already secured for budgeted staff and/or services; long-term financial support.

Geographic focus: Minnesota statewide.

Geographic limitations: We typically do not provide funding for programs outside of Minnesota.

Areas of interest:

CIVIL RIGHTS: Intergroup relations/race relations.

COMMUNITY IMPROVEMENT: Community/neighborhood development/improvement, Nonprofit management.

EDUCATION: Early childhood.

ENVIRONMENTAL QUALITY/PROTECTION/BEAUTIFICATION: Pollution abatement and control.

HEALTH - GENERAL/REHABILITATIVE: Public health programs/wellness education, Related to our priority areas: Healthy Together, a program aimed at reducing health disparities for immigrants and improving the health of the entire community, and Growing Up Healthy: Kids and Communities, designed to strengthen the capacity of communities to work across sectors to create an environment that nurtures the healthy growth and development of children.

HEALTH - MENTAL HEALTH/CRISIS INTERVENTION: Related to our priority areas: Healthy Together, a program aimed at reducing health disparities for immigrants and improving the health of the entire community, and Growing Up Healthy: Kids and Communities, designed to strengthen the capacity of communities to work across sectors to create an environment that nurtures the healthy growth and development of children.

HEALTH - RESEARCH: Related to our priority areas: Healthy Together, a program aimed at reducing health disparities for immigrants and improving the health of the entire community, and Growing Up Healthy: Kids and Communities, designed to strengthen the capacity of communities to work across sectors to create an environment that nurtures the healthy growth and development of children.

HOUSING/SHELTER.

HUMAN SERVICES: Children/youth services, Family services, Family services for adolescent parents, Multipurpose human service organizations, Services to specific groups, Related to our priority areas: Healthy Together, a program aimed at reducing health disparities for immigrants and improving the health of the entire community, and Growing Up Healthy: Kids and Communities, designed to strengthen the capacity of communities to work across sectors to create an environment that nurtures the healthy growth and development of children.

PUBLIC AFFAIRS/SOCIETY BENEFIT: Citizen participation, Leadership development/awards programs (other than youth), Public policy research and analysis.

Intended beneficiaries: General public/unspecified.

Types of support for organizations: PROGRAM DEVELOPMENT/PROJECT SUPPORT. RESEARCH.

Types of support for individuals: none.

Dollars for Doers: yes.

Exclusions: Capital & endowment campaigns, Individuals, Political organizations, Scholarships/loans.

Sample grants:

Heartland Community Action Agency Inc/MN/Further the work of the Willmar Area Multicultural Market's diverse task force on health outreach and social connection to reduce isolation, increase economic development and foster cultural exchanges/$50,000.

Korean Service Center/MN/Establish a culturally competent assisted living program for Somali elders in public housing in Minneapolis' Cedar-Riverside community/$50,000.

Little Earth Residents Association/MN/To improve access to early childhood development programs for American Indian children in the Little Earth Housing Community in South Minneapolis/$25,000.

National Center for Healthy Housing/DC/To demonstrate how green building principles and tenant education will improve health status for residents of a renovated apartment complex in Worthington, Minnesota/$150,000.

National Conference of State Legislatures/Washington, DC/Roundtable discussions for state policymakers and Minnesota's refugee and immigrant community leaders to inform policymaking and promote greater civic engagement for effective immigrant integration and better health/$50,000.

Riverview Place - MN (Pelican Rapids)/MN/Support for the Giving + Learning mentoring program, which matches new immigrants with retiree mentors who focus on English language skills to prepare new immigrants for jobs/$35,000.

University of MN - Regional Sustainable Development Partnership/MN/To reduce exposure to household pesticides for children and pregnant women in Minnesota's Red River Valley/$25,000.

Financial Information

Financial data for year ending: 12/31/2006
Foundation assets: $53,421,529
Grants paid: $1,382,300
Number of grants: 57
Largest/smallest: $82,000/$1,000

Application Information

Preferred form of initial contact: letter of inquiry, telephone inquiry, request for guidelines.

Public information available by request: proposal guidelines, application form, website.

Proposal deadlines: Please visit website. Deadlines not yet determined for 2008.

Contribution decisions made by: board of directors/trustees.

Frequency of contributions decisions: quarterly.

Typical time from application deadlines to notification: 5-6 months.

Special application procedures: Applicants will be given a proposal due date at the time that a full proposal is invited. Please check website for more information.

Staff/Trustees

Staff: Jocelyn Ancheta, program officer; Joan Cleary, vice president, foundation and community leadership; Carol M. Guse, corporate campaign project manager; Janet Jablonske, foundation coordinator; Julie Lee, program communications consultant; Thomas J. Lee, principal community affairs consultant; Regina Prather, administrative assistant; Terri S. Schultz, community affairs coordinator; Marsha Shotley, president; Lisa Simer, program officer; Monika Strom, media contact.

Directors/trustees: Kathleen Annette M.D.; Mark W. Banks M.D.; Karen Bohn; William Collins Jr.; Luz Maria Frias; Kathy Gaalswyk; Deborah B. Madson; Kathleen Mock; Nancy Nelson; Timothy M. Peterson; Steven Richards M.D.; Marsha Shotley, president; MaryAnn Stump R.N.

The Boss Foundation

5858 Centerville Road
St Paul, MN 55127-6804
County: Ramsey
Phone: (651) 653-0599
Fax: (651) 653-0989
E-mail: dwm@specialtymfg.com
Contact: Daniel W. McKeown, treasurer
Established: 01/01/1956
Funder type: Private foundation

Program Description

Program's purpose: To support qualified 501(c)(3) organizations furthering or engaged in the performing and fine arts.

Funding priorities: Generally support programs first, and operating second.

Program limitations/restrictions: Contributions to 501(c)(3) tax-exempt organizations only.

Geographic focus: Twin Cities Metropolitan Area.

Areas of interest:
ARTS, CULTURE, HUMANITIES: Arts/cultural multipurpose, Historical societies, Humanities, Media/communications, Museums, Performing arts, Visual arts.
COMMUNITY IMPROVEMENT: Community/neighborhood development/improvement.
EDUCATION: Libraries/library science.
HEALTH - MENTAL HEALTH/CRISIS INTERVENTION: Alcohol/drug/substance, prevention and treatment.

Intended beneficiaries: General public/unspecified.

Types of support for organizations:
CAPITAL CAMPAIGNS.
GENERAL PURPOSE/OPERATING SUPPORT: Annual campaigns.
PROGRAM DEVELOPMENT/PROJECT SUPPORT.

Sample grants:

Actors Theatre of MN/MN/general operating/$1,000.

Children's Home Society - MN/MN/annual appeal - child abuse/$5,000.

MN Dance Theatre and School, Inc/MN/annual fund/$2,000.

MN Youth Symphonies/MN/string studio fiscal year 2004/$2,500.

MN Zoo Foundation/MN/annual fund/$1,500.

People Inc - St Paul/MN/9th annual Artability exhibit/$5,000.

Textile Center of MN - St Paul/MN/capital campaign/$5,000.

Twin Cities Gay Men's Chorus/MN/general operating/$2,000.

Financial Information

Financial data for year ending: 06/30/2006
Foundation assets: $5,344,814
Grants paid: $300,500
Number of grants: 60
Largest/smallest: $40,000/$1,000

Application Information

Preferred form of initial contact: complete proposal.

Public information available by request: proposal guidelines, annual report.

Accept common grant application: yes.

Proposal deadlines: June 1.

Preferred time for receiving proposals: proposals received by June 1 will receive priority consideration.

Contribution decisions made by: board of directors/trustees.

Frequency of contributions decisions: annually.

Specific times board meets: June.

Special application procedures: proposal should consist of five pages and include one-page letter stating dollar amount of request, purpose for which the funds will be used and any special time constraints on the receipt of the contribution; evidence of 501(c)(3) status; and up to three pages of any supporting documentation you wish to include.

Staff/Trustees

Directors/trustees: W. Andrew Boss, chair; Daniel W. McKeown, treasurer; Heidi S. McKeown, secretary.

Boston Scientific Foundation - Cardiovascular

One Scimed Place
Maple Grove, MN 55311
County: Hennepin
Phone: (763) 494-1700
Alt. Phone: (763) 494-2127
Fax: (763) 494-2290
Website: www.bostonscientific.com
Established: 01/01/1971
Funder type: Corporate foundation and corporate giving program

Program Description

Program's purpose: The Boston Scientific Foundation supports organizations that focus on innovative and community-driven education and preventative health programs. As a manufacturer of minimally invasive medical devices, Boston Scientific values programs that emphasize meeting the unmet or undermet health and education needs of the community. In Minnesota, math, science and technology are the focus areas of educational grants. We look to support organizations that are addressing these issues and are able to document impact. From classrooms to field work to community health, the Boston Scientific Foundation's purpose is to help make a positive difference through organizations that are providing health or education opportunities for the underprivileged.

Funding priorities: The company has funding criteria that includes tax-exempt 501(c)(3) status, efforts that target communities with unmet needs, support of innovative or experimental approaches, refinement or improvement of existing approaches, cost-effective and results-orientated programs where our contributions can make a long-term measurable difference in the quality of people's lives, and community-based approaches that work to empower those who are involved.

Financial Information

Financial data for year ending: 12/31/2006
Grants paid: $400,000

Application Information

Preferred form of initial contact: request for guidelines.

Public information available by request: proposal guidelines, annual report, website.

Proposal deadlines: Proposals are generally reviewed quarterly and are accepted at any time throughout the year.

Contribution decisions made by: Foundation board from recommendations by employee committee.

Staff/Trustees

Staff: Karen Patton, senior specialist, employee communications.

W. Glen Boyd Charitable Foundation

PO Box 8128
Portland, OR 97207-8128
E-mail: WGBCF@ureach.com
Website: www.wgbcf.org
Funder type: Private foundation

Program Description

Program's purpose: The W. Glen Boyd Charitable Foundation (WGBCF) is a private, grantmaking foundation committed to significantly improving the lives of women and children, especially those living in poverty, violence or at-risk situations.

Funding priorities: WGBCF disperses grants to grassroots and other 501(c)(3) organizations that are committed to empowering women and children through direct service or a blend of direct service and progressive social/systems change.

Program limitations/restrictions: WGBCF is not currently accepting applications related to environmental issues. However, proposals may be considered if they can show a clear and legitimate link between addressing critical needs for women and/or children through involvement with the environment. Also, WGBCF does not fund individuals, research, fiscal agents, groups without 501(c)(3) status, chemical dependency, health care, political/capital/religious campaigns or multi-year grants.

Geographic focus: Minnesota statewide, Areas outside Minnesota, Oregon.

Geographic limitations: Minnesota, Oregon.

Areas of interest:

COMMUNITY IMPROVEMENT: Economic development.

EDUCATION: Adult/continuing education/literacy, Educational services, Graduate education/professional schools, Higher education, Pre-school/elementary, Secondary, Student services/organizations of students, Vocational/technical, Mentorships/leadership.

EMPLOYMENT/JOBS: Employment procurement/job training, Vocational rehabilitation, Women or youth only, Culturally specific programs.

HEALTH - MENTAL HEALTH/CRISIS INTERVENTION: Addiction disorders, Counseling/support groups, Hotline/crisis intervention.

HUMAN SERVICES: Children/youth services, Emergency assistance (food/clothing/cash), Family services, Family services for adolescent parents, Family violence shelters and services, Multipurpose human service organizations, Personal social services, Services to specific groups, Victims services, Women & Children; culturally specific programs.

PUBLIC AFFAIRS/SOCIETY BENEFIT: Leadership development/awards programs (other than youth), Women's and children's issues.

PUBLIC PROTECTION - CRIME/COURTS/LEGAL SERVICES: Legal services, Protection/prevention - neglect/abuse/exploitation.

RECREATION: Summer youth leadership camps, Culturally specific programs.

YOUTH DEVELOPMENT: Adult/child matching programs, Multipurpose youth centers/clubs, Scouting organizations, Youth development programs, Culturally specific programs.

Intended beneficiaries: African Americans/Blacks, Asian/Pacific Islanders, Blind/vision impaired, Children and youth (infants-19 years), Crime/abuse victims, Deaf/hearing impaired, Disabled - general or unspecified disability, Ethnic/racial minorities - other specified group(s), Ethnic/racial populations - general, Female adults, Female aging/elderly/senior citizens, Female children and youth (infants-19 years), Females - all ages or age unspecified, Gay/lesbian/bisexual/transgender, General public/unspecified, Hispanics/Latinos, Homeless, Immigrants/newcomers/refugees, Male children and youth (infants 0-19 years), Migrant workers, Native American/American Indians, Other minorities, People with HIV/AIDS, Physically disabled, Poor/economically disadvantaged, Single parents, Youth/adolescents (ages 14-19).

Types of support for organizations:

GENERAL PURPOSE/OPERATING SUPPORT.

PROGRAM DEVELOPMENT/PROJECT SUPPORT: Mentoring programs, Seed money/start-up funds.

STUDENT AID (GRANTS TO INSTITUTIONS): Internships, Scholarship funds.

Types of support for individuals: none.

Matching grants: any nonprofit organization.

Exclusions: Individuals, Non-501(c)(3), Political organizations, Religious organizations, Research, Chemical dependency treatment, Health care, Multi-year grants.

Sample grants:

Bridge for Runaway Youth, The/MN/provide housing and independent living skills/$15,000.

Centro Campesino/Owatonna, MN/improving Latino/Latina daycare options/$15,000.

First Witness Child Abuse Resource Center/Duluth, MN/investigative interview program and crisis counseling/$20,000.

Hmong American Partnership - MN/MN/Hmong women and children's domestic abuse program/$10,000.

Hoofbeats & Heartbeats, Inc./MN/purchase of lesson horse/$6,500.

MN Adoption Resource Network/MN/Our Voices Matter general program support/$15,000.

Parrott Creek Child & Family Service/OR/community safety net/$10,000.

St Gabriel's Church/Washington, DC/tuition assistance program/$10,000.

Financial Information

Financial data for year ending: 12/31/2005
Foundation assets: $2,054,704
Grants paid: $475,213
Number of grants: 38
Largest/smallest: $20,000/$5,000

Application Information

Preferred form of initial contact: letter of inquiry, telephone inquiry.

Public information available by request: proposal guidelines, application form, website.

Accept common grant application: yes.

Proposal deadlines: See website for most up-to-date information.

Preferred time for receiving proposals: Year-round, by invitation only.

Contribution decisions made by: board of directors/trustees.

Frequency of contributions decisions: quarterly; see website for up-to-date information.

Typical time from application deadlines to notification: 3 months.

Special application procedures: Submit letter of inquiry or telephone inquiry first.

Staff/Trustees

Staff: Diana Dokos, program officer.

Otto Bremer Foundation

445 Minnesota Street
Suite 2250
St Paul, MN 55101-2107
County: Ramsey
Phone: (651) 227-8036
Fax: (651) 312-3665
E-mail: obf@ottobremer.org
Website: www.ottobremer.org
Contact: John Kostishack, executive director
Established: 05/01/1944
Funder type: Private foundation

Program Description

Program's purpose: To fulfill various charitable purposes that are part of the Trust Instrument that established the foundation.

Funding priorities: In accordance with the principles set forth by Otto Bremer in his trust agreement, the mission of the Otto Bremer Foundation is to assist people in achieving full economic, civic and social participation in and for the betterment of their communities. Beneficiaries must reside in the states of Minnesota, Wisconsin, North Dakota or Montana, with preference given to those in regions served by Bremer banks.

Program limitations/restrictions: Grant recipients are to be public or private non-profit organizations. Grants are not made to individuals. The foundation discourages requests for annual fund drives, benefit events, camps, economic development, medical research, building endowments (other than community foundations), media projects and sporting activities. The foundation does not fund K-12 education.

Geographic focus: Twin Cities Metropolitan Area, Greater Minnesota, Minnesota statewide, Areas outside Minnesota.

Geographic limitations: Beneficiaries must be residents of Minnesota, Montana, North Dakota or Wisconsin.

Areas of interest:

CIVIL RIGHTS: Civil liberties advocacy, Civil rights/advocacy for specific groups, Equal opportunity and access, Intergroup relations/race relations, Voter education/registration.

COMMUNITY IMPROVEMENT: Community coalitions, Community/neighborhood development/improvement, Nonprofit management.

EDUCATION: Adult/continuing education/literacy, Graduate education/professional schools, Higher education, Limited to post-secondary schools in Minnesota.

EMPLOYMENT/JOBS: Employment procurement/job training, Labor unions/organizations, Vocational rehabilitation.

FOOD/NUTRITION/AGRICULTURE: Agricultural programs, Nutrition promotion, Soil and water conservation/farm land preservation.

HEALTH - GENERAL/REHABILITATIVE: Emergency medical services, Public health programs/wellness education.

HEALTH - MENTAL HEALTH/CRISIS INTERVENTION: Counseling/support groups, Mental health associations, Mental health treatment and services.

HOUSING/SHELTER: Homeless, temporary housing, Housing development/construction/management, Housing owners/renter organizations, Housing search assistance, Housing support services, Low-cost temporary housing.

HUMAN SERVICES: Children/youth services, Emergency assistance (food/clothing/cash), Family services, Family services for adolescent parents, Family violence shelters and services, Multipurpose human service organizations, Services to specific groups, Victims services.

INTERNATIONAL AFFAIRS: International human rights, Promotion of international understanding.

PHILANTHROPY/VOLUNTARISM: Federated Funds, Philanthropy associations, Public foundations and community foundations, Voluntarism promotion.

PUBLIC AFFAIRS/SOCIETY BENEFIT: Citizen participation, Government/public administration, Public policy research and analysis, Public transportation services.

PUBLIC PROTECTION - CRIME/COURTS/LEGAL SERVICES: Dispute/conflict resolution, Legal services, Protection/prevention - neglect/abuse/exploitation.

PUBLIC SAFETY/DISASTERS/RELIEF: Disaster preparedness and relief.

RELIGION/SPIRITUAL DEVELOPMENT: Interfaith issues.

Intended beneficiaries: General public/unspecified.

Types of support for individuals: none.

Sample grants:

African Assistance Program/MN/For the African immigrant job development project/$15,000.

Center for Training & Careers - MN (Twin Cities)/MN/To provide American citizenship training to refugee and immigrant youth/$10,000.

Como Park Living at Home/MN/To provide affordable professional home health and nursing services/$5,000.

Greater Frogtown Community Development Corporation/MN/For a communications and outreach initiative/$15,000.

HOME Line/MN/To support the statewide tenant services that include a toll-free hotline, organizing work and advocacy/$15,000.

Jewish Community Relations Council - MN/Dakotas/To support Tolerance MN, a program that will enable educators to teach tolerance and anti-bias/$50,000.

Southeast Asian Community Council Inc/MN/For the North Minneapolis Southeast Asian Initiative, a collaborative that empowers residents/$25,000.

Youth Investment Foundation/MN/ Timber Bay program that works with at-risk youth/$8,000.

Financial Information

Financial data for year ending: 12/31/2005
Foundation assets: $535,178,874
Grants paid: $28,037,818
Number of grants: 807
Largest/smallest: $500,000/$1,000
Typical grant amount: $33,632
Program related investments: $1,115,000
Number of program-related investments: 7

Application Information

Preferred form of initial contact: letter of inquiry, telephone inquiry, request for guidelines, complete proposal.

Public information available by request: proposal guidelines, annual report, website, video.

Accept common grant application: yes.

Proposal deadlines: none.

Preferred time for receiving proposals: Anytime.

Contribution decisions made by: board of directors/trustees.

Frequency of contributions decisions: monthly.

Typical time from application deadlines to notification: 6-8 weeks.

Staff/Trustees

Staff: Danielle Cheslog, grants manager; Kaying Hang, program officer; Lue Her, program officer; John Kostishack, executive director; Karen Starr, senior program officer; Kari Suzuki Bardy, director of operations; Anthony Vasquez, computer professional; Twana Williams, office administrator.

Directors/trustees: Charlotte Johnson; William H. Lipschultz; Daniel Reardon.

Bromelkamp Foundation

106 East 24 Street
Minneapolis, MN 55404
County: Hennepin
Phone: (612) 870-2601 x19
Fax: (612) 767-6709
E-mail: grants@bromelkamp.com
Website: www.bromelkamp.com/foundation.html
Contact: Sarah Geving
Established: 01/01/1997
Donor: Bromelkamp Company
Funder type: Corporate giving program

Program Description

Program's purpose: Bromelkamp Foundation is a program within Bromelkamp Company whose purpose is to address community and human needs in the Twin Cities area. The foundation provides grants of up to $1,000 as well as in-kind technical assistance.

Funding priorities: 1) Homelessness - Programming that helps to improve the quality of life of the homeless. This includes, but is not restricted to, food banks, shelters, job training or housing assistance. 2) Literacy - Educational programming that teaches new or enhances current language skills. This includes, but is not restricted to, speaking, writing and reading. 3) Technology - A range of technology-related issues including, but not restricted to, equipment, training, installation or accessibility concerns.

Geographic focus: Twin Cities Metropolitan Area, neighborhoods in which Bromelkamp Company employees reside, which currently includes downtown Minneapolis, South Minneapolis, St Paul (East Side), Maple Grove and Fridley.

Areas of interest:

EDUCATION: Adult/continuing education/literacy.

EMPLOYMENT/JOBS: Employment procurement/job training.

HOUSING/SHELTER: Homeless, temporary housing.

HUMAN SERVICES: Emergency assistance (food/clothing/cash).

SCIENCE/TECHNOLOGY.

Intended beneficiaries: Children and youth (infants-19 years), General public/unspecified, Homeless, Poor/economically disadvantaged.

Types of support for organizations:

IN-KIND SERVICES: Technical services such as training and support of the Microsoft Office products (including Word, Outlook, Excel and Access). This help should be limited in scope (approximately 7-10 hours of work) and not project work or ongoing technical issues.

Application Information

Preferred form of initial contact: complete proposal. Applications are accepted via website, mail, fax or e-mail; applicants are strongly encouraged to use the online grant application.

Public information available by request: proposal guidelines, application form, website.

Staff/Trustees

Staff: Sarah Geving.

Directors/trustees: Bromelkamp Company staff members.

Burdick-Craddick Family Foundation

PO Box 16348
Minneapolis, MN 55416-0348
County: Hennepin
Phone: (952) 807-2471
E-mail: BeckyElj@aol.com
Contact: Allan L. Burdick, chairman & CEO
Established: 06/01/1974
Paid Staff: Yes
Funder type: Private foundation

Program Description

Program's purpose: Annual support of community and social service organizations that address the needs of children, minorities and the disadvantaged, especially those programs that empower people to gain economic self-sufficiency.

Funding priorities: Human services organizations, primarily those programs having a direct impact on people in Hennepin County.

Program limitations/restrictions: No grants for medical research. Medical and Health requests considered only if a there is a social service aspect. Grants from organizations not previously funded will be accepted by invitation only in 2007.

Geographic focus: Twin Cities Metropolitan Area.

Geographic limitations: Limited to organizations in Minneapolis and its Hennepin County suburbs.

Areas of interest:

ARTS, CULTURE, HUMANITIES: We fund a very small number of arts organizations but only social service aspects of those programs.

HEALTH - MENTAL HEALTH/CRISIS INTERVENTION.

HOUSING/SHELTER.

HUMAN SERVICES: Focus on programs designed to help the chronically disadvantaged become self-supporting.

Intended beneficiaries: Poor/economically disadvantaged.

Types of support for organizations:
CAPITAL CAMPAIGNS.
GENERAL PURPOSE/OPERATING SUPPORT.

Types of support for individuals: none.

Exclusions: Individuals, Non-501(c)(3), Political organizations, Research, Scholarships/loans.

Sample grants:

Courage Center - MN/MN/$2,000.

Emergency Food Shelf Network - MN/MN/$1,000.

Friends of St Stephens/MN/$2,000.

Kids First - MN/MN/$1,000.

Mixed Blood Theatre Company/MN/$1,000.

MN Opera Company/MN/$750.

MN Public Radio - St Paul/MN/$1,500.

WomenVenture/MN/$1,000.

Financial Information

Financial data for year ending: 12/31/2006
Foundation assets: $646,107
Grants paid: $107,850
Number of grants: 85
Largest/smallest: $3,000/$750
Typical grant amount: $1,000
Largest multi-year grant approved: $5,000

Application Information

Preferred form of initial contact: request for guidelines, letter of inquiry via e-mail.

Public information available by request: proposal guidelines, annual report. All grants to be submitted on MN Common Grants Form.

Accept common grant application: yes.

Accept common report form: yes.

Will view video: yes.

Proposal deadlines: Ongoing.

Contribution decisions made by: CEO, board of directors/trustees.

Frequency of contributions decisions: quarterly.

Typical time from application deadlines to notification: within two months.

Special application procedures: The executive committee is authorized to review and award grants as they are received during the year. Funds are distributed quarterly. Grant requests submitted in the 4th quarter of the year must be received by November 1 to receive consideration during the current fiscal year. Keep proposal narratives short and to the point – no extra points for providing all the information available regardless of its relevance to your grant request.

Staff/Trustees

Staff: Rebecca Elj, secretary/treasurer.

Directors/trustees: Allan L. Burdick, chairman & CEO; Lou Brum Burdick, president & COO; Stephen Burdick; Helen S. Craddick; Susan C. Lott; Ralph Lott III.

Bush Foundation

332 Minnesota Street
Suite E-900
St Paul, MN 55101
County: Ramsey
Phone: (651) 227-0891
Fax: (651) 297-6485
E-mail: info@bushfoundation.org
Website: www.bushfoundation.org
Contact: Anita Pampusch Ph.D., president
Established: 02/01/1953
Paid Staff: Yes
Funder type: Private foundation

Program Description

Program's purpose: The Bush Foundation improves the quality of life in our geographic region of Minnesota, North Dakota and South Dakota through strengthening organizational, community and individual leadership.

Funding priorities: Our goals for the next several years include: supporting leadership that creates conditions to improve human health and sustain the environment to enhance the physical, mental, and social well-being of the populations in our region; supporting leadership that will create conditions to retain intellectual, financial, and social capital in local communities; supporting leadership that will create conditions for a vibrant, sustainable, and interdependent system of cultural activities that contribute to the well-being of the region. We accomplish this through the areas of interest listed below.

Program limitations/restrictions: No support for other private foundations, research in biomedical and health sciences, hospital construction, deficit financing, continuing operating support, loans, or individuals (outside of fellowship programs).

Geographic focus: Minnesota statewide, North Dakota, South Dakota.

Geographic limitations: Regional emphasis (Minnesota, North Dakota, South Dakota).

Areas of interest:

ARTS, CULTURE, HUMANITIES: Arts/cultural multipurpose, Humanities, Media/communications, Museums, Performing arts, Visual arts.

CIVIL RIGHTS: Civil rights/advocacy for specific groups, Equal opportunity and access.

COMMUNITY IMPROVEMENT: Economic development, Nonprofit management, Community capacity building.

EDUCATION: Higher education, Preschool/elementary, Secondary.

EMPLOYMENT/JOBS: Employment procurement/job training.

ENVIRONMENTAL QUALITY/PROTECTION/BEAUTIFICATION: Natural resources conservation/protection, Pollution abatement and control.

FOOD/NUTRITION/AGRICULTURE: Agricultural programs, Soil and water conservation/farm land preservation.

HEALTH - MENTAL HEALTH/CRISIS INTERVENTION: Alcohol/drug/

substance, prevention and treatment, Mental health treatment and services.
HOUSING/SHELTER: Housing support services.
HUMAN SERVICES: Children/youth services, Family services, Family violence shelters and services, Multipurpose human service organizations, Services to specific groups.
PHILANTHROPY/VOLUNTARISM: Nonprofit sector assistance, Philanthropy - general, Philanthropy associations.
PUBLIC PROTECTION - CRIME/COURTS/LEGAL SERVICES: Crime prevention, Dispute/conflict resolution, Legal services, Protection/prevention - neglect/abuse/exploitation, Rehabilitation of offenders.
YOUTH DEVELOPMENT: Youth development programs.

Types of support for organizations:
CAPITAL CAMPAIGNS: Building/renovation.
MANAGEMENT/TECHNICAL ASSISTANCE.
PROGRAM DEVELOPMENT/PROJECT SUPPORT: Faculty/staff development, Program evaluation, Public policy research/analysis.

Types of support for individuals: fellowships.

Exclusions: Individuals, Non-501(c)(3), Research, Scholarships/loans.

Sample grants:
Community Homes & Resources in Service to Many/ND/For a planning process and pilot programming for a community-based program working to resettle refugee youth/$50,000.
Cornucopia Arts Center/MN/Toward expenses for a curator and public relations coordinator/$70,000.
Great Plains Institute for Sustainable Development Inc/MN/To continue the Powering the Plains project/$180,000.
In The Heart of the Beast Puppet & Mask Theatre/MN/For entry-year support through the Regional Arts Development Program II/$96,000.
Latino Economic Development Center/MN/To add an assistant director and program manager for rural Minnesota/$190,000.
MN Historical Society/MN/To expand technological infrastructure and provide increased public access to cultural heritage resources as digital content in the Upper Midwest/$999,709.

Northern Great Plains, Inc./ND/To conduct the Meadowlark Project, a leadership laboratory on the future of the Northern Great Plains/$400,000.
Rapid City Area School District #51-4/SD/To support a middle school to high school student retention program/$859,200.

Financial Information

Financial data for year ending: 12/31/2006
Foundation assets: $866,466,601
Grants paid: $40,241,987
Number of grants: 419
Largest/smallest: $1,000,000/$5,000
Largest multi-year grant approved: $2,000,000
Note: Due to a fiscal year change, grants paid and number of grants are for a 13-month period.

Application Information

Preferred form of initial contact: Letter of inquiry required.
Public information available by request: proposal guidelines, application form, annual report, website, magazine.
Accept common report form: yes.
Proposal deadlines: March 1, July 1, November 1 for full proposals. Letters of inquiry deadlines are May 1, September 1, and January 1.
Contribution decisions made by: board of directors/trustees.
Specific times board meets: Three times a year: March, July, November.
Typical time from application deadlines to notification: Four months.
Special application procedures: Fellowship applications have different, annual due dates. See website for more information.

Staff/Trustees

Staff: John Archabal, senior program officer; Lee-Hoon Benson, program officer; Nancy Fushan, senior program officer; Jose Gonzalez, program officer; Rudy Guglielmo Jr., program officer; Jane Kretzmann, senior program officer; June Noronha, strategic planning officer; Anita Pampusch Ph.D., president.

Directors/trustees: Ivy S. Bernhardson; Wilson G. Bradshaw; Dudley Cocke; Roxanne Givens Copeland; Steve Goldstein; Dwight Gourneau; Esperanza Guerrero-Anderson; Robert B. Jones; Jan K. Malcolm; Tim Mathern; William P. Pierskalla; Catherine V. Piersol; Gordon M. Sprenger; Kathryn H. Tunheim.

Patrick and Aimee Butler Family Foundation

332 Minnesota Street
Suite E-1420
St Paul, MN 55101-1369
County: Ramsey
Phone: (651) 222-2565
E-mail: info@butlerfamilyfoundation.org
Website: www.butlerfamilyfoundation.org
Contact: Kerrie Blevins, foundation director
Established: 11/01/1951
Paid Staff: Yes
Funder type: Private foundation

Program Description

Program's purpose: The Patrick & Aimee Butler Family Foundation supports solid progressive ideas in the arts, social service, environment and social change.

Funding priorities: Arts & humanities; environment; human services; philanthropy & the nonprofit sector.

Program limitations/restrictions: Does not fund criminal justice, economic development, primary or secondary education, capital/endowment, employment/vocation programs, film/video, hospitals or medical research, dance/theater, projects outside the United States.

Geographic focus: Twin Cities Metropolitan Area, Minnesota statewide.

Geographic limitations: Geographic priority: St Paul and Minneapolis metropolitan area. Minnesota statewide for environment. The foundation does not fund projects outside the United States.

Areas of interest:
ARTS, CULTURE, HUMANITIES: Historical societies, Humanities, Museums, Music education.
ENVIRONMENTAL QUALITY/PROTECTION/BEAUTIFICATION: Environmental education/outdoor survival, Natural resources conservation/protection, No outdoor survival.
HOUSING/SHELTER: Homeless, temporary housing, Housing development/construction/management, Housing support services.

HUMAN SERVICES: Family services, Family services for adolescent parents, Family violence shelters and services, Multipurpose human service organizations.

PHILANTHROPY/VOLUNTARISM: Nonprofit sector assistance, Public foundations and community foundations.

Intended beneficiaries: Children and youth (infants-19 years), Deaf/hearing impaired, Ethnic/racial populations - general, Females - all ages or age unspecified, Homeless, Immigrants/newcomers/refugees, Poor/economically disadvantaged, Single parents, Substance abusers.

Types of support for organizations:
GENERAL PURPOSE/OPERATING SUPPORT.
PROGRAM DEVELOPMENT/ PROJECT SUPPORT.

Types of support for individuals: none.

Exclusions: Capital & endowment campaigns, Individuals, Non-501(c)(3), Political organizations, Research, Scholarships/loans.

Sample grants:
Domestic Abuse Project Inc - MN/MN/ $12,000.

Eagle Bluff Environmental Center - MN/MN/$10,000.

Graywolf Press/MN/$9,000.

Hmong American Partnership - MN/MN/Support for the Parent & Family Support Program/$10,000.

Mixed Blood Theatre Company/MN/ $7,500.

Project for Pride in Living/MN/General operating support for housing/$30,000.

Ramsey County Historical Society/MN/ $15,000.

Wayside House, Inc - MN/St Louis Park, MN/$15,000.

Financial Information

Financial data for year ending: 12/31/2005
Foundation assets: $61,236,731
Grants paid: $2,328,360
Number of grants: 121
Largest/smallest: $100,000/$1,000
Typical grant amount: $10,000

Application Information

Preferred form of initial contact: telephone inquiry, request for guidelines, e-mail.

Public information available by request: proposal guidelines, application form, annual report, website.

Accept common grant application: yes.

Accept common report form: yes.

Proposal deadlines: The 2007 deadline was February 7. Please check website for deadlines as they are subject to change.

Contribution decisions made by: board of directors/trustees.

Frequency of contributions decisions: semiannually.

Typical time from application deadlines to notification: 4 months.

Staff/Trustees

Staff: Kerrie Blevins, foundation director; Nora McKinnon, grants administrator.

Directors/trustees: Brigid M. Butler; Catherine C. Butler; Cecilia M. Butler; John K. Butler; Patricia M. Butler; Patrick Butler; Paul S. Butler; Peter M. Butler, president; Sandra K. Butler; Suzanne A. LeFevour.

Buuck Family Foundation

Suite 5300
90 South Seventh Street
Minneapolis, MN 55402
County: Hennepin
Contact: Robert E. Buuck, president
Established: 12/31/1994
Donor Robert & Gail Buuck Family
Funder type: Private foundation

Program Description

Program's purpose: The Buuck Family Foundation was established in 1994 to serve as a primary gifting vehicle for the Robert and Gail Buuck family in their charitable activities.

Funding priorities: Education, arts and culture, environmental, social and community.

Geographic focus: Twin Cities Metropolitan Area, Greater Minnesota, Minnesota statewide, National Areas, Phoenix Metropolitan area, where the family has an interest.

Geographic limitations: The principal focus for gifts from the foundation is the Twin Cities and Phoenix greater metropolitan areas. Limited funding will also be provided to national or international organizations that address issues of particular interest to the foundation.

Areas of interest:

ARTS, CULTURE, HUMANITIES: Arts/cultural multipurpose, Museums, Performing arts, Visual arts. Special emphasis will be given to programs that serve the broad community in Minnesota and Arizona.

EDUCATION: Graduate education/professional schools, Higher education, Preschool/elementary. Support will be given to financial aid and scholarship programs for the benefit of students in secondary, undergraduate and graduate-level institutions. Emphasis given to programs directed toward minority students or students with physical disabilities.

EMPLOYMENT/JOBS: Employment procurement/job training, Vocational rehabilitation.

ENVIRONMENTAL QUALITY/PROTECTION/BEAUTIFICATION: Environmental beautification/open spaces, Natural resources conservation/protection, including regional and national programs where emphasis is directed toward restoration and/or the saving of habitat otherwise lost to development.

HEALTH - DISEASES/MEDICAL DISCIPLINES: Nerve/muscle/bone diseases, Specific named diseases.

HEALTH - GENERAL/REHABILITATIVE: Rehabilitative medical services.

HEALTH - RESEARCH: Nerve, muscle and bone research, Specific named disease research, Programs that serve physically challenged individuals, to include research, disease management, rehabilitation and the use of new technology to empower people with disabilities to reach their full potential.

HOUSING/SHELTER: Homeless, temporary housing, Housing owners/renter organizations, Housing support services, Housing programs that help break the cycle of poverty.

HUMAN SERVICES: Emergency assistance (food/clothing/cash), Family violence shelters and services, Community programs directed toward providing emergency services to assist in the transition of individuals with special needs into a safer and more promising environment.

Intended beneficiaries: Adults, Blind/vision impaired, Deaf/hearing impaired, Disabled - general or unspecified disability, Ethnic/racial populations - general, Females - all ages or age unspecified, General public/unspecified, Infants/babies (under age 5), Males - all ages or age unspecified, Physically disabled, Poor/economically disadvantaged, Youth/adolescents (ages 14-19).

Types of support for organizations:
CAPITAL CAMPAIGNS: Land acquisitions.
GENERAL PURPOSE/OPERATING SUPPORT: Annual campaigns.
RESEARCH.
STUDENT AID (GRANTS TO INSTITUTIONS): Scholarship funds.

Types of support for individuals: none.

Exclusions: Individuals, Non-501(c)(3), Political organizations, Religious organizations, Fundraisers.

Sample grants:
Andre House of Arizona/AZ/$4,000.
Bridging, Inc/MN/$17,500.
Courage Center - MN/MN/$15,000.
Eye-Link Foundation/MN/$4,000.
Habitat for Humanity/MN/AZ/$25,000.
The Jeremiah Program/MN/$10,000.
Nature Conservancy/MN/AZ/$15,000.
Page Educational Foundation/MN/$10,000.

Financial Information

Financial data for year ending: 12/31/2006
Foundation assets: $11,665,000
Grants paid: $703,500
Number of grants: 85
Largest/smallest: $50,000/$2,500
Largest multi-year grant approved: $100,000

Application Information

Preferred form of initial contact: letter of inquiry.
Accept common grant application: yes.
Accept common report form: yes.
Preferred time for receiving proposals: April, July, October.
Contribution decisions made by: board of directors/trustees.
Frequency of contributions decisions: quarterly.
Typical time from application deadlines to notification: 1 month.

Staff/Trustees

Directors/trustees: David A. Buuck; Gail P. Buuck, vice president; John R. Buuck; Robert E. Buuck, president; Katherine Buuck Fratzke.

Cade Foundation

17642 Kettering Trail
Lakeville, MN 55044
County: Scott
Phone: (877) 571-4421
Contact: Kristin Carlson
Funder type: Private foundation

Program Description

Geographic focus: Twin Cities Metropolitan Area, Areas outside Minnesota.

Areas of interest:
EDUCATION: Higher education, Preschool/elementary, Secondary.
HEALTH - DISEASES/MEDICAL DISCIPLINES: Cancer.
HEALTH - RESEARCH: Cancer research.

Types of support for organizations:
GENERAL PURPOSE/OPERATING SUPPORT.

Sample grants:
Academy of Holy Angels - MN (Richfield)/MN/$1,450.
Anderson Cancer Center/Houston, TX/$30,000.
Catholic Central High School - WI (Marinette)/WI/$20,000.
Christian Children's Fund/MN/$2,400.
MN Ovarian Cancer Alliance/MN/$6,522.
University of St Thomas - MN/MN/$15,000.

Financial Information

Financial data for year ending: 12/31/2005
Foundation assets: $3,887,438
Grants paid: $238,037
Number of grants: 8
Largest/smallest: $105,000/$2,500

Application Information

Preferred form of initial contact: letter of inquiry.
Proposal deadlines: none.
Special application procedures: provide statement including the amount and purpose of funding needed.

Staff/Trustees

Directors/trustees: Brian Cade; Kevin Cade; Kristin Carlson; Julie Nelson.

Caliber Foundation

5032 Garfield Avenue South
Minneapolis, MN 55419
County: Hennepin
Contact: John Lavander, president
Established: 12/10/1997
Funder type: Private foundation

Program Description

Geographic focus: Twin Cities Metropolitan Area.

Areas of interest:
EDUCATION.
HUMAN SERVICES.

Intended beneficiaries: General public/unspecified.

Types of support for organizations:
GENERAL PURPOSE/OPERATING SUPPORT.

Sample grants:
Food Share - MN/MN/$55,000.
Friends of Pacer/MN/$10,000.
Minnehaha Academy/MN/$40,000.
Parents In Community Action (PICA)/MN/$5,000.
Project for Pride in Living/MN/$25,000.
Riverview Elementary School - MN/MN/$5,000.
St Cloud State University Foundation/MN/$10,000.
Twin Cities RISE!/MN/$6,000.

Financial Information

Financial data for year ending: 12/31/2005
Foundation assets: $1,357,089
Grants paid: $90,050
Number of grants: 12
Largest/smallest: $55,000/$3,000

Application Information

Preferred form of initial contact: No new applications are being accepted.

Staff/Trustees

Directors/trustees: John Lavander, president; Nancy F. Owen, treasurer; Nancy Lavander Seeger, secretary.

Martin and Esther Capp Foundation

7951 12th Avenue South
Bloomington, MN 55425
County: Hennepin
Phone: (952) 854-6608 x18
Contact: Lisa Capp
Established: 02/20/1961
Funder type: Private foundation

Program Description

Program's purpose: Environment and Jewish organizations, among others.

Geographic focus: Twin Cities Metropolitan Area, National Areas.

Areas of interest:

ANIMAL RELATED: Wildlife preservation/protection.

ENVIRONMENTAL QUALITY/ PROTECTION/BEAUTIFICATION.

RELIGION/SPIRITUAL DEVELOPMENT: Specific denomination.

Intended beneficiaries: General public/unspecified.

Types of support for individuals: none.

Exclusions: Individuals, Political organizations, Scholarships/loans.

Sample grants:

Arthritis Foundation - MN/MN/$1,750.

Jewish Community Center - St Paul/MN/ $20,327.

Sholom Home Auxiliary/MN/$1,000.

Temple of Aaron/MN/$30,108.

United Hospital Foundation/MN/$5,000.

United Jewish Fund & Council/MN/ $107,700.

World Wildlife Fund - DC/Washington, DC/$1,000.

Financial Information

Financial data for year ending: 12/31/2005
Foundation assets: $1,876,120
Grants paid: $382,960
Number of grants: 45
Largest/smallest: $200,000/$25
Matching gifts: $200,000
Largest multi-year grant approved: $1,000,000

Application Information

Preferred form of initial contact: letter of inquiry.

Accept common grant application: yes.

Proposal deadlines: none.

Contribution decisions made by: distribution committee.

Frequency of contributions decisions: quarterly.

Typical time from application deadlines to notification: 90 days.

Staff/Trustees

Directors/trustees: Lisa Capp; Leonard Horowitz; Cynthia Rosenblatt.

Cargill Citizenship Fund

PO Box 5650
Minneapolis, MN 55440-5690
County: Hennepin
Phone: (952) 742-4311
Fax: (952) 742-7224
E-mail: stacey_smida@cargill.com
Website: www.cargill.com/about/ citizenship/corpgiving.htm
Contact: Stacey Smida, grants manager, corporate citizenship
Established: 01/01/1963
Paid Staff: Yes
Funder type: Corporate giving program

Program Description

Program's purpose: The Cargill Citizenship Committee works in partnership with Cargill businesses to provide strategic grants to organizations serving communities where Cargill has a presence. The committee provides direct grants for regional, national and global partnerships and provides matching funds for selected local projects supported by our businesses.

Funding priorities: Cargill will seek to build sustainable communities by focusing our human and financial resources in three areas: 1) Nutrition and Wellness; 2) Promote innovation in education; 3) Environment.

Program limitations/restrictions: We will not fund organizations without 501(c)(3) status or the equivalent; organizations that do not serve communities where Cargill has a business presence; individuals or groups seeking support for research, planning, personal needs or travel; public service or political campaigns; lobbying, political or fraternal activities; benefit dinners or tickets to the same; fundraising campaigns, walk-a-thons, or promotions to eliminate or control specific diseases; athletic scholarships; advertising or event sponsorships; religious groups for religious purposes; publications, audio-visual productions or special broadcasts; endowments; medical equipment (ambulances, defibrillators).

Geographic focus: National Areas, International Areas, where Cargill business presence.

Geographic limitations: Communities with a Cargill business presence, areas outside Minnesota and international locations.

Areas of interest:

EDUCATION: Cargill will support innovative programs that improve academic achievement, develop logic and thinking skills, promote leadership development, and/or increase access to education for socio-economically disadvantaged children. Cargill also supports mutually beneficial partnerships with selected higher education institutions. (unsolicited proposals not accepted).

ENVIRONMENTAL QUALITY/ PROTECTION/BEAUTIFICATION: Cargill will support projects that protect and improve accessibility to water resources; promote biodiversity conservation in agricultural areas; and educate children about conservation and/or proper sanitation.

FOOD/NUTRITION/AGRICULTURE: Nutrition and wellness promotion, Cargill will support programs and projects that address long-term solutions to hunger, increase access to health education and/or basic health care in developing and emerging countries, and improve youth nutrition and wellness.

PHILANTHROPY/VOLUNTARISM: Employee/retiree community service projects.

PUBLIC SAFETY/DISASTERS/
RELIEF: Disaster relief.

Types of support for organizations:
PROGRAM DEVELOPMENT/
PROJECT SUPPORT: Cargill directs resources primarily to projects/programs serving Cargill communities and only under special circumstances may consider general operating or capital support for organizations that contact the staff before applying.
IN-KIND PRODUCTS: Cargill products, e.g. flour, meat.
IN-KIND SERVICES: Volunteer time.

Types of support for individuals: none.

Matching grants: higher education, disaster relief.

Sample grants:

Big Brothers/Big Sisters - PA/PA/School-based mentoring program and a Hispanic mentoring initiative/$250,000.

CARE - IL (International)/IL/To help the organization address education and maternal/child health issues in Central American countries and others/ $1,000,000.

Conservation International Foundation - VA/VA/Biodiversity and natural resources conservation projects/$750,000.

Global Foodbanking Network/IL/ Assisting Ghana with foodbanking resources focusing on extending shelf life of crops increasing and stabilizing farm income and food security; in Mexico provide nutrition education training and new technologies for farmers/$50,000.

Junior Achievement - CO (WorldWide)/ CO/Supporting programming in Cargill communities in China and Honduras/ $38,700.

Students In Free Enterprise, Inc/MO/ Supporting education program for college students to promote education in free enterprise/$50,000.

United Nations Foundation - DC/DC/ Global Water Challenge international program/$250,000.

Financial Information

Financial data for year ending: 05/31/2006
Grants paid: $12,489,582
Number of grants: 833
Largest/smallest: $1,000,000/$250
Matching gifts: $179,484
Largest multi-year grant approved: $1,000,000

Application Information

Preferred form of initial contact: telephone inquiry, request for guidelines, e-mail. We encourage organizations to submit a 2-3 page letter of inquiry via mail or e-mail including the following: name of organization and mission; description of project for which funds are requested; the project/program focus area; amount requested.

Public information available by request: proposal guidelines, application form, annual report, website. Applications are available on Cargill's website or by calling (952) 742-4311.

Proposal deadlines: Applications are reviewed on an ongoing basis.

Preferred time for receiving proposals: Cargill will review the letter of inquiry and determine whether the organization will be invited to submit a complete proposal. Those organizations invited to submit a proposal must complete the Cargill Citizenship Fund Grant Application form.

Contribution decisions made by: staff, board of directors.

Frequency of contributions decisions: quarterly.

Typical time from application deadlines to notification: within 90 days.

Special application procedures: The Cargill Citizenship Fund staff may request additional information or a site visit.

Staff/Trustees

Staff: Michelle Grogg, director, corporate citizenship; Emily Longaecker, administrative assistant; Suzanne McCarty, director, community relations; Mark Murphy, assistant vice president, corporate citizenship and secretary Cargill Citizenship Committee; Rebecca Oswald, community relations associate; Stacey Smida, grants manager, corporate citizenship.

Cargill Foundation

PO Box 5650
Minneapolis, MN 55440-5650
County: Hennepin
Phone: (952) 742-4311
Fax: (952) 742-7224
E-mail: stacey_smida@cargill.com
Website: www.cargill.com/about/citizenship/foundation.htm
Contact: Stacey Smida, grants manager
Established: 12/01/1951
Paid Staff: Yes
Funder type: Corporate foundation

Program Description

Program's purpose: Cargill Foundation uses its resources to fund organizations and programs that focus on educational success and the development of necessary life skills that enable socio-economically disadvantaged young people to work and thrive in a rapidly changing world.

Funding priorities: To help children learn in the following ways: 1) Prepare youth for school; 2) Improve academic achievement; 3) Build character; 4) Raise self-esteem; 5) Create healthy, supportive family systems.

Program limitations/restrictions: The foundation generally does not consider grants for the following: individuals; athletic scholarships; religious organizations for religious purposes; membership in civic organizations or trade associations; benefit fundraising events or tickets for the same; endowments or endowment campaigns; recognition or testimonial events; fundraising campaigns to eliminate or control specific diseases; medical research; fraternal, veterans' or professional associations; public service or political campaigns; political lobbying activities; participation in conferences; travel for groups or individuals. Because of limited funds, we have chosen not to focus on youth facing physical or mental challenges; programs that primarily serve adults; summer programs; juvenile offender programs; faith-based organizations; programs that serve children whose parents are incarcerated or have serious medical problems; homes for children including temporary shelters; foster care; emergency shelter; adoption; and organizations or programs that serve the medical or dental needs of children.

Geographic focus: West Metropolitan Area/Minneapolis only.

Geographic limitations: Northern and western suburbs of Minneapolis only.

Areas of interest:

EDUCATION: Organizations and programs that demonstrate leadership and effectiveness in educating socio-economically disadvantaged children and in eliminating barriers to their educational success.

Intended beneficiaries: Children only (5-14 years), Poor/economically disadvantaged.

Types of support for individuals: none.

Sample grants:

Achieve! Minneapolis/MN/Guys in Science and Engineering (GISE) an after-school and summer program (over 3 years)/$225,000.

Achieve! Minneapolis/MN/Implementing the AVID program into two Mpls Public Schools (over 4 years)/$367,000.

Alliance of Early Childhood Professionals/MN/Support for the Wicoie Nandagikendan Urban Early Childhood Immersion Project - Native American Language program/$25,000.

Family & Children's Services - MN/Minneapolis, MN/Support their School Success for new immigrants program (over 2 years)/$55,000.

YWCA - MN (Minneapolis)/MN/Support for an early childhood program at four centers/$100,000.

Financial Information

Financial data for year ending: 12/31/2006
Foundation assets: $103,748,000
Grants paid: $7,438,820
Number of grants: 81
Largest/smallest: $800,000/$1,500

Application Information

Preferred form of initial contact: review the content on website, telephone/e-mail inquiry.

Public information available by request: proposal guidelines, application form, website.

Proposal deadlines: Eliminating Barriers - once a year/March; Education - ongoing.

Preferred time for receiving proposals: ongoing.

Contribution decisions made by: board of directors.

Frequency of contributions decisions: quarterly.

Typical time from application deadlines to notification: 12-14 weeks.

Staff/Trustees

Staff: Mark Murphy, executive director, Cargill Foundation; Stacey Smida, grants manager; Kayla Yang, senior program officer.

Directors/trustees: Terri Barreiro; Robbin Johnson; Thomas Moe; Scott Portnoy; Frank Sims.

The Curtis L. Carlson Family Foundation

550 Tonkawa Road
Long Lake, MN 55356
County: Hennepin
Phone: (952) 404-5636
Fax: (952) 358-2437
Website: www.clcfamilyfoundation.com
Contact: C. David Nelson, executive director
Established: 12/01/1959
Funder type: Private foundation

Program Description

Program's purpose: Carlson Companies has traditionally fostered a deep commitment to education, humanitarian and community affairs through its charitable contributions, grants, donations and public service to nonprofit organizations.

Funding priorities: The Curtis L. Carlson Family Foundation seeks to support projects and organizations that address education, at-risk youth and mentoring needs in the community. Projects and organizations funded by the foundation meet one or more of the following guidelines: self-sufficiency; self-sustainability; performance; potential benefit to a particular population and the community as a whole; cooperation and coordination with other organizations.

Program limitations/restrictions: Does not fund dinners, benefits or conferences; travel costs; individual scholarships or requests; political activities or causes; support of athletic events; endowments; organizations that do not have a determined IRS 501(c)(3) status.

Geographic focus: Twin Cities Metropolitan Area, Communities where Carlson Companies has a substantial number of employees.

Geographic limitations: The foundation seeks to support projects and organizations within the Twin Cities Metropolitan area and communities where Carlson Companies has a substantial number of employees.

Areas of interest:

EDUCATION.

HUMAN SERVICES: Children/youth services.

YOUTH DEVELOPMENT: Adult/child matching programs, Multipurpose youth centers/clubs, Youth development programs.

Intended beneficiaries: General public/unspecified.

Types of support for individuals: none.

Exclusions: Individuals, Non-501(c)(3), Political organizations, Scholarships/loans, Endowment campaigns.

Financial Information

Financial data for year ending: 12/31/2005
Foundation assets: $85,862,091
Grants paid: $3,141,079
Number of grants: 125
Largest/smallest: $215,000/$100
Largest multi-year grant approved: $1,000,000

Application Information

Preferred form of initial contact: complete proposal.

Public information available by request: proposal guidelines, application form.

Proposal deadlines: January 15, April 15, August 15.

Contribution decisions made by: board of directors/trustees.

Frequency of contributions decisions: Three times per year.

Specific times board meets: March, June, October.

Typical time from application deadlines to notification: 2-4 months.

Special application procedures: We only accept online applications via our website. Please see website for guidelines, application form and list of required attachments.

Staff/Trustees

Staff: C. David Nelson, executive director.

Directors/trustees: Barbara C. Gage, president; Geoffrey C. Gage; Gina M. Gage; Richard C. Gage; Daisy Mitchell; Diana L. Nelson; Marilyn C. Nelson; Wendy M. Nelson.

Carolyn Foundation

706 Second Avenue South
760 Baker Building
Minneapolis, MN 55402
County: Hennepin
Phone: (612) 596-3266
Alt. Phone: (612) 596-3279
Fax: (612) 339-1951
E-mail: CMellin@carolynfoundation.org
Website: www.carolynfoundation.org
Contact: Becky Erdahl, executive director
Established: 01/01/1964
Paid Staff: Yes
Funder type: Private foundation

Program Description

Program's purpose: General purpose foundation whose primary areas of emphasis are economically disadvantaged children and youth, community & cultural vitality, & environmental grantmaking. Grants are made only to organizations that are classified by the IRS as 501(c)(3).

Funding priorities: 1) Community Grantmaking: Economically Disadvantaged Children & Youth; Community & Cultural Vitality; 2) Environment.

Program limitations/restrictions: No grants to individuals, political or veterans organizations, religious organizations, annual fund drives, for deficits already incurred, or for costs of litigation. No grants in consecutive years. Normally the foundation will not sponsor conferences or seminars, or projects carried on outside the United States. No grants to private foundations.

Geographic limitations: Accepts grant applications narrowly focused in New Haven, CT and Minneapolis, MN. Some environmental grants will be made outside of those areas.

Areas of interest:
ARTS, CULTURE, HUMANITIES.
COMMUNITY IMPROVEMENT: Community vitality through arts, civic & cultural organizations.
ENVIRONMENTAL QUALITY/ PROTECTION/BEAUTIFICATION: Renewable energy programs.
YOUTH DEVELOPMENT: Youth development programs, Empower economically disadvantaged children & youth to achieve long-term stability & well-being.

Intended beneficiaries: Children and youth (infants-19 years), Ethnic/racial populations - general, Infants/children (ages 0-14), Poor/economically disadvantaged, Youth/adolescents (ages 14-19).

Types of support for organizations:
GENERAL PURPOSE/OPERATING SUPPORT.
PROGRAM DEVELOPMENT/ PROJECT SUPPORT.

Types of support for individuals: none.

Exclusions: Individuals, Non-501(c)(3), Political organizations, Religious organizations, Tax-supported institutions, Annual fund drives, Multiple year grants, International.

Sample grants:
East Side Neighborhood Services/MN/ After School Academic Support program/$15,000.

Environmental Law & Policy Center of the Midwest/IL/Clean Energy Development Initiative in the upper Midwest/$35,000.

Genesis II For Families Inc/MN/New Beginnings program supporting families/$10,000.

Leadership, Education & Athletics in Partnership/CT/General operating support of the children's and youth development programs/$35,000.

Renewable Energy AMP - MA/MA/Phase II, for advancing renewable energy in the Midwest in order to reduce current greenhouse gas emission by 80% by 2030/ $25,000.

Southside Community Health Services - MN/MN/To establish a Plan Talk pregnancy prevention program in Minneapolis/$30,000.

Financial Information

Financial data for year ending: 12/31/2006
Foundation assets: $39,653,252
Grants paid: $1,650,327
Number of grants: 86
Largest/smallest: $150,000/$3,000
Typical grant amount: $20,000
Matching gifts: $42,000

Application Information

Preferred form of initial contact: telephone inquiry, complete proposal, see website for proposal coversheet & FAQs.

Public information available by request: website (application, guidelines and annual report available on website or upon request).

Accept common grant application: yes.

Accept common report form: yes.

Proposal deadlines: January 15 for June grants, July 15 for January grants.

Preferred time for receiving proposals: deadlines.

Contribution decisions made by: board of directors/trustees, distribution committee.

Frequency of contributions decisions: semiannually.

Specific times board meets: June, December.

Typical time from application deadlines to notification: 4 months.

Special application procedures: Procedures described in detail at www.carolynfoundation.org.

Staff/Trustees

Staff: Becky Erdahl, executive director; Cindy Mellin, foundation administrator.

Directors/trustees: Guido Calabresi, emeritus; Betsey Copp; Andrew Crosby; Harriett Crosby; Stewart F. Crosby, chair; Thomas M. Crosby Jr., emeritus; Timothy B. Crosby; Sumner McKnight Crosby III; Charles C. Dobson; Marguerite Goss; Edmund C. Graham, treasurer; Rosa Lizarde; Jennifer C. Phelps; Eleanor W. Smith.

Catholic Aid Association Foundation

3499 North Lexington Avenue
St Paul, MN 55126
County: Ramsey
Phone: (651) 765-4135
Alt. Phone: (877) 275-7145
Fax: (651) 765-4133
E-mail: pnaumann@catholicaid.org
Website: www.catholicaid.org
Established: 12/17/1997
Funder type: Community/public foundation

Program Description

Program's purpose: To support financially the spiritual, educational and social needs of the Catholic community where the Catholic Aid Association has a major presence.

Funding priorities: Catholic Education, Chastity and Abstinence and Disaster Relief.

Geographic focus: Minnesota statewide, areas outside Minnesota, Wisconsin, North Dakota, South Dakota and Iowa.

Geographic limitations: Minnesota, Iowa, North Dakota, South Dakota and Wisconsin.

Areas of interest:

EDUCATION: Secondary.

HEALTH - GENERAL/REHABILITATIVE: Health support services, Rehabilitative medical services.

HUMAN SERVICES: Family services.

RELIGION/SPIRITUAL DEVELOPMENT: Specific denomination.

Intended beneficiaries: General public/unspecified.

Sample grants:

Church, Catholic - IA/IA/Holy Name Parish, Rock Rapids/$500.

Church, Catholic - MN/MN/Church of St Mary, Foley/$250.

Diocese of St Cloud/MN/$800.

St Dominic School - MN/MN/Northfield/$500.

St Edwards School/MN/Mineota/$500.

St John's School/MN/Hopkins/$500.

St Mary's Mission/Red Lake, MN/$200.

Financial Information

Financial data for year ending: 12/31/2006
Foundation assets: $2,000,000
Grants paid: $18,700
Number of grants: 40
Largest/smallest: $1,000/$200

Application Information

Preferred form of initial contact: letter of inquiry.

Public information available by request: website.

Contribution decisions made by: staff, board of directors/trustees.

Frequency of contributions decisions: quarterly.

Staff/Trustees

Staff: Paul Naumann, executive director.

Directors/trustees: Frances M. Barten; Bernard Bastian; Kathy Hemmelgarn; Joseph F. Kueppers; Michael F. McGovern, chair; Dennis Olson; Deb Pauly; Peter Ryan; Tracy Skuza; Florbert L. Spanier.

Catholic Community Foundation in the Archdiocese of Saint Paul and Minneapolis

One Water Street West
Suite 200
St Paul, MN 55107
County: Ramsey
Phone: (651) 389-0878
Fax: (651) 389-0650
E-mail: info@catholiccommunityfoundation.org
Website: www.catholiccommunityfoundation.org
Established: 11/01/1992
Paid Staff: Yes
Funder type: Community/public foundation

Program Description

Program's purpose: To support financially the spiritual, educational and social needs of our Catholic community. Catholic Community Foundation (CCF) fulfills its mission by helping donors achieve their charitable and financial goals; helping parishes, schools and Catholic organizations meet their long-term financial needs; providing responsible and effective financial management for long-term and endowed funds; and distributing earnings according to community priorities and donor intent.

Funding priorities: Support for Catholic schools, religious education and youth; ministerial enrichment and pastoral outreach through social service programs; programs for elderly who have limited resources, very limited involvement with family and friends, and wish to live at home; afterschool programs for 5-14-year-old kids at risk; programs for young mothers striving to improve the quality of life for themselves and their families.

Program limitations/restrictions: We review the organizations recommended as grant recipients to ensure they are legitimate charities and that their missions do not conflict with the teachings of the Roman Catholic Church.

Geographic focus: Twin Cities Metropolitan Area, Greater Minnesota.

Geographic limitations: For permanent endowed funds: the 12-county area defined by the Archdiocese of Saint Paul and Minneapolis. CCF will support national and international tax-exempt and charitable organizations with gifts from donor-advised funds and remainders of charitable trusts and annuities.

Areas of interest:

EDUCATION: Educational services, Higher education, Pre-school/elementary, Secondary.

FOOD/NUTRITION/AGRICULTURE: Agricultural programs, Soil and water conservation/farm land preservation.

HUMAN SERVICES: Children/youth services, Multipurpose human service organizations, Residential/custodial care.

RELIGION/SPIRITUAL DEVELOPMENT: Specific denomination, Catholic parishes, schools or apostolates.

Intended beneficiaries: Adults, Aging/elderly/senior citizens, Children and youth (infants-19 years), Female adults.

Types of support for individuals: scholarships.

Exclusions: Individuals, Non-501(c)(3).

Sample grants:

Cookie Cart/MN/Kids at Risk/$2,500.

The Jeremiah Program/MN/Young Mothers with Children/$2,500.

Sisters Care - MN/MN/Elderly at Risk/$5,000.

St Joseph's Home for Children - MN/MN/$12,500.

Trinity Catholic School/MN/Kids at Risk/$2,500.

University of MN - Minneapolis/MN/Life Care Center - Young Mothers with Children/$2,000.

Financial Information

Financial data for year ending: 06/30/2006
Foundation assets: $167,834,733
Grants paid: $5,662,793
Number of grants: 1546
Largest/smallest: $500,000/$50

Application Information

Preferred form of initial contact: letter of inquiry.

Public information available by request: proposal guidelines, application form, annual report, website.

Accept common grant application: yes.

Accept common report form: yes.

Will view video: yes.

Proposal deadlines: End of August. (Deadline is subject to change. Please visit our website for current information.)

Preferred time for receiving proposals: April-June.

Contribution decisions made by: board of directors/trustees, grants distribution committee.

Frequency of contributions decisions: annually.

Typical time from application deadlines to notification: 3 months.

Special application procedures: See CCF website for more information.

Staff/Trustees

Staff: Becky Abbott, accountant; Nancy Borzo, vice president of finance & administration; Marilou Eldred, president; Jim Mullin, investment officer; Jeff Pedersen, planned giving officer; James Seidel, director of development; Carol A. Swanson, director of marketing and communications; Jules Vierling, grants manager.

Directors/trustees: Gerald D. Brennan; Mary Broderick; John K. Butler; Norbert Conzemius; Alfred O. Elder; Archbishop Harry Flynn, chair; Patricia Huber; Josie Johnson; Stewart Laird, vice chair; Maureen Lannan; Andrea Lee; Diane Liemandt-Reimann; Fr. Kevin McDonough; Lawrence McGough; Thomas McKeown; John Moore; Susan Morrison; Brian C. Murray; Bishop Richard Pates; John M. Pohlad; Gregory J. Pulles, treasurer; Gerald Rauenhorst, director emeritus; Molly Rumsey Park; Tim Scanlan, secretary; Roger Scherer; Roger Schnobrich; Roger Vasko.

The CCP Foundation

474 Cleveland Avenue
Suite 130
St Paul, MN 55104
County: Ramsey
Phone: (651) 356-1013
E-mail: jammihb@ccpfoundation.org
Website: www.ccpfoundation.org
Contact: Jammi Hansen Blair, foundation administrator
Funder type: Private foundation

Program Description

Program's purpose: The mission of The CCP Foundation is to instigate action that leads to better opportunities for people with developmental disabilities.

Funding priorities: A request must primarily serve persons with developmental disabilities. Modest grants, technical assistance and/or stipends and educational, conference or symposium sponsorships. Sponsorship opportunities for organizations related to or mission of better opportunities for people with developmental disabilities; educational events to bring new or innovative ideas to our area, conferences or speakers related to improved service delivery models, or symposiums to gather folks together to advance the field.

Program limitations/restrictions: Lobbying, advocacy, or political activities, ongoing general operating or existing deficits, endowments or fundraising events, programs outside Minnesota.

Geographic focus: Twin Cities Metropolitan Area, East Metropolitan Area/St Paul only.

Types of support for organizations:
MANAGEMENT/TECHNICAL ASSISTANCE.
PROGRAM DEVELOPMENT/ PROJECT SUPPORT.
PROGRAM-RELATED INVESTMENTS.

Application Information

Preferred form of initial contact: request for guidelines. Full guidelines, forms and deadlines on website at www.ccpfoundation.org.

Public information available by request: proposal guidelines, application form, website.

Will view video: yes.

Proposal deadlines: ongoing

Contribution decisions made by: staff, board of directors/trustees.

Frequency of contributions decisions: ongoing.

Typical time from application deadlines to notification: 1-2 months.

Staff/Trustees

Staff: Gerald Glomb, executive director; Mary Glomb; Jammi Hansen Blair, foundation administrator; Steve Miletich.

CDF Foundation

2100 Spruce Trail
Golden Valley, MN 55422-4169
County: Hennepin
Contact: Carolyn D. Fiterman, president
Established: 10/06/1992
Funder type: Private foundation

Program Description

Program's purpose: General charitable purposes.

Geographic focus: Twin Cities Metropolitan Area.

Areas of interest:
ARTS, CULTURE, HUMANITIES.
HEALTH - DISEASES/MEDICAL DISCIPLINES.
HUMAN SERVICES.
RELIGION/SPIRITUAL DEVELOPMENT.

Intended beneficiaries: General public/unspecified.

Sample grants:
Emergency Food Shelf - MN (Minneapolis)/MN/$1,000.
Susan G Komen Foundation - MN/MN/ $5,000.
March of Dimes - MN (Minneapolis)/MN/$1,000.
Minneapolis Jewish Federation/MN/ $27,500.
MN Orchestra/MN/$1,000.
Sholom Community Alliance/MN/$200.
Twin Cities Gay Men's Chorus/MN/ $1,000.
Twin Cities Opera Guild Inc/MN/$250.

Financial Information

Financial data for year ending: 09/30/2005
Foundation assets: $1,012,317
Grants paid: $11,475
Number of grants: 30
Largest/smallest: $1,000/$100

Application Information

Preferred form of initial contact: complete proposal.

Proposal deadlines: none.

Staff/Trustees

Directors/trustees: Roger Cone, vice president; Carolyn D. Fiterman, president; John Simon, vice president.

CenterPoint Energy

800 LaSalle Avenue
PO Box 59038
Minneapolis, MN 55459-0038
County: Hennepin
Website: www.centerpointenergy.com
Contact: Al Swintek, manager, local government relations
Established: 01/01/1955
Funder type: Corporate giving program

Program Description

Program's purpose: To enhance our strategic business plans by building relationships with grassroots, community-based organizations. The success of our business is dependent on the success of the communities we serve. Requests are considered for remaining funds on a quarterly basis.

Funding priorities: 1) Affordable housing; 2) Environment; 3) Post-Secondary Technical education.

Geographic focus: Twin Cities Metropolitan Area, Greater Minnesota, Communities within our service territory.

Geographic limitations: CenterPoint Energy Minnesota service area.

Areas of interest:

EDUCATION: Post-secondary technical education.

ENVIRONMENTAL QUALITY/PROTECTION/BEAUTIFICATION: Environmental beautification/open spaces, Natural resources conservation/protection.

HOUSING/SHELTER: Housing development/construction/management, Rehab and new construction affordable housing.

PUBLIC SAFETY/DISASTERS/RELIEF: Disaster preparedness and relief, Safety education, Other.

Intended beneficiaries: General public/unspecified.

Types of support for organizations:

GENERAL PURPOSE/OPERATING SUPPORT.

PROGRAM DEVELOPMENT/PROJECT SUPPORT.

CORPORATE SPONSORSHIP: Strategically focused events related to business initiatives. Affordable housing, environmental, post secondary technical education. No grants to religious, political, individuals, travel, conferences, athletics, national fund drives, capital campaigns.

Types of support for individuals: none.

Exclusions: Capital & endowment campaigns, Individuals, Non-501(c)(3), Political organizations, Religious organizations, Research, Scholarships/loans, Tax-supported institutions, Travel, Conferences, Athletics, National fund drives.

Financial Information

Financial data for year ending: 12/31/2006
Grants paid: $303,000

Application Information

Preferred form of initial contact: letter of inquiry, telephone inquiry, request for guidelines, e-mail.

Public information available by request: proposal guidelines, application form, website.

Accept common grant application: yes.

Accept common report form: yes.

Proposal deadlines: Quarterly.

Contribution decisions made by: staff.

Frequency of contributions decisions: quarterly.

Typical time from application deadlines to notification: 1-4 months.

Staff/Trustees

Staff: Suzanne Pierazek, manager, community relations; Al Swintek, manager, local government relations.

Central Minnesota Community Foundation

101 South Seventh Avenue
Suite 100
St Cloud, MN 56301
County: Stearns
Phone: (320) 253-4380
Fax: (320) 240-9215
E-mail: info@communitygiving.org
Website: www.CommunityGiving.org
Contact: Susan Lorenz, program officer
Established: 11/30/1985
Funder type: Community/public foundation

Program Description

Program's purpose: To build social capital.

Funding priorities: The foundation focuses on building social capital, bridging, and bonding. Please see www.communitygiving.com for more details.

Program limitations/restrictions: The foundation will not fund individuals; endowments; medical research; capital campaigns to which the foundation can contribute no more than a tiny fraction of the total need; debt retirement or deficit financing; dollar-for-dollar replacement of government funding that has been reduced or eliminated; religious organizations for direct religious activities; political organizations or political campaigns; fraternal organizations, societies or orders; telephone solicitations; national fundraising efforts; or grants for travel.

Geographic focus: Central Minnesota region.

Geographic limitations: Benton, Sherburne and Stearns counties, central Minnesota region.

Areas of interest:

ANIMAL RELATED: Animal protection/welfare, Wildlife preservation/protection.

ARTS, CULTURE, HUMANITIES: Arts/cultural multipurpose, Historical societies, Humanities, Museums, Performing arts, Visual arts.

CIVIL RIGHTS: Civil liberties advocacy, Civil rights/advocacy for specific groups, Equal opportunity and access, Intergroup relations/race relations.

COMMUNITY IMPROVEMENT: Community coalitions, Community/neighborhood development/improvement, Nonprofit management.

EDUCATION: Adult/continuing education/literacy, Educational services, Higher education, Pre-school/elementary, Secondary, Student services/organizations of students, Vocational/technical, Scholarships primarily - some special projects accepted.

ENVIRONMENTAL QUALITY/PROTECTION/BEAUTIFICATION: Botanical/horticultural/landscape, Environmental beautification/open spaces, Environmental education/outdoor survival, Natural resources conservation/protection.

HEALTH - GENERAL/REHABILITATIVE: Health support services, Public health programs/wellness education.

HEALTH - MENTAL HEALTH/CRISIS INTERVENTION: Counseling/support groups, Hotline/crisis intervention.

HOUSING/SHELTER: Housing development/construction/management, Housing support services.

HUMAN SERVICES: Children/youth services, Emergency assistance (food/clothing/cash), Family services, Family services for adolescent parents, Family violence shelters and services, Multipurpose human service organizations, Senior centers and services, Services to specific groups, Victims services.

PHILANTHROPY/VOLUNTARISM: Nonprofit sector assistance, Philanthropy - general, Philanthropy associations, Public foundations and community foundations, Voluntarism promotion.

PUBLIC AFFAIRS/SOCIETY BENEFIT: Citizen participation, Leadership development/awards programs (other than youth).

PUBLIC PROTECTION - CRIME/COURTS/LEGAL SERVICES: Crime prevention, Dispute/conflict resolution, Legal services, Protection/prevention - neglect/abuse/exploitation.

PUBLIC SAFETY/DISASTERS/RELIEF: Disaster preparedness and relief, Safety education.

RECREATION: Physical fitness/recreational facilities, Recreation and sporting camps.

RELIGION/SPIRITUAL DEVELOPMENT: Interfaith issues.

YOUTH DEVELOPMENT: Adult/child matching programs, Multipurpose youth centers/clubs, Scouting organizations, Youth development programs.

Intended beneficiaries: General public/unspecified.

Types of support for organizations:
GENERAL PURPOSE/OPERATING SUPPORT.
PROGRAM DEVELOPMENT/PROJECT SUPPORT: Conferences/seminars, Curriculum development, Exhibitions, Mentoring programs, Performance/production costs, Public awareness, Seed money/start-up funds, Leadership programs.
STUDENT AID (GRANTS TO INSTITUTIONS): Scholarship funds.

Types of support for individuals: scholarships.

Sample grants:
Boy Scouts of America - MN (Central MN Council)/MN/$69,388.
Caritas Family Services/MN/$10,500.
Central MN Task Force on Battered Women/MN/$2,700.
Church, Protestant - MN/MN/Calvary Lutheran/$8,565.
ISD Nissaw #181/MN/$6,000.
St Cloud Technical College/MN/$30,000.

Financial Information

Financial data for year ending: 06/30/2006
Foundation assets: $49,857,758
Grants paid: $5,855,718

Application Information

Preferred form of initial contact: request for guidelines, e-mail.
Public information available by request: proposal guidelines, application form, annual report, newsletter, website.
Accept common grant application: yes.
Accept common report form: yes.
Proposal deadlines: Check website for deadlines. Deadlines may change each year.
Contribution decisions made by: board of directors/trustees.
Frequency of contributions decisions: depends on grant funds.
Typical time from application deadlines to notification: 2 months.

Staff/Trustees

Staff: Duane Aldrich, Willmar Area Community Foundation affiliate coordinator; Michael Burton, affiliate coordinator, Brainerd Lakes Area Community Foundation; Barbara Carlson, development officer; Sandra Henley, financial assistant; Steven R. Joul, president; Susan Lorenz, program officer; April Rabbie, administrative assistant; Greta Stark-Kraker, office manager; Glen Tautges, associate development officer; Constance M. Viere, financial officer.

Directors/trustees: Dean Anderson; Alex Didier; Keith Finstad; Dennis Gregory; Loran Hall; Andy Hilger; Pete Hill; Kevin Hughes; Steven R. Joul, president; Janet Knoblach; Shelly Bauerly Kopel; Gary Marsden; Asha Morgan Moran; Brian Myres; John Sullivan; Don Watkins.

Charity, Inc.

5786 118th Avenue
Clear Lake, MN 55319
County: Sherburne
Phone: (320) 743-5466
Contact: Deanne Hulme
Established: 02/01/1962
Funder type: Private foundation

Program Description

Program's purpose: Primarily contributions to local religious organizations and Christian educational organizations; consideration also given to public charities.

Funding priorities: Christian organizations and schools and colleges, local religious organizations and to public charities.

Geographic focus: Twin Cities Metropolitan Area, Greater Minnesota, Areas outside Minnesota.

Areas of interest:
EDUCATION.
RELIGION/SPIRITUAL DEVELOPMENT.

Intended beneficiaries: General public/unspecified.

Types of support for organizations:
CAPITAL CAMPAIGNS: Building/renovation.
GENERAL PURPOSE/OPERATING SUPPORT.

Sample grants:
Church of Holy Cross/Minneapolis, MN/general charitable activity/$10,000.

East Side Neighborhood Services/MN/general charitable activity/$500.

Friends of the Orphans - MN/MN/general charitable activity/$5,000.

Life Teen Inc./AZ/general charitable activity/$5,000.

National Catholic Educational Association/DC/general charitable activity/$500.

NET Ministries Inc/MN/general charitable activity/$100,000.

Prison Fellowship - VA/VA/general charitable activity/$1,000.

Totino Grace High School/MN/building fund/$156,799.

Financial Information

Financial data for year ending: 02/28/2006
Foundation assets: $8,630,851
Grants paid: $343,739
Number of grants: 46
Largest/smallest: $156,799/$200

Application Information

Preferred form of initial contact: complete proposal.

Proposal deadlines: none.

Staff/Trustees

Directors/trustees: Bonita Brenny; Joanne Elwell, president; Donald Schwalm.

Charlson Foundation

5275 Edina Industrial Boulevard
Suite 111
Edina, MN 55439-2914
County: Hennepin
Phone: (952) 938-6968
Fax: (952) 938-0240
E-mail: info@charlsonfoundation.org
Website: www.charlsonfoundation.org
Contact: Karen K. McElrath
Established: 11/04/1977
Funder type: Private foundation

Program Description

Program's purpose: The Charlson Foundation invests in changing the lives and futures of at-risk youth and families.

Funding priorities: Youth development and supportive housing.

Program limitations/restrictions: The Charlson Foundation is not be accepting unsolicited grant requests.

Geographic focus: Twin Cities Metropolitan Area.

Geographic limitations: Giving restricted to the Twin Cities Metropolitan Area.

Areas of interest:
HOUSING/SHELTER: Supportive housing.
HUMAN SERVICES: Children/youth services, Family services, Family services for adolescent parents, Multipurpose human service organizations.
YOUTH DEVELOPMENT: Adult/child matching programs, Youth development programs.

Intended beneficiaries: Ethnic/racial populations - general, Migrant workers, Poor/economically disadvantaged, Single parents, Youth/adolescents (ages 14-19).

Types of support for organizations:
GENERAL PURPOSE/OPERATING SUPPORT: Annual campaigns.
PROGRAM DEVELOPMENT/PROJECT SUPPORT.

Types of support for individuals: none.

Sample grants:
Children's Hospital - MN (St Paul)/MN/Midwest Children's Resource Center - Home Health Intervention project/$15,000.

Dakota Woodlands/MN/$25,000.

Jeremiah Program (The)/MN/$50,000.

Learning Works Program/MN/$15,000.

St David's Child Development/Minnetonka, MN/Steep Program/$10,000.

St David's Child Development/Minnetonka, MN/STEEP program/$7,000.

Women's Foundation of MN/MN/girlsBEST program/$50,000.

YWCA - MN (St Paul)/MN/Transitional housing program/$12,000.

Financial Information

Financial data for year ending: 12/31/2005
Foundation assets: $13,918,528
Grants paid: $1,095,420

Application Information

Preferred form of initial contact: letter of inquiry, request for guidelines.

Public information available by request: proposal guidelines.

Accept common grant application: yes.

Accept common report form: yes.

Proposal deadlines: The Charlson Foundation is not currently accepting unsolicited grant requests.

Contribution decisions made by: board of directors/trustees.

Frequency of contributions decisions: semiannually.

Specific times board meets: May, October.

Typical time from application deadlines to notification: 2-3 months.

Staff/Trustees

Directors/trustees: Kim Herzog; Karen K. McElrath; Mary Rippy; Leslie H. Stiles.

CHS Foundation

5500 Cenex Drive
Inver Grove Heights, MN 55077
County: Dakota
Phone: (651) 355-5481
Fax: (651) 355-5073
E-mail: william.nelson@chsinc.com
Website: www.chsfoundation.org
Contact: William J. Nelson, president
Established: 12/05/1947
Funder type: Corporate foundation

Program Description

Program's purpose: The CHS Foundation is committed to investing in the future of rural America, agriculture and cooperative business through education and leadership development.

Funding priorities: Cooperative education, scholarships, rural youth leadership development and farm and agricultural safety.

Program limitations/restrictions: Giving is focused on programs and people.

Geographic focus: National areas.

Geographic limitations: Support is given for state, regional and national based programs fitting the CHS Foundation's purpose. Geographically, giving is done in the CHS trade area, which spans from the Great Lakes to the Pacific Northwest and from the Canadian border to Texas.

Areas of interest:

EDUCATION: Higher education, Vocational/technical, Related to agriculture and cooperative education.

FOOD/NUTRITION/AGRICULTURE: Agricultural programs, Farm and agricultural safety.

YOUTH DEVELOPMENT: Rural agricultural youth leadership development.

Intended beneficiaries: General public/unspecified.

Types of support for individuals: none.

Sample grants:

Ag in the Classroom - WA/WA/$2,500.

Farm Safety Just 4 Kids - IA/IA/Support of education programs that help keep farm families safe/$15,000.

Future Farmers of America Foundation - MN/MN/$4,800.

Iowa Farmers Union/IA/$9,049.

North Dakota State University/ND/Science Fair/$1,500.

Ridgewater College - Hutchinson/MN/$3,600.

South Dakota Farmers Union/SD/$88,475.

University of Wisconsin - Platteville Foundation/WI/$6,000.

Financial Information

Financial data for year ending: 12/31/2006
Foundation assets: $28,890,529
Grants paid: $1,351,853
Number of grants: 92
Largest/smallest: $158,500/$250

Application Information

Preferred form of initial contact: Online application at www.chsfoundation.org.

Public information available by request: proposal guidelines, application form.

Proposal deadlines: All grants are accepted on an ongoing basis, with the exception of the Cooperative Education Grants, which are due September 30 for the upcoming year.

Preferred time for receiving proposals: Applications should be submitted at least 60 to 90 days prior to requested deadline.

Contribution decisions made by: staff, board of directors/trustees.

Typical time from application deadlines to notification: 30-90 days.

Staff/Trustees

Staff: William J. Nelson, president; Leslie Shuler, senior editor; Jennifer Thatcher, manager.

Directors/trustees: Bruce Anderson; Don Anthony; Robert Bass; Dennis Carlson; Curt Eischens; Steve Fritel; Robert Grabarski; Jerry Hasnedl; David Kayser; James Kile; Randy Knecht; Michael Mulcahey; Richard Owen; Steve Riegel; Don Schurr; Duane Stenzel.

ClearWay Minnesota (fka Minnesota Partnership for Action Against Tobacco)

Two Appletree Square
Suite 400
8011 34th Avenue South
Minneapolis, MN 55425
County: Hennepin
Phone: (952) 767-1400
Fax: (952) 767-1422
Website: www.clearwaymn.org
Paid Staff: Yes
Funder type: Community/public foundation
Paid Staff: Yes

Program Description

Program's purpose: ClearWay Minnesota funds programs and activities to reduce tobacco use and exposure to secondhand smoke in Minnesota through research, action and collaboration.

Funding priorities: Areas of emphasis include providing intervention grants to support innovative programs and efforts to reduce tobacco's harm around the state of Minnesota; funding research that can be translated into effective interventions to reduce tobacco's harm; and working with priority populations to create strategies to reduce commercial tobacco use (as opposed to traditional/sacred use by indigenous peoples) and the harm it causes in their communities.

Program limitations/restrictions: ClearWay Minnesota does not fund ongoing general operating expenses; unapproved drug therapies or devices; direct support to individuals; operating deficits or debt service.

Geographic focus: Minnesota statewide.

Geographic limitations: State of Minnesota only.

Areas of interest:

COMMUNITY IMPROVEMENT: Community coalitions, Developing coalitions and capacity of community groups to work on tobacco use reduction.

HEALTH - MENTAL HEALTH/CRISIS INTERVENTION: Counseling/support groups, Hotline/crisis intervention, Tobacco use and cessation.

HEALTH - RESEARCH: Tobacco use reduction and treatment.

HUMAN SERVICES: Services to specific groups.

Intended beneficiaries: Adults, African Americans/Blacks, Asian/Pacific Islanders, Ethnic/racial minorities - other specified group(s), Ethnic/racial populations - general, Gay/lesbian/bisexual/transgender, Hispanics/Latinos, Immigrants/newcomers/refugees, Migrant workers, Native American/American Indians.

Types of support for individuals: none.

Sample grants:

Association of Asian Pacific Community Health Organizations/CA/Leadership Institute to advance Minnesota's parity for priority populations/$540,000.

Healthways Quitnet, Inc/MN/Provide Internet Cessation services (quitplan.com) for Minnesotans/$450,000.

Mayo Clinic/MN/Health Solutions/To operate the QUITPLAN Helpline to assist smokers to stop smoking/$1,000,000.

University of MN - Division of Epidemiology/MN/Community academic research project to prevent tobacco abuse in American Indian Nations/$488,747.

Financial Information

Financial data for year ending: 06/30/2006
Foundation assets: $166,503,972
Grants paid: $6,950,442
Number of grants: 75
Largest/smallest: $718,201/$1,000
Largest multi-year grant approved: $517,495

Application Information

Preferred form of initial contact: telephone inquiry, e-mail. Check website or call main number for current guidelines and application release dates.

Public information available by request: proposal guidelines, application form, annual report, website, Form 990.

Proposal deadlines: varies.

Contribution decisions made by: board of directors/trustees.

Frequency of contributions decisions: varies.

Specific times board meets: every other month, third Wednesday, 9am - noon.

Typical time from application deadlines to notification: 3-6 months.

Staff/Trustees

Staff: Jennifer Cash, intervention program manager; Joanne D'Silva, research program manager; Marietta Dreher, senior advertising manager; Kerri Gordon, public relations manager; Amy Henderson, executive assistant; Adam Kintopf, communications manager; Lindsey Knutson, administrative assistant; Lana Kopylov, finance manager; Kristin Lemke, office manager; Theresa Leonard, intervention program manager; Jaime Martinez, director of community development; Chris Matter, community development manager; Molly Moilanen, intervention program manager; Andrea Mowery, director of marketing & communications; Paul Orman, chief financial officer; Jeri Reinhardt, legal services manager; Jessie Saul, research program manager; Barbara Schillo, director of research programs; Michael Sheldon, communications manager; Ann St Claire, research program manager; Christine Tholkes, senior policy manager; Ann Wendling, director of intervention programs; Megan Whittet, research program manager; David Willoughby, chief executive officer; Gouzel Zhdanova, accounting specialist.

Directors/trustees: Colleen Aho; Blanton Bessinger; Nancy Brataas; Mitchell Davis Jr.; Ivan Dusek; Gary Eckenberg; Kirby Erickson; David Fisher; Vernae Hasbargen; Patricia Hoven; Sylvia Kaplan; Richard Mulder; Fred Nobrega; Michael Paymar; Charlie Rounds; Michael Scandrett.

Cloquet Educational Foundation

302 14th Street
Cloquet, MN 55720
County: Carlton
Phone: (218) 879-3806
Website: www.cloquet.k12.mn.us/Page918.aspx
Contact: Lorna Mangan, executive director
Established: 07/01/1984
Funder type: Community/public foundation

Program Description

Program's purpose: The foundation was created on the belief that children need a full range of activities, in the classroom and in the community, to develop into healthy, productive and responsible adults. The foundation supports activities that address the needs of our youth while providing the learning experiences necessary to develop essential life skills.

Funding priorities: Educational programs. We fund activities that serve children from birth to age 19.

Geographic focus: Greater Minnesota.

Geographic limitations: Only Cloquet, Minnesota.

Areas of interest:
EDUCATION: Pre-school/elementary, Secondary.
RECREATION.
YOUTH DEVELOPMENT.

Intended beneficiaries: Children and youth (infants-19 years).

Sample grants:
City of Cloquet - MN/MN/$2,000.
Cloquet Community Education/Cloquet, MN/$1,000.
Cloquet Public Schools/MN/$33,218.
Cloquet Youth Baseball/Cloquet, MN/$1,100.
Historical Society - Carlton County/MN/$1,500.

Financial Information

Financial data for year ending: 08/31/2006
Foundation assets: $887,911
Grants paid: $33,322

Application Information

Preferred form of initial contact: complete proposal.

Public information available by request: application form, website.

Proposal deadlines: April 5, September 5, December 5.

Contribution decisions made by: board of directors/trustees.

Frequency of contributions decisions: 3 times a year.

Specific times board meets: first Tuesday in Jan., May, Oct.

Staff/Trustees

Staff: Lorna Mangan, executive director.

Directors/trustees: Mike Acheson; Robin Anderson; Vivian Bergquist; Richard Brenner; Rhonda Johnson, president; Kim Josephson, treasurer, ex-officio; Lorna Mangan, executive director; David Minkkinen; Denny Modec; Rob Nelson; Sue Olson; Karrie Osvold, secretary, ex-officio; Jill Pertler; Patty Petite; Tom Proulx; Ken Scarbrough, superintendent, ex-officio; Russell Smith; Gail Wangen; James Yorston, vice president.

Comcast Cable Company

10 River Park Plaza
St Paul, MN 55107
County: Ramsey
Phone: (651) 493-5775
Fax: (651) 493-5288
Website: www.comcast.com/community
Contact: Mary Beth Schubert
Paid Staff: Yes
Funder type: Corporate foundation

Program Description

Program's purpose: The Comcast Foundation primarily funds organizations/programs that use communications technology effectively to address community needs in the areas of education, libraries, literacy, community service and volunteerism, and scholarships.

Program limitations/restrictions: The Comcast Foundation does not fund organizations without 501(c)(3) charitable status; organizations that practice discrimination by race, gender, religion, age, sexual preference or national origin; marketing sponsorships; sporting events (including golf outings, tournaments, teams and participant sponsorships); trips or tours; capital campaigns; private foundations; individuals; political candidates or organizations.

Geographic focus: Twin Cities Metropolitan Area, areas outside Minnesota, Comcast communities.

Geographic limitations: Only organizations operating within Comcast communities can be considered.

Areas of interest:
COMMUNITY IMPROVEMENT.
EDUCATION: Libraries/library science, Literacy, Scholarships.
YOUTH DEVELOPMENT: Youth leadership development.

Intended beneficiaries: General public/unspecified.

Types of support for organizations: PROGRAM DEVELOPMENT/PROJECT SUPPORT.

Types of support for individuals: none.

Exclusions: Capital & endowment campaigns, Non-501(c)(3), Political organizations.

Financial Information

Financial data for year ending: 12/31/2005
Grants paid: $65,000
Number of grants: 187
Largest/smallest: $20,000/$1,000

Application Information

Preferred form of initial contact: letter of inquiry.

Public information available by request: proposal guidelines, website, financial information.

Preferred time for receiving proposals: Letters of inquiry reviewed on a year-round basis.

Typical time from application deadlines to notification: 4-6 weeks.

Special application procedures: Letters of inquiry no more than 2 pages in length accompanied by confirmation of 501(c)(3) status; no faxes or e-mails; no videotapes or other extra materials unless requested; follow-up phone calls are strongly discouraged.

Staff/Trustees

Staff: Mary Beth Schubert.

The Constable Family Foundation

19455 Cedarhurst
Deephaven, MN 55391
County: Hennepin
Phone: (952) 473-8854
Contact: Donald M. Constable
Funder type: Private foundation

Program Description

Funding priorities: Religious, charitable, scientific, literary or educational activities.

Sample grants:
Bethel College & Seminary/MN/$20,000.
Church, Protestant - MN/MN/Ridgewood Church/$20,500.
Hill Cities, Inc/MN/$2,500.
Quiet Miracles - MN/MN/$350.
University of MN/Minneapolis, MN/$500.

Financial Information

Financial data for year ending: 12/31/2005
Foundation assets: $1,358,944
Grants paid: $45,049
Number of grants: 17
Largest/smallest: $20,000/$20

Application Information

Preferred form of initial contact: Applications may take any form.
Proposal deadlines: none.

Staff/Trustees

Directors/trustees: Donald M. Constable; Tracy B. Constable.

The Cooperative Foundation

PO Box 64047
St Paul, MN 55164-0047
County: Dakota
Phone: (651) 355-5481
Fax: (651) 355-5073
E-mail: william.nelson@chsinc.com
Website: www.thecooperativefoundation.org
Contact: William J. Nelson, president
Established: 01/01/1945
Paid Staff: Yes
Funder type: Private foundation

Program Description

Program's purpose: To expand and enhance cooperatives through research, teaching, extension, innovation and development.

Geographic focus: Twin Cities Metropolitan Area, Greater Minnesota, Minnesota statewide, Areas outside Minnesota, Minnesota, Wisconsin, North Dakota, South Dakota, Iowa.

Geographic limitations: Upper Midwest states of Minnesota, Iowa, North Dakota, South Dakota and Wisconsin.

Areas of interest:
COMMUNITY IMPROVEMENT: Economic development, Cooperative business approach to community development.
EDUCATION: Adult/continuing education/literacy, Graduate education/professional schools, Higher education, Libraries/library science, Secondary, Vocational/technical, on cooperative business economics and cooperative business development.
FOOD/NUTRITION/AGRICULTURE: Agricultural programs, related to cooperative business and rural development.
HOUSING/SHELTER: Development of cooperatively owned housing.
PUBLIC AFFAIRS/SOCIETY BENEFIT: Government/public administration, Leadership development/awards programs (other than youth), Public policy research and analysis, related to cooperative business and development.
SOCIAL SCIENCES: Interdisciplinary research/studies to improve understanding of particular populations/cultures, Interdisciplinary research on cooperative economics.

Intended beneficiaries: General public/unspecified.

Types of support for organizations:
PROGRAM DEVELOPMENT/PROJECT SUPPORT: Conferences/seminars, Curriculum development, Faculty/staff development, Film/video/radio production, Public policy research/analysis, Publications, Seed money/start-up funds, Leadership programs.
RESEARCH.
STUDENT AID (GRANTS TO INSTITUTIONS): Fellowships.
IN-KIND SERVICES: Speaking, workshops, educational resources.

Types of support for individuals: none.

Exclusions: Capital & endowment campaigns, Political organizations.

Sample grants:

Association of Co-op Education/MN/ education programs/$24,496.

Co-op Communicators Association/TX/ education program & fellowship project/ $5,000.

Cooperative Development Foundation/ DC/education program/$6,000.

MAC Education Foundation/MN/ education program/$22,500.

National Cooperative Business Association/DC/education program/ $2,929.

North Country Cooperative Foundation/ MN/training/education programs/$7,125.

South Dakota Association of Cooperatives - SD/SD/cooperative education/$1,500.

University of WI Center for Cooperatives/WI/education/research projects/$3,840.

Financial Information

Financial data for year ending: 12/31/2005
Foundation assets: $2,102,474
Grants paid: $107,334
Number of grants: 34
Largest/smallest: $5,000/$130

Application Information

Preferred form of initial contact: letter of inquiry, request for guidelines, complete proposal, e-mail, online form.

Public information available by request: proposal guidelines, application form, website.

Accept common grant application: yes.

Accept common report form: yes.

Proposal deadlines: open.

Contribution decisions made by: CEO, staff, board of directors/trustees.

Frequency of contributions decisions: monthly.

Typical time from application deadlines to notification: up to 6 months.

Staff/Trustees

Staff: Frank Blackburn; Leslie Mead; William J. Nelson, president; Jennifer Thatcher, manager.

Directors/trustees: Connie Cihak; Terri Dallas; Sheryl Doering Meshke; Brenda Forman; Gail Graham; Michael Gustafson; Patricia Keough-Wilson, chair; Jeff Nielsen; Anne Reynolds; Dan Stoltz; Jeffrey Swanhorst.

Arthur and David Cosgrove Memorial Fund

228 South Main Street
Le Sueur, MN 56058
County: Le Sueur
Phone: (507) 665-6363
Contact: Peter Schoeppner
Established: 11/01/1946
Funder type: Private foundation

Program Description

Geographic focus: Greater Minnesota, Area surrounding Le Sueur, Minnesota.

Geographic limitations: Restricted to Le Sueur, Minnesota.

Areas of interest:
ARTS, CULTURE, HUMANITIES.
EDUCATION.
HUMAN SERVICES.

Intended beneficiaries: General public/unspecified.

Types of support for organizations:
GRANTS TO INDIVIDUALS.
PROGRAM DEVELOPMENT/ PROJECT SUPPORT.

Types of support for individuals: scholarships.

Sample grants:

HAVE Inc/LeSueur, MN/school program/ $6,000.

Healthy Communities/LeSueur, MN/drug program/$3,000.

ISD LeSueur #2397/MN/$25,000.

LeSueur Museum/LeSueur, MN/tour program/$5,000.

Nursery School - LeSueur, MN/MN/ $40,000.

Financial Information

Financial data for year ending: 12/31/2006
Foundation assets: $1,500,000
Grants paid: $75,000
Number of grants: 8
Largest/smallest: $25,000/$3,000
Typical grant amount: $5,000

Application Information

Preferred form of initial contact: letter of inquiry, describe purpose of application in writing.

Staff/Trustees

Directors/trustees: Dodd Cosgrove; R.C. Cosgrove Jr.; June Curme; Neil R. Morem; Mary Scott Riviere; Peter Schoeppner; Ann Cosgrove Warner, chairman; Bradley Warner.

Cote Foundation

10179 Crosstown Circle
Eden Prairie, MN 55344-3301
County: Hennepin
Phone: (952) 925-0280
Contact: Jim Olson, executive director
Established: 03/01/1961
Funder type: Private foundation

Program Description

Program's purpose: Grant requests in the areas of Arts, Education, Health and Social Services are considered.

Funding priorities: Special consideration given to organizations that promote the positive development of youth.

Program limitations/restrictions: Only organizations with annual operating budgets of under $2 million and with recognized leadership are considered. The foundation does NOT make multi-year commitments, fund individuals, support endowment drives, conferences, seminars, tours or fundraising events.

Geographic focus: Grants are made only to organizations that serve people who reside in the Nisswa, Brainerd and Pequot Lakes areas of Minnesota, the Tucson area of Arizona, and to a lesser extent their surrounding communities.

Geographic limitations: Grants are made only to organizations that serve people who reside in the Nisswa, Brainerd and Pequot Lakes areas of Minnesota, the Tucson area of Arizona, and to a lesser extent their surrounding communities.

Areas of interest:
ARTS, CULTURE, HUMANITIES.
COMMUNITY IMPROVEMENT.
EDUCATION: Libraries/library science.
EMPLOYMENT/JOBS.

ENVIRONMENTAL QUALITY/
PROTECTION/BEAUTIFICATION.
FOOD/NUTRITION/AGRICULTURE:
Food service/free food distribution.
HEALTH - DISEASES/MEDICAL
DISCIPLINES.
HEALTH - GENERAL/
REHABILITATIVE.
HEALTH - MENTAL HEALTH/CRISIS
INTERVENTION.
HOUSING/SHELTER.
HUMAN SERVICES.
PUBLIC PROTECTION -
CRIME/COURTS/LEGAL SERVICES.
YOUTH DEVELOPMENT.

Types of support for organizations:
CAPITAL CAMPAIGNS: Building/renovation, Equipment.
EMERGENCY FUNDS.
GENERAL PURPOSE/OPERATING
SUPPORT.
PROGRAM DEVELOPMENT/PROJECT SUPPORT: Mentoring programs.

Types of support for individuals: none.

Exclusions: Individuals, Political organizations, Scholarships/loans.

Sample grants:
Brainerd Youth Orchestra/MN/$500.
Chamber of Commerce - MN (Nisswa)/MN/gazebo fund/$500.
Crow Wing Historical Society/Crow Wing, MN/$1,000.
Fellowship of Christian Athletes - MN/MN/$5,280.
Gull Lake Trail Association/MN/$500.
Lakeshore First Responders/Nisswa, MN/$3,500.
St Joseph Foundation - MN (Brainerd)/MN/$4,000.
Timber Bay Youth Investment Association/MN/$4,000.

Financial Information

Financial data for year ending: 12/31/2005
Foundation assets: $1,091,554
Grants paid: $27,500
Largest/smallest: $7,000/$1,000

Application Information

Preferred form of initial contact: letter of inquiry, complete proposal.
Public information available by request: proposal guidelines.
Accept common grant application: yes.

Proposal deadlines: Grant requests should arrive before close of business on April 1 to be considered for the June grantmaking meeting and October 1 to be considered for the December grantmaking meeting.
Contribution decisions made by: board of directors/trustees.
Frequency of contributions decisions: semiannually.

Staff/Trustees

Staff: Robert Cote, president; Jim Olson, executive director.
Directors/trustees: Mary C. Boos; James Randolph Cote; Robert Cote, president; Samual Ruggles Cote; Kelly Cote Jasper; Carolyn Jones; Jim Olson, executive director.

Cottonwood Foundation

PO Box 10803
White Bear Lake, MN 55110
County: Ramsey
Phone: (651) 426-8797
Fax: (651) 294-1012
E-mail: info@cottonwoodfdn.org
Website: www.cottonwoodfdn.org
Established: 01/31/1992
Funder type: Community/public foundation

Program Description

Program's purpose: Promoting empowerment of people, protection of the environment and respect for cultural diversity. The foundation focuses its funding on committed, grassroots organizations that rely strongly on volunteer efforts and where foundation support will make a significant difference.
Funding priorities: The foundation has a very limited amount of funding available, and will only award grants to organizations that meet all four of the following criteria: Protect the environment, promote cultural diversity, empower people to meet their basic needs, rely on volunteer efforts. Cottonwood Foundation currently provides grants only to preselected organizations called Cottonwood Partners.
Geographic focus: Twin Cities Metropolitan Area, Greater Minnesota, Minnesota statewide, areas outside Minnesota, national areas, international areas.

Geographic limitations: Cottonwood Foundation has no geographic restrictions.

Areas of interest:
ANIMAL RELATED: Wildlife preservation/protection.
CIVIL RIGHTS: Intergroup relations/race relations.
COMMUNITY IMPROVEMENT: Economic development.
ENVIRONMENTAL QUALITY/
PROTECTION/BEAUTIFICATION: Natural resources conservation/protection.
FOOD/NUTRITION/AGRICULTURE: Soil and water conservation/farm land preservation.
HUMAN SERVICES.
INTERNATIONAL AFFAIRS: Promotion of international understanding.

Intended beneficiaries: General public/unspecified.

Types of support for organizations:
CAPITAL CAMPAIGNS: Building/renovation, Computer systems/technology, Equipment, Land acquisitions.
GENERAL PURPOSE/OPERATING
SUPPORT.
PROGRAM DEVELOPMENT/
PROJECT SUPPORT: Seed money/start-up funds.

Types of support for individuals: none.

Exclusions: Individuals, Political organizations, Religious organizations, Tax-supported institutions, Universities, For-profit businesses.

Sample grants:
Dos Pueblos - NY/NY/$1,000.
Maka Foundation - SD/SD/$1,000.
Nepal Social Service Fund/MN/$1,000.
Porters Progress - NH/NH/$1,000.
Sustainable Harvest International/ME/$1,000.
Trees for the Future - MD/MD/$1,000.
White Earth Land Recovery Project/MN/$1,000.

Financial Information

Financial data for year ending: 12/31/2006
Foundation assets: $81,005
Grants paid: $45,000
Number of grants: 45
Largest/smallest: $1,000/$1,000
Typical grant amount: $1,000

Application Information

Preferred form of initial contact: e-mail.

Public information available by request: proposal guidelines, annual report, newsletter, website.

Contribution decisions made by: board of directors/trustees.

Special application procedures: Unsolicited grant applications are currently not being invited, although the foundation does plan to add a very small number of new organizations as Cottonwood Partners over time. See the foundation's website for details.

Staff/Trustees

Staff: Paul Moss, executive director.

Directors/trustees: Laura Bray, treasurer; Jamie Ford; Karissa Huntington, chair; Prabhakar Karri; Kathy Kinzig; Tom Meersman; Craig R. Miller, vice chair; Paul Moss, executive director; Erik Nelson, secretary; Joel Peterson; Caleb Werth.

Coughlan Companies

151 Good Counsel Drive
PO Box 669
Mankato, MN 56002-0669
County: Blue Earth
E-mail: mgustafson@coughlancompanies.com
Website: www.coughlan-companies.com/CommunityRelations.htm
Contact: Maureen Gustafson, director
Funder type: Corporate giving program

Program Description

Funding priorities: Environment, libraries, education.

Geographic focus: Greater Minnesota, Minnesota statewide.

Geographic limitations: Minnesota, mainly in Mankato area.

Areas of interest:
EDUCATION: Libraries/library science.
ENVIRONMENTAL QUALITY/PROTECTION/BEAUTIFICATION.

Types of support for organizations:
IN-KIND PRODUCTS: Limestone and Children's Books.

Types of support for individuals: aid to needy persons, scholarships.

Exclusions: Capital & endowment campaigns, Political organizations.

Staff/Trustees

Staff: Robert J. Coughlan, CEO; T. William Coughlan, senior vice president; Maureen Gustafson, director; Matt Keller, COO.

Charles and Kathryn Cunningham Family Foundation

U.S. Bank Trust, N.A.
101 East Fifth Street
St Paul, MN 55101
County: Ramsey
Phone: (651) 466-8738
Contact: Gary Westeen
Established: 01/01/1996
Funder type: Private foundation

Program Description

Program's purpose: Grants are made to charitable, religious, scientific, literary and education organizations under 501(c)(3).

Geographic focus: Twin Cities Metropolitan Area.

Areas of interest:
ARTS, CULTURE, HUMANITIES.
EDUCATION: Higher education.
HUMAN SERVICES.

Intended beneficiaries: Children and youth (infants-19 years), General public/unspecified.

Types of support for organizations:
GENERAL PURPOSE/OPERATING SUPPORT: Annual campaigns.
PROGRAM DEVELOPMENT/PROJECT SUPPORT.

Exclusions: Non-501(c)(3).

Sample grants:
DARE - MN/MN/general operating/$1,000.
Greater Twin Cities Youth Symphonies/MN/general operating/$5,000.
Gustavus Adolphus College - MN/MN/annual fund, Steuer Scholarship Fund/$26,500.
MacPhail Center for the Arts/MN/general operating/$2,000.
MN Orchestral Association/MN/general operating/$25,000.
MN Youth Symphony Inc/MN/general operating/$3,000.
PACER Center/MN/general operating/$5,000.
St Olaf College/MN/annual fund/$7,500.

Financial Information

Financial data for year ending: 12/31/2005
Foundation assets: $1,953,779
Grants paid: $82,500
Number of grants: 11
Largest/smallest: $25,000/$1,000

Application Information

Preferred form of initial contact: letter of inquiry.

Proposal deadlines: none.

Staff/Trustees

Directors/trustees: Charles G. Cunningham, president; Greg C. Cunningham, treasurer; Kathryn M. Cunningham, vice president; Dawn Ostrem, secretary; U.S. Bank, N.A.

Frances Curran Foundation, Inc.

Securian Trust Company
400 Robert Street North
St Paul, MN 55101-2098
County: Ramsey
Phone: (651) 665-4693
Alt. Phone: (651) 665-4667
Fax: (651) 665-5414
E-mail: bonnie.dougherty@securiantrust.com
Contact: Bonnie S. Dougherty, secretary
Established: 04/28/1972
Funder type: Private foundation

Program Description

Program's purpose: The Frances Curran Foundation is dedicated to the prevention of cruelty to animals and the improvement of their lot and well-being.

Funding priorities: Grants are provided to organizations with demonstrated history of service to, and on behalf of, animals with an emphasis on animals in shelters and foster homes and bolstering spay/neuter programs for companion animals.

Program limitations/restrictions: Applications are accepted from Minnesota organizations that provide services for, and on behalf of, companion animals and that have 501(c)(3) IRS tax-exempt status.

Geographic focus: Twin Cities Metropolitan Area, Greater Minnesota, Minnesota statewide.

Geographic limitations: Minnesota only.

Areas of interest:

ANIMAL RELATED: Spay/neuter for companion animals.

Types of support for individuals: none.

Exclusions: Individuals, Non-501(c)(3), Political organizations, Research, Scholarships/loans.

Sample grants:

Albert Lea Animal Control/MN/$3,000.

Cedar Riverside People's Center Veterinary Clinic/MN/$2,500.

Humane Society - MN (Brown County)/MN/$2,000.

Humane Society - MN (Lakes Area)/MN/$2,000.

Humane Society - MN (Minnesota Valley)/MN/$4,000.

Humane Society - MN (Pope County)/MN/$2,500.

Humane Society - MN (Wright County)/Buffalo, MN/$4,000.

Second Chance Animal Rescue/ MN/$2,500.

Financial Information

Financial data for year ending: 12/31/2005
Foundation assets: $1,132,880
Grants paid: $52,400
Number of grants: 21
Largest/smallest: $5,000/$1,000
Typical grant amount: $2,000

Application Information

Preferred form of initial contact: letter of inquiry, request for guidelines, e-mail.

Public information available by request: proposal guidelines, application form.

Proposal deadlines: Applications are due April 1 and September 1.

Preferred time for receiving proposals: March and August.

Contribution decisions made by: board of directors/trustees.

Frequency of contributions decisions: semiannually.

Specific times board meets: May and October.

Staff/Trustees

Directors/trustees: Bonnie S. Dougherty, secretary; Harold M. Johnson, president; Jan Mitchell; John A. Ritt, Treasurer; Jill Sherritt; Christa Treichel.

Dakota Medical Foundation/Dakota Medical Charities

4152 30th Avenue South
Suite 102
Fargo, ND 58104
Phone: (701) 271-0263
Fax: (701) 271-0408
E-mail: pattraynor@dakmed.org
Website: www.dakmed.org
Contact: J. Patrick Traynor J.D., president
Established: 11/01/1995
Paid Staff: Yes
Funder type: Community/public foundation

Program Description

Program's purpose: Measurably improving health and access to healthcare services by funding/managing innovative projects/programs.

Funding priorities: The foundation's current health focus is measurably improving health and access to health care services, especially for children. The foundation awards several types of grants: 1) Responsive grants, which are awarded in response to unsolicited requests that improve health and access to health care services or measurably address another significant health issue; 2) Initiative grants, which are foundation-sponsored strategic grant programs with specific measurable goals that address a particular health focus area; 3) Match grants, in which the foundation partners with others to leverage its existing investments and improve health and access to health care services. The foundation also awards grants through its donor-advised funds.

Geographic focus: Greater Minnesota, areas outside Minnesota, Generally, eastern North Dakota and northwest Minnesota.

Geographic limitations: Generally within the Red River Valley region (a 125-mile radius of Fargo, ND) – specifically the Minnesota counties of Pennington, Red Lake, Polk, Norman, Mahnomen, Clearwater, Hubbard, Clay, Becker, Wilkin, Ottertail and Wadena.

Areas of interest:

HEALTH - DISEASES/MEDICAL DISCIPLINES: Improve health and access to health care services.

HEALTH - GENERAL/REHABILITATIVE: Improve health and access to health care services.

HEALTH - MENTAL HEALTH/CRISIS INTERVENTION: Improve health and access to health care services.

Intended beneficiaries: Children and youth (infants-19 years), General public/unspecified.

Types of support for organizations:

PROGRAM DEVELOPMENT/ PROJECT SUPPORT.

Types of support for individuals: none.

Exclusions: Capital & endowment campaigns, Individuals, Non-501(c)(3).

Sample grants:

Altru Diabetes Management/ND/Diabetes Prevention Program/Worksite Wellness/$100,000.

American Heart Association - ND/North Dakota Goes Red Heart Health Initiative/$386,230.

Lake Region State College - ND/LPN Distance Education Program/$84,775.

St Joseph's Area Health Services - Park Rapids/MN/Community Dental Services for Low Income/Uninsured Persons/$115,000.

Financial Information

Financial data for year ending: 09/30/2005
Foundation assets: $106,665,038
Grants paid: $3,172,487
Number of grants: 117
Largest/smallest: $386,230/$100
Largest multi-year grant approved: $507,875

Application Information

Preferred form of initial contact: letter of inquiry, telephone inquiry, see website: www.dakmed.org/Grantmaking/Responsive to access eligibility questionnaire and online letter of intent form.

Public information available by request: proposal guidelines, application form, annual report, website.

Proposal deadlines: see website.

Contribution decisions made by: board of directors/trustees, grants committee, executive committee.

Frequency of contributions decisions: semiannually.

Typical time from application deadlines to notification: 3-4 months.

Staff/Trustees

Staff: Cynthia Eggl, executive assistant; David Gibb, director of finance; Joan Koperski, accountant; Kim Palm, grants and programs assistant; Jeana Peinovich, Lend-a-Hand program director; Jennifer Thompson J.D., director of development; J. Patrick Traynor J.D., president; Deb Watne, grants and programs manager.

Directors/trustees: John Bertel; David Clutter M.D.; Bruce Domm M.D.; Jay Eisenbeis; Tony Grindberg; Joel Haugen M.D.; Walter Johnson M.D., chair; Chris Kennelly; Deb Magnuson, B.S.N, R.N.; Ann Malmberg M.S., R.N.; Susan Mathison M.D.; Donald Matthees M.D.; Kevin Melicher O.D.; Curt Noyes; Richard Vetter M.D.; Jon Wanzek.

The Daulton Foundation

2925 Country Drive
St Paul, MN 55117
County: Ramsey
Phone: (651) 766-5110
Contact: Carrie Troske, program director
Established: 12/01/2003
Funder type: Private foundation

Program Description

Program's purpose: To improve the quality of lives of women, children and families through grants and programs that make systemic change in the communities in which we live and work. The Daulton Foundation envisions being a catalyst to get the broader community involved in creating a society where children and families have the housing and resources they need to succeed.

Intended beneficiaries: Children and youth (infants-19 years), Female adults, families.

Financial Information

Financial data for year ending: 12/31/2005
Foundation assets: $120,509
Grants paid: $83,932

Staff/Trustees

Staff: Carrie Troske, program director.

Directors/trustees: Patrick J. Daulton; Renee T. Daulton; Julie Daulton-Saad.

Edwin W. and Catherine M. Davis Foundation

2000 Wells Fargo Place
30 East Seventh Street
St Paul, MN 55101
County: Ramsey
Phone: (651) 215-4408
Contact: Gayle Roth, grants administrator
Established: 12/01/1956
Funder type: Private foundation

Program Description

Program's purpose: Amelioration of social problems, increasing opportunities available to disadvantaged people.

Funding priorities: Education, social welfare, mental health, the arts and environment.

Program limitations/restrictions: The foundation's directors prefer not to make long-term commitments, in order to preserve flexibility in the foundation's program to meet changing conditions from year to year.

Geographic focus: Twin Cities Metropolitan Area, Areas outside Minnesota.

Areas of interest:

ARTS, CULTURE, HUMANITIES: Historical societies, Museums, Performing arts.
EDUCATION.
ENVIRONMENTAL QUALITY/PROTECTION/BEAUTIFICATION.
HEALTH - MENTAL HEALTH/CRISIS INTERVENTION.
HUMAN SERVICES.

Intended beneficiaries: General public/unspecified, Poor/economically disadvantaged.

Types of support for organizations:
GENERAL PURPOSE/OPERATING SUPPORT.
PROGRAM DEVELOPMENT/PROJECT SUPPORT.
STUDENT AID (GRANTS TO INSTITUTIONS): Fellowships, Scholarship funds.

Types of support for individuals: none.

Exclusions: Capital & endowment campaigns, Individuals.

Sample grants:

Earth Island Institute/San Francisco, CA/general operating/$14,000.

Friends of the Library - MN (St Paul)/MN/Albert J. Moorman Fund/$50,000.

Fulfillment Fund - CA/CA/children's programs/$76,681.

MacPhail Center for the Arts/MN/scholarships/$2,000.

Ramsey County Historical Society/MN/Gibbs Farm Museum/$2,500.

Second Harvest Food Bank - IL (Chicago)/IL/general operating/$15,000.

University of California - Los Angeles Foundation/CA/pediatric cranial-facial institute/$20,000.

Youth Leadership, Inc - MN/MN/general operating/$5,000.

Financial Information

Financial data for year ending: 12/31/2005
Foundation assets: $21,471,687
Grants paid: $709,000
Number of grants: 44
Largest/smallest: $150,000/$1,000

Application Information

Preferred form of initial contact: letter of inquiry.

Public information available by request: annual report.

Accept common grant application: yes.

Accept common report form: yes.

Proposal deadlines: none.

Contribution decisions made by: board of directors/trustees.

Frequency of contributions decisions: monthly.

Typical time from application deadlines to notification: 4-6 weeks.

Staff/Trustees

Staff: Gayle Roth, grants administrator.

Directors/trustees: John L. Davis; Mary E. Davis; Lisa M. Fremont; Bette D. Moorman, president.

The Deikel Family Foundation

4400 Baker Road
Minnetonka, MN 55343
County: Hennepin
Phone: (952) 975-4813
Established: 01/01/1989
Funder type: Private foundation

Program Description

Program's purpose: To assist community in building and maintaining human service organizations.

Funding priorities: 1) Agencies demonstrating effectiveness in providing service to communities in need; 2) Selected health research areas; 3) Primary local support; 4) Education at primary and secondary levels.

Geographic focus: Twin Cities Metropolitan Area.

Areas of interest:
ANIMAL RELATED: Wildlife preservation/protection.
CIVIL RIGHTS: Civil rights/advocacy for specific groups.
COMMUNITY IMPROVEMENT: Community/neighborhood development/improvement, Nonprofit management.
ENVIRONMENTAL QUALITY/PROTECTION/BEAUTIFICATION: Environmental beautification/open spaces, Natural resources conservation/protection.
FOOD/NUTRITION/AGRICULTURE: Food service/free food distribution.
HEALTH - DISEASES/MEDICAL DISCIPLINES: AIDS/HIV, Allergy related diseases, Parkinson`s disease.
HEALTH - GENERAL/REHABILITATIVE: Health support services, Public health programs/wellness education.
HEALTH - MENTAL HEALTH/CRISIS INTERVENTION: Alcohol/drug/substance, prevention and treatment, Hotline/crisis intervention, Mental health treatment and services.
HOUSING/SHELTER: Homeless, temporary housing, Housing development/construction/management.
HUMAN SERVICES: Children/youth services, Emergency assistance (food/clothing/cash), Family services, Multipurpose human service organizations, Personal social services.
INTERNATIONAL AFFAIRS: International development/relief.
PHILANTHROPY/VOLUNTARISM: Federated Funds.
YOUTH DEVELOPMENT: Multipurpose youth centers/clubs.

Intended beneficiaries: General public/unspecified.

Types of support for organizations:
GENERAL PURPOSE/OPERATING SUPPORT.
PROGRAM DEVELOPMENT/PROJECT SUPPORT.

Sample grants:
B'nai Emet Synagogue/St Louis Park, MN/general operating/$5,000.
Community of Recovering People/Excelsior, MN/general operating/$5,000.
Fraser Community Services/MN/general operating/$3,000.
Minneapolis Jewish Day School/MN/general operating/$1,000.
MN AIDS Project Inc/MN/general operating/$500.
Parkinson Association of MN/MN/general operating/$500.
State of MN - Education/MN/citizens book/$6,735.
University of California - San Francisco/CA/R Glogau Teddy Bear Fund/$500.

Financial Information

Financial data for year ending: 12/31/2005
Foundation assets: $8,376,495
Grants paid: $467,475
Number of grants: 20
Largest/smallest: $150,000/$250

Application Information

Preferred form of initial contact: letter of inquiry, accompanied by financial statement, tax return or equivalent form indicating financial data.

Accept common grant application: yes.
Proposal deadlines: none.

Staff/Trustees

Directors/trustees: Theodore Deikel, president.

Roger L. and Agnes C. Dell Charitable Trust 1

U.S. Bank, N.A.
EP-MN-S14
St Paul, MN 55101
County: Ramsey
Phone: (651) 466-8443
Contact: Richard C. Hefte
Established: 12/01/1964
Funder type: Private foundation

Program Description

Geographic focus: Greater Minnesota.

Geographic limitations: Primarily funds programs in Fergus Falls and surrounding area.

Areas of interest:
ARTS, CULTURE, HUMANITIES.
COMMUNITY IMPROVEMENT.
EDUCATION.
HEALTH - DISEASES/MEDICAL DISCIPLINES.
PUBLIC AFFAIRS/SOCIETY BENEFIT.

Intended beneficiaries: General public/unspecified.

Types of support for organizations:
GENERAL PURPOSE/OPERATING SUPPORT.

Sample grants:
City of Parkers Prairie/MN/event center/$1,000.
Dollars for Scholars - MN (Fergus Falls)/Fergus Falls, MN/general operating/$1,000.
Fergus Falls Area College Foundation/Fergus Falls, MN/scholarships/$1,000.
Lake Region Hospital Foundation/Fergus Falls, MN/scholarships/$2,500.
Pioneer Public Television - MN/MN/operating/$750.
YMCA - MN (Fergus Falls)/MN/general operating/$7,500.

Financial Information

Financial data for year ending: 11/30/2005
Foundation assets: $930,972
Grants paid: $8,288
Number of grants: 14
Largest/smallest: $2,000/$288

Application Information

Preferred form of initial contact: complete proposal.

Proposal deadlines: none.

Special application procedures: applications should be submitted in written form outlining nature of the request.

Staff/Trustees

Directors/trustees: U.S. Bank Trust, N.A.; Richard C. Hefte; Richard L. Pemberton Jr.; Stephen F. Rufer.

Roger L. and Agnes C. Dell Charitable Trust 2

Law Office Building
110 North Mill
Fergus Falls, MN 56537
County: Otter Tail
Phone: (218) 998-3355
Contact: Richard C. Hefte
Established: 02/01/1956
Funder type: Private foundation

Program Description

Program's purpose: Exclusively for charitable, religious, scientific, literary and educational purposes.

Geographic focus: Greater Minnesota.

Geographic limitations: Limited mainly to Fergus Falls, Minnesota and its surrounding area.

Areas of interest:
ARTS, CULTURE, HUMANITIES.
EDUCATION.
HUMAN SERVICES.
PUBLIC AFFAIRS/SOCIETY BENEFIT.
RELIGION/SPIRITUAL DEVELOPMENT.
YOUTH DEVELOPMENT.

Intended beneficiaries: General public/unspecified.

Types of support for organizations:
CAPITAL CAMPAIGNS: Building/renovation.
GENERAL PURPOSE/OPERATING SUPPORT.
PROGRAM DEVELOPMENT/PROJECT SUPPORT.
STUDENT AID (GRANTS TO INSTITUTIONS).

Sample grants:
American Cancer Society - MN/MN/$3,000.
Fergus Falls Center for the Arts/MN/Kaddatz Arts Project/$10,000.
Fergus Falls Center for the Arts/MN/$22,500.
Fergus Falls Youth Sports Program/MN/$2,500.
Friends of Prairie Wetlands Learning Center - MN/MN/$4,500.
Salvation Army - MN (Fergus Falls)/MN/$5,000.
YMCA - MN (Fergus Falls)/MN/operating/$15,000.

Financial Information

Financial data for year ending: 03/23/2007
Foundation assets: $3,940,166
Grants paid: $118,933
Number of grants: 24
Largest/smallest: $22,500/$300

Application Information

Preferred form of initial contact: complete proposal.

Proposal deadlines: none.

Staff/Trustees

Directors/trustees: U.S. Bank Trust, N.A.. Richard C. Hefte; Richard L. Pemberton Jr.; Stephen F. Rufer.

Delta Dental of Minnesota

3560 Delta Dental Drive
Eagan, MN 55122
County: Dakota
Phone: (651) 994-5248
Fax: (651) 406-5975
E-mail: ajohnson@deltadentalmn.org
Website: www.deltadentalmn.org
Contact: Ann Johnson, director of community affairs
Paid Staff: Yes
Funder type: Corporate giving program

Program Description

Program's purpose: Delta Dental of Minnesota focuses its corporate philanthropic efforts on programs that promote health — particularly oral health — and educational initiatives that address effective and innovative solutions to the challenges of healthy living.

Funding priorities: Our commitment to solutions-oriented community investment requires that we go beyond simple checkbook philanthropy. Our goal is to work hand-in-hand with public and nonprofit organizations to identify and implement solutions that address specific problems, particularly in the area of oral health. This kind of partnership requires our partner organizations to go beyond business as usual, to set clear benchmarks and to focus on measurable results. Our philanthropic investments are based on four basic funding priorities that help us advance our mission and increase our impact, primarily in the area of oral health education and prevention. We direct funds to organizations and initiatives that address a unique and targeted community need related to: 1.) Oral & general health: Promote oral health and health education programs and activities that empower individual action and safety and those that can be leveraged to larger audiences; 2.) Children: Increase access to health services for underserved, low-income and at-risk children; 3.) Education: Support education institutions and initiatives focusing on oral health and health that strengthen the communities we serve; and 4.) Community: Build community capacity — particularly to improve the overall health and vitality of our communities. Note: Occasionally our Philanthropic Committee may make a funding decision outside of the above guidelines in response to an urgent, timely or significant community need.

Program limitations/restrictions: Delta Dental of Minnesota is a corporate giving program rather than a foundation, which can shape the types of giving we support. We do not typically fund multi-year programs. We prefer to form partnerships toward innovative solutions on oral health issues. In addition, the philanthropic program does not provide funds or grants for the following: general operating support or annual operating expenses, capital campaigns, endowments, religious groups for religious purposes, individuals, staff support, lobbying, political or fraternal activities, individual schools or school districts, sports events and athletic groups, payment of services or benefits reimbursable from other sources.

Geographic focus: Minnesota statewide.

Areas of interest:

COMMUNITY IMPROVEMENT: Community coalitions, Build community capacity - particularly to improve access to oral health and health care services.

EDUCATION: Support educational institutions and initiatives that strengthen our oral health mission.

HEALTH - DISEASES/MEDICAL DISCIPLINES.

HEALTH - GENERAL/REHABILITATIVE: Public health programs/wellness education, particularly oral health, Promote education programs and initiatives that empower individual awareness and action.

HUMAN SERVICES: Children/youth services, Improve children's access to oral health and health services for at-risk populations.

YOUTH DEVELOPMENT: Multipurpose youth centers/clubs, Youth development programs.

Types of support for organizations:

PROGRAM DEVELOPMENT/ PROJECT SUPPORT.

CORPORATE SPONSORSHIP: Contact: Ann Johnson, Community Affairs, ajohnson@deltadentalmn.org.

Exclusions: Capital & endowment campaigns, Individuals, Political organizations, Religious organizations, General operating support, Staff support, Fraternal activities, K-12 schools, Sports events, Athletic groups.

Financial Information

Financial data for year ending: 12/31/2006
Grants paid: $250,000
Largest/smallest: $55,000/$2,000
Typical grant amount: $10,000

Application Information

Preferred form of initial contact: letter of inquiry, e-mail.

Public information available by request: proposal guidelines, website.

Accept common grant application: yes.

Proposal deadlines: At the time that a full proposal is invited, applicants will be given the full proposal due date.

Preferred time for receiving proposals: Letters of inquiry are accepted by March 30 and September 28, 2007 (received in hand by 4:30 p.m. on the last working day of the month). Applicants will be notified of the status of their letter of inquiry within 2-4 weeks of receipt.

Contribution decisions made by: Philanthropy committee of the board of directors.

Typical time from application deadlines to notification: 10-12 weeks.

Special application procedures: The letter of inquiry should provide full contact information (name, organization, address, phone number, e-mail), specify the amount being requested, provide a brief overview of program or project, including any potential partnership or collaboration opportunities with Delta Dental of Minnesota.

Staff/Trustees

Staff: Ann Johnson, director of community affairs.

Deluxe Corporation Foundation/Deluxe Corporation

PO Box 64235
St Paul, MN 55164-0235
County: Ramsey
Phone: (651) 483-7842
Fax: (651) 481-4371
E-mail: jenny.anderson@deluxe.com
Website: www.deluxe.com/foundation
Contact: Pamela Bridger, grants & community affairs administrator
Established: 01/01/1952
Paid Staff: Yes
Funder type: Corporate foundation and corporate giving program

Program Description

Program's purpose: The Deluxe Corporation Foundation partners with nonprofit organizations to enrich the lives of people and communities through philanthropy and volunteerism.

Funding priorities: Students who struggle with reading, people with limited incomes, people with disabilities, professional arts, youth programs, people in crisis situations.

Program limitations/restrictions: No special events, individuals, sponsorships, programs that do not serve Deluxe communities, start-up organizations, athletic events, long-term housing, community arts groups, libraries, zoos, travel expenses, research, organizations designed for lobbying, religious organizations, national organizations.

Geographic focus: Twin Cities Metropolitan Area, Areas outside Minnesota.

Geographic limitations: Limit grants to the communities where Deluxe facilities are located.

Areas of interest:

ARTS, CULTURE, HUMANITIES: Arts/cultural multipurpose, Historical societies, Museums, Performing arts.

CIVIL RIGHTS: Voter education/registration.

COMMUNITY IMPROVEMENT: Nonprofit management, Volunteer bureaus.

EDUCATION: Limited to Deluxe's Reading Is For Life program and K-12 economic education programs.

EMPLOYMENT/JOBS: Vocational rehabilitation.

FOOD/NUTRITION/AGRICULTURE: Food service/free food distribution.

HEALTH - DISEASES/MEDICAL DISCIPLINES: AIDS/HIV, Prevention-education programs, Camping programs for children with disabilities.

HEALTH - GENERAL/REHABILITATIVE: Community health clinics.

HEALTH - MENTAL HEALTH/CRISIS INTERVENTION: Alcohol/drug/substance, prevention and treatment, Counseling/support groups, Hotline/crisis intervention, Mental health associations, Mental health disorders, Mental health treatment and services.

HOUSING/SHELTER: Homeless, temporary housing, Low-cost temporary housing.

HUMAN SERVICES: Children/youth services, Emergency assistance (food/clothing/cash), Family services, Family violence shelters and services, Multipurpose human service organizations, Services to specific groups, Victims services.

PHILANTHROPY/VOLUNTARISM: Philanthropy associations.

PUBLIC PROTECTION - CRIME/COURTS/LEGAL SERVICES: Crime prevention, Other.

PUBLIC SAFETY/DISASTERS/ RELIEF: Disaster preparedness and relief.

YOUTH DEVELOPMENT: Adult/child matching programs, Multipurpose youth centers/clubs, Scouting organizations, Youth development programs, Other.

Intended beneficiaries: Adults, African Americans/Blacks, Aging/elderly/senior citizens, Asian/Pacific Islanders, Blind/vision impaired, Children and youth (infants-19 years), Children only (5-14 years), Crime/abuse victims, Deaf/hearing impaired, Disabled - general or unspecified disability, Ethnic/racial minorities - other specified group(s), Ethnic/racial populations - general, Female adults, Female aging/elderly/senior citizens, Female children and youth (infants-19 years), Female infants/babies (under age 5), Female youth/adolescents (ages 14-19), Females - all ages or age unspecified, Gay/lesbian/bisexual/transgender, General public/unspecified, Hispanics/Latinos, Homeless, Immigrants/newcomers/refugees, Infants/babies (under age 5), Infants/children (ages 0-14), Male adults, Male aging/elderly/senior citizens, Male children and youth (infants 0-19 years), Male youth/adolescents (ages 14-19), Males - all ages or age unspecified, Mentally /emotionally disabled, Native American/ American Indians, No specified population groups, Other minorities, Physically disabled, Poor/economically disadvantaged, Single parents, Youth/adolescents (ages 14-19).

Types of support for organizations:

CAPITAL CAMPAIGNS: Building/renovation, Computer systems/technology, Equipment.

EMERGENCY FUNDS.

GENERAL PURPOSE/OPERATING SUPPORT: Annual campaigns.

PROGRAM DEVELOPMENT/PROJECT SUPPORT: Curriculum development, Mentoring programs, Publications.

Types of support for individuals: none.

Matching grants: elementary/secondary education, higher education, public broadcasting, historical societies, professional arts organizations.

Dollars for Doers: yes.

Exclusions: Individuals, Non-501(c)(3), Political organizations, Religious organizations, Research, Scholarships/loans.

Sample grants:

American Red Cross - DC/DC/Disaster Relief/$100,000.

Food Pantry - MA/$9,000.

Junior Achievement - CA/CA/$3,000.

MN Indian Women's Resource Center/MN/$5,000.

Music Academy - NC/NC/$3,500.

Reading Recovery Council - OH/OH/$100,000.

Schools - CO/CO/Denver Public Schools - Literacy grant/$15,000.

Somali Education Center - MN/MN/Special Program Grant/$10,000.

Financial Information

Financial data for year ending: 12/31/2005
Foundation assets: $34,159,765
Grants paid: $2,513,587
Number of grants: 251
Largest/smallest: $97,000/$539
Typical grant amount: $3,000
Matching gifts: $225,000

Application Information

Preferred form of initial contact: letter of inquiry, telephone inquiry, request for guidelines, complete proposal, e-mail.

Public information available by request: proposal guidelines, website.

Accept common grant application: yes.

Accept common report form: yes.

Will view video: yes.

Proposal deadlines: Will accept between February 1 and November 1.

Preferred time for receiving proposals: March through October.

Contribution decisions made by: employee committee.

Frequency of contributions decisions: annually, Minnesota contributions committee meets monthly.

Specific times board meets: typically meet twice each year.

Typical time from application deadlines to notification: 8 weeks.

Staff/Trustees

Staff: Jennifer A. Anderson, director of foundation & community affairs; Pamela Bridger, grants & community affairs administrator.

Directors/trustees: Jennifer A. Anderson, director of foundation & community affairs; Ronald E. Eilers; Katherine L. Miller; Lawrence J. Mosner; Anthony C. Scarfone; Brett E. Scribner; Douglas J. Treff; Luann E. Widener.

The Donaldson Foundation

PO Box 1299
Minneapolis, MN 55440-1299
County: Hennepin
Phone: (952) 887-3809
E-mail: Donaldsonfoundation@mail.donaldson.com
Website: www.donaldson.com/en/about/community/
Contact: Norman C. Linnell, president
Established: 07/07/1966
Funder type: Corporate foundation

Program Description

Program's purpose: We direct our contributions to the major community programs supporting social and human services and education. Our intent is to support important basic human services, as well as to maintain and improve the quality of life for those who live in the communities in which Donaldson operates.

Funding priorities: Economic self-sufficiency, education, scholarships for post-secondary education to children of employees.

Geographic focus: Minnesota statewide, areas outside Minnesota, other.

Geographic limitations: Local or regional agencies in those communities with concentrations of Donaldson Company, Inc. employees.

Areas of interest:

EDUCATION.

HUMAN SERVICES: Economic self-sufficiency.

Intended beneficiaries: General public/unspecified.

Types of support for individuals: none.

Matching grants: Education, United Way.

Exclusions: Individuals, Non-501(c)(3), Political organizations, Religious organizations, National drives, Private foundations.

Sample grants:

Bloomington Scholarship Foundation - MN/MN/scholarships/$3,000.

Community Action Council - MN/MN/self sufficiency/$40,000.

Grinnel Medical Center - IL/IL/health services/$6,100.

Junior Achievement - MN (Upper Midwest)/MN/economic education/$7,000.

Lime Springs Fire Station Project/IA/fire & rescue services/$1,000.

United Way - WI/WI/social services/$6,000.

Women in Transition/MO/self sufficiency/$35,000.

Financial Information

Financial data for year ending: 07/31/2005
Foundation assets: $2,409,293
Grants paid: $834,662
Number of grants: 62
Largest/smallest: $187,000/$500

Application Information

Preferred form of initial contact: Introductory letter.

Accept common grant application: yes.

Proposal deadlines: 1 month prior to board meeting.

Contribution decisions made by: employee committee.

Specific times board meets: August, January, May.

Typical time from application deadlines to notification: 4 months.

Staff/Trustees

Staff: Norman C. Linnell, president.

Directors/trustees: Jim Burrows; Becky Cahn; Karen Geronime; Dennis Grigal; Jeff May; Darnell McElveen; Julie Rumsey; Chris Valle; Kristin Wendel.

The Dorsey & Whitney Foundation

50 South Sixth Street
Suite 1500
Minneapolis, MN 55402-1498
County: Hennepin
Phone: (612) 340-2847
Fax: (612) 340-2643
E-mail: wilson.rose@dorsey.com
Website: www.dorsey.com/about/community.aspx
Contact: Rose Wilson, community & legislative affairs administrator
Established: 01/28/1982
Funder type: Corporate foundation

Program Description

Program's purpose: The foundation supports the communities in which Dorsey & Whitney LLP operates and organizations that reflect the diverse interests of its attorneys.

Funding priorities: Established arts, cultural and community service organizations in which attorneys are actively involved.

Geographic focus: Twin Cities Metropolitan Area, areas outside Minnesota, locations of branch offices.

Geographic limitations: Locations of U.S. offices: Minneapolis/St Paul, MN; Great Falls and Missoula, MT; Denver, CO; Des Moines, IA; Fargo, ND; New York, NY; Palo Alto and Southern CA; Seattle, WA; Washington, DC; Anchorage, AK; and Salt Lake City, UT. Also Hong Kong, London, Toronto, Vancouver and Shanghai.

Areas of interest:
ARTS, CULTURE, HUMANITIES.
COMMUNITY IMPROVEMENT.
EDUCATION.
HEALTH - GENERAL/REHABILITATIVE.
HUMAN SERVICES.
YOUTH DEVELOPMENT.

Intended beneficiaries: General public/unspecified.

Types of support for organizations:
GENERAL PURPOSE/OPERATING SUPPORT: Annual campaigns.
IN-KIND SERVICES: Pro bono legal services.

Exclusions: Individuals, Religious organizations, Private foundations, National fundraising campaigns, Ticket sales, Fundraising dinners, Endowment of chairs, Lobbying, Voter registration drives.

Sample grants:

Children's Home Society - MN/MN/$1,000.

Colorado Lawyers Committee/CO/$3,640.

High Five Tickets to the Arts/NY/$5,000.

MAP for NonProfits/MN/$5,000.

MN Advocates for Human Rights/MN/$10,000.

Southern MN Regional Legal Services/MN/$5,000.

University of MN - Law School/MN/$50,000.

Financial Information

Financial data for year ending: 12/31/2006
Foundation assets: $332,660
Grants paid: $1,793,848
Number of grants: 543
Largest/smallest: $200,000/$25

Application Information

Preferred form of initial contact: letter of inquiry, request for guidelines.

Public information available by request: proposal guidelines, application form.

Accept common grant application: yes.

Contribution decisions made by: board of directors/trustees.

Frequency of contributions decisions: quarterly.

Staff/Trustees

Staff: Tom Vander Molen, general counsel to the foundation; Rose Wilson, community & legislative affairs administrator.

Directors/trustees: Peter Hendrixson, chair; Bryce Holland; Kim Severson; Richard Silberberg; Jay Swanson.

Douglas Foundation

9650 Valley View Road
Eden Prairie, MN 55344-3507
County: Hennepin
Phone: (952) 941-2944
Established: 08/21/1980
Funder type: Corporate foundation

Program Description

Program's purpose: Associated with the Douglas Corporation.

Exclusions: Individuals, Non-501(c)(3).

Sample grants:

Junior League - MN (Minneapolis)/MN/$5,000.

University of MN Foundation/MN/$50,000.

Financial Information

Financial data for year ending: 09/30/2005
Foundation assets: $18,480
Grants paid: $156,744
Number of grants: 58

Staff/Trustees

Directors/trustees: C.A. Skanse; Douglas Skanse, president; Ronald D. Skanse.

Dovenberg Family Foundation

17110 Fifth Avenue North
Plymouth, MN 55447
County: Hennepin
Phone: (763) 473-0026
Contact: Dave Dovenberg, president
Funder type: Private foundation

Program Description

Program's purpose: General charitable purposes.

Geographic limitations: None.

Areas of interest:

HEALTH - DISEASES/MEDICAL DISCIPLINES: Cancer.

HUMAN SERVICES.

Sample grants:

American Cancer Society - MN/MN/$25,000.

Caring & Sharing Hands/Minneapolis, MN/$3,000.

Children's Cancer Research Fund - MN (Minneapolis)/MN/$4,000.

Dana Farber Cancer Institute/MA/$1,000.

Interfaith Outreach & Community Partners/MN/$12,000.

Minneapolis Heart Institute Foundation/MN/$3,000.

Salvation Army - MN (Northern Division)/Roseville, MN/$2,000.

Financial Information

Financial data for year ending: 12/31/2005
Foundation assets: $989,507
Grants paid: $49,490
Number of grants: 7
Largest/smallest: $25,000/$1,000

Application Information

Proposal deadlines: None.

Contribution decisions made by: board of directors/trustees.

Special application procedures: Requests must be received by mail.

Staff/Trustees

Directors/trustees: Dave Dovenberg, president; Jean Marie Dovenberg; Kirsten Dovenberg; Robert Dovenberg.

Driscoll Foundation

30 East Seventh Street
Suite 2000
St Paul, MN 55101-4930
County: Ramsey
Phone: (651) 228-0935
Fax: (651) 228-0776
Contact: W. John Driscoll, president
Established: 07/01/1963
Funder type: Private foundation

Program Description

Program's purpose: The Driscoll Foundation is concerned primarily with people and values. The foundation's emphasis and focus is on supporting activities and programs of established nonprofit organizations that are of importance to human welfare. The foundation prefers to participate with other donors rather than committing a major portion of the amount to be raised.

Funding priorities: Priority is given to the support of organizations whose programs and projects receive little or no support from public tax funds.

Geographic focus: Twin Cities Metropolitan Area, Areas outside Minnesota.

Geographic limitations: The foundation confines its grants largely, but not exclusively, to the metropolitan areas of St Paul and Minneapolis, MN, and San Francisco, CA.

Areas of interest:

ARTS, CULTURE, HUMANITIES.

EDUCATION: Higher education, Preschool/elementary, Secondary.

ENVIRONMENTAL QUALITY/PROTECTION/BEAUTIFICATION: Natural resources conservation/protection.

HUMAN SERVICES.

Intended beneficiaries: General public/unspecified.

Types of support for organizations:

CAPITAL CAMPAIGNS: Building/renovation, Endowment funds.

GENERAL PURPOSE/OPERATING SUPPORT: Annual campaigns.

PROGRAM DEVELOPMENT/PROJECT SUPPORT.

Types of support for individuals: none.

Exclusions: Individuals, Scholarships/loans, Organizations that conduct propaganda and lobbying programs, Voter registration programs, Conferences and seminars, Travel by individuals or groups, Publication of books, periodicals and monographs, Production of films.

Sample grants:

Minneapolis Institute of Arts/MN/endowment fund, annual fund/$80,000.

MN Landscape Arboretum Foundation/MN/Slade Perennial Gardens/$20,000.

Neighborhood House - MN (St Paul)/MN/general operating/$5,000.

Palo Alto Players/CA/general operating/$10,000.

Shanti Project/San Francisco, CA/endowment/$50,000.

St Paul Academy & Summit School/MN/Driscoll Maintenance Fund/$20,000.

United Way - MN (Twin Cities, Greater)/MN/2003 campaign/$50,000.

Vassar College/NY/reunion fund/$150,000.

Financial Information

Financial data for year ending: 02/28/2006
Foundation assets: $20,004,385
Grants paid: $903,000
Number of grants: 20
Largest/smallest: $250,000/$2,000

Application Information

Preferred form of initial contact: complete proposal, no set format for applications.

Public information available by request: proposal guidelines.

Accept common grant application: yes.

Accept common report form: yes.

Proposal deadlines: none.

Contribution decisions made by: board of directors/trustees.

Special application procedures: applications should be concise and submitted in typewritten form, and include a clear statement of purpose of the project or program, a complete budget, a statement of qualifications of person who will have major responsibilities for the project, and a copy of the organization's tax-exemption letter from the IRS.

Staff/Trustees

Directors/trustees: Elizabeth S. Driscoll; W. John Driscoll, president; Michael J. Giefer.

Joseph C. and Lillian A. Duke Foundation

U.S. Bank Philanthropic Services
EP-MN-S12
101 East Fifth Street
St Paul, MN 55101
County: Ramsey
Phone: (651) 466-8443
Established: 11/01/1963
Funder type: Private foundation

Program Description

Program's purpose: Primarily makes grants to youth support organizations in Minnesota.

Funding priorities: The foundation does not have explicit guidelines but it primarily makes grants to youth organizations in Minnesota.

Program limitations/restrictions: No grants to individuals or to organizations that would require expenditure responsibility.

Geographic focus: East Metropolitan Area/St Paul only.

Areas of interest:
YOUTH DEVELOPMENT.

Intended beneficiaries: Youth/adolescents (ages 14-19).

Types of support for organizations:
GENERAL PURPOSE/OPERATING SUPPORT.
PROGRAM DEVELOPMENT/PROJECT SUPPORT.

Sample grants:
Ain Dah Yung - MN (St Paul)/St Paul, MN/Ninijanisag program/$5,000.
Eco Education/St Paul, MN/urban stewards program/$2,500.
Girl Scout Council - MN (St Croix Valley)/MN/math, science & technology initiative/$2,500.
Junior Achievement Foundation - Upper Midwest/MN/general operating/$5,000.
Neighborhood House - MN (St Paul)/MN/Summer Adventures program/$2,500.
Ramsey County Historical Society/MN/Gibbs Museum of Pioneer & Dakota Life Project/$2,500.
St Paul Chamber Orchestra/MN/Connect program/$2,500.
YWCA - MN (St Paul)/MN/Two-gether Mentoring/$3,500.

Financial Information

Financial data for year ending: 12/31/2005
Foundation assets: $1,050,619
Grants paid: $30,000
Number of grants: 13
Largest/smallest: $10,000/$2,500

Application Information

Preferred form of initial contact: telephone inquiry, request for guidelines.

Public information available by request: proposal guidelines, application form.

Accept common grant application: yes.

Proposal deadlines: September 1 (October meeting).

Special application procedures: Call for guidelines and application forms.

Staff/Trustees

Staff: Tina Holgin.

Duluth Superior Area Community Foundation

Medical Arts Building
324 West Superior Street
Suite 212
Duluth, MN 55802-1707
County: St Louis
Phone: (218) 726-0232
Fax: (218) 726-0257
E-mail: grantsinfo@dsacommunityfoundation.com
Website: www.dsacommunityfoundation.com
Established: 07/01/1982
Paid Staff: Yes
Funder type: Community/public foundation

Program Description

Program's purpose: Administers a broad range of unrestricted, field of interest, donor-advised and restricted funds and makes grants for a variety of purposes. Unrestricted funds are granted for initiatives that meet the changing needs of the community.

Funding priorities: Projects that create connections between diverse people that increase bridging social capital; are newly developed collaborative efforts that strengthen service results; address underlying causes of community problems or are preventive in nature; are new and require start-up funds; undertake studies on matters that impact civic issues or public policy; help organizations resolve crisis situations within our community; build the organization's program and/or management capacity or quality; or respond to well-documented community needs and/or require a moderate amount of grant money but produce significant results in the service area.

Program limitations/restrictions: No grants for endowments, religious organizations, medical research, debt retirement, individuals (except for scholarships), political organizations, benefits, fundraising, phone solicitation. Grants are not made for re-granting purposes. Capital and equipment requests are a very low priority.

Geographic focus: Limited to organizations located in or providing services to seven counties of northeastern Minnesota (Aitkin, Carlton, Cook, Itasca, Koochiching, Lake and St Louis) and Douglas and Bayfield counties in northwestern Wisconsin.

Geographic limitations: Grants limited to the seven counties in northeastern Minnesota, and Douglas and Bayfield counties in Wisconsin.

Areas of interest:

ANIMAL RELATED: Animal protection/welfare, Wildlife preservation/protection, Zoo/zoological societies.

ARTS, CULTURE, HUMANITIES: Arts services, Arts/cultural multipurpose, Historical societies, Humanities, Media/communications, Museums, Performing arts, Visual arts.

CIVIL RIGHTS: Civil rights/advocacy for specific groups, Intergroup relations/race relations, Voter education/registration.

COMMUNITY IMPROVEMENT: Community coalitions, Community/neighborhood development/improvement, Economic development, Nonprofit management, Volunteer bureaus.

EDUCATION: Adult/continuing education/literacy, Educational services, Graduate education/professional schools, Higher education, Libraries/library science, Pre-school/elementary, Secondary, Student services/organizations of students, Vocational/technical.

EMPLOYMENT/JOBS: Employment procurement/job training, Vocational rehabilitation.

ENVIRONMENTAL QUALITY/PROTECTION/BEAUTIFICATION: Environmental beautification/open spaces, Environmental education/outdoor survival, Natural resources conservation/protection, Pollution abatement and control.

FOOD/NUTRITION/AGRICULTURE: Agricultural programs, Food service/free food distribution, Nutrition promotion, Soil and water conservation/farm land preservation.

HEALTH - DISEASES/MEDICAL DISCIPLINES: AIDS/HIV.

HEALTH - GENERAL/REHABILITATIVE: Health treatment facilities - primarily outpatient, Public health programs/wellness education, Reproductive health care.

HEALTH - MENTAL HEALTH/CRISIS INTERVENTION: Addiction disorders, Alcohol/drug/substance, prevention and treatment, Counseling/support groups, Hotline/crisis intervention, Mental health associations, Mental health disorders, Mental health treatment and services.

HEALTH - RESEARCH: Specific named disease research.

HOUSING/SHELTER: Homeless, temporary housing, Housing owners/renter organizations, Housing search assistance, Housing support services, Low-cost temporary housing.

HUMAN SERVICES: Children/youth services, Emergency assistance (food/clothing/cash), Family services, Family services for adolescent parents, Family violence shelters and services, Multipurpose human service organizations, Personal social services, Residential/custodial care, Senior centers and services, Services to specific groups, Victims services.

INTERNATIONAL AFFAIRS: International human rights, International peace/security, Promotion of international understanding.

PHILANTHROPY/VOLUNTARISM: Voluntarism promotion.

PUBLIC AFFAIRS/SOCIETY BENEFIT: Citizen participation, Military/veterans' organizations, Welfare policy and reform.

PUBLIC PROTECTION - CRIME/COURTS/LEGAL SERVICES: Correctional facilities and prisoner services, Crime prevention, Dispute/conflict resolution, Legal services, Protection/prevention - neglect/abuse/exploitation, Rehabilitation of offenders.

PUBLIC SAFETY/DISASTERS/RELIEF: Disaster preparedness and relief

RECREATION: Recreation and sporting camps, Recreational opportunities for disabled people.

RELIGION/SPIRITUAL DEVELOPMENT: Interfaith issues.

SOCIAL SCIENCES: Interdisciplinary research/studies to improve understanding of particular populations/cultures.

YOUTH DEVELOPMENT: Adult/child matching programs, Multipurpose youth centers/clubs, Scouting organizations, Youth development programs.

Intended beneficiaries: Adults, African Americans/Blacks, Aging/elderly/senior citizens, Asian/Pacific Islanders, Blind/vision impaired, Children and youth (infants-19 years), Children only (5-14 years), Crime/abuse victims, Deaf/hearing impaired, Disabled - general or unspecified disability, Ethnic/racial minorities - other specified group(s), Ethnic/racial populations - general, Female adults, Female aging/elderly/senior citizens, Female children and youth (infants-19 years), Female infants/babies (under age 5), Female youth/adolescents (ages 14-19), Females - all ages or age unspecified, Gay/lesbian/bisexual/transgender, General public/unspecified, Hispanics/Latinos, Homeless, Immigrants/newcomers/refugees, Infants/babies (under age 5), Infants/children (ages 0-14), Male adults, Male aging/elderly/senior citizens, Male children and youth (infants 0-19 years), Male youth/adolescents (ages 14-19), Males - all ages or age unspecified, Mentally/ emotionally disabled, Migrant workers, Military/veterans, Native American/ American Indians, No specified population groups, Offenders/ex-offenders, Other minorities, Other named groups, People with HIV/AIDS, Physically disabled, Poor/economically disadvantaged, Single parents, Substance abusers, Youth/adolescents (ages 14-19).

Types of support for organizations: PROGRAM DEVELOPMENT/PROJECT SUPPORT.

Types of support for individuals: scholarships.

Sample grants:

Duluth Art Institute/MN/Ceramics Studio Relocation/$5,000.

Environmental Association for Great Lakes Education/MN/Volunteer Coordinator/$5,000.

Hearing and Service Dog Program of MN/MN/Hearing Dog Field Training and Placement/$2,050.

ISD - MN/MN/Silver Bay Parent Teacher Student Organization - Transportation for After School Activities/$6,500.

MN Ballet/MN/$2,000.

Reach - ND (Fargo/Moorhead)/MN/Mother-Daughter Program/$4,000.

Financial Information

Financial data for year ending: 12/31/2005
Foundation assets: $43,064,025
Grants paid: $1,989,044

Application Information

Preferred form of initial contact: e-mail.

Public information available by request: proposal guidelines, application form, annual report, newsletter, website.

Accept common grant application: yes.

Proposal deadlines: February 1, March 1, April 1, May 1, July 1, August 1, September 1, October 1.

Preferred time for receiving proposals: Required to be in our office by 5:00 p.m. on the deadline date or if holiday/weekend, 5:00 p.m. the following business day.

Contribution decisions made by: board of directors/trustees.

Frequency of contributions decisions: End of March, June, September, December.

Typical time from application deadlines to notification: 2-3 months.

Special application procedures: Submit inquiry.

Staff/Trustees

Staff: Lois Albrecht, donor services officer; Nora Breems, office assistant; Becky Byers Strand, development officer; Barb Chapin, financial officer; Claudia Lundquist, executive assistant; Julie Munger, community initiatives officer; Holly C. Sampson, president; Brenda Sproat, scholarship and program officer.

Directors/trustees: Abbot G. Apter, chair; Peter L. Boman, secretary; Paul R. Buckley; Jennifer L. Carey; Michael A. Cowles; Helena E. Jackson, treasurer; Howard T. Klatzky; John P. Lawien; Ilene F. Levin; Lyle W. Northey; Donald L. Wallgren, vice chair; Thomas B. Wheeler, immediate past chair.

Eagan Foundation, Incorporated

PO Box 211192
Eagan, MN 55121
County: Dakota
Phone: (651) 895-2203
E-mail: info@eaganfoundation.org
Website: www.eaganfoundation.org
Established: 01/01/1992
Funder type: Community/public foundation

Program Description

Program's purpose: To raise funds and generate resources to support and encourage worthy community, charitable, literary and cultural needs in Eagan.

Funding priorities: Scholarship programs for seniors residing in Eagan; Community organization support.

Geographic focus: Twin Cities Metropolitan Area, East Metropolitan Area/St Paul only.

Geographic limitations: Eagan, Minnesota.

Types of support for individuals: scholarships.

Financial Information

Financial data for year ending: 12/31/2006
Foundation assets: $32,270
Grants paid: $45,000

Staff/Trustees

Staff: Lesley A. Chester, executive director.

Directors/trustees: Ruthe Batulis; Barb Blumer; Christine Cassellius; John Curlee; Joe Dwyer; Sandy Erickson; Tom Hedges; Susan Larkin; Barry Minsker; Trixie Newman; Anna Paulson; Kathy Pollock; Ann Styx; Arleen Sullivan; Doreen Ulrich; Jane Vanderpoel; Janelle Waldock.

Ecolab Foundation and Corporation

370 Wabasha Street North
ECC-5
St Paul, MN 55102-1307
County: Ramsey
Phone: (651) 293-2923
Fax: (651) 225-3191
E-mail: Ecolabfoundation@ecolab.com
Website: www.ecolab.com/Company Profile/Foundation/
Established: 01/01/1987
Funder type: Corporate foundation

Program Description

Funding priorities: Youth development and education, job readiness, arts organizations where Ecolab associates serve on boards.

Program limitations/restrictions: No grants to individuals; disease-specific organizations; sectarian/denominational religious organizations; sports or athletic programs.

Geographic focus: Twin Cities Metropolitan Area, East Metropolitan Area/St Paul only, Limited areas outside Minnesota.

Geographic limitations: St Paul, MN; City of Industry, CA; Elk Grove Village, IL; McDonough, GA; So. Beloit, IL; Garland, TX; Grand Forks, ND; Greensboro, NC; Hebron, OH; Huntington, IN; Joliet, IL; Martinsburg, WV; San Jose, CA.

Areas of interest:

ARTS, CULTURE, HUMANITIES: Arts services, Arts/cultural multipurpose, Museums, Performing arts.

COMMUNITY IMPROVEMENT: Community/neighborhood development/improvement, Economic development.

EDUCATION: Educational services, Preschool/elementary, Secondary.

EMPLOYMENT/JOBS: Employment procurement/job training, Vocational rehabilitation.

ENVIRONMENTAL QUALITY/PROTECTION/BEAUTIFICATION: Natural resources conservation/protection.

HOUSING/SHELTER: Homeless, temporary housing, Housing development/construction/management, Housing support services.

HUMAN SERVICES: Children/youth services, Emergency assistance (food/clothing/cash), Family services, Multipurpose human service organizations.

PUBLIC SAFETY/DISASTERS/RELIEF: Disaster preparedness and relief.

SCIENCE/TECHNOLOGY: Engineering/technology research.

YOUTH DEVELOPMENT: Multipurpose youth centers/clubs, Youth development programs, Early childhood programs.

Intended beneficiaries: Adults, African Americans/Blacks, Asian/Pacific Islanders, Children and youth (infants-19 years), Disabled - general or unspecified disability, Ethnic/racial populations - general, Females - all ages or age unspecified, Hispanics/Latinos, Homeless, Immigrants/newcomers/refugees, Infants/babies (under age 5), Male children and youth (infants 0-19 years), Native American/American Indians,

Offenders/ex-offenders, Poor/economically disadvantaged, Single parents, Youth/adolescents (ages 14-19).

Types of support for organizations:
CAPITAL CAMPAIGNS: Building/renovation.
GENERAL PURPOSE/OPERATING SUPPORT.
PROGRAM-RELATED INVESTMENTS.

Types of support for individuals: none.

Matching grants: employee matching, higher education, public broadcasting.

Sample grants:
CLUES (Chicanos/Latinos Unidos En Servicio)/MN/$15,000.
Como Zoo/MN/$7,500.
East Side Learning Center - MN/MN/$5,000.
Habitat for Humanity - MN/MN/$20,000.
Penumbra Theatre Company/MN/$15,000.

Financial Information

Financial data for year ending: 12/31/2006
Grants paid: $3,865,235
Number of grants: 1,200
Largest/smallest: $60,000/$100
Typical grant amount: $7,500
Matching gifts: $151,000
Largest multi-year grant approved: $500,000

Application Information

Preferred form of initial contact: telephone inquiry, request for guidelines, website.

Public information available by request: proposal guidelines, website, annual giving report.

Proposal deadlines: Deadline for 2007 funding has now passed. We will no longer be accepting any proposals for 2007 funding. The 2008 funding deadline is September 21, 2007.

Contribution decisions made by: staff, employee committee, board of directors/trustees.

Frequency of contributions decisions: annually.

Typical time from application deadlines to notification: 3 months.

Special application procedures: Apply online only through www.ecolab.com.

Staff/Trustees

Staff: Lisa Maloney-Vinz, community relations specialist; Kris Taylor, vice president, Ecolab Foundation; Shannon Toren, grants manager & volunteer coordinator.

Directors/trustees: Lawrence Bell; Jim Franklin; Diana Lewis; Michael Monahan, president; Susan Nestegard; Tom Schnack; Al Schuman.

Eddy (Edwin H.) Foundation

Wells Fargo Bank Minnesota, N.A.
230 West Superior Street
Duluth, MN 55802
County: St Louis
Phone: (218) 723-2765
Established: 09/08/1982
Funder type: Private foundation

Program Description

Program's purpose: The Eddy Foundation makes grants directly to institutions, organizations or individuals for the purpose of performing services to residents of the City of Duluth and surrounding areas in the general area of communicative disorders and the related fields of neuropathology.

Funding priorities: Research educational work treatment and rehabilitation in the field of communicative disorders and related fields of neuropathology; financial assistance in testing, interpreting tests and treatment of individuals who have communication disorders, with special consideration given to stuttering; scholarships to students in the field of communicative disorders; funding of projects, programs and research that have application to helping individuals with communicative disorders; assistance to help in the rehabilitation of individuals with speech and/or hearing disorders. Special consideration given for funding to institutions, organizations or faculties jointly sponsoring projects or programs.

Program limitations/restrictions: Scholarships limited to Duluth-area residents attending any accredited institution and to non-Duluth residents attending University of Minnesota-Duluth.

Geographic focus: Greater Minnesota.

Geographic limitations: Duluth area.

Areas of interest:
HEALTH - GENERAL/REHABILITATIVE: Rehabilitative medical services, communicative disorders.
HEALTH - RESEARCH: Specific named disease research, communicative disorders.

Intended beneficiaries: Deaf/hearing impaired, General public/unspecified, People with speech and hearing disorders.

Types of support for organizations:
PROGRAM DEVELOPMENT/PROJECT SUPPORT.
RESEARCH.

Types of support for individuals: scholarships.

Sample grants:
Confidence Learning Center Inc/MN/$1,500.
Courage Center - Greater MN/MN/$7,000.
ISD #316 Greenway Schools/MN/$3,415.
ISD #319/MN/$3,408.
ISD Duluth #709/MN/$32,050.
Northeast Service Cooperative/MN/$3,675.
Scottish Rite Clinic/Duluth, MN/$7,000.
University of MN - Duluth/MN/$87,422.

Financial Information

Financial data for year ending: 06/30/2006
Foundation assets: $4,412,270
Grants paid: $251,863
Number of grants: 42
Largest/smallest: $87,422/$750

Application Information

Preferred form of initial contact: request for guidelines.

Public information available by request: proposal guidelines, application form.

Proposal deadlines: scholarship applications due by July 10.

Staff/Trustees

Directors/trustees: Rodney E. Edwards; Wells Fargo Bank Minnesota, N.A.; Elizabeth Simonson; Barbara A. Spencer.

Edina Community Foundation

5280 Grandview Square
Suite 101
Edina, MN 55436
County: Hennepin
Phone: (952) 833-9573
Alt. Phone: (952) 833-9575
E-mail: edinacommunityfoundation@ci.edina.mn.us
Website: www.edinacommunityfoundation.org
Contact: Dick Crockett, executive director
Established: 11/04/1977
Paid Staff: Yes
Funder type: Community/public foundation

Program Description

Program's purpose: We strive to strengthen the Edina community as a premier place for living, learning, raising families and nurturing leadership.

Funding priorities: Support for City of Edina projects through its Senior Center, Art Center, Park & Recreation Department, Fire Department and Police Department; support for independent nonprofits in the community with programs and activities related to Designated Funds we have established; community-wide programs that we sponsor or co-host, such as Edina Reads, the Edina Dialogue, Holiday Home Tour, Senior Health Expo, Torchlight Concert and the Edina 4th of July Parade.

Geographic focus: Edina.

Geographic limitations: Organizations and projects outside of Edina are not likely to be funded.

Areas of interest:
ARTS, CULTURE, HUMANITIES: Arts services, Arts/cultural multipurpose, Historical societies, Humanities, Media/communications, Museums, Performing arts, Visual arts.
CIVIL RIGHTS: Equal opportunity and access, Intergroup relations/race relations.
COMMUNITY IMPROVEMENT: Community coalitions, Community service clubs, Community/neighborhood development/improvement, Nonprofit management.
EDUCATION: Higher education, Pre-school/elementary, Other.
ENVIRONMENTAL QUALITY/PROTECTION/BEAUTIFICATION: Botanical/horticultural/landscape, Environmental beautification/open spaces, Environmental education/outdoor survival, Natural resources conservation/protection, Pollution abatement and control.
HUMAN SERVICES: Children/youth services, Emergency assistance (food/clothing/cash), Family services, Multipurpose human service organizations, Personal social services.
PHILANTHROPY/VOLUNTARISM: Nonprofit sector assistance, Philanthropy - general, Public foundations and community foundations, Voluntarism promotion.
PUBLIC AFFAIRS/SOCIETY BENEFIT: Citizen participation.
PUBLIC PROTECTION - CRIME/COURTS/LEGAL SERVICES: Law enforcement agencies.
PUBLIC SAFETY/DISASTERS/RELIEF: Disaster preparedness and relief.
RECREATION: Amateur sports clubs/leagues, Amateur sports competitions, Physical fitness/recreational facilities, Recreational/pleasure/social clubs, Sports training facilities/agencies.
YOUTH DEVELOPMENT: Adult/child matching programs, Multipurpose youth centers/clubs, Youth development programs.

Intended beneficiaries: No specified population groups.

Types of support for organizations:
CAPITAL CAMPAIGNS: Collections acquisitions, Equipment.
PROGRAM DEVELOPMENT/PROJECT SUPPORT: Conferences/seminars, Exhibitions, Film/video/radio production, Mentoring programs, Performance/production costs, Seed money/start-up funds, Leadership programs.
STUDENT AID (GRANTS TO INSTITUTIONS): Scholarship funds.

Types of support for individuals: aid to needy persons, scholarships.

Sample grants:
Country Club Neighborhood Association - MN (Edina)/MN/community activities and events/$1,375.

Edina Chorale/MN/Mozart concert professional musicians/$3,000.

Edina Park and Recreation Department/Edina, MN/Arneson Acres fountain/$51,139.

Friends of the Edina Library/MN/Martin Luther King Day speaker honorarium/$200.

Financial Information

Financial data for year ending: 06/30/2006
Foundation assets: $425,748
Grants paid: $175,295
Number of grants: 45
Largest/smallest: $51,000/$50

Application Information

Preferred form of initial contact: e-mail.

Public information available by request: application form, annual report, website, IRS Form 990.

Accept common grant application: yes.

Accept common report form: yes.

Will view video: yes.

Proposal deadlines: September 15, January 15, and May 15

Contribution decisions made by: staff, board of directors/trustees.

Frequency of contributions decisions: October, February and June.

Typical time from application deadlines to notification: 6 weeks from application deadline.

Staff/Trustees

Staff: Mary Brindle, program coordinator; Dick Crockett, executive director.

Directors/trustees: Al Alexander; Otto Bang, secretary; Brad Beard; Grethe Langeland Dillon; James B. Hovland, president; George Klus, treasurer; Dennis Maetzold; Bonnie McGrath; Brenda Quaye; Frederick S. Richards; Kevin Ries, vice president; Carolyn Schroeder; James Van Valkenburg, assistant treasurer; Geof Workinger.

Edina Realty Foundation

6800 France Avenue South
Suite 670
Edina, MN 55435-2017
County: Hennepin
Phone: (952) 928-5356
Website: www.edinarealty.com
Contact: Susan Cowsert, marketing/community relations manager
Funder type: Corporate foundation

Program Description

Program's purpose: All of the foundation's funds are donated to nonprofit organizations that support homeless individuals, children and families and/or homelessness prevention.

Funding priorities: Homelessness. The foundation extends financial support to organizations that provide housing and related services such as counseling and medical care to homeless children, families and individuals. Grant examples include funds to support those nonprofit organizations working in the areas of providing safe shelter, food and clothing to those fleeing domestic violence; aiding families facing financial crisis with help in forestalling mortgage foreclosures; providing clinical services, medical supplies, outreach services and social services; and providing on-the-street medical care and crisis nursery support.

Geographic focus: Twin Cities Metropolitan Area, Greater Minnesota, Minnesota statewide, Areas outside Minnesota, Western Wisconsin and Fargo, North Dakota.

Areas of interest:

COMMUNITY IMPROVEMENT: Community/neighborhood development/improvement.

EMPLOYMENT/JOBS: Employment procurement/job training.

FOOD/NUTRITION/AGRICULTURE: Food service/free food distribution.

HEALTH - DISEASES/MEDICAL DISCIPLINES: Medical services for the homeless.

HEALTH - GENERAL/REHABILITATIVE: Emergency medical services.

HOUSING/SHELTER: Homeless, temporary housing, Housing support services, Low-cost temporary housing.

HUMAN SERVICES: Emergency assistance (food/clothing/cash), Family violence shelters and services.

Intended beneficiaries: Adults, Children and youth (infants-19 years), Children only (5-14 years), Homeless, Poor/economically disadvantaged.

Types of support for organizations:

CAPITAL CAMPAIGNS: Equipment.

EMERGENCY FUNDS.

GENERAL PURPOSE/OPERATING SUPPORT: Annual campaigns.

PROGRAM-RELATED INVESTMENTS.

CORPORATE SPONSORSHIP: Contact: Susan Cowsert, Marketing, (952) 928-5556, susancowsert@edinarealty.com.

Types of support for individuals: aid to needy persons, homeless.

Sample grants:

ARC - MN (Anoka & Ramsey Counties Inc)/MN/$200.

Central MN Task Force on Battered Women/MN/$1,800.

Clare Housing/MN/$4,000.

Faribault Food Shelf/MN/$1,000.

Greater Minneapolis Crisis Nursery/MN/$7,300.

MN Teen Challenge/MN/$14,575.

Safe Haven Shelter for Youth - Prior Lake/MN/$16,000.

Simpson Housing Services/MN/$3,113.

Financial Information

Financial data for year ending: 09/30/2006
Foundation assets: $626,487
Grants paid: $556,749
Number of grants: 127
Largest/smallest: $32,225/$90
Typical grant amount: $4,384

Application Information

Preferred form of initial contact: request for guidelines, complete proposal, e-mail, Send proposals to foundation representative in Edina Realty office.

Public information available by request: proposal guidelines, application form, website.

Accept common grant application: yes.

Accept common report form: yes.

Proposal deadlines: none.

Preferred time for receiving proposals: August through September. Funds are available annually beginning October 1, and grant application forms may be submitted at any time.

Contribution decisions made by: staff, the decision-making process is by office consensus.

Frequency of contributions decisions: monthly. Each Edina Realty office has its own foundation funds that they direct themselves.

Typical time from application deadlines to notification: depends on when grants are submitted.

Staff/Trustees

Staff: Susan Cowsert, marketing/community relations manager.

Directors/trustees: Mark Christopherson; Michele Fremming; Todd Johnson, president, Edina Realty Mortgage; Amy Kleinschmidt; Marc Kuhnley; Deb Stumne.

Edwards Memorial Trust

U.S. Bank, N.A.
EP-MN-S14
101 East Fifth Street
St Paul, MN 55101
County: Ramsey
Phone: (651) 466-8443
Contact: Tina Holgin
Established: 07/01/1961
Funder type: Private foundation

Program Description

Program's purpose: The Edwards Memorial Trust is dedicated to the grantor's expressed interest in health care for persons with very limited access to affordable services.

Funding priorities: Primarily health care in the east metro area.

Program limitations/restrictions: Nonprofit organizations with budgets of $1.5 million or more may not apply for general operating support grants.

Geographic focus: East Metropolitan Area/St Paul and Ramsey, Washington and Dakota counties only.

Geographic limitations: Most grantmaking serves individuals in Ramsey, Washington and Dakota counties.

Areas of interest:

HEALTH - DISEASES/MEDICAL DISCIPLINES.

HEALTH - GENERAL/REHABILITATIVE: Trustees welcome requests from organizations that provide direct health care services to vulnerable populations (low-income, young, elderly, or persons with disabilities). The services can be: Preventive care to promote healthy early childhood development, Intervention care to aid healing (both physical and mental), Long-term care to reduce suffering, Empowering programs to assist persons with disabilities to manage their lives.

Types of support for individuals: none.

Exclusions: Individuals, Non-501(c)(3), Political organizations, Research, Scholarships/loans.

Sample grants:

Center for Asians & Pacific Islanders - MN/Minneapolis, MN/Asian Elders with Limited English Skills/$5,000.

Freeport West/MN/StreetWorks/$7,500.

MetroEast Program for Health/MN/ $15,000.

Model Cities Health Center Inc/MN/ Facility at 409 Dunlap Ave/$25,000.

Sight & Hearing Association/MN/ Preschool Screening Program/$5,000.

Volunteer Resource Center - MN/MN/ Ability to Serve Program/$2,500.

Women's Cancer Resource Center - MN/ MN/Woman to Woman Targeted Outreach Project/$7,500.

Financial Information

Financial data for year ending: 12/31/2005
Foundation assets: $20,098,631
Grants paid: $759,000
Number of grants: 72
Largest/smallest: $50,000/$2,500

Application Information

Preferred form of initial contact: letter of inquiry, request for guidelines.

Public information available by request: proposal guidelines, application form.

Accept common grant application: yes.

Accept common report form: yes.

Proposal deadlines: Spring cycle-May 1 for June meeting. Fall cycle-October 1 for November meeting.

Preferred time for receiving proposals: no more than 1 month prior to deadline is preferable.

Contribution decisions made by: trustee distribution committee.

Frequency of contributions decisions: semiannually.

Specific times board meets: June, November.

Typical time from application deadlines to notification: 2 months.

Special application procedures: Many more proposals are received than can be funded. Proposals for certain purposes will not be considered: Film and video production, Lobbying or political activities including legislative advocacy, Debt reduction, Endowment, Research, Support of individuals, Travel, Activities that do not benefit communities in the St Paul or East metropolitan area, Fundraising for the purposes of re-granting to other organizations.

Staff/Trustees

Staff: Tina Holgin.

Directors/trustees: U.S. Bank Trust, N.A.

ELEOS Foundation

430 Lake Virginia Trail
Excelsior, MN 55331
County: Hennepin
Phone: (952) 474-7643
Contact: Harry Evert, co-manager
Established: 11/28/1990
Funder type: Private foundation

Program Description

Funding priorities: Support of ministries administered by other 501(c)(3) organizations.

Program limitations/restrictions: 501(c)(3) organizations only.

Geographic focus: National Areas, International Areas.

Geographic limitations: Fund primarily outside Minnesota.

Areas of interest:
RELIGION/SPIRITUAL DEVELOPMENT.

Intended beneficiaries: General public/unspecified.

Sample grants:

Dallas Theological Seminary/TX/support for ministries/$200.

Everlasting Reach/Pineville, MO/support for ministries/$600.

Hand in Hand Together/Maple Grove, MN/support for ministries/$450.

International Airport Church/Stillwater, MN/support for ministries/$2,500.

Mississippi Partnership/Jackson, MS/ support for ministries/$800.

Rose Price Ministries/Sunrise, FL/support for ministries/$5,000.

Teen Missions/Merrit Island, FL/support for ministries/$3,535.

Financial Information

Financial data for year ending: 06/30/2006
Foundation assets: $2,482
Grants paid: $67,406
Number of grants: 14
Largest/smallest: $31,000/$100

Application Information

Preferred form of initial contact: complete proposal.

Proposal deadlines: none.

Special application procedures: applicants must submit a statement verifying status as a 501(c)(3) if applicable, and must describe how the funds will be used as it relates to the goals.

Staff/Trustees

Directors/trustees: Diana Evert, co-manager; Harry Evert, co-manager.

Charles Engasser Memorial Foundation, Inc.

7000 Dakota Avenue
Chanhassen, MN 55317
County: Carver
Phone: (612) 934-5070
Contact: Mark Engasser
Established: 12/23/1986
Funder type: Private foundation

Program Description

Geographic focus: Minnesota statewide, Areas outside Minnesota.

Areas of interest:
EDUCATION.
HUMAN SERVICES.

Intended beneficiaries: General public/unspecified.

Types of support for organizations:
GENERAL PURPOSE/OPERATING SUPPORT.

Sample grants:

Blake School/MN/general operating/ $12,102.

Common Hope, Inc/MN/general operating/$1,500.

Courage Center - MN/MN/general operating/$500.

Habitat for Humanity - MN/MN/general operating/$1,000.

Orthopedic Research & Education Foundation/IL/general operating/$1,500.

Sharing & Caring Hands, Inc/MN/general operating/$500.

Williams College/MA/general operating/ $1,000.

Financial Information

Financial data for year ending: 12/31/2005
Foundation assets: $602,607
Grants paid: $38,800
Number of grants: 11
Largest/smallest: $15,000/$200

Application Information

Preferred form of initial contact: letter of inquiry.
Proposal deadlines: none.

Staff/Trustees

Directors/trustees: Mark Engasser.

Otto C. and Elsie Ewert Charitable Trust

110 North Mill Street
Box 866
Fergus Falls, MN 56537
County: Otter Tail
Phone: (218) 736-5493
Established: 09/01/1984
Funder type: Private foundation

Program Description

Program's purpose: General charitable purposes.
Program limitations/restrictions: 501(c)(3) organizations.
Geographic focus: Greater Minnesota.
Geographic limitations: Funding limited to organizations located in Otter Tail and Wilkin counties of Minnesota.
Areas of interest:
ARTS, CULTURE, HUMANITIES.
EDUCATION.
HUMAN SERVICES.
RELIGION/SPIRITUAL DEVELOPMENT.
Intended beneficiaries: General public/unspecified.

Types of support for organizations:
GENERAL PURPOSE/OPERATING SUPPORT.
PROGRAM DEVELOPMENT/ PROJECT SUPPORT.
STUDENT AID (GRANTS TO INSTITUTIONS).
Exclusions: Political organizations, organizations that directly or indirectly conduct activities of propaganda, or otherwise attempt to influence legislation or participate in or intervene in any political campaign on behalf of any candidate for public office.
Sample grants:
Campus Crusade for Christ - MN/MN/ $1,200.
Dollars for Scholars - MN (Fergus Falls)/ Fergus Falls, MN/scholarships/ $922.
Fergus Falls Area College Foundation/ Fergus Falls, MN/scholarships/$5,000.
Lake and Hospice Inc/MN/$3,000.
Otter Tail Historical Society/Fergus Falls, MN/$1,300.
Wilkin County - Historical Society/MN/ $1,300.
YMCA - MN (Fergus Falls)/MN/$3,000.
Young Life - MN (Fergus Falls)/Fergus Falls, MN/$5,000.

Financial Information

Financial data for year ending: 09/30/2005
Foundation assets: $917,835
Grants paid: $72,535
Number of grants: 14
Largest/smallest: $12,000/$1,000

Application Information

Preferred form of initial contact: letter of inquiry, request for guidelines.
Proposal deadlines: August 1 of each year.
Special application procedures: application must be submitted by the proper authority of the requesting organization Include proof of tax-exempt status and explain in detail the purpose and use of funds that are subject to the application.

Staff/Trustees

Directors/trustees: Phil Frederick; Lawrence Kremeier; Paul Lindholm; David L. Schneeberger; Oscar J. Sorlie Jr.

Extendicare Foundation

111 West Michigan Street
Milwaukee, WI 53203
Phone: (414) 908-8230
Fax: (414) 908-8507
E-mail: lbehling@extendicare.com
Website: www.extendicarefoundation.org
Established: 01/01/1985
Funder type: Corporate foundation

Program Description

Program's purpose: Funds Alzheimer's research, caregiver education, and quality care of life in long-term care.
Funding priorities: States and communities where Extendicare facilities are located.
Geographic focus: Minnesota statewide, areas outside Minnesota.
Geographic limitations: Arkansas, Delaware, Idaho, Indiana, Kentucky, Minnesota, Ohio, Oregon, Pennsylvania, Washington, West Virginia and Wisconsin.
Areas of interest:
EDUCATION: Caregiver education in long-term care.
HEALTH - DISEASES/MEDICAL DISCIPLINES: Specific named diseases, Alzheimer's disease.
HEALTH - GENERAL/REHABILITATIVE: Nursing care/services, Quality of life.
HEALTH - RESEARCH: Specific named disease research, Alzheimer's disease.
Intended beneficiaries:
Aging/elderly/senior citizens.
Types of support for organizations:
PROGRAM DEVELOPMENT/ PROJECT SUPPORT: Curriculum development, Faculty/staff development, Seed money/start-up funds.
RESEARCH.
Exclusions: Capital & endowment campaigns, Individuals, Non-501(c)(3), Political organizations, Scholarships/ loans, Administrative/overhead expenses.
Sample grants:
American Society on Aging/CA/$13,556.
Arthritis Foundation - WI/WI/$2,250.
French Foundation for Alzheimer Research, The/CA/$17,500.
Institute for Caregiver Education/PA/ $10,000.

Medical College of Wisconsin/WI/ $15,000.

Milwaukee Public Theatre/Milwaukee, WI/$9,375.

Residents Council of Washington/WA/ $7,500.

Wisconsin Geriatric Center/WI/$5,000.

Financial Information

Financial data for year ending: 12/31/2005
Foundation assets: $834,397
Grants paid: $275,231
Number of grants: 17
Largest/smallest: $35,408/$2,000

Application Information

Preferred form of initial contact: letter of inquiry, telephone inquiry, request for guidelines, complete proposal, e-mail.

Public information available by request: proposal guidelines, application form, annual report, website.

Accept common grant application: yes.

Proposal deadlines: March 31, June 30, September 30, December 31.

Contribution decisions made by: board of directors/trustees.

Frequency of contributions decisions: quarterly.

Staff/Trustees

Staff: Lisa Behling, secretary.

Directors/trustees: Lisa Behling, secretary; Dwayne Dabbs; Kelly Daugherty; Bill Dowd; Mark Eberhage; Tom Gerdes; Holly Gould; Diana Kerwin; Wally Levonowich, treasurer; Hugh McManus; LaRae Nelson, president; Rick Parker, vice president; Patrick Shaughnessy; Kay Weidner.

Faegre & Benson Foundation

2200 Wells Fargo Center
90 South Seventh Street
Minneapolis, MN 55402-3901
County: Hennepin
Phone: (612) 766-7000
Fax: (612) 766-1600
E-mail: cgiardina@faegre.com
Website: www.faegre.com/firm_about_ community.aspx
Contact: Carmela F. Giardina, legal administrative assistant
Established: 01/01/1993
Funder type: Corporate foundation and corporate giving program

Program Description

Program's purpose: The foundation supports communities in which Faegre & Benson LLP maintains offices.

Funding priorities: Organizations that provide legal aid, or that help the community through social service, cultural, environmental or educational activities. Special consideration is given to organizations involved with the judicial system and in providing legal services to those to whom such services are not readily available. In recent years we have given special emphasis to the legal needs of children.

Program limitations/restrictions: Programs receiving United Way funds are usually not considered. The foundation's largest social services and community grant is made to the United Way.

Geographic focus: Twin Cities Metropolitan Area, areas outside Minnesota.

Geographic limitations: The foundation is unlikely to fund organizations in states other than Minnesota, Iowa and Colorado.

Areas of interest:
ARTS, CULTURE, HUMANITIES.
EDUCATION.
ENVIRONMENTAL QUALITY/ PROTECTION/BEAUTIFICATION.
HUMAN SERVICES.
PUBLIC PROTECTION - CRIME/COURTS/LEGAL SERVICES: Legal services.

Intended beneficiaries: General public/unspecified.

Types of support for organizations:
CAPITAL CAMPAIGNS.
GENERAL PURPOSE/OPERATING SUPPORT.
IN-KIND SERVICES: pro bono legal services.

Types of support for individuals: none.

Exclusions: Individuals, Religious organizations, Neighborhood organizations, Service clubs, Lobbying efforts, Fundraising benefits or events.

Sample grants:

American Refugee Committee/MN/ $2,500.

Children's Law Center - MN/MN/$5,000.

Children's Theater Company - Twin Cities/MN/$10,000.

Family Housing Fund - MN (Minneapolis & St Paul)/MN/$5,000.

Legal Aid Society - MN (Minneapolis)/ MN/$18,000.

Minority Lawyers in Large Law Firms/MN/$5,000.

Wilderness Inquiry/MN/$2,000.

William Mitchell College of Law/MN/ $50,000.

Financial Information

Financial data for year ending: 12/31/2005
Foundation assets: $2,380,646
Grants paid: $1,418,787
Number of grants: 277
Largest/smallest: $247,540/$50

Application Information

Preferred form of initial contact: letter of inquiry.

Public information available by request: proposal guidelines, website.

Accept common grant application: yes.

Proposal deadlines: November 15.

Contribution decisions made by: board of directors/trustees.

Frequency of contributions decisions: annually.

Specific times board meets: December.

Typical time from application deadlines to notification: 3 months.

Staff/Trustees

Staff: Carmela F. Giardina, legal administrative assistant; Gina Kastel, partner.

Directors/trustees: Thomas M. Crosby Jr., president; Charles S. Ferrell; Thomas G. Morgan.

Arlin Falck Foundation

110 East Grove Street
Caledonia, MN 55921-1304
County: Houston
Phone: (507) 724-3348
Contact: Kathleen V. Nelson
Established: 08/26/1998
Funder type: Private foundation

Program Description

Program's purpose: To receive and administer funds to assist the residents of Houston and Fillmore counties in Minnesota, and Allamakee and Winneshiek Counties in Iowa, to improve their living conditions.

Funding priorities: Provide scholarships for deserving students who reside in the four-county area and intend to study business subjects; provide funds for 501(c)(3) organizations or municipalities in the four-county area, for community projects.

Geographic focus: Greater Minnesota, areas outside Minnesota.

Geographic limitations: Houston and Fillmore counties in Minnesota; Allamakee and Winneshiek counties in Iowa.

Areas of interest:
ARTS, CULTURE, HUMANITIES.
EDUCATION.
HUMAN SERVICES.
RELIGION/SPIRITUAL DEVELOPMENT.

Intended beneficiaries: General public/unspecified.

Types of support for organizations:
GENERAL PURPOSE/OPERATING SUPPORT.
PROGRAM DEVELOPMENT/ PROJECT SUPPORT.
STUDENT AID (GRANTS TO INSTITUTIONS): Scholarship funds.

Sample grants:
Caledonia Fire Department/MN/$5,000.
Decorah Public Library/IA/$2,850.
Hesper-Mabel Area Historical Society/MN/$3,300.
Houston High School/MN/scholarships/$925.
La Crescent High School/La Crescent, MN/scholarships/$3,125.
Lanesboro High School/Lanesboro, MN/scholarships/$675.
Laura Ingalls Wilder Museum/MN/$3,500.
Northland Agency on Aging/IA/$2,500.

Financial Information

Financial data for year ending: 12/31/2005
Foundation assets: $4,576,199
Grants paid: $55,688
Number of grants: 26
Largest/smallest: $5,000/$375

Application Information

Preferred form of initial contact: request for guidelines.

Public information available by request: proposal guidelines, application form.

Proposal deadlines: November 1.

Staff/Trustees

Directors/trustees: Alan C. Anderson, treasurer; Dale Evavold, secretary; Kathleen V. Nelson, president.

Fargo-Moorhead Area Foundation

502 First Avenue North
Suite 202
Fargo, ND 58102
Phone: (701) 234-0756
Fax: (701) 234-9724
E-mail: office@areafoundation.org
Website: www.areafoundation.org
Established: 05/10/1960
Paid Staff: Yes
Funder type: Community/public foundation

Program Description

Program's purpose: A regional community foundation with broad interests in arts and culture, education, health, civic betterment and human services.

Funding priorities: Education, human services, arts, health, community improvement and youth.

Program limitations/restrictions: Our grants are awarded to tax exempt organizations classified as 501(c)(3) public charities as defined by the Internal Revenue Service, religious institutions and governmental agencies. The organizations must be located in or directly benefit the residents of Cass County, North Dakota and/or Clay County, Minnesota. Grant seekers outside of Cass and Clay Counties must provide information on Cass and Clay residents served. If your organization/program does not have a tax-exempt ruling from the IRS, please complete the Fiscal Sponsor Information Form. Types of programs/projects normally NOT funded by the FMAF: Annual appeals or membership drives; Capital debt reduction; Capital Campaigns, Individuals or for-profit organizations; Organizations with outstanding final reports from previous FMAF grants; Organizations with outstanding due diligence reports from FMAF; Political projects; Religious groups for religious purposes; Travel for groups and Retroactive funding for any project expenses incurred before the decision date.

Geographic focus: Greater Minnesota, Clay County, MN, and Cass County, ND, only.

Geographic limitations: Grants only to Cass County, ND; Clay County, MN.

Areas of interest:
ANIMAL RELATED.
ARTS, CULTURE, HUMANITIES.
CIVIL RIGHTS: Civil rights/advocacy for specific groups.
COMMUNITY IMPROVEMENT: Economic development.
EDUCATION.
EMPLOYMENT/JOBS.
ENVIRONMENTAL QUALITY/ PROTECTION/BEAUTIFICATION: Environmental beautification/open spaces.
FOOD/NUTRITION/AGRICULTURE.
HEALTH - DISEASES/MEDICAL DISCIPLINES.
HEALTH - GENERAL/REHABILITATIVE: Rehabilitative medical services.
HEALTH - MENTAL HEALTH/CRISIS INTERVENTION: Mental health associations.

HEALTH - RESEARCH.
HOUSING/SHELTER.
HUMAN SERVICES: Children/youth services, Residential/custodial care.
INTERNATIONAL AFFAIRS.
PHILANTHROPY/VOLUNTARISM.
PUBLIC AFFAIRS/SOCIETY BENEFIT: Public policy research and analysis.
PUBLIC PROTECTION - CRIME/COURTS/LEGAL SERVICES: Legal services.
PUBLIC SAFETY/DISASTERS/ RELIEF: Disaster preparedness and relief.
RECREATION.
SCIENCE/TECHNOLOGY: Science - general, Other.
SOCIAL SCIENCES.
YOUTH DEVELOPMENT.

Intended beneficiaries: General public/unspecified.

Types of support for individuals: none.

Sample grants:

Children's Museum at Yunker Farm/ ND/Thinking Outside of the "Sand Box" create and educate through play/$6,795.

Fargo-Moorhead Opera/MN/Family night at the opera/$10,500.

Habitat for Humanity - MN (Lake Agassiz)/MN/Women Build/$6,000.

Learning Bank/MN/Fine arts series for all K-6 children/$3,000.

Moorhead Healthy Community Initiative/ MN/Healthy Community partnership/ $10,000.

New Sudanese Community Association/ MN/Organizational effectiveness and capacity building program/$7,000.

Rape & Abuse Crisis Center - MN/ND/ Computer network expansion and completion for counseling staff/$10,000.

River Keepers - Fargo/Moorhead/MN/ Wild bird/native plant demonstration garden signs/$8,500.

Financial Information

Financial data for year ending: 12/31/2006
Foundation assets: $46,130,637
Grants paid: $1,853,644
Number of grants: 455
Largest/smallest: $200,000/$50

Application Information

Preferred form of initial contact: see www.areafoundation.org for guidelines.

Public information available by request: proposal guidelines, newsletter, website.

Accept common report form: yes.

Proposal deadlines: See website - www.areafoundation.org.

Contribution decisions made by: Fargo-Moorhead Area Foundation Grants Committee.

Frequency of contributions decisions: annually.

Specific times board meets: Feb., April, June, Aug., Oct., Dec.

Typical time from application deadlines to notification: 45 days.

Special application procedures: See website - www.areafoundation.org.

Staff/Trustees

Staff: Karla Aaland, executive director; Carol Gustad, finance director; Michael Hannaher, development director; Wendy DeLane Milligan, gifts & grants specialist; Nyla Olson, administrative assistant.

Directors/trustees: Sue Andrews; Kelly Boyum; Matt Butler; Roland Dille; William Guy; Tracy Hartmann; Neil Jordheim; Sandy Kobel; Mary Lokken; Phyllis May-Machunda; Tracey Moorhead; Beth Renner; Paul Sather; Tom Schaffer; James Stenerson; John Stibbe; Joyce Wallman.

Farmers Union Marketing and Processing Foundation

PO Box 319
Redwood Falls, MN 56283-0319
County: Redwood
Phone: (507) 637-2938
Contact: Dwight Bassingthwaite, president
Established: 01/01/1998
Funder type: Private foundation

Program Description

Program's purpose: The purposes of the corporation are to support, initiate and operate programs of research and education designed to enhance and develop practices of agricultural production and management and cooperative ventures.

Funding priorities: Protect and maximize producer income and returns; promote and apply the principles of cooperative organization to the advantage of producers; secure the viability of family farming; develop processes and applications to add value to agricultural products to the benefit of producers; stimulate the development and growth of new and experimental cooperative ventures.

Geographic focus: Minnesota statewide, areas outside Minnesota.

Geographic limitations: Five-state region of Minnesota, Montana, North Dakota, South Dakota and Wisconsin.

Areas of interest:
ANIMAL RELATED.
FOOD/NUTRITION/AGRICULTURE.

Intended beneficiaries: General public/unspecified.

Sample grants:

Dakota Beef Cooperative/Mandan, ND/ $5,000.

Dakota Pride Cooperative/Jamestown, ND/$15,000.

National Enterprise Development Center/Huron, SD/$5,000.

North Dakota State University/ND/ $1,750.

Ultimate Value Added Co-op/Jamestown, ND/$15,000.

Financial Information

Financial data for year ending: 06/30/2006
Foundation assets: $3,478,814
Grants paid: $184,000
Largest/smallest: $50,000/$1,000
Typical grant amount: $1,500

Application Information

Preferred form of initial contact: letter of inquiry, request for guidelines.

Proposal deadlines: none.

Contribution decisions made by: board of directors/trustees.

Frequency of contributions decisions: quarterly.

Staff/Trustees

Staff: Duane Roger Anderson, treasurer.

Directors/trustees: Dwight Bassingthwaite, president; Robert Carlson; Doug Peterson; Dennis Rosen; Rollie Schlepp.

Federated Insurance Foundation, Inc.

121 East Park Square
Owatonna, MN 55060
County: Steele
Phone: (507) 455-5200
Established: 04/01/1972
Funder type: Corporate foundation

Program Description

Program's purpose: Primarily makes contributions to Steele County in the following areas: education, human services, youth, health and wellness, environment, civic and community, arts and humanities.

Geographic focus: Twin Cities Metropolitan Area, Greater Minnesota, Areas outside Minnesota, Steele County, Minnesota; Atlanta, Georgia; Phoenix, Arizona.

Geographic limitations: Funding limited primarily to areas where large numbers of company employees are located.

Areas of interest:
ARTS, CULTURE, HUMANITIES: Arts/cultural multipurpose, Historical societies, Museums, Performing arts, Visual arts.
COMMUNITY IMPROVEMENT: Community nonprofits.
EDUCATION: Higher education, Secondary, Vocational/technical.
ENVIRONMENTAL QUALITY/PROTECTION/BEAUTIFICATION: Natural resources conservation/protection.
FOOD/NUTRITION/AGRICULTURE: Food shelf.
HEALTH - GENERAL/REHABILITATIVE: Public health programs/wellness education.
HUMAN SERVICES: Children/youth services, Emergency assistance (food/clothing/cash), Family services, Personal social services, Other.
PHILANTHROPY/VOLUNTARISM: Voluntarism promotion.
PUBLIC SAFETY/DISASTERS/RELIEF: Disaster preparedness and relief, Safety education.
YOUTH DEVELOPMENT: Adult/child matching programs, Youth development programs.

Intended beneficiaries: General public/unspecified.

Types of support for organizations:
CAPITAL CAMPAIGNS: Building/renovation.
EMERGENCY FUNDS.
GENERAL PURPOSE/OPERATING SUPPORT.
STUDENT AID (GRANTS TO INSTITUTIONS): Fellowships, Scholarship funds.

Types of support for individuals: none.

Sample grants:
Ducks Unlimited - MN (Steele County)/MN/$350.
Melpomene Institute for Women's Health Research/MN/$750.
MN Orchestral Association/MN/$1,000.
MN State University - Mankato Foundation/MN/$2,700.
Owatonna Arts Center/MN/$4,500.
Owatonna Hospice/MN/$25,000.
Public Library - Owatonna/MN/children's summer reading program/$5,000.
Women's Resource Center - MN (Steele County)/Owatonna, MN/$500.

Financial Information

Financial data for year ending: 12/31/2005
Foundation assets: $379,188
Grants paid: $927,273
Number of grants: 100
Largest/smallest: $300,000/$250

Application Information

Preferred form of initial contact: letter of inquiry, complete proposal, no specific format requirements.

Public information available by request: proposal guidelines.

Accept common grant application: yes.

Proposal deadlines: none.

Frequency of contributions decisions: annually.

Staff/Trustees

Directors/trustees: Jonathon R. Hanson; Michael N. Keller; Richard J. Sherwood; Ray Stawarz; Gregory J. Stroik, president.

Fidelis Foundation

3189 Fernbrook Lane North
Plymouth, MN 55447
County: Hennepin
Phone: (763) 201-1268
Funder type: Community/public foundation

Program Description

Program's purpose: The foundation provides resources to help ministries to maximize their effectiveness by providing strategic planning assistance, administrative, legal and tax services.

Areas of interest:
RELIGION/SPIRITUAL DEVELOPMENT.

Sample grants:
City Sites Ministry/$25,000.
Crystal Evangelical - MN/MN/$10,000.
Lighthouse Ministry - MN/MN/$10,000.
Mission Moving Mountains - MN/MN/$10,000.
MN Family Institute/MN/$17,500.
New Life Services/$20,000.
Teen Challenge - MN/MN/$100,000.

Financial Information

Financial data for year ending: 09/30/2006
Foundation assets: $17,131,209
Grants paid: $2,789,571

Staff/Trustees

Staff: Joseph L. Smith, president.

Directors/trustees: L. John Buyse; Sam Crabtree; G. Craig Howse, chair; Bruce Pearson; Joseph L. Smith, president; Garth Warren, vice president.

Fingerhut Family Foundation

5354 Parkdale Drive
Suite 310
Minneapolis, MN 55416
County: Hennepin
Phone: (952) 545-3000
Fax: (952) 545-9381
Contact: Beverly Deikel
Established: 08/01/1960
Funder type: Private foundation

Program Description

Program's purpose: To promote the self-sufficiency, health and well-being of low-income communities in Minneapolis and its suburbs, and to strengthen Jewish communities in Minneapolis and Israel.

Funding priorities: Assistance to organizations serving low-income communities in Minneapolis and its suburbs.

Geographic focus: West Metropolitan Area/Minneapolis only, International Areas.

Geographic limitations: Minneapolis and its suburbs.

Sample grants:

Avenues for Homeless Youth - MN/MN/$1,500.

Emergency Food Shelf Network/MN/$5,000.

Person to Person/MN/$1,500.

Sholom Foundation - MN/MN/$17,000.

Tubman Family Alliance - MN/MN/$1,000.

Youth Farm & Market Project/Minneapolis, MN/$1,500.

Financial Information

Financial data for year ending: 12/31/2006
Foundation assets: $27,532
Grants paid: $223,875
Number of grants: 67
Largest/smallest: $70,000/$100

Application Information

Preferred form of initial contact: The Fingerhut Family Foundation is not currently accepting unsolicited applications.

Staff/Trustees

Staff: Donna Sherlock, consultant.

Directors/trustees: Beverly Deikel; Ronald Fingerhut, president; Rose Fingerhut.

First National Bank of Bemidji Foundation

PO Box 670
Bemidji, MN 56619-0670
County: Beltrami
Phone: (218) 333-4312
Fax: (218) 759-4355
E-mail: pwelle@fnbbemidji.com
Website: www.fnbbemidji.com/about comm.htm
Contact: Paul N. Welle, president
Established: 12/23/1993
Funder type: Corporate foundation

Program Description

Program's purpose: Established to assist in grantmaking to qualified nonprofit organizations within Bemidji and surrounding community that help to enhance, strengthen and improve the quality of life for the area's children and their families.

Funding priorities: Primary grantmaking focus is on children and families – programs that work to prevent problems rather than to correct them after the fact.

Geographic focus: Greater Minnesota.

Geographic limitations: Greater Bemidji area, Beltrami County.

Areas of interest:

ARTS, CULTURE, HUMANITIES: Arts/cultural multipurpose.

COMMUNITY IMPROVEMENT: Economic development.

EDUCATION: Higher education.

ENVIRONMENTAL QUALITY/PROTECTION/BEAUTIFICATION: Natural resources conservation/protection.

FOOD/NUTRITION/AGRICULTURE: Soil and water conservation/farm land preservation.

HEALTH - MENTAL HEALTH/CRISIS INTERVENTION: Alcohol/drug/substance, prevention and treatment.

HOUSING/SHELTER: Homeless, temporary housing, Housing development/construction/management.

HUMAN SERVICES: Children/youth services, Senior centers and services.

RECREATION: Amateur sports clubs/leagues, Physical fitness/recreational facilities.

YOUTH DEVELOPMENT: Adult/child matching programs, Multipurpose youth centers/clubs, Youth development programs.

Intended beneficiaries: Ethnic/racial populations - general, Females - all ages or age unspecified, Homeless, Infants/babies (under age 5), Males - all ages or age unspecified, Native American/American Indians, Poor/economically disadvantaged, Substance abusers, Youth/adolescents (ages 14-19).

Types of support for organizations:

CAPITAL CAMPAIGNS: Building/renovation, Computer systems/technology, Equipment, Land acquisitions.

GENERAL PURPOSE/OPERATING SUPPORT.

PROGRAM DEVELOPMENT/PROJECT SUPPORT: Mentoring programs, Seed money/start-up funds.

STUDENT AID (GRANTS TO INSTITUTIONS): Scholarship funds.

Types of support for individuals: none.

Exclusions: Individuals, Political organizations, Organizations already receiving support from the United Way, National causes outside our market area.

Sample grants:

American Indian Center/MN/construction costs/$12,500.

Boys & Girls Club - MN (Red Lake Nation)/MN/equipment purchase/$2,800.

Concordia Language Village/MN/general operating/$5,000.

Headwaters Science Center/Bemidji, MN/general operating/$2,000.

ISD Bemidji #31/MN/general operating/$500.

Paul Bunyan Playhouse/Bemidji, MN/general operating/$7,500.

Public Television - MN (Bemidji KAWE)/MN/general operating/$2,500.

Special Olympics - MN/MN/general operating/$2,500.

Financial Information

Financial data for year ending: 12/31/2005
Foundation assets: $910,386
Grants paid: $45,000
Number of grants: 10
Largest/smallest: $12,500/$500

Application Information

Preferred form of initial contact: telephone inquiry.

Public information available by request: proposal guidelines, application form.

Accept common grant application: yes.

Accept common report form: yes.
Proposal deadlines: semi-annual meetings.
Contribution decisions made by: board of directors/trustees.
Frequency of contributions decisions: semiannually.

Staff/Trustees

Directors/trustees: Ron Cuperus; B. Scott Curb; Susan S. Engel; E. Joseph Welle; Paul N. Welle, president; Robert J. Welle; Kyle Young, trustee.

The Jack and Bessie Fiterman Foundation

PO Box 62053
St Louis Park, MN 55426
County: Hennepin
Phone: (763) 545-7213
Contact: Linda Fiterman, treasurer
Established: 05/01/1966
Funder type: Private foundation

Program Description

Geographic focus: Minnesota statewide, areas outside Minnesota.
Areas of interest:
ARTS, CULTURE, HUMANITIES.
HEALTH - DISEASES/MEDICAL DISCIPLINES.
HUMAN SERVICES.
PHILANTHROPY/VOLUNTARISM.
Intended beneficiaries: Children and youth (infants-19 years), General public/unspecified.
Exclusions: Individuals, Political organizations, Lobbying or advocacy groups.
Sample grants:
Big Brothers/Big Sisters - MN (Minneapolis)/MN/$1,000.
Cornerhouse/MN/$300.
Family & Children's Services - MN (Mpls)/Minneapolis, MN/$5,500.
Jewish Community Action/MN/$1,000.
Loaves & Fishes/MN/$500.
Minnetonka Center for the Arts/MN/$12,500.
Ronald McDonald House - MN (Minneapolis)/MN/$6,000.
United Way - MN (Olmsted County)/MN/$500.

Financial Information

Financial data for year ending: 05/31/2006
Foundation assets: $7,445,335
Grants paid: $1,042,113
Number of grants: 77
Largest/smallest: $452,000/$100

Application Information

Preferred form of initial contact: request for guidelines.
Public information available by request: application form.
Proposal deadlines: none.

Staff/Trustees

Directors/trustees: Ben Fiterman, vice president; Linda Fiterman, treasurer; Michael Fiterman, president; David Lenzen, secretary.

Flint Hills Resources

PO Box 64596
St Paul, MN 55164
County: Dakota
Phone: (651) 438-1260
Fax: (651) 437-0868
Website: www.fhr.com
Paid Staff: Yes
Funder type: Corporate foundation and corporate giving program

Staff/Trustees

Staff: Heather Rein, manager, community investment.

Fredrikson & Byron Foundation

200 South Sixth Street
4000 Pillsbury Center
Minneapolis, MN 55402
County: Hennepin
Phone: (612) 492-7000
Fax: (612) 492-7077
E-mail: twind@fredlaw.com
Website: www.fredlaw.com/probono/
Contact: Todd Wind, president
Established: 01/01/1974
Funder type: Corporate foundation

Program Description

Program's purpose: The foundation's mission is to support law-related institutions and events, organizations that complement the rule of law in our society and a small number of cultural activities that are of special interest to the lawyers of Fredrikson & Byron.
Funding priorities: Professional, law and justice, arts and culture.
Geographic focus: Twin Cities Metropolitan Area.
Geographic limitations: Primarily Twin Cities focus.
Areas of interest:
ARTS, CULTURE, HUMANITIES.
PUBLIC PROTECTION - CRIME/COURTS/LEGAL SERVICES.
Intended beneficiaries: General public/unspecified.
Types of support for organizations:
IN-KIND SERVICES: pro bono legal services.
Types of support for individuals: scholarships, Minority Scholarship Program to promote the legal training of minority lawyers.

Financial Information

Financial data for year ending: 05/31/2005
Foundation assets: $35,471
Grants paid: $229,193

Application Information

Contribution decisions made by: board of directors/trustees.

Staff/Trustees

Staff: Nilla Christiansen, administrative support.
Directors/trustees: R. J. Hamilton; Ronalee Haugen; Todd Wind, president.

Fremont Foundation

U.S. Bank, N.A.
101 East Fifth Street
EP MN S14
St Paul, MN 55101
County: Ramsey
Phone: (651) 466-8735
Contact: Jeffrey T. Peterson, secretary
Established: 11/24/2000
Funder type: Private foundation

Program Description

Program's purpose: General charitable purposes.

Funding priorities: The foundation does not have explicit guidelines, but it primarily makes grants to education, cultural, youth, environmental, education and community support organizations.

Program limitations/restrictions: The foundation does not make grants to individuals or organizations that would require expenditure responsibility.

Geographic focus: Minnesota statewide.

Geographic limitations: Organizations must be located in Minnesota.

Areas of interest:
ARTS, CULTURE, HUMANITIES.
EDUCATION.
ENVIRONMENTAL QUALITY/PROTECTION/BEAUTIFICATION.
HUMAN SERVICES.
YOUTH DEVELOPMENT.

Intended beneficiaries: General public/unspecified.

Types of support for organizations:
GENERAL PURPOSE/OPERATING SUPPORT.

Exclusions: Individuals.

Sample grants:

Cable Natural History Museum/WI/general operating/$1,000.

Free Arts MN/MN/general operating/$1,500.

Independent Feature Project - MN (Minneapolis)/MN/Wayward Girls/$1,000.

MN Medical Foundation/MN/general operating/$2,000.

Partnership for Choice in Education/MN/general operating/$1,000.

Wilderness Inquiry/Minneapolis, MN/general operating/$500.

Financial Information

Financial data for year ending: 12/31/2005
Foundation assets: $1,875,534
Grants paid: $64,000
Number of grants: 13
Largest/smallest: $20,000/$1,000

Application Information

Preferred form of initial contact: letter of inquiry.

Proposal deadlines: November 1.

Staff/Trustees

Directors/trustees: Bruce A. Lilly, president; David M. Lilly; Mary P. Lilly; Jeffrey T. Peterson, secretary.

Frey Foundation

5000 Wells Fargo Center
90 South Seventh Street
Minneapolis, MN 55402
County: Hennepin
Phone: (612) 359-6215
Fax: (612) 359-6210
E-mail: joann@freyfoundationmn.org
Website: freyfoundationmn.org
Contact: Jo Ann Gruesner, executive assistant
Established: 01/01/1988
Funder type: Private foundation

Program Description

Program's purpose: The Frey family has long believed in investing in the community. The goals are to help others become self-sufficient and to reach their full potential.

Funding priorities: Supportive affordable housing, education, human services, health, disability issues.

Program limitations/restrictions: No endowments or funding to individuals; arts by invitation only.

Geographic focus: Twin Cities Metropolitan Area.

Geographic limitations: Nonprofit organizations located within the Twin Cities metropolitan area are the primary beneficiaries of the foundation.

Areas of interest:
ARTS, CULTURE, HUMANITIES: Historical societies, Museums.
COMMUNITY IMPROVEMENT: Community/neighborhood development/improvement.
EDUCATION: Educational reform, Educational services, Pre-school/elementary, Secondary.
EMPLOYMENT/JOBS: Employment procurement/job training.
FOOD/NUTRITION/AGRICULTURE: Food service/free food distribution.
HEALTH - GENERAL/REHABILITATIVE: Health support services, Health treatment facilities - primarily outpatient, Rehabilitative medical services.
HOUSING/SHELTER: Housing development/construction/management, Housing support services, Other.
HUMAN SERVICES: Children/youth services, Emergency assistance (food/clothing/cash), Family services, Multipurpose human service organizations.
RELIGION/SPIRITUAL DEVELOPMENT: Specific denomination.
YOUTH DEVELOPMENT: Adult/child matching programs, Scouting organizations, Youth development programs.

Intended beneficiaries: Disabled - general or unspecified disability, General public/unspecified, Homeless.

Types of support for organizations:
GENERAL PURPOSE/OPERATING SUPPORT.
PROGRAM DEVELOPMENT/PROJECT SUPPORT.

Sample grants:

Admission Possible/St Paul, MN/General operating support/$25,000.

HOPE Community - MN/Minneapolis, MN/New models to strengthen affordable housing initiatives/$100,000.

MN Historical Society/MN/Mill City Museum/$9,606.

Second Harvest - MN (Heartland, St Paul)/MN/Service improvement plan/$190,000.

Financial Information

Financial data for year ending: 06/30/2006
Foundation assets: $22,730,904
Grants paid: $964,565
Number of grants: 27
Largest/smallest: $200,000/$1,000

Application Information

Preferred form of initial contact: e-mail letter of inquiry (must be e-mailed).

Public information available by request: See guidelines and other info on website: www.freyfoundationmn.org.

Accept common grant application: no.

Accept common report form: yes.

Proposal deadlines: Letters of Inquiry are due March 15, June 15 and December 15. The board meets 3 times per year; deadlines coincide with these meetings. Applicants will be invited to submit for appropriate meeting date.

Contribution decisions made by: board of directors/trustees.

Frequency of contributions decisions: 3 times per year.

Typical time from application deadlines to notification: 8 weeks.

Special application procedures: We do not accept Common Grant Applications. Request for guidelines/letter of inquiry are first steps in process. See website: www.freyfoundationmn.org for details.

Staff/Trustees

Staff: Jo Ann Gruesner, executive assistant.

Directors/trustees: Eugene U. Frey, chair; James R. Frey; John J. Frey; Mary F. Frey, vice-chair; Mary W. Frey; Jane E. Letourneau; Carol F. Wolfe; Daniel T. Wolfe.

H.B. Fuller Company Foundation

PO Box 64683
Corporate Office
St Paul, MN 55164-0683
County: Ramsey
Phone: (651) 236-5217
Fax: (651) 236-5056
E-mail: christine.meyer@hbfuller.com
Website: www.hbfuller.com/About-Us/Community
Established: 12/01/1986
Paid Staff: Yes
Funder type: Corporate foundation and corporate giving program

Program Description

Program's purpose: H.B. Fuller Company Foundation, through its contributions program, is committed to building strong communities that create educational and economic opportunities for children and their families. In 2007, the foundation will continue to be a community partner in building and strengthening a system for delivering early childhood and family literacy services while transitioning to include targeted programs that support increased involvement and educational opportunities in science literacy and STEM (Science, Technology, Engineering and Math) education.

Funding priorities: For grants in Minnesota, the foundation will consider proposals only from organizations that advance the objectives outlined above. Within the categories of early childhood and family literacy, the foundation focuses on three types of grants: direct service, capacity-building and advocacy. In the areas of science literacy and STEM education, the foundation will consider support for programs/organizations that support STEM education, and encourage young people to become proficient in science, technology, engineering and math. This includes organization(s) that leverage H.B. Fuller Company expertise and employee involvement in science. For grants in other H.B. Fuller plant communities, priorities are in general, set by Community Affairs Councils following the principals listed below. HBF Invest (matching gifts) program encourages employees and retirees in the U.S. to support educational institutions and arts and cultural public charities.

Program limitations/restrictions: General priorities that guide decision-making: 1) Contributions will be made only to tax-exempt 501(c)(3) public charities. Organizations incorporated in countries other than the U.S. must qualify for tax-exempt status according to U.S. tax regulations and comply with national and/or state charity laws; 2) Grants will be made to organizations serving the communities where H.B. Fuller Company has its operations. Since most H.B. Fuller Company operations are located in urban areas, urban programs will be given priority; 3) Generally, the company will make contributions directly to organizations in the countries where services are provided rather than through multinational or U.S.-based intermediaries; 4) H.B. Fuller Company will not provide contributions to programs that appear to be the responsibility of governments unless the program is a community-based effort directed at improving the delivery of government-funded services; 5) Currently requests for capital campaigns and endowments will not be considered.

Geographic focus: Twin Cities Metropolitan Area, Minnesota statewide, Areas outside Minnesota, National Areas, Plant communities worldwide.

Geographic limitations: Limited to communities where H.B. Fuller Company has its operations.

Areas of interest:

ANIMAL RELATED: Wildlife preservation/protection, Zoo/zoological societies.

ARTS, CULTURE, HUMANITIES: Arts services, Arts/cultural multipurpose, Historical societies, Humanities, Media/communications, Museums, Performing arts, Visual arts.

EDUCATION: Adult/continuing education/literacy, Educational services, Graduate education/professional schools, Higher education, Libraries/library science, Pre-school/elementary, Secondary, Vocational/technical, Early Childhood and Family Literacy, Science Literacy, STEM education.

ENVIRONMENTAL QUALITY/PROTECTION/BEAUTIFICATION: Natural resources conservation/protection.

FOOD/NUTRITION/AGRICULTURE: Soil and water conservation/farm land preservation.

HUMAN SERVICES: United Way.

Intended beneficiaries: Infants/babies (under age 5), for Early Childhood Literacy and parents for Family Literacy, Children from K-12 for Science Literacy and STEM education.

Types of support for organizations:

CAPITAL CAMPAIGNS: Building/renovation, Equipment.

GENERAL PURPOSE/OPERATING SUPPORT.

PROGRAM DEVELOPMENT/PROJECT SUPPORT: Advocacy, capacity-building and direct service in the focus area of Early Childhood and Family Literacy.

IN-KIND PRODUCTS: adhesives.

Types of support for individuals: none.

Exclusions: Capital & endowment campaigns, Individuals, Non-501(c)(3), Political organizations, Religious organizations, Research, Scholarships/loans, Fraternal or veterans' organizations except for programs that are of direct benefit to the broader community, Travel, Disease-specific organizations, Courtesy or public service advertisements, Fundraising events or sponsorships.

Sample grants:

Children's Home Society - MN/MN/nutrition and medical programs in China/$50,000.

Habitat for Humanity/Costa Rica/$12,000.

Kentucky Sheriffs Ranch/KY/$11,500.

Lao Family Community of MN/MN/$10,000.

MN Literacy Council/MN/$20,000.

Schools - WA/WA/Chinook Elementary School - math enrichment program/$5,000.

Financial Information

Financial data for year ending: 11/30/2006
Foundation assets: $1,634,272
Grants paid: $612,531
Number of grants: 337
Largest/smallest: $100,000/$50

Application Information

Preferred form of initial contact: letter of inquiry, telephone inquiry, request for guidelines, e-mail.

Public information available by request: proposal guidelines, application form, annual report, website.

Accept common grant application: yes.

Accept common report form: yes.

Proposal deadlines: February 2, June 4, October 5.

Contribution decisions made by: employee committee, board of directors/trustees.

Frequency of contributions decisions: contributions committee meets 3 times per year.

Specific times board meets: 2 times per year.

Typical time from application deadlines to notification: 45 days.

Staff/Trustees

Staff: Keralyn Groff, executive director and secretary; Christine Meyer, administrative assistant.

Directors/trustees: Norbert Berg, director; Archie Givens Jr., director; Keralyn Groff, executive director and secretary; Rich Kastner, president of foundation; Al Longstreet, vice president; Jodie Monson, treasurer; Ann Parriott, ex-officio director; Michele Riemersma, assistant secretary; Sandy Swanson, director; Kathleen Vallenga, director; Michele Volpi, president and CEO.

G&K Services Foundation

5995 Opus Parkway
Minnetonka, MN 55343
County: Hennepin
Phone: (952) 912-5633
Fax: (952) 912-5537
Website: www.gkservices.com
Established: 09/02/2005
Funder type: Corporate foundation and corporate giving program

Program Description

Program's purpose: G&K Services Foundation focuses on helping people reach their full potential by supporting innovative approaches to developing self-esteem and cultivating life and leadership skills.

Funding priorities: Education and human services.

Program limitations/restrictions: Individual; Capital & Endowment campaigns; Non 501(c)(3); Political organizations; Religious organizations; Research; Diseases; Travel; Conferences; Fundraisers; Scholarships/Loans; Individual K-12 schools; Fraternal, Social, Labor, Alumni, Veterans or Military organizations; Advocacy and Lobbying efforts to influence legislation; Sports events or Athletic groups.

Geographic focus: Twin Cities Metropolitan Area, Communities where G&K Services has facilities.

Areas of interest:
EDUCATION.
HUMAN SERVICES.

Intended beneficiaries: General public/unspecified.

Types of support for organizations:
GENERAL PURPOSE/OPERATING SUPPORT.
PROGRAM DEVELOPMENT/PROJECT SUPPORT.

Types of support for individuals: none.

Financial Information

Financial data for year ending: 12/31/2006
Grants paid: $262,000

Application Information

Preferred form of initial contact: complete proposal.

Public information available by request: proposal guidelines, application form, annual report, website.

Accept common grant application: yes.

Proposal deadlines: January 15.

Contribution decisions made by: staff, employee committee, board of directors/trustees.

Frequency of contributions decisions: annually.

Typical time from application deadlines to notification: 4-5 months.

Special application procedures: All requests must be submitted in writing via U.S. Mail.

Staff/Trustees

Staff: Michelle Zirbes, community relations manager.

Directors/trustees: David Fisher, vice president, general counsel & corporate secretary; Richard Marcantonio, chairman & CEO; Jackie Punch, senior vice president, human resources; Jeff Wright, senior vice president & CFO.

Donald G. Gardner Humanities Trust

PO Box 720
Ely, MN 55731
County: St Louis
Phone: (218) 365-2639
Fax: (218) 365-2639
E-mail: info@dgght.org
Website: www.dgght.org
Established: 01/01/1989
Paid Staff: Yes
Funder type: Private foundation

Program Description

Program's purpose: The trust seeks to further any activities in the area of the enhancement, growth and improvement of the fine arts within the community as it relates to the arts and artisans, visual and performing arts and literature, including educational and artistic grants, and as it relates to the cultural and aesthetic environment of the Ely Area.

Funding priorities: The trust provides: 1) Project grants to help organizations produce or present a fine arts activity; 2) Operational funding grants to fund high-quality, established Ely-area arts organizations that produce or present fine arts activities or provide services to artists; 3) Scholarships to Ely-area students majoring in one of the disciplines of the fine arts or library science; 4) Individual artists grants to recognize and encourage developing and established Ely-area artists with funding to take advantage of an impending, concrete opportunity or specific development activity.

Geographic focus: Greater Minnesota, Ely-area residents.

Geographic limitations: Open to Ely-area residents and organizations only.

Areas of interest:
ARTS, CULTURE, HUMANITIES: Performing arts, Visual arts.
EDUCATION: Libraries/library science.

Intended beneficiaries: General public/unspecified.

Types of support for organizations:
GENERAL PURPOSE/OPERATING SUPPORT.
GRANTS TO INDIVIDUALS.
PROGRAM DEVELOPMENT/PROJECT SUPPORT: Conferences/seminars, Exhibitions, Faculty/staff development, Film/video/radio production, Performance/production costs, Publications.
STUDENT AID (GRANTS TO INSTITUTIONS): Scholarship funds.

Types of support for individuals: scholarships, individual artist grants.

Sample grants:
CAPP/MN/$1,600.
Northern Lakes Arts Association/Ely, MN/$8,250.
Voyageur Winter Festival - Ely/MN/$2,000.

Financial Information

Financial data for year ending: 12/31/2004
Foundation assets: $368,694
Grants paid: $306,300
Number of grants: 12
Largest/smallest: $8,250/$250

Application Information

Preferred form of initial contact: complete proposal.

Public information available by request: proposal guidelines, application form, annual report, website.

Proposal deadlines: March 1, July 1, November 1.

Contribution decisions made by: staff, board of directors/trustees.

Frequency of contributions decisions: annually.

Staff/Trustees

Staff: Keiko L. Williams, executive director.

Directors/trustees: Linda Dally, chairperson.

The Janice Gardner Foundation

11580 K-Tel Drive
Minnetonka, MN 55343-8855
County: Hennepin
Phone: (651) 714-2306
Contact: Elizabeth Glaeser, secretary/treasurer
Established: 12/22/1987
Funder type: Private foundation

Program Description

Program's purpose: For religious, charitable, scientific, literary or educational purposes, including the encouragement of art and the prevention of cruelty to animals.

Program limitations/restrictions: No specific restrictions.

Geographic focus: Twin Cities Metropolitan Area, Areas outside Minnesota.

Areas of interest:
ANIMAL RELATED: Animal protection/welfare.
ARTS, CULTURE, HUMANITIES.
HUMAN SERVICES.
RELIGION/SPIRITUAL DEVELOPMENT.

Intended beneficiaries: General public/unspecified.

Types of support for organizations:
GENERAL PURPOSE/OPERATING SUPPORT.

Sample grants:
Basilica of St Mary/MN/general operating/$29,780.
Jeremiah Program (The)/MN/general operating/$2,000.
League of Catholic Women - Minneapolis/MN/general operating/$10,900.

MN Sinfonia/MN/general operating/$13,500.
Opportunity Partners/MN/general operating/$7,400.
Park Nicollet Medical Foundation/MN/general operating/$45,000.
St David's Child Development/Minnetonka, MN/general operating/$5,750.
University of St Thomas - MN/MN/general operating/$25,350.

Financial Information

Financial data for year ending: 12/31/2005
Foundation assets: $4,466,112
Grants paid: $470,803
Number of grants: 24
Largest/smallest: $157,000/$1,000

Application Information

Preferred form of initial contact: letter of inquiry, telephone inquiry, complete proposal, no specific format required.

Proposal deadlines: none.

Staff/Trustees

Directors/trustees: George W. Gardner; Jacqui Gardner; Elizabeth Glaeser, secretary/treasurer; Susan M. Khaury.

General Mills Community Action

PO Box 1113
Minneapolis, MN 55440
County: Hennepin
Phone: (763) 764-2211
Fax: (763) 764-4114
Website: www.generalmills.com/foundation
Contact: Ellen Goldberg Luger, executive director, General Mills Foundation, and vice president, General Mills
Established: 01/01/1954
Funder type: Corporate foundation and corporate giving program

Program Description

Program's purpose: To improve and maintain the quality of life in communities with General Mills facilities; to initiate innovative solutions and approaches to problems in targeted areas of interest; to support and reinforce personal involvement of employees and retirees; and to reinforce General Mills' image and reputation as a top corporate citizen.

Funding priorities: Youth Nutrition & Fitness, Education, Social Services, and Arts & Culture.

Geographic focus: Twin Cities Metropolitan Area, General Mills manufacturing communities in the U.S. and Canada. Champions for Healthy Kids is a national program to improve Youth Nutrition and Fitness.

Geographic limitations: General Mills plant communities.

Areas of interest:

ARTS, CULTURE, HUMANITIES: Arts/cultural multipurpose, Museums, Performing arts, Visual arts, Public Broadcasting.

CIVIL RIGHTS: Diversity.

COMMUNITY IMPROVEMENT: Community/neighborhood development/improvement.

EDUCATION: Higher education, Pre-school/elementary, Secondary, Vocational/technical.

FOOD/NUTRITION/AGRICULTURE: Food service/free food distribution.

HUMAN SERVICES: Children/youth services, Family services, Multipurpose human service organizations.

PUBLIC SAFETY/DISASTERS/RELIEF: Disaster relief.

YOUTH DEVELOPMENT: Nutrition and fitness programs for youth.

Intended beneficiaries: General public/unspecified.

Types of support for organizations:

CAPITAL CAMPAIGNS.

GENERAL PURPOSE/OPERATING SUPPORT.

PROGRAM DEVELOPMENT/PROJECT SUPPORT.

Exclusions: Individuals, Political organizations, Religious organizations, Research, Travel, Conferences, Fundraisers.

Sample grants:

Achieve! Minneapolis/MN/$25,000.

Boys & Girls Club - MN (Twin Cities)/MN/$25,000.

Greater Minneapolis Crisis Nursery/MN/$15,000.

Juxtaposition Arts/MN/West Broadway Gateway project/$10,000.

Mixed Blood Theatre Company/MN/$25,000.

MN Children's Museum/MN/$30,000.

Peta Wakan Tipi (Sacred Fire Lodge)/MN/Dream of Wild Health/$10,000.

Private Schools - MN/MN/NA-WAY-EE Center School, Healthy Choices Project/$15,000.

Financial Information

Financial data for year ending: 05/31/2006
Foundation assets: $55,270,506
Grants paid: $53,331,232

Application Information

Preferred form of initial contact: complete proposal. Prefer completion of foundation application found on website at www.generalmills.com/foundation.

Public information available by request: proposal guidelines, application form, annual report, website: www.generalmills.com/foundation.

Accept common grant application: yes.

Proposal deadlines: Ongoing. February 1 for Champions for Healthy Kids.

Contribution decisions made by: board of directors/trustees, staff committee.

Typical time from application deadlines to notification: 4-6 weeks.

Staff/Trustees

Staff: Ruth Barlow, administrative assistant; Adrienne Jordan, program manager; Ellen Goldberg Luger, executive director, General Mills Foundation, and vice president, General Mills; Mary Jane Melendez, program and operations manager; Donna Nicholson Svendsen, associate director; Chris Shea, president, General Mills Foundation, and senior vice president, external relations; Cynthia Ann Thelen, coordinator, financial & administrative services; Jan Thon, grants administrator.

Directors/trustees: Y.M. Belton; R.G. Darcy; J.A. Lawrence; S.S. Marshall; M.A. Peel; K.J. Powell; J.J. Rotsch; S.W. Sanger, chairman & CEO.

Getsch Charitable Trust

PO Box 385258
Bloomington, MN 55438
County: Hennepin
Phone: (952) 893-3863
Funder type: Private foundation

Program Description

Geographic focus: Twin Cities Metropolitan Area, Areas outside Minnesota, International Areas.

Areas of interest:

RELIGION/SPIRITUAL DEVELOPMENT.

Sample grants:

Colonial Church of Edina/MN/$2,000.

Evangelical Free Church of America - MN/MN/Missions/$2,300.

Haiti Outreach/MN/$7,000.

Metro Women's Center/MN/$1,000.

Normandale Baptist Church/Bloomington, MN/$3,000.

Westwood Lutheran Church/MN/$23,000.

Young Life - Minneapolis South/MN/$1,000.

Financial Information

Financial data for year ending: 12/31/2005
Foundation assets: $2,740,199
Grants paid: $106,920
Number of grants: 39
Largest/smallest: $23,000/$300

Application Information

Preferred form of initial contact: Applications should be in written form with reason for grant or donation.

Proposal deadlines: Applications are accepted at anytime.

Staff/Trustees

Directors/trustees: David D. Getsch, executive director; Dianne H. Getsch; Edward W. Getsch; John H. Getsch; Marilyn Getsch; Marjorie D. Getsch.

Fanny S. Gilfillan Memorial, Incorporated

c/o Redwood County Human Services
PO Box 510
Redwood Falls, MN 56283
County: Redwood
Established: 06/16/1964
Funder type: Private foundation

Program Description

Program's purpose: To assist with medical bills for families who are otherwise unable to pay and for individuals who do not qualify for government-sponsored medical assistance programs. The foundation also provides donations to other charitable organizations.

Program limitations/restrictions: Must demonstrate financial need and be a resident of Redwood County, Minnesota.

Geographic focus: Greater Minnesota.

Geographic limitations: Redwood County, Minnesota.

Areas of interest:
HEALTH - GENERAL/REHABILITATIVE.

Intended beneficiaries: Poor/economically disadvantaged.

Types of support for organizations: GRANTS TO INDIVIDUALS.

Types of support for individuals: aid to needy persons.

Financial Information

Financial data for year ending: 12/31/2005
Foundation assets: $858,111
Grants paid: $42,726
Number of grants: 29
Largest/smallest: $5,000/$127

Application Information

Preferred form of initial contact: request for guidelines.

Public information available by request: application form.

Proposal deadlines: none.

Special application procedures: application forms available at Redwood County Human Services, Redwood Falls, Minnesota.

Staff/Trustees

Directors/trustees: Richard Aakre, president; Arliss Becker, director; Vera Doidge, director; Doris Petracek, director.

The Graco Foundation

PO Box 1441
Minneapolis, MN 55440-1441
County: Hennepin
Phone: (612) 623-6684
Fax: (612) 623-6944
Website: www.graco.com
Contact: Kristin Ridley, grants administration manager
Established: 01/01/1957
Funder type: Corporate foundation

Program Description

Program's purpose: The foundation's goal is to help organizations grow their ability to serve community needs through grants specifically aimed at expanding or enhancing services to clients, including capital projects and capacity-building grants.

Funding priorities: The foundation addresses the needs of the community in the following areas: 1) Productivity and Self-Sufficiency – Priority given to organizations that have a proven track record in enabling people to be self-sufficient and more productive. Emphasis will be placed on educational programs, human service programs that promote self-sufficiency, and sports/youth development programs; 2) Civic Projects – Business depends on healthy communities, as communities thrive around healthy businesses. Projects that improve the community will be given special consideration.

Program limitations/restrictions: The foundation focus usually does not allow grants for organizations or causes that do not directly impact Graco communities.

Geographic focus: Twin Cities Metropolitan Area, Areas outside Minnesota.

Geographic limitations: Awards are limited to the Twin Cities area, and in particular north and northeast Minneapolis, Sioux Falls, South Dakota and North Canton, Ohio.

Areas of interest:
COMMUNITY IMPROVEMENT: Community/neighborhood development/improvement.
EDUCATION: Adult/continuing education/literacy, Educational services, Graduate education/professional schools, Higher education, Libraries/library science, Secondary, Vocational/technical.
EMPLOYMENT/JOBS: Employment procurement/job training, Vocational rehabilitation.
HUMAN SERVICES.
RECREATION: Youth sports.
YOUTH DEVELOPMENT.

Intended beneficiaries: General public/unspecified.

Types of support for organizations:
CAPITAL CAMPAIGNS: Building/renovation, Computer systems/technology.
STUDENT AID (GRANTS TO INSTITUTIONS): Scholarship funds.

Types of support for individuals: none.

Matching grants: Education.

Exclusions: Individuals, Non-501(c)(3), Political organizations, Religious organizations, Fundraising, Travel, Special events, Dinners, Courtesy advertising, Fraternal organizations, National or local campaigns for disease research, Product donations.

Sample grants:

Admission Possible/St Paul, MN/Facilities improvements/$65,000.

ARC - MN (Greater Twin Cities)/MN/Technology upgrade/$25,000.

Cristo Rey - MN (Minneapolis)/MN/Capital campaign/$100,000.

Minneapolis Community & Technical College Foundation/MN/Power of You Initiative/$75,000.

MN Children's Museum/MN/Technology upgrade/$50,000.

Vail Place/Minneapolis, MN/Technology and building upgrades/$36,810.

Financial Information

Financial data for year ending: 12/31/2006
Foundation assets: $5,091,000
Grants paid: $2,249,866
Number of grants: 50
Largest/smallest: $100,000/$2,000

Application Information

Preferred form of initial contact: complete proposal.

Public information available by request: website.

Accept common grant application: yes.

Proposal deadlines: none.

Preferred time for receiving proposals: one month prior to board meetings.

Contribution decisions made by: board of directors/trustees.

Frequency of contributions decisions: quarterly.

Specific times board meets: March, June, September, December.

Typical time from application deadlines to notification: three months.

Special application procedures: include list of clients served, budget information, program evaluation methods and results, board of directors list, 501(c)(3) or other tax-exempt confirmation and most recent tax return.

Staff/Trustees

Staff: Kristin Ridley, grants administration manager.

Directors/trustees: Trudy L. Berggren, director; Janel W. French, treasurer; Karen P. Gallivan, vice president; Debra J. Hall, director; David Lowe, director; David A. Roberts, president; Mark Sheahan, director; Fred A. Sutter, director; Angie Wordell, director.

Grand Rapids Area Community Foundation

PO Box 543
201 NW Fourth Street
Suite 111
Grand Rapids, MN 55744-0543
County: Itasca
Phone: (218) 327-8855
Fax: (218) 327-8856
E-mail: info@gracf.org
Website: www.gracf.org
Contact: Wendy Roy, executive director
Established: 01/01/1994
Funder type: Community/public foundation

Program Description

Program's purpose: The foundation's express purpose is to provide opportunities to individuals and organizations that wish to invest in the community to improve the quality of life.

Program limitations/restrictions: Donor-advised grants and designated grants.

Geographic focus: Itasca County and surrounding communities.

Geographic limitations: Itasca County and surrounding communities.

Areas of interest:
ARTS, CULTURE, HUMANITIES: Arts services, Arts/cultural multipurpose, Historical societies, Humanities, Media/communications, Museums, Performing arts, Visual arts.
COMMUNITY IMPROVEMENT: Community coalitions, Economic development, Nonprofit management.
EDUCATION: Libraries/library science, Pre-school/elementary, Secondary, Vocational/technical.
ENVIRONMENTAL QUALITY/PROTECTION/BEAUTIFICATION: Environmental education/outdoor survival, Natural resources conservation/protection, Pollution abatement and control.
HOUSING/SHELTER: Homeless, temporary housing, Housing development/construction/management, Housing support services, Low-cost temporary housing.
HUMAN SERVICES: Children/youth services, Emergency assistance (food/clothing/cash), Family services, Family services for adolescent parents, Family violence shelters and services, Multipurpose human service organizations, Personal social services, Residential/custodial care, Senior centers and services, Victims services.
PHILANTHROPY/VOLUNTARISM: Voluntarism promotion.
PUBLIC AFFAIRS/SOCIETY BENEFIT: Leadership development/awards programs (other than youth).
PUBLIC PROTECTION - CRIME/COURTS/LEGAL SERVICES: Crime prevention.
RECREATION: Amateur sports clubs/leagues, Physical fitness/recreational facilities.
YOUTH DEVELOPMENT: Adult/child matching programs, Multipurpose youth centers/clubs, Youth development programs.

Intended beneficiaries: General public/unspecified.

Types of support for organizations:
CAPITAL CAMPAIGNS: Endowment funds, Equipment.
EMERGENCY FUNDS.
GRANTS TO INDIVIDUALS.
PROGRAM DEVELOPMENT/PROJECT SUPPORT.

Types of support for individuals: scholarships.

Sample grants:

Alzheimer's Family Support Fund/MN/Alzheimer's family support/$1,000.

Economic Development Projects/MN/leverage low-interest loans to businesses/$50,000.

Friends of Grand Rapids Youth Hockey/MN/$2,621.

Grand Rapids Public Library - MN/MN/books and expenses/$6,800.

Hill Lake Trail Association/MN/distribution for maintenance/$2,500.

Northern MN Builders/MN/scholarship/$500.

Peace & Safety/MN/$750.

Voice of Democracy/MN/scholarship/$50.

Financial Information

Financial data for year ending: 12/31/2005
Foundation assets: $7,200,000
Grants paid: $1,020,000
Number of grants: 500
Largest/smallest: $65,000/$200

Application Information

Preferred form of initial contact: letter of inquiry, telephone inquiry.

Public information available by request: proposal guidelines, application form, annual report, newsletter, website.

Accept common grant application: yes.

Proposal deadlines: March 15, September 15.

Contribution decisions made by: board of directors/trustees.

Frequency of contributions decisions: quarterly.

Typical time from application deadlines to notification: eight weeks.

Staff/Trustees

Staff: Sarah Copeland, program director; Wendy Roy, executive director; Kimberly Thompson, accountant.

Directors/trustees: Philip Anderson; Lynn DeGrio; Tom Fasteland, vice chair; Kris Ferraro; Peg Greenside; Cricket Guyer, secretary; Kelly Hain; Larke Huntley, chair; Al Kruger; Carolyn Liebe; Jean MacDonell; Pat Medure; Tom Osborn; Pam Rajala; Mike Rourke; Rex Sala; Ed Sorrentino; Jeff Stampohar; Joe Stauffer, second vice chair; Noah Wilcox.

Gray Plant Mooty Foundation

500 IDS Center
80 South Eighth Street
Minneapolis, MN 55402-5383
County: Hennepin
Phone: (612) 632-3000
Alt. Phone: (612) 632-3345
Fax: (612) 632-4000
Website: www.gpmlaw.com
Contact: Linda M. Spotts, executive secretary
Established: 07/21/1982
Funder type: Corporate foundation

Program Description

Program's purpose: Legal-related and other charitable purposes.

Geographic focus: Twin Cities Metropolitan Area, Greater Minnesota.

Areas of interest:
ARTS, CULTURE, HUMANITIES.
EDUCATION.
HEALTH - DISEASES/MEDICAL DISCIPLINES.
HEALTH - GENERAL/REHABILITATIVE.
HUMAN SERVICES.
PUBLIC PROTECTION - CRIME/COURTS/LEGAL SERVICES: Legal services.

Intended beneficiaries: General public/unspecified.

Types of support for organizations:
IN-KIND SERVICES: Pro bono legal services.

Sample grants:
Children's Hospital & Clinics Foundation/MN/$5,000.
Dunwoody Institute/MN/College of Technology/$2,000.
Fund for the Legal Aid Society - Mpls/MN/$10,000.
Greater Minneapolis Metropolitan Housing Corporation/MN/$2,250.
Guthrie Theater Foundation/Minneapolis, MN/$3,000.

Financial Information

Financial data for year ending: 03/31/2006
Foundation assets: $2,380
Grants paid: $192,834
Number of grants: 90
Largest/smallest: $60,000/$100

Application Information

Preferred form of initial contact: letter of inquiry.

Frequency of contributions decisions: quarterly.

Staff/Trustees

Staff: Linda M. Spotts, executive secretary.

Directors/trustees: Albert Andrews Jr.; Sarah Duniway; Julie A. Frommelt, chair; Nevin R. Harwood; Malcolm D. Reid; C. Steven Wilson; Quentin R. Wittrock.

Mary S. Gray Charitable Trust

U.S. Bank, N.A.
800 Nicollet Mall
Minneapolis, MN 55402
County: Hennepin
Phone: (612) 303-3209
Contact: Joyce James
Established: 03/23/1987
Funder type: Private foundation

Program Description

Program's purpose: Religious, charitable, scientific, literary and educational purposes.

Program limitations/restrictions: A majority of the recipients are specifically designated in establishment of foundation.

Intended beneficiaries: General public/unspecified.

Sample grants:
Children's Home Society - MN/MN/general operating/$27,500.
Courage Center - MN (Golden Valley)/MN/Camp Courage/$27,500.
Planned Parenthood - MN/MN/general operating/$55,000.
Presbyterian Homes of MN/MN/general operating/$90,000.
Walker Methodist Foundation/MN/general operating/$75,000.

Financial Information

Financial data for year ending: 08/31/2006
Foundation assets: $5,356,634
Grants paid: $250,000
Number of grants: 5
Largest/smallest: $1,000/$25,000

Application Information

Proposal deadlines: none.

Special application procedures: applications should be submitted in written form outlining the nature of the request.

Staff/Trustees

Directors/trustees: U.S. Bank Private Client Group; Glenn Bartsch.

Mary Livingston Griggs and Mary Griggs Burke Foundation

55 East Fifth Street
Suite 1400
St Paul, MN 55101-1792
County: Ramsey
Phone: (651) 227-7683
Contact: Marvin Pertzik, treasurer/secretary
Established: 06/01/1966
Funder type: Private foundation

Program Description

Geographic focus: Twin Cities Metropolitan Area, Areas outside Minnesota, New York, NY.

Areas of interest:
ARTS, CULTURE, HUMANITIES: Historical societies, Humanities, Museums, Performing arts, Visual arts.
EDUCATION: Higher education, Libraries/library science.
ENVIRONMENTAL QUALITY /PROTECTION/BEAUTIFICATION.
HUMAN SERVICES.

Intended beneficiaries: General public/unspecified.

Types of support for organizations:
GENERAL PURPOSE/OPERATING SUPPORT.
PROGRAM DEVELOPMENT/ PROJECT SUPPORT.

Sample grants:
Guthrie Theater, The/Minneapolis, MN/$40,000.
Mixed Blood Theatre Company/MN/$2,000.
MN Landscape Arboretum/MN/Annual Garden/$200,000.
MN Museum of American Art/MN/$3,150.

MN Zoo/MN/$2,000.

Planned Parenthood - MN/SD/MN/$7,500.

St Paul Academy & Summit School/MN/$4,500.

Twin Cities Public Television/St Paul, MN/$3,150.

Financial Information

Financial data for year ending: 06/30/2006
Foundation assets: $25,484,728
Grants paid: $1,478,538

Application Information

Preferred form of initial contact: complete proposal.

Proposal deadlines: none.

Special application procedures: The form of application is a comprehensive letter outlining the amount, purpose, time period and other relevant data; additional materials are a budget, a copy of the last audited financial statements and a copy of the federal exemption letter.

Staff/Trustees

Directors/trustees: Eleanor Briggs; Mary Griggs Burke; Gale Lansing Davis, vice president; C. E. Bayliss Griggs, president; Marvin Pertzik, treasurer/secretary.

Virginia A. Groot Foundation

PO Box 1050
Evanston, IL 60204-1050
County: Hennepin
Phone: (763) 550-9003
Fax: (763) 550-7921
E-mail: virginia@virginiaagroot foundation.org
Website: www. virginiaagroot foundation.org
Contact: Patrice Olander-Quamme, bookkeeper
Established: 12/01/1986
Funder type: Private foundation

Program Description

Program's purpose: Each year the foundation offers a grant of up to $35,000 to an artist who has exceptional talent and demonstrated ability in ceramic arts. The foundation also awards annual scholarships to recognize outstanding achievement in the ceramic arts.

Program limitations/restrictions: Grant: Applicants must be 21 years or older, at any stage of career development; students are ineligible; teachers are eligible if their program plan is for their development as artists rather than teachers; the grant does not support continued academic training. Scholarships: Applicants must be currently enrolled in an accredited four-year liberal arts program and have a demonstrated interest and ability in ceramic arts.

Geographic focus: Minnesota statewide, national areas.

Geographic limitations: Grant: No geographic restrictions. Scholarships: Applicants must be enrolled in a liberal arts program in Illinois, Iowa, Minnesota, North Dakota, South Dakota or Wisconsin.

Areas of interest:
ARTS, CULTURE, HUMANITIES: Visual arts, Ceramic arts.

Intended beneficiaries: Adults.

Types of support for organizations:
GRANTS TO INDIVIDUALS.
STUDENT AID (GRANTS TO INSTITUTIONS): Scholarship funds.

Types of support for individuals: scholarships, postgraduate pursuit of ceramic arts.

Financial Information

Financial data for year ending: 12/31/2005
Foundation assets: $551,007
Grants paid: $65,000
Number of grants: 5
Largest/smallest: $35,000/$1,500

Application Information

Preferred form of initial contact: complete proposal.

Public information available by request: proposal guidelines, application form.

Proposal deadlines: grant: March 1; scholarships: October 1.

Contribution decisions made by: panel of mostly prior top recipients.

Frequency of contributions decisions: annually.

Special application procedures: Grant: applicants must submit up to 20 35mm slides of their work along with the application form. Scholarships: applicants must submit eight 35mm slides of their work along with the application form.

Staff/Trustees

Directors/trustees: Bruce Blackburn; Christine Federighi; Candice B. Groot, president; Stanley Shetka.

N. Bud and Beverly Grossman Foundation

4670 Wells Fargo Center
90 South Seventh Street
Minneapolis, MN 55402
County: Hennepin
Phone: (612) 337-8192
Contact: Larry Waller
Established: 07/31/1973
Funder type: Private foundation

Program Description

Program's purpose: General charitable purposes.

Geographic focus: Minnesota statewide, Areas outside Minnesota.

Geographic limitations: Preference given to Minnesota projects.

Areas of interest:
ARTS, CULTURE, HUMANITIES: Museums, Performing arts, Visual arts.
COMMUNITY IMPROVEMENT.
EDUCATION.
HEALTH - GENERAL/REHABILITATIVE.
HUMAN SERVICES.

Intended beneficiaries: General public/unspecified.

Types of support for organizations:
GENERAL PURPOSE/OPERATING SUPPORT.

Sample grants:

Adath Jeshurun Congregation/MN/$47,400.

Guthrie Theater, The/Minneapolis, MN/$42,000.

Jewish Federation - AZ/AZ/$50,000.

MN Opera Company/MN/$8,000.

MN Orchestral Association/MN/$121,500.

United Way - MN (Minneapolis Area)/MN/$27,000.

University of MN - Foundation/MN/$50,000.

Walker Art Center/MN/$37,000.

Financial Information

Financial data for year ending: 12/31/2005
Foundation assets: $2,995,128
Grants paid: $1,999,503

Application Information

Preferred form of initial contact: complete proposal. Note: phone solicitations and form letters will not be considered.

Proposal deadlines: April 15 for consideration within the fiscal year.

Preferred time for receiving proposals: Requests are accepted throughout the year.

Frequency of contributions decisions: annually.

Special application procedures: Formal applications are not required, but in order to process a proposal, the foundation asks for the following information: description of the organization requesting support; statement of objectives; details of how the objectives will be maintained; evidence of the need for the activity or project; a proposed budget; a specific dollar amount requested; information about other sources of support and current list of major donors; the most recent annual financial statement; list of officers and board members; proposed method of evaluating how well objectives are met and how the evaluation will be reported; project scope, geographic area and population served; copy of the most recent tax-exempt 501(c)(3) ruling from the IRS.

Staff/Trustees

Staff: Larry Waller.

Directors/trustees: Beverly N. Grossman; N. Bud Grossman, president; Morris M. Sherman.

Grotto Foundation, Inc.

5323 Lakeland Avenue North
Suite 100
Minneapolis, MN 55429-3115
County: Hennepin
Phone: (763) 277-3434
Fax: (763) 277-3444
E-mail: info@grottofoundation.org
Website: www.grottofoundation.org
Contact: Sarah Marquardt, grants manager
Established: 12/01/1964
Paid Staff: Yes
Funder type: Private foundation

Program Description

Program's purpose: The mission of the Grotto Foundation is to benefit society by improving the education and the economic, physical and social well-being of citizens, with a special focus on families and culturally diverse groups.

Funding priorities: The Grotto Foundation supports projects that promote communities, families and understanding. The Grotto Foundation board continues to explore the role of language and culture in keeping families together, building strength in communities, and assisting young people to achieve established academic learner outcomes in math and reading. Great importance is placed on projects that are primarily initiated by, and have the full support of, the respective communities involved.

Program limitations/restrictions: Does not typically make grants to individuals; for scholarships; for capital fund programs/projects; to subsidize the writing and publishing of most publications; for multiple years; to organizations outside of Minnesota; for travel, study and conference attendance; for undergraduate and graduate student research; to non-operating foundations; for general operation of large organizations; nor to subsidize programs primarily supported by government agencies.

Geographic focus: Minnesota statewide.

Areas of interest:
ARTS, CULTURE, HUMANITIES.
CIVIL RIGHTS: Civil rights/advocacy for specific groups, Intergroup relations/race relations.
COMMUNITY IMPROVEMENT: Community/neighborhood development/improvement, Nonprofit management, Programs that address specific needs of Native Americans and other ethnic populations.
EDUCATION: Mentoring, Tutoring, After-school programs, Remedial education.
EMPLOYMENT/JOBS: Employment procurement/job training, Labor unions/organizations.
ENVIRONMENTAL QUALITY/PROTECTION/BEAUTIFICATION: Sustainability, particularly related to preservation of the life of a cultural group.
HEALTH - DISEASES/MEDICAL DISCIPLINES: AIDS/HIV, Other.
HEALTH - GENERAL/REHABILITATIVE: Health support services, Health treatment facilities - primarily outpatient, Public health programs/wellness education.
HEALTH - MENTAL HEALTH/CRISIS INTERVENTION: Alcohol/drug/substance, prevention and treatment, Mental health treatment and services, Other.
HOUSING/SHELTER: Housing support services, Low-cost temporary housing.
HUMAN SERVICES: Children/youth services, Family services, Services to specific groups.
PUBLIC AFFAIRS/SOCIETY BENEFIT: Leadership development/awards programs (other than youth).
PUBLIC PROTECTION - CRIME/COURTS/LEGAL SERVICES: Protection/prevention - neglect/abuse/exploitation.
SOCIAL SCIENCES.
YOUTH DEVELOPMENT: Youth development programs.

Intended beneficiaries: Ethnic/racial populations - general, General public/unspecified, Native American/American Indians.

Types of support for organizations:
GENERAL PURPOSE/OPERATING SUPPORT.
PROGRAM DEVELOPMENT/PROJECT SUPPORT: Curriculum development, Faculty/staff development, Public awareness, Seed money/start-up funds.

Types of support for individuals: none.

Exclusions: Capital & endowment campaigns, Individuals, Scholarships/loans, Arts, Organizations with budgets over $1 million.

Sample grants:

Admission Possible/St Paul, MN/to support capacity-building for this organization dedicated to helping low-income high school students in the Twin Cities achieve admission to higher education/$7,500.

Ain Dah Yung Shelter Center/MN/to support the Oyate Nawajin (Stand with the People) Counseling and Support Project, a new program that uses both mainstream therapeutic models and traditional American-Indian culture and wellness concepts to understand and treat American-Indian youth and families/$10,000.

Breaking Free, Inc (MN)/St Paul, MN/to support its Building Strong Families program/$10,000.

Greater Frogtown Community Development Corporation/MN/to partially fund a Hmong Language Program Assistant position for one year/$5,000.

Greater Minneapolis Council of Churches/MN/to focus specifically on fostering leadership in Indian youth in the context of community awareness, social change, service, and personal development/$7,500.

Little Earth Neighborhood Early Learning Center Co/MN/to support its Little Earth/Phillips Early Childhood Language Revitalization Project/$35,000.

Native American Community Board - SD/SD/to support its Native American Language Revitalization & School Retention Program/$30,000.

Upper Sioux Indian Community/MN/to support the family-based Master/Apprentice Language Project during which a family cluster will engage in Dakota language instruction/immersion with an elderly master speaker/relative for one year/$40,000.

Financial Information

Financial data for year ending: 04/30/2006
Foundation assets: $25,118,050
Grants paid: $745,510
Number of grants: 43
Largest/smallest: $464,000/$3,500
Largest multi-year grant approved: $464,000

Application Information

Preferred form of initial contact: request for guidelines, complete proposal.

Public information available by request: proposal guidelines, application form, annual report, website.

Proposal deadlines: January 15, March 15, July 15 and November 15.

Frequency of contributions decisions: quarterly.

Specific times board meets: April, June, October, February.

Typical time from application deadlines to notification: 3 months.

Staff/Trustees

Staff: Ellis Bullock, executive director and secretary; LaVon Lee, program officer; Sarah Marquardt, grants manager.

Directors/trustees: Ellis Bullock, executive director and secretary; Kathrine E. Hill; Louis Fors Hill, president; Louis Shea Hill; Scott Hill; Mary Manuel, treasurer; Malcolm W. McDonald, second vice-president; Elizabeth A. Pegues-Smart, first vice-president; Nancy Randall Dana; Cris Stainbrook.

Haggerty Family Foundation

5816 Long Brake Trail
Edina, MN 55439
County: Hennepin
Established: 10/22/1996
Funder type: Private foundation

Program Description

Program's purpose: General charitable purposes.

Geographic focus: Twin Cities Metropolitan Area, Minnesota statewide, Areas outside Minnesota.

Areas of interest:
HEALTH - MENTAL HEALTH/CRISIS INTERVENTION.
HUMAN SERVICES.

Intended beneficiaries: General public/unspecified, Mentally/emotionally disabled, Physically disabled.

Types of support for organizations:
GENERAL PURPOSE/OPERATING SUPPORT.
PROGRAM DEVELOPMENT/PROJECT SUPPORT.

Sample grants:
Appalachia Service Project Inc/Johnson City, TN/$8,000.
Catholic Charities - MN (Minneapolis)/MN/general operating/$10,000.
Exceptional Children's Assistance Network/Davidson, NC/general operating/$7,000.
Family Hope Services Inc - MN (Plymouth)/MN/general operating/$5,000.
The Jeremiah Program/MN/general operating/$10,500.
MN Landscape Arboretum/MN/general operating/$10,000.
NAMI-MN/MN/general operating/$10,000.
Outward Bound - MN/MN/voyageur program/$5,000.

Financial Information

Financial data for year ending: 12/31/2005
Foundation assets: $2,311,961
Grants paid: $100,500
Number of grants: 19
Largest/smallest: $12,000/$250

Application Information

Preferred form of initial contact: complete proposal.

Staff/Trustees

Directors/trustees: Daniel J. Haggerty; John Haggerty; Ruth Haggerty, president; Kathleen Malone; Maureen L. Mischinski; Laurie Rivard.

Hardenbergh Foundation (fka St Croix Foundation)

U.S. Bank, N.A.
101 East Fifth Street
EP MN S14
St Paul, MN 55101
County: Ramsey
Phone: (651) 466-8735
Alt. Phone: (651) 466-8707
Contact: Jeffrey T. Peterson
Established: 12/01/1950
Funder type: Private foundation

Program Description

Program's purpose: Grants are made to charitable institutions, institutions of learning, hospitals, sanitariums, churches and other religious organizations to aid and assist needy and oppressed persons.

Geographic focus: East Metropolitan Area/St Paul only.

Geographic limitations: Grants to organizations located in the St Paul/Stillwater area only.

Intended beneficiaries: General public/unspecified, Poor/economically disadvantaged.

Types of support for organizations:
CAPITAL CAMPAIGNS.
GENERAL PURPOSE/OPERATING SUPPORT: Annual campaigns.

Sample grants:
Boys & Girls Club - MN (Twin Cities)/MN/$5,000.
Family Means/MN/$30,000.

HealthEast Foundation/St Paul, MN/ $10,000.

Hope House - MN (St Croix Valley)/ MN/$2,000.

MN Historical Society/MN/$5,000.

St Croix Concert Series/MN/$2,000.

Stillwater Public Library/MN/Additional capital Grant Library Renovation/$300,000.

YMCA Camp St Croix/MN/$10,000.

Financial Information

Financial data for year ending: 12/31/2005
Foundation assets: $67,231,908
Grants paid: $2,527,500
Number of grants: 97
Largest/smallest: $25,000/$1,000
Largest multi-year grant approved: $150,000

Application Information

Preferred form of initial contact: complete proposal.

Proposal deadlines: none.

Staff/Trustees

Directors/trustees: Edgerton Bronson; Robert S. Davis, president; Quentin O. Heimerman; Jeffrey T. Peterson; Jon Theobald.

Olga B. Hart Education Foundation

2094 Miller Creek Drive
Duluth, MN 55811-1805
County: St Louis
Phone: (218) 723-7814
Funder type: Private foundation

Program Description

Funding priorities: Educational activities.

Geographic focus: Twin Cities Metropolitan Area, Minnesota statewide.

Areas of interest:
EDUCATION.

Sample grants:
ISD St Paul #625/MN/$15,000.

Normandale Lutheran Church/MN/ $5,000.

St Cloud State University/MN/$22,500.

University of MN Foundation/MN/ $20,000.

Financial Information

Financial data for year ending: 12/31/2005
Foundation assets: $4,382,720
Grants paid: $175,000
Number of grants: 11
Largest/smallest: $25,000/$2,500

Staff/Trustees

Directors/trustees: Robert J. Wasko.

Hartz Foundation

13773 W. M. Davis Parkway
Jacksonville, FL 32224
Contact: Onealee Hartz
Established: 02/14/1975
Funder type: Private foundation

Program Description

Program limitations/restrictions: Contributions to 501(c)(3) tax-exempt organizations only.

Geographic focus: Greater Minnesota, Minnesota statewide, areas outside Minnesota.

Geographic limitations: Primary consideration given to northern Minnesota and northeastern North Dakota.

Areas of interest:
ARTS, CULTURE, HUMANITIES: Historical societies, Media/communications, Museums.
EDUCATION: Adult/continuing education/literacy, Graduate education/professional schools, Higher education, Libraries/library science, Pre-school/elementary, Secondary, Vocational/technical.
ENVIRONMENTAL QUALITY/ PROTECTION/BEAUTIFICATION: Botanical/horticultural/landscape, Environmental beautification/open spaces, Environmental education/outdoor survival, Natural resources conservation/protection.
FOOD/NUTRITION/AGRICULTURE: Food service/free food distribution.
HUMAN SERVICES: Senior centers and services.
PUBLIC PROTECTION - CRIME/ COURTS/LEGAL SERVICES: Law enforcement agencies.

RECREATION: Physical fitness/ recreational facilities, Recreation and sporting camps, Sports training facilities/agencies.
YOUTH DEVELOPMENT: Scouting organizations.

Intended beneficiaries: Adults, Aging/ elderly/senior citizens, Deaf/hearing impaired, General public/unspecified, Mentally/emotionally disabled.

Types of support for organizations:
CAPITAL CAMPAIGNS: Building/ renovation, Computer systems/ technology, Equipment.
PROGRAM DEVELOPMENT/ PROJECT SUPPORT.
STUDENT AID (GRANTS TO INSTITUTIONS): Scholarship funds.

Exclusions: Non-501(c)(3).

Sample grants:
Boy Scouts of America - ND (Northern Lights)/Fargo, ND/programming/$4,000.

City of Thief River Falls/MN/complete Hartz Park/$1,352.

ISD Roseau #682/MN/construction of tennis courts/$15,000.

ISD Thief River Falls #564/MN/portable computers/$10,000.

MN Public Radio/MN/programming/ $2,000.

Moorhead State University/MN/ scholarships/$2,500.

Northland Community College - MN/ MN/scholarships/$30,000.

Roseau County Historical Society/MN/ flood recovery expense/$10,000.

Financial Information

Financial data for year ending: 07/31/2006
Foundation assets: $4,724,788
Grants paid: $216,900
Number of grants: 23
Largest/smallest: $30,000/$200

Application Information

Preferred form of initial contact: letter of inquiry, include purpose for funds, copy of exemption letter and project budget.

Proposal deadlines: none.

Contribution decisions made by: board of directors/trustees.

Frequency of contributions decisions: annually.

Staff/Trustees

Directors/trustees: Onealee Hartz; Richard Sjoberg, president; Dwight Tanquist.

Hatlen Foundation

13141 Hannover Court
Apple Valley, MN 55124
County: Dakota
Phone: (952) 432-1403
Contact: Roe Hatlen
Established: 11/14/1989
Donor: Roe & Beverly Hatlen
Funder type: Private foundation

Program Description

Geographic focus: Twin Cities Metropolitan Area, Greater Minnesota, Areas outside Minnesota.

Areas of interest:
ARTS, CULTURE, HUMANITIES.
EDUCATION: Higher education, Secondary.
RELIGION/SPIRITUAL DEVELOPMENT.

Intended beneficiaries: General public/unspecified.

Types of support for organizations:
GENERAL PURPOSE/OPERATING SUPPORT: Annual campaigns.

Types of support for individuals: scholarships.

Sample grants:

Augsburg College/MN/annual fund/ $2,500.

Christ Lutheran Church - MN (Eagan)/ MN/scholarship fund/$10,000.

Sons of Norway Foundation/MN/Norway Fund/$1,000.

Financial Information

Financial data for year ending: 11/30/2006
Foundation assets: $230,000
Grants paid: $23,000

Application Information

Preferred form of initial contact: The foundation's funds are currently committed. No new applications are being taken.

Staff/Trustees

Directors/trustees: Beverly J. Hatlen, president; Kari Hatlen; Roe Hatlen.

Headwaters Foundation for Justice

2801 21st Avenue South
Suite 132B
Minneapolis, MN 55407
County: Hennepin
Phone: (612) 879-0602
Fax: (612) 879-0613
E-mail: info@headwatersfoundation.org
Website: www.headwatersfoundation.org
Established: 12/27/1984
Funder type: Community/public foundation

Program Description

Program's purpose: Headwaters Foundation for Justice is a catalyst for social change that supports grassroots communities working to create social, economic and racial justice.

Funding priorities: Constituent-led social change organizations that address the root causes of problems in our society, work in a cooperative manner with other groups in the community, and have limited access to traditional funding sources.

Geographic focus: Twin Cities Metropolitan Area, Minnesota statewide.

Geographic limitations: Twin Cities of Minneapolis and St Paul, Greater Minnesota, Wisconsin.

Areas of interest:
CIVIL RIGHTS: Civil liberties advocacy, Civil rights/advocacy for specific groups, Equal opportunity and access, Intergroup relations/race relations, Voter education/registration.
EDUCATION: Educational reform, Organizing components for social change.
EMPLOYMENT/JOBS: Labor unions/organizations.
ENVIRONMENTAL QUALITY/PROTECTION/BEAUTIFICATION: Pollution abatement and control, Equitable Development, Land Preservation, Organizing components for social change.
FOOD/NUTRITION/AGRICULTURE: Food production and preservation, Organizing components for social change.
HEALTH - DISEASES/MEDICAL DISCIPLINES: Health issues related to social and environmental issues and organizing for social change.
HOUSING/SHELTER: Housing owners/renter organizations, Affordable Housing issues.
PUBLIC AFFAIRS/SOCIETY BENEFIT: Citizen participation, Welfare policy and reform.
PUBLIC PROTECTION - CRIME/COURTS/LEGAL SERVICES: Judicial reform, Neglect/abuse/exploitation, Organizing components for social change.
RELIGION/SPIRITUAL DEVELOPMENT: Faith-based groups organizing for social justice.

Intended beneficiaries: Adults, African Americans/Blacks, Aging/elderly/senior citizens, Asian/Pacific Islanders, Disabled - general or unspecified disability, Ethnic/racial populations - general, Females - all ages or age unspecified, Gay/lesbian/bisexual/transgender, Hispanics/Latinos, Homeless, Immigrants/newcomers/refugees, Infants/babies (under age 5), Males - all ages or age unspecified, Migrant workers, Native American/American Indians, People with HIV/AIDS, Poor/economically disadvantaged.

Types of support for individuals: none.

Exclusions: Capital & endowment campaigns, Individuals, Social service organizations.

Sample grants:

Centro Campesino/Owatonna, MN/ $10,000.

ISAIAH/MN/St Paul Caucus/$10,000.

Little Earth Residents Association/MN/ $5,000.

MN Alliance for Progressive Action/MN/ $10,000.

Outfront MN/MN/Community Services/ $10,000.

People Escaping Poverty Project/MN/ $10,000.

West Side Citizens Organization/MN/ $10,000.

Women's Environmental Institute/MN/ $10,000.

Financial Information

Financial data for year ending: 06/30/2006
Foundation assets: $4,375,624
Grants paid: $792,412
Number of grants: 190
Largest/smallest: $15,000/$1,000

Application Information

Preferred form of initial contact: telephone inquiry, request for guidelines, e-mail.

Public information available by request: proposal guidelines, application form, annual report, website.

Proposal deadlines: Social Change Fund-February 1; Democracy Fund-June 1; Fund of the Sacred Circle-August 1; Environmental Justice Fund-August 1.

Contribution decisions made by: board of directors/trustees, activist-guided grants committees.

Frequency of contributions decisions: annually.

Typical time from application deadlines to notification: General - 4 months.

Special application procedures: Identify which fund – Social Change Fund or Fund of the Sacred Circle Environmental Justice Fund, Democracy Fund – and apply in appropriate timeframe.

Staff/Trustees

Staff: Monica Bryand, program officer; Julia Kashaeva, administrative associate; Carol Mollner, development director; Cynthia Moothart, communications manager; David Nicholson, program director; Kelly Perkins, development officer; Jim Sauder, operations director; Senay Yargici, administrative associate.

Directors/trustees: John R. Farrish; Anne Haddad; Daniel Hawkins; Carol McGee Johnson; Chuck Koosman; Brandon Lacy-Campos; Arif Mamdani; Dave Mann; Cecilia Martinez; Ron McKinley; Munir Meghjee; Elaine Salinas; Mai Thor; Ann Tobin; Friendly Vang-Johnson; David Waterbury; Barbra Wiener; Perry Wilson; Beth Zemsky.

Healthier Minnesota Community Clinic Fund

PO Box 241236
St Paul, MN 55124-1236
County: Ramsey
Phone: (651) 599-1921
E-mail: healthiermnccfund@msn.com
Website: www.minnesotacommunityclinicfund.org
Contact: Kristen Gloege, executive director
Established: 09/05/2001
Funder type: Private foundation

Program Description

Program's purpose: Support primary care services offered by safety net providers.

Program limitations/restrictions: No past debt payment.

Geographic focus: Minnesota statewide.

Areas of interest:
HEALTH - GENERAL/REHABILITATIVE: Health care financing activities, Health support services, Hospitals and related primary medical care facilities, Nursing care/services, Public health programs/wellness education, Reproductive health care, Primary medical care.

Intended beneficiaries: Ethnic/racial populations - general, Poor/economically disadvantaged, Medically underserved.

Types of support for organizations:
CAPITAL CAMPAIGNS: Building/renovation, Computer systems/technology, Equipment.
PROGRAM DEVELOPMENT/PROJECT SUPPORT: Primary care service delivery.

Types of support for individuals: none.

Sample grants:
Community University Health Care Center/MN/fund 2 dentist positions/$100,000.

Lake Superior Community Health Center/Duluth, MN/fund physician/$100,000.

Leech Lake Band of Ojibwe/MN/capital/$100,000.

Open Door Health Center - MN/MN/primary care service delivery/$100,000.

Financial Information

Financial data for year ending: 12/31/2005
Foundation assets: $28,044,046
Grants paid: $1,146,971
Number of grants: 26
Largest/smallest: $100,000/$10,000

Application Information

Preferred form of initial contact: telephone inquiry.

Public information available by request: proposal guidelines, application form, website.

Accept common grant application: yes.

Accept common report form: yes.

Proposal deadlines: Letters of inquiry accepted year round.

Contribution decisions made by: board of directors/trustees.

Frequency of contributions decisions: annually.

Typical time from application deadlines to notification: variable.

Staff/Trustees

Staff: Kristen Gloege, executive director.

Directors/trustees: Jim Bernstein; Ray Christensen M.D.; Mike Finch, chair; Cindy Goff; Gayle Hallin; Deborah Madson; Gretchen Musicant; Karl Self; Cheryl Stevens.

HealthPartners

Community Relations, M.S. 21103A
8100 34th Ave South
Bloomington, MN 55425
County: Hennepin
Phone: (952) 883-5393
Fax: (952) 883-7761
Website: www.healthpartners.com
Paid Staff: Yes
Funder type: Corporate giving program

Program Description

Program's purpose: Community health improvement.

Funding priorities: Activities that prevent health problems: prevention related to heart disease, cancer and diabetes; promotion of healthy eating and physical activity; reduction of health disparities.

Program limitations/restrictions: Does not fund political organizations or fundraisers for specific families or individuals; gives low priority to religious causes, capital campaigns, endowments, arts and humanities.

Geographic focus: Twin Cities Metropolitan Area.

Geographic limitations: Priority is Twin Cities metropolitan area.

Areas of interest:
FOOD/NUTRITION/AGRICULTURE: Nutrition promotion.
HEALTH - DISEASES/MEDICAL DISCIPLINES: Cancer, Diabetes, Heart disease.
HEALTH - GENERAL/REHABILITATIVE: Public health programs/wellness education, Eliminating health disparities.
PHILANTHROPY/VOLUNTARISM: Federated Funds.

Intended beneficiaries: General public/unspecified.

Types of support for organizations:
GENERAL PURPOSE/OPERATING SUPPORT.
PROGRAM DEVELOPMENT/PROJECT SUPPORT.
PROGRAM-RELATED INVESTMENTS.
CORPORATE SPONSORSHIP: Limited funds for sponsorships. Activities that prevent health problems: prevention related to heart disease, cancer and diabetes; promotion of healthy eating and physical activity; reduction of health disparities. Does not sponsor political events or fundraisers for specific families or individuals; gives low priority to religious events, arts and humanities. Contact: Donna Zimmerman, Community Relations.

Types of support for individuals: none.

Dollars for Doers: yes.

Exclusions: Individuals, Political organizations, Scholarships/loans.

Sample grants:
American Diabetes Association - MN/MN/$1,000.
Multilingual Health Resources Exchange/MN/$3,500.
Southside Community Health Services - MN/MN/Research on obesity/$2,500.
Youth Farm & Market Project/Minneapolis, MN/$3,000.

Financial Information

Financial data for year ending: 12/31/2004
Grants paid: $350,000
Number of grants: 250
Largest/smallest: $80,000/$25
Typical grant amount: $2,000

Application Information

Public information available by request: proposal guidelines, website.
Proposal deadlines: ongoing.
Contribution decisions made by: staff.
Frequency of contributions decisions: ongoing.
Typical time from application deadlines to notification: one month.

Staff/Trustees

Staff: Jordana Schmidt, community relations sr. administrative assistant; Donna Zimmerman, vice president.

Anna M. Heilmaier Charitable Foundation

U.S. Bank, N.A.
EP-MN-S14
101 East Fifth Street
St Paul, MN 55101
County: Ramsey
Phone: (651) 466-8443
Contact: Tina Holgin
Established: 11/05/1993
Funder type: Private foundation

Program Description

Program's purpose: Emphasis on promotion of chamber and other classical music, programs for treatment of cancer and diseases of the eye, and cultural preservation for the East Metro/St Paul area.

Program limitations/restrictions: Nonprofit organizations with budgets of $1.5 million or more may not apply for general operating support grants.

Geographic focus: East Metropolitan Area/St Paul only.

Areas of interest:
ARTS, CULTURE, HUMANITIES: Performing arts, Chamber and classical music, Cultural preservation.
HEALTH - DISEASES/MEDICAL DISCIPLINES: Cancer, diseases of the eye.
HEALTH - GENERAL/REHABILITATIVE.
HEALTH - RESEARCH: Cancer research, diseases of the eye.

Intended beneficiaries: Blind/vision impaired, General public/unspecified.

Types of support for organizations:
CAPITAL CAMPAIGNS.
GENERAL PURPOSE/OPERATING SUPPORT.
PROGRAM DEVELOPMENT/PROJECT SUPPORT.

Sample grants:
Chamber Music Society of MN/MN/general operating/$5,000.
East Metro Music Academy/MN/general operating/$5,000.
Gillette Children's Hospital Foundation/MN/capital campaign, focus on special children/$25,000.
Lifetrack Resources/MN/rehabilitation therapies division services for low income & elderly/$20,000.
MN Sinfonia/MN/six free concerts for east St Paul area/$25,000.
Music in the Park Series/MN/general operating/$5,000.
Sight & Hearing Association/MN/preschool screening program/$7,500.
Women's Cancer Resource Center - MN/MN/woman-to-woman cancer support programs/$10,000.

Financial Information

Financial data for year ending: 12/31/2005
Foundation assets: $7,508,862
Grants paid: $288,000
Number of grants: 19
Largest/smallest: $125,000/$5,000

Application Information

Preferred form of initial contact: letter of inquiry, telephone inquiry.
Public information available by request: proposal guidelines, application form.
Accept common grant application: yes.
Accept common report form: yes.
Proposal deadlines: August 1 of each year with notification mailed by September 30 of each year.
Contribution decisions made by: trustee distribution committee.
Typical time from application deadlines to notification: 2 months.

Staff/Trustees

Staff: Tina Holgin.
Directors/trustees: U.S. Bank, N.A.

Hennepin County Bar Foundation

600 Nicollet Mall
Suite 390
Minneapolis, MN 55402
County: Hennepin
Phone: (612) 752-6600
Alt. Phone: (612) 752-6610
Fax: (612) 752-6601
E-mail: larry@hcba.org
Website: www.hcba.org/about-hcba/hcbf-home.htm
Established: 01/01/1968
Funder type: Community/public foundation

Program Description

Program's purpose: The Hennepin County Bar Foundation is a charitable corporation that derives virtually all of its funds from lawyers who are members of the Hennepin County Bar Association. Its objective is to provide financial assistance to Hennepin County projects that are educational or charitable in nature and are related to the law or the American jurisprudence system.

Funding priorities: The foundation contributes to projects in the following general areas: improving the administration of justice, increasing public understanding of the law and facilitating the delivery of legal services.

Geographic focus: Twin Cities Metropolitan Area, Hennepin County.

Geographic limitations: The foundation's focus is on programs serving the residents of Hennepin County.

Areas of interest:

PUBLIC PROTECTION - CRIME/COURTS/LEGAL SERVICES: Administration of justice/courts, Legal services, Access to legal services, Education.

Types of support for organizations:

GENERAL PURPOSE/OPERATING SUPPORT.

MANAGEMENT/TECHNICAL ASSISTANCE.

PROGRAM DEVELOPMENT/ PROJECT SUPPORT.

Financial Information

Financial data for year ending: 06/30/2005
Foundation assets: $235,000
Grants paid: $74,000
Number of grants: 19
Largest/smallest: $30,000/$500
Typical grant amount: $3,895

Application Information

Preferred form of initial contact: letter of inquiry, telephone inquiry, request for guidelines, e-mail.

Public information available by request: proposal guidelines, application form.

Proposal deadlines: March 15.

Preferred time for receiving proposals: January until March of each year.

Contribution decisions made by: board of directors/trustees. The foundation's grant committee submits a report to the board of directors for approval.

Frequency of contributions decisions: annually.

Typical time from application deadlines to notification: April/May.

Special application procedures: Application forms become available in early January of each year, and decisions and distributions are made by late spring early summer.

Staff/Trustees

Staff: Laurence R. Buxbaum, executive director.

Directors/trustees: Lee Brennan; Gary Debele; Paul Floyd, vice president; David Forro; Marlene Garvis; Tom Johnson; Marshall Lichty; Kate MacKinnon; Glen McCluskey; Sonia Miller-Van Oort; Andrew Mohring; Steve Pincus; Richard Pins, Judy Rogosheske, president; Brent Routman; Miriam Rykken; Joan Schulkers; Tim Shields; Christina Szitta; Mary Vasaly; Courtney Ward-Reichard, secretary; Tom Wilson; Elizabeth Wons Kappenman, treasurer.

The Hermundslie Foundation

3762 North Harrison Road
Tucson, AZ 85749
Phone: (520) 749-0793
Contact: Gerold Hermundslie, president
Established: 11/01/1968
Funder type: Private foundation

Program Description

Geographic focus: Twin Cities Metropolitan Area, Tucson, AZ.

Geographic limitations: Minnesota and Arizona.

Areas of interest:

EDUCATION.

HEALTH - RESEARCH.

RELIGION/SPIRITUAL DEVELOPMENT.

Intended beneficiaries: General public/unspecified.

Sample grants:

Alzheimer's Association - MN (Minneapolis)/MN/further research/ $130,000.

American Diabetes Association - MN/MN/further research/$150,000.

Benilde-St Margaret's High School/ MN/educational grants/$15,500.

Desert Christian School/Tucson, AZ/ educational grants/$100,000.

Educational Special Needs Services - AZ/Tucson, AZ/educational grants/$20,200.

Minneapolis Medical Research Foundation, Inc/MN/medical research/ $18,637.

Sight & Hearing Association/MN/ medical research/$100,000.

Financial Information

Financial data for year ending: 12/31/2005
Foundation assets: $21,434,263
Grants paid: $983,971
Number of grants: 12
Largest/smallest: $160,000/$15,500

Application Information

Preferred form of initial contact: complete proposal, no specific format.

Proposal deadlines: none.

Staff/Trustees

Directors/trustees: Gloria Fitzgerald; Carol Hermundslie; Gerold Hermundslie, president; John Hibbard.

Hiawatha Education Foundation

360 Vila Street
Winona, MN 55987
County: Winona
Phone: (507) 453-8765
E-mail: pknee@hefwinona.org
Contact: Patricia A. Knee, managing director
Established: 03/07/1987
Donor: Directors
Paid Staff: Yes
Funder type: Private foundation

Program Description

Program's purpose: Grants for start-up pre-school Montessori programs for at-risk children. Most grants are to particular institutions as specified by the donor, although there are a limited number of discretionary grants each year.

Funding priorities: Education.

Program limitations/restrictions: Limited to nonprofit education or education-related activity.

Geographic focus: Greater Minnesota.

Geographic limitations: Minnesota.

Areas of interest:
EDUCATION: Pre-school/elementary, Secondary.

Intended beneficiaries: Types of support for individuals: none.

Sample grants:
ISD Winona #861/MN/$16,000.
Private Schools - MN/MN/$25,000.
Private Schools - MN/MN/$5,000.
St Elizabeth's - MN/MN/$20,000.
St Mary's University - MN/MN/$22,000.
University of St Thomas - MN/MN/$50,000.

Financial Information

Financial data for year ending: 12/31/2005
Foundation assets: $13,822,235
Grants paid: $554,177

Application Information

Preferred form of initial contact: letter of inquiry, telephone inquiry.

Public information available by request: annual report.

Proposal deadlines: June 1.

Preferred time for receiving proposals: by June 1.

Contribution decisions made by: board of directors/trustees.

Frequency of contributions decisions: annually.

Staff/Trustees

Directors/trustees: Lara Kierlin; Monique Kierlin; Robert Kierlin.

Hickory Tech Corporation Foundation

PO Box 3248
Mankato, MN 56002-3248
County: Blue Earth
Phone: (507) 387-3355
Established: 12/01/1962
Funder type: Corporate foundation

Program Description

Program's purpose: To help support the community of Mankato and build a strong, educated workforce pool of candidates.

Funding priorities: Higher education in specific areas supporting our corporate hiring needs. Benefits should be focused in the service areas of Hickory Tech Corporation's subsidiaries.

Program limitations/restrictions: No grants to organizations without a 501(c)(3) IRS exempt status, except for some government organizations such as schools. No grants to individuals; travel; religious organizations for sectarian purposes; political activities or organizations; fraternal, veteran or labor groups when serving only their membership; special or goodwill advertising; general operating purposes; loans or loan guarantees; cause-related marketing; organizations that practice discrimination by race, color, creed, gender, sexual preference or national origin; hospital operating funds or capital funds unless a unique community need can be demonstrated.

Geographic focus: Greater Mankato area, MN, and HickoryTech's Iowa serving areas.

Geographic limitations: Focus in service areas of Hickory Tech's subsidiaries.

Areas of interest:
ARTS, CULTURE, HUMANITIES: Performing arts.
COMMUNITY IMPROVEMENT: Community/neighborhood development/improvement.
EDUCATION: Higher education, Libraries/library science, Secondary.

Intended beneficiaries: General public/unspecified.

Types of support for organizations:
PROGRAM DEVELOPMENT/PROJECT SUPPORT: Faculty/staff development, Performance/production costs.
STUDENT AID (GRANTS TO INSTITUTIONS): Scholarship funds.

Types of support for individuals: none.

Matching grants: employee matching, higher education, scholarships.

Exclusions: Individuals, Non-501(c)(3), Political organizations, Religious organizations.

Sample grants:
Blue Earth Historical Society/MN/Hubbard House renovation/$1,250.
Boy Scouts of America - MN (Twin Valley)/Mankato, MN/new building project/$10,000.
Echo Food Shelf/Mankato, MN/funds for Thanksgiving baskets/$2,500.
Mankato Symphony Orchestra Association/MN/partially underwrite a symphony production/$5,000.
MN State University - Mankato Foundation/MN/scholarships/$20,000.

Financial Information

Financial data for year ending: 02/28/2007
Foundation assets: $2,999,000
Grants paid: $100,000
Number of grants: 29
Largest/smallest: $23,000/$500
Matching gifts: $34,000

Application Information

Preferred form of initial contact: letter of inquiry, telephone inquiry.

Public information available by request: proposal guidelines.

Proposal deadlines: November 10.

Preferred time for receiving proposals: early November.

Contribution decisions made by: board of directors/trustees.

Frequency of contributions decisions: annually.

Typical time from application deadlines to notification: End of first quarter.

Staff/Trustees

Staff: Jennifer Spaude, administrator.

Directors/trustees: Robert D. Alton Jr.; Lyle T. Bosacker; James W. Bracke; Myrita P. Craig; James H. Holdrege; Lyle G. Jacobson; R. Wynn Kearney Jr.; Starr J. Kirklin; Dale E. Parker.

Honeywell Hometown Solutions

101 Columbia Road
Morristown, NJ 07962
Phone: (973) 455-2010
Website: www.honeywell.com/sites/hhs
Established: 11/25/1957
Funder type: Corporate giving program

Program Description

Funding priorities: Community support, education, housing and child safety.

Program limitations/restrictions: HHS does not make loans or grants to political organizations, religious organizations or individuals. The organization does not generally make grants for conferences, travel or public relations-related activities.

Geographic focus: Twin Cities Metropolitan Area, national areas.

Geographic limitations: Requesting organizations should send proposals to the nearest Honeywell facility.

Areas of interest:
COMMUNITY IMPROVEMENT.
EDUCATION.
HOUSING/SHELTER.
PUBLIC SAFETY/DISASTERS/RELIEF: Child safety.

Intended beneficiaries: General public/unspecified.

Sample grants:

Dunwoody Institute/MN/general support/$20,000.

Greater Minneapolis Metropolitan Housing Corporation/MN/general operating/$15,000.

Habitat for Humanity (Twin Cities)/MN/general operating/$20,000.

Innovations in Science & Technology Education/MN/general operating/$10,000.

MN Rebuilding Together/MN/$10,000.

Project for Pride in Living/MN/$25,000.

Urban Ventures - Minneapolis/MN/$25,000.

Application Information

Preferred form of initial contact: complete proposal.

Staff/Trustees

Staff: Paul Boudreau, executive director; Maureen Delp-Cassidy; Sheila McBride.

George A. Hormel Testamentary Trust

301 North Main Street
Austin, MN 55912-3680
County: Mower
Phone: (507) 437-9800
Fax: (507) 434-6731
Contact: John J. Gray Jr., assistant secretary-treasurer
Established: 12/27/1946
Donor: George A. Hormel
Paid Staff: Yes
Funder type: Private foundation

Program Description

Program's purpose: To provide financial support for capital and program budgets of local organizations.

Funding priorities: Primary emphasis on youth programs, educational programs and local economic development.

Program limitations/restrictions: Grants made to local federally tax-exempt organizations, for charitable, educational or scientific purposes.

Geographic focus: Austin, MN, area.

Geographic limitations: Organizations must be located in or affect the Austin, MN, area.

Areas of interest:

ANIMAL RELATED: Animal protection/welfare.

ARTS, CULTURE, HUMANITIES: Arts/cultural multipurpose, Performing arts.

CIVIL RIGHTS: Equal opportunity and access.

COMMUNITY IMPROVEMENT: Community/neighborhood development/improvement, Economic development.

EDUCATION: Adult/continuing education/literacy, Libraries/library science, Pre-school/elementary.

HEALTH - GENERAL/REHABILITATIVE: Hospitals and related primary medical care facilities, Public health programs/wellness education.

HEALTH - MENTAL HEALTH/CRISIS INTERVENTION: Counseling/support groups, Hotline/crisis intervention, Mental health treatment and services.

HUMAN SERVICES: Children/youth services, Family services, Multipurpose human service organizations, Senior centers and services, Victims services.

PUBLIC AFFAIRS/SOCIETY BENEFIT: Leadership development/awards programs (other than youth), Public transportation services.

PUBLIC PROTECTION - CRIME/COURTS/LEGAL SERVICES: Dispute/conflict resolution, Law enforcement agencies.

RECREATION: Amateur sports clubs/leagues, Physical fitness/recreational facilities.

SCIENCE/TECHNOLOGY: Science - general.

YOUTH DEVELOPMENT: Multipurpose youth centers/clubs, Scouting organizations, Youth development programs.

Intended beneficiaries: General public/unspecified.

Types of support for organizations:

CAPITAL CAMPAIGNS: Computer systems/technology, Equipment.

PROGRAM DEVELOPMENT/PROJECT SUPPORT: Performance/production costs.

Types of support for individuals: none.

Sample grants:

Austin Sesquicentennial - MN/MN/community celebration/$12,500.

Austin Symphony Orchestra - MN/MN/operating/$5,000.

Austin Youth Baseball - MN/MN/equipment and field maintenance/$5,000.

Community Child Care Center/MN/equipment for Applelane in Austin/$1,000.

Girl Scout Council - MN (River Trails)/MN/building maintenance/$2,500.

Hormel Historic Home/MN/maintenance/$2,500.

Math Masters of MN/MN/operating/$3,000.

Visitors & Convention Bureau - MN (Austin)/MN/media box, printer, laptop/$2,000.

Financial Information

Financial data for year ending: 12/31/2006
Foundation assets: $1,464,727
Grants paid: $62,500
Number of grants: 15
Largest/smallest: $12,500/$1,000

Application Information

Preferred form of initial contact: letter of inquiry.

Public information available by request: application form.

Proposal deadlines: September 1.

Contribution decisions made by: contributions committee.

Frequency of contributions decisions: annually.

Typical time from application deadlines to notification: 3 months.

Staff/Trustees

Staff: John J. Gray Jr., assistant secretary-treasurer.

Directors/trustees: M. K. Anderson, director; J. A. Anfinson, treasurer; M. T. Bjorlie, director; D. R. Brezicka, director; Z. Dong, director; J. M. Ettinger, director; K. F. Hoversten, director; J. W. Johnson, vice chairman; R. L. Knowlton, chairman; M. D. Lighthizer-Schmidt, director; J. R. Mueller, director; J. D. Myers, director; J. E. O'Rourke, director; G. J. Ray, director; S. T. Rizzi Jr., secretary; M. C. Schneider, director; R. J. Thatcher, director.

HRK Foundation

345 Saint Peter Street
Suite 1200
St Paul, MN 55102
County: Ramsey
Phone: (651) 293-9001
Fax: (651) 298-0551
E-mail: info@hrkfoundation.org
Website: www.hrkfoundation.org
Contact: Kathleen Fluegel, executive director
Established: 10/31/1962
Paid Staff: Yes
Funder type: Private foundation

Program Description

Program's purpose: Family philanthropy: HRK Foundation is a family foundation defined and sustained by a sense of spirituality, creativity and stewardship. Through quiet leadership and philanthropy, the board seeks to promote healthy families and communities, to enhance the quality of and access to education, and to improve the fabric of our society.

Funding priorities: Arts: People and organizations that nourish the human spirit and encourage our connectedness. Health: Programs that strengthen families and promote healthy lives for children and/or provide services for people affected by HIV/AIDS. Community Building: Efforts that increase adequate and affordable housing; encourage responsible land use; promote conservation and preservation of community resources; advance the work of neighbors who reach across their differences for the common good. Education: Educational approaches and institutions that promote holistic personal development – intellectual, social, emotional and spiritual. Grants in the education area are board-directed, and new applications are not accepted.

Program limitations/restrictions: HRK Foundation has a commitment to long-term relationships with grantees and accepts only a limited number of new, capital or project requests in each calendar year. Prior to submitting a proposal, please call or e-mail the foundation's director to discuss your request.

Geographic focus: Twin Cities Metropolitan Area.

Geographic limitations: Historically, the foundation's geographic service area has included the Twin Cities metro area, the St Croix Valley, and Ashland and Bayfield counties in Wisconsin. In evaluating new requests, the board's primary focus is St Paul.

Areas of interest:

ANIMAL RELATED: Animal protection/welfare.

ARTS, CULTURE, HUMANITIES: Arts services, Arts/cultural multipurpose, Historical societies, Humanities, Museums, Performing arts, Visual arts, people and organizations that nourish the human spirit and encourage our connectedness.

CIVIL RIGHTS: Civil rights/advocacy for specific groups, Voter education/registration.

COMMUNITY IMPROVEMENT: Community coalitions, Community/neighborhood development/improvement, Economic development, Community building - efforts that advance the work of neighbors who reach across their differences for the common good.

EDUCATION: Higher education, Libraries/library science, Pre-school/elementary. Grants in this area are board-directed, and new applications are not accepted.

ENVIRONMENTAL QUALITY/PROTECTION/BEAUTIFICATION: Environmental beautification/open spaces, Environmental education/outdoor survival, Natural resources conservation/protection, Community building – efforts that encourage responsible land use and promote conservation and preservation of community resources.

FOOD/NUTRITION/AGRICULTURE: Food service/free food distribution, Soil and water conservation/farm land preservation.

HEALTH - DISEASES/MEDICAL DISCIPLINES: AIDS/HIV, Programs that provide services for people affected by HIV/AIDS.

HEALTH - GENERAL/REHABILITATIVE: Public health programs/wellness education, Reproductive health care.

HOUSING/SHELTER: Homeless, temporary housing, Housing support services, Community building – efforts that increase adequate and affordable housing.

HUMAN SERVICES: Children/youth services, Family services, Health – programs that strengthen families and promote healthy lives for children.

PHILANTHROPY/VOLUNTARISM: Philanthropy – general.

RELIGION/SPIRITUAL DEVELOPMENT: Interfaith issues.

SOCIAL SCIENCES: Interdisciplinary research/studies to improve understanding of particular populations/cultures.

Intended beneficiaries: General public/unspecified, Military/veterans.

Types of support for organizations:
CAPITAL CAMPAIGNS.
PROGRAM DEVELOPMENT/PROJECT SUPPORT: Fundraising.
STUDENT AID (GRANTS TO INSTITUTIONS): Scholarship funds.

Types of support for individuals: none.

Exclusions: Individuals, Non-501(c)(3).

Sample grants:

Highpoint Center for Printmaking/MN/$2,500.

The Jeremiah Program/MN/$25,000.

Madeline Island Music Camp - MN/MN/$35,000.

MN Historical Society/MN/$10,000.

Penumbra Theatre Company/MN/Special gifts/$5,000.

Planned Parenthood - MN/SD/MN/$20,000.

Rondo Community Land Trust/MN/$20,000.

St Paul Academy & Summit School/MN/$10,000.

Financial Information

Financial data for year ending: 12/31/2005
Foundation assets: $31,334,865
Grants paid: $2,281,143
Number of grants: 281
Largest/smallest: $200,000/$1,000

Application Information

Preferred form of initial contact: letter of inquiry, telephone inquiry or e-mail. Before submitting a proposal, please call our executive director and visit our website.

Public information available by request: proposal guidelines, application form, website.

Accept common grant application: yes.

Proposal deadlines: March 15, September 15.

Contribution decisions made by: staff, board of directors/trustees.

Frequency of contributions decisions: semiannually.

Specific times board meets: May, November.

Typical time from application deadlines to notification: 8-10 weeks.

Special application procedures: HRK Foundation has a commitment to long-term relationships with grantees and accepts only a limited number of new, capital or project requests in each calendar year.

Staff/Trustees

Staff: Katy Davis, executive assistant; Kathleen Fluegel, executive director; Stephanie Hynes, foundation assistant; Jeff Masco, grants consultant.

Directors/trustees: Jim Hayes; Katherine D. R. Hayes; Eric M. Hynnek; Julia L. Hyrnek; Arthur W. Kaemmer, chair; Frederick C. Kaemmer; Martha H. Kaemmer; Dan Priebe; Mary H. Rice; Molly E. Rice; Katherine R. Tilney.

The Hubbard Broadcasting Foundation

3415 University Avenue
St Paul, MN 55114
County: Ramsey
Phone: (651) 642-4305
Contact: Kathryn Hubbard Rominski, executive director
Established: 08/01/1958
Funder type: Private foundation

Program Description

Program's purpose: General charitable purposes.

Geographic focus: Twin Cities Metropolitan Area, Greater Minnesota, Areas outside Minnesota.

Geographic limitations: Primarily, but not exclusively, greater Twin Cities metro area of Minnesota; Alexandria, MN; Austin, MN; Duluth, MN; Albuquerque, NM; Farmington, NM; Roswell, NM; Albany, NY; Rochester, NY.

Areas of interest:

ANIMAL RELATED: Zoo/zoological societies.

ARTS, CULTURE, HUMANITIES: Historical societies, Museums, Performing arts, Visual arts.

COMMUNITY IMPROVEMENT.

EDUCATION: Adult/continuing education/literacy, Higher education, Libraries/library science.

HEALTH - DISEASES/MEDICAL DISCIPLINES.
HEALTH - GENERAL/REHABILITATIVE.
HEALTH - MENTAL HEALTH/CRISIS INTERVENTION.
HEALTH - RESEARCH.
HUMAN SERVICES: Children/youth services, Family services.
PUBLIC SAFETY/DISASTERS/RELIEF: Disaster preparedness and relief.
SCIENCE/TECHNOLOGY.
YOUTH DEVELOPMENT.

Intended beneficiaries: General public/unspecified.

Types of support for organizations:
CAPITAL CAMPAIGNS.
GENERAL PURPOSE/OPERATING SUPPORT.

Types of support for individuals: none.

Exclusions: Individuals, Non-501(c)(3), Political organizations.

Sample grants:

Big Brothers/Big Sisters - MN (Greater Twin Cities)/MN/$4,000.

Breck School/MN/$100,000.

Broadcasters Foundation/$5,000.

Gillette Children's Hospital/MN/$75,000.

MN Zoo Foundation/MN/$3,000.

Ocean Reef Community Foundation/FL/$20,000.

Second Harvest Food Bank - MN (St Paul)/MN/$2,500.

WAMSO - MN Orchestra Volunteer Association/MN/$6,000.

Financial Information

Financial data for year ending: 12/31/2005
Foundation assets: $20,293,637
Grants paid: $1,165,496
Number of grants: 300
Largest/smallest: $75,000/$100
Typical grant amount: $1,000

Application Information

Preferred form of initial contact: letter of inquiry, request for guidelines.

Public information available by request: proposal guidelines, application form.

Accept common grant application: yes.

Proposal deadlines: October 1 of each year.

Preferred time for receiving proposals: Prefer NOT to receive proposals in January, November, December.

Contribution decisions made by: board of directors/trustees.

Frequency of contributions decisions: annually. Grants are primarily made at the end of the year with occasional grants throughout the year.

Typical time from application deadlines to notification: end of year.

Special application procedures: Please summarize your organization's history and mission and provide specifics about the project you are applying for. Include budget and supporting fiscal info, and be certain to include a copy of your IRS 501(c)(3) letter indicating tax-exempt status.

Staff/Trustees

Staff: Kathryn Hubbard Rominski, executive director.

Directors/trustees: Julia D. Coyte; Gerald D. Deeney; Karen H. Hubbard; Robert W. Hubbard; Stanley S. Hubbard, president; Stanley E. Hubbard; Virginia H. Morris; Kathryn Hubbard Rominski, executive director.

Nevin Huested Foundation for Handicapped Children, Inc.

9100 West Bloomington Freeway
Suite 137
Bloomington, MN 55431
County: Hennepin
Phone: (952) 884-7004
Contact: Vernon A. Schultz, president
Established: 06/01/1961
Funder type: Private foundation

Program Description

Program's purpose: Serve children and youth up to age 21 with disabilities who are residents of Minnesota. Focus on the needs of special disability groups or special services, and not on a disabled individual. Priority is given to new or alternative approaches to meeting the needs of children and youth with disabilities.

Funding priorities: Grants focused on the needs of children and youth who are severely disabled with measurable outcomes and/or published findings. Grants with shared funding or in partnership with other resources. Short-term grants, preferably one year. Grants with statewide impact and potential.

Geographic focus: Minnesota statewide.

Geographic limitations: Minnesota only.

Areas of interest:
HEALTH - GENERAL/REHABILITATIVE: Rehabilitative medical services.
HUMAN SERVICES: Children/youth services, Services to specific groups, Children and youth with disabilities.

Intended beneficiaries: Blind/vision impaired, Children and youth (infants-19 years), Deaf/hearing impaired, Disabled - general or unspecified disability, Mentally/emotionally disabled, Physically disabled.

Types of support for organizations:
PROGRAM DEVELOPMENT/PROJECT SUPPORT: Conferences/seminars, Curriculum development, Faculty/staff development, Mentoring programs, Program evaluation, Public awareness, Publications, Seed money/start-up funds, Leadership programs.

Financial Information

Financial data for year ending: 12/31/2006
Foundation assets: $615,000
Grants paid: $25,000
Number of grants: 8
Largest/smallest: $5,000/$500

Application Information

Preferred form of initial contact: letter of inquiry, telephone inquiry, request for guidelines, complete proposal.

Public information available by request: proposal guidelines, brochure and letters.

Accept common grant application: yes.

Accept common report form: yes.

Will view video: yes.

Proposal deadlines: none.

Contribution decisions made by: board of directors/trustees.

Frequency of contributions decisions: quarterly.

Typical time from application deadlines to notification: 2-3 months.

Staff/Trustees

Directors/trustees: Elizabeth Bassett; Mary Dybvig, Ph.D.; Elaine Hartman, Ph.D.; Dennis LaRogue; Sharon Lund, vice president; Florence M. Schultz, secretary/treasurer; Vernon A. Schultz, president.

Imation

1 Imation Place
301-2E-114
Oakdale, MN 55128-3414
County: Washington
Phone: (651) 704-4762
Fax: (651) 704-4688
Website: www.imation.com/about_imation/company_info/community_involvement.html
Contact: Patty Kovacs, community affairs manager
Paid Staff: Yes
Funder type: Corporate giving program

Program Description

Program's purpose: Imation's community affairs and corporate contributions guidelines are designed to reflect Imation's corporate commitment to the health and vitality of the communities in which the company employs people and conducts business. Contributions fund worthy nonprofit charitable and educational organizations as they work to improve opportunities and expand access to technology.

Funding priorities: Priority given to: 1) Arts: Major arts and cultural organizations in the Twin Cities area with an emphasis on organizations with strong outreach to diverse audiences; Established, mid-sized organizations with budgets between $200,000 and $2.5 million; The Imation Computer Arts Scholarship Program. 2) Education: Grants focus on K-12 education, business/education partnerships, special education programs and inner city schools that create opportunities and encourage the use of technology as tools to gain and retain knowledge; Public and private educational institutions that produce people and services that fit Imation's interests and needs; Economic education and organizations that help improve the climate for private industry and the public understanding of the role of business in the community. 3) Human Services: Priority given to programs that focus on life and job development skills for youth;

Programs that encourage the disadvantaged and those with significant barriers to employment to become self-sufficient through the creative use of technology.

Geographic focus: Twin Cities Metropolitan Area, Areas outside Minnesota.

Geographic limitations: Organizations will be considered for funding if they are located in major Imation locations, including the Twin Cities, MN; Nekoosa, WI; Weatherford, OK; Wahpeton, ND and Camarillo, CA. For those Twin Cities organizations that serve a specific neighborhood or a more narrowly focused community, priority will be given to those located in St Paul and the eastern suburbs. Contributions to national organizations will be considered if they have strong employee involvement and/or strongly enhance Imation's community affairs objectives and guidelines in Imation locations.

Areas of interest:
ARTS, CULTURE, HUMANITIES.
EDUCATION.
HUMAN SERVICES.

Types of support for organizations:
PROGRAM DEVELOPMENT/ PROJECT SUPPORT.
STUDENT AID (GRANTS TO INSTITUTIONS): Scholarship funds.
CORPORATE SPONSORSHIP: Imation will consider proposals to fund community events in key company locations, when there is significant economic impact on that local community. The organization hosting the event must qualify as a 501(c) (3) and fit Imation's charitable giving priorities. Excluded are professional sporting events, marathons and fundraisers.

Exclusions: Capital & endowment campaigns, Individuals, Political organizations, Religious organizations, Scholarships/loans, Regranting organizations, Industry, trade or professional association memberships, Professional sporting events, marathons and fundraisers (bowl-a-thons, bike-a-thons, etc.).

Financial Information

Financial data for year ending: 12/31/2005
Grants paid: $350,000

Application Information

Preferred form of initial contact: complete proposal.

Public information available by request: website.

Accept common grant application: yes.

Proposal deadlines: funding proposals are accepted on an ongoing basis and will be acknowledged within 90 days of receipt.

Frequency of contributions decisions: quarterly.

Staff/Trustees

Staff: Patty Kovacs, community affairs manager.

Impact Foundation, Inc.

355 South Garfield Street
Cambridge, MN 55008
County: Isanti
Established: 12/05/1997
Funder type: Private foundation

Program Description

Program's purpose: The corporation shall be primarily dedicated to the preservation and dissemination of Biblically based truth and values and, as such, may be directly involved in ministries designed to fulfill its stated purpose or may provide support for other ministries and institutions whose purposes shall be aligned with those of the corporation. The corporation shall also be available to act as a channel for directing humanitarian aid.

Funding priorities: Preservation and dissemination of Biblically based truth and values.

Geographic focus: Twin Cities Metropolitan Area, Greater Minnesota, Areas outside Minnesota.

Areas of interest:
RELIGION/SPIRITUAL DEVELOPMENT.

Intended beneficiaries: General public/unspecified.

Sample grants:
First Baptist Church - Cambridge/Cambridge, MN/local religious ministry/$16,000.
MN Baptist Conference/MN/Ukraine religious ministry/$6,000.
MN Family Institute/MN/religious family ministry/$11,000.
READ Ministries/$25,000.

Financial Information

Financial data for year ending: 12/31/2006
Foundation assets: $200,000
Grants paid: $40,000

Application Information

Preferred form of initial contact: All current and anticipated funds that are or will be available to the next five years are committed. No applications can be processed.

Staff/Trustees

Staff: Rob Eastlund, president.

Directors/trustees: Mark J. Anderson, secretary; Timothy A. Johnson, vice president.

Indian Land Tenure Foundation

151 East County Road B2
Little Canada, MN 55117-1523
County: Ramsey
Phone: (651) 766-8999
Fax: (651) 766-0012
E-mail: info@indianlandtenure.org
Website: www.indianlandtenure.org
Paid Staff: Yes
Funder type: Community/public foundation

Program Description

Program's purpose: The foundation's mission is "land within the original boundaries of every reservation and other areas of high significance where tribes retain aboriginal interest are in Indian ownership and management."

Funding priorities: Educate every Indian landowner about Indian land management, ownership and transference issues; increase economic assets of Indian landowners; use Indian land to help Indian people discover and maintain their culture; and reform legal mechanisms related to recapturing the physical, cultural and economic assets for Indian people and strengthening sovereignty of Indian land.

Program limitations/restrictions: Program activities are focused on facilitating and strengthening land-related projects that work to recover, restore and preserve Indian lands.

Geographic focus: Minnesota statewide, areas outside Minnesota.
Geographic limitations: National.
Areas of interest:
CIVIL RIGHTS: Civil rights/advocacy for specific groups.
COMMUNITY IMPROVEMENT: Community/neighborhood development/improvement.
EDUCATION: Indian land curriculum development and implementation for Head Start, K-12, colleges and adult education.
Intended beneficiaries: Native American/American Indians.
Types of support for organizations:
PROGRAM DEVELOPMENT/ PROJECT SUPPORT: Conferences/seminars, Curriculum development, Public awareness, Public policy research/analysis, Seed money/start-up funds.
Types of support for individuals: none.
Exclusions: Individuals.

Financial Information

Financial data for year ending: 12/31/2006
Foundation assets: $23,699,166
Grants paid: $2,919,479
Number of grants: 53
Largest/smallest: $194,309/$3,000
Typical grant amount: $55,000
Largest multi-year grant approved: $653,026

Application Information

Preferred form of initial contact: Submit proposals according to Request for Proposal announcements on the website.
Public information available by request: General information requests on Indian land issues, proposal guidelines, internal publications, current news and events posted on the website.
Proposal deadlines: Varies according to each Request for Proposals. Interested applicants must check the website.
Contribution decisions made by: board of directors/trustees.
Frequency of contributions decisions: quarterly.
Typical time from application deadlines to notification: 4 months.
Special application procedures: The original proposal and attachments must be complete and follow the format established in the application and proposal outline. Proposals will not be accepted via e-mail or fax.

Staff/Trustees

Staff: D'Arcy Bordeaux, accountant/human resources director; Cecelia Burke, deputy director of IIEPP; Patricia Chase, administrative assistant; Eileen J. Grundstrom, development associate; Terry Janis, program officer; Douglas Nash, executive director of IIEPP; Cris Stainbrook, president; Jo-Anne E. Stately, vice president of development; Howard D. Valandra, vice president of grants & programs.

Directors/trustees: Ben Black Bear Jr.; Brian Collins; Virgil Dupuis, chair; Eric Giles; Arvel Hale; Margie Hutchinson; Ross Racine, secretary/treasurer; John Sirois, vice chair; David Tovey; Emily White Hat.

ING Foundation

5780 Powers Ferry Road NW
Atlanta, GA 30327
Phone: (770) 980-4517
Website: www.ing-usa.com/us/aboutING/communityconnections
Established: 01/01/1980
Funder type: Corporate foundation and corporate giving program

Program Description

Program's purpose: ING grants are intended to assist nonprofit organizations in motivating individuals to assume personal responsibility for their financial well-being.
Funding priorities: Focus areas are arts/culture, financial literacy, education, and health/wellness.
Program limitations/restrictions: ING does not consider grant requests under $5,000.
Geographic focus: Twin Cities Metropolitan area, areas outside Minnesota, national areas.
Geographic limitations: Although ING provides funding to national initiatives, our contribution program primarily focuses its community resources in the areas where employees are based and customers live.

Areas of interest:
ARTS, CULTURE, HUMANITIES.
EDUCATION: Adult/continuing education/literacy, Educational reform, Educational services, Graduate education/professional schools, Higher education, Pre-school/elementary, Secondary, Vocational/technical.
EMPLOYMENT/JOBS: Employment procurement/job training, Vocational rehabilitation.
HEALTH - DISEASES/MEDICAL DISCIPLINES.
HEALTH - GENERAL/ REHABILITATIVE.
HUMAN SERVICES: Children/youth services, Multipurpose human service organizations.
PHILANTHROPY/VOLUNTARISM: Philanthropy associations, Voluntarism promotion, United Way.
YOUTH DEVELOPMENT: Multipurpose youth centers/clubs, Youth development programs.

Intended beneficiaries: General public/unspecified.
Types of support for organizations:
GENERAL PURPOSE/OPERATING SUPPORT.
Matching grants: employee matching, scholarships.
Exclusions: Individuals, Political organizations, Religious organizations, Fraternities and sororities, Organizations outside the United States, Organizations representing conflicts of interest for employees and/or ING.
Sample grants:
BestPrep/MN/$15,000.
Breck School/MN/$5,000.
Catholic Charities - MN (St Cloud Diocese)/MN/$5,000.
College of St Catherine/MN/$20,000.
Girl Scout Council - ND (Northwest)/Minot, ND/$8,000.
Hammer Residences Inc/MN/$5,000.
Learning Disabilities Association - MN (Mpls)/MN/$7,500.
MN Orchestral Association/MN/$20,000.

Financial Information

Financial data for year ending: 12/31/2005
Foundation assets: $2,109,100
Grants paid: $3,298,500

Application Information

Preferred form of initial contact: online application.

Public information available by request: proposal guidelines, application form, website.

Proposal deadlines: February 15, 2007 (committee reviews on March 13), May 25, 2007 (committee reviews on June 12), September 14, 2007 (committee reviews on October 2).

Contribution decisions made by: employee committee, board of directors/trustees.

Frequency of contributions decisions: 3 times per year.

Specific times board meets: April, July, October

Typical time from application deadlines to notification: 1-2 months.

Staff/Trustees

Directors/trustees: Kevin P. Brown; Timothy W. Brown; B. Scott Burton; Robert Crispin; Thomas J. McInerney; Rhonda Mims Simpson, president; Kathleen Murphy; Dawn Peck; David S. Pendergrass.

Initiative Foundation

405 First Street SE
Little Falls, MN 56345-3042
County: Morrison
Phone: (320) 632-9255
Fax: (320) 632-9258
E-mail: info@ifound.org
Website: www.ifound.org
Contact: Kathy Gaalswyk, president
Established: 03/17/1986
Funder type: Community/public foundation

Program Description

Program's purpose: The Initiative Foundation supports innovative projects that identify and mobilize existing resources, build capacity and involve local people in creative problem-solving. Core programs encourage citizen participation in social issues through a volunteer coalition model buoyed by leadership training, resource referral, staff assistance and funding. Our grant awards eliminate barriers to economic development and foster asset-based community development.

Funding priorities: Projects that identify and mobilize the existing resources of communities with emphasis on diversity as a resource, family economic stability, strengthening children, youth and families, preservation of space, place and resources, increase utilization of technology and build capacity of nonprofit organizations. Priority consideration is given to projects originating from integrated community and organizational planning efforts such as the Healthy Communities Partnership program.

Program limitations/restrictions: Grants are made only to 501(c)(3) nonprofit organizations, local units of government and school districts. Our average grant amount is $5,000.

Geographic focus: Central Minnesota.

Geographic limitations: The Initiative Foundation serves the central Minnesota counties of Benton, Cass, Chisago, Crow Wing, Isanti, Kanabec, Mille Lacs, Morrison, Pine, Sherburne, Stearns, Todd, Wadena and Wright.

Areas of interest:

COMMUNITY IMPROVEMENT: Community coalitions, Community/neighborhood development/improvement, Economic development, Nonprofit management, Volunteer bureaus.
EDUCATION: Community/school partnerships only.
EMPLOYMENT/JOBS: Workforce development, Technology planning.
ENVIRONMENTAL QUALITY/PROTECTION/BEAUTIFICATION: Natural resources conservation/protection.
HUMAN SERVICES: Children/youth services, Multipurpose human service organizations, Senior centers and services, Services to specific groups, Build capacity of nonprofits.
PHILANTHROPY/VOLUNTARISM: Voluntarism promotion.
PUBLIC AFFAIRS/SOCIETY BENEFIT: Citizen participation, Government/public administration, Leadership development/awards programs (other than youth), Public transportation services.
PUBLIC SAFETY/DISASTERS/RELIEF: Disaster relief.
RELIGION/SPIRITUAL DEVELOPMENT: Interfaith issues, Non-ecumenical, faith-based initiatives only.
YOUTH DEVELOPMENT: Adult/child matching programs, Youth development programs.

Intended beneficiaries: General public/unspecified.

Types of support for individuals: none.

Exclusions: Capital & endowment campaigns, Individuals, Religious organizations.

Sample grants:

Benton County/MN/Economic development strategies/$5,000.

City of Cold Spring - MN/MN/Farmers' market startup/$4,800.

City of Melrose - MN/MN/Healthy Communities partnership/$10,000.

Hands of Hope Resource Center, Inc/MN/Healthy Organizations partnership multi-year program/$5,500.

ISD Sauk Rapids/Rice #47/MN/First Start early education program/$10,000.

Lutheran Social Services - MN (St Cloud)/MN/St Cloud refugee collaboration/$2,000.

Mille Lacs Band of Ojibwe Indians/MN/Third annual Business Development summit/$1,000.

St Cloud State University/MN/Mediation program development in the central Minnesota area/$10,000.

Financial Information

Financial data for year ending: 06/30/2006
Foundation assets: $40,664,676
Grants paid: $1,042,920
Number of grants: 219
Largest/smallest: $60,000/$250
Largest multi-year grant approved: $10,000

Application Information

Preferred form of initial contact: letter of inquiry, e-mail, website.

Public information available by request: proposal guidelines, application form, annual report, newsletter, website, grant inquiry via e-mail.

Proposal deadlines: open, call for information on specific programs.

Preferred time for receiving proposals: none; applications are accepted on an ongoing basis.

Contribution decisions made by: CEO, staff, board of directors/trustees.

Frequency of contributions decisions: monthly.

Typical time from application deadlines to notification: within 90 days.

Staff/Trustees

Staff: Bethany Carlton, donor services clerk; Chris Fastner, VISTA program manager; Dan Frank, program manager for community development; Kathy Gaalswyk, president; Sharon Gottwalt, business finance assistant; Curt Hanson, vice president for donor services; Cathy Hartle, senior program manager for organizational development; Don Hickman, program manager for planning & preservation; Anita Hollenhorst, communications associate; Lynn Houle, director of finance and operations; Jolene Howard, program assistant for grants & training; Karin Ihnen, early childhood specialist; John Kaliszewski, vice president for economic development; Lois Kallsen, office and facilities coordinator; Linda Kaufmann, senior program manager for children, youth and families; Matt Kilian, director of communications; Kris Kowalzek, finance assistant; Mark Lease, donor services officer; MaryAnn Lindell, executive assistant; Geri Pohlkamp, meth & youth development specialist; Leah Posterick, program assistant for grants & training; MaryAnn Schefers, finance assistant; Ashley Vargo, business finance officer; Sandy Voigt, program manager for technology finance; Tina Yorek, program assistant for grants & training.

Directors/trustees: Barb Anderson; Jim Anderson; Chuck Christian; Gloria Contreras Edin; Dave Gruenes; Lee Hanson; Janet Moran, secretary/treasurer; Mary Sam; John Schlagel; Steve Shelley; Patricia Spence; Gene Waldorf, vice-chair; George Wallin; Warren Williams, chair.

Italian American Club Foundation, Inc.

2221 Central Avenue NE
Minneapolis, MN 55418
County: Hennepin
Phone: (612) 781-0625
Funder type: Community/public foundation

Program Description

Program's purpose: The Italian American Club Foundation provides scholarships and grants to individuals and charitable organizations in the community through an application process.

Program limitations/restrictions: Grants are provided to charitable organizations that qualify as exempt under Sections 170(c)(2) and 501(c)(3). Although Italian heritage is a consideration, it is not used as an exclusion for scholarships.

Geographic focus: Twin Cities Metropolitan Area.

Areas of interest:

EDUCATION: Higher education, Secondary.

HUMAN SERVICES: Emergency assistance (food/clothing/cash), Senior centers and services.

RECREATION: Amateur sports clubs/leagues, Amateur sports competitions.

YOUTH DEVELOPMENT: Youth development programs.

Intended beneficiaries:
Aging/elderly/senior citizens, Children and youth (infants-19 years), General public/unspecified, Poor/economically disadvantaged.

Types of support for organizations:
GENERAL PURPOSE/OPERATING SUPPORT.
GRANTS TO INDIVIDUALS.
PROGRAM DEVELOPMENT/PROJECT SUPPORT.
STUDENT AID (GRANTS TO INSTITUTIONS).

Types of support for individuals: scholarships.

Sample grants:

Business Professional of America - Anoka Chapter/Anoka, MN/program support/$1,500.

Edison High School/Minneapolis, MN/youth programs/$2,200.

Fridley High School/MN/national fire safety/$500.

Metropolitan Council - St Paul/MN/programs for youth/$3,300.

Mount Carmel Church/Minneapolis, MN/donation for programs/$2,000.

Northeast Senior Citizen Resource Center - Mpls/MN/$1,500.

Teamsters Food Shelf/Minneapolis, MN/food shelf donation/$6,800.

Financial Information

Financial data for year ending: 06/30/2006
Foundation assets: $915,048
Grants paid: $156,320
Number of grants: 114
Largest/smallest: $3,500/$300

Application Information

Preferred form of initial contact: complete proposal.

Public information available by request: application form, for scholarships.

Contribution decisions made by: committee. Requests from nonprofits go through committees to the general membership, which vote on the requests.

Staff/Trustees

Directors/trustees: Frank Balma; Sam Iaquinto; James Livingston; James Marino, president; James Montury; Mike Scavo; Harry Villella; Jerry Villella.

Jennings Family Foundation (fka Prophet Corporation Foundation)

220 24th Avenue NW
Owatonna, MN 55060-1000
County: Steele
Phone: (507) 451-7470
Contact: Joel C. Jennings, president
Funder type: Corporate foundation

Program Description

Geographic focus: Twin Cities Metropolitan Area, Greater Minnesota, Minnesota statewide, Areas outside Minnesota.

Areas of interest:

COMMUNITY IMPROVEMENT.

HEALTH - DISEASES/MEDICAL DISCIPLINES.

HUMAN SERVICES: Children/youth services, Emergency assistance (food/clothing/cash), Family services, Multipurpose human service organizations.

RELIGION/SPIRITUAL DEVELOPMENT.

YOUTH DEVELOPMENT.

Intended beneficiaries: General public/unspecified.

Sample grants:

Admission Possible/St Paul, MN/youth ministries/$1,000.

Alzheimer's Association - MN (Minneapolis)/MN/public health/$26,000.

Children's HeartLink/MN/children's health issues/$1,000.

Food Shelf - MN (Steele County)/MN/local hunger relief/$14,000.

Riverland Community College/Austin, MN/community development/$7,500.

Women's Resource Center - MN (Steele County)/Owatonna, MN/funding for women at risk/$3,000.

Financial Information

Financial data for year ending: 12/31/2005
Foundation assets: $1,431,387
Grants paid: $329,681
Number of grants: 50
Largest/smallest: $39,560/$500

Application Information

Proposal deadlines: none.

Staff/Trustees

Directors/trustees: Joel C. Jennings, president; Mary Lee Jennings.

Jerome Foundation

400 Sibley Street
Suite 125
St Paul, MN 55101-1928
County: Ramsey
Phone: (651) 224-9431
Fax: (651) 224-3439
E-mail: info@jeromefdn.org
Website: www.jeromefdn.org
Contact: Cynthia A. Gehrig, president
Established: 12/31/1964
Donor: Jerome Hill
Paid Staff: Yes
Funder type: Private foundation

Program Description

Program's purpose: The Jerome Foundation makes grants that support emerging artists in the creation, development and production of new works.

Funding priorities: Creation of new works of art by emerging artists.

Program limitations/restrictions: Capital and endowment grants are not funded.

Geographic focus: Minnesota statewide, New York City.

Geographic limitations: New York City and state of Minnesota only.

Areas of interest:

ARTS, CULTURE, HUMANITIES: Arts services, Arts/cultural multipurpose, Media/communications, Museums, Performing arts, Visual arts.

PHILANTHROPY/VOLUNTARISM: Philanthropy associations.

Intended beneficiaries: Adults, No specified population groups.

Types of support for organizations: GRANTS TO INDIVIDUALS. PROGRAM DEVELOPMENT/PROJECT SUPPORT: Exhibitions, Film/video/radio production, Mentoring programs, Performance/production costs, Publications, Seed money/start-up funds.

Types of support for individuals: production grants for media artists, travel and study.

Exclusions: Capital & endowment campaigns, Scholarships/loans.

Sample grants:

Art Center - NY/NY/Special Projects Program/$10,000.

Blacklock Nature Sanctuary/MN/Emerging Artist Residency Program/$22 000.

Cave Canem/NY/New York City workshops for emerging African-American poets/$15,000.

Pillsbury United Communities/MN/Non-English Speaking Spoken Here: The Late Nite Series/$22,500.

Roulette Intermedium - NY/NY/Emerging Composer Commissioning program/$44,000.

Soap Factory - MN/MN/Participation of emerging artists in the Exhibition Program/$22,000.

Southern Theater Foundation/MN/TU Dance/$17,000.

Financial Information

Financial data for year ending: 04/30/2006
Foundation assets: $90,292,673
Grants paid: $3,121,341
Number of grants: 70
Largest/smallest: $117,000/$750

Application Information

Preferred form of initial contact: letter of inquiry, telephone inquiry, request for guidelines, complete proposal, e-mail, will accept any.

Public information available by request: proposal guidelines, application form, website, customized information packets, i.e. by discipline, grant, etc.

Will view video: yes.

Proposal deadlines: No deadlines for general program grants. Deadlines apply for New York City and Minnesota Media Arts Program and Travel and Study Grant Program. See www.jeromefdn.org for details.

Contribution decisions made by: board of directors/trustees.

Specific times board meets: 5 times a year.

Typical time from application deadlines to notification: 4 months.

Staff/Trustees

Staff: Robert Byrd, senior program officer; Karen Fjorden, controller; Cynthia A. Gehrig, president; Linda Gilbert, computer professional; Rush Merchant III, secretary/receptionist.

Directors/trustees: W. Andrew Boss, treasurer; Laurie Carlos; Jessica Hagedorn, chair; Catherine Jordan; Libby Larsen, secretary; Cynthia Mayeda.

JNM 1966 Gift Trust U/A

Wells Fargo Bank MN, N.A.
230 West Superior Street
Suite 400
Duluth, MN 55802
County: St Louis
Contact: Lisa Mandelin
Established: 03/01/1966
Funder type: Private foundation

Program Description

Program's purpose: General charitable purposes.

Funding priorities: Assist in carrying out projects of civic beautification of the city of Duluth or elsewhere. Make charitable gifts or render financial assistance to any worthy individual objects of charity.

Geographic focus: Greater Minnesota.

Areas of interest:
ARTS, CULTURE, HUMANITIES.
COMMUNITY IMPROVEMENT.
EDUCATION.
HEALTH - GENERAL/REHABILITATIVE.

Intended beneficiaries: General public/unspecified.

Types of support for organizations:
GENERAL PURPOSE/OPERATING SUPPORT.

Sample grants:
Historical Society - MN (St Louis County)/Duluth, MN/general operating/$14,000.
Sacred Heart Music Center/Duluth, MN/general operating/$7,000.
Scottish Rite Foundation - MN/Duluth, MN/general operating/$20,000.

Financial Information

Financial data for year ending: 12/31/2005
Foundation assets: $950,926
Grants paid: $80,000
Number of grants: 4

Application Information

Preferred form of initial contact: letter of inquiry, request for guidelines.
Proposal deadlines: none.

Staff/Trustees

Directors/trustees: Wells Fargo Trust Department.

Lewis H. Johnson Family Foundation

689 Maple Park Drive
St Paul, MN 55118-1711
County: Dakota
Contact: Scott W. Johnson, president
Established: 09/01/1964
Funder type: Private foundation

Program Description

Program's purpose: General charitable purposes.
Geographic focus: Twin Cities Metropolitan Area, areas outside Minnesota.

Areas of interest:
ARTS, CULTURE, HUMANITIES: Media/communications.
EDUCATION: Higher education, Secondary.
HEALTH - GENERAL/REHABILITATIVE.
HUMAN SERVICES.
RELIGION/SPIRITUAL DEVELOPMENT.

Intended beneficiaries: General public/unspecified.

Types of support for organizations:
CAPITAL CAMPAIGNS.
GENERAL PURPOSE/OPERATING SUPPORT.

Sample grants:
Center of the American Experiment/MN/general operating/$10,500.
Chant Music Society/Minneapolis, MN/general operating/$500.
Claremont Institute for the Study of Statesmanship/CA/general operating/$1,000.
Mounds Park Academy/MN/general operating/$2,480.
St Paul Academy & Summit School/MN/annual fund/$200.
Temple of Aaron/MN/general operating/$7,041.
Torah Academy - MN (St Paul)/St Paul, MN/rabbis discretionary fund/$200.
United Jewish Fund/St Paul, MN/general operating/$5,000.

Financial Information

Financial data for year ending: 12/31/2005
Foundation assets: $540,863
Grants paid: $23,435
Number of grants: 17
Largest/smallest: $10,500/$75

Application Information

Preferred form of initial contact: letter of inquiry.
Proposal deadlines: none.

Staff/Trustees

Directors/trustees: Salome Z. Johnson; Scott W. Johnson, president.

Lloyd K. Johnson Foundation

130 West Superior Street
Suite 520
Duluth, MN 55802
County: St Louis
Phone: (218) 726-9000
Fax: (218) 726-9002
E-mail: jgardner@lloydkjohnsonfoundation.org
Website: www.lloydkjohnsonfoundation.org
Contact: Joan Gardner-Goodno, executive director
Established: 09/01/1975
Funder type: Private foundation

Program Description

Program's purpose: To enhance educational opportunities in Cook County and to significantly improve the quality of life in the North Shore communities of Cook, Lake and southern St Louis counties in Minnesota.

Funding priorities: Arts & culture, community & economic development, education, environment, and social welfare programs.

Program limitations/restrictions: telephone solicitations, support for individuals, activities whose purpose is to influence legislation, political campaigns, medical research, fundraising drives or activities, debt retirement, endowments, re-granting, religious organizations for direct religious activities.

Geographic limitations: Any locations outside of Cook County, Lake County and southern St Louis County are not eligible.

Areas of interest:
ARTS, CULTURE, HUMANITIES: Arts/cultural multipurpose, Historical societies, Museums, Performing arts.
COMMUNITY IMPROVEMENT: Community/neighborhood development/improvement, Economic development.
EDUCATION: Adult/continuing education/literacy, Pre-school/elementary, Secondary, Vocational/technical.
ENVIRONMENTAL QUALITY/PROTECTION/BEAUTIFICATION: Natural resources conservation/protection.
HUMAN SERVICES: Children/youth services, Emergency assistance (food/clothing/cash), Family services, Family services for adolescent parents, Family violence shelters and services,

Multipurpose human service organizations, Senior centers and services, Victims services.

YOUTH DEVELOPMENT: Adult/child matching programs, Multipurpose youth centers/clubs, Scouting organizations, Youth development programs.

Intended beneficiaries: General public/unspecified.

Types of support for organizations:
CAPITAL CAMPAIGNS.
EMERGENCY FUNDS.
GENERAL PURPOSE/OPERATING SUPPORT.
PROGRAM DEVELOPMENT/ PROJECT SUPPORT: Mentoring programs, Seed money/start-up funds.

Sample grants:

Boys & Girls Club - MN (Duluth)/MN/ general operating/$2,500.

Cook County Community Center/Grand Marais, MN/general operating/$1,000.

Duluth Superior Symphony Orchestra/ MN/general operating/$1,000.

First Witness Child Abuse Resource Center/Duluth, MN/general operating/ $500.

Grand Marais Art Colony/Grand Marais, MN/general operating/$1,000.

Soup Kitchen - Duluth/MN/general operating/$4,000.

Union Gospel Mission - MN (Duluth)/ MN/general operating/$2,500.

YMCA - MN (Duluth)/MN/general operating/$2,500.

Financial Information

Financial data for year ending: 12/31/2005
Foundation assets: $1,367,184
Grants paid: $83,000
Number of grants: 30
Largest/smallest: $5,000/$100

Application Information

Preferred form of initial contact: letter of inquiry, telephone inquiry.

Public information available by request: website.

Accept common grant application: yes.

Proposal deadlines: Yet to be determined. Please check website.

Contribution decisions made by: board of directors/trustees.

Typical time from application deadlines to notification: 2-3 months.

Staff/Trustees

Staff: Joan Gardner-Goodno, executive director.

Directors/trustees: Darryl Coons, vice president, CFO, treasurer; Betty Fitzgibbons, secretary; Tom Johnson, president.

The Lynn Johnson Family Foundation

1999 Shepard Road
St Paul, MN 55116-3210
County: Ramsey
Phone: (651) 649-5800
Contact: Lynn Johnson, president/ treasurer
Established: 09/02/1982
Funder type: Private foundation

Program Description

Program's purpose: General charitable purposes.

Geographic focus: Twin Cities Metropolitan Area, National Areas.

Areas of interest:
ARTS, CULTURE, HUMANITIES.
COMMUNITY IMPROVEMENT.
EDUCATION.
HEALTH - DISEASES/MEDICAL DISCIPLINES.
RELIGION/SPIRITUAL DEVELOPMENT.

Intended beneficiaries: General public/unspecified.

Sample grants:

American Cancer Society - MN/MN/ $100.

Empire Arts Center/Grand Forks, ND/ $800.

Hawaii Pacific University/HI/$5,220.

Mount Zion Temple/St Paul, MN/$4,806.

Ordway Music Theatre/MN/$1,000.

University of South Dakota - Women's Athletics/SD/$100.

University of South Dakota Foundation/ SD/$500.

Financial Information

Financial data for year ending: 09/30/2005
Foundation assets: $3,872,684
Grants paid: $22,563
Number of grants: 20
Largest/smallest: $8,580/$100

Application Information

Preferred form of initial contact: letter of inquiry, on applicant's letterhead with board listed.

Proposal deadlines: none.

Staff/Trustees

Directors/trustees: Gloria Johnson; Lynn Johnson, president/treasurer; Michael Johnson.

Mitchell and Lois Johnson Charitable Foundation

136 Groveland Terrace
Minneapolis, MN 55403
County: Hennepin
Phone: (612) 381-1000
Established: 07/03/1995
Funder type: Private foundation

Program Description

Program's purpose: General charitable purposes.

Geographic focus: Twin Cities Metropolitan Area, Areas outside Minnesota.

Areas of interest:
CIVIL RIGHTS.
EDUCATION.
HEALTH - DISEASES/MEDICAL DISCIPLINES.
HEALTH - GENERAL/ REHABILITATIVE.
HUMAN SERVICES.
RELIGION/SPIRITUAL DEVELOPMENT.

Intended beneficiaries: General public/unspecified.

Types of support for organizations:
GENERAL PURPOSE/OPERATING SUPPORT.

Sample grants:

American Diabetes Association - MN (Minneapolis)/MN/general operating/ $500.

City of Hope - MN Chapters/MN/general operating/$700.

Jewish Community Center - Greater Minneapolis/MN/general operating/$250.

Leukemia & Lymphoma Society - MN/ MN/general operating/$250.

Mount Zion Hebrew Congregation/St Paul, MN/$3,600.

Philanthrofund Foundation/MN/general operating/$750.

Servicemembers Legal Defense Network/MN/general operating/$250.

United Jewish Fund/St Paul, MN/general operating/$1,000.

Financial Information

Financial data for year ending: 12/31/2005
Foundation assets: $396,933
Grants paid: $41,445
Number of grants: 13
Largest/smallest: $15,100/$30

Application Information

Preferred form of initial contact: letter of inquiry, on applicant's letterhead with the board of directors listed.

Proposal deadlines: none.

Staff/Trustees

Directors/trustees: Lois Johnson; Mitchell Johnson, president.

The Jostens Foundation

3601 Minnesota Drive
Minneapolis, MN 55435
County: Hennepin
Phone: (952) 830-3235
E-mail: foundation@jostens.com
Website: www.jostens.com/company/community
Contact: Teresa Olson, foundation director
Established: 01/01/1976
Paid Staff: Yes
Funder type: Corporate foundation

Program Description

Program's purpose: The foundation supports organizations in their work to create strong communities and healthy families and children, and is committed to ensuring that its strategy best serves the needs of its customers and plant communities, as well as its employees and sales representatives.

Funding priorities: Guiding the foundation's giving and support is its focus on youth and education and programs that help young people become healthy, productive adults. Requests for funding are given priority if there is direct participation of Jostens employees. The foundation's primary funding is through its Community Grants program, which provides support to organizations that enhance the lives of youth and promote educational opportunities that significantly and positively impact children from birth through college. The company also provides funding through an employee gift matching program and employee contributions committees at 16 plants.

Program limitations/restrictions: Because of company policies or federal tax law, the foundation cannot consider grants for schools, school districts, school programs or school foundations; organizations involved in highly political or controversial issues; churches, religious groups or programs primarily sponsored by religious organizations; individual applicants or groups for support of their personal needs, including travel; political campaigns or political lobbying activities; benefit fundraisers or tickets to fundraisers; recognition or testimonial events; fundraising campaigns to eliminate or control specific diseases; fraternal, veterans or professional associations; athletic scholarships or activities; advertising sponsorships; endowment campaigns; capital funding.

Geographic focus: Twin Cities Metropolitan Area, Greater Minnesota, Areas outside Minnesota. Priority to organizations where Jostens facilities and employees are located.

Geographic limitations: United States only.

Areas of interest:
ARTS, CULTURE, HUMANITIES: Youth in arts, Arts in the classroom.
EDUCATION: Educational services, Student services/organizations of students, Programs specifically for youth.
HUMAN SERVICES: Children/youth services.
PHILANTHROPY/VOLUNTARISM: Voluntarism promotion.
YOUTH DEVELOPMENT: Adult/child matching programs, Multipurpose youth centers/clubs, Youth development programs.

Intended beneficiaries: Children and youth (infants-19 years), Infants/babies (under age 5), Poor/economically disadvantaged, Youth/adolescents (ages 14-19).

Types of support for organizations:
GENERAL PURPOSE/OPERATING SUPPORT.

IN-KIND SERVICES: Jostens provides in-kind gifts to worthy causes when possible.

Types of support for individuals: none.

Matching grants: any nonprofit organization, higher education.

Sample grants:

African American Mentor Program/St Paul, MN/general operating/$2,500.

Cookie Cart/MN/general operating/$2,000.

Free Arts for Abused Children - MN/MN/general operating/$3,000.

Lauj Youth Society of MN/MN/general operating/$5,000.

Nancy Hauser Dance Company/MN/general operating/$1,000.

Page Educational Foundation/MN/general operating/$5,000.

Search Institute/MN/general operating/$45,000.

Suicide Awareness Voices of Education (SAVE) - MN/MN/general operating/$2,500.

Financial Information

Financial data for year ending: 12/31/2005
Foundation assets: $34,084
Grants paid: $527,098
Number of grants: 55
Largest/smallest: $45,000/$1,000
Matching gifts: $179,010

Application Information

Preferred form of initial contact: telephone inquiry, request for guidelines, e-mail.

Public information available by request: proposal guidelines, website.

Accept common grant application: yes.

Proposal deadlines: Community Grants: March 5, 2007, June 4, 2007, September 4, 2007, and December 3, 2007. Must be on administrator's desk by 5:00 p.m. on the deadline date.

Contribution decisions made by: board of directors/trustees.

Frequency of contributions decisions: quarterly, for Community Grants.

Staff/Trustees

Staff: Teresa Olson, foundation director.

Directors/trustees: M. J. Bauer; Kent Gilmore, president; Julie Goetz; Paula Johnson; Claire Klaus; Tim Larson; Charley Nelson; Lance Novak; Al Nuness; Bonnie Severson; Bill Sheehan; Ron Somerville; Kris Thompson; Tim Wolfe.

Jundt Family Foundation

7342 East Alta Sierra Drive
Scottsdale, AZ 85262
Phone: (952) 404-2503
Contact: Romy P. Jundt Erlandson
Established: 01/01/1992
Funder type: Private foundation

Program Description

Program's purpose: General charitable purposes.

Geographic focus: Twin Cities Metropolitan Area.

Areas of interest:
ARTS, CULTURE, HUMANITIES: Museums, Performing arts.
EDUCATION: Higher education, Preschool/elementary, Secondary.
HUMAN SERVICES.

Intended beneficiaries: General public/unspecified.

Types of support for organizations:
CAPITAL CAMPAIGNS.
GENERAL PURPOSE/OPERATING SUPPORT.

Sample grants:

Basilica of St Mary/MN/restoration/ $20,000.

Common Bond Communities - MN/ MN/general operating/$375.

Guthrie Theater Foundation/Minneapolis, MN/general operating/$15,000.

Minneapolis Institute of Arts/MN/general operating/$24,000.

MN Orchestra/MN/Guarantee Fund/ $15,000.

MN Zoo Foundation/MN/general operating/$20,000.

St David's Child Development & Family Services/MN/capital campaign/$10,000.

University of St Thomas - MN Law School/MN/general operating/$10,000.

Financial Information

Financial data for year ending: 12/31/2005
Foundation assets: $984,791
Grants paid: $129,150
Number of grants: 12
Largest/smallest: $35,000/$150

Application Information

Preferred form of initial contact: letter of inquiry, complete proposal, no special form required.

Proposal deadlines: none.

Staff/Trustees

Directors/trustees: Celeste Argento; James R. Jundt, president; Marcus E. Jundt; Mary Jundt; Romy P. Jundt Erlandson.

George Kaplan Memorial Foundation, Incorporated

PO Box 4412
St Paul, MN 55104
County: Ramsey
Phone: (952) 925-9121
Contact: Allan Baumgarten, secretary/treasurer
Established: 01/01/1952
Funder type: Private foundation

Program Description

Funding priorities: Efforts focus on educational programs serving the Minneapolis/St Paul Jewish community.

Geographic focus: Twin Cities Metropolitan Area.

Geographic limitations: Minneapolis/St Paul.

Areas of interest:
EDUCATION.
RELIGION/SPIRITUAL DEVELOPMENT.

Intended beneficiaries: Other named groups.

Types of support for organizations:
GENERAL PURPOSE/OPERATING SUPPORT.

Sample grants:

Herzl Camp/Minneapolis, MN/Hebrew education/$30,000.

Financial Information

Financial data for year ending: 12/31/2005
Foundation assets: $583,363
Grants paid: $43,500
Number of grants: 7
Largest/smallest: $26,500/$1,000

Application Information

Preferred form of initial contact: complete proposal. Include cover letter with program description, budget, personnel, etc. attached.

Proposal deadlines: none; however, most grants issued in spring.

Staff/Trustees

Directors/trustees: Allan Baumgarten, secretary/treasurer; Bruce Fink; Jerry Ingber; Jerry Lavin; Sol Minsberg; David Touchin, president.

Margaret H. and James E. Kelley Foundation, Inc.

408 St Peter Street
Suite 425 Hamm Building
St Paul, MN 55102-1187
County: Ramsey
Phone: (651) 222-7463
Contact: Timothy J. Dwyer, treasurer
Established: 11/23/1960
Funder type: Private foundation

Program Description

Program's purpose: General charitable purposes.

Funding priorities: Women's issues, reproductive health, human rights, local social services, education, medical/mental health, and the arts.

Geographic focus: Twin Cities Metropolitan Area, national areas, international areas.

Areas of interest:
ARTS, CULTURE, HUMANITIES.
CIVIL RIGHTS: Civil rights/advocacy for specific groups.
EDUCATION.
ENVIRONMENTAL QUALITY/PROTECTION/BEAUTIFICATION.
HEALTH - GENERAL/REHABILITATIVE: Reproductive health care.
HUMAN SERVICES: Multipurpose human service organizations.

INTERNATIONAL AFFAIRS: International human rights.

Intended beneficiaries: Female adults, General public/unspecified.

Types of support for organizations:
GENERAL PURPOSE/OPERATING SUPPORT.
PROGRAM DEVELOPMENT/PROJECT SUPPORT.
STUDENT AID (GRANTS TO INSTITUTIONS): Scholarship funds.

Types of support for individuals: none.

Exclusions: Individuals.

Sample grants:
The Bridge for Runaway Youth/MN/general operating/$4,000.

Center for Reproductive Rights/New York, NY/general operating/$3,500.

Girl Scout Council (St Croix Valley)/MN/general operating/$2,000.

MN Children's Museum/MN/Teen Mom Program/$2,000.

MN Coalition for Battered Women/MN/general operating/$2,000.

MN Medical Foundation/MN/Dr. Donald Hastings Memorial Fund/$20,000.

WATCH (Women at the Court House)/MN/general operating/$2,000.

Financial Information

Financial data for year ending: 11/30/2005
Foundation assets: $12,628,100
Grants paid: $640,000
Largest/smallest: $35,000/$1,000

Application Information

Preferred form of initial contact: letter of inquiry.

Public information available by request: 990 tax return.

Accept common grant application: yes.

Proposal deadlines: October 1.

Contribution decisions made by: board of directors/trustees.

Frequency of contributions decisions: annually.

Specific times board meets: November.

Special application procedures: Information and purpose of organization, purpose of grant requested, and IRS exemption letter.

Staff/Trustees

Directors/trustees: Timothy J. Dwyer, treasurer; James C. O'Neill, president; Mr. & Mrs. Hampton K. O'Neill; Mr. & Mrs. James W. O'Neill; Mr. & Mrs. Kelley McC. O'Neill.

W.K. Kellogg Foundation

One Michigan Avenue East
Battle Creek, MI 49017-4058
County: Calhoun
Phone: (269) 968-1611
Fax: (269) 968-0413
Website: www.wkkf.org
Donor: W.K. Kellogg
Paid Staff: Yes
Funder type: Private foundation

Program Description

Program's purpose: To help people help themselves through the practical application of knowledge and resources to improve their quality of life and that of future generations. The W.K. Kellogg Foundation is a nonprofit organization whose mission is to apply knowledge to solve the problems of people. Its founder, W.K. Kellogg, the cereal industry pioneer, established the foundation in 1930. Since its beginning, the foundation has focused continuously on building the capacity of individuals, communities and institutions to solve their own problems.

Funding priorities: Current U.S. programming goals are as follows: health, food systems and rural development, youth and education, philanthropy and volunteerism, Greater Battle Creek, cross-programming work: devolution.

Program limitations/restrictions: The foundation does not make loans and does not provide grants for operational phases of established programs; capital facilities; separate budget line items labeled as indirect or overhead costs; equipment; conferences; films, television or radio programs unless an integral part of a project or program already being funded; endowments or development campaigns; religious purposes; or individuals.

Geographic focus: Minnesota statewide, areas outside Minnesota, national areas, international areas.

Geographic limitations: Most grants are awarded in the United States, Latin America and the Caribbean, and six southern Africa countries.

Areas of interest:
EDUCATION.
FOOD/NUTRITION/AGRICULTURE: Food systems and rural development.
HEALTH - GENERAL/REHABILITATIVE.
PHILANTHROPY/VOLUNTARISM.
PUBLIC AFFAIRS/SOCIETY BENEFIT: Cross-programming work: devolution.
YOUTH DEVELOPMENT: Youth and education.

Intended beneficiaries: General public/unspecified.

Types of support for individuals: none.

Sample grants:
MIGIZI Communications Inc/MN/develop diverse community leadership that can work across geographic, racial, cultural, class or faith boundaries by mobilizing collective action to build public will for improved teaching and learning in their communities./$279,000.

National Youth Leadership Council/MN/support capacity-building through the creation of marketing and fund development plans./$95,000.

White Earth Land Recovery Project/MN/increase production and distribution of traditional Native American foods to those on the White Earth Reservation who have limited access and who will benefit from a health perspective/$55,086.

Amherst H. Wilder Foundation/MN/improve the capacity of intermediaries by providing management assistance to the large network of nonprofit organizations working with immigrant- and refugee-led organizations/$200,000.

Women's Foundation of MN/MN/promote and build the leadership and economic security of young women throughout Minnesota by expanding the Girls as Grantmakers model (GirlsBEST)/$600,000.

Financial Information

Financial data for year ending: 08/31/2005
Foundation assets: $432,965,318
Grants paid: $219,862,847

Application Information

Preferred form of initial contact: letter of inquiry, online application.

Public information available by request: proposal guidelines, annual report, website. Website review encouraged.

Accept common grant application: yes.

Proposal deadlines: none.

Preferred time for receiving proposals: proposals accepted on an ongoing basis.

Contribution decisions made by: staff, board of directors/trustees.

Frequency of contributions decisions: monthly, regularly.

Typical time from application deadlines to notification: 3 months for initial review.

Staff/Trustees

Directors/trustees: Shirley D. Bowser; Roderick D. Gillum; Dorothy A. Johnson; Fred P. Keller; Hanmin Liu; Cynthia H. Milligan, president; Sterling K. Speirn; Joseph M. Stewart; Wenda Weekes Moore.

Elizabeth Callender King Foundation

PO Box 499
c/o Winona National Bank
Winona, MN 55987
County: Winona
Phone: (507) 454-9218
Established: 01/29/1991
Funder type: Private foundation

Program Description

Program limitations/restrictions: Those qualifying under IRC Section 501(c)(3).

Geographic focus: Greater Minnesota, Minnesota statewide, Winona area.

Areas of interest:
ARTS, CULTURE, HUMANITIES: Historical societies, Performing arts.
EDUCATION: Higher education, Preschool/elementary, Secondary.
HUMAN SERVICES.

Intended beneficiaries: General public/unspecified.

Sample grants:
Cotter High School - Winona/MN/$350.
Family Service - MN (Winona)/MN/$5,400.
Hiawatha Valley Education District/MN/$1,000.
Southern MN Regional Legal Services/MN/$10,000.
Theatre du Mississippi - MN/MN/$2,500.
Winona County DAC/MN/$5,000.
Winona Oratorio Chorus/MN/$1,500.
Winona Symphony Orchestra Association, Inc/MN/$500.

Financial Information

Financial data for year ending: 12/31/2005
Foundation assets: $1,792,212
Grants paid: $66,650
Number of grants: 31
Largest/smallest: $10,000/$100
Typical grant amount: $1,000

Application Information

Preferred form of initial contact: letter of inquiry.

Proposal deadlines: none.

Staff/Trustees

Directors/trustees: Sue Cornwall; Kent A. Gernander, president; Tom Graham; Pauline Knight; Pat Mutter; Kenneth Seebold; Edith Tschumper.

Hess Kline Foundation, Inc.

8800 Highway 7
Suite 480
St Louis Park, MN 55426
County: Hennepin
Phone: (952) 931-9580
Contact: Hess Kline, president
Established: 12/01/1956
Funder type: Private foundation

Program Description

Program's purpose: General charitable purposes.

Geographic focus: Twin Cities Metropolitan Area, Areas outside Minnesota.

Areas of interest:
ARTS, CULTURE, HUMANITIES: Museums, Performing arts.
EDUCATION.
HEALTH - DISEASES/MEDICAL DISCIPLINES: Diabetes.
HEALTH - RESEARCH.
HUMAN SERVICES.
RELIGION/SPIRITUAL DEVELOPMENT: Specific denomination.

Intended beneficiaries: General public/unspecified.

Types of support for organizations: GENERAL PURPOSE/OPERATING SUPPORT.

Sample grants:
American Diabetes Association - MN (Minneapolis)/MN/$500.
B'nai B'rith Foundation - Washington, DC/DC/$100.
Brandeis University/MA/$35.
Camp Discovery Challenge/Schaumburg, IL/$1,000.
Jewish Community Center - St Paul/MN/$500.
Kravis, Raymond F Center for the Performing Arts/West Palm Beach, FL/$1,150.
Norton Museum & School of Art - FL/West Palm Beach, FL/$125.
Temple Israel/Minneapolis, MN/memorial book fund/$120.

Financial Information

Financial data for year ending: 12/31/2005
Foundation assets: $18,510
Grants paid: $55,491
Number of grants: 14
Largest/smallest: $75,000/$25

Application Information

Preferred form of initial contact: complete proposal.

Proposal deadlines: June 30.

Special application procedures: provide written details of charitable, religious, educational or medical use; include amounts required and details of benefit to mankind.

Staff/Trustees

Directors/trustees: James R. Greupner; Hess Kline, president; Renee Kline.

John S. and James L. Knight Foundation

c/o Otto Bemer Foundation
445 Minnesota Street
Suite 2250
St Paul, MN 55101
County: Ramsey
Phone: (651) 312-3519
Fax: (651) 312-3665
E-mail: talen@knightfdn.org
Website: www.knightfdn.org
Contact: Polly M. Talen, for Minnesota
Paid Staff: Yes
Funder type: Private foundation

Program Description

Program's purpose: Through the Community Partners Program, we seek to work with local organizations capable of helping our Knight communities realize their potential.

Funding priorities: Economic development in Duluth; affordable housing and health and mental health and oral health of very young children in St Paul.

Program limitations/restrictions: The foundation prefers not to fund requests for support of fundraising events; requests to cover operating deficits; charities operated by service clubs; activities that are normally the responsibility of government (the foundation will, in selective cases, join with units of government in supporting special projects); medical research; organizations or projects whose mission is to prevent, eradicate and/or alleviate the effects of a specific disease; requests from hospitals (unless they are for community-wide capital campaigns with a stated goal and beginning and ending dates or for specific projects that meet foundation goals); activities to propagate a religious faith or restricted to one religion or denomination; support of political candidates; memorials; international programs and organizations, except U.S.-based organizations supporting a free press around the world; a second request for a capital campaign for which the foundation previously approved a grant; conferences; group travel; honoraria for distinguished guests — except in initiatives of the foundation in all three cases; scholarships for individuals.

Geographic focus: East Metropolitan Area/St Paul only, Duluth.

Geographic limitations: Only the 26 Knight communities. In Minnesota: Duluth and St Paul. Also Grand Forks, North Dakota, and Aberdeen, South Dakota.

Areas of interest:
COMMUNITY IMPROVEMENT: Economic development.
HEALTH - MENTAL HEALTH/CRISIS INTERVENTION: Young children's mental health screening.
HOUSING/SHELTER.
HUMAN SERVICES: Children/youth services.

Intended beneficiaries: Ethnic/racial populations - general, Hispanics/Latinos, Immigrants/newcomers/refugees, Infants/babies (under age 5), Poor/economically disadvantaged.

Types of support for individuals: none.

Exclusions: Individuals, Political organizations, Religious organizations, Scholarships/loans.

Financial Information

Financial data for year ending: 12/31/2005
Foundation assets: $2,071,507,291
Grants paid: $92,577,162
Number of grants: 534
Largest/smallest: $4,800,000/$5,000
Typical grant amount: $250,000
Largest multi-year grant approved: $4,405,000
Purpose: press freedom

Application Information

Preferred form of initial contact: letters of inquiry, which must be submitted online. Proposals that have not been invited will not be accepted.

Public information available by request: annual report, newsletter, website.

Proposal deadlines: Ongoing in Duluth, Grand Forks and Aberdeen. In St Paul, foundations funds are already committed in 2007.

Preferred time for receiving proposals: First six months of the year for consideration in this calendar year.

Contribution decisions made by: board of directors/trustees.

Frequency of contributions decisions: quarterly.

Typical time from application deadlines to notification: 6 months.

Special application procedures: Knight requires all inquiries to come through our online inquiry system at www.knightfdn.org.

Staff/Trustees

Staff: Ann Corriston, for North and South Dakota; Eric Newton, for journalism; Polly M. Talen, for Minnesota.

Knitcraft - St Croix Foundation, Inc.

4020 West Sixth Street
Winona, MN 55987-1596
County: Winona
Phone: (507) 454-1163
Contact: Mary J. Bergin
Established: 01/01/1994
Funder type: Corporate foundation

Program Description

Program's purpose: Grants awarded primarily for handicapped, health and social organizations.

Geographic focus: Greater Minnesota, Minnesota statewide.

Areas of interest:
EDUCATION.
HEALTH - GENERAL/REHABILITATIVE.
HUMAN SERVICES.

Intended beneficiaries: Physically disabled.

Sample grants:

American Red Cross - MN (Winona County)/MN/$100.
ARC - MN (Winona County)/MN/$150.
Camp Winnebago Inc/MN/$200.
GameHaven Council/MN/$150.
St Mary's University - Winona/MN/$1,250.
Winona Health Foundation/MN/$1,500.
Winona ORC/MN/$6,667.
Winona Volunteer Services Inc/MN/$250.

Financial Information

Financial data for year ending: 06/30/2005
Foundation assets: $78,649
Grants paid: $16,391
Number of grants: 29
Largest/smallest: $5,000/$50

Application Information

Preferred form of initial contact: request for guidelines.

Public information available by request: application form.

Proposal deadlines: ongoing.

Staff/Trustees

Directors/trustees: Mary J. Bergin; Bernard J. Brenner, president; Colleen Brenner; Wilfried J. Hahn; Tom Kabat, treasurer; Samuel P. Shea.

Knox Foundation

U.S. Bank, N.A.
101 East Fifth Street
EP MN S14
St Paul, MN 55101
County: Ramsey
Phone: (651) 466-8735
Alt. Phone: (651) 466-8707
Fax: (651) 466-8741
Contact: Jeffrey T. Peterson
Established: 11/24/2000
Funder type: Private foundation

Program Description

Program's purpose: General charitable purposes.

Funding priorities: The foundation does not have explicit grant guidelines, but it primarily makes grants to education, cultural, youth, environmental, education and community support organizations located in Minnesota.

Geographic focus: Minnesota statewide.

Geographic limitations: Organizations located in Minnesota.

Intended beneficiaries: General public/unspecified.

Types of support for individuals: none.

Exclusions: Individuals, Organizations that would require expenditure responsibility.

Sample grants:
Juvenile Diabetes Foundation - MN/MN/$400.
MN Medical Foundation/MN/$2,000.
Nantucket Yacht Club Foundation/MA/$500.
Wilderness Inquiry/Minneapolis, MN/$500.

Financial Information

Financial data for year ending: 12/31/2005
Foundation assets: $1,876,925
Grants paid: $84,000
Number of grants: 14
Largest/smallest: $25,000/$500
Typical grant amount: $500

Application Information

Preferred form of initial contact: complete proposal.

Public information available by request: application form.

Proposal deadlines: November 1.

Staff/Trustees

Directors/trustees: Susanne L. Hutcheson; Zenas W. Hutcheson; David M. Lilly; Jeffrey T. Peterson.

Kopp Family Foundation

7701 France Avenue South
Suite 500
Edina, MN 55435-3201
County: Hennepin
Phone: (952) 841-0438
Fax: (952) 841-0460
E-mail: foundation@koppinvestments.com
Contact: Lindsey R. Lang, administrator
Established: 11/01/1986
Funder type: Private foundation

Program Description

Program's purpose: To benefit local organizations that impact our community in a positive, proactive way.

Funding priorities: Spiritual Growth, Emergency Service/Shelter, Education, Health & Wellness.

Program limitations/restrictions: Each application is reviewed for merit; no restrictions.

Geographic focus: Twin Cities Metropolitan Area, Greater Minnesota.

Areas of interest:
ANIMAL RELATED.
ARTS, CULTURE, HUMANITIES.
COMMUNITY IMPROVEMENT: Community/neighborhood development/improvement.
EDUCATION: Adult/continuing education/literacy, Higher education, Libraries/library science, Pre-school/elementary. We give scholarships only through local high schools.
ENVIRONMENTAL QUALITY/PROTECTION/BEAUTIFICATION: Environmental beautification/open spaces.
HEALTH - GENERAL/REHABILITATIVE: Health support services, Public health programs/wellness education.
HEALTH - MENTAL HEALTH/CRISIS INTERVENTION: Counseling/support groups, Hotline/crisis intervention, Mental health treatment and services.
HOUSING/SHELTER.
HUMAN SERVICES.
RELIGION/SPIRITUAL DEVELOPMENT.
YOUTH DEVELOPMENT.

Intended beneficiaries: Adults, Aging/elderly/senior citizens, Children and youth (infants-19 years), Female adults, General public/unspecified, Homeless, Immigrants/newcomers/refugees, Mentally/emotionally disabled, Poor/economically disadvantaged, Youth/adolescents (ages 14-19).

Types of support for organizations:
CAPITAL CAMPAIGNS.
EMERGENCY FUNDS.
GENERAL PURPOSE/OPERATING SUPPORT.
PROGRAM DEVELOPMENT/PROJECT SUPPORT.

Types of support for individuals: none.

Financial Information

Financial data for year ending: 12/31/2005
Foundation assets: $38,352,000
Grants paid: $1,676,740
Number of grants: 584
Largest/smallest: $100,000/$100

Application Information

Preferred form of initial contact: letter of inquiry, request for guidelines, e-mail.

Public information available by request: proposal guidelines, annual report.

Accept common grant application: yes.

Proposal deadlines: The Kopp Family Foundation has no deadlines; we meet every other month.

Contribution decisions made by: board of directors/trustees.

Frequency of contributions decisions: monthly.

Typical time from application deadlines to notification: 2 weeks.

Staff/Trustees

Staff: Lindsey R. Lang, administrator.

Directors/trustees: Jim Berbee; Barbara Kopp; Brian Kopp; Debbie Kopp; Debra Kopp; Kristin Kopp; Leroy C. Kopp; Missy Kopp; Terry Kopp.

Ethel Mae Kreutz Private Foundation

152 West Third Street
Winona, MN 55987-3101
County: Winona
Phone: (507) 452-8313
Contact: Ralph P. Ruben Jr.
Established: 01/01/2002
Donor: Ethel Mae Kreutz
Funder type: Private foundation

Program Description

Program's purpose: General charitable purposes.

Geographic focus: Greater Minnesota, Areas outside Minnesota, Winona, Minnesota region.

Sample grants:

Big Brothers/Big Sisters - MN (Winona County)/MN/$1,250.

CASA - WI (La Crosse)/WI/$13,093.

Cochrane-Fountain City Schools/Fountain City, WI/$500.

Home and Community Options/Winona, MN/$1,000.

Lions Club - MN (Winona)/MN/$668.

Public Library - WI (Alma)/WI/$2,520.

Winona Area Industrial Development Association/MN/$1,000.

Winona ORC/MN/$1,000.

Financial Information

Financial data for year ending: 12/31/2005
Foundation assets: $1,441,398
Grants paid: $78,777
Number of grants: 16
Largest/smallest: $30,000/$500

Application Information

Accept common grant application: yes.
Proposal deadlines: none.

Staff/Trustees

Directors/trustees: Doris Ruben; Ralph P. Ruben Jr.

Lahti Family Foundation

c/o Brenda Pearson
60 South Sixth Street
Minneapolis, MN 55402
County: Hennepin
Phone: (612) 215-3603
Funder type: Private foundation

Program Description

Program limitations/restrictions: No scholarships.

Geographic focus: Twin Cities Metropolitan Area, Greater Minnesota, Duluth area.

Geographic limitations: Grants to organizations in Duluth, and the Twin Cities.

Areas of interest:
YOUTH DEVELOPMENT.

Sample grants:

Boys & Girls Club - MN (Duluth)/MN/$20,000.

Boys Club - MN (Duluth)/MN/$10,000.

First Witness Child Abuse Resource Center/Duluth, MN/$15,000.

Life House - MN (Duluth)/MN/$15,000.

University of MN - Duluth/MN/Glensheen summer program/$11,000.

YWCA - MN (Duluth)/MN/$5,000.

Financial Information

Financial data for year ending: 12/31/2005
Foundation assets: $2,194,645
Grants paid: $145,500
Number of grants: 12
Largest/smallest: $20,000/$1,000

Application Information

Proposal deadlines: None.

Land O'Lakes Foundation

4001 Lexington Avenue North
PO Box 64150
St Paul, MN 55164-0150
County: Ramsey
Phone: (651) 481-2222
Fax: (651) 481-2000
E-mail: MLAtkins-Sakry@landolakes.com
Website: www.foundation.landolakes.com
Contact: Lydia Botham, executive director
Established: 11/01/1996
Funder type: Corporate foundation

Program Description

Program's purpose: The foundation's five programs provide support through cash grants to nonprofit organizations that are working to improve the quality of life in communities where Land O'Lakes has a significant concentration of farmer-members or employees.

Funding priorities: These include federated campaigns supporting community human services, organizations that work to alleviate hunger; programs designed to build leadership skills of rural youth; civic organizations active in addressing community problems or capturing opportunities; quality artistic endeavors - especially those in under-served rural areas, or those with touring or outreach programs. 90% of donations made to rural communities.

Program limitations/restrictions: Community Grants limited to one per year per organization; no funds for lobbying, religious, political, veterans, fraternal or labor organizations; fundraising events, dinners or benefits; capital campaigns at public or private colleges and universities; racing/sports sponsorships; advertising; individuals; scholarships; travel expenses; disease/medical research or treatment.

Geographic focus: Twin Cities Metropolitan Area, Greater Minnesota, Minnesota statewide, Areas outside Minnesota, National Areas.

Geographic limitations: Areas outside Minnesota including Arkansas, California, Idaho, Illinois, Indiana, Iowa, Kansas, Michigan, Mississippi, Missouri, Nebraska, North Dakota, Ohio,

Oklahoma, Oregon, Pennsylvania, South Dakota, Texas, Washington and Wisconsin. 90% rural, 10% urban.

Areas of interest:
ARTS, CULTURE, HUMANITIES: Arts services, Arts/cultural multipurpose, Historical societies, Humanities, Museums, Performing arts, Visual arts.
COMMUNITY IMPROVEMENT: Community coalitions, Community funds/federated giving programs, Community/neighborhood development/improvement.
EDUCATION: Ag in the Classroom, Matching gifts to education program (employees, corporate board members and member-leaders only).
ENVIRONMENTAL QUALITY/PROTECTION.
FOOD/NUTRITION/AGRICULTURE: Agricultural programs, Food service/free food distribution, Nutrition promotion, Soil and water conservation/farm land preservation, America's Second Harvest.
HUMAN SERVICES: Emergency assistance (food/clothing/cash), United Way.
YOUTH DEVELOPMENT: Youth development programs, 4-H and FFA, LEAD.

Intended beneficiaries: General public/unspecified.

Types of support for organizations:
CAPITAL CAMPAIGNS.
GENERAL PURPOSE/OPERATING SUPPORT.
PROGRAM DEVELOPMENT/PROJECT SUPPORT.

Types of support for individuals: none.

Matching grants: elementary/secondary education, employee matching, higher education, public broadcasting.

Dollars for Doers: yes.

Exclusions: Individuals, Non-501(c)(3), Political organizations, Religious organizations, Scholarships/loans, Tax-supported institutions, Medical or disease-related causes.

Sample grants:
4-H Foundation - IA/IA/State Volunteer Development/$2,000.
Agricultural Leadership Council - NE/NE/Project Lead/$1,500.
Fire Department - PA/PA/The Keystone Hook & Ladder Company #1 - Firefighting equipment/$2,000.
Gleanings for the Hungry - CA/CA/$5,000.
Indiana Agricultural Leadership Institute/IN/$1,500.
Public Library - NE/NE/Battle Creek Library Foundation - Matching Battle Creek Co-op's donation to capital campaign/$1,204.
Southwest State University Foundation/MN/MARL Program Class III/$2,000.
United Way - WI/WI/$9,135.

Financial Information

Financial data for year ending: 12/31/2005
Foundation assets: $3,121,719
Grants paid: $1,005,183
Largest/smallest: $115,500/$25
Matching gifts: $193,023

Application Information

Preferred form of initial contact: request for guidelines, e-mail.

Public information available by request: proposal guidelines, application form, website.

Accept common grant application: yes.

Proposal deadlines: First of month prior to board meeting date: July 1, September 1, December 1.

Contribution decisions made by: staff, board of directors/trustees.

Frequency of contributions decisions: quarterly, Requests under $10,000 reviewed as received.

Specific times board meets: Four times per year, generally quarterly.

Typical time from application deadlines to notification: Up to 3 months.

Special application procedures: Check website for 2007 giving information.

Staff/Trustees

Staff: Martha Atkins-Sakry, executive assistant/arts program manager; Lydia Botham, executive director.

Directors/trustees: Lynn Boadwine; Jim Fife; Lawrence Hooks; Jane Kleinkramer; Manuel Maciel Jr., chairman; Bob Marley.

Lang Family Charitable Trust

U.S. Bank Philanthropic Services
101 East Fifth Street, EP-MN-S12
St Paul, MN 55101
County: Ramsey
Phone: (651) 466-8443
Funder type: Private foundation

Program Description

Areas of interest:
EDUCATION: Secondary.
ENVIRONMENTAL QUALITY/PROTECTION/BEAUTIFICATION: Botanical/horticultural/landscape, Natural resources conservation/protection.
HEALTH - DISEASES/MEDICAL DISCIPLINES: Cancer.
HEALTH - MENTAL HEALTH/CRISIS INTERVENTION: Mental health treatment and services.

Sample grants:
Academy of Holy Angels - MN (Richfield)/MN/Scholarship fund/$2,500.
Annunciation School/MN/$3,262.
Friends of the Mississippi River/MN/$3,500.
Hamm Memorial Psychiatric Clinic/MN/$35,000.
Institute for Local Self-Reliance/MN/$10,000.
Land Stewardship Project/MN/$3,000.
MN Landscape Arboretum Foundation/MN/Support Lang-Ankeny memorial gardens/$40,762.
Organic Consumers Association/Little Marais, MN/$1,000.

Financial Information

Financial data for year ending: 12/31/2005
Foundation assets: $2,209,095
Grants paid: $118,048
Number of grants: 17
Largest/smallest: $40,000/$1,000

Application Information

Preferred form of initial contact: complete proposal.

Accept common grant application: yes.

Proposal deadlines: none.

Special application procedures: Applicants should use the Minnesota Common Grant Application Form.

Staff/Trustees

Directors/trustees: Jeremy T. Lang; Phoebe Hamm Lang; William Scheffer Lang; Sarah F. Sponheim.

Leonette M. and Fred T. Lanners Foundation

12805 Highway 55
Suite 102
Plymouth, MN 55441
County: Hennepin
Phone: (763) 550-9892
Fax: (763) 550-9630
E-mail: alanners@lannersfoundation.org
Website: www.lannersfoundation.org
Contact: Alan Lanners, president
Established: 04/27/1991
Donor: Fred T. Lanners
Funder type: Private foundation

Program Description

Program's purpose: The foundation supports charitable organizations whose activities are consistent with our belief in God, Catholicism, Judeo/Christian principles, family, morality, individual responsibility, economic freedom and constitutional government.

Program limitations/restrictions: No grants to individuals, endowments, annual fund appeals, political campaigns, capital campaigns, medical research, environmental organizations, purchase of educational supplies or physical plant used for education, or the arts.

Geographic focus: Twin Cities Metropolitan Area, Greater Minnesota, Areas outside Minnesota.

Geographic limitations: Most grants made to Minnesota based programs. No grants outside United States.

Areas of interest:
ARTS, CULTURE, HUMANITIES: Historical societies.
COMMUNITY IMPROVEMENT: Community/neighborhood development/improvement.
EDUCATION: Educational reform, Higher education, Pre-school/elementary, Secondary.
HEALTH - DISEASES/MEDICAL DISCIPLINES: Birth defects/genetic disorders.
HOUSING/SHELTER: Homeless, temporary housing.
HUMAN SERVICES: Children/youth services, Family services.
SOCIAL SCIENCES: Social science research institutes/services.

Intended beneficiaries: General public/unspecified.

Types of support for organizations:
GENERAL PURPOSE/OPERATING SUPPORT.
PROGRAM DEVELOPMENT/PROJECT SUPPORT.

Types of support for individuals: none.

Sample grants:

Center of the American Experiment/MN/general operating/$10,000.

Cradle of Hope/MN/general operating/$4,000.

Gopher State Railway Museum Inc/MN/general operating/$250.

Hillsdale College/MI/general operating/$8,000.

Jay Phillips Center for Jewish Christian Learning/St Paul, MN/general operating/$5,000.

Little Sisters of the Poor - MN (St Paul)/MN/general operating/$1,000.

MN Family Institute/MN/general operating/$5,000.

St John's University - MN/MN/general operating/$5,000.

Financial Information

Financial data for year ending: 12/31/2005
Foundation assets: $2,771,576
Grants paid: $115,150
Number of grants: 20
Largest/smallest: $10,000/$250

Application Information

Preferred form of initial contact: letter of inquiry, complete proposal.

Public information available by request: proposal guidelines, application form, website.

Accept common grant application: yes.

Accept common report form: yes.

Will view video: yes.

Proposal deadlines: Ongoing, but proposals are evaluated from March through May.

Preferred time for receiving proposals: first half of calendar year.

Contribution decisions made by: board of directors/trustees.

Frequency of contributions decisions: annually.

Specific times board meets: July 31, usually.

Staff/Trustees

Directors/trustees: Carol T. Hockert; Alan Lanners, president; F. Thomas Lanners; John J. Lanners; Leonette Lanners.

Lawson

380 Saint Peter Street
St Paul, MN 55102
County: Ramsey
Phone: (651) 767-4803
Fax: (651) 767-4920
Website: www.lawson.com
Paid Staff: Yes
Funder type: Corporate giving program

Program Description

Program's purpose: At Lawson, we recognize the significant role nonprofit organizations play in strengthening our communities and the people in them. That's why each year, Lawson offers support to several nonprofit organizations through our giving program, Lawson Lends a Hand.

Funding priorities: Priority will be given to proposals whose mission is aligned with Lawson's mission; that propose unique and innovative solutions focusing on the needs of youth in the areas of education and mentoring; that are for programs and/or activities that provide ongoing involvement/participation by Lawson employees; from organizations that devote a high percentage of their budget (including Lawson's donation) to direct services rather than administrative overhead; that are direct and of high quality; and that emphasize use of computer-based technology.

Geographic focus: Twin Cities Metropolitan Area.

Geographic limitations: While proposals from the Minneapolis-St Paul communities receive priority, the Lawson Lends a Hand committee will accept proposals from national organizations for programs that complement Lawson's funding priorities.

Areas of interest:
EDUCATION: Mentoring.
SCIENCE/TECHNOLOGY: Use of computer-based technology.
YOUTH DEVELOPMENT.

Intended beneficiaries: Children and youth (infants-19 years).

Exclusions: Non-501(c)(3), Political organizations, Religious organizations, Scholarships/loans, Underwriting for advertising, Affiliates of labor organizations, Organizations that discriminate based on race, color, gender, creed or country of origin.

Financial Information

Financial data for year ending: 12/31/2004
Grants paid: $469,542

Application Information

Preferred form of initial contact: complete proposal.

Public information available by request: proposal guidelines, website.

Proposal deadlines: The Lawson Lends a Hand committee review process is continuous, and proposals are welcome at any time.

Contribution decisions made by: employee committee.

Staff/Trustees

Staff: Kathleen Stringfield.

Helen Sperry Lea Foundation

3534 Fulton Street NW
Washington, DC 20007
Phone: (202) 337-5448
Contact: Sperry Lea, president
Funder type: Private foundation

Program Description

Geographic focus: Twin Cities Metropolitan Area, Areas outside Minnesota.

Areas of interest:
ARTS, CULTURE, HUMANITIES.
EDUCATION.
ENVIRONMENTAL QUALITY/PROTECTION/BEAUTIFICATION.

Financial Information

Financial data for year ending: 12/31/2005
Foundation assets: $2,668,760
Grants paid: $86,000
Number of grants: 19

Application Information

Preferred form of initial contact: No specific format required.

Staff/Trustees

Directors/trustees: Anna L. Lea, treasurer; Brooke Lea; Helena A. Lea; Sperry Lea, president; Catherine W. Wilkinson, secretary.

Leonard, Street and Deinard Foundation

150 South Fifth Street
Suite 2300
Minneapolis, MN 55402-4238
County: Hennepin
Phone: (612) 335-1500
Fax: (612) 335-1657
Website: www.leonard.com/about/foundation.aspx
Contact: Jill Weber, administrative director
Established: 10/29/1982
Funder type: Corporate foundation

Program Description

Program's purpose: Provides general operating support for established nonprofit 501(c)(3) organizations that are good citizens of the communities in which we operate and make a positive and significant impact on diverse populations within that community.

Funding priorities: Major charitable and cultural institutions, legal and pro bono organizations. The Leonard, Street and Deinard Foundation makes contributions in four primary categories: 1) Major legal organizations: Grants are awarded to worthy causes directly related to the practice of law, including law schools, bar associations, and organizations committed to improving legal aid to the poor, the administration of justice, and to supporting minority lawyers. 2) Major charitable and cultural institutions that are generally recognized as such in the communities in which we have offices. Included in this category is an annual contribution to the United Way. Organizations that are part of the United Way funding system are considered funded through our United Way contribution; additional requests directly from those organizations are not considered. 3) Nonprofit organizations on which our attorneys serve as directors or officers. 4) Nonprofit organizations requiring our support for tactical client relations reasons.

Geographic focus: Minnesota statewide, areas outside Minnesota.

Geographic limitations: Minnesota statewide; secondarily the five-state region (Iowa, North Dakota, South Dakota, Wisconsin).

Intended beneficiaries: General public/unspecified.

Types of support for organizations:
GENERAL PURPOSE/OPERATING SUPPORT: Annual campaigns.

Financial Information

Financial data for year ending: 12/31/2006
Grants paid: $399,604
Number of grants: 121
Largest/smallest: $57,000/$100

Application Information

Preferred form of initial contact: letter of inquiry.

Accept common grant application: yes.

Proposal deadlines: December 1 of each year for the following calendar year.

Contribution decisions made by: staff, board of directors/trustees.

Staff/Trustees

Staff: Sara Springan, administrative assistant; Jill Weber, administrative director.

Directors/trustees: Joseph M. Finley, director; Timothy J. Pabst, foundation board president; Byron E. Starns, director.

Lerner Foundation

241 First Avenue North
Minneapolis, MN 55401-1607
County: Hennepin
Phone: (612) 332-3344
Contact: Lynn Burow
Established: 09/01/1968
Funder type: Private foundation

Program Description

Program's purpose: General charitable purposes.

Geographic focus: Twin Cities Metropolitan Area, Areas outside Minnesota.

Areas of interest:
ARTS, CULTURE, HUMANITIES: Historical societies, Humanities, Media/communications, Museums, Performing arts.
EDUCATION: Higher education, Libraries/library science.
HEALTH - DISEASES/MEDICAL DISCIPLINES.
HEALTH - RESEARCH.
HUMAN SERVICES.
RELIGION/SPIRITUAL DEVELOPMENT.

Intended beneficiaries: General public/unspecified.

Types of support for organizations:
GENERAL PURPOSE/OPERATING SUPPORT.

Sample grants:
American Heart Association - IL/IL/ general operating/$1,000.
Anderson Center for Interdisciplinary Studies/Red Wing, MN/general operating/$400.
Brady Center to Prevent Gun Violence/ Washington, DC/general operating/$100.
Coffee House Press/MN/general operating/$2,000.
Hamline University/MN/general operating/$8,800.
MN Library Association/MN/general operating/$600.
United Way - CT/CT/general operating/ $400.
University Film Society/MN/general operating/$3,000.

Financial Information

Financial data for year ending: 08/31/2005
Foundation assets: $1,125,180
Grants paid: $71,337
Number of grants: 71
Largest/smallest: $10,000/$10

Application Information

Preferred form of initial contact: letter of inquiry, no formal form or format; letter should state organization's charitable function and purpose for which money will be used.

Proposal deadlines: none.

Staff/Trustees

Directors/trustees: Harry J. Lerner, president.

Steven C. Leuthold Family Foundation

100 North Sixth Street
412A Butler Square
Minneapolis, MN 55403
County: Hennepin
Phone: (612) 332-1567
Contact: Steven C. Leuthold
Established: 09/14/1990
Funder type: Private foundation

Program Description

Program's purpose: We want to make the world a better place by helping people, animals and the environment.

Geographic focus: Twin Cities Metropolitan Area, Greater Minnesota, Minnesota statewide, Areas outside Minnesota.

Areas of interest:
ANIMAL RELATED: Animal protection/welfare, Wildlife preservation/ protection.
ARTS, CULTURE, HUMANITIES: Historical societies, Media/communications.
ENVIRONMENTAL QUALITY/ PROTECTION/BEAUTIFICATION: Environmental education/outdoor survival, Natural resources conservation/protection, Pollution abatement and control.
HEALTH - DISEASES/MEDICAL DISCIPLINES.
HEALTH - RESEARCH.
HUMAN SERVICES: Children/youth services, Multipurpose human service organizations.

Types of support for organizations:
GENERAL PURPOSE/OPERATING SUPPORT.
PROGRAM DEVELOPMENT/ PROJECT SUPPORT.
RESEARCH.

Types of support for individuals: none.

Exclusions: Individuals, music, arts.

Sample grants:
ALS Association - MN/MN/ research/ $13,000.
Animal Human Society - MN (Freeborn County)/Albert Lea, MN/general operating/$15,000.
Common Bond Communities - MN/MN/ general operating/$1,000.
English Learning Center/Minneapolis, MN/general operating/$5,000.
KBEM - FM Radio/MN/general operating/$2,000.
National Resources Defense Council/ MN/general operating/$33,000.
Nature Conservancy - VA/VA/rescue the reef/$10,000.
Vision Loss Resources/MN/general operating/$3,000.

Financial Information

Financial data for year ending: 12/31/2005
Foundation assets: $21,760,325
Grants paid: $1,004,000
Number of grants: 125
Largest/smallest: $60,000/$1,000

Application Information

Preferred form of initial contact: letter of inquiry. Letter should state purpose for which funds are requested and relevant information on activities of organization.

Accept common grant application: yes.

Preferred time for receiving proposals: ongoing.

Contribution decisions made by: board of directors/trustees.

Frequency of contributions decisions: annually.

Staff/Trustees

Directors/trustees: Linda Leuthold Donerkiel; Kurt A. Leuthold; Michael S. Leuthold; Russell C. Leuthold; Steven C. Leuthold.

Liebhaber Family Foundation

4509 Minnetonka Boulevard
Minneapolis, MN 55416-4027
County: Hennepin
Phone: (952) 259-5228
Contact: Marc Liebhaber, president
Established: 05/05/1983
Funder type: Private foundation

Program Description

Program's purpose: General charitable purposes.

Geographic focus: Twin Cities Metropolitan Area, Areas outside Minnesota.

Areas of interest:
ARTS, CULTURE, HUMANITIES.
EDUCATION.
HUMAN SERVICES.
RELIGION/SPIRITUAL DEVELOPMENT.

Intended beneficiaries: General public/unspecified.

Sample grants:
Anti-Defamation League - NY/NY/$500.
Brandeis University/MA/$10,000.
Hadassah - FL/Pompano Beach, FL/$100.
Jewish Federation - Minneapolis/MN/$1,000.
Jewish Theological Seminary/New York, NY/$31,000.
United Jewish Communities - FL (Boca Raton)/FL/$100.
World Council of Synagogues/New York, NY/$2,000.

Financial Information

Financial data for year ending: 12/31/2005
Foundation assets: $542,992
Grants paid: $65,079
Number of grants: 15
Largest/smallest: $31,000/$25

Application Information

Preferred form of initial contact: complete proposal.

Proposal deadlines: none.

Special application procedures: provide applicant's name and address, statement as to whether applicant is organized as a nonprofit organization, dollar amount requested, detailed explanation of how requested amount will be used.

Staff/Trustees

Directors/trustees: Henia Liebhaber; Marc Liebhaber, president; Sharon F. Liebhaber.

R. C. Lilly Foundation

U.S. Bank, N.A.
101 East Fifth Street
EP MN S14
St Paul, MN 55101
County: Ramsey
Phone: (651) 466-8735
Alt. Phone: (651) 466-8707
Contact: Jeffrey T. Peterson
Established: 05/24/1968
Funder type: Private foundation

Program Description

Funding priorities: Educational, cultural, youth, environmental, education and community support organizations.

Program limitations/restrictions: No grants to individuals or organizations that would require expenditure responsibility.

Geographic focus: Minnesota statewide.

Geographic limitations: Minnesota.

Areas of interest:
ARTS, CULTURE, HUMANITIES.
COMMUNITY IMPROVEMENT.
EDUCATION.
ENVIRONMENTAL QUALITY/PROTECTION/BEAUTIFICATION.
YOUTH DEVELOPMENT.

Intended beneficiaries: General public/unspecified.

Exclusions: Individuals.

Sample grants:
Children's Home Society - MN/MN/general operating/$5,000.
Dartmouth College Alumni Fund/NH/$5,500.
Hofstra University/NY/F Scott Fitzgerald Society/$1,000.
Metropolitan State University/MN/general operating/$10,000.
MN AIDS Project Inc/MN/general operating/$3,000.
Nantucket Athenaeum Library/MA/general operating/$2,000.
St Paul Academy & Summit School/MN/general operating/$35,000.
University of MN/Minneapolis, MN/grant for new building/$25,000.

Financial Information

Financial data for year ending: 12/31/2005
Foundation assets: $14,947,743
Grants paid: $533,000
Number of grants: 84
Largest/smallest: $35,000/$300

Application Information

Preferred form of initial contact: letter of inquiry, complete proposal.

Proposal deadlines: none.

Staff/Trustees

Directors/trustees: Susanne L. Hutcheson, vice president; Bruce A. Lilly, treasurer; David M. Lilly Jr., vice president; David M. Lilly, president; Jeffrey T. Peterson, secretary.

Carl and Aune Lind Family Foundation

18371 Bearpath Trail
Eden Prairie, MN 55347-3471
County: Hennepin
Contact: Dennis A. Lind, president
Established: 12/06/1983
Funder type: Private foundation

Program Description

Program's purpose: General charitable purposes.

Geographic focus: Twin Cities Metropolitan Area, Greater Minnesota, Minnesota statewide, Areas outside Minnesota, Arizona.

Areas of interest:
ARTS, CULTURE, HUMANITIES: Historical societies, Media/communications.
HEALTH - DISEASES/MEDICAL DISCIPLINES.
HUMAN SERVICES: Children/youth services, Emergency assistance (food/clothing/cash), Family services, Multipurpose human service organizations.
PHILANTHROPY/VOLUNTARISM.

Intended beneficiaries: General public/unspecified.

Sample grants:
ALS Association - MN/MN/$1,000.
Barnesville Area Community Fund/MN/$1,250.

Catholic Charities - MN/MN/$1,000.

Courage Center - MN (Golden Valley)/MN/$2,000.

Greater Minneapolis Crisis Nursery/MN/$1,000.

Lutheran Social Services - MN/MN/$1,000.

MN Historical Society - Verndale/MN/$100.

Salvation Army - MN/MN/$1,000.

Financial Information

Financial data for year ending: 12/31/2005
Foundation assets: $380,417
Grants paid: $60,350
Number of grants: 45
Largest/smallest: $3,100/$100

Application Information

Preferred form of initial contact: letter of inquiry; no specific form, information or material requirement.

Proposal deadlines: none.

Staff/Trustees

Directors/trustees: Kristin Richard Armstrong; Joseph Brazas; Karen S. Brazas; Aune E. Lind; Carl V. Lind, chair; Dennis A. Lind, president; Jeanne M. Lind; David Richard; Ethel A. Richard.

The Charles A. and Anne Morrow Lindbergh Foundation

2150 Third Avenue North
Suite 310
Anoka, MN 55303-2200
County: Anoka
Phone: (763) 576-1596
Fax: (763) 576-1664
E-mail: info@lindberghfoundation.org
Website: www.lindberghfoundation.org
Contact: Shelley Nehl, grants administrator
Established: 01/01/1977
Paid Staff: Yes
Funder type: Community/public foundation

Program Description

Program's purpose: The Lindbergh Foundation supports research or educational projects that address technological solutions to improve our environment for a sustainable future, balancing the advancement of technology with the preservation of the human/natural environment.

Funding priorities: We have 14 funding categories that are considered: aviation, conservation of plant, conservation of animal, conservation of water, agriculture, health, adaptive technology, biomedical engineering, intercultural communications, education, waste management, general conservation, arts and exploration.

Program limitations/restrictions: The work must exhibit a balance of technological advancements with the preservation of the environment. We do not fund overhead expenses.

Geographic focus: National areas, international areas.

Areas of interest:

ANIMAL RELATED: Wildlife preservation/protection, Conservation of animal resources.

ARTS, CULTURE, HUMANITIES: Humanities.

EDUCATION: Intercultural communication.

ENVIRONMENTAL QUALITY/PROTECTION/BEAUTIFICATION: Natural resources conservation/protection, Conservation of plant, water and land, air, energy, etc., Waste minimization and management.

FOOD/NUTRITION/AGRICULTURE: Agricultural programs.

HEALTH - DISEASES/MEDICAL DISCIPLINES: Biomedical research, Health & population sciences.

HEALTH - GENERAL/REHABILITATIVE: Adaptive technology.

HEALTH - RESEARCH.

SCIENCE/TECHNOLOGY: Biological/life science, Physical sciences/earth sciences.

Intended beneficiaries: Adults, General public/unspecified.

Types of support for organizations: Research.

Types of support for individuals: research.

Financial Information

Financial data for year ending: 12/31/2006
Foundation assets: $1,681,844
Grants paid: $125,808
Number of grants: 12
Largest/smallest: $10,580/$10,000

Application Information

Preferred form of initial contact: request for guidelines, complete proposal, e-mail.

Public information available by request: application form, annual report, newsletter, website.

Proposal deadlines: Second Thursday of June.

Contribution decisions made by: board of directors/trustees, grants committee of the board.

Frequency of contributions decisions: annually.

Specific times board meets: March, May, October.

Typical time from application deadlines to notification: 9-10 months.

Staff/Trustees

Staff: Shelley Nehl, grants administrator; Kelley Welf, communications manager.

Directors/trustees: J. D. Anding; Daniel Bennett; John Knox Bridges, president and CEO; Clare Hallward, vice chairman, grants program; Greg Herrick; John King; Martha King, secretary; Erik R. Lindbergh, chairman; Kristina Lindbergh; Lars Lindbergh; Reeve Lindbergh, honorary chairman; Wendy R. Lindbergh; Gregg Maryniak; Miles O'Brien; John L. Petersen; Judith A. Schiff; Daniel E. Stoltz, treasurer; David E. Treinis, vice chairman, award selection program; Steven R. Whitley.

James G. Lindell Irrevocable Charitable Trust

U.S. Bank, N.A.
101 East 5th Street, 14th Floor
St Paul, MN 55101-1860
County: Ramsey
Phone: (651) 466-8738
Contact: Gary Westeen
Established: 12/19/1991
Funder type: Private foundation

Program Description

Program's purpose: Grants for educational and other charitable purposes.

Geographic focus: Twin Cities Metropolitan Area, areas outside Minnesota.

Areas of interest:
EDUCATION.
HEALTH - DISEASES/MEDICAL DISCIPLINES.
RELIGION/SPIRITUAL DEVELOPMENT.

Intended beneficiaries: General public/unspecified.

Types of support for organizations:
GENERAL PURPOSE/OPERATING SUPPORT.
PROGRAM DEVELOPMENT/ PROJECT SUPPORT.

Sample grants:

Alzheimer's Association - MN (Minneapolis)/MN/general operating/ $2,000.

Center for the Visually Impaired/Atlanta, GA/Begin and Stars programs/$5,000.

Dodge Nature Center, Thomas Irvine/St Paul, MN/general operating/$1,500.

Hazelden Foundation/MN/youth recovery program/$4,000.

New Life Academy/MN/general operating/$2,000.

Northern Pines Methodist Camp/Park Rapids, MN/general operating/$2,500.

Peace Lutheran Church - MN (Inver Grove Heights)/MN/general operating/ $3,000.

Woodbury United Methodist Church/MN/ general operating/$2,500.

Financial Information

Financial data for year ending: 10/31/2005
Foundation assets: $591,396
Grants paid: $26,500
Number of grants: 9
Largest/smallest: $5,000/$1,500

Application Information

Preferred form of initial contact: letter of inquiry; submit organization's determination letter.

Proposal deadlines: none.

Staff/Trustees

Directors/trustees: U.S. Bank, N.A.

Longview Foundation

601 Carlson Parkway
Suite 800
Attn: Jon Crow
Minnetonka, MN 55343
County: Hennepin
Phone: (952) 835-2577
Contact: Carol Fetzer, secretary
Established: 12/19/1999
Funder type: Private foundation
fka: Lydiard Foundation

Program Description

Geographic focus: Twin Cities Metropolitan Area, areas outside Minnesota.

Intended beneficiaries: General public/unspecified.

Sample grants:

Carleton College/MN/$6,000.

Greater Minneapolis Crisis Nursery/MN/ $600.

Minnetonka Center for the Arts/MN/ $5,100.

MN Historical Society/MN/$51,000.

MN Landscape Arboretum Foundation/ MN/$2,750.

MN Orchestral Association/MN/$2,600.

MN Zoo Foundation/MN/$500.

Walker Art Center/MN/$1,750.

Financial Information

Financial data for year ending: 12/31/2005
Foundation assets: $352,941
Grants paid: $171,042
Number of grants: 75
Largest/smallest: $65,050/$20

Application Information

Preferred form of initial contact: letter of inquiry, no standard form requirement.

Proposal deadlines: none.

Staff/Trustees

Staff: Carol Fetzer, secretary.

Directors/trustees: David P. Crosby, treasurer; Ella P. Crosby, president; Thomas M. Crosby Jr., vice president; Lucy C. Mitchell, vice president.

Russell T. Lund Charitable Trust

U.S. Bank
101 East Fifth Street
St Paul, MN 55101
County: Ramsey
Phone: (651) 466-8744
Contact: Ted Olsen
Established: 12/01/1950
Funder type: Private foundation

Program Description

Program's purpose: Religious, charitable, scientific, literary or educational purposes.

Geographic focus: Twin Cities Metropolitan Area, Greater Minnesota, Minnesota statewide, Areas outside Minnesota.

Geographic limitations: Within the United States.

Areas of interest:
ARTS, CULTURE, HUMANITIES: Media/communications, Museums, Performing arts.
EDUCATION.
HEALTH - DISEASES/MEDICAL DISCIPLINES: Cancer.
HUMAN SERVICES: Children/youth services, Emergency assistance (food/clothing/cash), Family services, Multipurpose human service organizations.
YOUTH DEVELOPMENT: Multipurpose youth centers/clubs.

Intended beneficiaries: Children and youth (infants-19 years), General public/unspecified.

Types of support for organizations:
GENERAL PURPOSE/OPERATING SUPPORT.

Sample grants:

Arthritis Foundation - MN/MN/general operating/$10,000.

Boys & Girls Club - MN (Minneapolis)/ MN/general operating/$9,250.

Children's Cancer Research Fund - MN/ MN/general operating/$3,000.

Friends of FANA MN/MN/general operating/$500.

Gustavus Adolphus College - MN/MN/ general operating/$60,000.

Ordway - Circle of Stars/MN/general operating/$4,500.

The Science Museum of MN/MN/ general operating/$1,000.

Youth Performance Company/MN/ general operating/$2,500.

Financial Information

Financial data for year ending: 12/31/2005
Foundation assets: $760,839
Grants paid: $117,576
Number of grants: 29
Largest/smallest: $60,000/$300

Application Information

Preferred form of initial contact: letter of inquiry.

Proposal deadlines: none.

Preferred time for receiving proposals: applications may be submitted at any time.

Staff/Trustees

Directors/trustees: U.S. Bank Trust, N.A.; Russell T. Lund III.

The Luther Family Foundation

701 Xenia Avenue South
Suite 220
Golden Valley, MN 55416-1029
County: Hennepin
Phone: (763) 593-5755
Contact: Charles D. Luther
Established: 12/05/1994
Funder type: Private foundation

Program Description

Program's purpose: Organized and operated exclusively for religious, charitable, scientific, literary and educational purposes for fostering of national and international amateur sports competitions (other than providing athletic facilities or equipment) and for the purpose of preventing cruelty to children.

Geographic focus: Twin Cities Metropolitan Area, Areas outside Minnesota.

Areas of interest:
ARTS, CULTURE, HUMANITIES.
EDUCATION.
HEALTH - GENERAL/
REHABILITATIVE.

HUMAN SERVICES: Children/youth services, Family services, Family violence shelters and services.
RECREATION: Amateur sports competitions.
YOUTH DEVELOPMENT.

Intended beneficiaries: Children and youth (infants-19 years), General public/unspecified.

Types of support for organizations:
GENERAL PURPOSE/OPERATING SUPPORT.

Sample grants:
Abbott Northwestern Hospital/MN/ $1,005,720.
Children's Cancer Research Fund - MN/ MN/$3,000.
Children's Home - MN (St Cloud)/MN/ $8,000.
HEART (Help Enable Alcoholics Receive Treatment)/MN/$6,000.
Hospitality House Boys & Girls Clubs - MN/MN/Youth Directions/$3,000.
Risen Christ Catholic School/ Minneapolis, MN/$2,000.
Salvation Army - MN/MN/$3,500.
Twin Cities Public Television/St Paul, MN/$2,500.

Financial Information

Financial data for year ending: 12/31/2005
Foundation assets: $7,192,632
Grants paid: $97,525
Number of grants: 18
Largest/smallest: $15,000/$500

Application Information

Preferred form of initial contact: letter of inquiry; requests for contributions should contain a brief description of the applicant and proposed use of funds.

Proposal deadlines: none.

Staff/Trustees

Directors/trustees: Charles D. Luther; Rudy D. Luther.

Luverne Area Community Foundation

PO Box 623
Luverne, MN 56156
County: Rock
Phone: (507) 220-2424
E-mail: vandykem@sanfordhealth.org
Website: www.luvacf.org
Funder type: Community/public foundation

Program Description

Program's purpose: LACF will be a leader in enhancing the community by focusing on programs and services that build long-term solutions to meet the current and future needs in the Luverne community area.

Funding priorities: Each year, the Luverne Area Community Foundation invites applications that will enhance the quality of life in the following areas: Arts & Humanities, Community & Civic Affairs, Social & Economic Growth, Environment and Youth.

Geographic focus: Luverne Area community only.

Geographic limitations: Luverne Area community only.

Areas of interest:
ARTS, CULTURE, HUMANITIES.
COMMUNITY IMPROVEMENT.
EMPLOYMENT/JOBS.
ENVIRONMENTAL QUALITY/PROTECTION/BEAUTIFICATION.
HEALTH - DISEASES/MEDICAL DISCIPLINES.
HEALTH - GENERAL/
REHABILITATIVE.
HEALTH - MENTAL HEALTH/CRISIS INTERVENTION.
HEALTH - RESEARCH.
HUMAN SERVICES.
PHILANTHROPY/VOLUNTARISM.
PUBLIC AFFAIRS/SOCIETY BENEFIT.
PUBLIC SAFETY/DISASTERS/
RELIEF.
RECREATION.
SCIENCE/TECHNOLOGY.
SOCIAL SCIENCES.
YOUTH DEVELOPMENT.

Financial Information

Financial data for year ending: 12/31/2005
Grants paid: $366,619

Application Information

Public information available by request: application form, website.

Staff/Trustees

Staff: Michele Van Dyke, executive director.

The M.B. Foundation

8400 Normandale Lake Boulevard
Suite 920
Bloomington, MN 55437
County: Hennepin
Phone: (952) 921-3994
Fax: (952) 833-1358
Contact: H.M. Baskerville Jr., chair
Established: 12/27/1996
Donor: H.B. Baskerville Jr.
Funder type: Private foundation

Program Description

Program's purpose: Community betterment by individual and family education, training and programs.

Funding priorities: Primarily youth development.

Program limitations/restrictions: Give only to organizations that are exempt from federal income taxation under IRC 501(a) by virtue of being described in IRC 501(c)(3) or to organizations to which contributions are deductible under IRC 170(c)(2), 2055(a) and 2522(a).

Geographic focus: Twin Cities Metropolitan Area, Greater Minnesota, Areas outside Minnesota.

Areas of interest:
EDUCATION.
HEALTH - DISEASES/MEDICAL DISCIPLINES.
YOUTH DEVELOPMENT.

Types of support for organizations:
GENERAL PURPOSE/OPERATING SUPPORT: Annual campaigns.

Sample grants:
Boy Scouts of America - MN (Viking - Minneapolis)/MN/annual sustaining/$500.
Brain Injury Association - MN/MN/general operating/$500.
Lake Minnetonka Sailing School/MN/general operating/$3,200.
Minneapolis Rotary Community Service Foundation/MN/general operating/$200.
Palm Springs Air Museum/Palm Springs, CA/general operating/$10,500.
Parkinson's Resource Organization/Palm Desert, CA/general operating/$500.
Shattuck-St Mary's School/Faribault, MN/general operating/$41,800.
Summit Academy OIC/MN/general operating/$1,000.

Financial Information

Financial data for year ending: 12/31/2005
Foundation assets: $1,467,202
Grants paid: $43,821
Number of grants: 9
Largest/smallest: $41,800/$200

Staff/Trustees

Directors/trustees: H.M. Baskerville Jr., chair.

Macy's North

700 Nicollet Mall
MS-859
Minneapolis, MN 55402
County: Hennepin
E-mail: macys.gives@macys.com
Website: www.macys.com
Funder type: Corporate giving program

Program Description

Program's purpose: Macy's believes in giving back to the communities where we live and work. Macy's Gives, the community giving program at Macy's North, supports this commitment by engaging in charitable giving and employee volunteerism at the local level. Macy's Community Grants provide the opportunity for each Macy's North store to partner with local nonprofit organizations in the immediate community by providing programming funding, volunteers and additional fundraising opportunities throughout the year.

Funding priorities: Building on a 150-year history of community giving, Macy's Gives supports local causes in the areas of arts and culture, childhood education and women's health, with a special emphasis on diversity across all areas.

Program limitations/restrictions: Macy's North grants will not be awarded for purposes of general operating costs including salaries; verbal requests for support or requests with incomplete documentation; projects outside of our focus areas; individuals; private foundations; fraternal organizations; programs located outside of Macy's North communities; endowment funds or capital campaigns; advocacy groups; charities with a primarily international focus or operation; conferences, trips or tours; places of worship devoted solely to religious instruction (church/synagogue); athletic teams or events; fundraisers or gala events; multi-year requests (grants must be reviewed on an annual basis); politically or socially controversial projects; fiscal agents and other "umbrella" organizations that provide funding to nonprofits.

Geographic limitations: Nonprofits located in the Minneapolis, Detroit and Chicago metro areas may apply, as well as those located in the following Macy's North communities: Joliet, Rockford, IL; Merrillville, IN; Ann Arbor, Flint, Grand Rapids, Grandville, Kalamazoo/Battle Creek, Lansing, Port Huron, Saginaw, Traverse City, MI; Rochester, St Cloud, MN; Fargo, Grand Forks, ND; Toledo, OH; Sioux Falls, SD; Appleton/Fox River Valley, Eau Claire, La Crosse, Madison, Milwaukee, WI.

Areas of interest:
ARTS, CULTURE, HUMANITIES.
EDUCATION: Childhood education.
HEALTH - GENERAL/REHABILITATIVE: Women's health.

Intended beneficiaries: Children and youth (infants-19 years), Ethnic/racial populations - general, Females - all ages or age unspecified, General public/unspecified.

Financial Information

Financial data for year ending: 01/31/2007
Grants paid: $950,000

Application Information

Preferred form of initial contact: e-mail, application.

Public information available by request: proposal guidelines, application form, website.

Staff/Trustees

Staff: Tim Showalter-Loch, community relations manager.

Mall of America Foundation for Youth

Simon MOA Management Co. Inc.
60 East Broadway
Bloomington, MN 55425-5550
County: Hennepin
Phone: (952) 883-8845
Fax: (952) 883-8801
Website: www.mallofamerica.com/adults_moa_foundation_youth.aspx
Paid Staff: Yes
Funder type: Corporate foundation

Program Description

Program's purpose: The Mall of America Foundation for Youth (MOAFY) supports local programs which promote self-development, well-being and education of youth, their families and their communities.

Funding priorities: Each year the foundation awards college scholarships to Twin Cities high school seniors. MOAFY also awards grants to organizations that support area youth.

Geographic focus: Twin Cities Metropolitan Area.

Areas of interest:
EDUCATION: Higher education.
YOUTH DEVELOPMENT.

Intended beneficiaries: Children and youth (infants-19 years).

Types of support for organizations:
PROGRAM DEVELOPMENT/PROJECT SUPPORT.
STUDENT AID (GRANTS TO INSTITUTIONS): Scholarship funds.

Sample grants:

Ascension Place/MN/$2,000.

Augsburg College/MN/scholarship/$2,000.

Bridging, Inc/MN/$5,000.

Hamline University/MN/scholarship/$3,000.

Minneapolis Community & Technical College/MN/scholarship/$3,000.

Normandale Community College/MN/scholarship/$1,000.

PACER Center/ MN/$2,500.

Streetworks/Minneapolis, MN/$10,000.

Financial Information

Financial data for year ending: 04/30/2006
Foundation assets: $37,368
Grants paid: $100,000
Number of grants: 24
Largest/smallest: $10,000/$500

Staff/Trustees

Staff: Casey Feigh, community relations coordinator.

Directors/trustees: Maureen Bausch, treasurer; John Wheeler, chairman.

Mankato Area Foundation

PO Box 999
122 Riverfront Drive
Mankato, MN 56002-0999
County: Blue Earth
Phone: (507) 345-4519
Fax: (507) 345-4551
E-mail: info@greatermankato.com
Website: www.mankatoareafoundation.com
Contact: Shelly Langworthy
Established: 01/01/1974
Funder type: Community/public foundation

Program Description

Program's purpose: The mission of the Mankato Area Foundation is to encourage and support projects that enrich the quality of life in the Mankato area.

Funding priorities: Education, culture, recreation, aesthetics, civic, capital projects and other projects that meet the needs of the community.

Program limitations/restrictions: Must be for or benefit the Mankato area.

Geographic focus: Greater Minnesota, Mankato area.

Geographic limitations: Within the geographic boundaries of Mankato School District #77.

Areas of interest:
ARTS, CULTURE, HUMANITIES.
COMMUNITY IMPROVEMENT.
EDUCATION.
PUBLIC AFFAIRS/SOCIETY BENEFIT.
RECREATION.

Intended beneficiaries: General public/unspecified.

Sample grants:

Leave a Legacy/MN/$6,664.

Mankato Area Sesquicentennial/MN/$93,904.

Mankato Ballet/MN/$5,000.

Mankato Symphony Orchestra Association/MN/ $1,659.

Mankato West High School/MN/Academic Decathlon/$8,269.

Martin Luther King Board/MN/$2,000.

MN Valley Chorale/MN/$500.

YMCA - MN (Mankato)/MN/Youth in Government/$370.

Financial Information

Financial data for year ending: 06/30/2005
Foundation assets: $2,518,349
Grants paid: $215,117
Number of grants: 19
Largest/smallest: $93,904/$370

Application Information

Public information available by request: proposal guidelines, application form, annual report, website.

Proposal deadlines: April 1 for events/projects beginning no earlier than June 1. October 1 for events/projects beginning no earlier than December 1.

Frequency of contributions decisions: semiannually.

Staff/Trustees

Staff: Janie Berndt.

Directors/trustees: John Brady; David Christensen; Tony Filipovitch; Curt Fisher; Andrew Foster; Anne Ganey; Michael Jacobs; Bob Kitchenmaster; Marcia Koepp; Erik Leagjeld; Troy Leiferman; Tom Lietha; Todd Loosbrock; Fred Lutz; Dave Schooff, president; Ann Splinter; Stacey Straka; Steve Suir; Dave Sunderman; Kathy Trauger.

Ted and Roberta Mann Foundation

19550 Cedarhurst
Wayzata, MN 55391-3010
County: Hennepin
Phone: (952) 475-2000
Fax: (952) 475-3153
E-mail: joanne@mannfoundation.com
Contact: Roberta L. Mann, president
Established: 10/21/2001
Funder type: Private foundation

Program Description

Program's purpose: The mission of the Ted and Roberta Mann Foundation is to keep alive the legacy established by Ted Mann, to be carried out through future generations by continuing the Mann family tradition of making a positive difference.

Funding priorities: The ongoing mission of the foundation is to make a difference principally in the areas of the Arts, Education, Health, Religion, and Social Services.

Geographic focus: Twin Cities Metropolitan Area, Select areas outside Minnesota.

Areas of interest:

ARTS, CULTURE, HUMANITIES: Arts/cultural multipurpose, Visual arts, Art, Music and Drama.

EDUCATION: Higher education, Learning disabilities.

HEALTH - DISEASES/MEDICAL DISCIPLINES: Other.

HEALTH - GENERAL/REHABILITATIVE: Integrative medicine.

HEALTH - MENTAL HEALTH/CRISIS INTERVENTION.

HUMAN SERVICES: Community Services, Programs working toward self-sufficiency.

RELIGION/SPIRITUAL DEVELOPMENT: Christian, Jewish.

YOUTH DEVELOPMENT.

Types of support for individuals: scholarships.

Sample grants:

Greater Minneapolis Crisis Nursery/MN/ $3,000.

Heart Institute Foundation - MN (Minneapolis)/MN/$5,000.

Menninger Foundation/KS/$1,000.

St Mary's University - MN/MN/$10,000.

Financial Information

Financial data for year ending: 12/31/2006
Foundation assets: $47,224,899
Grants paid: $2,046,966
Largest/smallest: $200,000/$1,000

Application Information

Preferred form of initial contact: letter of inquiry, telephone inquiry.

Public information available by request: proposal guidelines, application form.

Accept common grant application: yes.

Accept common report form: yes.

Contribution decisions made by: CEO, board of directors/trustees.

Frequency of contributions decisions: monthly.

Staff/Trustees

Directors/trustees: Margaret M. Adams; Donald E. Benson, vice president; Blythe A. Brenden, secretary; John T. Brenden, vice president; Thomas M. Crosby Jr.; Roberta L. Mann, president; Michael F. Sullivan.

Marbrook Foundation

1300 U.S. Trust Building
730 Second Avenue South
Minneapolis, MN 55402
County: Hennepin
Phone: (612) 752-1783
Fax: (512) 752-1780
E-mail: jhara@marbrookfoundation.org
Website: www.marbrookfoundation.org
Contact: Julie Hara, executive director
Established: 11/01/1948
Paid Staff: Yes
Funder type: Private foundation

Program Description

Program's purpose: To promote broad philanthropic objectives through grants and investments in the areas of the environment, education, mind and spirit, the arts, social empowerment and health.

Funding priorities: Programmatic funding priorities are (in order of priority): environment, education, mind and spirit, arts, social empowerment, health.

Program limitations/restrictions: Generally does not give to individuals, political organizations, start-up organizations, recreational programs, to retire debt or cover operating losses, memorials, fundraising dinners, testimonials, national ceremonies and conferences or other similar events. Also, does not usually give to specific disease organizations, the elderly, diabetes, domestic abuse, programs serving the physically or mentally disabled.

Geographic focus: Twin Cities Metropolitan Area.

Geographic limitations: Generally restricted to Minneapolis-St Paul area.

Areas of interest:

ARTS, CULTURE, HUMANITIES: Arts services, Arts/cultural multipurpose, Historical societies, Museums, Performing arts, Visual arts.

COMMUNITY IMPROVEMENT: Community/neighborhood development/improvement, Economic development, Nonprofit management.

EDUCATION: Higher education, Preschool/elementary, Secondary, Vocational/technical.

EMPLOYMENT/JOBS: Employment procurement/job training.

ENVIRONMENTAL QUALITY/ PROTECTION/BEAUTIFICATION: Environmental beautification/open spaces, Environmental education/outdoor survival, Natural resources conservation/protection.

HEALTH - GENERAL/REHABILITATIVE: Health support services, Wellness education.

HOUSING/SHELTER: Housing development/construction/management, Housing support services.

HUMAN SERVICES: Children/youth services, Family services, Multipurpose human service organizations.

RELIGION/SPIRITUAL DEVELOPMENT: Mind and Spirit.

Intended beneficiaries: General public/unspecified.

Types of support for organizations:

CAPITAL CAMPAIGNS.

GENERAL PURPOSE/OPERATING SUPPORT.

PROGRAM DEVELOPMENT/ PROJECT SUPPORT.

STUDENT AID (GRANTS TO INSTITUTIONS).

Types of support for individuals: none.

Exclusions: Individuals, Non-501(c)(3), Political organizations.

Sample grants:

The Children's Theatre Company,/MN/ capital campaign/$50,000.

Common Ground Meditation Center/ MN/capital campaign/$10,000.

Eco Education/St Paul, MN/Urban Environmental Education Initiative/ $6,000.

Friends of the Minneapolis Public Library/MN/capital campaign/$50,000.

Friends of the Mississippi River/MN/ general operating support/$6,000.

Lao Family Community of MN/MN/ English education program/$5,000.

Project for Pride in Living/MN/general operating support/$7,500.

United Theological Seminary of the Twin Cities/MN/general operating support/ $5,000.

Financial Information

Financial data for year ending: 12/31/2006
Foundation assets: $16,687,019
Grants paid: $798,500
Number of grants: 118
Largest/smallest: $97,000/$200
Typical grant amount: $5,000

Application Information

Preferred form of initial contact: letter of inquiry, telephone inquiry, complete proposal; review website before inquiry.

Public information available by request: proposal guidelines, annual report, website.

Accept common grant application: yes.

Proposal deadlines: generally June 1 and December 1.

Contribution decisions made by: staff, board of directors/trustees.

Frequency of contributions decisions: semiannually.

Specific times board meets: June and December.

Typical time from application deadlines to notification: 1 week after board meeting.

Staff/Trustees

Staff: Julie Hara, executive director.

Directors/trustees: Conley Brooks Jr., chair; Conley Brooks; Markell Brooks; Stephen B. Brooks; Markell Kiefer; Katherine M. Leighton; Julie B. Zelle.

Mardag Foundation

55 Fifth Street East
Suite 600
St Paul, MN 55101-1797
County: Ramsey
Phone: (651) 224-5463
Fax: (651) 224-8123
E-mail: inbox@mardag.org
Website: www.mardag.org
Contact: John G. Couchman, administrative director
Established: 05/01/1969
Donor: Agnes E. Ober
Funder type: Private foundation

Program Description

Program's purpose: The Mardag Foundation is committed to making grants to nonprofit organizations and public entities located within and serving residents of the State of Minnesota. The foundation will consider grant applications for capital projects, program expansion and special projects of a time-limited nature; start-up costs for promising new programs that demonstrate sound management and clear goals relevant to community needs; support for established agencies that have temporary or transitional needs; and funds to match contributions received from other sources or to provide a challenge to raise new contributions.

Funding priorities: The primary focus of our grantmaking is on improving the lives of at-risk families and children, supporting seniors to live independently, promoting arts and humanities, addressing human service needs of at-risk populations, and supporting community development throughout St Paul.

Program limitations/restrictions: The foundation will not consider grant applications for scholarships and grants to individuals; ongoing annual operating expenses; sectarian religious programs; medical research; federated campaigns; conservation or environmental programs; events and conferences; programs serving the physically, developmentally or mentally disabled; capital campaigns of private secondary schools; capital and endowment campaigns of private colleges and universities. The Mardag Foundation does not make grants through fiscal agents.

Geographic focus: East metro area of Ramsey, Washington and Dakota counties, as well as Greater Minnesota.

Geographic limitations: The foundation will not consider grant applications for programs serving Minneapolis and the surrounding west metro area.

Areas of interest:

ARTS, CULTURE, HUMANITIES.

COMMUNITY IMPROVEMENT: Community/neighborhood development/improvement.

EDUCATION: Pre-school/elementary, Secondary, Vocational/technical.

HUMAN SERVICES: Senior centers and services.

YOUTH DEVELOPMENT.

Intended beneficiaries: Types of support for organizations:

CAPITAL CAMPAIGNS.

PROGRAM DEVELOPMENT/ PROJECT SUPPORT.

Types of support for individuals: none.

Exclusions: Individuals, Non-501(c)(3), Political organizations, Research, Scholarships/loans, 509(a)(3) Type III non-functionally integrated organizations.

Sample grants:

Barnesville Child Care Center/MN/For the 2006 Building Project/$35,000.

Big Brothers/Big Sisters - MN (Greater Twin Cities)/MN/To help finance the budget of the Big Families Program/ $40,000.

Children's Law Center - MN/MN/To help finance the budget of the Guardianship Pilot Project in Ramsey County/$15,000.

First Witness Child Abuse Resource Center/Duluth, MN/To help finance the budget to expand services to victims of child physical abuse and severe neglect/ $20,000.

History Theatre/MN/To help finance the position of Director of Individual Giving/ $50,000.

Metropolitan Area Agency on Aging/ MN/To help finance the budget of the Sustaining Minority Elders in their Communities Project/$20,000.

Minnesota Senior Federation/MN/To help finance the budget for building statewide effectiveness and capacity/$30,000.

Northwoods Interfaith Volunteer Caregivers Program/MN/To help finance the budget of the Senior Care Outreach and Coordination Project/$20,000.

Financial Information

Financial data for year ending: 12/31/2006
Foundation assets: $60,134,724
Grants paid: $2,537,655
Number of grants: 96
Largest/smallest: $100,000/$500

Application Information

Preferred form of initial contact: request for guidelines.

Public information available by request: proposal guidelines, application form, annual report, website.

Proposal deadlines: For April grantmaking meeting, postmarked by December 31; for August grantmaking meeting, postmarked by May 1; for November grantmaking meeting, postmarked by August 1.

Preferred time for receiving proposals: Full proposals must be received by the following dates to be considered for a grant: December 31, May 1, August 1. Applications that are not received in time for a grantmaking meeting are carried forward to the next one.

Contribution decisions made by: board of directors/trustees.

Specific times board meets: April, August, November.

Typical time from application deadlines to notification: 4-5 months.

Staff/Trustees

Staff: John G. Couchman, administrative director; Jack H. Pohl, finance director.

Directors/trustees: Janice K. Angell; Gretchen D. Davidson; Cornelia Ober Eberhart; Phyllis Rawls Goff; James R. Heltzer; Gayle M. Ober, vice president; Richard B. Ober, treasurer; Timothy M. Ober, president; Wilhelmina M. Wright, secretary.

Marquette Financial Companies Community Support Program

60 South Sixth Street
Suite 3900
Minneapolis, MN 55402
County: Hennepin
Phone: (612) 661-3903
Fax: (612) 661-3715
E-mail: rpeterson@pohladfamilygiving.org
Website: www.marquette.com/giving
Established: 01/01/1999
Funder type: Corporate giving program

Program Description

Program's purpose: Marquette dedicates 5% of pre-tax profits to support nonprofits and community involvement programs. Community support is provided through employee-led regional grantmaking, corporate and operating business giving programs, and in support of employee interests.

Funding priorities: Affordable housing, community economic development, financial literacy, and human services where basic needs are addressed.

Geographic focus: Twin Cities Metropolitan Area; Chicago, IL; Phoenix, AZ; Inland Empire, CA; Dallas, Houston, Fort Worth, TX.

Areas of interest:

COMMUNITY IMPROVEMENT: Economic development, Financial literacy.

HOUSING/SHELTER: Affordable housing.

HUMAN SERVICES: Direct service, Basic needs.

Types of support for organizations:

GENERAL PURPOSE/OPERATING SUPPORT.

PROGRAM DEVELOPMENT/PROJECT SUPPORT: limited project support available.

Sample grants:

Arizona Saves/AZ/General operating/$7,500.

BestPrep/MN/General operating/$15,000.

Food Bank - TX/TX/North Texas Food Bank of Dallas/General operating/$10,000.

Greater Chicago Food Depository/IL/General operating/$15,000.

MN Housing Partnership/MN/General operating/$3,000.

Texas Low Income Housing Information Services/TX/General operating/$15,000.

Financial Information

Financial data for year ending: 12/31/2006
Grants paid: $1,713,000
Number of grants: 123
Largest/smallest: $75,000/$100

Application Information

Preferred form of initial contact: Review guidelines posted on www.marquette.com/giving. Submit proposal if work aligns with giving priorities. Decisions based on community impact, and demonstration of strong financial and management practices.

Public information available by request: Guidelines and application form posted on website.

Proposal deadlines: March 15 and August 15, 2007.

Contribution decisions made by: employee committee.

Staff/Trustees

Staff: Terry Egge, senior program officer; Marina Muñoz Lyon, vice president; Rose Peterson, grants manager.

Martinson Clinic Foundation

317 East Wayzata Boulevard
Wayzata, MN 55391
County: Hennepin
Phone: (952) 471-9019
Contact: Elmer Martinson, president
Established: 09/08/1958
Funder type: Private foundation

Program Description

Program's purpose: Carry on medical educational activities, promote and carry on scientific research, participate in promoting general health of community.

Funding priorities: Field of medicine.

Program limitations/restrictions: Awards are made in the field of medicine.

Geographic focus: Areas outside Minnesota, Minnetonka area.

Areas of interest:
HEALTH - DISEASES/MEDICAL DISCIPLINES.
HEALTH - GENERAL/REHABILITATIVE: Preventative medicine, Healthful living.

Intended beneficiaries: General public/unspecified.

Types of support for organizations:
CAPITAL CAMPAIGNS: Equipment.
GENERAL PURPOSE/OPERATING SUPPORT.
RESEARCH.

Sample grants:
Hammer Residences Inc/MN/group home assistance/$3,000.
Interfaith Outreach & Community Partners/MN/charity medical clinic assistance/$3,000.
Loma Linda University/CA/education, expanding, providing health care globally/$30,000.
St David's Child Development & Family Services/MN/$2,500.

Financial Information

Financial data for year ending: 09/30/2005
Foundation assets: $782,173
Grants paid: $39,500
Number of grants: 6
Largest/smallest: $15,000/$3,000

Application Information

Preferred form of initial contact: request for guidelines.

Proposal deadlines: August 1.

Staff/Trustees

Directors/trustees: Wyman Haberer; Bruce Martinson; Elmer Martinson, president; Tom Martinson; John B. McKellip.

The Martinson Foundation

239 North Miles
Farmers & Merchants State Bank
Appleton, MN 56208
County: Swift
Phone: (320) 289-1454
Contact: Leonard Massee, secretary & treasurer
Established: 04/23/1983
Funder type: Private foundation

Program Description

Program's purpose: General charitable purposes.

Geographic limitations: Appleton, Minnesota area.

Areas of interest:
ARTS, CULTURE, HUMANITIES: Historical societies, Media/communications.
COMMUNITY IMPROVEMENT: Community coalitions, Community/neighborhood development/improvement.
EDUCATION: Libraries/library science, Pre-school/elementary, Secondary.
HEALTH - GENERAL/REHABILITATIVE.
HUMAN SERVICES.
PUBLIC AFFAIRS/SOCIETY BENEFIT.
RELIGION/SPIRITUAL DEVELOPMENT.
YOUTH DEVELOPMENT: Multipurpose youth centers/clubs, Scouting organizations, Youth development programs.

Intended beneficiaries: Children and youth (infants-19 years), General public/unspecified.

Types of support for organizations:
GENERAL PURPOSE/OPERATING SUPPORT: Annual campaigns.
PROGRAM DEVELOPMENT/PROJECT SUPPORT.
STUDENT AID (GRANTS TO INSTITUTIONS).

Sample grants:
Appleton Hospital/MN/general operating/$5,000.
Appleton Library Foundation/WI/general operating/$2,000.
Boy Scouts of America - MN (Appleton)/MN/general operating/$1,000.
Camp Buckskin/MN/general operating/$1,000.
Chamber of Commerce - MN (Appleton)/MN/Applefest/$1,200.
Girl Scout Council - MN (Appleton)/MN/general operating/$1,000.
MN Historical Society - Swift County/MN/marker/$1,500.
Pioneer Public Television - MN/MN/general fund/$4,500.

Financial Information

Financial data for year ending: 11/30/2006
Foundation assets: $1,077,021
Grants paid: $48,682
Number of grants: 37
Largest/smallest: $5,000/$250

Application Information

Preferred form of initial contact: complete proposal; applications should be in letter form and should provide information on the applicant's charitable proposal and funding requirements.

Proposal deadlines: none.

Staff/Trustees

Directors/trustees: Leonard Massee, secretary & treasurer; H. Rudy Ronning, president.

Mayo Clinic

200 First Street SW
Rochester, MN 55905
County: Olmsted
Phone: (507) 284-5549
Website: www.mayo.edu
Funder type: Corporate giving program

Program Description

Program's purpose: Mayo Clinic's community value-driven contributions are based on the following cornerstone strategies: to be a responsible corporate citizen; to support programs providing a needed community service; to support programs that make the community a better place to live and work; to support broad-based programs.

Funding priorities: Mayo Clinic's community contributions are value-driven and focus on such topics as diversity, housing, education/workforce development, youth (especially at-risk youth). The community contribution program supports the core principle of social commitment and ensures that Mayo Clinic contributes a fair share as a responsible member of the community.

Areas of interest:

ARTS, CULTURE, HUMANITIES: Arts/cultural multipurpose, Humanities, Museums, Performing arts, Visual arts.

COMMUNITY IMPROVEMENT: Community/neighborhood development/improvement, Economic development, Nonprofit management, Volunteer bureaus.

EDUCATION: Educational services, Higher education, Libraries/library science, Pre-school/elementary, Secondary.

HEALTH - DISEASES/MEDICAL DISCIPLINES: Cancer.

HEALTH - GENERAL/REHABILITATIVE: Health support services.

HEALTH - RESEARCH: Other.

HOUSING/SHELTER: Housing development/construction/management.

HUMAN SERVICES: Children/youth services, Emergency assistance (food/clothing/cash), Family services, Multipurpose human service organizations.

PUBLIC AFFAIRS/SOCIETY BENEFIT: Citizen participation, Leadership development/awards programs (other than youth), Public policy research and analysis, Telecommunications services.

RELIGION/SPIRITUAL DEVELOPMENT: Interfaith issues.

YOUTH DEVELOPMENT: Adult/child matching programs, Multipurpose youth centers/clubs, Scouting organizations, Youth development programs.

Intended beneficiaries: Adults, African Americans/Blacks, Asian/Pacific Islanders, Children and youth (infants-19 years), Disabled - general or unspecified disability, Ethnic/racial populations - general, Gay/lesbian/bisexual/transgender, Hispanics/Latinos, Homeless, Immigrants/newcomers/refugees, Native American/American Indians, Physically disabled, Poor/economically disadvantaged.

Types of support for organizations:

CAPITAL CAMPAIGNS: Building/renovation.

GENERAL PURPOSE/OPERATING SUPPORT.

Financial Information

Financial data for year ending: 12/31/2006
Grants paid: $1,800,000
Number of grants: 125
Largest/smallest: $250,000/$25
In-kind gifts: $304,994

Application Information

Preferred form of initial contact: letter of inquiry, complete proposal.
Will view video: yes.
Contribution decisions made by: employee committee.
Frequency of contributions decisions: monthly.
Typical time from application deadlines to notification: varies.

Staff/Trustees

Staff: Karel M. Weigel, administrator, community relations.

Directors/trustees: Michael L. Blute, M.D.; Richard Ehman, vice chair; Glenn S Forbes, chair; Sherine E. Gabriel, M.D.; Morrie A. Gertz, M.D.; David C. Herman, M.D.; Diane F. Jelinek, Ph.D.; Jeffrey O. Korsmo, secretary; John H. Noseworthy, vice chair; Teresa A. Rummans, M.D.; Nan B. Sawyer; Mark A. Warner, M.D.; Walter R. Wilson, M.D.

McGough Foundation

2737 North Fairview Avenue
St Paul, MN 55113
County: Ramsey
Phone: (651) 633-5050
Contact: Richard E. Opitz
Established: 12/05/1991
Funder type: Private foundation

Program Description

Program's purpose: General charitable purposes.

Funding priorities: Foundation hopes to provide assistance to Midwest-based organizations that are exempt under section 501(c)(3).

Geographic focus: Minnesota statewide, Midwest.

Geographic limitations: Midwest.

Intended beneficiaries: General public/unspecified.

Types of support for organizations:
GENERAL PURPOSE/OPERATING SUPPORT.

Sample grants:
Dominician Sisters of St Cecilia/MN/$50,000.
St John Vianney Seminary/MN/$5,000.

Financial Information

Financial data for year ending: 12/31/2005
Foundation assets: $3,050,412
Grants paid: $178,500
Number of grants: 7
Largest/smallest: $50,000/$1,000

Application Information

Preferred form of initial contact: complete proposal, no special form required.
Proposal deadlines: none.

Staff/Trustees

Directors/trustees: L.B. McGough; L.J. McGough, president; T.J. McGough; Richard E. Opitz.

The McKnight Foundation

710 South Second Street
Suite 400
Minneapolis, MN 55401
County: Hennepin
Phone: (612) 333-4220
Fax: (612) 332-3833
E-mail: info@mcknight.org
Website: www.mcknight.org
Established: 08/06/1953
Donor: William and Maude McKnight
Funder type: Private foundation

Program Description

Program's purpose: The McKnight Foundation, a Minnesota-based private philanthropic organization, seeks to improve the quality of life for present and future generations. Through grantmaking, coalition-building and encouragement of strategic policy reform, we use our resources to attend, unite and empower those we serve.

Funding priorities: We support efforts to strengthen communities, families and individuals, particularly those in need. We contribute to the arts, encourage preservation of our natural environment and promote research in selected fields. Please refer to individual program guidelines for specific funding priorities within each area of grantmaking.

Program limitations/restrictions: Work in the fields of mental health or disabilities; Chemical dependency treatment; Services for seniors; Health services or policy; Assistance for individuals, including scholarships; Attendance at or travel to conferences or costs related to conferences; Travel, except when related to other McKnight support of an organization; Scientific research outside established McKnight research programs; Endowments, except in rare cases; Activities that have a specific religious purpose.

Geographic focus: Twin Cities Metropolitan Area, Greater Minnesota, Minnesota statewide, International Areas.

Areas of interest:

ARTS, CULTURE, HUMANITIES: Arts services, Arts/cultural multipurpose, Media/communications, Museums, Performing arts, Visual arts.

COMMUNITY IMPROVEMENT: Community coalitions, Community/neighborhood development/improvement, Economic development.

ENVIRONMENTAL QUALITY/PROTECTION/BEAUTIFICATION: Environmental beautification/open spaces, Natural resources conservation/protection, Pollution abatement and control, Mississippi River Program.

FOOD/NUTRITION/AGRICULTURE: Soil and water conservation/farm land preservation, Crop Research Program.

HOUSING/SHELTER: Affordable housing development.

HUMAN SERVICES: Children/youth services, Multipurpose human service organizations, Family services to build parenting skills.

INTERNATIONAL AFFAIRS: International economic and community development.

YOUTH DEVELOPMENT: Youth development programs.

Intended beneficiaries: Adults, Children and youth (infants-19 years), Ethnic/racial populations - general, Females - all ages or age unspecified, Immigrants/newcomers/refugees, Males - all ages or age unspecified, Poor/economically disadvantaged, Single parents.

Types of support for organizations:

CAPITAL CAMPAIGNS: Building/renovation, Equipment.

GENERAL PURPOSE/OPERATING SUPPORT.

PROGRAM DEVELOPMENT/PROJECT SUPPORT.

Types of support for individuals: none.

Sample grants:

ACTS of St Paul/MN/For year-round academic enrichment programs for Hmong youth in St Paul/$30,000.

American Red Cross - MN (Minneapolis)/MN/For the Street Survival Program, which offers health and safety information and supplies to homeless youth/$20,000.

Ballet of the Dolls Inc/MN/For a professional dance theater company/$50,000.

Center for Independent Artists/MN/For an organization that provides resources and services to independent artists/$12,500.

Center for Rural Policy & Development/MN/To expand and enhance policy and research development efforts on salient issues facing rural MN/$125,000.

Child Care WORKS/MN/To help improve the quality and accessibility of early childcare in MN/$50,000.

East Side Neighborhood Development Company Inc/MN/To support a comprehensive approach to revitalizing St Paul's East Side neighborhood/$35,000.

Housing Preservation Project, Inc/MN/To conduct community case studies that will advance balanced growth and housing policies/$75,000.

Financial Information

Financial data for year ending: 12/31/2006
Foundation assets: $2,200,000,000
Grants paid: $93,482,513
Number of grants: 939
Largest/smallest: $6,225,000/$2,000

Application Information

Preferred form of initial contact: letter of inquiry.

Public information available by request: annual report, newsletter, website, funding guidelines.

Proposal deadlines: Africa: Jan. 1, Jul. 1; Children & Families: Feb. 15, May 15, Aug. 15, Nov. 15; Arts and Region & Communities: Jan. 15, Apr. 15, Jul. 15, Oct. 15; Youth Out-of-School Time: Feb. 1; Multiservice: May 1; Environment: Feb. 1, May 1, Aug. 1, Nov. 1; SE Asia: Jun. 1, Dec. 1.

Contribution decisions made by: board of directors/trustees.

Frequency of contributions decisions: quarterly.

Specific times board meets: Feb., May, Aug., Nov.

Typical time from application deadlines to notification: 4 months.

Staff/Trustees

Staff: Susan Baker, accounting assistant; Jeannine Balfour, program officer, children and families; Dan Bartholomay, program director, region and communities and international; Vickie Benson, program director, arts; Gretchen Bonfert, program director, environment; Kathy Bonnifield, program assistant, international; Bernadette Christiansen, vice president of human resources and administration; Neal Cuthbert, vice president of program; Stephanie Duffy, grants administration manager; Christine Ganzlin, program director, children and families; Jamie Hagerty, accountant; Tim Hanrahan, communications director; Jennifer Harshner, communications/administrative assistant; Sarah Hernandez, program officer, region and communities; Louis Hohlfeld, senior program officer, greater Minnesota; David Kennedy-Logan, communications production manager; Shawn Kinniry, operations manager; Kathryn Koenigsmark, executive assistant; Ron Kroese, program officer, environment; Brenda Krotzer, grants administration associate; Shannon Lee, program assistant, environment; Cosandra Lloyd, IT and program associate; Sarah Lovan, program assistant, arts; Tom Miller, program officer, children and families; Mariam Mohamed, program officer, children and families; Eric Muschler, program officer, region and communities; Kevin Overson, program assistant, children and families; Janet Peterson, grants administration assistant; Renee Richie, program assistant, region and communities; Kathleen Rysted, director of research programs; Karyn Sciortino, program associate, children and families; Richard J. Scott, vice president for finance and compliance; Therese Simmons, controller; Janine Steffens, receptionist/administrative assistant; Lori Todd, meeting and travel coordinator; Alla Vaynberg, accountant; Kate Wolford, president; Laura Zimmermann, program officer, arts.

Directors/trustees: Anne Binger; Ben Binger; Erika L. Binger, chair; James M. Binger; Patricia S. Binger; Peg Birk; Cynthia Binger Boynton; Meghan Binger Brown; Richard D. McFarland; Ted Staryk; Robert Struyk.

McNeely Foundation

444 Pine Street
St Paul, MN 55101-2453
County: Ramsey
Phone: (651) 228-4503
Fax: (651) 228-4506
E-mail: kreynolds@meritex.com
Contact: Karen Reynolds, foundation administrator
Established: 12/19/1980
Funder type: Private foundation

Program Description

Program's purpose: The McNeely Foundation makes grants in the areas of education, human services, the environment, the arts and community betterment.

Funding priorities: Community development, education programs, environmental education, human services.

Geographic focus: East Metropolitan Area/St Paul only, other.

Geographic limitations: The foundation has a special interest in funding projects that benefit the St Paul community, especially East Side St Paul neighborhoods.

Areas of interest:
ARTS, CULTURE, HUMANITIES: Arts/cultural multipurpose.
COMMUNITY IMPROVEMENT: Community/neighborhood development/improvement, Economic development.
EDUCATION: Educational services, Preschool/elementary, Secondary.
EMPLOYMENT/JOBS: Employment procurement/job training.
ENVIRONMENTAL QUALITY/PROTECTION/BEAUTIFICATION: Environmental education/outdoor survival, Natural resources conservation/protection.
HOUSING/SHELTER: Housing support services.
HUMAN SERVICES: Children/youth services, Family services, Multipurpose human service organizations.
YOUTH DEVELOPMENT: Youth development programs.

Intended beneficiaries: Children and youth (infants-19 years), No specified population groups, Youth/adolescents (ages 14-19).

Types of support for organizations:
PROGRAM DEVELOPMENT/PROJECT SUPPORT: Curriculum development, Mentoring programs.

Types of support for individuals: none.

Exclusions: Individuals, Non-501(c)(3), Political organizations, Tax-supported institutions.

Sample grants:

American Indian Family Center - MN/MN/$15,000.

Breakthrough Saint Paul/MN/$10,000.

Face to Face Health & Counseling Services/MN/$15,000.

Lower Phalen Creek Project/MN/$10,000.

Merrick Community Services/MN/$15,000.

Neighborhood Development Center - MN/MN/$25,000.

Opportunity Neighborhood Development Corp/MN/$10,000.

Project SUCCESS/MN/$10,000.

Financial Information

Financial data for year ending: 12/31/2005
Foundation assets: $20,990,453
Grants paid: $853,190
Number of grants: 217
Largest/smallest: $125,000/$50
Typical grant amount: $15,000
Matching gifts: $70,070
Largest multi-year grant approved: $125,000

Application Information

Preferred form of initial contact: request for guidelines, complete proposal, e-mail.

Public information available by request: proposal guidelines.

Accept common grant application: yes.

Accept common report form: yes.

Proposal deadlines: ongoing.

Contribution decisions made by: board of directors/trustees.

Frequency of contributions decisions: quarterly.

Typical time from application deadlines to notification: 180 days.

Staff/Trustees

Staff: Karen Reynolds, foundation administrator.

Directors/trustees: Armar A. Archbold; W.E. Barsness; Gregory McNeely; Kevin McNeely; Paddy McNeely; Shannon McNeely Whitaker, chair.

Medica Foundation

Mail Route CP585
PO Box 9310
Minneapolis, MN 55440-9310
County: Hennepin
Phone: (952) 992-2060
Fax: (952) 992-2060
E-mail: foundation@medica.com
Website: www.medica.com/C10/Medica Foundation1/
Contact: JoAnn M. Birkholz, manager
Paid Staff: Yes
Funder type: Community/public foundation

Program Description

Program's purpose: The Medica Foundation funds programs and community-based initiatives that support the needs of Medica's customers and the greater community by improving their health and removing barriers to heath care services.

Funding priorities: The Medica Foundation funds proposals that support and further Medica's mission, and benefit Medica's members and the community it serves. These include initiatives to improve the availability of, access to and/or quality of health care, with the ability to achieve success or demonstrate effectiveness through measurable outcomes. Funding will be directed toward programs initiatives that are true innovations in how health care is delivered; have a high likelihood of creating systematic change, which in turn will increase sustainability; reduce health care disparities and address social issues that drive health care costs; build partnerships and collaborations between Medica and other community organizations and/or that build collaborations between community organizations. In 2007, the Medica Foundation is offering the following funding opportunities in the first funding cycle: Behavioral Health: Filling the Gaps and Empowerment and Self Management of Chronic Diseases. The focus areas for the second funding cycle in 2007 are: Healthy Living for Children and Partnership for Prevention. Descriptions for each funding area and additional information can be found on our website.

Program limitations/restrictions: Only single-year grant requests will be considered.

Geographic focus: Minnesota statewide, areas outside Minnesota limited to western Wisconsin, North Dakota and South Dakota.

Areas of interest:

FOOD/NUTRITION/AGRICULTURE: Nutrition promotion.

HEALTH - DISEASES/MEDICAL DISCIPLINES: Funding priority areas determined on an annual basis.

HEALTH - GENERAL/REHABILITATIVE: Funding priority areas determined on an annual basis.

HEALTH - MENTAL HEALTH/CRISIS INTERVENTION: Funding priority areas determined on an annual basis.

HEALTH - RESEARCH: Funding priority areas determined on an annual basis.

Intended beneficiaries: No specified populations. Funding priorities determined on an annual basis.

Types of support for organizations: PROGRAM DEVELOPMENT/PROJECT SUPPORT.

Types of support for individuals: none.

Exclusions: Capital & endowment campaigns, Political organizations, Religious organizations, General and/or ongoing operational support, Long-term financial support, Projects where other viable funding sources are available, Projects in which administrative expenses exceed 10% of total grant, Sports events and athletic groups.

Financial Information

Financial data for year ending: 12/31/2006
Foundation assets: $16,650,881
Grants paid: $1,503,515

Application Information

Preferred form of initial contact: letter of inquiry.

Public information available by request: proposal guidelines, annual report, website, letter of inquiry form, past grant recipients.

Proposal deadlines: March 23 and June 22 for letters in inquiry. Check website for deadlines and LOI process. Requests must be sent electronically and received by 5:00 p.m. on the deadline date, and followed by a hard copy with the appropriate authorizing signatures.

Contribution decisions made by: Grant review committee.

Frequency of contributions decisions: semiannually.

Typical time from application deadlines to notification: Applicants will be notified whether or not a full proposal is requested 6-8 weeks from the LOI deadline date. The complete process will likely take 4-6 months.

Special application procedures: See website at www.medica.com/C10/Medica Foundation1 for Letter of Inquiry form, procedures and specific requirements.

Staff/Trustees

Staff: JoAnn M. Birkholz, manager; Heather Craig, project coordinator; Robert M. Longendyke, senior vice president and executive director.

The Medtronic Foundation

710 Medtronic Parkway
MS LC110
Minneapolis, MN 55432-5604
County: Anoka
Phone: (763) 505-2639
Fax: (763) 505-2648
Website: www.medtronic.com/foundation
Contact: David Etzwiler, vice president, community affairs and the foundation
Established: 01/01/1977
Donor: Medtronic, Inc.
Paid Staff: Yes
Funder type: Corporate foundation and corporate giving program

Program Description

Program's purpose: Our mission is to improve the health of people and communities.

Funding priorities: The priorities of the Medtronic Foundation are health and education organizations serving socio-economically disadvantaged populations. These programs include Patient Link - supports national patients associations that provide education, support and advocacy to patients with chronic cardiovascular and neurological conditions; HeartRescue - funds community-based education related to sudden cardiac death.

Program limitations/restrictions: The Medtronic Foundation does not fund capital or operating projects; clinical/scientific research; fiscal agents; fundraising events/activities; social events or goodwill advertising; general support of education institutions; individuals, including scholarships for individuals; lobbying, political or fraternal activities; long-term counseling or personal development; program endowments; religious groups for religious purposes; programs supported by United Way of Twin Cities.

Geographic focus: Twin Cities Metropolitan area, areas outside Minnesota, national areas, international areas.

Geographic limitations: Medtronic communities in Minnesota: Twin Cities seven-county metro area. Areas outside Minnesota: Tempe, AZ; Goleta, Northridge, Santa Ana and Santa Rosa, CA; Louisville and Parker, CO; Jacksonville, FL; Warsaw, IN; Danvers, MA; Humacao, Juncos and Villalba, PR; Memphis, TN; Ft. Worth, TX.

Areas of interest:

ARTS, CULTURE, HUMANITIES: Arts/cultural multipurpose, Arts access program funding through COMPAS.

EDUCATION: Graduate education/professional schools, Higher education, Preschool/elementary, Secondary, Vocational/technical, Science education K-12.

HEALTH - DISEASES/MEDICAL DISCIPLINES: AIDS/HIV, Cancer, Diseases of specific organs, Nerve/muscle/bone diseases, Specific named diseases.

HEALTH - GENERAL/REHABILITATIVE: Health support services, Nursing care/services, Public health programs/wellness education, Rehabilitative medical services.

HUMAN SERVICES: Funding through the United Way.

SCIENCE/TECHNOLOGY: K-12 STAR (Science and Technology are Rewarding) program.

Intended beneficiaries: Ethnic/racial populations - general, General public/unspecified, Poor/economically disadvantaged.

Types of support for organizations: PROGRAM DEVELOPMENT/PROJECT SUPPORT.

CORPORATE SPONSORSHIP: Where the Medtronic Foundation has a relationship or organizations where are employees are involved. Twin Cities organizations. Contact: Tammi Gabbert, Community Affairs, (505) 550-5505, tammi.gabbert@medtronic.com.

Types of support for individuals: none.

Matching grants: elementary/secondary education, employee matching, higher education, scholarships.

Dollars for Doers: yes.

Exclusions: Capital & endowment campaigns, Individuals, Non-501(c)(3), Political organizations, Research, Scholarships/loans, Tax-supported institutions.

Sample grants:

Access Works - MN/MN/Syringe Exchange/$15,000.

Children's Cardiomyopathy Foundation - NJ/NJ/Patient outreach initiative/$30,000.

ISD Minneapolis #282/MN/GEMS - Girls in Engineering, Mathematics and Science/$80,000.

Leonardo's Basement - MN/MN/ Curriculum and staff development: training teachers for an informal hands-on science and math program/$10,000.

Minneapolis Medical Research Foundation, Inc/MN/CPR/AED Training/$30,000.

North Memorial Medical Center/MN/ North Memorial Community Heart Hero Program/$25,000.

Taking Control of Your Diabetes - CA/ CA/$25,000.

West Side Community Health Center/ MN/Health Start Como Park School-based Clinic/$50,000.

Financial Information

Financial data for year ending: 04/30/2006
Foundation assets: $83,737,643
Grants paid: $40,865,798
Number of grants: 714
Largest/smallest: $1,038,434/$300
Typical grant amount: $15,000
Matching gifts: $888,010
Largest multi-year grant approved: $1,000,000
Purpose: capital

Application Information

Preferred form of initial contact: website.

Public information available by request: proposal guidelines, application form, website, online grant application.

Proposal deadlines: Deadlines vary by program and location. Check website for specific program guidelines.

Contribution decisions made by: staff, employee committee, board of directors/trustees.

Frequency of contributions decisions: quarterly.

Specific times board meets: varies.

Typical time from application deadlines to notification: 90 days.

Staff/Trustees

Staff: Marty Allen, consultant - patient link program; Deb Anderson, grants administrator; Christy Eichers, manager, employee involvement; David Etzwiler, vice president, community affairs and the foundation; Emily Haugen, employee involvement specialist; Juan Jackson, consultant - Twin Cities Health in the Community; Joan Mellor, consultant - HeartRescue; Kathleen O'Keefe, consultant - education; Amy Peterson, employee involvement specialist.

Directors/trustees: Arthur D. Collins, director; Gary Ellis, director; Steve Mahle, chair; Stephen N. Oesterle, M.D.; Oern R. Stuge, director; Scott R. Ward, director.

Donald and Marjorie Meredith Foundation

26001 South Glenburne Drive
Sun Lakes, AZ 85248-6646
Phone: (480) 895-7670
Contact: Donald C. Meredith
Established: 12/27/1994
Funder type: Private foundation

Program Description

Program's purpose: The foundation will primarily use trust property to make grants to organizations that are described in section 501(c)(3) and paragraph (1), (2), (3) of section 509(a) of the Internal Revenue Code.

Program limitations/restrictions: Grants are limited to charitable, scientific, literary, religious and educational purposes, all within the meaning of sections 170(c)(2) and 501(c)(3) of the Internal Revenue Code.

Geographic focus: Minnesota statewide, areas outside Minnesota.

Intended beneficiaries: General public/unspecified.

Sample grants:

Habitat for Humanity - MN (Mankato)/ MN/general funding/$1,500.

Joachim Regional Museum/ND/general funding/$1,100.

Mankato Area 77 Lancers Marching Band/MN/Band instrument funding/ $1,000.

MN State University - Mankato/MN/ scholarships/$31,250.

New England Community Arts/ND/ general funding/$1,500.

Salvation Army - MN (Mankato)/MN/ general funding/$1,000.

Valley City State University/ND/general funding/$2,000.

Washington University - St Louis/MO/ general funding/$3,000.

Financial Information

Financial data for year ending: 09/30/2006
Foundation assets: $703,112
Grants paid: $17,295
Number of grants: 28
Largest/smallest: $5,900/$35

Application Information

Preferred form of initial contact: complete proposal.

Proposal deadlines: none.

Preferred time for receiving proposals: applications are accepted at any time.

Staff/Trustees

Directors/trustees: Nancy Belland; Bruce Meredith; Donald C. Meredith II; Donald C. Meredith; Marjorie Meredith; Janet Stromborg; Barbara Woodford.

Martin and Esther Miller Foundation

1908 Cedar Lake Parkway
Minneapolis, MN 55416-3614
County: Hennepin
Phone: (612) 926-9850
Contact: Esther Miller, president
Established: 01/01/1996
Funder type: Private foundation

Program Description

Program's purpose: General charitable purposes.

Geographic focus: Twin Cities Metropolitan Area.

Areas of interest:
ARTS, CULTURE, HUMANITIES: Media/communications.
COMMUNITY IMPROVEMENT.
EDUCATION.
HEALTH - DISEASES/MEDICAL DISCIPLINES: Cancer.
HEALTH - GENERAL/REHABILITATIVE.

Intended beneficiaries: General public/unspecified.

Sample grants:
Adath Jeshurun Congregation/MN/ $5,000.
Jewish Federation - Minneapolis/MN/ $10,000.
Minneapolis Jewish Day School/MN/ $11,200.
MN Public Radio - St Paul/MN/$1,200.
Multiple Sclerosis Society - MN/MN/ $1,000.
Public Television - MN (Twin Cities)/ MN/$900.
Race for the Cure - MN/MN/$1,000.
Struthers Parkinsons Center/MN/$6,000.

Financial Information

Financial data for year ending: 12/31/2005
Foundation assets: $190,435
Grants paid: $36,550
Number of grants: 9
Largest/smallest: $11,200/$250

Application Information

Preferred form of initial contact: letter of inquiry, any reasonable form.
Proposal deadlines: none.

Staff/Trustees

Directors/trustees: Esther Miller, president; Michael Miller; Teresa Miller; Louise Ribnick.

Minneapolis Area Association of Realtors Foundation, Inc.

5750 Lincoln Drive
Minneapolis, MN 55436-1694
County: Hennepin
Phone: (952) 988-3124
Website: www.mplsrealtor.com/MRC/Foundation.htm
Established: 10/21/1987
Funder type: Private foundation

Program Description

Program's purpose: The foundation supports housing and housing-related programs directed or organized for low-income or underserved individuals and families living in counties in Minnesota within the jurisdiction of the Minneapolis Area Association of Realtors.

Geographic focus: West Metropolitan Area/Minneapolis only, Greater Minnesota.

Geographic limitations: Funding limited to organizations and programs benefiting people living in Carver, Hennepin, McLeod, Scott and Sibley counties.

Areas of interest:
HOUSING/SHELTER.

Intended beneficiaries: General public/unspecified, Poor/economically disadvantaged.

Types of support for organizations:
GENERAL PURPOSE/OPERATING SUPPORT.

Sample grants:
City of Lakes Community Land Trust/MN/general operating/$2,500.
Greater Metropolitan Housing Corporation Twin Cities/MN/general operating/$2,500.
Habitat for Humanity - MN (Twin Cities)/MN/general operating/$5,000.
HOPE Community - MN/Minneapolis, MN/general operating/$2,000.
Life's Missing Link/MN/general operating/$2,500.
St Joseph's Home for Children - MN/MN/general operating/$4,000.

Financial Information

Financial data for year ending: 12/31/2006
Foundation assets: $769,966
Grants paid: $33,000
Number of grants: 12
Largest/smallest: $6,000/$2,000

Application Information

Preferred form of initial contact: letter of inquiry, request for guidelines, business letter stating intent to receive award.

Public information available by request: proposal guidelines.

Accept common grant application: yes.

Proposal deadlines: the 2007 deadline was May 18. See website for updated information.

Contribution decisions made by: board of directors/trustees, committee.

Frequency of contributions decisions: annually.

Typical time from application deadlines to notification: 3 months.

Special application procedures: Use the Minnesota Common Grant Application Form. The foundation will not approve grants for general budget or administrative costs. To validate each request, the foundation committee submits the name of each organization to the Charities Review Council of Minnesota.

Staff/Trustees

Staff: Mark Allen, CEO; Donnie Brown, executive administrator; Bill Gerst, vice president public affairs.

Directors/trustees: Stephen Dieringer; Lee Doucette; Gina Dumas; Trace Edwards; Maura Kolars, 2007 committee chair; Kathy Maas; Mary Thorpe-Mease; John Walsh; Tracey Wilson.

The Minneapolis Foundation

800 IDS Center
80 South Eighth Street
Minneapolis, MN 55402
County: Hennepin
Phone: (612) 672-3878
Fax: (612) 672-3846
E-mail: grants@mplsfoundation.org
Website: www.minneapolisfoundation.org
Established: 01/01/1915
Paid Staff: Yes
Funder type: Community/public foundation

Program Description

Program's purpose: The Minneapolis Foundation and its funding partners are committed to addressing underlying issues and to effecting long-term change to improve the lives of people in our community.

Funding priorities: Community Grants are awarded for policy or systems change activities in the areas of affordable housing, economic opportunity, educational achievement, and the health and well-being of children, youth and families. While these goals direct our grantmaking, the foundation remains open to unique opportunities in other areas, e.g. the arts, seniors and disabilities. The Connections program presents an opportunity for Minnesota nonprofits to connect with other funding sources through The Minneapolis Foundation. Nonprofits may submit a standardized letter of inquiry for possible consideration by foundation donors. Periodically, The Minneapolis Foundation also publishes Requests for Proposals on behalf of its donors.

Program limitations/restrictions: Community grantmaking will not fund individuals; endowments;scholarships; participation in conferences; direct religious activities; financial deficits; memberships in organizations; political organizations or candidates; courtesy advertising or benefit tickets; national fundraising efforts; fundraising expenses or telephone solicitations.

Geographic focus: Twin Cities Metropolitan Area, Greater Minnesota, Minnesota statewide.

Geographic limitations: State of Minnesota only.

Areas of interest:
CIVIL RIGHTS: Civil liberties advocacy, Civil rights/advocacy for specific groups, Equal opportunity and access, Intergroup relations/race relations, Voter education/registration.
COMMUNITY IMPROVEMENT: Community/neighborhood development/improvement, Economic development, Grants to programs that can clearly demonstrate how they will accomplish long-term change in the availability of economic opportunities.
EDUCATION: Adult/continuing education/literacy, Educational reform, Preschool/elementary, Secondary, Vocational/technical, Grants to programs that can clearly demonstrate how they will accomplish long-term change in the area of educational achievement of children and youth.
EMPLOYMENT/JOBS: Employment procurement/job training, Economic development. Grants to programs that can clearly demonstrate how they will accomplish long-term change in the availability of economic opportunities.
ENVIRONMENTAL QUALITY/PROTECTION/BEAUTIFICATION.
HEALTH - GENERAL/REHABILITATIVE: Public health programs/wellness education, Reproductive health care, Grants to programs that can clearly demonstrate how they will accomplish long-term change in the area of health and well-being of children, youth and families.
HOUSING/SHELTER: Housing advocacy, Grants to programs that can clearly demonstrate how they will accomplish long-term change in the area of affordable housing.
HUMAN SERVICES: Children/youth services, Family services, Family services for adolescent parents, Family violence shelters and services, Multipurpose human service organizations, Grants to programs that can clearly demonstrate how they will accomplish long-term change in the area of health and well-being of children, youth and families.
PHILANTHROPY/VOLUNTARISM: Nonprofit sector assistance, Philanthropy associations.
PUBLIC AFFAIRS/SOCIETY BENEFIT.
PUBLIC PROTECTION - CRIME/COURTS/LEGAL SERVICES: Dispute/conflict resolution, Legal services, Protection/prevention - neglect/abuse/exploitation, Rehabilitation of offenders.
YOUTH DEVELOPMENT: Youth development programs, Grants to programs that can clearly demonstrate how they will accomplish long-term change in the area of health and well-being of children, youth and families.

Intended beneficiaries: General public/unspecified.

Types of support for organizations:
CAPITAL CAMPAIGNS: Building/renovation, Computer systems/technology, Equipment, Land acquisitions.
GENERAL PURPOSE/OPERATING SUPPORT.
PROGRAM DEVELOPMENT/PROJECT SUPPORT: Public awareness, Public policy research/analysis.

Types of support for individuals: none.

Exclusions: Capital & endowment campaigns, Individuals, Political organizations, Religious organizations, Scholarships/loans.

Sample grants:

Children's Advocacy Network - MN (Minneapolis)/MN/For a campaign to establish a commitment to children's issues among candidates participating in the Minneapolis mayoral and city council races/$75,000.

Immigrant Development Center/To organize and expand micro-enterprise opportunities for immigrant and refugee communities in the Fargo-Moorhead area, over three years to organize and expand micro-enterprise opportunities for immigrant and refugee communities in the Fargo-Moorhead area, over 3 years/$90,000.

MN Community Land Trust Coalition/MN/For policy advocacy to protect existing affordable housing and provide for more permanently affordable housing held in Minnesota community land trusts, over 2 years/$50,000.

Organizing Apprenticeship Project/MN/For the transformation of a grassroots community-organizing nonprofit to address racial justice and racial equity issues across Minnesota, over 2 years/$100,000.

Parents United Network/MN/To solidify support and increase momentum among parents and community groups to advocate for restoration of adequate state funding for Minnesota Public Schools, over 2 years/$100,000.

Financial Information

Financial data for year ending: 03/31/2006
Foundation assets: $654,649,964
Grants paid: $36,054,903

Application Information

Preferred form of initial contact: request for guidelines; check website for guidelines and submit request as appropriate.

Public information available by request: proposal guidelines, application form, annual report, newsletter, website.

Accept common grant application: yes.

Accept common report form: yes.

Proposal deadlines: ongoing.

Contribution decisions made by: Community Philanthropy Committee of TMF and other funding bodies.

Frequency of contributions decisions: Twice per year.

Typical time from application deadlines to notification: up to 6 months.

Special application procedures: use Minnesota Common Grant Application Form for Community grant applications (system change requests, Minnesota only).

Staff/Trustees

Staff: Jean Adams, vice president, finance and administration; Gregory E. Allen, controller; Eric L. Anderson, community philanthropy officer; Stuart Appelbaum, vice president, development; Jeana Aubinger, senior accountant; Paul Bachleitner, development associate; Lisa Bachman, human resources manager; Daniel Berg, senior asset development officer; Becky Borsheim, communications coordinator; Jennifer Brink, senior accountant; Colleen Byrne, administrative services manager; Marigrace Deters, associate vice president, community philanthropy; Donald Flower, information services manager; Brenda Hayden, senior administrative assistant, community philanthropy; Desiree Heller, vice president, consulting services; Steve Hosier, investment associate; Robert Hybben, community philanthropy associate; Donjia Johnson, community philanthropy assistant; Karen Kelley-Ariwoola, vice president, community philanthropy; Christelle Langer, vice president, marketing and communications; Valerie Lee, community philanthropy officer; Jennifer Lick, student resource coordinator, Destination 2010; Jodi Maly, information services technician; Tahasha McDonald, accounting clerk; Kristine Migely, communications and events associate; Sandy 'Ci Moua, senior administrative assistant, Destination 2010; Kathleen O'Donnell, program manager, Destination 2010; Angelines Pabon, National Urban fellow; Mary Ellis Peterson, gift planning officer; Denise Ryan, administrative services supervisor; Kate Sattler, communications officer; Nick Scheibel, fund administrator; Robyn Schein, philanthropic advisor; Lillian Steadman, senior administrative assistant, development; William M. Sternberg, professional advisor development officer; Bette Theisen, fund administration supervisor; Jenifer Thompson, executive assistant; Jan Tusler, senior accountant; Sandra Vargas, president and CEO; Connie Volcke, senior administrative assistant, consulting services; Joanne Walz, community philanthropy officer; Jo Young, information services technician.

Directors/trustees: Pamela G. Alexander; Albert Andrews Jr.; Marshall K. Besikof; Dorothy J. Bridges, secretary; Lynn Casey; Yvonne Cheung Ho; Mark Chronister; Brother Louis Dethomasis; John F. Eisberg, vice chair; Jesse Bethke Gomez; Morris Goodwin Jr.; Sima Griffith; Joan Anderson Growe, treasurer; Katherine Hadley; Eric J. Jolly Ph.D.; John M. Lavander; Weiming Lu; Lee Mitau; Russell C. Nelson; James Pohlad; James W. Rockwell; Stephen Roszell, chair; Hussein Samatar; Nancy Siska; Gerald Stenson.

Minneapolis Kiwanis Foundation

400 Robert Street North
c/o Securian Trust Company
St Paul, MN 55101
County: Ramsey
Phone: (612) 436-2314
Established: 01/01/1941
Funder type: Community/public foundation

Program Description

Program's purpose: The foundation's sole function is to support nonprofit organizations and individuals in the field of health, education and social welfare.

Funding priorities: Minneapolis children and youth.

Program limitations/restrictions: Scholarships to individuals and grants to social welfare organizations.

Geographic focus: West Metropolitan Area/Minneapolis only.

Geographic limitations: None, though beneficiaries of grants must be citizens of Minneapolis.

Areas of interest:
EDUCATION.
HEALTH - GENERAL/ REHABILITATIVE.
HUMAN SERVICES.

Intended beneficiaries: Children and youth (infants-19 years), General public/unspecified.

Types of support for organizations:
GENERAL PURPOSE/OPERATING SUPPORT.

Exclusions: Capital & endowment campaigns, Individuals, Non-501(c)(3), Political organizations.

Sample grants:

Bundles of Love/MN/general operating/ $1,500.

Catholic Youth Camps/MN/general operating/$4,000.

Greater Minneapolis Crisis Nursery/MN/ general operating/$3,000.

Kinship of Greater Minneapolis/MN/ general operating/$2,500.

Life Time Transition, Inc./MN/general operating/$500.

MN Computers for Schools/MN/general operating/$3,000.

St Joseph's Home for Children - MN/MN/general operating/$3,000.

Volunteers of America - MN/MN/general operating/$2,000.

Financial Information

Financial data for year ending: 09/30/2006
Foundation assets: $1,157,191
Grants paid: $52,500
Number of grants: 19
Largest/smallest: $4,000/$500

Staff/Trustees

Directors/trustees: Charles T. Aycock; Duane Bell; Ted Ferrara, treasurer; Carl Hanson; Henry Hayden, vice president; Kelly McCrary; Paul Sortland; Robert F. Thompson, secretary; Leonard J. Washko, president.

Minneapolis Rotary Community Service Foundation

Local Community Service Committee
650 Third Avenue South
Suite 100
Minneapolis, MN 55402
County: Hennepin
Phone: (612) 673-0166
Fax: (612) 673-0164
E-mail: tami@mplsrotary.org
Website: www.rotarympls9.org
Established: 01/01/1961
Funder type: Community/public foundation

Program Description

Program's purpose: The foundation represents the members of the Rotary Club of Minneapolis in their support of local community service projects, funding nonprofit organizations that work toward improving the quality of life within the Twin Cities metropolitan area.

Funding priorities: The foundation generally favors: 1) Organizations that deal with basic human needs, especially those that are directed toward helping the socially or economically disadvantaged become more self-sufficient; 2) Projects or programs that are of a demonstration nature and preferably could be carried on by others at the conclusion of Rotary support (i.e., a pilot program, start-up, or special need). We are not adverse to high-risk programs with potential for significant leverage; 3) Grant requests for small identified capital improvement or special purpose. We prefer projects where a small grant from Rotary makes an impact on a discreet project, whether the applicant organization is large or small. For example, we will not contribute a small percentage of an applicant's large capital campaign. Successful applicants generally ask us for a significant or defined share of a small, focused element of their program; 4) Grant requests that would benefit many individuals rather than a few; 5) Programs that serve people in the City of Minneapolis.

Geographic focus: West Metropolitan Area/Minneapolis only.

Areas of interest:

COMMUNITY IMPROVEMENT: Volunteer bureaus.

EDUCATION: Adult/continuing education/literacy, Educational services, Higher education, Pre-school/elementary, Secondary, Vocational/technical.

HEALTH - GENERAL/REHABILITATIVE: Health care financing activities, Health support services, Hospitals and related primary medical care facilities, Nursing care/services, Public health programs/wellness education, Rehabilitative medical services.

HEALTH - MENTAL HEALTH/CRISIS INTERVENTION: Alcohol/drug/substance, prevention and treatment, Counseling/support groups, Mental health associations, Mental health treatment and services.

HUMAN SERVICES: Children/youth services, Family services, Multipurpose human service organizations, Residential/custodial care.

INTERNATIONAL AFFAIRS: Promotion of international understanding.

PUBLIC PROTECTION - CRIME/COURTS/LEGAL SERVICES: Protection/prevention - neglect/abuse/exploitation.

RECREATION: Physical fitness/recreational facilities.

YOUTH DEVELOPMENT: Adult/child matching programs, Multipurpose youth centers/clubs, Scouting organizations, Youth development programs.

Intended beneficiaries:
Aging/elderly/senior citizens, Children only (5-14 years), Crime/abuse victims, Disabled - general or unspecified disability, Infants/babies (under age 5), Poor/economically disadvantaged, Single parents, Youth/adolescents (ages 14-19).

Types of support for organizations:
CAPITAL CAMPAIGNS: Building/renovation, Computer systems/technology, Equipment.

PROGRAM DEVELOPMENT/PROJECT SUPPORT: Seed money/start-up funds.

STUDENT AID (GRANTS TO INSTITUTIONS): Scholarship funds.

Types of support for individuals: none.

Exclusions: Capital & endowment campaigns, Individuals, Political organizations, Religious organizations, Research, Operating expenses; Support travel; Special events, tickets or benefits.

Sample grants:

The Bridge for Runaway Youth/MN/education program/$2,000.

Frank Gray Scholarship Program/MN/financial aid to six colleges for six students/$6,000.

Groups Study Exchange Program/MN/expenses of hosting international group/$1,612.

House of Charity Inc/MN/refrigeration equipment/$1,650.

Kenya Children's Fund Inc/MN/education equipment/$2,000.

Minneapolis Public Schools Economic Learning Center/MN/teaching of economics K-12/$9,000.

Walker Cityview/MN/senior healthcare center hospital beds/$1,000.

Financial Information

Financial data for year ending: 06/30/2006
Foundation assets: $1,519,968
Grants paid: $99,102

Application Information

Preferred form of initial contact: request for guidelines, complete proposal.

Public information available by request: proposal guidelines, application form, website.

Proposal deadlines: November 30.

Preferred time for receiving proposals: requests for grants are accepted from September 1 through November 30 of each year.

Contribution decisions made by: board of directors/trustees, committees.

Frequency of contributions decisions: annually.

Typical time from application deadlines to notification: decisions made on or around May 1.

Staff/Trustees

Staff: Tami Hagen, executive director; Susan A. Holton, assistant director.

Directors/trustees: Erick Ajaz; Theodore Bather; Fred Friswold; James Hancock; Thomas Hubler; Judy Kirk; George Koblas; Bob Laskey; James Martin; Lucy Mattson; Leslie Ogg; Lynn Swon; Maureen Tubbs; Vicki Turnquist, president; Michael Weber.

Minnesota Business and Professional Women's Foundation

8014 Highway 55
Suite 186
Golden Valley, MN 55427-4712
County: Hennepin
E-mail: bmleinin@smig.net
Website: www.bpwmn.org/files/index.php?id=14
Contact: Barb Leining, president
Established: 01/01/1956
Funder type: Community/public foundation

Program Description

Program's purpose: To provide resources that empower women to achieve economic self-sufficiency.

Funding priorities: BPW assists adult women who are faced with internal and external challenges while they are striving to achieve economic self-sufficiency. Through scholarships, grants and partnering with other organizations, women are enabled to improve their education, improve their employability, develop their careers and develop leadership skills.

Program limitations/restrictions: Scholarship program: annually awards several $500 scholarships to women 25 years or older who are pursuing higher education degrees or professional certification programs: Women at Crossroads: grant program designed to help eliminate barriers to employment. These grants give limited financial assistance to women age 25 years or older for immediate job-related expenses that will have a long-term impact on the individual's economic self-sufficiency: Step Up to Leadership: partners with local community organizations to provide financial support for seminars or programs that help participants identify and develop leadership skills that can be used in their personal and professional life.

Areas of interest:
COMMUNITY IMPROVEMENT: Support for seminars that help identify and develop leadership skills.
EDUCATION: Graduate education/professional schools, Higher education, Professional certification programs.
EMPLOYMENT/JOBS: Employment procurement/job training.

Intended beneficiaries: Female adults.

Types of support for organizations:
GRANTS TO INDIVIDUALS.
PROGRAM DEVELOPMENT/PROJECT SUPPORT: Conferences/seminars.

Types of support for individuals: aid to needy persons, scholarships, grants to limit barriers to employment.

Financial Information

Financial data for year ending: 05/31/2005
Foundation assets: $65,406

Application Information

Preferred form of initial contact: letter of inquiry.

Public information available by request: website.

Staff/Trustees

Staff: Anne Andreasen; Barb Leining, president.

Minnesota Early Learning Foundation

2233 University Avenue
Suite 424
St Paul, MN 55114
County: Ramsey
Phone: (651) 287-9005
Fax: (651) 645-0946
E-mail: yates@melf.us
Website: www.melf.us
Contact: Barbara Yates, director of programs & operations
Funder type: Community/public foundation

Program Description

Program's purpose: Identify cost-effective ways of ensuring that Minnesota's children ages 0-5, from low income or challenged families, are ready for success in kindergarten.

Funding priorities: The Minnesota Early Learning Foundation will support programs and initiatives that educate, inform and empower parents, particularly in Minnesota's fast-growing immigrant communities and other under-served communities. MELF will support programs and initiatives that will – through measurement, demonstration, collaboration and evaluation – guide development of an effective early learning system.

Program limitations/restrictions: Funds are not available for on-going operations/programs. Unfortunately, MELF is not a source of funding to make up for previous funding cuts, or to expand your service delivery.

Areas of interest:
EDUCATION: Early childhood learning.

Intended beneficiaries: Infants/babies (under age 5).

Financial Information

Financial data for year ending: 12/31/2005
Foundation assets: $1,886,223

Application Information

Preferred form of initial contact: letter of inquiry.

Public information available by request: proposal guidelines, application form, annual report, website.

Proposal deadlines: May 1.

Contribution decisions made by: staff.

Staff/Trustees

Staff: Duane Benson, executive director; Barbara Yates, director of programs & operations.

Minnesota Power Foundation

30 West Superior Street
Duluth, MN 55802
County: St Louis
Phone: (218) 720-2518
Fax: (218) 723-3915
E-mail: mhanson@mnpower.com
Website: www.mnpowerfoundation.org
Contact: Peggy Hanson, community relations administrator & foundation director
Funder type: Corporate giving program

Program Description

Program's purpose: Minnesota Power Foundation provides funding to select organizations that demonstrate commitment to improving the region's quality of life.

Funding priorities: Education, the environment, community service, youth development, arts and culture, health, and human services.

Program limitations/restrictions: Funding is considered only to 501(c)(3) organizations.

Geographic focus: Greater Minnesota. Service area only: central and northern Minnesota.

Geographic limitations: Within the Minnesota Power service area only.

Areas of interest:
ARTS, CULTURE, HUMANITIES: Arts/cultural multipurpose, Performing arts.
COMMUNITY IMPROVEMENT: Community coalitions, Community/neighborhood development/improvement, Economic development, Volunteer bureaus.
EDUCATION: Higher education, Preschool/elementary, Secondary, Other.
ENVIRONMENTAL QUALITY/PROTECTION/BEAUTIFICATION: Botanical/horticultural/landscape, Environmental beautification/open spaces, Natural resources conservation/protection.
FOOD/NUTRITION/AGRICULTURE: Food service/free food distribution.
HEALTH - DISEASES/MEDICAL DISCIPLINES: Other.
HEALTH - GENERAL/REHABILITATIVE: Public health programs/wellness education.
HEALTH - MENTAL HEALTH/CRISIS INTERVENTION.
HOUSING/SHELTER: Homeless, temporary housing, Low-cost temporary housing.
HUMAN SERVICES: Children/youth services, Emergency assistance (food/clothing/cash), Multipurpose human service organizations, Victims services.
PHILANTHROPY/VOLUNTARISM: Voluntarism promotion.
PUBLIC PROTECTION - CRIME/COURTS/LEGAL SERVICES: Crime prevention.
PUBLIC SAFETY/DISASTERS/RELIEF: Disaster preparedness and relief, Safety education.
RECREATION: Other.
YOUTH DEVELOPMENT: Multipurpose youth centers/clubs, Scouting organizations, Youth development programs.

Intended beneficiaries: General public/unspecified.

Types of support for organizations:
GENERAL PURPOSE/OPERATING SUPPORT.
PROGRAM DEVELOPMENT/PROJECT SUPPORT.
STUDENT AID (GRANTS TO INSTITUTIONS): Scholarship funds.
CORPORATE SPONSORSHIP: Contact: Peggy Hanson, Community Relations, (218) 722-2641 x3380, mhanson@mnpower.com.

Types of support for individuals: none.

Financial Information

Financial data for year ending: 12/31/2006
Grants paid: $820,770

Application Information

Preferred form of initial contact: complete proposal.
Public information available by request: proposal guidelines, website.
Accept common grant application: yes.
Proposal deadlines: ongoing.
Contribution decisions made by: employee committee, board of directors/trustees.
Specific times board meets: 6 times a year.

Staff/Trustees

Staff: Peggy Hanson, community relations administrator & foundation director.

Minnesota Research Fund (fka SOTA TEC Fund)

1000 Westgate Drive
Suite 251
St Paul, MN 55108
County: Ramsey
Phone: (651) 486-7041
E-mail: info@mnresearchfund.org
Website: www.mnresearchfund.org
Established: 05/25/1993
Funder type: Private foundation

Program Description

Program's purpose: To develop economic opportunities in Minnesota through technology transfer.

Funding priorities: Fund research projects at the University of Minnesota, Mayo Clinic, and MnSCU private colleges and universities with the intent of commercializing the technology to increase job opportunities in Minnesota.

Program limitations/restrictions: Projects must have commercialization ability and Minnesota economic enhancement opportunities.

Areas of interest:
ENVIRONMENTAL QUALITY/PROTECTION/BEAUTIFICATION: Pollution abatement and control.
FOOD/NUTRITION/AGRICULTURE: Agricultural programs.
HEALTH - DISEASES/MEDICAL DISCIPLINES: Digestive diseases/disorders.
HEALTH - RESEARCH: Birth defects & genetic diseases research, Digestive disease/disorder research, Specific named disease research.
SCIENCE/TECHNOLOGY: Biological/life science, Engineering/technology research, Physical sciences/earth sciences, Science - general.

Intended beneficiaries: Other named groups, Minnesota institutions of higher learning.

Types of support for organizations: Research.

Types of support for individuals: research.

Financial Information

Financial data for year ending: 12/31/2005
Foundation assets: $1,610,073
Grants paid: $11,000

Application Information

Preferred form of initial contact: letter of inquiry; potential applicants are asked to provide a brief preliminary summary.

Public information available by request: proposal guidelines, application form, website.

Contribution decisions made by: board of directors/trustees.

Frequency of contributions decisions: quarterly.

Typical time from application deadlines to notification: 3 months.

Staff/Trustees

Staff: Peter A. Birkeland, chief financial officer; Patricia M. Blaisdell, vice president of operations; Gerald (Jerry) A. Okerman, president and CEO.

Directors/trustees: M. James Bensen; Robert W. Hatch, chair; Russell J. McNaughton; John A. Meslow; Charles C. Muscoplat; Gerald (Jerry) A. Okerman, president and CEO; Steven P. VanNurden.

Minnesota State Bar Foundation

600 Nicollet Mall
Suite 380
Minneapolis, MN 55402
County: Hennepin
Phone: (612) 333-1183
Alt. Phone: (800) 882-6722
Fax: (612) 333-4927
E-mail: cpalmer@mnbar.org
Website: www.mnbar.org/foundat.htm
Contact: Caroline Palmer, staff director
Established: 12/01/1932
Paid Staff: Yes
Funder type: Community/public foundation

Program Description

Program's purpose: Support law-related, community and bar-related programs and activities including legal assistance to the disadvantaged, law-related education and improvements in the administration of justice. The foundation recognizes that its existence and its ability to carry out its assigned mission are due to the cooperation and support that it receives from the Minnesota State Bar Association and its individual members, who are the primary source of all funds available to the foundation. The foundation therefore feels deeply obligated to pursue policies and make grants to such programs and causes as it believes would attract the special interest and support of the lawyers of the state of Minnesota.

Program limitations/restrictions: Must be directly law-related.

Geographic focus: Twin Cities Metropolitan Area, Greater Minnesota, Minnesota statewide.

Geographic limitations: Minnesota only.

Areas of interest:
EDUCATION: Law-related.
HUMAN SERVICES: Children/youth services, Family services, Family violence shelters and services, Senior centers and services, Law-related.
PUBLIC PROTECTION - CRIME/COURTS/LEGAL SERVICES: Courts and administration of justice, Crime prevention, Legal services, Protection/prevention - neglect/abuse/exploitation.

Intended beneficiaries: General public/unspecified, Immigrants/newcomers/refugees, Poor/economically disadvantaged.

Types of support for organizations:
CAPITAL CAMPAIGNS: Equipment.
GENERAL PURPOSE/OPERATING SUPPORT.
PROGRAM DEVELOPMENT/PROJECT SUPPORT.

Types of support for individuals: none.

Sample grants:

Battered Women's Legal Advocacy Project/Minneapolis, MN/Battered Women's Defense Initiative/$3,000.

Immigrant Law Center of MN, Inc/MN/supervision for direct legal services in immigration matters/$3,000.

Indian Child Welfare Law Center/MN/culturally appropriate legal services to low-income American Indian families/$1,000.

Koochiching County Sexual Assault Program/MN/legal advocacy program for sexual assault and domestic abuse victims/$1,500.

Sojourner Project Inc - MN/MN/legal advocacy services for survivors of domestic violence in western Hennepin County/$1,000.

Southeast Asian Refugee Community Home (SEARCH)/MN/law-related education for low-income immigrants and refugees/$1,500.

Southern MN Regional Legal Services/MN/equipment for a new Hotline service/$3,200.

Storefront Group, The/MN/update divorce education curriculum/$500.

Financial Information

Financial data for year ending: 06/30/2006
Foundation assets: $1,218,177
Grants paid: $99,750
Number of grants: 46
Largest/smallest: $7,500/$1,000
Typical grant amount: $2,700

Application Information

Preferred form of initial contact: complete proposal.

Public information available by request: proposal guidelines, application form, annual report, website.

Proposal deadlines: applications must be received by 5:00 p.m. on the first business day of month in which meeting is held (September, December, March, June).

Contribution decisions made by: board of directors/trustees.

Frequency of contributions decisions: quarterly.

Specific times board meets: Mid-month in September, December, March and June

Typical time from application deadlines to notification: 4-6 weeks.

Special application procedures: must use our application form, which can be found on our website; must limit to four pages and required attachments.

Staff/Trustees

Staff: Caroline Palmer, staff director.

Directors/trustees: Linda C. Barbe; James P. Barone, president; Edward Blomme; Judy Harris Brown; Robert Enger; Richard Hendrickson; Juan Hoyos; Nancy Kiskis; Cynthia Jokela Moyer; Erin O'Toole-Tomczik; Warren Ortland; Honorable Jon Stafsholt; Gary Voegele; Pamela Waggoner; Honorable Lloyd B. Zimmerman.

The Minnesota Timberwolves FastBreak Foundation

600 First Avenue North
Minneapolis, MN 55403
County: Hennepin
Phone: (612) 673-1600
Website: www.nba.com/timberwolves/community
Established: 12/08/1988
Funder type: Community/public foundation

Program Description

Program's purpose: To positively impact the lives of the youth in Minnesota communities, enabling them to make responsible decisions and helping them to contribute to their own future.

Funding priorities: Recipients' goals should be consistent with the foundation's mission. The foundation works hand-in-hand to support youth-related programs and initiatives, coinciding with seven monthly themes. The foundation also develops and implements unique programming through out the state, including Read to Achieve, Making Money Matter, Timberwolves Ten, high school scholarships, Lunch Learners and basketball court refurbishments.

Program limitations/restrictions: Excluded from consideration: fraternal organizations; religious organizations for religious purposes; political campaigns; organizations designed primarily for lobbying; requests for debt financing or endowments.

Geographic focus: Minnesota statewide.

Geographic limitations: Recipients should be a Minnesota-based or Upper Midwest nonprofit organization, or the project should primarily benefit Minnesotans.

Areas of interest:
HEALTH - DISEASES/MEDICAL DISCIPLINES.
HUMAN SERVICES: Children/youth services.
RECREATION: Basketball focus or community gathering spaces.
YOUTH DEVELOPMENT: Multipurpose youth centers/clubs, Youth development programs.

Intended beneficiaries: Children and youth (infants-19 years).

Sample grants:
Boys & Girls Club - MN (St Paul)/MN/Mt. Airy/$25,000.
Camp Odayin/MN/$10,000.
Cookie Cart/MN/$10,000.
Hope for the City - MN/MN/$10,000.
MN Military Family Foundation/MN/$10,000.
Parenting with Purpose/MN/$10,000.
YouthCARE/MN/$10,000.

Financial Information

Financial data for year ending: 09/30/2005
Foundation assets: $408,128
Grants paid: $280,744
Number of grants: 21
Largest/smallest: $25,000/$1,000

Application Information

Preferred form of initial contact: e-mail fastbreakfoundation@timberwolves.com to receive grant application.

Public information available by request: proposal guidelines, application form.

Proposal deadlines: Applications accepted August 15-September 15, 2007.

Typical time from application deadlines to notification: Monthly grants will be notified 30 days prior to announcement of monthly grant.

Staff/Trustees

Staff: Katie Mattis, manager of community relations.

Directors/trustees: Roger Griffith, CFO; Robert K. Moor, president; Glen A. Taylor, majority owner.

Minnesota Twins Community Fund

34 Kirby Puckett Place
Minneapolis, MN 55415
County: Hennepin
Phone: (612) 375-1366
Website: www.twinsbaseball.com
Contact: Kevin Smith, executive director
Established: 02/01/1991
Funder type: Community/public foundation

Program Description

Program's purpose: The Twins Community Fund is a private, nonprofit organization whose mission is to enrich local and regional communities by providing resources for the healthy development of children and families through an association with baseball, softball and the Minnesota Twins.

Funding priorities: Healthy development of children is its focus. The fund provides financial support to organizations that operate baseball and softball recreation programs for young people. Select educational programs are a secondary focus.

Geographic focus: Twin Cities Metropolitan Area, Greater Minnesota, Minnesota statewide, Areas outside Minnesota, National Areas.

Geographic limitations: Upper Midwest (Minnesota, Iowa, North Dakota, South Dakota and Wisconsin) and Southwest Florida.

Areas of interest:
ARTS, CULTURE, HUMANITIES.
COMMUNITY IMPROVEMENT: Community/neighborhood development/improvement.
EDUCATION: Educational services, Higher education, Libraries/library science, Pre-school/elementary, Secondary.
ENVIRONMENTAL QUALITY/PROTECTION/BEAUTIFICATION: Environmental beautification/open spaces.
HEALTH - GENERAL/REHABILITATIVE: Public health programs/wellness education.
HUMAN SERVICES: Children/youth services.
PHILANTHROPY/VOLUNTARISM: Public foundations and community foundations.

RECREATION: Amateur sports clubs/leagues, Amateur sports competitions, Physical fitness/recreational facilities, Professional athletic leagues, Recreation and sporting camps, Recreational/pleasure/social clubs, Sports training facilities/agencies, Baseball/softball.

YOUTH DEVELOPMENT: Youth development programs.

Intended beneficiaries: Children and youth (infants-19 years), Ethnic/racial populations - general, Physically disabled, Poor/economically disadvantaged.

Types of support for organizations:

CAPITAL CAMPAIGNS: Building/renovation.

STUDENT AID (GRANTS TO INSTITUTIONS): Scholarship funds.

Types of support for individuals: scholarships.

Sample grants:

Brooklyn Park Spring Invitational/MN/Summer baseball tournament/$1,000.

Chisholm Parks & Recreation Department/MN/Fields for Kids grant/$5,000.

City of Hull/IA/Fields for Kids grant/$5,000.

Minneapolis Park & Recreation Board/MN/Rookie League and RBI grant/$60,000.

St Paul Parks & Recreation/MN/Rookie League and RBI grant/$60,000.

Financial Information

Financial data for year ending: 12/31/2006
Foundation assets: $291,095
Grants paid: $397,600
Number of grants: 90
Largest/smallest: $60,000/$200

Application Information

Preferred form of initial contact: letter of inquiry, request for guidelines, review guidelines/applications on www.twinsbaseball.com (follow Community Link).

Public information available by request: proposal guidelines, application form, newsletter, website.

Proposal deadlines: Multiple deadlines - depends on program.

Contribution decisions made by: board of directors/trustees.

Frequency of contributions decisions: quarterly.

Typical time from application deadlines to notification: Varies, depending on program.

Staff/Trustees

Staff: Kevin Smith, executive director.

Directors/trustees: Julianne Bye; Kevin Cattoor; Billy Collins; Julie Craven; Michael Cuddyer; Mark Dienhart; Corri Ford; Brent Gish; Ginny Hubbard Morris; William LeClaire; Kyle Markland; Roger Moe; Ron Nelson; Lea B. Olsen; Jim Senske; Mark Shiffman; Dave St Peter; David Stead; Jodie Tanaka; Kevin Tapani; Kate Walker.

Marjorie Weil and Marvin Edward Mitchell Foundation

3832 Richfield Road
Minneapolis, MN 55410-1222
County: Hennepin
Phone: (612) 922-0343
Fax: (612) 922-3403
E-mail: emgallaghe@aol.com
Contact: Ellen Mitchell Gallagher, president
Established: 03/26/1996
Donor: Ellen Mitchell Gallagher
Funder type: Private foundation

Program Description

Program's purpose: General charitable purposes.

Funding priorities: The focus is on programs that are approaching issues systemically. Organizations supported approach their work based on a resilient view of people. Most of the funding to date has been for youth serving organizations. However, the foundation does not limit its commitment to one age group.

Geographic focus: Twin Cities Metropolitan Area.

Areas of interest:

ARTS, CULTURE, HUMANITIES: Humanities, Media/communications, Performing arts.

CIVIL RIGHTS: Equal opportunity and access.

COMMUNITY IMPROVEMENT: Community coalitions.

EDUCATION: Educational reform, Preschool/elementary, Secondary, Literacy.

ENVIRONMENTAL QUALITY/PROTECTION/BEAUTIFICATION.

HEALTH - GENERAL/REHABILITATIVE: Innovative collaborations.

HEALTH - MENTAL HEALTH/CRISIS INTERVENTION: Preventive Services.

HOUSING/SHELTER: Homeless, temporary housing, Affordable Housing.

HUMAN SERVICES: Children/youth services, Emergency assistance (food/clothing/cash), Family services, Services to specific groups.

YOUTH DEVELOPMENT: Youth development programs.

Intended beneficiaries: General public/unspecified.

Types of support for organizations:

PROGRAM DEVELOPMENT/PROJECT SUPPORT: Capacity building.

Types of support for individuals: none.

Exclusions: Non-501(c)(3), Political organizations.

Sample grants:

Chrysalis, A Center for Women - MN/MN/general operating/$1,500.

Creatives for Causes - MN/MN/general operating/$15,000.

Emergency Food Shelf Network - MN/MN/general operating/$3,000.

Eye of the Storm Theatre/MN/general operating/$100.

Family Service Inc - MN/MN/general operating/$1,000.

Graywolf Press/MN/general operating/$2,000.

Perspectives, Inc - MN/St Louis Park, MN/general operating/$500.

St Paul Chamber Orchestra/MN/general operating/$100.

Financial Information

Financial data for year ending: 12/31/2005
Foundation assets: $828,696
Grants paid: $42,250
Number of grants: 20
Largest/smallest: $15,000/$50

Application Information

Preferred form of initial contact: The Foundation initiates contact to organizations that are of interest. Any letter of inquiry should be in letter form and provide brief information on the applicant's charitable proposal and funding requirements.

Proposal deadlines: none.

Preferred time for receiving proposals: We do not accept unsolicited proposals.

Contribution decisions made by: CEO.

Frequency of contributions decisions: Ongoing.

Staff/Trustees

Directors/trustees: Ellen Mitchell Gallagher, president.

MoneyGram International

1550 Utica Avenue South
Suite 100, MS 8065
Minneapolis, MN 55416
County: Hennepin
Phone: (952) 591-3839
Fax: (952) 591-3860
E-mail: giving@moneygram.com
Website: www.moneygram.com/MGICorp/CompanyInformation/CommunityGiving
Funder type: Corporate giving program

Program Description

Program's purpose: MoneyGram supports organizations that strengthen the global communities served by the company.

Funding priorities: Basic needs and affordable housing; Education; Global healthcare and disaster relief.

Program limitations/restrictions: Does not offer corporate contributions for individuals; religious organizations not related to social services; political, labor or veterans organizations; private foundations or public broadcasting companies; fraternal organizations; environmental or animal rights organizations; arts, recreation or athletic events or programs.

Geographic limitations: Contributes to local, national and international programs.

Areas of interest:

EDUCATION: Adult/continuing education/literacy, Basic education programs at all levels, Community education programs, Programs teaching basic parenting skills.
HEALTH - GENERAL/REHABILITATIVE: Programs supporting immunization and disease prevention in children throughout the world, Programs supporting prenatal and other preventative healthcare.
HOUSING/SHELTER: Homeless, temporary housing, Housing development/construction/management, Affordable home ownership.
HUMAN SERVICES: Children/youth services, Food pantries and/or food shelves, Services for the elderly, Neighborhood and after-school programs.
INTERNATIONAL AFFAIRS: Programs supporting disease and famine prevention on a global scale.
PUBLIC SAFETY/DISASTERS/RELIEF: Disaster preparedness and relief.

Financial Information

Financial data for year ending: 12/31/2006
Grants paid: $850,000

Application Information

Preferred form of initial contact: application (available on website).

Public information available by request: proposal guidelines, application form, website.

Proposal deadlines: March 15, July 15, November 15.

Contribution decisions made by: MoneyGram Global Giving Board.

Frequency of contributions decisions: 3 times a year.

Typical time from application deadlines to notification: 4 weeks.

Staff/Trustees

Staff: Jody Hinkle, MoneyGram Global Giving manager.

Jane N. Mooty Foundation Trust

PO Box 24628
Edina, MN 55424
County: Hennepin
Phone: (952) 829-0890
Contact: Kenneth C. Glaser
Established: 12/24/1990
Funder type: Private foundation

Program Description

Program's purpose: Awards made for religious, charitable, scientific, literary or educational programs. No other restrictions apply.

Geographic focus: Twin Cities Metropolitan Area, Greater Minnesota, Minnesota statewide, Areas outside Minnesota.

Areas of interest:

ARTS, CULTURE, HUMANITIES: Historical societies, Media/communications.
EDUCATION: Higher education.
HEALTH - GENERAL/REHABILITATIVE.
HUMAN SERVICES.
RELIGION/SPIRITUAL DEVELOPMENT.
YOUTH DEVELOPMENT.

Intended beneficiaries: General public/unspecified.

Sample grants:

Concordia College - MN (Moorhead)/MN/$1,000.
Foothills Community Foundation Inc/AZ/$100.
Gethsemane Lutheran Church - MN (Hopkins)/MN/$10,000.
MN Historical Society/MN/$1,000.
Saratoga Springs Open Space Project/Saratoga Springs, NY/$2,000.
University of MN Foundation/MN/Aave Gopher Sports/$25,000.
Wilderness Inquiry/Minneapolis, MN/$500.
YMCA, Minneapolis/MN/$10,000.

Financial Information

Financial data for year ending: 12/31/2005
Foundation assets: $4,048,713
Grants paid: $188,450
Number of grants: 16
Largest/smallest: $75,000/$100

Application Information

Preferred form of initial contact: letter of inquiry.

Proposal deadlines: none.

Preferred time for receiving proposals: application may be made at any time and will be acted upon periodically.

Staff/Trustees

Directors/trustees: Barbara L. Glaser; Kenneth C. Glaser.

John W. Mooty Foundation Trust

80 South Eighth Street
Suite 500
Minneapolis, MN 55402-5363
County: Hennepin
Phone: (612) 632-3200
Contact: Bruce W. Mooty
Established: 12/26/1990
Funder type: Private foundation

Program Description

Program's purpose: Awards made for religious, charitable, scientific, literary or educational purposes. No other restrictions apply.

Geographic focus: Twin Cities Metropolitan Area.

Areas of interest:
COMMUNITY IMPROVEMENT: Community coalitions, Community funds/federated giving programs, Community service clubs.
EDUCATION: Graduate education/professional schools, Higher education.
HEALTH - DISEASES/MEDICAL DISCIPLINES.
HEALTH - GENERAL/REHABILITATIVE.
HEALTH - RESEARCH.
HUMAN SERVICES: Children/youth services.
YOUTH DEVELOPMENT: Multipurpose youth centers/clubs, Scouting organizations, Youth development programs.

Intended beneficiaries: General public/unspecified.

Sample grants:
Citizens League - MN (Minneapolis)/MN/$10,000.
Council on Crime & Justice/MN/$1,000.
Minneapolis Heart Institute Foundation/MN/$5,000.
MN Organization on Fetal Alcohol Syndrome/MN/$1,000.
Prayer Ventures/MN/$250.
Rotary International Foundation - MN/MN/$600.
United Way - MN (Minneapolis Area)/MN/$10,000.
University of MN - Law School/MN/$105,000.

Financial Information

Financial data for year ending: 12/31/2005
Foundation assets: $4,252,054
Grants paid: $177,650
Number of grants: 22
Largest/smallest: $30,000/$250

Application Information

Preferred form of initial contact: letter of inquiry, complete proposal; application may take any form.

Proposal deadlines: none.

Preferred time for receiving proposals: application may be made at any time and will be acted on periodically.

Staff/Trustees

Directors/trustees: Bruce W. Mooty; Charles W. Mooty; David N. Mooty.

Moscoe Family Foundation

6600 City West Parkway
Suite 100
Eden Prairie, MN 55344
County: Hennepin
Phone: (952) 829-7850
Contact: Thomas Moscoe
Funder type: Private foundation

Program Description

Program's purpose: General charitable purposes.

Program limitations/restrictions: None.

Geographic focus: Twin Cities Metropolitan Area, Areas outside Minnesota.

Areas of interest:
ARTS, CULTURE, HUMANITIES.
HEALTH - DISEASES/MEDICAL DISCIPLINES: Cancer.
HEALTH - GENERAL/REHABILITATIVE.
HUMAN SERVICES.
RELIGION/SPIRITUAL DEVELOPMENT.

Intended beneficiaries: General public/unspecified.

Types of support for organizations: GENERAL PURPOSE/OPERATING SUPPORT.

Sample grants:
American Cancer Society - MN/MN/general operating/$250.
American Diabetes Association - MN (Minneapolis)/MN/general operating/$1,000.
Friends of Dana Farber Cancer Institute/Boston, MA/general operating/$100.
Jewish Federation - Greater Miami/FL/general operating/$2,135.
Public Television - MN (Twin Cities)/MN/general operating/$100.
Simon Wiesenthal Center/CA/general operating/$200.
Sister Kenny Institute/MN/general operating/$100.
Walker Art Center/MN/general operating/$30.

Financial Information

Financial data for year ending: 12/31/2005
Foundation assets: $193,078
Grants paid: $97,316
Number of grants: 26
Largest/smallest: $58,000/$10

Application Information

Preferred form of initial contact: letter of inquiry, complete proposal.

Proposal deadlines: none.

Special application procedures: state purpose of organization and intended use of grant.

Staff/Trustees

Directors/trustees: Cathy Broms; Thomas Moscoe.

Kingsley H. Murphy Family Foundation

6311 Wayzata Blvd Suite 100
St Louis Park, MN 55416
County: Hennepin
Phone: (763) 486-1748
Fax: (763) 486-1749
Contact: Kingsley H. Murphy Jr., president
Established: 06/11/1969
Funder type: Private foundation

Program Description

Program's purpose: General charitable purposes.

Program limitations/restrictions: None.

Geographic focus: Twin Cities Metropolitan Area, Areas outside Minnesota.

Intended beneficiaries: General public/unspecified.

Sample grants:

Columbia University/NY/$500.

Guthrie Theater/Minneapolis, MN/$1,500.

Minneapolis Institute of Arts/MN/$1,500.

MN Historical Society/MN/$1,000.

St John's University - MN/MN/$500.

United Way (Minneapolis Area)/MN/$3,000.

Walker Art Center/MN/$3,000.

Financial Information

Financial data for year ending: 12/31/2005
Foundation assets: $1,510,682
Grants paid: $185,450
Number of grants: 49
Largest/smallest: $19,000/$50

Application Information

Preferred form of initial contact: letter of inquiry, complete proposal, no specific form.

Proposal deadlines: none.

Staff/Trustees

Directors/trustees: Katherine B. Murphy; Kingsley H. Murphy Jr., president.

The Laura Jane Musser Fund

318 West 48th Street
Minneapolis, MN 55419
County: Hennepin
Phone: (612) 825-2024
E-mail: ljmusser@earthlink.net
Website: www.musserfund.org
Contact: Mary Karen Lynn Klimenko, managing consultant
Established: 10/18/1984
Funder type: Private foundation

Program Description

Program's purpose: To carry on the philanthropy that Laura Jane Musser started in her lifetime.

Funding priorities: 1) Building a community-based approach to solving environmental problems and encouraging environmental stewardship; 2) Participatory smaller arts programs for underserved children K-12; 3) Promoting intercultural harmony.

Program limitations/restrictions: No grants for general operating or ongoing programs, no endowments and no scholarships.

Geographic focus: Minnesota statewide, areas outside Minnesota, national areas.

Geographic limitations: Projects submitted by organizations in Colorado, Hawaii, Minnesota, New York, Wyoming and Ohio only will be considered for the Rural Initiative program. In the areas of Intercultural Harmony or the Environmental Initiative, proposals are restricted to organizations within the United States.

Areas of interest:

ARTS, CULTURE, HUMANITIES.

CIVIL RIGHTS: Intergroup relations/race relations.

COMMUNITY IMPROVEMENT: Community coalitions in the environment.

ENVIRONMENTAL QUALITY/PROTECTION/BEAUTIFICATION: Community-based.

HUMAN SERVICES: Children/youth services, Non-violence in schools.

INTERNATIONAL AFFAIRS: International peace/security, Promotion of international understanding.

PUBLIC AFFAIRS/SOCIETY BENEFIT: Citizen participation in the environment.

RELIGION/SPIRITUAL DEVELOPMENT: Intercultural harmony.

Intended beneficiaries: Children and youth (infants-19 years), Ethnic/racial populations - general, Other named groups.

Types of support for organizations:
PROGRAM DEVELOPMENT/PROJECT SUPPORT: Seed money/start-up funds.

Types of support for individuals: none.

Exclusions: Capital & endowment campaigns, Individuals, Scholarships/loans.

Sample grants:

Battered Women's Legal Advocacy Project/Minneapolis, MN/agents of change institute/$2,000.

College of St Benedict/MN/$15,000.

Forest History Science Publications/Durham, NC/program in forest history/$25,000.

Green Institute - MN (Minneapolis)/MN/market produce program/$10,000.

Little Falls Community Schools/MN/$5,000.

Metropolitan State College Center for Visual Arts/MN/$6,600.

Nature Conservancy - CO/CO/$25,000.

Ramsey County Historical Society/MN/Gibbs Farm Museum/$2,500.

Financial Information

Financial data for year ending: 12/31/2005
Foundation assets: $18,293,382
Grants paid: $515,662
Number of grants: 56

Application Information

Preferred form of initial contact: e-mail, website.

Public information available by request: proposal guidelines, application form, website.

Proposal deadlines: October 10, 2007 for Intercultural Harmony funding. October 27, 2007 for Rural Initiative. November 28, 2007 for Environmental funding.

Contribution decisions made by: board of directors/trustees.

Frequency of contributions decisions: semiannually.

Typical time from application deadlines to notification: 3 months.

Staff/Trustees

Staff: Kerrie Blevins, program consultant; Mary Karen Lynn Klimenko, managing consultant.

Directors/trustees: Sarah Godfrey; Joseph S. Micallef, chair; Ivy Parish; Robert Strasburg; Jane Taylor; Drew Walker; Meg Walker.

The Nash Foundation

Lowry Hill
90 South 7th Street
Suite 5300
Minneapolis, MN 55402
County: Hennepin
Phone: (612) 667-1762
Fax: (612) 667-1791
E-mail: info@nashfoundation.org
Website: www.nashfoundation.org
Contact: Nicolas Atwood, president
Established: 04/01/1922
Donor: Fred Nash and Willis Nash
Paid Staff: Yes
Funder type: Private foundation

Program Description

Program's purpose: To provide charitable support that reflects the interests of family members.

Funding priorities: Media and performing arts, environmental preservation, conservation and protection, at-risk children and youth, and human services benefiting families and communities in need.

Geographic focus: Twin Cities Metropolitan Area, Minnesota statewide.

Geographic limitations: Minnesota, with a focus on the Twin Cities.

Areas of interest:
ARTS, CULTURE, HUMANITIES: Arts/cultural multipurpose, Performing arts, Visual arts.
ENVIRONMENTAL QUALITY/PROTECTION/BEAUTIFICATION: Natural resources conservation/protection.
HUMAN SERVICES: Children/youth services, Emergency assistance (food/clothing/cash), Family services, Multipurpose human service organizations, Services to specific groups.
YOUTH DEVELOPMENT: Multipurpose youth centers/clubs, Youth development programs.

Intended beneficiaries: Children and youth (infants-19 years), Homeless, Poor/economically disadvantaged, Youth/adolescents (ages 14-19).

Types of support for organizations:
GENERAL PURPOSE/OPERATING SUPPORT: Annual campaigns.
PROGRAM DEVELOPMENT/PROJECT SUPPORT: Mentoring programs, Seed money/start-up funds, Other.

Types of support for individuals: none.

Exclusions: Individuals, Non-501(c)(3), Political organizations, Religious organizations, Scholarships/loans.

Sample grants:
1000 Friends - MN/MN/$2,500.
Ballet of the Dolls Inc/MN/$2,000.
Cedar Cultural Center/MN/$2,000.
Cookie Cart/MN/$2,500.
Life's Missing Link/MN/$2,500.

Financial Information

Financial data for year ending: 06/30/2006
Foundation assets: $4,618,091
Grants paid: $160,685
Number of grants: 50
Largest/smallest: $5,000/$500

Application Information

Preferred form of initial contact: complete proposal, e-mail.

Public information available by request: proposal guidelines, website.

Proposal deadlines: July 1.

Preferred time for receiving proposals: not before April 1 and not after July 1.

Contribution decisions made by: board of directors/trustees.

Frequency of contributions decisions: annually.

Specific times board meets: November.

Typical time from application deadlines to notification: 4-6 months.

Special application procedures: only accept online applications through the foundation's website.

Staff/Trustees

Staff: Peggie Van Wychen, consultant - management & administration.

Directors/trustees: Barbara Atwood; Nicolas Atwood, president; Thomas Atwood; Steven Brautigam; William Dietz; Christine B. Evans; Jason Kochevar; Rebecca Nash.

George W. Neilson Foundation

PO Box 692
Bemidji, MN 56619-0692
County: Beltrami
Website: www.gwnf.org
Contact: Suzanne Liapis, secretary
Established: 01/01/1962
Funder type: Private foundation

Program Description

Funding priorities: The George W. Neilson Foundation will continue to support community development projects by making grants to programs and projects that will improve the lives of the area's children, adults and senior citizens. Projects that improve the quality of community life; contribute to community cohesion; provide for community revitalization; help to create a positive community image; respond to specific community needs; assist in economic development.

Program limitations/restrictions: The foundation does not fund propaganda, attempts to influence legislation or the outcome of any public election or political activity; individual travel or study; promotion of any sectarian religious activity; general purpose grants; sustaining grants whose purpose is to meet continuing operating costs such as salaries, rent, supplies or maintenance, etc.; works of art whose primary function is of a decorative nature; publications or advertising; feasibility studies, employment of consultants, or support of advisory committees; camping programs or field trips; basic research (defined as pursing the advancement of knowledge.); projects that are commonly supported by tax dollars.

Geographic focus: Greater Minnesota.

Geographic limitations: City of Bemidji and surrounding area.

Types of support for individuals: none.

Sample grants:
Boys & Girls Club - MN (Bemidji)/MN/Building Pledge/$100,000.

Courage Center - MN (Golden Valley)/MN/Van for Transportation/$25,000.

Family Adocacy Center/MN/Start-up costs/$29,000.

ISD Bemidji #31/MN/Northern Elementary PTO - Playground Equipment/$15,000.

Lakeland Public Television/MN/Equipment/$45,000.

Meals on Wheels - MN/Greater Minnesota/ $10,000.

Northern Artists Association/MN/CPTR Systems/$2,853.

Opportunities in Science - MN/MN/Headwaters Science Center - Indian Culture & Science/$7,500.

Financial Information

Financial data for year ending: 12/31/2005
Foundation assets: $25,611,402
Grants paid: $1,158,536

Application Information

Preferred form of initial contact: letter of inquiry, complete proposal.

Public information available by request: proposal guidelines, website.

Contribution decisions made by: board of directors/trustees.

Frequency of contributions decisions: monthly.

Specific times board meets: third Thursday of the month.

Staff/Trustees

Staff: Suzanne Liapis, secretary.

Directors/trustees: Lowell Gillett, chair; Charles Naylor; Marcus Weichmann; Paul Welle, treasurer.

The Nelson Family Foundation

301 Carlson Parkway
Suite 102
Minnetonka, MN 55305
County: Hennepin
Phone: (952) 404-5656
Fax: (952) 404-5051
Contact: C. David Nelson, secretary
Established: 05/29/1997
Funder type: Private foundation

Program Description

Program limitations/restrictions: No restrictions or limitations on awards at this time.

Geographic focus: Twin Cities Metropolitan Area, areas outside Minnesota.

Areas of interest:
ARTS, CULTURE, HUMANITIES: Museums, Performing arts, Visual arts.
EDUCATION: Graduate education/professional schools, Higher education, Libraries/library science, Pre-school/elementary, Secondary.
HUMAN SERVICES.

Intended beneficiaries: General public/unspecified.

Types of support for organizations:
CAPITAL CAMPAIGNS.
GENERAL PURPOSE/OPERATING SUPPORT: Annual campaigns.
PROGRAM DEVELOPMENT/PROJECT SUPPORT.
STUDENT AID (GRANTS TO INSTITUTIONS): Scholarship funds.

Financial Information

Financial data for year ending: 12/31/2005
Foundation assets: $1,039,675
Grants paid: $483,847
Number of grants: 16
Largest/smallest: $299,847/$100

Application Information

Preferred form of initial contact: Does not accept unsolicited proposals at this time.

Staff/Trustees

Directors/trustees: C. David Nelson, secretary; Glen D. Nelson, vice president; Marilyn C. Nelson, president.

Richard A. Newman Foundation

c/o Larson, Allen, Weishair
220 South Sixth Street
Suite 300
Minneapolis, MN 55402-1436
County: Hennepin
Established: 09/01/1967
Funder type: Private foundation

Program Description

Program's purpose: To support grassroots organizations that utilize volunteerism; to offer educational support to people learning the plumbing trades; to foster entrepreneurs; to support community programs that utilize volunteerism.

Funding priorities: Assist women and children.

Geographic focus: Twin Cities Metropolitan Area.

Geographic limitations: Rarely any greater Minnesota giving.

Areas of interest:
ANIMAL RELATED: Animal protection/welfare.
EDUCATION: Student services/organizations of students, Vocational/technical.
HOUSING/SHELTER: Housing support services.
HUMAN SERVICES: Children/youth services.
YOUTH DEVELOPMENT: Youth development programs.

Intended beneficiaries: Adults, Females - all ages or age unspecified, Youth/adolescents (ages 14-19).

Types of support for organizations:
GENERAL PURPOSE/OPERATING SUPPORT.

Sample grants:

Ascension Place/MN/general operating/$10,000.

East Side Learning Center - MN/MN/general operating/$5,000.

Search Institute/MN/childcare provider training/$3,000.

Sharing & Caring Hands, Inc/MN/general operating/$5,000.

Turning Point - MN/MN/general operating/$5,000.

Union Gospel Mission - MN (St Paul)/MN/general operating/$2,500.

YMCA - MN (St Paul)/MN/Partners with Youth/$1,000.

Financial Information

Financial data for year ending: 12/31/2006
Foundation assets: $4,698,404
Grants paid: $160,000
Number of grants: 25
Largest/smallest: $75,000/$500

Application Information

Preferred form of initial contact: letter of inquiry.

Proposal deadlines: No later than November 1.

Contribution decisions made by: board of directors/trustees.

Frequency of contributions decisions: annually.

Typical time from application deadlines to notification: 45 days.

Staff/Trustees

Directors/trustees: Robert Newman, president; Sarah C. Newman, secretary; Mary Wright, treasurer.

NFC Foundation

PO Box 355
Minneapolis, MN 55440-0355
County: Hennepin
Phone: (952) 844-1201
Website: www.nashfinch.com/about_corpgiving.html
Contact: Brian Numainville, chair
Established: 06/05/1997
Donor: Nash Finch Company
Funder type: Corporate foundation

Program Description

Program's purpose: The foundation has been established by the Nash Finch Company to help feed the hungry and assist families and their children, within the communities we service, who are in need or find themselves in a time of crisis.

Geographic focus: Twin Cities Metropolitan Area, areas outside Minnesota.

Areas of interest:
EDUCATION.
FOOD/NUTRITION/AGRICULTURE: Food service/free food distribution.
HEALTH - DISEASES/MEDICAL DISCIPLINES.
HUMAN SERVICES: Children/youth services, Emergency assistance (food/clothing/cash), Family services.
PUBLIC SAFETY/DISASTERS/RELIEF: Disaster preparedness and relief, Safety education.

Intended beneficiaries: Children and youth (infants-19 years), General public/unspecified, Poor/economically disadvantaged.

Types of support for organizations:
PROGRAM DEVELOPMENT/PROJECT SUPPORT.
STUDENT AID (GRANTS TO INSTITUTIONS): Scholarship funds.

Sample grants:
Loaves & Fishes/MN/$25,000.
Perspectives Family Center - MN/MN/$12,000.
United Way (Twin Cities, Greater)/MN/relief for needy/$42,409.
University of MN Foundation/MN/community support/$4,950.
Wilderness Inquiry/Minneapolis, MN/disability relief/$5,000.

Financial Information

Financial data for year ending: 12/31/2005
Foundation assets: $610,654
Grants paid: $95,315
Number of grants: 11
Largest/smallest: $50,000/$120

Application Information

Preferred form of initial contact: letter of inquiry.
Proposal deadlines: none.

Staff/Trustees

Directors/trustees: Alec Covington; Bob Dimond; Kathleen Mahoney; Brian Numainville, chair.

Noel Foundation

13310 Coral Drive
Fort Myers, FL 33908
Phone: (941) 472-0194
Contact: Richard E. Jacker, vice president
Established: 12/18/1985
Funder type: Private foundation

Program Description

Geographic focus: Twin Cities Metropolitan Area, Greater Minnesota, Areas outside Minnesota.

Areas of interest:
ENVIRONMENTAL QUALITY/PROTECTION/BEAUTIFICATION.
HEALTH - GENERAL/REHABILITATIVE: Reproductive health care.
HUMAN SERVICES: Children/youth services, Family services, Family violence shelters and services.

Intended beneficiaries: General public/unspecified.

Exclusions: Non-501(c)(3).

Sample grants:
ACT/Fort Myers, FL/$500.
Brightest Horizons Daycare/Fort Myers, FL/$7,500.
Center for Family Crisis - Grand Marais/MN/$1,000.
Episcopal Community Services Inc - MN/MN/$2,000.
Family Tree Clinic/St Paul, MN/$1,000.
Human Development Services - NY/Port Chester, NY/$1,000.
MN Historical Society/MN/$1,000.
Planned Parenthood - MN/SD/MN/$1,000.

Financial Information

Financial data for year ending: 11/30/2005
Foundation assets: $439,829
Grants paid: $54,500
Number of grants: 20
Largest/smallest: $10,000/$500

Application Information

Preferred form of initial contact: letter of inquiry, complete proposal, any written form.
Proposal deadlines: none.

Staff/Trustees

Directors/trustees: William J. Berens; Neil Bettencourt; Carol Daniels, president; Richard E. Jacker, vice president; Amelia Spruill; Kevin Spruill; John P. Toombs; Polly Toombs.

Roger and Violet Noreen Charitable Trust

U.S. Bank, N.A.
101 East Fifth Street
St Paul, MN 55101
County: Ramsey
Phone: (651) 466-8444
Contact: Sally A. Mullen
Established: 04/07/1989
Funder type: Private foundation

Program Description

Funding priorities: Primarily to charitable, educational, religious or scientific purposes.

Geographic focus: Twin Cities Metropolitan Area.

Areas of interest:
ARTS, CULTURE, HUMANITIES.
HUMAN SERVICES.
RELIGION/SPIRITUAL DEVELOPMENT.

Intended beneficiaries: General public/unspecified.

Types of support for organizations:
CAPITAL CAMPAIGNS.
GENERAL PURPOSE/OPERATING SUPPORT.

Sample grants:

Casa de Esperanza/Minneapolis, MN/general operating/$7,500.

Children's Hospitals & Clinics Foundation/MN/NICU Expansion Project/$10,000.

Community Action Council - MN (Eagan)/MN/third installment of four-year pledge/$100,000.

DARTS Inc/MN/capital campaign/$40,000.

Loaves & Fishes/MN/St Mathew's site/$5,000.

Minneapolis Institute of Arts/MN/general operating/$3,000.

St Stephens Lutheran Church - W St Paul/MN/Lutheran Orient Mission/$40,000.

VIBE Urban Youth Ministries/MN/general operating/$7,000.

Financial Information

Financial data for year ending: 12/31/2005
Foundation assets: $7,061,710
Grants paid: $465,000
Number of grants: 21
Largest/smallest: $100,000/$500

Application Information

Preferred form of initial contact: letter of inquiry.

Proposal deadlines: ongoing.

Staff/Trustees

Directors/trustees: U.S. Bank, N.A.

North Star Charitable Foundation

2701 University Avenue SE
Minneapolis, MN 55414
County: Hennepin
Phone: (612) 617-6113
Fax: (612) 617-6001
Contact: Karen Johnson
Established: 09/02/2004
Funder type: Corporate foundation

Program Description

Program's purpose: Focus on supporting research, education, and information activities for breast cancer Alzheimer's disease and cystic fibrosis.

Areas of interest:
HEALTH - DISEASES/MEDICAL DISCIPLINES: Breast cancer, Alzheimer's disease, Cystic Fibrosis.
HEALTH - RESEARCH: Breast cancer, Alzheimer's disease, Cystic Fibrosis.

Sample grants:

American Cancer Society - MN (Minneapolis)/MN/$5,000.

Breast Cancer Awareness Association/MN/$18,000.

Regents of the University of California/CA/Medical research/$25,000.

Financial Information

Financial data for year ending: 12/31/2005
Foundation assets: $108,800
Grants paid: $97,185
Number of grants: 11
Largest/smallest: $25,000/$500

Application Information

Preferred form of initial contact: Standard grant request.

Proposal deadlines: None.

Staff/Trustees

Staff: Karen Johnson.

Directors/trustees: Phillip Richards, president; Scott Richards; Susan Richards.

North Suburban Community Foundation

2233 North Hamline Avenue
Suite 511
Roseville, MN 55113
County: Ramsey
Phone: (651) 633-3623
Contact: Donald F. Zibell, treasurer
Established: 08/12/1981
Funder type: Community/public foundation

Program Description

Program's purpose: Conduit for charitable gifts, comprised primarily of donor-designated funds.

Funding priorities: Any Roseville-based community charity.

Geographic focus: North suburban St Paul only.

Geographic limitations: Roseville-based charities, due to donor restrictions.

Areas of interest:
ARTS, CULTURE, HUMANITIES: Historical societies, Performing arts.
EDUCATION: Libraries/library science, Pre-school/elementary, Secondary.
RECREATION: Senior programs.
YOUTH DEVELOPMENT.

Intended beneficiaries: Children and youth (infants-19 years), General public/unspecified.

Types of support for organizations:
GENERAL PURPOSE/OPERATING SUPPORT.
PROGRAM DEVELOPMENT/PROJECT SUPPORT.
STUDENT AID (GRANTS TO INSTITUTIONS): Scholarship funds.

Sample grants:

ISD Moundsview #621/MN/Mounds View Senior High Local Scholarship Association/$3,500.

Resources for Child Caring/MN/$1,250.

Roseville Area Schools - District #623/MN/Middle School/$1,000.

Roseville Area Senior Program/MN/$2,500.

Roseville Arts Council/Roseville, MN/$2,500.

Roseville String Ensemble/Roseville, MN/$2,500.

SteppingStone Theatre for Youth Development/MN/$2,500.

Store to Door/MN/$2,500.

Financial Information

Financial data for year ending: 06/30/2006
Foundation assets: $601,631
Grants paid: $55,400
Number of grants: 33
Largest/smallest: $3,500/$100

Application Information

Preferred form of initial contact: letter of inquiry, telephone inquiry.

Accept common grant application: yes.

Proposal deadlines: February 15, May 17, August 23, November 15.

Preferred time for receiving proposals: February, May, August, November.

Contribution decisions made by: board of directors/trustees, committees.

Frequency of contributions decisions: quarterly.

Typical time from application deadlines to notification: 1 month.

Special application procedures: Grants: recipients are determined by broad-based grant committee from grant applications of qualifying organizations, except restricted gifts, which are made by advisory committees selected by donors. Scholarships: PTA committees select all scholarship winners at area high schools based on need, ability, potential, and service to school and community.

Staff/Trustees

Directors/trustees: George H. Krienke, president; Herbert Mischke; Jan Parker; Tammy Pust; Ronald J. Riach; Don Salverda; Gust Zahariades; Donald F. Zibell, treasurer.

North Suburban Youth Foundation

1970 Oakcrest Avenue
Suite 118
Roseville, MN 55113-2624
County: Ramsey
Phone: (651) 638-4600
E-mail: bmatson@nsyf.net
Website: www.nsyf.net
Contact: Robert Matson, CEO, executive director
Established: 10/01/1987
Funder type: Private foundation

Program Description

Program's purpose: The foundation is a community-based organization dedicated to the enhancement and enrichment of the lives of youth in the North Suburban community, by creating programs and providing assistance to youth through scholarships and grants.

Funding priorities: Grants must be going to a youth-related program or organization.

Geographic focus: East Metropolitan Area/St Paul only.

Geographic limitations: Grants restricted to the North Suburban area, which includes school districts 621, 623 (except the City of Maplewood) and a portion of 625.

Areas of interest:
COMMUNITY IMPROVEMENT.
EDUCATION.
RECREATION: Amateur sports clubs/leagues, Amateur sports competitions.
YOUTH DEVELOPMENT: Multipurpose youth centers/clubs, Scouting organizations, Youth development programs.

Intended beneficiaries: Children only (5-14 years), Youth/adolescents (ages 14-19).

Types of support for organizations:
PROGRAM DEVELOPMENT/PROJECT SUPPORT.

Types of support for individuals: scholarships.

Sample grants:
Arden Hills Soccer Club/MN/activities to promote youth participation in soccer/$1,142.
City of Arden Hills - MN/MN/community event sponsorship/$3,000.
Irondale High School/MN/activities to promote youth participation in skiing/$150.
ISD Roseville #623/MN/funds to provide all-day kindergarten/$5,000.
Little Canada Parks and Recreation/Little Canada, MN/community event sponsorship/$125.
Northwest Youth & Family Services/MN/health education services at schools/$5,000.
Ramsey County Public Library Foundation/MN/funding for bleachers/$8,000.
Roseville Parks & Recreation/MN/community event sponsorship/$2,500.

Financial Information

Financial data for year ending: 12/31/2005
Foundation assets: $380,538
Grants paid: $36,823
Number of grants: 21
Largest/smallest: $8,000/$125

Application Information

Preferred form of initial contact: letter of inquiry.

Public information available by request: proposal guidelines, application form, website.

Contribution decisions made by: board of directors/trustees.

Frequency of contributions decisions: monthly, June and November meetings are reserved for business meetings only.

Staff/Trustees

Staff: Robert Matson, CEO, executive director.

Directors/trustees: Bruce Bonine; Kerri Engholm; Jeff Johnson; Maggie Kahler; David Kill; Mike Kirschner; Perry Lofquist; Dale Maristuen, president; Barb Mastel; Betty Matson; Robert Matson, CEO, executive director; Gale Pederson; Greg Quitter; Christie Schmidt.

Northland Foundation

202 West Superior Street
Suite 610
Duluth, MN 55802
County: St Louis
Phone: (218) 723-4040
Alt. Phone: (800) 433-4045
Fax: (218) 723-4048
E-mail: info@northlandfdn.org
Website: www.northlandfdn.org
Established: 03/01/1986
Funder type: Community/public foundation

Program Description

Program's purpose: To strengthen families, grow a sustainable regional economy, cultivate leadership and philanthropy, and foster respect for all to achieve prosperity through economic and social justice.

Funding priorities: 1) Connecting Kids & Communities/Strengthening Families – To help communities build positive, caring environments for children, youth and families; 2) Aging with Independence – To foster independence, dignity, and respect for the growing number of older adults in our region; 3) Opportunities for Self-Reliance – To create opportunities for people to become self-sufficient and self-reliant by reducing social, institutional, and economic barriers.

Program limitations/restrictions: Grants to nonprofit organizations only. No grants to religious organizations for religious purposes, endowments, individuals, private foundations, national fundraising campaigns, capital, ticket sales, benefits or to replace government funding.

Geographic focus: Northeastern Minnesota.

Geographic limitations: Aitkin, Carlton, Cook, Itasca, Lake, Koochiching and St Louis Counties.

Areas of interest:
CIVIL RIGHTS: Civil rights/advocacy for specific groups, Equal opportunity and access, Intergroup relations/race relations.
COMMUNITY IMPROVEMENT: Economic development, Nonprofit management, Volunteer bureaus.
HEALTH - MENTAL HEALTH/CRISIS INTERVENTION: Counseling/support groups, Hotline/crisis intervention.
HOUSING/SHELTER: Housing support services, Homeless, Transitional housing.
HUMAN SERVICES: Children/youth services, Family services, Multipurpose human service organizations, Personal social services.
PUBLIC PROTECTION - CRIME/COURTS/LEGAL SERVICES: Crime prevention, Dispute/conflict resolution, Protection/prevention - neglect/abuse/exploitation.
YOUTH DEVELOPMENT: Adult/child matching programs, Multipurpose youth centers/clubs, Youth development programs.

Intended beneficiaries: General public/unspecified.

Types of support for organizations:
GENERAL PURPOSE/OPERATING SUPPORT.
MANAGEMENT/TECHNICAL ASSISTANCE.
PROGRAM DEVELOPMENT/PROJECT SUPPORT: Mentoring programs, Seed money/start-up funds.

Sample grants:

Action Through Churches Together - MN/MN/To expand community awareness on the issues and needs of young children through advocacy, outreach and education in the Itasca County area/$15,000.

ANGELS - MN/MN/To support a Living At Home/Block Nurse Program that assists older adults and people with disabilities to remain independent in their own homes/$20,000.

Ely Community Resource Inc/MN/To offer a variety of youth-led out-of-school time activities for young people, grades 7-12/$955.

ISD Duluth #709/MN/Denfield High School/To implement the LINK Crew transition program for incoming ninth-grade students/$6,000.

Kids Closet - Duluth/MN/To provide basic winter clothing to low-income families with pre-school through elementary-aged children/$5,000.

KIDS PLUS - MN (Esko)/MN/To implement the Esko Youth Leadership & Service Learning Program for incoming ninth-grade students/$5,000.

Northern Lights Community School - MN (Warba)/MN/To support a youth-developed Peace Garden and community beautification project/$1,000.

Range Women's Advocates/MN/To strengthen organizational capacity and improve service delivery to women and families in the Range Communities/$5,000.

Financial Information

Financial data for year ending: 06/30/2006
Foundation assets: $50,736,386
Grants paid: $1,027,789
Number of grants: 203
Largest/smallest: $25,000/$100

Application Information

Preferred form of initial contact: telephone inquiry, request for guidelines and preapplication form.

Public information available by request: proposal guidelines application form, annual report, newsletter, website.

Accept common grant application: yes.
Proposal deadlines: 15th of each month.

Contribution decisions made by: board of directors/trustees.
Frequency of contributions decisions: monthly.
Typical time from application deadlines to notification: 4 months.

Staff/Trustees

Staff: Jan Amys, program associate; Zane Bail, director of special projects; Heather Brouse, chief financial officer; Carol Chipman, receptionist/administrative assistant; Jeanine Dahl, director of communications; John Elden, director of business finance; Lynn Haglin, vice president/KIDS PLUS director; Kurt Johnson, senior loan officer; Shari McCorison, program associate; Beth Olson, administrative assistant/receptionist; Suzanne Rauvola, administrative assistant; Thomas S. Renier, president; Mary Robillard, grant program manager; Carole Saylor, grants coordinator.

Directors/trustees: David Clusiau; Jeff Corey; Ed Crawford, chair; Barbara Dorry, vice chair; Cindy Hansen, secretary/treasurer; Edwina Hertzberg; Kenneth A. Johnson; Rachel Kincade; Nancy Norr; Claudia Otos; Mark Phillips; Chuck Walt.

Northwest Minnesota Foundation

4225 Technology Drive NW
Bemidji, MN 56601-5118
County: Beltrami
Phone: (218) 759-2057
Fax: (218) 759-2328
E-mail: nwmf@nwmf.org
Website: www.nwmf.org
Contact: John S. Ostrem, president
Established: 04/01/1986
Funder type: Community/public foundation

Program Description

Program's purpose: To support regional economic growth and build individual, organizational and community capacity through a variety of grants, business loans, technical assistance, philanthropic services and educational opportunities.

Funding priorities: Caring Communities grants are awarded for inter-agency efforts that focus on issues affecting children, families and the elderly.

Community Planning grants are awarded for the design and implementation of plans that address affordable housing, community or economic development or effective management of community growth. Natural Resources grants are awarded for research leading to new strategies and/or technologies that add value to local resources and that promote the sustainable use and preservation of the natural resource base.

Program limitations/restrictions: Grants limited to nonprofit, tax-exempt organizations and governmental units. Ineligible activities include fundraising campaigns, religious, lobbying, equipment and building construction.

Geographic focus: Greater Minnesota.

Geographic limitations: Greater Northwest Minnesota: Beltrami, Clearwater, Hubbard, Kittson, Lake-of-the-Woods, Mahnomen, Marshall, Norman, Pennington, Polk, Red Lake and Roseau counties.

Areas of interest:
COMMUNITY IMPROVEMENT: Business services, Community/neighborhood development/improvement, Economic development, Nonprofit management, Community planning, Growth management.
EDUCATION: Youth leadership.
ENVIRONMENTAL QUALITY/PROTECTION/BEAUTIFICATION: Environmental beautification/open spaces, Natural resources conservation/protection, Research leading to the development of new strategies and/or technologies that add value to local resources, including agricultural and forest products.
FOOD/NUTRITION/AGRICULTURE: Agricultural programs.
HOUSING/SHELTER: Housing support services, Convening.
HUMAN SERVICES: Children/youth services, Emergency assistance (food/clothing/cash), Multipurpose human service organizations, Senior centers and services.
PHILANTHROPY/VOLUNTARISM: Philanthropy - general, Public foundations and community foundations, component and community fund development.
PUBLIC AFFAIRS/SOCIETY BENEFIT: Leadership development/awards programs (other than youth).
YOUTH DEVELOPMENT: Youth development programs.

Intended beneficiaries: General public/unspecified.

Types of support for organizations:
EMERGENCY FUNDS.
MANAGEMENT/TECHNICAL ASSISTANCE.
PROGRAM DEVELOPMENT/PROJECT SUPPORT.

Types of support for individuals: none.

Exclusions: Capital and endowment campaigns, Individuals, Non-501(c)(3), Religious organizations, Major equipment purchases, Annual fund drives, Building construction, Past operating deficits, General operating expenses, Lobbying, Publicity or advertising.

Sample grants:
Ada Area Promotions Committee - MN/MN/To increase the economic development capacity of the community by creating an improved business support system/$25,000.
Bi County CAP, Inc./MN/To help develop mental health services for children from birth to age 5/$5,000.
City of Park Rapids - MN/MN/To negotiate an agreement that will create a new growth management and service delivery model for the area/$5,000.
Family Advocacy Center - MN (Northern)/MN/For aid to victims of child abuse, domestic violence and sexual assault/$25,000.
International Water Institute - ND/ND/To develop a community Watershed Watch model by building on the existing River Watch program/$25,000.

Financial Information

Financial data for year ending: 06/30/2006
Foundation assets: $39,657,000
Grants paid: $923,408
Number of grants: 275
Largest/smallest: $50,000/$150
Typical grant amount: $10,000

Application Information

Preferred form of initial contact: telephone inquiry.
Public information available by request: proposal guidelines, application form, annual report, newsletter, website.
Accept common grant application: yes.
Accept common report form: yes.
Will view video: yes.
Proposal deadlines: Pre-proposals may be submitted at any time. Those received by the last Friday of each month will be reviewed at the next board meeting.
Contribution decisions made by: staff, board of directors/trustees.
Frequency of contributions decisions: monthly.
Specific times board meets: Third Friday of each month.
Typical time from application deadlines to notification: 2 weeks for pre-proposals.

Staff/Trustees

Staff: Lin Backstrom, early childhood development specialist; Peggy Crandall, grants services associate; Samantha Hedin, administrative assistant; Ritchie Houge, vice president for philanthropic services; Sandra Kamnikar, accounting associate; LaRae Maddox, office/systems manager; Diane Morey, business development specialist; John Ostrem, president; Lisa Peterson, communications specialist; Marty Sieve, vice president for programs; Jim Steenerson, grants specialist; Holly Tri, administrative assistant; Caryl Turnow, fund development specialist; Tim Wang, finance director; Rebecca Weir, training specialist; David West, business finance specialist.

Directors/trustees: Terri Anderson; Ann Beck; Eric Bergeson, board chair; David Bergman; Robert Hager; Mark Hewitt; Dean Johnson; Roger Malm; Gary Purath; Anne Sand; Kim Wilson.

Alice M. O'Brien Foundation

480 Grand Hill
St Paul, MN 55102
County: Ramsey
Contact: Thomond R. O'Brien, president
Established: 12/01/1951
Funder type: Private foundation

Program Description

Program limitations/restrictions: Preference given to Minnesota charitable organizations, but not limited to Minnesota.

Geographic focus: Twin Cities Metropolitan Area, Greater Minnesota, Minnesota statewide, Areas outside Minnesota.

Areas of interest:

ARTS, CULTURE, HUMANITIES: Historical societies, Museums, Performing arts, Visual arts.

EDUCATION.

HEALTH - RESEARCH.

HUMAN SERVICES.

Intended beneficiaries: General public/unspecified.

Types of support for organizations:

CAPITAL CAMPAIGNS: Building/renovation.

GENERAL PURPOSE/OPERATING SUPPORT.

RESEARCH.

Sample grants:

Archdiocesan AIDS Ministry Program/MN/general operating/$1,000.

Cathedral of St Paul/MN/roof project/$25,000.

Little Sisters of the Poor - MN (St Paul)/MN/general operating/$15,000.

Parks & Trails Council of MN/MN/general operating/$1,000.

Regions Hospital/MN/Alzheimer's research/$5,000.

Twin Cities Opera Guild Inc/MN/general operating/$2,000.

University of MN Hospital & Clinic/MN/lung disease research/$20,000.

University of MN Hospital & Clinic/MN/diabetes research/$20,000.

Financial Information

Financial data for year ending: 12/31/2006
Foundation assets: $3,900,000
Grants paid: $199,000
Number of grants: 27
Largest/smallest: $25,000/$1,000

Application Information

Preferred form of initial contact: complete proposal, no specific form, should include statement of exempt status, use of requested funds, short history of organization and financial statements.

Proposal deadlines: May 1 of each year.

Staff/Trustees

Directors/trustees: Alice Berquist; Alvina O'Brien, secretary; Eleanor O'Brien; Terrence O'Brien Jr.; Thomond R. O'Brien, president; Thomas P. Wilcox.

Casey Albert T. O'Neil Foundation

U.S. Bank, N.A.
101 East Fifth Street
St Paul, MN 55101
County: Ramsey
Phone: (651) 466-8718
Contact: Nancy Frankenberry
Established: 02/02/1965
Funder type: Private foundation

Program Description

Program's purpose: For religious purposes associated with the Roman Catholic Church or any religious order affiliated therewith, or for charitable, scientific, literary or education purposes or the prevention of cruelty to children or animals.

Geographic focus: Twin Cities Metropolitan Area, Greater Minnesota, Minnesota statewide, areas outside Minnesota.

Areas of interest:

ARTS, CULTURE, HUMANITIES: Historical societies, Media/communications, Museums, Performing arts.

EDUCATION.

ENVIRONMENTAL QUALITY/PROTECTION/BEAUTIFICATION.

HEALTH - DISEASES/MEDICAL DISCIPLINES.

HEALTH - GENERAL/REHABILITATIVE.

HUMAN SERVICES: Children/youth services, Emergency assistance (food/clothing/cash), Family services, Multipurpose human service organizations.

Intended beneficiaries: General public/unspecified.

Types of support for organizations:

GENERAL PURPOSE/OPERATING SUPPORT.

Types of support for individuals: none.

Exclusions: Individuals.

Sample grants:

Bridging, Inc/MN/general operating/$4,000.

Cystic Fibrosis Foundation - MN (Mpls)/MN/general operating/$20,000.

International Wolf Center/St Joseph, MN/general operating/$10,000.

La Oportunidad-Opportunity/St Paul, MN/general operating/$4,000.

Milwaukee Road Heritage Center/Montevideo, MN/general operating/$30,000.

MN Land Trust/MN/general operating/$5,000.

MN Museum of American Art/MN/general operating/$8,000.

Red Cloud Indian School - SD/Pine Ridge, SD/general operating/$10,000.

Financial Information

Financial data for year ending: 06/30/2006
Foundation assets: $13,069,726
Grants paid: $656,000
Number of grants: 82
Largest/smallest: $30,000/$1,000

Application Information

Preferred form of initial contact: letter of inquiry, a letter outlining the nature of the request and a copy of the IRS exemption letter.

Accept common grant application: yes.

Proposal deadlines: none.

Staff/Trustees

Directors/trustees: U.S. Bank, N.A.; Thomas Dwight; John Kelley; Casey Albert O'Neil.

O'Shaughnessy Foundation

1150 Friesen Drive
PO Box 923
Angwin, CA 55318
Established: 12/31/1996
Funder type: Private foundation

Program Description

Program's purpose: The foundation's mission is to educate patients, families, professionals and the public concerning the nature of depressive and manic-depressive illness as medical diseases; to foster self-help for patients and families; to eliminate discrimination and stigma associated with these illnesses; to improve the availability and quality of help and support; and to advocate for research toward the treatment and elimination of these illnesses. Formerly known as Five-O Foundation.

Geographic focus: Minnesota statewide, Areas outside Minnesota.

Areas of interest:
HEALTH - MENTAL HEALTH/CRISIS INTERVENTION: Mental health disorders, Mental health treatment and services.
HEALTH - RESEARCH: Mental health research.

Sample grants:
ALDEA - CA/Napa, CA/group home & counseling services for abused children/$15,000.
Family Service of the North Bay/Napa, CA/mental health counseling services and housing/$15,000.
Kindling Group, The/Chicago, IL/mental health education/$50,000.
Mayo Foundation/MN/medical research/$80,000.

Financial Information

Financial data for year ending: 10/31/2005
Foundation assets: $3,483,054
Grants paid: $550,000
Number of grants: 5
Largest/smallest: $40,000/$15,000

Staff/Trustees

Directors/trustees: Linda Bagaason; Betty O'Shaughnessy, president; Susan O'Shaughnessy; Dr. Dan Peters; Jack Thomas.

I. A. O'Shaughnessy Foundation, Incorporated

W-1271 First Bank Building
332 Minnesota Street
St Paul, MN 55101
County: Ramsey
Phone: (651) 222-2323
Fax: (651) 222-3638
E-mail: info@iaoshaughnessyfdn.org
Website: www.iaoshaughnessyfdn.org
Contact: Brenda Lommen, administrator
Established: 12/01/1941
Donor: I.A. O'Shaughnessy
Funder type: Private foundation

Program Description

Program's purpose: Support high-quality education that prepares students, Preschool-Grade 12, in disadvantaged communities for educational and life success.

Funding priorities: Students in high poverty areas who have low achievement scores, higher drop-out rates and low rates of college graduation. Low-income families who lack the resources to choose better schools. Schools that lack sufficient resources.

Geographic focus: National areas.

Areas of interest:
EDUCATION: Graduate education/professional schools, Higher education, Preschool/elementary, Secondary.

Intended beneficiaries: General public/unspecified.

Types of support for organizations: PROGRAM DEVELOPMENT/PROJECT SUPPORT.

Types of support for individuals: none.

Exclusions: Individuals, Non-501(c)(3), Political organizations.

Sample grants:
Boys Hope/Girls Hope - MO/MO/5-year grant/$1,000,000.
Cristo Rey Network - IL/IL/5-year grant/$1,000,000.
Foundation for the Nativity & Miguel Schools/DC/5-year grant/$1,000,000.
Lasallian Volunteer Program/MD/3-year grant/$300,000.
Montessori Training Center of MN/MN/3-year grant/$300,000.
SEED Academy/Harvest Preparatory School/Minneapolis, MN/3-year grant/$450,000.
Summerbridge Kent Denver/CO/3 year grant/$150,000.

Financial Information

Financial data for year ending: 12/31/2006
Foundation assets: $103,000,000
Grants paid: $4,017,982

Application Information

Preferred form of initial contact: letter of inquiry.

Public information available by request: proposal guidelines, website, letter of inquiry form.

Contribution decisions made by: board of directors/trustees.

Frequency of contributions decisions: quarterly.

Typical time from application deadlines to notification: 3-6 months.

Staff/Trustees

Staff: Brenda Lommen, administrator; Jane Stamstad, program and board consultant.

Directors/trustees: Teresa O'Shaughnessy Duggan; Charles Lyman; Eileen A. O'Shaughnessy, secretary; John F. O'Shaughnessy Jr.; Kathleen E. O'Shaughnessy; Michael W. O'Shaughnessy; Terence P. O'Shaughnessy; Timothy J. O'Shaughnessy, president; Michele O'Shaughnessy Traeger; Kathryn Wysong.

E.O. Olson Trust U/A Water Resources

U.S. Bank, N.A.
101 East Fifth Street
St Paul, MN 55101
County: Ramsey
Phone: (651) 466-8744
Contact: Ted Olsen
Established: 08/19/1964
Funder type: Private foundation

Program Description

Program's purpose: For the development of an adequate water supply for the city of Worthington, MN and surrounding territory.

Geographic focus: Greater Minnesota; Worthington area.

Areas of interest:
ENVIRONMENTAL QUALITY/ PROTECTION/BEAUTIFICATION: Natural resources conservation/protection.

Intended beneficiaries: General public/unspecified.

Sample grant:
City of Worthington/MN/$16,096.

Financial Information

Financial data for year ending: 12/31/2005
Foundation assets: $372,513
Grants paid: $16,317
Number of grants: 1

Application Information

Preferred form of initial contact: letter of inquiry.

Contribution decisions made by: advisory board.

Staff/Trustees

Staff: Ted Olsen.
Directors/trustees: U.S. Bank, N.A.

Dwight D. Opperman Foundation

225 South Sixth Street
Suite 5250
Minneapolis, MN 55402
County: Hennepin
Established: 09/18/1996
Funder type: Private foundation

Program Description

Intended beneficiaries: General public/unspecified.

Sample grants:
Breck School/MN/$25,000.
East Metro Music Academy/MN/$10,000.
Greater Twin Cities Youth Symphonies/MN/$5,000.
Latin Athletes Education Fund/MN/$10,000.
MN Business Academy/MN/$10,000.
PACER Center (Parent Advoc Coalition Edu Rights)/MN/$25,000.
Second Harvest - MN/MN/$500.
St Paul Chamber Orchestra/MN/$10,000.

Financial Information

Financial data for year ending: 12/31/2005
Foundation assets: $17,322,424
Grants paid: $790,100
Number of grants: 37
Largest/smallest: $150,000/$500

Application Information

Preferred form of initial contact: letter of inquiry.

Proposal deadlines: none.

Staff/Trustees

Staff: Julie R. Nelson, executive director.

Directors/trustees: Cathy Farrell; Dwight D. Opperman, president; Fane W. Opperman; Vance K. Opperman.

Ordean Foundation

501 Ordean Building
Duluth, MN 55802
County: St Louis
Phone: (218) 726-4787
Fax: (218) 726-4848
Contact: Joe E. Everett, program director
Established: 12/19/1933
Paid Staff: Yes
Funder type: Private foundation

Program Description

Program's purpose: Services for low-income people; treatment, care and rehabilitation services for mentally and physically challenged people, elderly, and chemically dependent people; youth services to prevent delinquency.

Funding priorities: Food, clothing, shelter, medical care, individual and family counseling, and programs for youths.

Program limitations/restrictions: Must serve low-income and/or mentally or physically challenged populations. No grants for political campaigns or lobbying, direct religious purposes; research; or national fundraising. In order to support Duluth's critically needed basic needs and youth programs during the current nonprofit financial crisis, the Ordean Foundation will not accept unsolicited proposals in 2007.

Geographic focus: Greater Duluth area only.

Areas of interest:
EDUCATION: Higher education, Vocational/technical, Pre-school, Literacy.
EMPLOYMENT/JOBS: Career path development.
FOOD/NUTRITION/AGRICULTURE: Food service/free food distribution, Nutrition promotion.
HEALTH - GENERAL/REHABILITATIVE: Emergency medical services, Health support services, Public health programs/wellness education, Rehabilitative medical services.
HEALTH - MENTAL HEALTH/CRISIS INTERVENTION: Addiction disorders, Alcohol/drug/substance, prevention and treatment, Counseling/support groups, Hotline/crisis intervention, Mental health associations, Mental health disorders, Mental health treatment and services.
HOUSING/SHELTER: Homeless, temporary housing, Housing development/construction/management, Housing search assistance, Housing support services, Low-cost temporary housing.
HUMAN SERVICES: Children/youth services, Emergency assistance (food/clothing/cash), Family services, Family services for adolescent parents, Family violence shelters and services, Multipurpose human service organizations, Personal social services, Residential/custodial care, Victims services.
PUBLIC PROTECTION - CRIME/COURTS/LEGAL SERVICES: Legal services, Protection/prevention - neglect/abuse/exploitation, Rehabilitation of offenders.
YOUTH DEVELOPMENT: Adult/child matching programs, Multipurpose youth centers/clubs, Youth development programs.

Intended beneficiaries: Adults, Homeless, Mentally/emotionally disabled, Physically disabled, Poor/economically disadvantaged, Single parents, Children and youth (infants-22 years).

Types of support for organizations:
GENERAL PURPOSE/OPERATING SUPPORT.
PROGRAM DEVELOPMENT/PROJECT SUPPORT: Mentoring programs.
STUDENT AID (GRANTS TO INSTITUTIONS): Scholarship funds.

Sample grants:
Boys & Girls Club - MN (Duluth)/MN/ $55,000.

Lake Superior Community Health Center/Duluth, MN/$350,000.

Life House - MN (Duluth)/MN/$40,000.

Residential Services of Northeastern MN Inc/MN/Fetal alcohol syndrome program/$15,000.

Safe Haven Shelter for Battered Women/MN/$80,000.

Second Harvest Northern Lakes Food Bank/MN/$10,000.

Women's Community Development Organization - MN (Duluth)/MN/$50,000.

YMCA - MN (Duluth)/MN/Mentor Duluth/$150,000.

Financial Information

Financial data for year ending: 12/31/2005
Foundation assets: $38,761,351
Grants paid: $1,888,270
Number of grants: 40
Largest/smallest: $150,000/$5,000
Typical grant amount: $40,000

Application Information

Preferred form of initial contact: telephone inquiry.

Public information available by request: proposal guidelines, application form.

Accept common grant application: yes.

Accept common report form: yes.

Proposal deadlines: middle of each month.

Contribution decisions made by: board of directors/trustees.

Frequency of contributions decisions: monthly.

Typical time from application deadlines to notification: 30 days.

Special application procedures: Please note that in order to help maintain critically needed services in Duluth during the current nonprofit financial crisis, the Ordean Foundation will not accept unsolicited proposals in 2007.

Staff/Trustees

Staff: Joe E. Everett, program director; Peggy Hom, administrative assistant; Stephen A. Mangan, executive director.

Directors/trustees: Larry Fortner; JoAnn Hoag, vice-president; Beth Kelly, treasurer; Lauren Larsen; Mark Melhus, president; Carol Person, secretary; Mary Beth Santori; Lonnie Swartz; Anntionette D. Thorstad.

OSilas Foundation

309 Pondfield Road
Bronxville, NY 10708
Phone: (914) 337-4044
Contact: Silas M. Ford III, president
Established: 01/01/1999
Funder type: Private foundation

Program Description

Program's purpose: General charitable purposes.

Program limitations/restrictions: Awards are made for religious, charitable, scientific, literary or educational purposes. No other restrictions apply.

Geographic focus: Twin Cities Metropolitan Area, Greater Minnesota, Areas outside Minnesota.

Areas of interest:
ARTS, CULTURE, HUMANITIES.
EDUCATION: Higher education, Libraries/library science, Pre-school/elementary, Secondary.
ENVIRONMENTAL QUALITY/PROTECTION/BEAUTIFICATION.

Intended beneficiaries: General public/unspecified.

Types of support for organizations:
CAPITAL CAMPAIGNS: Endowment funds.
GENERAL PURPOSE/OPERATING SUPPORT: Annual campaigns.
STUDENT AID (GRANTS TO INSTITUTIONS): Scholarship funds.

Sample grants:

American Ballet Theater Foundation/New York, NY/general operating/$3,000.

American Whitewater/MD/general operating/$500.

Blake School/MN/centennial fund/$20,000.

Circus Juventas - MN/MN/general operating/$1,000.

Concordia College - MN (Moorhead)/MN/Russian scholarship fund/$1,000.

Dodge Nature Center, Thomas Irvine/St Paul, MN/capital improvements/$207,500.

Sarah Lawrence College/Bronxville, NY/Fund for Sarah Lawrence/$2,500.

St Paul Academy & Summit School/MN/general operating/$1,500.

Financial Information

Financial data for year ending: 12/31/2005
Foundation assets: $6,091,988
Grants paid: $264,850
Number of grants: 32
Largest/smallest: $80,000/$200

Application Information

Preferred form of initial contact: applications may take any form.

Proposal deadlines: none.

Staff/Trustees

Directors/trustees: Francios Bertschy; Nannette Bertschy; Christopher Ford; David C. Ford; Durand G. Ford; Margaret Ford; Olivia C. Ford; Silas M. Ford III, president; Kimberly Ford-Werling; Bruce Genereaux; Olivia J. Genereaux; Robert Werling.

Osterud-Winter Foundation

909 South Broadway
Spring Valley, MN 55975
County: Fillmore
Phone: (507) 285-7045
Established: 01/01/1993
Funder type: Private foundation

Program Description

Program limitations/restrictions: Grants are restricted to the Kingsland Scholarship fund. Grants to select local nonprofits are at the discretion of the trustees.

Geographic limitations: Grants only to organizations within 15 miles of Spring Valley, MN.

Sample grants:

City of Spring Valley/MN/$9,500.

Community Memorial Nursing Home/MN/$4,500.

Good Earth Village Log Cabin/MN/$2,600.

Kingsland School/MN/$38,600.

Spring Valley Ambulance/MN/$2,600.

Spring Valley Cemetery Association/MN/$4,500.

Spring Valley Historical Society/MN/ $7,100.

St John's Food Shelf/MN/$2,600.

Financial Information

Financial data for year ending: 12/31/2006
Foundation assets: $1,400,000
Grants paid: $68,050
Number of grants: 8
Largest/smallest: $38,600/$1,000

Staff/Trustees

Directors/trustees: Mary Jo Dathe; Rita Hartert; James McCabe.

Otter Tail Power Company

Community Connections program
215 South Cascade Street
Fergus Falls, MN 56537
County: Otter Tail
Phone: (218) 739-8206
Fax: (218) 739-8218
E-mail: bluhning@otpco.com
Website: www.otpco.com
Contact: Becky Luhning, executive assistant
Funder type: Corporate giving program

Program Description

Program's purpose: Our mission is to connect with rural communities to help them support young minds, invest in our current and future workforce, create vibrant culture and vital communities, improve health and human services, and protect our natural resources.

Funding priorities: Education, Health and Human Services, Arts and Culture, Community Enhancement, Environment.

Program limitations/restrictions: We do not fund organizations without 501(c)(3) status, requests from outside Otter Tail Power Company's service area, individuals, lobbying, political, or fraternal organizations, religious organizations.

Geographic limitations: Limited to the Otter Tail Power Company's service areas in MN, ND, and SD.

Areas of interest:

ANIMAL RELATED: Wildlife preservation/protection, Zoo/zoological societies.

ARTS, CULTURE, HUMANITIES: Arts/cultural multipurpose, Historical societies, Museums, Performing arts.

COMMUNITY IMPROVEMENT: Community/neighborhood development/improvement, Economic development.

EDUCATION: Graduate education/professional schools, Higher education, Libraries/library science, Vocational/technical.

ENVIRONMENTAL QUALITY/PROTECTION/BEAUTIFICATION: Natural resources conservation/protection, Research.

HEALTH - GENERAL/REHABILITATIVE: Health care financing activities, Hospitals and related primary medical care facilities, Public health programs/wellness education.

HEALTH - RESEARCH: Cancer research.

HOUSING/SHELTER: Habitat for Humanity.

HUMAN SERVICES: Children/youth services, Emergency assistance (food/clothing/cash), Family violence shelters and services, Multipurpose human service organizations, Senior centers and services.

PHILANTHROPY/VOLUNTARISM: Nonprofit sector assistance, Voluntarism promotion.

PUBLIC PROTECTION - CRIME/COURTS/LEGAL SERVICES: Crime prevention, Law enforcement agencies.

PUBLIC SAFETY/DISASTERS/RELIEF: Disaster preparedness and relief, Safety education.

SCIENCE/TECHNOLOGY: Engineering/technology research.

YOUTH DEVELOPMENT: Multipurpose youth centers/clubs, Scouting organizations.

Intended beneficiaries: General public/unspecified.

Types of support for organizations:

CAPITAL CAMPAIGNS: Building/renovation.

GENERAL PURPOSE/OPERATING SUPPORT: Annual campaigns.

PROGRAM DEVELOPMENT/PROJECT SUPPORT: Conferences/seminars.

STUDENT AID (GRANTS TO INSTITUTIONS): Scholarship funds.

IN-KIND SERVICES: Printing.

Types of support for individuals: none.

Matching grants: employee matching, higher education.

Exclusions: Individuals, Non-501(c)(3), Political organizations, Religious organizations.

Sample grants:

Anne Carlson Center for Children - ND/ND/general operating/$5,000.

Bismarck State College/ND/scholarships/$32,000.

Center for the Arts - MN (White Bear Lake)/MN/general operating/$5,000.

Girl Scout Council - MN/MN/scholarships/$2,500.

Habitat for Humanity - MN/MN/in-kind printing/$3,500.

International Music Camp/ND/scholarships/$4,500.

MeritCare Foundation - ND/ND/general operating/$3,000.

Mitchell Area Technical Institute/SD/scholarships/$6,000.

Financial Information

Financial data for year ending: 12/31/2006
Grants paid: $400,000
Number of grants: 200
Largest/smallest: $20,000/$200
Largest multi-year grant approved: $200,000
Purpose: capital campaign

Application Information

Preferred form of initial contact: complete proposal.

Public information available by request: proposal guidelines, application form, website.

Proposal deadlines: March 1, June 1, September 1, December 1.

Contribution decisions made by: employee committee.

Frequency of contributions decisions: quarterly, March 15, June 15, September 15 and December 15.

Typical time from application deadlines to notification: 3 weeks after meeting.

Staff/Trustees

Staff: Matt Bucher, manager, customer service; Nancy Heck, market research/financial analyst; Mark Helland, vice president, customer service; Cris Kling, director, public relations; Becky Luhning, executive assistant.

Ben and Jeanne Overman Charitable Trust

131 West Superior Street
North Shore Bank Commerce
Duluth, MN 55802
County: St Louis
Phone: (218) 722-4784
Contact: Jeffrey Cadwell
Established: 09/01/1980
Funder type: Private foundation

Program Description

Funding priorities: 501(c)(3) organizations authorized to carry on religious, charitable, scientific, literary or educational activities.
Geographic focus: Greater Minnesota, primarily in Duluth region.
Areas of interest:
EDUCATION: Higher education.
HUMAN SERVICES: Children/youth services, Emergency assistance (food/clothing/cash), Family services, Family violence shelters and services, Multipurpose human service organizations.
RELIGION/SPIRITUAL DEVELOPMENT.
YOUTH DEVELOPMENT: Multipurpose youth centers/clubs, Youth development programs.
Intended beneficiaries: General public/unspecified.
Types of support for organizations:
CAPITAL CAMPAIGNS.
GENERAL PURPOSE/OPERATING SUPPORT.
PROGRAM DEVELOPMENT/PROJECT SUPPORT.
STUDENT AID (GRANTS TO INSTITUTIONS): Scholarship funds.
Exclusions: Non-501(c)(3).
Sample grants:
Boys & Girls Club - MN (Duluth)/MN/scholarships/$7,500.
Churches United in Ministry/Duluth, MN/general operating/$1,000.
First Witness Child Abuse Resource Center/Duluth, MN/general operating/$2,000.
Lake Superior Center/Duluth, MN/general operating/$5,000.
Northwood Children's Home/Duluth, MN/general operating/$5,000.
Temple Israel, Duluth/MN/general operating/$15,000.
Union Gospel Mission - MN (Duluth)/MN/soup kitchen/$2,000.
University of MN - Duluth/MN/general operating/$33,500.

Financial Information

Financial data for year ending: 12/31/2005
Foundation assets: $2,882,482
Grants paid: $138,000
Number of grants: 26
Largest/smallest: $33,500/$250

Application Information

Preferred form of initial contact: telephone inquiry, request for guidelines.
Proposal deadlines: May 31.

Staff/Trustees

Directors/trustees: North Shore Bank of Commerce; Beverly Goldfine; Manley Goldfine; Steve Goldfine; Jane Overman; James Sher.

Owatonna Foundation

PO Box 642
Owatonna, MN 55060
County: Steele
Phone: (507) 455-2995
E-mail: info@owatonnafoundation.com
Website: www.owatonnafoundation.com
Established: 12/24/1957
Paid Staff: Yes
Funder type: Community/public foundation

Program Description

Program's purpose: Provide grants to 501(c)(3) agencies to purchase equipment for the community betterment, educational, health, literary, recreational, scientific, musical or cultural benefit of the residents of the Steele County area. Also provide scholarships to local high school graduates and others for continuing secondary education.
Program limitations/restrictions: Grants are for nothing other than capital expenditures in Steele County area.
Geographic focus: Greater Minnesota, Steele County area only.
Areas of interest:
ARTS, CULTURE, HUMANITIES: Arts services, Arts/cultural multipurpose, Historical societies, Humanities, Media/communications, Museums, Performing arts, Visual arts.
COMMUNITY IMPROVEMENT: Community coalitions, Community service clubs, Community/neighborhood development/improvement, Economic development.
EDUCATION: Adult/continuing education/literacy, Educational services, Higher education, Libraries/library science, Preschool/elementary, Secondary, Student services/organizations of students, Vocational/technical.
EMPLOYMENT/JOBS: Employment procurement/job training, Vocational rehabilitation.
ENVIRONMENTAL QUALITY/PROTECTION/BEAUTIFICATION.
FOOD/NUTRITION/AGRICULTURE.
HEALTH - DISEASES/MEDICAL DISCIPLINES.
HEALTH - GENERAL/REHABILITATIVE.
HEALTH - MENTAL HEALTH/CRISIS INTERVENTION.
HEALTH - RESEARCH.
HOUSING/SHELTER.
HUMAN SERVICES.
PUBLIC AFFAIRS/SOCIETY BENEFIT.
PUBLIC PROTECTION - CRIME/COURTS/LEGAL SERVICES.
PUBLIC SAFETY/DISASTERS/RELIEF.
RECREATION.
SCIENCE/TECHNOLOGY.
SOCIAL SCIENCES.
YOUTH DEVELOPMENT.
Intended beneficiaries: General public/unspecified.
Types of support for organizations:
CAPITAL CAMPAIGNS: Building/renovation.
STUDENT AID (GRANTS TO INSTITUTIONS): Scholarship funds.
Types of support for individuals: none.
Sample grants:
Citizens Scholarship Foundation of America - MN/MN/scholarships/$30,000.
Civil Air Patrol - MN (Owatonna)/MN/$3,448.
Little Theatre of Owatonna/MN/$8,504.

Owatonna Arts Council/MN/$14,783.
Owatonna Gun Club/MN/$10,000.
Owatonna Skate Park/MN/$82,867.
Owatonna Soccer Fields/MN/$140,000.
Steele County 2nd Arena/MN/$8,000.

Financial Information

Financial data for year ending: 12/31/2005
Foundation assets: $6,387,505
Grants paid: $357,143
Number of grants: 8
Largest/smallest: $122,840/$6,030

Application Information

Preferred form of initial contact: letter of inquiry, telephone inquiry, request for guidelines.
Public information available by request: proposal guidelines, application form, annual report, newsletter.
Proposal deadlines: May 1 and September 1 each calendar year.
Contribution decisions made by: board of directors/trustees, executive committee.
Frequency of contributions decisions: semiannually.
Typical time from application deadlines to notification: 1-3 months.

Staff/Trustees

Staff: Jim Brunner, asst secretary/treasurer.
Directors/trustees: Chad S. Lange, president; Timothy McManimon; Kenneth E. Wilcox.

P.G.N. Foundation

c/o U.S. Bank
155 First Avenue SW
Rochester, MN 55902
County: Olmsted
Phone: (507) 285-7925
Contact: Duane Feragen
Established: 09/15/1961
Funder type: Private foundation

Program Description

Geographic focus: Twin Cities Metropolitan Area, Minnesota statewide, Areas outside Minnesota, Montana.
Geographic limitations: Primarily in the states of Minnesota and Montana.
Areas of interest:
ARTS, CULTURE, HUMANITIES.
COMMUNITY IMPROVEMENT.
EDUCATION.
ENVIRONMENTAL QUALITY/PROTECTION/BEAUTIFICATION.
HEALTH - DISEASES/MEDICAL DISCIPLINES.
HEALTH - GENERAL/REHABILITATIVE.
HUMAN SERVICES.
RELIGION/SPIRITUAL DEVELOPMENT.
YOUTH DEVELOPMENT.
Intended beneficiaries: General public/unspecified.
Exclusions: PGN Foundation grants are focused on organizations in which board member(s) are actively involved or personally support.
Sample grants:
Boys & Girls Club - MN (Minneapolis)/MN/general operating/$500.
Citizens League - MN (Minneapolis)/MN/general operating/$400.
Learning Disabilities Association - MN (Mpls)/MN/general operating/$500.
MN Orchestra/MN/general operating/$2,000.
Montana Fish, Wildlife and Parks Foundation/Helena, MT/partners in life/$10,000.
New Prague Gymnastics Club/MN/general operating/$1,200.
Pillsbury Neighborhood Services Inc/MN/general operating/$500.
St Paul Episcopal Church/Minneapolis, MN/general operating/$2,500.

Financial Information

Financial data for year ending: 08/31/2006
Foundation assets: $1,569,298
Grants paid: $67,000
Number of grants: 71
Largest/smallest: $10,000/$200

Application Information

Preferred form of initial contact: letter of inquiry, written form only.
Contribution decisions made by: board of directors/trustees.

Staff/Trustees

Directors/trustees: Andrea C. Anderson; John D. Curtin; John S. Curtin; Paula S. Curtin, president.

Pagel Foundation

2940 Gale Road
Wayzata, MN 55391
County: Hennepin
Phone: (952) 475-2084
Contact: Jack W. Pagel, president
Established: 12/29/1986
Funder type: Private foundation

Program Description

Program's purpose: To promote Christian and educational values and institutions.
Geographic focus: Twin Cities Metropolitan Area, Greater Minnesota, Areas outside Minnesota.
Areas of interest:
EDUCATION.
RELIGION/SPIRITUAL DEVELOPMENT.
Sample grants:
Augustana Lutheran Church - Minneapolis/MN/$1,000.
City of Minnetonka - MN/MN/recreation department/$1,000.
Faith Studies International/Chanhassen, MN/$5,000.
Focus on the Family/Colorado Springs, CO/$10,000.
Grace Lutheran Church - MN (Wayzata)/MN/$5,000.
Gustavus Adolphus College - MN/MN/$9,575.
Lutheran Orient Mission Society/MN/$1,000.
University of MN/MN/$1,140.

Financial Information

Financial data for year ending: 12/31/2005
Foundation assets: $3,086,803
Grants paid: $45,355
Number of grants: 8
Largest/smallest: $10,000/$350

Application Information

Preferred form of initial contact: letter of inquiry; no formal form or format for submitting applications.

Proposal deadlines: none.

Typical time from application deadlines to notification: 3 weeks.

Special application procedures: send a letter stating the organization's function and purpose for using the funds, and attach a copy of the organization's IRS letter stating its tax-exempt status.

Staff/Trustees

Directors/trustees: Jack W. Pagel, president.

Pajor Family Foundation

380 Ridge Circle
Wayzata, MN 55391
County: Hennepin
Phone: (480) 595-7516
Contact: Robert E. Pajor
Established: 12/12/1994
Funder type: Private foundation

Program Description

Geographic focus: Twin Cities Metropolitan Area, Greater Minnesota, Areas outside Minnesota.

Areas of interest:
EDUCATION.
HEALTH - DISEASES/MEDICAL DISCIPLINES.
HUMAN SERVICES.
RELIGION/SPIRITUAL DEVELOPMENT.
YOUTH DEVELOPMENT.

Intended beneficiaries: General public/unspecified.

Types of support for organizations:
GENERAL PURPOSE/OPERATING SUPPORT.

Sample grants:

Archdiocese - AZ/AZ/general operating/$500.

Family Hope Services Inc - MN (Plymouth)/ MN/general operating/ $1,500.

Hearing and Service Dog Program of MN/MN/general operating/$5,000.

Holy Name of Jesus of Medina/MN/ general operating/$6,025.

Interfaith Outreach - Wayzata/MN/ general operating/$3,700.

Quakerdale/IA/general operating/ $13,100.

St Mary's College - MN (Winona)/MN/ general operating/$1,000.

University of MN Foundation/MN/ general operating/$50.

Financial Information

Financial data for year ending: 12/31/2005
Foundation assets: $1,309,691
Grants paid: $61,362
Number of grants: 42
Largest/smallest: $12,500/$20

Application Information

Preferred form of initial contact: complete proposal.

Proposal deadlines: none.

Special application procedures: no specific requirements for form of application.

Staff/Trustees

Directors/trustees: Michaeline D. Pajor; Robert E. Pajor; Scott R. Pajor; Steven M. Pajor; Wendy R. Pajor.

Lewis and Annie F. Paper Foundation, Inc.

197 Woodlawn Avenue
St Paul, MN 55105-1143
County: Ramsey
Phone: (651) 699-6106
Contact: Deborah Arrigoni
Established: 12/01/1947
Funder type: Private foundation

Program Description

Program's purpose: General charitable purposes.

Funding priorities: Public charities serving fields of health, education, culture, history.

Geographic focus: Twin Cities Metropolitan Area.

Areas of interest:
ARTS, CULTURE, HUMANITIES.
EDUCATION.
HEALTH - GENERAL/ REHABILITATIVE.

Intended beneficiaries: General public/unspecified.

Types of support for organizations:
CAPITAL CAMPAIGNS.

GENERAL PURPOSE/OPERATING SUPPORT: Annual campaigns.

Sample grants:

Mount Zion Hebrew Congregation/St Paul, MN/capital campaign/$20,000.

The Science Museum of MN/MN/building campaign/$5,000.

St Paul Academy & Summit School/ MN/building fund/$10,000.

Temple Sinai/St Paul, MN/$1,650.

United Jewish Fund & Council/MN/ $30,000.

Financial Information

Financial data for year ending: 12/31/2005
Foundation assets: $554,898
Grants paid: $57,935
Number of grants: 8
Largest/smallest: $26,000/$1,650

Application Information

Preferred form of initial contact: complete proposal, include audited financial statements.

Proposal deadlines: November 15.

Staff/Trustees

Directors/trustees: Deborah F. Arrigoni; Carolyn D. Forman; James D. Forman; Willis M. Forman; Barney W. Harris; Lewis R. Harris.

Park Nicollet Foundation

6500 Excelsior Boulevard
St Louis Park, MN 55426
County: Hennepin
Phone: (952) 993-5023
Fax: (952) 993-6745
Website: www.parknicollet.com/ foundation
Contact: Michael J. Johnson, president, Park Nicollet Foundation & senior vice president, PNHS
Established: 01/01/1973
Funder type: Supporting organization

Program Description

Program's purpose: Respond to the health care needs of the community. Healthy Community grants focus on improving the health of children and families, and increasing developmental assets of children and decreasing their risk factors. Internal grants distribute designated funds to programs and services of Park Nicollet that support patient needs.

Funding priorities: Improved health of children and families/research and education/clinical areas of designation (cancer, diabetes, hospice, Parkinson's, eating disorder).

Geographic focus: West Metropolitan Area/Minneapolis only, areas where Park Nicollet Clinics are located.

Geographic limitations: western, south, northwest Twin Cities.

Areas of interest:
COMMUNITY IMPROVEMENT: Community/neighborhood development/improvement.
HEALTH - DISEASES/MEDICAL DISCIPLINES: In partnership with Park Nicollet Health Services.
HEALTH - GENERAL/REHABILITATIVE: Health support services, Health treatment facilities - primarily outpatient, Public health programs/wellness education, In partnership with Park Nicollet Health Services.
HEALTH - MENTAL HEALTH/CRISIS INTERVENTION: Counseling/support groups, Hotline/crisis intervention, Mental health treatment and services, in partnership with Park Nicollet Health Services.
HEALTH - RESEARCH: In partnership with Park Nicollet Health Services.
HOUSING/SHELTER: Housing support services.
HUMAN SERVICES: Children/youth services, Emergency assistance (food/clothing/cash), Family services, Family services for adolescent parents, Family violence shelters and services, Multipurpose human service organizations, Services to specific groups.
PUBLIC PROTECTION - CRIME/COURTS/LEGAL SERVICES: Crime prevention.
SOCIAL SCIENCES: Interdisciplinary research/studies to improve understanding of particular populations/cultures.
YOUTH DEVELOPMENT: Multipurpose youth centers/clubs, Youth development programs.

Intended beneficiaries: Adults, African Americans/Blacks, Aging/elderly/senior citizens, Asian/Pacific Islanders, Blind/vision impaired, Children and youth (infants-19 years), Crime/abuse victims, Deaf/hearing impaired, Ethnic/racial minorities - other specified group(s), Ethnic/racial populations - general, Hispanics/Latinos, Immigrants/newcomers/refugees, Infants/children (ages 0-14), Mentally/emotionally disabled, Physically disabled, Poor/economically disadvantaged, Youth/adolescents (ages 14-19).

Types of support for organizations: PROGRAM DEVELOPMENT/PROJECT SUPPORT.

Types of support for individuals: none.

Exclusions: Capital and endowment campaigns, Individuals, Non-501(c)(3), Political organizations, Religious organizations, individual scholarships/loans.

Sample grants:
Central Clinic/MN/Primary care, mental health and personal health services for St Louis Park youth — infancy through high school/$48,500.

Family Hope Services/TreeHouse - MN/MN/Services Expansion project: expand at-risk youth program services into St Louis Park and launch youth program services in Plymouth and Wayzata/$10,000.

Hopkins Area Family Resource Center/MN/Human service programs for families in turmoil providing housing information, employment search assistance, emergency food programs, back-to-school supply drive, winter warm-wear, toy chest and tax preparation assistance; Project Starfish: one-to-one human service support; Smart Money 101: financial classes/$15,000.

Park Nicollet Clinic/MN/Children's Reading Initiative, promote developmental assets of literacy by giving books to children after visiting Park Nicollet clinics or Methodist Hospital/$25,000.

Park Nicollet Clinic/MN/Growing Through Grief, grief school support program (serving 9 school districts: Minnetonka, Edina, St Louis Park, Hopkins, Wayzata, Mound-Westonka, Prior Lake, Burnsville and Edina)/$73,400.

Teens Alone, Inc - MN/MN/Free counseling for middle, junior and high school youth and their families in the Eden Prairie, Hopkins, Orono, St Louis Park and Wayzata school districts/$15,000.

Washburn Child Guidance Center/MN/Chemical Health Family Services program: provide parenting skills to mothers and fathers recovering from chemical abuse; provide prevention services for youth at risk for drug abuse/$3,000.

YMCA - MN (Ridgedale Branch)/MN/Minnetonka Heights program: connecting seniors to needed health services; after-school and summer youth program/$5,000.

Financial Information

Financial data for year ending: 12/31/2005
Grants paid: $2,002,709

Application Information

Preferred form of initial contact: website for current Healthy Community guidelines and application; telephone inquiry only if additional assistance is needed.

Public information available by request: Website for Healthy Community guidelines and application form; annual report available upon request.

Proposal deadlines: Healthy Community grant requests for $5,000 or less can be submitted at any time during the year; Healthy Community grant requests greater than $5,000 must be submitted by noon the first Friday in May.

Contribution decisions made by: board of directors/trustees, community members and Park Nicollet Foundation president.

Frequency of contributions decisions: annually for Healthy Community requests of greater than $5,000; monthly for requests less than $5,000.

Typical time from application deadlines to notification: Between 3-5 weeks for requests of $5,000 or less; up to 14 weeks for requests of more than $5,000.

Staff/Trustees

Staff: Joan Bjergen, data management assistant; Judy Burdick, data management assistant; Kelly Codega, senior major gifts officer; Nadia Facey, special events & community coordinator; Chris Johnson, M.D., medical director of development; Michael J. Johnson, president, Park Nicollet Foundation & senior vice president, PNHS; Susan Knollenberg, director, resource development; Sharon Messler, database management specialist; Sherril Mozey, executive assistant; Colleen C. Simpson, director, community partnerships; Paula Slocum, administrative assistant; Veronica Theobald, grants specialist.

Directors/trustees: Carol Bergenstol, chair; John Byom; Barbara Z. Carlson; Nancy Erickson; Steven J. Frank; Bridget Gothberg; Robin Harmon; Robert E. Haselow, M.D.; Marlys Jenson; Chris Johnson M.D.; Michael J. Johnson; Mike Kahler; William O. Kenney; Cindy Koch; Marilyn Kreutz; Elizabeth McClure, M.D.; William W. McReavy; Betsy Packard; Carolyn Pratt; James Rhodes; Beth Schneider; Marty Siegel; David St Peter; Roger Storms; Paul E. Terry; Robert M. Weiss; David K. Wessner; Christopher Williams M.D.; Liz Wynne; Joan Ziemer.

Patterson Foundation

1031 Mendota Heights Road
St Paul, MN 55120
County: Ramsey
Phone: (651) 686-1775
Website: www.pattersoncompanies.com
Established: 07/18/2000
Funder type: Private foundation

Program Description

Geographic focus: National Areas.
Areas of interest:
ANIMAL RELATED: Veterinary services.
HEALTH - DISEASES/MEDICAL DISCIPLINES: Dental and Oral healthcare.
HEALTH - GENERAL/REHABILITATIVE: Rehabilitative medical services.
Intended beneficiaries: Children and youth (infants-19 years), Homeless, Poor/economically disadvantaged.
Types of support for organizations:
CAPITAL CAMPAIGNS: Building/renovation, Endowment funds.
PROGRAM DEVELOPMENT/PROJECT SUPPORT: Curriculum development, Faculty/staff development, Mentoring programs, Performance/production costs, Public awareness, Public policy research/analysis.
STUDENT AID (GRANTS TO INSTITUTIONS): Scholarship funds.
Types of support for individuals: scholarships.
Exclusions: Individuals, Non-501(c)(3), Political organizations, Religious organizations, Tax-supported institutions, More than 10% of annual budget or campaign goal.

Financial Information

Financial data for year ending: 12/31/2006
Foundation assets: $15,915,000
Grants paid: $775,000
Number of grants: 19
Largest/smallest: $100,000/$5,000

Application Information

Preferred form of initial contact: letter of inquiry.
Public information available by request: application form.
Accept common grant application: yes.
Proposal deadlines: Generally 45 days prior to each quarterly Board of Directors meeting.
Contribution decisions made by: board of directors/trustees.
Frequency of contributions decisions: quarterly.

Staff/Trustees

Staff: Steve Armstrong, executive president & CFO.

The Pentair Foundation

5500 Wayzata Boulevard
Suite 800
Golden Valley, MN 55416-1261
County: Hennepin
Phone: (763) 545-1730
Fax: (763) 656-5404
Website: www.pentair.com/foundation.html
Funder type: Corporate foundation

Program Description

Program's purpose: To enrich and advance the communities in which Pentair operates by funding local programs that promote education, vocational readiness, cultural understanding, self-sufficiency and general well-being.
Program limitations/restrictions: Pentair does not support individuals; political, lobbying or fraternal activities; religious groups for religious purposes; medical research by individuals; scholarships to individuals; fundraising events, sponsorships or advertising support; travel or tour expenses; conferences, seminars, workshops or symposiums; athletic or sports-related organizations.
Geographic focus: Twin Cities Metropolitan Area, West Metropolitan Area/Minneapolis only, East Metropolitan Area/St Paul only.
Geographic limitations: Only fund where there is a Pentair operating location with more than 100 employees. National initiatives are handled at foundation headquarters only.
Areas of interest:
ARTS, CULTURE, HUMANITIES: Arts services, Museums, Performing arts, Visual arts, Other.
COMMUNITY IMPROVEMENT: Community/neighborhood development/improvement.
EDUCATION: Adult/continuing education/literacy, Educational services, Higher education, Pre-school/elementary, Secondary, Vocational/technical.
EMPLOYMENT/JOBS: Employment procurement/job training, Vocational rehabilitation.
HEALTH - GENERAL/REHABILITATIVE: Emergency medical services, Health care financing activities, Health support services, Public health programs/wellness education, Rehabilitative medical services, Reproductive health care.
HEALTH - MENTAL HEALTH/CRISIS INTERVENTION: Addiction disorders, Alcohol/drug/substance, prevention and treatment, Counseling/support groups, Hotline/crisis intervention, Mental health treatment and services.
HOUSING/SHELTER: Homeless, temporary housing, Housing owners/renter organizations, Housing support services.
HUMAN SERVICES: Children/youth services, Emergency assistance (food/clothing/cash), Family services, Family violence shelters and services, Multipurpose human service organizations.
PUBLIC SAFETY/DISASTERS/RELIEF: Disaster preparedness and relief, Safety education.
SCIENCE/TECHNOLOGY: Science - general.
YOUTH DEVELOPMENT: Multipurpose youth centers/clubs, Scouting organizations, Youth development programs.
Intended beneficiaries: Adults, African Americans/Blacks, Aging/elderly/senior citizens, Asian/Pacific Islanders, Blind/vision impaired, Children and youth (infants-19 years), Crime/abuse victims, Deaf/hearing impaired, Disabled - general or unspecified disability, Ethnic/racial minorities - other specified

group(s), Ethnic/racial populations - general, Females - all ages or age unspecified, Gay/lesbian/bisexual/transgender, General public/unspecified, Hispanics/Latinos, Homeless, Immigrants/newcomers/refugees, Males - all ages or age unspecified, Mentally/emotionally disabled, Migrant workers, Military/veterans, Native American/American Indians, Offenders/ex-offenders, People with HIV/AIDS, Physically disabled, Poor/ economically disadvantaged, Single parents, Substance abusers.

Types of support for organizations:
GENERAL PURPOSE/OPERATING SUPPORT.
PROGRAM DEVELOPMENT/PROJECT SUPPORT.

Types of support for individuals: none.

Matching grants: Education only.

Sample grants:

Bridge for Runaway Youth, The/MN/$20,000.

Dunwoody Institute/MN/General operating $8K, Capital support $50K/$58,000.

Guthrie Theater Foundation/Minneapolis, MN/$20,000.

House of Charity Inc/MN/$15,000.

MN Independent School Forum/MN/Project Support/$15,000.

Neighborhood House - MN/MN/$15,000.

Project for Pride in Living/MN/$15,000.

Financial Information

Financial data for year ending: 12/31/2006
Foundation assets: $5,528,320
Grants paid: $2,345,412
Number of grants: 148
Largest/smallest: $25,000/$5,000

Application Information

Preferred form of initial contact: telephone inquiry, request for guidelines, complete proposal, e-mail.

Public information available by request: proposal guidelines, application form, annual report, website.

Accept common grant application: yes.

Accept common report form: yes.

Proposal deadlines: March 1, June 1, October 1.

Contribution decisions made by: staff, employee committee, board of directors/trustees.

Frequency of contributions decisions: 3 times a year.

Typical time from application deadlines to notification: 2 -3 months.

Staff/Trustees

Staff: Rachael Jarosh, president; Michelle Murphy, foundation administrator.

Directors/trustees: Jack Dempsey; Steve Duea; Pete Dyke; Susan Harrison; Randall J. Hogan; Fred Koury; Michael G. Meyer; Joan Swartz.

People in Business Care, Inc.

PO Box 977
Chanhassen, MN 55317
County: Carver
Phone: (952) 486-6306
Established: 07/25/1983
Funder type: Corporate foundation

Program Description

Program's purpose: Make a positive impact on those we help, so they can in turn help others.

Funding priorities: Individuals and organizations in a desperate situation.

Geographic focus: Twin Cities Metropolitan Area, Greater Minnesota, Minnesota statewide, Areas outside Minnesota, National Areas, International Areas.

Areas of interest:
COMMUNITY IMPROVEMENT.
EDUCATION.
HEALTH - DISEASES/MEDICAL DISCIPLINES.
HEALTH - GENERAL/REHABILITATIVE.
HEALTH - MENTAL HEALTH/CRISIS INTERVENTION.
HOUSING/SHELTER.
HUMAN SERVICES.
PUBLIC PROTECTION - CRIME/COURTS/LEGAL SERVICES.
PUBLIC SAFETY/DISASTERS/RELIEF.
RELIGION/SPIRITUAL DEVELOPMENT.
YOUTH DEVELOPMENT.

Intended beneficiaries: General public/unspecified.

Types of support for organizations:
EMERGENCY FUNDS.

GENERAL PURPOSE/OPERATING SUPPORT.
PROGRAM DEVELOPMENT/PROJECT SUPPORT.

Types of support for individuals: aid to needy persons.

Sample grants:

American Red Cross - MN (Mankato)/MN/ $500.

Campus Crusade for Christ - MN/MN/$12,750.

Deer River Endowment/Deer River, MN/$250.

Kosovo Project/MN/$1,000.

Navigators/MN/$2,400.

Santa's Mitten Maids/MN/$500.

Student Venture/MN/$1,000.

Union Gospel Mission - MN (St Paul)/MN/$1,500.

Financial Information

Financial data for year ending: 07/31/2005
Foundation assets: $1,960,507
Grants paid: $653,334
Number of grants: 100
Largest/smallest: $14,800/$17.93

Application Information

Preferred form of initial contact: letter of inquiry.

Contribution decisions made by: employee committee.

Frequency of contributions decisions: monthly.

Staff/Trustees

Directors/trustees: LeRoy Morgan.

Peravid Foundation

U S Bank
101 East Fifth Street
WP MN S14
St Paul, MN 55101
County: Ramsey
Phone: (651) 466-8735
Alt. Phone: (651) 466-8707
Fax: (651) 466-8741
Contact: Jeffrey T. Peterson
Established: 11/24/2000
Funder type: Private foundation

Program Description

Program's purpose: General charitable purposes.

Sample grants:

Academy of Holy Angels/MN/$2,000.

Boston College/MA/$1,500.

Common Bond Communities - MN/MN/$2,000.

Hazelden Foundation/MN/$5,000.

HOPE Community - MN/Minneapolis, MN/$5,000.

MN Medical Foundation/MN/$2,000.

Plymouth Congregational Church/Minneapolis, MN/$3,000.

Plymouth Music Series/MN/$2,703.

Financial Information

Financial data for year ending: 12/31/2005
Foundation assets: $1,871,617
Grants paid: $67,000
Number of grants: 19
Largest/smallest: $15,000/$500

Application Information

Preferred form of initial contact: letter of inquiry.

Proposal deadlines: November 1.

Staff/Trustees

Directors/trustees: David M. Lilly; Diane P. Lilly; David M. Lilly Jr., president; Jeffrey T. Peterson.

Perkins Foundation

730 East Lake Street
Wayzata, MN 55391-1713
County: Hennepin
Phone: (952) 473-8367
Fax: (952) 473-4702
E-mail: perk@perkinscap.com
Contact: Richard W. Perkins, president
Established: 02/11/1969
Donor: Richard W. Perkins
Funder type: Private foundation

Program Description

Program's purpose: Primarily supports projects helping youth face the various forces that affect their lives in a modern society; especially drug and alcohol abuse.

Geographic focus: Twin Cities Metropolitan Area, Greater Minnesota, Minnesota statewide.

Areas of interest:

HEALTH - MENTAL HEALTH/CRISIS INTERVENTION: Alcohol/drug/substance, prevention and treatment.

HUMAN SERVICES: Children/youth services.

YOUTH DEVELOPMENT: Youth development programs.

Intended beneficiaries: Substance abusers, Youth/adolescents (ages 14-19).

Types of support for organizations: GENERAL PURPOSE/OPERATING SUPPORT.

Types of support for individuals: fellowships, scholarships.

Exclusions: Capital & endowment campaigns, Individuals, Non-501(c)(3), Political organizations, Religious organizations, Research, Scholarships/loans, Tax-supported institutions, Other.

Sample grants:

The Bridge/Minneapolis, MN/$1,000.

Face to Face Health & Counseling Services/MN/$1,000.

PACER Center /MN/$5,000.

Tranquility Farm/$5,000.

Trumpeter Swan Society/MN/$250.

Financial Information

Financial data for year ending: 12/31/2006
Foundation assets: $1,339,995
Grants paid: $51,835
Number of grants: 30
Largest/smallest: $10,000/$50

Application Information

Preferred form of initial contact: letter of inquiry, request for guidelines.

Public information available by request: proposal guidelines, annual report.

Accept common grant application: yes.

Proposal deadlines: November 15.

Contribution decisions made by: CEO, board of directors/trustees.

Frequency of contributions decisions: annually.

Specific times board meets: December.

Typical time from application deadlines to notification: 30 days.

Staff/Trustees

Directors/trustees: Pamela L. Brown; Daniel S. Perkins; Richard C. Perkins; Richard W. Perkins, president.

The Lawrence and Linda Perlman Family Foundation

1818 Oliver Avenue South
Minneapolis, MN 55405
County: Hennepin
Phone: (612) 377-8400
Established: 01/01/1997
Funder type: Private foundation

Program Description

Geographic focus: Twin Cities Metropolitan Area.

Areas of interest:

ARTS, CULTURE, HUMANITIES.

COMMUNITY IMPROVEMENT.

EDUCATION.

HEALTH - GENERAL/REHABILITATIVE.

HUMAN SERVICES.

PUBLIC AFFAIRS/SOCIETY BENEFIT.

Intended beneficiaries: General public/unspecified.

Sample grants:

Admission Possible/St Paul, MN/$8,250.

Blake School/MN/$7,429.

The Bridge for Runaway Youth/MN/$2,000.

Children's Defense Fund - MN/MN/$8,250.

PACER Center/MN/$500.

Park Nicollet Medical Foundation/MN/$1,000.

Rise Inc -Twin Cities/MN/$1,500.

WomenVenture/MN/$5,000.

Financial Information

Financial data for year ending: 12/31/2005
Foundation assets: $1,318,799
Grants paid: $477,302
Number of grants: 19
Largest/smallest: $15,000/$250

Application Information

Preferred form of initial contact: letter of inquiry.

Staff/Trustees

Staff: Sara Perlman Barrow, executive director.

Directors/trustees: Justin Barrow; Sara Perlman Barrow, executive director; David M. Perlman; Lawrence Perlman; Linda Peterson Perlman, president.

Petters Group Worldwide, LLC

4400 Baker Road
Minnetonka, MN 55343
County: Hennepin
Phone: (952) 936-5090
Fax: (952) 975-4088
Website: www.pettersgroup.com
Funder type: Corporate giving program

Staff/Trustees

Staff: DeAnne Anderson, program manager.

John T. Petters Foundation

4400 Baker Road
Minnetonka, MN 55343
County: Hennepin
Phone: (800) 532-1407
E-mail: info@jtpfoundation.org
Website: www.jtpfoundation.org
Funder type: Private foundation

Program Description

Program's purpose: To endow the leaders of tomorrow with an opportunity to advance their educational experience at home and abroad for ongoing knowledge.

Funding priorities: Scholarships are awarded to college students pursuing international business study abroad programs.

Geographic focus: Twin Cities Metropolitan Area, Minnesota statewide, areas outside Minnesota.

Geographic limitations: Students must be attending select universities or be involved with a few select nonprofit organizations. This list will be continually growing; check the website for the current list.

Areas of interest:
EDUCATION: Higher education, International business and study abroad in business.

Types of support for organizations:
STUDENT AID (GRANTS TO INSTITUTIONS): Scholarship funds.

Types of support for individuals: scholarships.

Financial Information

Financial data for year ending: 12/31/2006
Foundation assets: $2,359,697
Grants paid: $30,000

Application Information

Preferred form of initial contact: request for guidelines.

Public information available by request: application form, website.

Proposal deadlines: December 15.

Contribution decisions made by: CEO, staff, board of directors/trustees.

Frequency of contributions decisions: annually.

Typical time from application deadlines to notification: check website.

Staff/Trustees

Staff: Dawn Fish, executive director; Mollie O'Brien, foundation administrator.

Philanthrofund Foundation (PFund)

1409 Willow Street
Suite 210
Minneapolis, MN 55403
County: Hennepin
Phone: (612) 870-1806
Fax: (612) 821-6587
E-mail: info@PFundOnline.org
Website: www.PFundOnline.org
Contact: Gregory Grinley, executive director
Established: 12/21/1987
Paid Staff: Yes
Funder type: Community/public foundation

Program Description

Program's purpose: Philanthrofund is a vital resource and community builder for gay, lesbian, bisexual, transgender and allied communities by providing grants and scholarships, developing leaders and inspiring giving.

Funding priorities: Preventing discrimination and ending violence and harassment against GLBT persons; celebrating the contributions of the GLBT and allied communities and promoting visibility that will lead to greater understanding; supporting organizations that promote advocacy, education and work toward achieving social and systems change; reducing the isolation of members of the GLBT and allied communities, particularly in rural areas and small cities and amongst seniors; building the capacity of the GLBT community to achieve the goals outlined above, including developing the philanthropy of the community.

Program limitations/restrictions: Philanthrofund does not fund religious organizations for religious purposes; political campaigns and lobbying activities; individual persons; fundraising events; for-profit organizations; public agencies for mandated services; projects for the fulfillment of requirement toward a degree-granting program.

Geographic focus: Twin Cities Metropolitan Area, Greater Minnesota, Minnesota statewide, areas outside Minnesota.

Geographic limitations: Philanthrofund makes annual grants in the states of Minnesota, Iowa, North Dakota, South Dakota and in western Wisconsin.

Areas of interest:
CIVIL RIGHTS: Civil liberties advocacy, Civil rights/advocacy for specific groups, Equal opportunity and access, Intergroup relations/race relations. Must relate specifically to GLBT communities.

COMMUNITY IMPROVEMENT: Community coalitions. Must relate specifically to GLBT communities.

EDUCATION: Student services/organizations of students, Scholarships. Must relate specifically to GLBT communities.

PHILANTHROPY/VOLUNTARISM: Voluntarism promotion. Must relate specifically to GLBT communities.

PUBLIC AFFAIRS/SOCIETY BENEFIT: Citizen participation, Leadership development/awards programs (other than youth). Must relate specifically to GLBT communities.

YOUTH DEVELOPMENT: Youth development programs, Scholarships. Must relate specifically to GLBT communities.

Intended beneficiaries: Adults, African Americans/Blacks, Aging/elderly/senior citizens, Asian/Pacific Islanders, Ethnic/racial populations - general, Females - all ages or age unspecified, Gay/lesbian/bisexual/transgender, Hispanics/Latinos, Males - all ages or age unspecified, Native American/American Indians, Youth/adolescents (ages 14-19).

Types of support for organizations:

CAPITAL CAMPAIGNS: Building/renovation, Computer systems/technology, Equipment.

GENERAL PURPOSE/OPERATING SUPPORT: Annual campaigns.

MANAGEMENT/TECHNICAL ASSISTANCE.

PROGRAM DEVELOPMENT/PROJECT SUPPORT: Conferences/seminars, Curriculum development, Exhibitions, Film/video/radio production, Mentoring programs, Performance/production costs, Program evaluation, Public awareness, Public policy research/analysis, Publications, Seed money/start-up funds.

STUDENT AID (GRANTS TO INSTITUTIONS): Scholarship funds.

Types of support for individuals: scholarships.

Exclusions: Individuals are not eligible to apply for grants.

Financial Information

Financial data for year ending: 06/30/2006
Foundation assets: $954,464
Grants paid: $90,000

Application Information

Preferred form of initial contact: telephone inquiry, request for guidelines, complete proposal, e-mail.

Public information available by request: proposal guidelines, application form, annual report, newsletter, website.

Proposal deadlines: September 15 for grants, February 1 for scholarships.

Contribution decisions made by: Review Committee – Community members and PFund BOD members.

Frequency of contributions decisions: annually.

Specific times board meets: December.

Typical time from application deadlines to notification: 3 months.

Special application procedures: Must include a certificate of nondiscrimination.

Staff/Trustees

Staff: John Buchholz, programs manager; Susan Cogger, director of development and communications; Lois Epstein, accountant; Gregory Grinley, executive director; Sarah Quick, administrative assistant.

Directors/trustees: John Brentnall; Bill Burleson; Lupe Castillo; Kim Coleman; Debra Davis; Donald Whipple Fox; Amy Johnson; Cindy Kaiser; Tom Knabel; Richard LaFortune; Barry Lau; Ron Linde; Mindy Nakamoto; Diane Napper; Connie Nyman; Kathy Robinson; Roderic Southall; Shane Swanson; Bill Venne.

The Jay and Rose Phillips Family Foundation

10 Second Street NE
Suite 200
Minneapolis, MN 55413
County: Hennepin
Phone: (612) 623-1654
Fax: (612) 623-1653
E-mail: phillipsfnd@phillipsfnd.org
Website: www.phillipsfnd.org
Established: 01/01/1944
Donor: Jay and Rose Phillips
Paid Staff: Yes
Funder type: Private foundation

Program Description

Program's purpose: The mission of the Jay and Rose Phillips Family Foundation is to honor the legacy of its founders, Jay and Rose Phillips, by continuing the family tradition of sharing resources for the public good, while exercising leadership and flexibility in responding to emerging community needs.

Funding priorities: Primary concern: during times of severe economic hardship and financial distress, the foundation's primary concern is in providing support for projects that address unmet human and social needs. Special concerns: self-sufficiency; strengthening families; improvement of quality of health care; quality education; independent living for disabled and elderly; promoting good relations among people of all races and religions and actively opposing discrimination; arts that address social issues.

Program limitations/restrictions: No grants in support of individuals, for political campaigns, for lobbying efforts to influence legislation. No application from an organization previously funded by the foundation will be reviewed until a full report on the previous grant has been received.

Geographic focus: Twin Cities Metropolitan Area.

Geographic limitations: Primarily in the Twin Cities Metropolitan Area.

Areas of interest:

ARTS, CULTURE, HUMANITIES: Arts services, Arts/cultural multipurpose, Museums, Performing arts, Visual arts. The arts should be supported primarily as a vehicle to address social issues.

CIVIL RIGHTS: Civil liberties advocacy, Civil rights/advocacy for specific groups, Equal opportunity and access, Intergroup relations/race relations. Good relations among people of all races and religions should be fostered and discrimination should be actively opposed.

EDUCATION: Adult/continuing education/literacy, Educational services, Higher education, Pre-school/elementary, Secondary, Student services/organizations of students. Quality education as the key to individual success should be promoted.

EMPLOYMENT/JOBS: Employment procurement/job training, Vocational rehabilitation.

HEALTH - DISEASES/MEDICAL DISCIPLINES: AIDS/HIV, Medical disciplines. The quality of health care should be continually improved for the benefit of all people.

HEALTH - GENERAL/REHABILITATIVE: Health support services, Public health programs/wellness education, Reproductive health care. The quality of health care should be continually improved for the benefit of all people.

HEALTH - MENTAL HEALTH/CRISIS INTERVENTION: Mental health treatment and services. The quality of health care should be continually improved for the benefit of all people.

HOUSING/SHELTER: Housing support services, Low-cost temporary housing. Self-sufficiency should be the goal of all efforts to assist people.

HUMAN SERVICES: Children/youth services, Family services, Family services for adolescent parents, Family violence shelters and services, Multipurpose human service organizations, Senior centers and services, Services to specific groups. Families should be strengthened as nurturing and financially stable environments for children.

PUBLIC AFFAIRS/SOCIETY BENEFIT: Citizen participation, Leadership development/awards programs (other than youth), Public policy research and analysis, Welfare policy and reform. Self-sufficiency should be the goal of all efforts to assist people.

PUBLIC PROTECTION - CRIME/COURTS/LEGAL SERVICES: Crime prevention.

RELIGION/SPIRITUAL DEVELOPMENT: Interfaith issues. Good relations among people of all races and religions should be fostered, and discrimination should be actively opposed.

YOUTH DEVELOPMENT: Adult/child matching programs, Multipurpose youth centers/clubs, Youth development programs.

Intended beneficiaries:
Aging/elderly/senior citizens, Disabled - general or unspecified disability, Ethnic/racial populations - general, Gay/lesbian/bisexual/transgender, Homeless, Immigrants/newcomers/refugees, Infants/babies (under age 5), Mentally/emotionally disabled, People with HIV/AIDS, Physically disabled, Poor/economically disadvantaged, Single parents, Youth/adolescents (ages 14-19).

Types of support for organizations:
CAPITAL CAMPAIGNS: Building/renovation, Computer systems/technology, Equipment, Land acquisitions.
MANAGEMENT/TECHNICAL ASSISTANCE.
PROGRAM DEVELOPMENT/PROJECT SUPPORT: Curriculum development, Faculty/staff development, Fundraising, Mentoring programs, Performance/production costs, Program evaluation, Public awareness, Public policy research/analysis, Publications, Seed money/start-up funds.

Types of support for individuals: none.

Exclusions: Individuals, Non-501(c)(3), Political organizations.

Sample grants:
Family Housing Fund - MN (Minneapolis & St Paul)/MN/Start-up support for the Healthy Families Network Program/$50,000.

Greater Minneapolis Council of Churches/MN/Capital support for the new Anpa-Waste Numpa (New Beginnings II) program/$100,000.

Hearing & Service Dog Program of MN/MN/The feasibility for the capital campaign/$35,000.

Jewish Family & Children's Service - MN (Mpls)/MN/The Mental Health Education Project/$18,000.

Park Square Theatre Company/MN/Production and outreach support for Constant Star/$10,000.

Volunteers of America - MN/MN/The redesigned, competency-based Adult Diploma Program for Somali refugees/$10,000.

YWCA - MN (Minneapolis)/MN/The Public Policy and Racial Justice programs/$15,000.

Financial Information

Financial data for year ending: 12/31/2006
Foundation assets: $194,650,096
Grants paid: $9,766,565
Number of grants: 391
Largest/smallest: $500,000/$1,000
Typical grant amount: $15,000
Largest multi-year grant approved: $250,000

Application Information

Preferred form of initial contact: telephone inquiry, request for guidelines, e-mail.

Public information available by request: proposal guidelines, annual report, website.

Accept common grant application: yes.

Accept common report form: yes.

Proposal deadlines: March 15, July 15, November 15.

Preferred time for receiving proposals: ongoing.

Contribution decisions made by: board of directors/trustees.

Specific times board meets: 3 times a year.

Typical time from application deadlines to notification: 3-4 months.

Staff/Trustees

Staff: Amy K. Crawford, executive director; Dana L. Jensen, grants manager; Joel Luedtke, program officer; Arlene M. Reed, administrative/financial assistant; Patrick J. Troska, senior program officer.

Directors/trustees: Erik P. Bernstein; Paula P. Bernstein Ph.D., chair; William E. Bernstein M.D.; John P. Levin, co-chair; Suzan Levin; Terryl A. Levin; Dean Phillips; Edward J. Phillips, co-chair; Jeanne Phillips; Morton Phillips, trustee and chair emeritus; Pauline Phillips, trustee emeritus.

Piper Jaffray

800 Nicollet Mall
J13N03
Minneapolis, MN 55402
County: Hennepin
E-mail: communityrelations@pjc.com
Website: www.piperjaffray.com
Contact: Connie McCuskey, vice president, community and brand relations
Funder type: Corporate giving program

Program Description

Program's purpose: Piper Jaffray contributes 5 percent of pre-tax earnings to the community through the Piper Jaffray foundation, corporate giving and sponsorship.

Funding priorities: 1) Community Investment 2) Economic Education; 3) Arts and Cultural Sponsorship.

Program limitations/restrictions: Piper Jaffray corporate giving will not fund organizations that are not tax-exempt under Internal Revenue Code section 501(c)(3) or the equivalent; organizations that do not serve communities where Piper Jaffray has a business presence; individuals or groups seeking support for research, planning, personal needs or travel; public service or political campaigns; lobbying, political or fraternal activities; organizations receiving primary funding from United Way; fundraising campaigns; scholarships; religious groups for religious purposes; publications, audio-visual productions or special broadcasts; endowment campaigns.

Geographic focus: Twin Cities Metropolitan Area, Areas outside Minnesota.

Areas of interest:
ARTS, CULTURE, HUMANITIES: Arts/cultural multipurpose.
COMMUNITY IMPROVEMENT: Community/neighborhood development/improvement, Economic development.

EDUCATION: Economic, math and science.
PHILANTHROPY/VOLUNTARISM: Philanthropy - general.
SCIENCE/TECHNOLOGY.
YOUTH DEVELOPMENT.

Intended beneficiaries: Poor/economically disadvantaged, Youth/adolescents (ages 14-19).

Types of support for organizations:
GENERAL PURPOSE/OPERATING SUPPORT.
PROGRAM DEVELOPMENT/ PROJECT SUPPORT.

Exclusions: Individuals, Non-501(c)(3), Political organizations, Religious organizations, Research, Lobbying; Organizations receiving primary funding from United Way; golf tournaments; Fundraising campaigns.

Financial Information

Financial data for year ending: 12/31/2006
Grants paid: $2,078,000

Application Information

Preferred form of initial contact: www.piperjaffray.com. Please comply with predetermined and published guidelines.

Public information available by request: annual report, website.

Proposal deadlines: Proposals received between Jan. 1 - March 15.

Contribution decisions made by: staff, board of directors/trustees.

Frequency of contributions decisions: annually.

Typical time from application deadlines to notification: distributions in June.

Staff/Trustees

Staff: Connie McCuskey, vice president, community and brand relations; Diane Newes, administrative assistant.

Carl and Eloise Pohlad Family Foundation

60 South Sixth Street
Suite 3900
Minneapolis, MN 55402
County: Hennepin
Phone: (612) 661-3910
Fax: (612) 661-3715
E-mail: info@pohladfamilygiving.org
Website: www.pohladfamilygiving.org
Established: 01/01/1995
Funder type: Private foundation

Program Description

Program's purpose: To improve the lives of economically disadvantaged children and youth and to participate in projects that positively impact the quality of life in the Minneapolis/St Paul metropolitan area.

Funding priorities: We carry out our mission by creating our own grantmaking initiatives; providing support to private nonprofit organizations through a proactive grants program that provides operating support; making family-directed grants; making matching grants to nonprofit organizations supported by employees and Pohlad-owned businesses.

Program limitations/restrictions: Check the website for the most current information on the foundation's application guidelines.

Geographic focus: Twin Cities Metropolitan Area, Minnesota statewide, (two programs have statewide focus).

Geographic limitations: Service locations within the state of Minnesota (highest priority is given to organizations located and serving clients who reside in the Minneapolis/St Paul metropolitan area).

Areas of interest:
ARTS, CULTURE, HUMANITIES.
HUMAN SERVICES: Children/youth services, Multipurpose human service organizations.
YOUTH DEVELOPMENT.

Sample grants:

The Bridge for Runaway Youth/MN/ Capital/$100,000.

Guthrie Theater/Minneapolis, MN/ General operating/$33,000.

Lutheran Social Services - MN/ MN/Summer camp scholarship/$15,000.

Minneapolis Institute of Arts/MN/ Capital/$39,000.

MN Newspaper Foundation/MN/Summer youth employment program/$149,422.

United Way - (Greater Twin Cities)/MN/ Hurricane Katrina/$15,000.

Walker Art Center/MN/Capital/ $1,100,000.

Wilderness Inquiry/Minneapolis, MN/Capital/$25,000.

Financial Information

Financial data for year ending: 12/31/2006
Foundation assets: $56,200,000
Grants paid: $7,317,322
Number of grants: 316
Largest/smallest: $600,000/$100

Application Information

Preferred form of initial contact: e-mail, mlyon@pohladfamilygiving.org.

Public information available by request: annual report, website.

Proposal deadlines: Program RFPs include application deadlines.

Preferred time for receiving proposals: Visit website for foundation initiatives and other program RFPs.

Contribution decisions made by: board of directors/trustees.

Frequency of contributions decisions: dependent on RFP deadlines.

Staff/Trustees

Staff: Terry Egge, senior program officer; Ilse Ekechuku, program assistant; Kristen Keran, grants manager; Marina M. Lyon, vice president; Pamela E. Omann, treasurer; Rose A. Peterson, program manager.

Directors/trustees: Marina M. Lyon, vice president; Pam Omann, secretary and treasurer; Carl R. Pohlad; James O. Pohlad; Robert C. Pohlad; William M. Pohlad, president.

The Polaris Foundation

2100 Highway 55
Medina, MN 55340
County: Hennepin
Phone: (763) 542-0516
Alt. Phone: (218) 463-4580
Website: www.polarisindustries.com/en-us/OurCompany/AboutPolaris/Polaris Foundation
Contact: John Corness, president
Established: 12/20/1995
Funder type: Corporate foundation

Program Description

Program's purpose: The Polaris Foundation is dedicated to long-term investment in the communities in which we do business. Providing Polaris Industries with a quality workforce and creating healthy communities where we work and live are central to our vision.

Funding priorities: Grants are made in the following priority areas: Youth, Community Development and the Environment. The Polaris Foundation also considers in-kind requests.

Program limitations/restrictions: The Polaris Foundation will not consider requests for the following: Individuals; Private Charity or Foundations; Politically affiliated programs; Fraternal or veterans organizations; For-profit organizations; Research projects; Discretionary or emergency requests; Capital campaigns; State agencies; Religious affiliated organizations or programs; International or foreign-based programs; Social service programs; Courtesy advertising; Incomplete Grant Application; Organizations that have received a grant from the Polaris Foundation in the last three consecutive years; Organizations that discriminate on the basis of age, color, citizenship, disability, disabled veteran status, gender, race, religion, national origin, marital status, sexual orientation, military service or status or Vietnam-era veteran status.

Geographic focus: Twin Cities Metropolitan Area, Greater Minnesota, Areas outside Minnesota.

Geographic limitations: Priority given to organizations in Polaris, Inc. locations: Osceola, WI; Spirit Lake, IA; Roseau, MN; Wyoming, MN; Vermillion, SD; Winnipeg.

Areas of interest:
COMMUNITY IMPROVEMENT: Community/neighborhood development/improvement.
ENVIRONMENTAL QUALITY/PROTECTION/BEAUTIFICATION.
YOUTH DEVELOPMENT: Multipurpose youth centers/clubs, Scouting organizations, Youth development programs.

Intended beneficiaries: General public/unspecified.

Types of support for organizations:
IN-KIND PRODUCTS: ATVs, snowmobiles.

Types of support for individuals: none.

Sample grants:
District 284 Youth Hockey/MN/$2,000.
Roseau Area Senior Citizens Center/MN/$2,500.
Tri-K Sports/MN/$525.
University of Minnesota - Minneapolis/MN/veterinary research/$5,000.
YMCA - IA/IA/facility construction/$10,000.

Financial Information

Financial data for year ending: 12/31/2005
Foundation assets: $7,256
Grants paid: $52,150
Number of grants: 123
Largest/smallest: $50,000/$800

Application Information

Preferred form of initial contact: complete proposal. Application is only available online, and must be completed in its entirety in one sitting.

Public information available by request: proposal guidelines, application form, annual report, website.

Proposal deadlines: February 1, May 1, August 1, November 1.

Contribution decisions made by: board of directors/trustees.

Frequency of contributions decisions: quarterly.

Typical time from application deadlines to notification: 2 months.

Staff/Trustees

Staff: Melinda Walter, secretary.
Directors/trustees: John Corness, president; Paul Moe, treasurer; Tom Tiller, director.

The Irwin Andrew Porter Foundation

PO Box 580057
Minneapolis, MN 55458-0057
County: Hennepin
Phone: (612) 343-5994
Fax: (612) 343-5995
E-mail: iapfoundation@iapfoundation.org
Website: www.iapfoundation.org
Contact: Amy L. Hubbard, chair
Established: 09/09/1996
Donor: Amy L. Hubbard
Funder type: Private foundation

Program Description

Program's purpose: To offer support to projects and programs fostering connections to ourselves, our community, our environment, our world.

Funding priorities: IAP is looking for projects that foster connections between communities and individuals, create partnerships with multiple organizations and enable beneficiaries to give as well as receive. The foundation provides funding for a variety of interest areas. The quality, innovation, thoughtfulness and effectiveness of a project are of more importance than the specific interest area. Areas of interest for IAP are the arts, education, environment and social programs.

Program limitations/restrictions: The foundation accepts a limited number of proposals for multi-year and matching grants.

Geographic focus: Minnesota statewide, areas outside Minnesota, international areas.

Geographic limitations: Preferences given to projects within Minnesota, Wisconsin, Illinois and Michigan. This preference reflects the board's desire to be able to have personal contact with the grant applicants and the beneficiaries of the specific programs.

Areas of interest:
ANIMAL RELATED: Wildlife preservation/protection.
ARTS, CULTURE, HUMANITIES.

CIVIL RIGHTS: Intergroup relations/race relations.
EDUCATION: Pre-school/elementary, Secondary.
ENVIRONMENTAL QUALITY/PROTECTION/BEAUTIFICATION: Environmental education/outdoor survival, Natural resources conservation/protection.
HOUSING/SHELTER.
HUMAN SERVICES: Children/youth services, Family services, Multipurpose human service organizations, Personal social services.
INTERNATIONAL AFFAIRS: International development/relief, International peace/security, Promotion of international understanding.
PHILANTHROPY/VOLUNTARISM: service learning.
PUBLIC AFFAIRS/SOCIETY BENEFIT: Citizen participation.
YOUTH DEVELOPMENT: Youth development programs.

Intended beneficiaries: General public/unspecified.

Types of support for organizations: PROGRAM DEVELOPMENT/PROJECT SUPPORT.

Types of support for individuals: none.

Exclusions: Capital & endowment campaigns, Individuals, Political organizations, Religious organizations, Scholarships/loans, General operating expenses, Fundraising events or activities, Social events, Goodwill advertising or marketing, Travel for individuals or groups, Fraternal, athletic, social or veterans organizations.

Sample grants:

Anoka County Community Action - Minneapolis/MN/$2,493.

Eco Education/St Paul, MN/$2,413.

LEAP! to Language/Chicago, IL/$12,928.

Rivers Council of MN/MN/$5,000.

SASE : The Write Place/MN/$2,000.

SteppingStone Theatre for Youth Development/MN/$6,250.

Wild Swan Theatre/Ann Arbor, MI/$3,200.

Youth Farm & Market Project/Minneapolis, MN/LEAD program/$7,500.

Financial Information

Financial data for year ending: 08/31/2006
Foundation assets: $3,819,872
Grants paid: $140,564
Number of grants: 23
Largest/smallest: $12,928/$740

Application Information

Preferred form of initial contact: complete proposal, all questions and applications must be submitted in writing via the U.S. postal system; do not send videos or e-mails.

Public information available by request: proposal guidelines, website.

Proposal deadlines: second Friday in April for a June review and second Friday in October for a December review.

Contribution decisions made by: board of directors/trustees.

Frequency of contributions decisions: semiannually; annual for international.

Specific times board meets: June and December.

Typical time from application deadlines to notification: 1-3.5 months.

Staff/Trustees

Directors/trustees: Arta Cheney; Scott Elkins; Gleason E. Glover; Jay Goldberg; Amy L. Hubbard, chair; Geoffrey James Kehoe; Dipankar Mukherjee; Gloria Perez Jordan.

Prospect Creek Foundation

4900 IDS Center
80 South Eighth Street
Minneapolis, MN 55402
County: Hennepin
Phone: (612) 672-9603
Contact: Martha Atwater
Established: 12/23/1992
Funder type: Private foundation

Program Description

Geographic focus: Twin Cities Metropolitan Area, Areas outside Minnesota.

Areas of interest:
ARTS, CULTURE, HUMANITIES.
COMMUNITY IMPROVEMENT.
EDUCATION.
ENVIRONMENTAL QUALITY/PROTECTION/BEAUTIFICATION.
HEALTH - DISEASES/MEDICAL DISCIPLINES.
HUMAN SERVICES.

Intended beneficiaries: General public/unspecified.

Types of support for organizations: GENERAL PURPOSE/OPERATING SUPPORT.

Sample grants:

Abbott Northwestern Hospital/MN/$2,500.

Afton Historical Society Press - MN/MN/$10,000.

Bolder Options - MN/Minneapolis, MN/$5,000.

Guthrie Theater/Minneapolis, MN/$30,500.

Princeton University/NJ/$10,000.

St Helena Hospital - CA/CA/$20,178.

St Paul Chamber Orchestra/MN/$2,000.

Walker Art Center/MN/$30,500.

Financial Information

Financial data for year ending: 12/31/2005
Foundation assets: $36,581,244
Grants paid: $1,377,365
Number of grants: 134
Largest/smallest: $101,000/$100

Application Information

Preferred form of initial contact: letter of inquiry.

Staff/Trustees

Directors/trustees: Martha Atwater; H. Brewster Atwater Jr.; Elizabeth A. Connolly.

Quetico Superior Foundation

50 South Sixth Street
Suite 1500
Minneapolis, MN 55402-1498
County: Hennepin
Phone: (612) 340-2934
Established: 10/01/1947
Funder type: Private foundation

Program Description

Program's purpose: Preservation of the wilderness character of the border lakes canoe country.

Geographic focus: Minnesota's border lakes canoe country - The BWCA.

Geographic limitations: Quetico-Superior region, which includes the Boundary Waters Canoe Area and Quetico Provincial Park.

Areas of interest:

ENVIRONMENTAL QUALITY/PROTECTION/BEAUTIFICATION: Natural resources conservation/protection.

Sample grants:

MN Land Trust/MN/$10,000.

Quetico Foundation/MN/$5,000.

Voyageurs Region National Park Association/MN/$12,000.

Warner Nature Center/MN/$750.

Financial Information

Financial data for year ending: 12/31/2005
Foundation assets: $1,589,726
Grants paid: $26,000
Number of grants: 4
Largest/smallest: $12,000/$750

Application Information

Preferred form of initial contact: letter of inquiry, complete proposal.

Staff/Trustees

Directors/trustees: Frederick Winston; James C. Wyman.

The Elizabeth C. Quinlan Foundation, Inc.

5701 Kentucky Avenue North
Suite 201
Crystal, MN 55428-3370
County: Hennepin
Phone: (763) 535-1550
Established: 11/01/1945
Funder type: Private foundation

Program Description

Program's purpose: To make donations to tax-exempt organizations within the state of Minnesota; primarily the Twin Cities metropolitan area.

Geographic focus: Twin Cities Metropolitan Area, Greater Minnesota, Minnesota statewide.

Geographic limitations: In accordance with its articles of incorporation, the foundation is required to restrict its donations to organizations that will use them wholly within the state of Minnesota. Emphasis is placed on Twin Cities metropolitan area and limited Greater Minnesota.

Areas of interest:

ANIMAL RELATED: Wildlife preservation/protection, Zoo/zoological societies.

ARTS, CULTURE, HUMANITIES: Arts services, Arts/cultural multipurpose, Historical societies, Humanities, Media/communications, Museums, Performing arts, Visual arts.

CIVIL RIGHTS: Civil liberties advocacy, Equal opportunity and access, Voter education/registration.

COMMUNITY IMPROVEMENT: Community/neighborhood development/improvement.

EDUCATION: Adult/continuing education/literacy, Higher education, Libraries/library science.

EMPLOYMENT/JOBS: Employment procurement/job training.

ENVIRONMENTAL QUALITY/PROTECTION/BEAUTIFICATION: Botanical/horticultural/landscape, Natural resources conservation/protection.

HEALTH - DISEASES/MEDICAL DISCIPLINES: AIDS/HIV, Alzheimer's disease.

HEALTH - GENERAL/REHABILITATIVE: Nursing care/services.

HEALTH - MENTAL HEALTH/CRISIS INTERVENTION: Mental health treatment and services.

HOUSING/SHELTER.

HUMAN SERVICES: Multipurpose human service organizations.

PHILANTHROPY/VOLUNTARISM: Philanthropy associations.

RECREATION: Recreation and sporting camps.

RELIGION/SPIRITUAL DEVELOPMENT: Specific denomination: Catholic.

Intended beneficiaries: General public/unspecified.

Types of support for organizations:

CAPITAL CAMPAIGNS: Building/renovation, Computer systems/technology, Debt reduction, Endowment funds, Equipment, Land acquisitions.

GENERAL PURPOSE/OPERATING SUPPORT: Annual campaigns.

PROGRAM DEVELOPMENT/PROJECT SUPPORT: Conferences/seminars, Faculty/staff development, Seed money/start-up funds.

RESEARCH.

STUDENT AID (GRANTS TO INSTITUTIONS): Fellowships, Internships, Scholarship funds.

Types of support for individuals: none.

Sample grants:

The Bridge for Runaway Youth/MN/$2,000.

Children's Home Society - MN/MN/$5,000.

Fraser, LTD/ND/$2,000.

The Jeremiah Program/MN/$2,000.

Project for Pride in Living/MN/$3,000.

St David's Child Development & Family Services/MN/$3,000.

Tree Trust - Twin Cities/MN/$1,500.

Washburn Child Guidance Center/MN/$2,000.

Financial Information

Financial data for year ending: 12/31/2005
Foundation assets: $5,230,723
Grants paid: $180,950
Number of grants: 24
Largest/smallest: $15,000/$250

Application Information

Preferred form of initial contact: letter of inquiry, request for guidelines.

Public information available by request: proposal guidelines, application form, annual report.

Accept common grant application: yes.

Accept common report form: yes.

Proposal deadlines: September 1.

Contribution decisions made by: board of directors/trustees.

Frequency of contributions decisions: annually.

Specific times board meets: fall.

Typical time from application deadlines to notification: notification by mid-December.

Staff/Trustees

Staff: Kathryn H. Iverson, office manager.

Directors/trustees: Kathleen L. Budge; Lucia L. Crane; Mari Geis, trustee; Vincent Grundman; Richard A. Klein, president; David R. Leslie, trustee; Kathleen Leslie.

Rahr Foundation

800 West First Avenue
Shakopee, MN 55379
County: Hennepin
Phone: (952) 496-7003
E-mail: mtech@rahr.com
Contact: Marilyn Tech, secretary
Established: 01/01/1942
Funder type: Corporate foundation

Program Description

Funding priorities: Arts, Environment, Social Services.

Program limitations/restrictions: Scholarships are limited to children of employees of Rahr Malting Company and its affiliates.

Geographic focus: Twin Cities Metropolitan Area.

Geographic limitations: Primarily organizations in Minneapolis/St Paul area.

Areas of interest:

ANIMAL RELATED: Animal protection/welfare, Wildlife preservation/protection.
ARTS, CULTURE, HUMANITIES: Performing arts.
COMMUNITY IMPROVEMENT: Community/neighborhood development/improvement.
EDUCATION: Higher education.
ENVIRONMENTAL QUALITY/PROTECTION/BEAUTIFICATION: Botanical/horticultural/landscape, Environmental education/outdoor survival, Natural resources conservation/protection.
FOOD/NUTRITION/AGRICULTURE.
HEALTH - GENERAL/REHABILITATIVE: Hospitals and related primary medical care facilities.
HEALTH - RESEARCH: Birth defects & genetic diseases research.
HOUSING/SHELTER: Homeless, temporary housing.
HUMAN SERVICES: Children/youth services, Family violence shelters and services.
YOUTH DEVELOPMENT: Scouting organizations, Youth development programs.

Intended beneficiaries: General public/unspecified.

Types of support for organizations:

CAPITAL CAMPAIGNS: Building/renovation.
EMERGENCY FUNDS.
GENERAL PURPOSE/OPERATING SUPPORT: Annual campaigns.
PROGRAM DEVELOPMENT/PROJECT SUPPORT: Fundraising.
RESEARCH.
STUDENT AID (GRANTS TO INSTITUTIONS): Scholarship funds.

Types of support for individuals: scholarships.

Sample grants:

American Red Cross - MN (Minneapolis, Greater)/MN/general operating/$5,000.
ARC - MN (Greater Twin Cities)/MN/general operating/$3,000.
Boys & Girls Club - MN (Twin Cities)/MN/general operating/$5,000.
Emergency Food Shelf - MN (Minneapolis)/MN/general operating/$1,000.
Gillette Children's Hospital Foundation/MN/Motion Analyis laboratory/$3,750.
MacPhail Center for the Arts/MN/general operating/$3,000.
Minneapolis Heart Institute/MN/general operating/$2,500.
YMCA - MN (Minneapolis, Metropolitan Branch)/MN/campership program & Back to School fund/$1,500.

Financial Information

Financial data for year ending: 12/31/2005
Foundation assets: $5,101,188
Grants paid: $245,521
Number of grants: 41
Largest/smallest: $25,500/$150
Largest multi-year grant approved: $50,000

Application Information

Preferred form of initial contact: letter of inquiry, complete proposal.
Accept common grant application: yes.
Proposal deadlines: May and October.
Preferred time for receiving proposals: one month before board meetings.
Contribution decisions made by: board of directors/trustees.
Frequency of contributions decisions: semiannually.
Specific times board meets: June and November.

Staff/Trustees

Directors/trustees: George D. Gackle, treasurer; Laurel Mallon; Frederick W. Rahr, president; Heid Rahr, director; William Rahr, vice president.

Rappaport Family Foundation

11115 Excelsior Boulevard
Hopkins, MN 55343
County: Hennepin
Phone: (952) 931-2470
E-mail: RAPPJD@aol.com
Contact: Jon D. Rappaport
Established: 01/01/1998
Funder type: Private foundation

Program Description

Program's purpose: To support a variety of social service organizations.

Funding priorities: Smaller, entrepreneurial social service organizations.

Geographic focus: Greater Minnesota, National Areas, International Areas.

Areas of interest:

HEALTH - GENERAL/REHABILITATIVE: Hospitals and related primary medical care facilities.
HEALTH - MENTAL HEALTH/CRISIS INTERVENTION: Mental health treatment and services, Mental health disorders.
HUMAN SERVICES: Children/youth services, Family services, Family services for adolescent parents.
INTERNATIONAL AFFAIRS: International development/relief.
PHILANTHROPY/VOLUNTARISM: Public foundations and community foundations.
RELIGION/SPIRITUAL DEVELOPMENT.
YOUTH DEVELOPMENT: Youth development programs.

Intended beneficiaries: General public/unspecified.

Types of support for organizations:
CAPITAL CAMPAIGNS.
GENERAL PURPOSE/OPERATING SUPPORT.
PROGRAM DEVELOPMENT/ PROJECT SUPPORT.

Sample grants:

Adath Jeshurun Synagogue/Minnetonka, MN/$4,700.

Jewish Family & Children's Service - MN (Mpls)/MN/$5,000.

Jewish National Fund - MN/MN/$100.

Juvenile Diabetes Foundation - MN/MN/ $360.

MN Orchestra/MN/$100.

NECHAMA - Jewish Response to Disaster/MN/$5,000.

Sholom Home West/St Louis Park, MN/$400.

Teens Alone, Inc - MN/MN/$300.

Financial Information

Financial data for year ending: 04/30/2006
Foundation assets: $163,414
Grants paid: $16,373
Number of grants: 20
Largest/smallest: $6,000/$100

Application Information

Preferred form of initial contact: letter of inquiry.

Public information available by request: application form, annual report.

Accept common grant application: yes.

Proposal deadlines: December 31.

Contribution decisions made by: board of directors/trustees.

Frequency of contributions decisions: quarterly.

Typical time from application deadlines to notification: 90 days.

Staff/Trustees

Directors/trustees: Diane S. Rappaport; Fred J. Rappaport; Jon D. Rappaport; Naomi R. Rappaport; Shira J. Rappaport.

RBC Dain Rauscher Foundation

60 South Sixth Street
P20
Minneapolis, MN 55402-4422
County: Hennepin
Phone: (612) 371-2765
Alt. Phone: (612) 371-2936
Fax: (612) 371-7933
E-mail: sherry.koster@rbcdain.com
Website: www.rbcdain.com/community involvement
Contact: Sherry R. Koster, manager
Established: 01/01/1987
Paid Staff: Yes
Funder type: Corporate foundation

Program Description

Program's purpose: To improve the quality of life in the communities where we do business by supporting nonprofit organizations that make a positive difference.

Funding priorities: Youth Education: with emphasis on helping young people understand our country's economic system and effective education programs (K-12) that help students of color or those who are economically disadvantaged. Arts and Culture: Preeminent cultural institutions that enrich the quality of life in the communities where our employees and clients live; arts programs that generate an appreciation of the arts. Human Services: with an emphasis on fostering economic independence and strengthening families.

Program limitations/restrictions: No fundraising events; no religious, political, fraternal or veterans' organizations; no grants for travel, tours or conferences, athletic groups, academic, medical or scientific research, charitable sponsorships, recreational programs.

Geographic focus: Twin Cities Metropolitan Area, RBC Dain Rauscher communities in the 40 states where we are located. Please check our corporate website for locations.

Areas of interest:

ARTS, CULTURE, HUMANITIES: Arts services, Arts/cultural multipurpose, Humanities, Museums, Performing arts, Visual arts.

EDUCATION: Educational services, Secondary, Youth (K-12).

EMPLOYMENT/JOBS: Employment procurement/job training.

HOUSING/SHELTER: Homeless, temporary housing.

HUMAN SERVICES: Children/youth services, Family services, Family violence shelters and services, Multipurpose human service organizations, Personal social services, Human services (not health services).

RECREATION: No recreational programs.

YOUTH DEVELOPMENT: Adult/child matching programs, Youth education.

Intended beneficiaries: Adults, African Americans/Blacks, Asian/Pacific Islanders, Children only (5-14 years), Ethnic/racial minorities - other specified group(s), Ethnic/racial populations - general, Female adults, Female youth/adolescents (ages 14-19), Gay/lesbian/bisexual/ transgender, General public/unspecified, Hispanics/Latinos, Homeless, Immigrants/newcomers/refugees, Male adults, Male youth/adolescents (ages 14-19), Native American/American Indians, Poor/economically disadvantaged, Single parents, Youth/adolescents (ages 14-19).

Types of support for organizations:
GENERAL PURPOSE/OPERATING SUPPORT.

PROGRAM DEVELOPMENT/ PROJECT SUPPORT: Mentoring programs, Leadership programs.

CORPORATE SPONSORSHIP: Contact: Martha Baumbach, Community Affairs and Sponsorships, (612) 371-7753, martha.baumbach@rbcdaincom.

Types of support for individuals: none.

Matching grants: employee matching.

Dollars for Doers: yes.

Exclusions: Individuals, Non-501(c)(3), Political organizations, Religious organizations, Research, Scholarships/loans.

Sample grants:

Admission Possible/St Paul, MN/ Programming costs/$6,000.

BestPrep/MN/$15,000.

Cornerstone Advocacy Service - MN/ MN/The Family and Youth Services program/$6,500.

MN Children's Museum/MN/The Access Program/$5,000.

The Park Square Theatre Company/MN/ Educational services/$6,000.

Project for Pride in Living/MN/The Self-Sufficiency Program/$7,000.

Southeast Asian Refugee Community Home (SEARCH)/MN/The Refugee Employment Services/$5,000.

Financial Information

Financial data for year ending: 10/31/2006
Foundation assets: $273,000
Grants paid: $2,647,835
Number of grants: 1543
Largest/smallest: $100,000/$1,000
Matching gifts: $387,000
Largest multi-year grant approved: $100,000

Application Information

Preferred form of initial contact: Please visit our website for our online letter of inquiry.

Public information available by request: proposal guidelines, application form, annual report, website: www.rbcdain.com/communityinvolvement.

Proposal deadlines: Online letter of inquiry (if not funded in 2006) due by 1/12/07; proposal deadline: 1/31/07. Online letter of inquiry (if not funded in 2006) due by 6/8/07; proposal deadline: 6/29/07.

Preferred time for receiving proposals: January and June.

Contribution decisions made by: employee committee.

Frequency of contributions decisions: twice a year.

Specific times board meets: spring - March/April; fall - Aug./Sept.

Typical time from application deadlines to notification: 90 days.

Special application procedures: We no longer accept hard copy grant requests. Please refer to website for online letter of inquiry and online grant application procedures and requirements.

Staff/Trustees

Staff: Liz Anderson, grants administrator; Sherry R. Koster, manager; Andre Lewis, senior vice president & director, community affairs.

Horst M. Rechelbacher Foundation

220 South Sixth Street
Suite 300
Minneapolis, MN 55402
County: Hennepin
Phone: (612) 376-4500
Established: 01/01/1999
Funder type: Private foundation

Program Description

Program's purpose: The foundation is a philanthropic organization dedicated to social and environmental preservation projects that operate on a grassroots level.

Geographic focus: Twin Cities Metropolitan Area, National Areas, International Areas.

Areas of interest:
ARTS, CULTURE, HUMANITIES.
ENVIRONMENTAL QUALITY/PROTECTION/BEAUTIFICATION: Natural resources conservation/protection.
INTERNATIONAL AFFAIRS.

Sample grants:
American Botanical Council/Austin, TX/$10,000.
Defending Farm Animals/Minneapolis, MN/$5,000.
Greenpeace USA Incorporated/DC/$10,000.
MN Dance Theatre and School, Inc/MN/$10,000.
National Foundation for Alternative Medicine/DC/$20,000.
Organic Consumers Association/Little Marais, MN/$10,000.
St Croix Center for the Arts/Taylors Falls, MN/$1,000.
Tibetan Education Action/New Brighton, MN/$35,000.

Financial Information

Financial data for year ending: 12/31/2005
Foundation assets: $73,500
Grants paid: $362,500
Number of grants: 19
Largest/smallest: $50,000/$1,000

Staff/Trustees

Directors/trustees: James Greupner; Horst Rechelbacher, president; Peter Rechelbacher; Nicole Thomas.

Red Wing Shoe Company Foundation

314 Main Street
Red Wing, MN 55066-2300
County: Goodhue
Phone: (651) 388-8211
Contact: Stacy Crownhart
Established: 01/01/1954
Funder type: Corporate foundation

Program Description

Program's purpose: Contributions made to organizations whose activities have a direct impact on Red Wing, MN; Danville, K;, and Potosi, MO areas.

Geographic focus: Greater Minnesota especially the Red Wing area; areas outside Minnesota,

Geographic limitations: Red Wing, MN; Danville, KY; Potosi, MO areas.

Areas of interest:
ARTS, CULTURE, HUMANITIES.
COMMUNITY IMPROVEMENT.
EDUCATION: Pre-school/elementary, Secondary.
YOUTH DEVELOPMENT.

Intended beneficiaries: General public/unspecified.

Types of support for organizations:
CAPITAL CAMPAIGNS.
GENERAL PURPOSE/OPERATING SUPPORT.
PROGRAM DEVELOPMENT/PROJECT SUPPORT.

Exclusions: Individuals.

Sample grants:
BestPrep/MN/business education/$2,500.
Boy Scouts of America - MN (Gamehaven Council)/MN/general operating/$1,500.
Courage Center - MN (Golden Valley)/MN/general operating/$3,400.
Guthrie Theater/Minneapolis, MN/capital campaign/$10,000.
ISD Red Wing #256/MN/Arts Alive sponsorship/$2,500.
Preservation Alliance of MN, Inc/MN/general operating/$1,000.
Sheldon Performing Arts Theatre/MN/general operating/$40,000.
United Way - (Red Wing Inc)/MN/general operating/$25,000.

Financial Information

Financial data for year ending: 12/31/2005
Foundation assets: $161,024
Grants paid: $483,321
Number of grants: 37
Largest/smallest: $240,000/$500

Application Information

Preferred form of initial contact: letter of inquiry.

Staff/Trustees

Directors/trustees: Suzanne Blue; Stacy Crownhart; Silas B. Foot III; William J. Sweasy.

Redwood Area Communities Foundation, Inc.

200 South Mill Street
PO Box 481
Redwood Falls, MN 56283
County: Redwood
Phone: (507) 637-4004
Fax: (507) 637-4082
E-mail: radc@redwoodfalls.org
Website: www.radc.org/racf.html
Contact: Patricia Dingels, executive director
Established: 08/02/1988
Funder type: Community/public foundation

Program Description

Funding priorities: Youth and community.

Geographic focus: Greater Minnesota, Redwood County only.

Geographic limitations: Redwood County and 10-mile radius of Redwood County.

Areas of interest:
EDUCATION: Scholarships, Student loans.
YOUTH DEVELOPMENT.

Intended beneficiaries: Adults, Children and youth (infants-19 years), Youth/adolescents (ages 14-19).

Types of support for organizations:
STUDENT AID (GRANTS TO INSTITUTIONS): Scholarship funds.

Types of support for individuals: educational loans, scholarships.

Financial Information

Financial data for year ending: 12/31/2005
Foundation assets: $1,847,740
Grants paid: $55,500

Application Information

Preferred form of initial contact: e-mail.

Public information available by request: website.

Preferred time for receiving proposals: not receiving applications at this time.

Contribution decisions made by: board of directors/trustees.

Specific times board meets: 2 times per year.

Staff/Trustees

Staff: Patricia Dingels, executive director.

Directors/trustees: Duane Heiling, secretary/treasurer; Glen McKay, president; Don Yrjo, vice president.

Regis Foundation

7201 Metro Boulevard
Minneapolis, MN 55439-2103
County: Hennepin
Phone: (952) 947-7777
Contact: Myron Kunin, president
Established: 10/15/1981
Funder type: Corporate foundation

Program Description

Geographic focus: Twin Cities Metropolitan Area, Greater Minnesota, Areas outside Minnesota.

Areas of interest:
ARTS, CULTURE, HUMANITIES: Media/communications, Museums, Performing arts, Visual arts.
EDUCATION: Higher education, Preschool/elementary, Secondary.

Intended beneficiaries: General public/unspecified.

Types of support for organizations:
CAPITAL CAMPAIGNS.
GENERAL PURPOSE/OPERATING SUPPORT: Annual campaigns.
PROGRAM DEVELOPMENT/PROJECT SUPPORT.
STUDENT AID (GRANTS TO INSTITUTIONS): Scholarship funds.

Sample grants:
Children's Theatre Company - MN (Twin Cities)/MN/$5,000.
In The Heart of the Beast Puppet & Mask Theatre/MN/$17,500.
ISD Minneapolis #282/MN/$140,000.
Oxfam America/MA/$25,000.
Sholom Foundation - MN/MN/$20,000.
St Cloud State University/MN/Holocaust Education Incentive/$40,000.
Walker Art Center/MN/Regis Dialogues and general contribution/$82,000.

Financial Information

Financial data for year ending: 06/30/2005
Foundation assets: $1,434,166
Grants paid: $1,807,460

Application Information

Preferred form of initial contact: letter of inquiry.

Proposal deadlines: none.

Staff/Trustees

Directors/trustees: Eric Bakken; Paul Finkelstein; David B. Kunin; Myron Kunin, president; Randy Pearce.

Luther I. Replogle Foundation

PO Box 33873
Washington, DC 20033-3873
Phone: (202) 679-0677
Fax: (202) 580-6579
E-mail: info@lirf.org
Website: www.lirf.org
Contact: Gwenn Gebhard, executive director
Established: 01/01/1966
Funder type: Private foundation

Program Description

Program's purpose: Luther I. Replogle, a distinguished businessman, diplomat and philanthropist, established the foundation to support organizations and institutions whose goals were humanitarian, religious, scholarly and cultural.

Funding priorities: Programs addressing the needs of youth and children living in, or at risk of, long-term poverty (especially children of inner-city residents and migrant workers). Of particular interest are programs for teen pregnancy prevention, counseling, broad-spectrum social services, and other programs that help young people improve their own lives. Programs to improve educational opportunities for inner-city children, including enrichment programs in the arts and sciences, alternative schools, after-school tutoring and mentoring, and scholarship programs. Programs for affordable and supportive housing that reach groups of people frequently left out of traditional shelter programs, including single mothers and families with children, the elderly, ex-offenders and youth. An emphasis is placed on programs that enable individuals to help themselves and become self-sufficient over the long-term. Projects, lectures and fellowships in classical archaeology, particularly in efforts to enable scholars to cross disciplines and specialties, and thus broaden their horizons. Projects and institutions working for the conservation of maps and globes, and dissemination and education in the area of geography. Luther I. Replogle Award for Management Improvement at the U.S. Department of State to reward individuals who, through their managerial ability, have contributed to the effective administration of the department and its programs. The Replogle Foundation also has a modest budget for support of the arts. In addition, the directors are able to make a small number of discretionary grants.

Geographic focus: West Metropolitan Area/Minneapolis only, Chicago, Palm Beach County, FL, and Washington, DC.

Geographic limitations: Chicago, Minneapolis, Palm Beach County, FL, and Washington, DC.

Areas of interest:

EDUCATION: Pre-school/elementary, Secondary, Student services/organizations of students, Classical archaeology, Geography, Map and Globe conservation and related-projects.

HOUSING/SHELTER.

HUMAN SERVICES: Children/youth services.

Types of support for organizations:
GENERAL PURPOSE/OPERATING SUPPORT.

PROGRAM DEVELOPMENT/ PROJECT SUPPORT.

Types of support for individuals: none.

Exclusions: Non-501(c)(3).

Sample grants:
Banyan Foundation/MN/$5,000.
Bright Beginnings/DC/$5,000.
Chicago Youth Centers/IL/$5,000.
Hope and A Home/DC/$7,000.
Metropolitan Interfaith Council on Affordable Housing/MN/$5,000.
Planned Parenthood - DC/DC/$7,000.
Planned Parenthood - IL/IL/$7,000.

Financial Information
Financial data for year ending: 12/31/2005
Foundation assets: $12,408,137
Grants paid: $425,000

Application Information
Preferred form of initial contact: online form.

Public information available by request: proposal guidelines, website.

Proposal deadlines: March 15 and September 15.

Contribution decisions made by: board of directors/trustees.

Frequency of contributions decisions: semiannually, April and October.

Special application procedures: Letters of inquiry and proposals are accepted only online at www.lirf.org. Any other mail should be addressed to Gwenn Gebhard, executive director, Luther I. Replogle Foundation, 1900 L Street NW, Suite 205, Washington, DC 20036-5002.

Staff/Trustees
Staff: Gwenn Gebhard, executive director.

Directors/trustees: Sophia Gebhard Anema; Virginia Cobb; Elizabeth Dickie; Paul R.S. Gebhard; William O. Petersen; David Replogle; Anne Witkowsky.

Richfield Community Foundation

PO Box 23077
Richfield, MN 55423
County: Hennepin
Phone: (612) 869-8057
Fax: (612) 861-8348
E-mail: schoo017@tc.umn.edu
Contact: Lynn Schoonmaker
Established: 01/01/1989
Funder type: Community/public foundation

Program Description
Program's purpose: To provide the means to develop resources that support and fund new and existing organizations and groups to improve the quality of life for Richfield's diverse population.

Funding priorities: Vulnerable and at-risk youth, immigrant populations and housing.

Geographic focus: Twin Cities Metropolitan Area, Community of Richfield.

Areas of interest:

EDUCATION: Pre-school/elementary, Secondary.

HUMAN SERVICES: Children/youth services, Immigrant support.

YOUTH DEVELOPMENT: Adult/child matching programs.

Intended beneficiaries:
Aging/elderly/senior citizens, Children and youth (infants-19 years), Immigrants/newcomers/refugees, Infants/babies (under age 5), Youth/adolescents (ages 14-19).

Types of support for organizations:
GENERAL PURPOSE/OPERATING SUPPORT.

PROGRAM DEVELOPMENT/ PROJECT SUPPORT: Mentoring programs.

Sample grants:
Bridging, Inc/MN/free furniture program/ $1,250.

Cornerstone Advocacy Service/MN/ services to youth program/$1,250.

Family & Children's Services - MN (Mpls)/Minneapolis, MN/activities for Latino youth/$1,000.

Fraser Community Services/MN/help purchase multicultural and anti-bias equipment and learning tools for children with disabilities and disorders/$1,000.

Richfield Community Center/MN/older adult computer program/$1,250.

Richfield Public Schools/MN/outdoor play equipment for Richfield Middle School/$1,500.

Senior Community Services/MN/Household and Outside Maintenance for Elderly (HOME) program/$1,000.

YMCA - MN (Southdale)/MN/after-school program/$530.

Financial Information

Financial data for year ending: 12/31/2005
Foundation assets: $280,260
Grants paid: $25,200
Number of grants: 10
Largest/smallest: $10,200/$250

Application Information

Preferred form of initial contact: request for guidelines.

Public information available by request: proposal guidelines, application form, annual report.

Accept common grant application: yes.

Preferred time for receiving proposals: October.

Contribution decisions made by: board of directors/trustees.

Frequency of contributions decisions: annually.

Specific times board meets: October.

Typical time from application deadlines to notification: 1 month from due date.

Staff/Trustees

Directors/trustees: David Brown; Barbara Devlin; Raphael Dufresne-Harden; Debbie Goettel, chair; Joshua Hanley; Gordon Hanson; Joan Helmberger; Martin Kirsch; Michael Morris; Todd Nollenberger; Larry Olson; Dave Reinert; Mike Sandahl; Jon Schoonmaker; Lynn Schoonmaker; Frank White; Nancy Wigchers.

Ripley Memorial Foundation, Inc.

c/o KC Connors CFA
43 Main Street SE
Suite 148
Minneapolis, MN 55414
County: Hennepin
Phone: (612) 252-7114
Website: www.ripleymemorial.org
Established: 01/01/1957
Funder type: Private foundation

Program Description

Program's purpose: Funding is provided for direct service programs focused on teen pregnancy prevention.

Funding priorities: To be eligible for consideration for a grant, programs must provide direct services; demonstrate teen pregnancy prevention as a primary objective; include a process for evaluating the program's effectiveness; serve youth (up to 19 years of age) and operate within Hennepin or Ramsey counties. Priority is given to programs employing best practices in teen pregnancy prevention and serving populations experiencing the highest rates of teen pregnancy.

Program limitations/restrictions: Grants submitted for agency programming must demonstrate an intent to prevent adolescent pregnancies and have a process for evaluating program effectiveness. No funding for public or private schools or government entities; for solely research or for capital improvements.

Geographic focus: Twin Cities Metropolitan Area, Hennepin and Ramsey Counties.

Geographic limitations: Only within Hennepin or Ramsey counties within Minnesota.

Areas of interest:
EDUCATION: Related to agency programming that has adolescent pregnancy prevention as a goal.
HEALTH - GENERAL/REHABILITATIVE: Reproductive health care, Related to agency programming that has adolescent pregnancy prevention as a goal.
HEALTH - MENTAL HEALTH/CRISIS INTERVENTION: Counseling/support groups, Related to agency programming that has adolescent pregnancy prevention as a goal.
HUMAN SERVICES: Children/youth services, Related to agency programming that has adolescent pregnancy prevention as a goal.
YOUTH DEVELOPMENT: Youth development programs, Must state adolescent pregnancy prevention as a primary goal.

Intended beneficiaries: Youth/adolescents (ages 14-19).

Types of support for organizations:
PROGRAM DEVELOPMENT/PROJECT SUPPORT: Curriculum development.

Types of support for individuals: none.

Exclusions: Capital & endowment campaigns, Individuals, Non-501(c)(3), Research, Scholarships/loans.

Sample grants:

Camphor Foundation - MN/MN/$2,000.

Division of Indian Work - MN/MN/$5,000.

Employment Action Center/MN/$8,000.

Girl Scout Council (St Croix Valley)/MN/$3,500.

Midwest Health Center for Women/MN/$7,500.

Neighborhood House/MN/$10,000.

Plymouth Christian Youth Center/MN/$8,000.

Southside Community Health Services - MN/MN/$4,000.

Financial Information

Financial data for year ending: 12/31/2006
Foundation assets: $1,512,238
Grants paid: $53,000
Number of grants: 9
Largest/smallest: $10,000/$2,000

Application Information

Preferred form of initial contact: letter of inquiry, telephone inquiry, request for guidelines, complete proposal.

Public information available by request: proposal guidelines, annual report.

Accept common grant application: yes.

Proposal deadlines: September 1.

Contribution decisions made by: board of directors/trustees.

Frequency of contributions decisions: annually, by November.

Specific times board meets: January, April, July and October.

Typical time from application deadlines to notification: 3 months.

Special application procedures: Grants awarded in 2006 will cover programming conducted from January 1, 2007 to December 31, 2007. A final report will be due by January 31, 2008.

Staff/Trustees

Directors/trustees: Jean Adams, president; Stephanie Andrews; Catherine Asta; Carol C. Broback; Suzanne Busta; Gina Ciganik; KC Connors; Mari Oyanagi Eggum; Jacqui Catherine Gardner; Janel M. Goff; Aretha Green-Rupert; Audrey Hogan; Anne Mootz; Ginny Orth; Anita Patel; Gloria Perez Jordan; Saundra Rowell; Judie Russell; Robin B. Schoenwetter; Ann Scovil; Susan Sorenson; Renee Vanman Wixon.

Ritt Family Foundation

Securian Trust Company
400 Robert Street North
St Paul, MN 55101-2098
County: Ramsey
Phone: (651) 665-4867
Fax: (651) 665-5414
Contact: Harold M. Johnson
Established: 01/01/1988
fka: Midway National Bank of St Paul Foundation
Funder type: Private foundation

Program Description

Intended beneficiaries: General public/unspecified.

Sample grants:

Century College Foundation/MN/endowed scholarship/ $6,000.

Como Zoo & Conservatory Society/MN/ improve plant & animal collection/$500.

Dakota Woodlands/MN/women & children emergency transitional housing fund/$3,000.

Gillette Children's Hospital Foundation/ MN/free healthcare fund/$1,000.

HEART (Help Enable Alcoholics Receive Treatment)/MN/$2,500.

Merriam Park Community Services/MN/ $1,000.

St Paul Urban Tennis Program/MN/ general operating/$1,000.

United Hospital Foundation/MN/partners in health care careers program/$1,000.

Financial Information

Financial data for year ending: 12/31/2005
Foundation assets: $413,353
Grants paid: $33,050
Number of grants: 10

Application Information

Preferred form of initial contact: letter of inquiry.
Accept common grant application: yes.
Accept common report form: yes.
Proposal deadlines: none.
Contribution decisions made by: board of directors/trustees.
Special application procedures: written request stating the purpose, requested amount, and tax-exempt status of requesting organization.

Staff/Trustees

Directors/trustees: Harold M. Johnson; Lisa Meyers, president; John A. Ritt; Steven Ritt.

Margaret Rivers Fund

PO Box 197
Stillwater, MN 55082
County: Washington
Phone: (651) 430-3935
Contact: David Pohl, president
Established: 10/23/1948
Funder type: Private foundation

Program Description

Program's purpose: General charitable purposes.
Geographic focus: Twin Cities Metropolitan Area, Areas outside Minnesota.
Areas of interest:
ANIMAL RELATED.
ARTS, CULTURE, HUMANITIES: Arts services, Arts/cultural multipurpose, Historical societies, Media/communications, Museums, Performing arts, Visual arts.
COMMUNITY IMPROVEMENT.
EDUCATION.
HEALTH - DISEASES/MEDICAL DISCIPLINES.
HEALTH - GENERAL/ REHABILITATIVE.
HUMAN SERVICES: Children/youth services, Emergency assistance (food/clothing/cash), Family services.
YOUTH DEVELOPMENT: Multipurpose youth centers/clubs, Scouting organizations, Youth development programs.

Intended beneficiaries: General public/unspecified.

Sample grants:

Camp Heartland - MN/MN/$2,500.

Croixdale Residence & Apartments/MN/ $40,000.

Duck Soup Players Inc/MN/$3,000.

Girl Scout Council - MN (St Croix Valley)/MN/$10,000.

Graffiti Teen Center - Stillwater/MN/ $22,000.

Learning Disabilities Association - MN (Mpls)/MN/$8,000.

St Croix Festival Theatre/MN/$5,000.

Stillwater Public Library/MN/$100,000.

Financial Information

Financial data for year ending: 12/31/2005
Foundation assets: $32,675,832
Grants paid: $1,932,850

Application Information

Preferred form of initial contact: letter of inquiry; letters should include the charity's name, address, federal I.D. number and a written description of the charity and its intended use of the grant.
Accept common grant application: yes.
Frequency of contributions decisions: monthly.

Staff/Trustees

Directors/trustees: Jean M. Barry; Robert Briggs; David Pohl, president; Lawrence Severson.

The Riverway Foundation

8400 Normandale Lake Boulevard
Suite 920
Bloomington, MN 55437
County: Hennepin
Phone: (952) 921-3994
Fax: (952) 921-3992
E-mail: smoen@riverway.com
Contact: Shirley A. Moen, executive secretary
Established: 01/01/1996
Donor: The Riverway Company
Funder type: Corporate foundation

Program Description

Program's purpose: Improve community by assisting youth and family development; promote better health for residents.

Geographic focus: Twin Cities Metropolitan Area.

Areas of interest:
HEALTH - DISEASES/MEDICAL DISCIPLINES: Cancer, Alzheimer's.
HEALTH - RESEARCH: Cancer research.
HUMAN SERVICES: Children/youth services, Family services, Family services for adolescent parents, Family violence shelters and services, Senior centers and services.
PUBLIC SAFETY/DISASTERS/RELIEF: Disaster preparedness and relief.
YOUTH DEVELOPMENT: Adult/child matching programs, Multipurpose youth centers/clubs, Scouting organizations, Youth development programs.

Intended beneficiaries: Adults, Aging/elderly/senior citizens, Children and youth (infants-19 years), Poor/economically disadvantaged, Single parents.

Types of support for organizations:
CAPITAL CAMPAIGNS: Building/renovation, Endowment funds, Equipment.
EMERGENCY FUNDS.
GENERAL PURPOSE/OPERATING SUPPORT: Annual campaigns.
RESEARCH.

Sample grants:
Alzheimer's Association - MN (Minneapolis)/MN/General operating/$2,500.
Big Brothers/Big Sisters - MN (Minneapolis)/MN/General operating/$2,000.
Boy Scouts of America - MN/MN/$5,000.
Dunwoody Institute/MN/YCAP program/$2,000.
Friends of Children, Inc/Foster child enrichment program/$1,500.
Greater Minneapolis Crisis Nursery/MN/Program support/$2,500.
Living Lands & Waters Restoration Organization/IL/River clean up/$25,000.
Mayo Foundation/MN/General operating/$25,000.

Financial Information

Financial data for year ending: 12/31/2006
Foundation assets: $4,264,635
Grants paid: $114,000
Number of grants: 17
Largest/smallest: $25,000/$1,000

Application Information

Preferred form of initial contact: e-mail, letter of inquiry with IRS determination letter.

Contribution decisions made by: board of directors/trustees.

Frequency of contributions decisions: annually.

Staff/Trustees

Staff: Shirley A. Moen, executive secretary.

Directors/trustees: H.M. Baskerville Jr., chair; Laura Lee Becker; Terry R. Becker.

Robins, Kaplan, Miller & Ciresi, L.L.P. Foundation for Education, Public Health & Social Justice

800 LDS Center
80 South Eighth Street
Minneapolis, MN 55402-2015
County: Hennepin
Phone: (612) 672-3861
Fax: (612) 339-4181
Website: www.rkmc.com/EPHSJ_foundation.asp
Paid Staff: Yes
Funder type: Community/public foundation

Program Description

Program's purpose: The Robins, Kaplan, Miller & Ciresi L.L.P. Foundation for Education, Public Health and Social Justice was established to carry out the firm's commitment to contribute to the common good in the geographic regions in which it practices. The foundation is primarily dedicated to children in the areas of education, public health and social justice. Through the foundation, the firm is able to join with others in making a visible and meaningful commitment to the common good of our nation. That commitment is one of the core values of the firm and is supported by the entire Robins, Kaplan, Miller & Ciresi family.

Geographic focus: Twin Cities Metropolitan Area, Greater Minnesota.

Financial Information

Financial data for year ending: 03/31/2006
Foundation assets: $31,008,691
Grants paid: $1,599,900

Staff/Trustees

Directors/trustees: Michael V. Ciresi; John F. Eisberg; Rev. Albert Gallmon Jr.; Elliot S. Kaplan; Father Michael O'Connell; Kathleen Flynn Peterson; Roberta Walburn; Rabbi Marcia Zimmerman.

Rochester Area Foundation

2200 Second Street SW
Suite 300
Rochester, MN 55902-4125
County: Olmsted
Phone: (507) 282-0203
Alt. Phone: (507) 287-7117
Fax: (507) 282-4938
E-mail: info@RochesterArea.org
Website: www.RochesterArea.org
Contact: Steve Thornton, executive director
Established: 11/29/1944
Paid Staff: Yes
Funder type: Community/public foundation

Program Description

Program's purpose: The primary purpose of the foundation is to establish and promote activities of a social, moral, educational, religious and benevolent nature in greater Rochester area, Minnesota.

Funding priorities: Strengthen children and families; build capacity of nonprofit organizations.

Geographic focus: Greater Rochester area.

Geographic limitations: Greater Rochester area.

Areas of interest:

ANIMAL RELATED: Animal protection/welfare.

ARTS, CULTURE, HUMANITIES: Arts services, Arts/cultural multipurpose, Historical societies, Museums, Performing arts, Visual arts.

CIVIL RIGHTS: Civil liberties advocacy, Civil rights/advocacy for specific groups, Equal opportunity and access, Intergroup relations/race relations.

COMMUNITY IMPROVEMENT: Community coalitions, Community/neighborhood development/improvement, Economic development, Nonprofit management, Volunteer bureaus.

EDUCATION: Adult/continuing education/literacy, Educational reform, Educational services, Higher education, Libraries/library science, Pre-school/elementary, Secondary, Vocational/technical.

ENVIRONMENTAL QUALITY/PROTECTION/BEAUTIFICATION: Environmental education/outdoor survival, Natural resources conservation/protection.

FOOD/NUTRITION/AGRICULTURE: Food service/free food distribution.

HEALTH - DISEASES/MEDICAL DISCIPLINES: AIDS/HIV.

HEALTH - GENERAL/REHABILITATIVE: Health support services, Health treatment facilities - primarily outpatient, Nursing care/services, Public health programs/wellness education.

HEALTH - MENTAL HEALTH/CRISIS INTERVENTION: Addiction disorders, Alcohol/drug/substance, prevention and treatment, Counseling/support groups, Mental health treatment and services.

HOUSING/SHELTER: Homeless, temporary housing, Housing development/construction/management.

HUMAN SERVICES: Children/youth services, Emergency assistance (food/clothing/cash), Family services, Family services for adolescent parents, Family violence shelters and services, Multipurpose human service organizations, Residential/custodial care, Senior centers and services, Services to specific groups, Victims services.

PHILANTHROPY/VOLUNTARISM: Nonprofit sector assistance, Voluntarism promotion.

PUBLIC AFFAIRS/SOCIETY BENEFIT: Citizen participation.

PUBLIC PROTECTION - CRIME/COURTS/LEGAL SERVICES: Crime prevention, Dispute/conflict resolution, Protection/prevention - neglect/abuse/exploitation, Rehabilitation of offenders.

RECREATION: Amateur sports clubs/leagues, Physical fitness/recreational facilities.

YOUTH DEVELOPMENT: Adult/child matching programs, Multipurpose youth centers/clubs, Scouting organizations, Youth development programs.

Intended beneficiaries: Asian/Pacific Islanders, General public/unspecified.

Types of support for organizations:

CAPITAL CAMPAIGNS: Building/renovation, Equipment.

MANAGEMENT/TECHNICAL ASSISTANCE.

PROGRAM DEVELOPMENT/PROJECT SUPPORT: Mentoring programs, Seed money/start-up funds, Leadership programs.

Sample grants:

Boys & Girls Club - MN (Rochester)/MN/$3,000.

Lourdes High School - Rochester, MN/MN/$8,000.

Mayo Clinic/MN/$10,000.

Rochester Area Disabled Athletics and Recreation Inc./MN/$7,500.

Rochester Art Center/MN/$1,250.

Rochester Civic Theatre, Inc/MN/$500.

Ronald McDonald House - MN (Rochester)/MN/$10,000.

Financial Information

Financial data for year ending: 12/31/2006
Foundation assets: $30,000,000
Grants paid: $2,500,000
Number of grants: 162
Largest/smallest: $50,000/$250

Application Information

Preferred form of initial contact: telephone inquiry, request for guidelines, e-mail.

Public information available by request: proposal guidelines, application form, annual report, newsletter, website.

Accept common grant application: yes.

Accept common report form: yes.

Will view video: yes.

Proposal deadlines: January 1, May 1, September 1.

Contribution decisions made by: board of directors/trustees.

Frequency of contributions decisions: three times per year.

Specific times board meets: monthly.

Typical time from application deadlines to notification: four months.

Staff/Trustees

Staff: Sean Allen, assistant executive director; Allison Anderson, administrative assistant; Jane Campion, grants administrator; Al DeBoer, development director; Chris Flood, First Homes program officer; Sheila Kiscaden, First Steps director; Shirley Lee, First Homes program officer; Chris Mart, administrative assistant; Cheryl Richardson, First Homes program officer; Steve Thornton, executive director; Sarah Van Niewaal, First Steps program officer.

Directors/trustees: Nancy Brubaker; Nancy Domaille; Joe Duffy; Paul Harkess; Robert Hill; Leigh Johnson; Carol Kamper, secretary; Jean Locke; Michael McNeil, vice chair; Joe Powers; Alan Schafer, treasurer; David Stenhaug, chair; John Wade; Craig Wendland, vice chair.

Rochester Post Bulletin Charities

18 First Avenue SE
Rochester, MN 55904
County: Olmsted
Phone: (507) 285-7600
Established: 01/01/1987
Funder type: Community/public foundation

Program Description

Funding priorities: Newspaper in Education, a partnership program with area schools and the Earth Day, Every Day program.

Geographic focus: Greater Minnesota.

Geographic limitations: Rochester, Minnesota area.

Intended beneficiaries: Children and youth (infants-19 years).

Sample grants:

City of Rochester - MN/MN/independence day fireworks/$14,880.

Newspaper In Education/MN/newspapers for use in classroom study/$54,309.

Financial Information

Financial data for year ending: 12/31/2005
Foundation assets: $29,431
Grants paid: $52,398

Staff/Trustees

Directors/trustees: Christy Blade; Robert L. Hill.

Rukavina Family Foundation

802 Prairie Meadows
Hudson, WI 54016
Phone: (715) 386-6358
Funder type: Private foundation

Program Description

Funding priorities: Educational, civic, or religious activities.

Geographic limitations: Grants primarily to the Winona, MN, area.

Areas of interest:
EDUCATION.
RELIGION/SPIRITUAL DEVELOPMENT.

Sample grants:

American Red Cross - MN (Winona)/MN/$10,000.

Catholic Schools - MN (Greater)/MN/$10,000.

Heartland Montessori School/MN/$12,500.

Mayo Foundation/MN/$10,000.

Sisters of St Benedict/MN/$20,000.

St Anne Foundation/MN/$20,000.

YMCA - MN (Winona)/MN/$12,500.

Financial Information

Financial data for year ending: 12/31/2005
Foundation assets: $2,673,304
Grants paid: $100,000
Number of grants: 8
Largest/smallest: $20,000/$2,000

Application Information

Preferred form of initial contact: Amount requested and purpose of grant.

Proposal deadlines: none.

Staff/Trustees

Directors/trustees: John Rukavina, president.

Runestone Electric Association Community Trust

PO Box 9
Alexandria, MN 56308-0009
County: Douglas
Phone: (320) 762-1121
Alt. Phone: (800) 473-1722
E-mail: hultman@rea-alp.com
Website: www.runestoneelectric.com
Contact: Jim Hultman, manager of marketing and customer services
Funder type: Community/public foundation

Program Description

Program's purpose: Disbursement of funds from the Operation Round Up voluntary contribution program for charitable and educational purposes primarily in the area served by Runestone Electric Association.

Funding priorities: Grants for groups in the community for purposes such as fire department equipment, food shelves, disability programs, youth activities and college scholarships.

Program limitations/restrictions: Lobbying, political and religious organizations; veteran, fraternal and labor organizations; fundraising dinners, raffles and other events; individuals; capital fund campaigns; national fund drives; advertising; ongoing operational expenses.

Geographic focus: Greater Minnesota, Alexandria, area served by Runestone Electric Association.

Geographic limitations: Grants to the area served by Runestone Electric Association.

Areas of interest:
COMMUNITY IMPROVEMENT.
EDUCATION.
FOOD/NUTRITION/AGRICULTURE: Food service/free food distribution.
YOUTH DEVELOPMENT.

Sample grants:

4-H Club - MN (Douglas County)/MN/Summer programming /$500.

Alexandria Technical College/MN/Scholarships/$1,000.

Grant County Food Shelf/MN/$1,500.

Listening Ear Crisis Center/Alexandria, MN/PLUS Kids Safe exchange/$500.

Financial Information

Financial data for year ending: 12/31/2005
Foundation assets: $12,853
Grants paid: $65,180
Number of grants: 125
Largest/smallest: $1,500/$200

Application Information

Preferred form of initial contact: telephone inquiry, complete proposal, e-mail.

Public information available by request: proposal guidelines, application form, website.

Contribution decisions made by: board of directors/trustees.

Frequency of contributions decisions: quarterly.

Staff/Trustees

Staff: Jim Hultman, manager of marketing and customer services.

Directors/trustees: John Beem, president; Thomas Burquest, secretary/treasurer; Jeffrey Dreier; Bruce Ferris; Jerome Hagen, vice president; Gerald Johnson; Kathy Nelson.

Sacred Portion Foundation

8692 Tenth Street SE
Buffalo, MN 55313
County: Wright
Contact: David A. Clark
Funder type: Private foundation

Program Description

Program's purpose: The Sacred Portion foundation promotes the Gospel of Jesus Christ through the following endeavors: verbal, broadcast and printed proclamation of the Gospel; the training and equipping of ministers of the Gospel; acts of mercy and compassion to the poor, the disabled, the homeless, the sick, orphans, refugees, persecuted Christians; displaced persons and any person or group of people with an emergency need; the defense of the unborn; the promotion of family stability; Christian nurture and Christian education for children; the support and encouragement of Christian ministers; the advancement and maintenance of the material infrastructure needed by Christian ministries to accomplish their purposes; the promotion of Christian spiritual renewal.

Geographic focus: Twin Cities Metropolitan Area, Greater Minnesota, Areas outside Minnesota.

Areas of interest:
RELIGION/SPIRITUAL DEVELOPMENT.

Intended beneficiaries: General public/unspecified, Poor/economically disadvantaged.

Types of support for organizations:
PROGRAM DEVELOPMENT/PROJECT SUPPORT.

Sample grants:

Campus Crusade for Christ - FL/FL/missionaries/$3,000.

Community Christian School/Willmar, MN/$5,000.

International Ministerial Fellowship/Minneapolis, MN/$44,900.

King's Kids - MN (Cambridge)/MN/missionaries/$4,200.

Lutheran Hour/St Louis, MO/mission projects/$10,000.

People To People - MO/Manchester, MO/missionaries/$3,600.

Youth with a Mission - MN (Cambridge)/MN/missionary training/$70,000.

Financial Information

Financial data for year ending: 12/31/2005
Foundation assets: $4,755,688
Grants paid: $167,500
Number of grants: 11
Largest/smallest: $70,000/$2,100

Application Information

Preferred form of initial contact: request for guidelines.

Public information available by request: application form.

Proposal deadlines: none.

Staff/Trustees

Directors/trustees: David A. Clark; John L. Clark, president; Nancy E. Clark.

The Saint Paul Foundation

55 East Fifth Street
Suite 600
St Paul, MN 55101-1797
County: Ramsey
Phone: (651) 224-5463
Fax: (651) 224-8123
E-mail: inbox@saintpaulfoundation.org
Website: www.saintpaulfoundation.org
Established: 01/01/1940
Funder type: Community/public foundation

Program Description

Program's purpose: Vision: A healthy and vital community in which all people have the opportunity to enhance the quality of their lives and the lives of others. Values: We believe that the well-being of each person is connected to that of every other; all members of the community share responsibility for achieving a healthy and vital community; the community is strengthened when people of diverse backgrounds participate in meaningful partnerships; the cultural and ethnic diversity of our community should be reflected in all of its institutions and processes; all people must be treated with fairness, dignity and respect; achieving positive community change requires long-term investment and thoughtful, considered risk-taking. Mission: The Saint Paul Foundation actively serves the people of the greater St Paul area by building permanent charitable capital, making philanthropic grants, and providing services that contribute to the health and vitality of the community. We do this by working with donors to achieve their philanthropic goals; managing responsibly the foundation's assets; encouraging and participating in community initiatives and partnerships; broadening the base of effective leadership in the community; building awareness of the role of philanthropy in meeting the needs of the community; and providing services to other charitable organizations.

Funding priorities: The Saint Paul Foundation accepts applications for grants from unrestricted and field of interest funds. Areas of interest for funding include education, human services, humanities, the arts and community development. In November 1998, the foundation approved a new strategic plan for grantmaking that directs the foundation to pay special attention to helping achieve the following goals over the next decade: an anti-racist community; economic development for all segments of the East Metro area; strong families that provide healthy beginnings for children and youth; quality education for all. Proposals that address one or more of these goals are strongly encouraged. Proposals that address other community needs will also be considered. The foundation will consider grant applications for start-up costs for promising new programs that demonstrate sound management and clear goals relevant to community needs; support for established agencies that have temporary or transitional needs; multi-year funding; funds to match contributions received from other sources or to provide a challenge to help raise new contributions; capital projects, program expansion or special projects of a time-limited nature.

Program limitations/restrictions: Grants are authorized to nonprofit organizations and public entities. The foundation will not consider grant applications for annual operating expenses; sectarian religious programs; agency endowment funds; grants to individuals; capital projects located outside the East Metro area; and programs not serving the residents of the East Metro area.

Geographic focus: East Metropolitan Area/St Paul only, Dakota, Ramsey and Washington counties.

Geographic limitations: Grants are authorized to nonprofit organizations and public entities primarily serving residents of the East Metro area of Ramsey, Washington and Dakota counties. The foundation will not consider grant applications for capital projects located outside the East Metro area; and programs not serving the residents of the East Metro area.

Areas of interest:

ARTS, CULTURE, HUMANITIES: Arts services, Arts/cultural multipurpose, Historical societies, Humanities, Media/communications, Museums, Performing arts, Visual arts.

CIVIL RIGHTS: Civil rights/advocacy for specific groups, Equal opportunity and access, Intergroup relations/race relations, Voter education/registration, Anti-racism: reduce racism at both individual and institutional levels through education, direct-action and/or increased dialogue and understanding.

COMMUNITY IMPROVEMENT: Community coalitions, Community/neighborhood development/improvement, Economic development, Nonprofit management.

EDUCATION: Adult/continuing education/literacy, Educational services, Libraries/library science, Pre-school/elementary, Secondary, Vocational/technical.

EMPLOYMENT/JOBS: Employment procurement/job training.

ENVIRONMENTAL QUALITY/PROTECTION/BEAUTIFICATION: Environmental education/outdoor survival, Natural resources conservation/protection.

FOOD/NUTRITION/AGRICULTURE: Food service/free food distribution, Nutrition promotion, Soil and water conservation/farm land preservation.

HEALTH - GENERAL/REHABILITATIVE: Health support services, Health treatment facilities - primarily outpatient, Public health programs/wellness education.

HEALTH - MENTAL HEALTH/CRISIS INTERVENTION: Alcohol/drug/substance, prevention and treatment, Counseling/support groups, Hotline/crisis intervention, Mental health disorders, Mental health treatment and services.

HOUSING/SHELTER: Homeless, temporary housing, Housing development/construction/management, Housing support services, Low-cost temporary housing.

HUMAN SERVICES: Children/youth services, Emergency assistance (food/clothing/cash), Family services, Family services for adolescent parents, Family violence shelters and services, Multipurpose human service organizations, Personal social services, Residential/custodial care, Senior centers and services, Services to specific groups, Victims services.

PHILANTHROPY/VOLUNTARISM: Nonprofit sector assistance.

PUBLIC AFFAIRS/SOCIETY BENEFIT: Citizen participation.

PUBLIC PROTECTION - CRIME/COURTS/LEGAL SERVICES: Crime prevention, Legal services, Protection/prevention - neglect/abuse/exploitation.

YOUTH DEVELOPMENT: Adult/child matching programs, Multipurpose youth centers/clubs, Scouting organizations, Youth development programs.

Intended beneficiaries: General public/unspecified.

Types of support for organizations:

CAPITAL CAMPAIGNS: Building/renovation, Computer systems/technology, Endowment funds, Equipment.

MANAGEMENT/TECHNICAL ASSISTANCE.

PROGRAM DEVELOPMENT/PROJECT SUPPORT: Faculty/staff development, Mentoring programs, Seed money/start-up funds.

Types of support for individuals: none.

Matching grants: employee matching.

Exclusions: Individuals, Non-501(c)(3), Political organizations, Research, Scholarships/loans.

Sample grants:

Centro Legal Inc/MN/To help finance the budget to expand the Employment Readiness Project/$75,000.

Community Dental Care - MN/MN/To help finance the budget of the Oral Health Care Outreach and Education Project/$25,000.

Eftin Innovative - MN/MN/To help finance the budget of the Immigrant Student Achieving Program/$25,000.

Episcopal Homes Foundation - MN/MN/To help finance the budget for constructing the Carty Heights low-income housing development/$100,000.

Merrick Community Services/MN/To help finance the budget of the Middle School Street Youth Specialist Program/$25,000.

University UNITED Local Development Company/MN/For the District Councils Collaborative of Saint Paul and Minneapolis/$50,000.

Volunteers of America - MN/MN/To help finance the budget of Experience Corps – Minnesota in Public Schools in Saint Paul/$15,000.

Amherst H. Wilder Foundation/MN/For construction of the Wilder Center/$750,000.

Financial Information

Financial data for year ending: 12/31/2006
Foundation assets: $909,456,743
Grants paid: $51,018,719
Number of grants: 6485
Largest/smallest: $1,500,000/$5

Application Information

Preferred form of initial contact: request for guidelines.

Public information available by request: proposal guidelines, application form, annual report, website.

Preferred time for receiving proposals: Full proposals must be received approximately 3-1/2 months prior to a meeting date. Capital projects are considered only at the November grantmaking meeting.

Contribution decisions made by: board of directors/trustees.

Specific times board meets: April, August, November.

Typical time from application deadlines to notification: 4-5 months.

Staff/Trustees

Staff: Lori A. Berg-Kirsch, program officer; Claire J. Chang, director, program planning and special initiatives; John G. Couchman, vice president, grants and program; Sharon DeMark, program officer; Lisa M. Hansen, program assistant grants & special projects; Trista Harris, program officer; Heather Hinke, administrative assistant, grants & program; Sonja A. Moore, donor relations officer; Donna Paulson, administrative assistant; Carleen Rhodes, president; Jean Vukas Roberts, vice president, development; Carrie Jo Short, senior program officer; Gerald C. Timian, program officer.

Directors/trustees: Wilson G. Bradshaw; Mary K. Brainerd; John Cowles III; Jacqueline A. Dorsey; Robert A. Engebretsen; James R. Frey; Joan A. Grzywinski; Ann Huntrods; R. Scott Jones, chair; Thomas W. Kingston; Cynthia Lesher; Nancy E. Lindahl; Manuel Mariano Lopez; Wendy H. Rubin; John R. Ryan Jr.; Cris E. Stainbrook; Louise K. Thoreson; Judith L. Titcomb; Elsa Vega-Perez; Mark L. Wilson.

Salem Foundation, Inc.

2181 Springwood Road
Wayzata, MN 55391
County: Hennepin
Phone: (952) 476-6292
Contact: Robert S. Parish, president
Established: 08/01/1967
Funder type: Private foundation

Program Description

Program's purpose: For charitable, educational, religious, medical and scientific organizations.

Geographic focus: Twin Cities Metropolitan Area, areas outside Minnesota.

Areas of interest:
ARTS, CULTURE, HUMANITIES.
EDUCATION: Higher education, Preschool/elementary, Secondary.
ENVIRONMENTAL QUALITY/PROTECTION/BEAUTIFICATION.
HEALTH - GENERAL/REHABILITATIVE.
HUMAN SERVICES.
RELIGION/SPIRITUAL DEVELOPMENT.
YOUTH DEVELOPMENT.

Intended beneficiaries: General public/unspecified.

Exclusions: Individuals, Non-501(c)(3), Political organizations, Tax-supported institutions.

Sample grants:
Arthritis Foundation - MA/MA/$3,000.
Greater Yellowstone Coalition/MT/$600.
People, Inc/St Paul, MN/$2,000.
Plymouth Congregational Church/Minneapolis, MN/$2,000.
The Science Museum of MN/MN/$6,000.
Special Olympics - MN/MN/$1,500.
St Paul Academy & Summit School/MN/$300.
University of St Thomas - MN/MN/$600.

Financial Information

Financial data for year ending: 12/31/2005
Foundation assets: $904,965
Grants paid: $40,950
Number of grants: 27
Largest/smallest: $10,000/$500

Application Information

Preferred form of initial contact: no unsolicited applications accepted.

Contribution decisions made by: board of directors/trustees.

Staff/Trustees

Directors/trustees: Judith Diedrich; John C. Parish Jr.; Michael Parish; Robert S. Parish, president.

Samsara Foundation

2620 Glenhurst Avenue
Minneapolis, MN 55416-3957
County: Hennepin
Phone: (952) 920-6962
Contact: Tineka Kurth, president
Established: 11/20/1990
Funder type: Private foundation

Program Description

Program's purpose: Self-help for people and children living in poverty.

Funding priorities: Religious, charitable, scientific and educational only; inner city is highest priority.

Geographic focus: Twin Cities Metropolitan Area, areas outside Minnesota.

Areas of interest:
CIVIL RIGHTS.
EDUCATION.
FOOD/NUTRITION/AGRICULTURE: Food service/free food distribution.
HEALTH - RESEARCH.
HOUSING/SHELTER: Homeless, temporary housing.
HUMAN SERVICES: Children/youth services, Emergency assistance (food/clothing/cash), Family services.

Intended beneficiaries: General public/unspecified, Poor/economically disadvantaged.

Sample grants:
Advocating Change Together Inc/MN/$5,000.
American Foundation for AIDS Research - NY/NY/$2,000.
City Inc, The/MN/$1,500.
Food for Survival/NY/$5,000.
Greater Minneapolis Crisis Nursery/MN/$1,000.
Lambda Legal - NY/New York, NY/$2,000.
MN News Council/MN/$4,000.
We Win Institute Inc - Minneapolis/MN/$20,000.

Financial Information

Financial data for year ending: 12/31/2005
Foundation assets: $5,306,245
Grants paid: $196,000
Number of grants: 21
Largest/smallest: $50,000/$1,000

Application Information

Preferred form of initial contact: letter of inquiry.

Proposal deadlines: none.

Staff/Trustees

Directors/trustees: Tineka Kurth, president; Kera Messinger; William Messinger.

Sauer Children's Renew Foundation

2655 North Innsbruck Drive
Suite A
New Brighton, MN 55112
County: Ramsey
Phone: (651) 633-6165
Website: www.scrfmn.org
Contact: Colleen O'Keefe, executive director
Established: 01/01/1996
Funder type: Private foundation

Program Description

Program's purpose: To improve the lives of disadvantaged children in the state of Minnesota.

Funding priorities: Children.

Geographic focus: Minnesota statewide.

Areas of interest:
EDUCATION.
HUMAN SERVICES: Children/youth services.
YOUTH DEVELOPMENT.

Intended beneficiaries: Children and youth (infants-19 years).

Sample grants:
Children's Safety Center Network, Inc/MN/$10,000.

Greater Minneapolis Crisis Nursery/MN/$10,000.

The Jeremiah Program/MN/$10,000.

Life's Missing Link/MN/$10,000.

Risen Christ Catholic School/Minneapolis, MN/$10,000.

Sharing & Caring Hands, Inc/MN/$10,000.

St Joseph's Home for Children - MN/MN/$20,000.

Financial Information

Financial data for year ending: 12/31/2005
Foundation assets: $3,287,657
Grants paid: $200,600
Number of grants: 20
Largest/smallest: $20,000/$2,500

Staff/Trustees

Staff: Colleen O'Keefe, executive director; Corey D. Sauer, administrative assistant.

Directors/trustees: Carl Carlson; Carol J. Gallivan; Mary-Megan McMahon; Stephanie A. Morrissey; Jessica Nickelson; Chad B. Sauer; Gary B. Sauer; Kay Sauer; Patricia A. Sauer, president.

Saunders Family Foundation

PO Box 2187
Minneapolis, MN 55402
County: Hennepin
Phone: (612) 359-4481
Fax: (612) 359-4499
E-mail: bsaunders@worldnet.att.net
Contact: W. B. Saunders
Established: 01/31/1987
Funder type: Private foundation

Program Description

Program's purpose: The Saunders Family Foundation believes in responding to the needs of the community in a way that can effect change and ameliorate a problem. The goals are to help others become self-sufficient and to reach their full potential.

Funding priorities: Education, social programs with emphasis on children, health, organizations with direct links to foundation members.

Program limitations/restrictions: No endowments, funding to individuals, political campaigns; arts by invitation only.

Geographic focus: Twin Cities Metropolitan Area, Burnett County, WI.

Areas of interest:

ANIMAL RELATED: Animal protection/welfare, Wildlife preservation/protection.

ARTS, CULTURE, HUMANITIES: Historical societies, Performing arts, Visual arts.

COMMUNITY IMPROVEMENT: Community/neighborhood development/improvement.

EDUCATION: Higher education, Preschool/elementary, Secondary, Vocational/technical.

HEALTH - DISEASES/MEDICAL DISCIPLINES: AIDS/HIV, Cancer.

HEALTH - MENTAL HEALTH/CRISIS INTERVENTION: Alcohol/drug/substance, prevention and treatment.

HEALTH - RESEARCH: Cancer research, Specific named disease research.

HOUSING/SHELTER: Homeless, temporary housing.

HUMAN SERVICES: Children/youth services, Family services, Services to specific groups.

PHILANTHROPY/VOLUNTARISM: Philanthropy associations.

PUBLIC PROTECTION - CRIME/COURTS/LEGAL SERVICES: Correctional facilities and prisoner services, Rehabilitation of offenders.

YOUTH DEVELOPMENT: Multipurpose youth centers/clubs, Youth development programs.

Intended beneficiaries: Adults, Children and youth (infants-19 years), Ethnic/racial populations - general, General public/unspecified, Hispanics/Latinos, Homeless.

Types of support for organizations:

CAPITAL CAMPAIGNS: Building/renovation, Equipment.

GENERAL PURPOSE/OPERATING SUPPORT.

STUDENT AID (GRANTS TO INSTITUTIONS): Scholarship funds.

Exclusions: Individuals, Political organizations, endowments, funding to invidu-als, political campaigns; arts by invitation only.

Sample grants:
Jabbok Foundation/MN/$3,000.
Jungle Theater/MN/$2,000.
Project Regina - MN (Minneapolis)/MN/$1,500.
Rebuild Resources Inc/MN/$2,000.
Webster High School/Webster, WI/$10,000.
Youth Frontiers Inc/MN/$3,000.

Financial Information

Financial data for year ending: 12/31/2006
Foundation assets: $1,064,746
Grants paid: $68,250
Number of grants: 30
Largest/smallest: $10,000/$1,000

Application Information

Preferred form of initial contact: letter of inquiry.

Public information available by request: proposal guidelines, application form.

Accept common grant application: yes.

Accept common report form: yes.

Proposal deadlines: September 1.

Contribution decisions made by: board of directors/trustees.

Frequency of contributions decisions: annually.

Specific times board meets: early December.

Typical time from application deadlines to notification: notified in December.

Staff/Trustees

Staff: Nancy Dostal, executive assistant; Sallie Saunders March, president/director.

Directors/trustees: Arthur W. Saunders, treasurer; John D. Saunders, secretary; W. B. Saunders; Susan Saunders Zoidis, vice president.

Carl and Verna Schmidt Foundation

PO Box 638
Rochester, MN 55903-0638
County: Olmsted
Phone: (507) 285-2517
Established: 01/01/1958
Funder type: Private foundation

Program Description

Geographic focus: Greater Minnesota.

Areas of interest:

ANIMAL RELATED: Animal protection/welfare, Wildlife preservation/protection.

ARTS, CULTURE, HUMANITIES: Arts/cultural multipurpose, Historical societies, Performing arts.

COMMUNITY IMPROVEMENT.

EDUCATION: Libraries/library science.

ENVIRONMENTAL QUALITY/PROTECTION/BEAUTIFICATION: Botanical/horticultural/landscape, Environmental beautification/open spaces, Natural resources conservation/protection.

HEALTH - DISEASES/MEDICAL DISCIPLINES.

HEALTH - GENERAL/REHABILITATIVE.

HOUSING/SHELTER.

PUBLIC SAFETY/DISASTERS/RELIEF.

RELIGION/SPIRITUAL DEVELOPMENT.

Intended beneficiaries: General public/unspecified.

Exclusions: Non-501(c)(3).

Sample grants:

Friends of the Library - MN (LeSueur)/MN/$15,000.

Habitat for Humanity - MN (St Peter)/MN/$20,000.

MN Land Trust/MN/$10,000.

Nicollet County/MN/Public Works Dept., Seven Mile Creek Park/$115,000.

Paramount Theatre/Austin, MN/$25,000.

Rice County Historical Society/Faribault, MN/$6,500.

Senior Citizens of Rochester/MN/$15,000.

Shriners Children's Hospital - MN (Twin Cities)/MN/$25,000.

Financial Information

Financial data for year ending: 12/31/2005
Foundation assets: $27,284,058
Grants paid: $1,125,233
Number of grants: 79
Largest/smallest: $60,000/$250

Application Information

Preferred form of initial contact: complete proposal, by grant applications only, with brief description of purposes, location and amount of request; telephone applications are not acceptable.

Proposal deadlines: none.

Special application procedures: in writing only.

Staff/Trustees

Directors/trustees: Alan C. Anderson; Jonathan Anderson.

Schmoker Family Foundation

6616 Biscayne Boulevard
Edina, MN 55436
County: Hennepin
Phone: (952) 933-6590
Contact: Richard C. Schmoker
Established: 12/04/1986
Funder type: Private foundation

Program Description

Geographic focus: Twin Cities Metropolitan Area, areas outside Minnesota.

Areas of interest:

ARTS, CULTURE, HUMANITIES: Museums, Performing arts, Visual arts, Fine arts.

COMMUNITY IMPROVEMENT: Inner city.

EDUCATION: Higher education, Libraries/library science, Pre-school/elementary, Secondary.

HUMAN SERVICES.

Sample grants:

The Children's Theater Company & School/MN/theatre education/$10,000.

The Jeremiah Program/MN/general operating/$37,500.

Library Foundation of Hennepin County/MN/$3,000.

United Theological Seminary of the Twin Cities/MN/$5,000.

University of Nebraska Foundation/NE/$105,000.

VocalEssence/MN/general operating/$2,500.

Voyageur Outward Bound School/MN/$3,000.

YMCA - MN (Minneapolis)/MN/general operating/$1,500.

Financial Information

Financial data for year ending: 12/31/2005
Foundation assets: $3,019,346
Grants paid: $134,500
Number of grants: 16
Largest/smallest: $105,000/$1,000

Application Information

Preferred form of initial contact: complete proposal.

Proposal deadlines: none.

Typical time from application deadlines to notification: 2 months.

Staff/Trustees

Directors/trustees: Lisa Schmoker Hesdorffer; Catherine S. Hunnewell; Catherine S. Schmoker, president; Richard C. Schmoker; William C. Schmoker.

Arlan Schonberg Irrevocable Trust

U.S. Bank, N.A.
EP-MN-S14
101 East Fifth Street
St Paul, MN 55101
County: Ramsey
Phone: (651) 466-8443
Established: 10/05/1999
Funder type: Private foundation

Program Description

Program's purpose: Grants are made for charitable and educational purposes.

Geographic focus: Twin Cities Metropolitan Area.

Areas of interest:

EDUCATION.

Sample grants:
Dunwoody Institute/MN/$2,000.
Hennepin Technical College/MN/$14,000.
St Paul Technical College/MN/$14,000.

Financial Information

Financial data for year ending: 06/30/2006
Foundation assets: $862,444
Grants paid: $30,000
Number of grants: 2
Largest/smallest: $14,000/$2,000

Application Information

Preferred form of initial contact: complete proposal, standard grant proposal.
Public information available by request: proposal guidelines, application form.
Accept common grant application: yes.
Accept common report form: yes.
Proposal deadlines: December 15 of each year, with notification mailed by February 15 of the following year.

Staff/Trustees

Staff: Tina Holgin.

Schott Foundation

9350 Foxford Road
Chanhassen, MN 55317
County: Hennepin
Phone: (952) 475-1173
Contact: Owen W. Schott
Established: 12/01/1980
Funder type: Private foundation

Program Description

Program's purpose: Obtaining and/or disseminating education, knowledge and learning, or for promoting science and technology and programs to protect our natural heritage.

Program limitations/restrictions: Educational institutions awarding scholarships to students should make no preference to students who are employed by Schott Corporation or whose parents are employed or otherwise affiliated with Schott Corporation.

Areas of interest:
EDUCATION.
SCIENCE/TECHNOLOGY.

Intended beneficiaries: General public/unspecified.

Sample grants:
Bell Museum of Natural History - University of MN/MN/$86,000.
Business Economics Education Foundation of MN/MN/$7,000.
Marshall Public Schools Trust Fund/MN/scholarship/$2,000.
MN Professional Engineers Foundation/MN/Mathcounts/$1,000.
Northland Foundation/MN/$1,000.
Park Nicollet Institute - MN/MN/$55,000.
Twin Cities Public Television/St Paul, MN/$25,000.
University of MN - Duluth/MN/engineering scholarship/$2,500.

Financial Information

Financial data for year ending: 03/31/2006
Foundation assets: $4,248,724
Grants paid: $240,500

Application Information

Preferred form of initial contact: letter of inquiry, complete proposal.

Staff/Trustees

Directors/trustees: D. James Nielsen; Owen W. Schott; Wendell Schott.

The Schulze Family Foundation

14 Paddock Road
Edina, MN 55436
County: Hennepin
Phone: (952) 929-8014
Contact: Arthur R. Schulze Jr., president
Established: 12/10/1996
Funder type: Private foundation

Program Description

Program's purpose: Grants reflect the interests of the Schulze family members.
Intended beneficiaries: General public/unspecified.
Types of support for individuals: none.

Sample grants:
Carleton College/MN/general operating/$25,000.
Jabbok Foundation/MN/general operating/$5,000.
United Way - MN (Minneapolis Area)/MN/general operating/$10,000.

Financial Information

Financial data for year ending: 11/30/2005
Foundation assets: $1,083,496
Grants paid: $53,532
Number of grants: 3
Largest/smallest: $25,000/$5,000

Application Information

Preferred form of initial contact: letter of inquiry, complete proposal.
Proposal deadlines: none.

Staff/Trustees

Directors/trustees: Joan M. Schulze; Arthur R. Schulze Jr., president.

Securian Foundation/Securian Financial Group

400 North Robert Street
St Paul, MN 55101-2098
County: Ramsey
Phone: (651) 665-3501
Fax: (651) 665-3551
E-mail: lori.koutsky@securian.com
Website: www.securian.com/About/giveguide.asp
Contact: Lori J. Koutsky, manager, community relations and the foundation
Established: 08/01/1988
Paid Staff: Yes
Funder type: Corporate foundation and corporate giving program

Program Description

Program's purpose: To enhance the quality of life and vitality of our community by investing in nonprofit organizations that make a positive difference.

Funding priorities: Economic independence - employment training and placement; higher education; the arts; human services and special community needs.

Program limitations/restrictions: Grants to tax-exempt organizations only. No grants to individuals; benefits; trips; tours; political activities; services limited to one religious group; United Way agencies except special programs not embraced by United Way, because of the major support given to the United Way.

Geographic limitations: Greater Twin Cities metro area, with an emphasis on the corporate headquarters community in the East Metro.

Areas of interest:

ARTS, CULTURE, HUMANITIES: Arts/cultural multipurpose, Historical societies, Museums, Performing arts, Visual arts.

EDUCATION: Graduate education/professional schools, Higher education, Literacy programs.

EMPLOYMENT/JOBS: Employment procurement/job training, Vocational rehabilitation.

HEALTH - GENERAL/REHABILITATIVE: Public health programs/wellness education, Research.

HEALTH - MENTAL HEALTH/CRISIS INTERVENTION: Alcohol/drug/substance, prevention and treatment.

HOUSING/SHELTER: Housing development/construction/management, Low-cost temporary housing.

HUMAN SERVICES: Children/youth services, Family services, Multipurpose human service organizations, Services to specific groups.

PUBLIC AFFAIRS/SOCIETY BENEFIT: Education about free enterprise.

PUBLIC PROTECTION - CRIME/COURTS/LEGAL SERVICES: Crime prevention, Protection/prevention - neglect/abuse/exploitation.

PUBLIC SAFETY/DISASTERS/RELIEF: Disaster preparedness and relief, Safety education.

YOUTH DEVELOPMENT: Multipurpose youth centers/clubs.

Intended beneficiaries: General public/unspecified.

Types of support for organizations:

CAPITAL CAMPAIGNS: Building/renovation, Computer systems/technology, Equipment.

GENERAL PURPOSE/OPERATING SUPPORT: Annual campaigns.

Types of support for individuals: none.

Matching grants: employee matching, for education, arts and hospitals.

Dollars for Doers: yes.

Exclusions: Individuals, Non-501(c)(3), Political organizations, Religious organizations, Scholarships/loans.

Sample grants:

Admission Possible/St Paul, MN/Assist talented economically disadvantaged students to attend college/$4,000.

Boys & Girls Club - MN (Twin Cities)/MN/Building program & annual support/$10,000.

Employment Action Center/MN/Women Achieving New Directions/$3,000.

Junior Achievement - MN (St Paul)/MN/$13,000.

Metropolitan Economic Development Association/MN/$4,000.

MN Children's Museum/MN/$5,000.

Twin Cities RISE!/MN/$5,000.

Financial Information

Financial data for year ending: 12/31/2006
Foundation assets: $36,191,877
Grants paid: $1,633,243
In-kind gifts: $870,630
Matching gifts: $175,162

Application Information

Preferred form of initial contact: letter of inquiry, telephone inquiry, complete proposal, e-mail, visit website.

Public information available by request: proposal guidelines, application form, website.

Accept common grant application: yes.

Accept common report form: yes.

Will view video: yes.

Proposal deadlines: Four deadlines each year: February 15, May 15, August 15, November 15.

Contribution decisions made by: board of directors/trustees.

Frequency of contributions decisions: quarterly.

Specific times board meets: March, June, September, December.

Typical time from application deadlines to notification: 6-8 weeks.

Special application procedures: When using the common grant application, please list other funders and amounts.

Staff/Trustees

Staff: Mary Daily, administrative assistant; Lori J. Koutsky, manager, community relations and the foundation.

Directors/trustees: Keith Campbell, vice president; Dwayne Radel, secretary; Robert L. Senkler, president; Gregory Strong, treasurer.

Sewell Family Foundation

5200 West 73rd Street
Edina, MN 55439
County: Hennepin
Phone: (952) 841-2222
Fax: (952) 841-2223
Contact: Kathy Longo
Established: 01/09/1997
Donors: Fred & Gloria Sewell
Funder type: Private foundation

Program Description

Intended beneficiaries: General public/unspecified.

Sample grants:

Ballet Works, Inc/MN/$50,000.

Fraser School/MN/$5,000.

Global Grassroots - NH/NH/$10,000.

Headwaters School of Music and the Arts/MN/$5,500.

Humane Society for Companion Animals/MN/$5,000.

Pathways - MN (Minneapolis)/MN/$5,000.

Schubert Club, Inc/MN/$5,000.

St Paul Chamber Orchestra/MN/$100,000.

Financial Information

Financial data for year ending: 12/31/2006
Foundation assets: $3,689,570
Grants paid: $206,100
Number of grants: 17
Largest/smallest: $100,000/$600

Application Information

Preferred form of initial contact: letter of inquiry; not accepting new requests.

Proposal deadlines: ongoing.

Frequency of contributions decisions: semi-annual meeting.

Staff/Trustees

Directors/trustees: Sally Rousse; Frederick Sewell; Gloria Sewell, president; James Sewell; Laura Sewell.

Sexton Foundation

2225 Chelmsford Lane
St Cloud, MN 56301-9012
County: Stearns
Phone: (320) 230-9171
Contact: Yvonne Sexton, president
Established: 08/01/1977
Funder type: Private foundation

Program Description

Funding priorities: Preference is given to civic organizations in central Minnesota.

Program limitations/restrictions: Preference given to religious and civic organizations. Grants to 501(c)(3) organizations only.

Geographic focus: Twin Cities Metropolitan Area, Greater Minnesota, Areas outside Minnesota, central Minnesota.

Areas of interest:

ARTS, CULTURE, HUMANITIES.

EDUCATION: Higher education, Pre-school/elementary, Secondary.

ENVIRONMENTAL QUALITY/PROTECTION/BEAUTIFICATION.

HOUSING/SHELTER.

HUMAN SERVICES: Children/youth services, Emergency assistance (food/clothing/cash), Family services.

RELIGION/SPIRITUAL DEVELOPMENT.

YOUTH DEVELOPMENT.

Intended beneficiaries: General public/unspecified.

Types of support for organizations:

GENERAL PURPOSE/OPERATING SUPPORT.

Exclusions: Non-501(c)(3).

Sample grants:

Amicus Inc/Minneapolis, MN/general operating/$1,000.

Big Brothers/Big Sisters - MN (St Cloud)/MN/general operating/$5,000.

Bridge for Runaway Youth, The/MN/general operating/$10,000.

Habitat for Humanity - MN (St Cloud)/MN/general operating/$10,000.

Interfaith Outreach - Wayzata/MN/general operating/$10,000.

Land Stewardship Project/MN/general operating/$15,000.

Red Cloud Indian School - SD/Pine Ridge, SD/general operating/$23,000.

St Cloud Symphony Orchestra/MN/general operating/$1,500.

Financial Information

Financial data for year ending: 11/30/2006
Foundation assets: $10,021,750
Grants paid: $438,940
Number of grants: 33
Largest/smallest: $61,000/$1,000

Application Information

Preferred form of initial contact: no particular form required; need proof of 501(c)(3) status and audited financials.

Proposal deadlines: none.

Staff/Trustees

Directors/trustees: James W. Sexton; Thomas Sexton; Yvonne Sexton, president.

Shakopee Mdewakanton Sioux Community

2330 Sioux Trail NW
Prior Lake, MN 55372
County: Scott
Phone: (952) 445-8900
Fax: (952) 445-8906
Website: www.ShakopeeDakota.org
Funder type: Tribal giving program

Program Description

Program's purpose: Since our federal recognition in 1969, the SMSC has worked diligently to achieve a significant level of self-sufficiency. Along with self-sufficiency, we have gained a meaningful level of self-determination. The SMSC utilizes its financial resources from gaming and non-gaming enterprises to first and foremost meet our responsibilities to our tribal membership. All internal infrastructure, including but not limited to housing, roads, water and sewer systems and essential services to individuals regarding education, health and welfare, are met by tribal resources. The tribe also makes payments to city and county governments to cover the cost of services provided by those local jurisdictions to the tribe. When our needs are met, we have the good fortune to assist others. The business council is grateful that the tribal membership has authorized sharing financial assistance with other tribes and Indian and non-Indian organizations and individuals. There are overwhelming unmet needs in Indian country. It is our cultural and social tradition to assist those in need.

Funding priorities: Focus on support for Native American organizations and schools/education.

Geographic focus: Twin Cities Metropolitan Area, Great Plains tribes.

Areas of interest:

COMMUNITY IMPROVEMENT: Community coalitions, Community/neighborhood development/improvement, Economic development, Nonprofit management.

EDUCATION: Pre-school/elementary, Secondary, American Indian Education, Schools in Scott county.

HEALTH - DISEASES/MEDICAL DISCIPLINES: Cancer, Diabetes.

HEALTH - GENERAL/REHABILITATIVE: Hospitals and related primary medical care facilities, Public health programs/wellness education.

HEALTH - MENTAL HEALTH/CRISIS INTERVENTION: Alcohol/drug/substance, prevention and treatment.

HUMAN SERVICES: Children/youth services, Emergency assistance (food/clothing/cash), Family services, Multipurpose human service organizations, Personal social services, Services to specific groups.

YOUTH DEVELOPMENT: Multipurpose youth centers/clubs, Youth development programs.

Intended beneficiaries: Native American/American Indians.

Types of support for organizations:

CAPITAL CAMPAIGNS: Building/renovation.

PROGRAM DEVELOPMENT/PROJECT SUPPORT.

STUDENT AID (GRANTS TO INSTITUTIONS): Scholarship funds.

Sample grants:

Boise Forte Band of Ojibwe/MN/Lake Vermilion Community Wellness Center/$1,000,000.

CAP Agency - MN (Shakopee)/MN/For their annual Thanksgiving and Christmas program for families needing assistance/ $20,000.

Habitat for Humanity - MN (Twin Cities)/MN/$10,000.

Indian Youth of America/$45,000.

Minneapolis Public Schools/MN/St Paul Public Schools/MN/Winter wear and school supplies for students in the Indian Education programs/$120,050.

Susan G Komen Breast Cancer Foundation - MN/MN/Race for the Cure/$10,000.

United Tribes Technical College/ Bismarck, ND/For construction of a 28,000 square foot, two-story dormitory/ $500,000.

University of MN - Cancer Center/MN/ For medical research and education to the University of MN Cancer Center/ $50,000.

Financial Information

Financial data for year ending: 09/30/2006
Grants paid: $18,051,634

Application Information

Public information available by request: annual report.

Staff/Trustees

Directors/trustees: Keith Anderson, secretary/treasurer; Glynn A. Crooks, vice-chairman; Stanley R. Crooks, chairman.

Shamrock Foundation

21955 Minnetonka Boulevard
Suite 5
Excelsior, MN 55391
County: Hennepin
Phone: (952) 470-8635
Contact: Joan Slattery, president
Established: 12/17/1997
Donor: William & Joan Slattery
Funder type: Private foundation

Program Description

Program's purpose: To provide financial support to groups/services committed to education, faith and family.

Funding priorities: Education, faith, family and health.

Program limitations/restrictions: Foundation does not accept new grant proposals, as it is totally committed to those programs it is currently involved in and knows.

Areas of interest:
EDUCATION.
HEALTH - DISEASES/MEDICAL DISCIPLINES.
HEALTH - MENTAL HEALTH/CRISIS INTERVENTION.
HUMAN SERVICES.
RELIGION/SPIRITUAL DEVELOPMENT.

Types of support for organizations:
CAPITAL CAMPAIGNS.
GENERAL PURPOSE/OPERATING SUPPORT.

Sample grants:
Holy Family Catholic High School/ Victoria, MN/educational assistance/ $20,000.

International Village Clinic/Minneapolis, MN/health assistance/$5,000.

Perspectives, Inc - MN/St Louis Park, MN/$5,000.

Risen Christ Catholic School/ Minneapolis, MN/educational assistance/ $5,000.

Suicide Awareness Voices of Education (SAVE) - MN/MN/suicide prevention/ $4,000.

Financial Information

Financial data for year ending: 01/30/2007
Foundation assets: $850,000
Grants paid: $45,000
Number of grants: 7
Largest/smallest: $20,000/$2,000

Application Information

Preferred form of initial contact: see limitations.

Contribution decisions made by: board of directors/trustees.

Frequency of contributions decisions: annually.

Staff/Trustees

Directors/trustees: Joan Slattery, president; John P. Slattery; Kevin J. Slattery; Linda Slattery; Robert M. Slattery; William Slattery; W. Daniel Slattery Jr.

Shapiro Family Philanthropic Foundation

1660 South Highway 100
Parkdale Plaza
Suite 304
St Louis Park, MN 55416-1529
County: Hennepin
Phone: (952) 544-8715
Contact: Sidney K. Shapiro
Established: 12/28/1984
Funder type: Private foundation

Program Description

Geographic focus: Twin Cities Metropolitan Area, Areas outside Minnesota.

Areas of interest:
ARTS, CULTURE, HUMANITIES: Media/communications, Museums, Performing arts, Visual arts.
ENVIRONMENTAL QUALITY/ PROTECTION/BEAUTIFICATION.
HEALTH - DISEASES/MEDICAL DISCIPLINES.
HUMAN SERVICES.
RELIGION/SPIRITUAL DEVELOPMENT.

Intended beneficiaries: General public/unspecified.

Sample grants:
Arizona Theatre Company/Phoenix, AZ/$3,000.

Boulder Jewish Community Foundation/CO/$100.

Minneapolis Heart Institute Foundation/MN/$100.

Minneapolis Institute of Arts/MN/$2,500.

Minnetonka Choral Society/MN/$500.

MN Orchestral Association/MN/$1,500.

Public Television - MN (Twin Cities)/ MN/$150.

Scottsdale Center for the Arts/AZ/$500.

Financial Information

Financial data for year ending: 12/31/2005
Foundation assets: $406,157
Grants paid: $39,436
Number of grants: 62
Largest/smallest: $5,500/$25

Application Information

Preferred form of initial contact: complete proposal.

Proposal deadlines: none.

Special application procedures: must be in writing.

Staff/Trustees

Directors/trustees: Jane Shapiro; Peter Shapiro; Richard Shapiro; Sidney K. Shapiro.

The Shared Fund

6550 York Avenue South
Suite 402
Edina, MN 55435
County: Hennepin
Contact: Howard Weiner, president
Established: 12/27/1994
Funder type: Private foundation

Program Description

Geographic focus: Twin Cities Metropolitan Area, Areas outside Minnesota.

Areas of interest:

ARTS, CULTURE, HUMANITIES: Museums, Performing arts.

EDUCATION: Higher education, Pre-school/elementary, Secondary.

HUMAN SERVICES.

RELIGION/SPIRITUAL DEVELOPMENT.

Intended beneficiaries: General public/unspecified.

Types of support for organizations:

CAPITAL CAMPAIGNS.

GENERAL PURPOSE/OPERATING SUPPORT: Annual campaigns.

Sample grants:

Center for Jewish/Christian Learning/St Paul, MN/general operating/$1,000.

Courage Center - MN (Golden Valley)/MN/capital campaign and annual fund/$30,000.

Family & Children's Services - MN (Mpls)/Minneapolis, MN/general operating/$500.

Minneapolis Institute of Arts/MN/general operating/$3,000.

San Diego Museum of Art/CA/general operating/$1,250.

Waldorf School - City of the Lakes/Minneapolis, MN/capital campaign/$1,000.

Washington Institute for Near East Policy/DC/general operating/$1,000.

Weisman Art Museum/Minneapolis, MN/general operating/$500.

Financial Information

Financial data for year ending: 12/31/2005
Foundation assets: $2,640,003
Grants paid: $287,942
Number of grants: 20
Largest/smallest: $30,000/$250

Application Information

Preferred form of initial contact: letter of inquiry, request for guidelines.

Public information available by request: proposal guidelines, application form.

Special application procedures: request application and instructions by letter only.

Staff/Trustees

Directors/trustees: Frederick Weiner; Howard Weiner, president.

The Sheltering Arms Foundation

430 Oak Grove Street
Suite 214
Minneapolis, MN 55403
County: Hennepin
Phone: (612) 871-9210
Fax: (612) 871-1004
E-mail: info@sheltering-arms.org
Website: www.sheltering-arms.org
Established: 06/28/1983
Paid Staff: Yes
Funder type: Community/public foundation

Program Description

Program's purpose: To enhance the lives of children and help them reach their full potential, especially those experiencing barriers to success.

Funding priorities: The foundation's primary focus is on strengthening the lives of children ages 12 and under and their families. The foundation will consider applications for program start-up costs or program expansion, planning efforts or advocacy initiatives. The funding priorities: Supportive Housing - to support efforts that help to stabilize children and families in safe and affordable housing environments. Access to Early Childhood Education & Child Care - to enhance children's access and participation in culturally responsive, high-quality and affordable child care and early childhood education experiences. Strengthen Family Relationships - to strengthen families so that children can grow up in nurturing and violence-free environments and have opportunities for positive parent or caregiver/child interaction. Support Educational Enrichment - to provide support for school-aged youth who have limited access to after-school or non-school hour enrichment activities that enhance their academic and social skills development.

Geographic focus: Minnesota statewide.

Areas of interest:

EDUCATION: Pre-school/elementary, After-school programs, Parenting education, Early childhood and family education, Academic enrichment/skill building opportunities.

HOUSING/SHELTER: Housing support services.

HUMAN SERVICES: Children/youth services, Family services, Family services for adolescent parents, Family violence shelters and services, Multipurpose human service organizations, Human Services organizations.

PUBLIC AFFAIRS/SOCIETY BENEFIT: Public policy research and analysis.

Intended beneficiaries: African Americans/Blacks, Asian/Pacific Islanders, Disabled - general or unspecified disability, Ethnic/racial populations - general, Hispanics/Latinos, Homeless, Immigrants/newcomers/refugees, Infants/babies (under age 5), Migrant workers, Native American/American Indians, Poor/economically disadvantaged, Single parents, Infants/children (ages 0-12).

Types of support for organizations:

PROGRAM DEVELOPMENT/PROJECT SUPPORT: Mentoring programs, Public awareness, Public policy research/analysis, Seed money/start-up funds.

Types of support for individuals: none.

Exclusions: Capital & endowment campaigns, Individuals, Non-501(c)(3), Scholarships/loans, Fundraising or sponsorship of events, General operations of organizations.

Sample grants:

Centro Campesino/Owatonna, MN/ $15,000.

Cornerstone/MN/$20,000.

HOPE Community - MN/Minneapolis, MN/$10,000.

Plymouth Christian Youth Center/MN/ $10,000.

Financial Information

Financial data for year ending: 06/30/2006
Foundation assets: $16,426,105
Grants paid: $490,000
Number of grants: 35
Largest/smallest: $20,000/$5,000
Typical grant amount: $10,000

Application Information

Preferred form of initial contact: telephone inquiry, request for guidelines, e-mail.

Public information available by request: proposal guidelines, application form, annual report, website.

Accept common grant application: yes.

Accept common report form: yes.

Proposal deadlines: January 18, 2008.

Preferred time for receiving proposals: grant guidelines available November 1.

Contribution decisions made by: board of directors/trustees.

Frequency of contributions decisions: annually.

Specific times board meets: late May.

Typical time from application deadlines to notification: 5 months.

Staff/Trustees

Staff: Diane Grossman, associate director; Denise Mayotte, executive director.

Directors/trustees: Myra Barrett, president; Cara Gould, treasurer; Lisa Holmberg; Jane Hopkins; Sandy Hull; Barbara Kirby; Katherine Lewis; Anne Love-Mickelson; Edie Meissner; Juanita Palmerhall; Fiona Pradhan; Denise Reilly; Lindsay Strand, secretary; Lynne Teckman, president-elect; Joyce Walker.

The Shiebler Family Foundation

12219 Wood Lake Drive
Burnsville, MN 55337
County: Dakota
Phone: (952) 894-9711
Contact: William Perron
Established: 12/15/1999
Funder type: Private foundation

Program Description

Geographic focus: Twin Cities Metropolitan Area, areas outside Minnesota.

Areas of interest:
ARTS, CULTURE, HUMANITIES.
HEALTH - DISEASES/MEDICAL DISCIPLINES.
HEALTH - GENERAL/ REHABILITATIVE.
HUMAN SERVICES.
RECREATION.

Sample grants:

Cystic Fibrosis Foundation - NY/NY/ $28,300.

Friends of the Animals/Park City, UT/ $500.

Nature Conservancy - UT/Salt Lake City, UT/$5,000.

Ronald McDonald House - MN (Minneapolis)/MN/$250.

Salvation Army - MN (Northern Division)/Roseville, MN/$250.

Sharing & Caring Hands, Inc/MN/$300.

US Ski Team Foundation/Park City, UT/ $51,200.

Utah Symphony/UT/$62,650.

Financial Information

Financial data for year ending: 12/31/2005
Foundation assets: $1,320,996
Grants paid: $409,469
Number of grants: 12
Largest/smallest: $25,000/$250

Application Information

Preferred form of initial contact: letter of inquiry.

Staff/Trustees

Directors/trustees: William Perron; Christina Shiebler; Jason Shiebler; Joanne Shiebler; William Shiebler.

Gertrude R. Shiely Charitable Trust

U.S. Bank, N.A.
101 East Fifth Street
St Paul, MN 55101
County: Ramsey
Phone: (651) 466-8444
Contact: Sally Mullen
Established: 03/03/2000
Funder type: Private foundation

Program Description

Program's purpose: General charitable purposes, favoring Catholic organizations in the St Paul area.

Funding priorities: Grants will be mainly directed toward education, health and human services, and environmental organizations.

Geographic focus: East Metropolitan Area/St Paul only.

Areas of interest:
EDUCATION.
ENVIRONMENTAL QUALITY/ PROTECTION/BEAUTIFICATION.
HUMAN SERVICES.
RELIGION/SPIRITUAL DEVELOPMENT.

Intended beneficiaries: General public/unspecified.

Types of support for organizations:
GENERAL PURPOSE/OPERATING SUPPORT.

Sample grants:

HealthEast Foundation/St Paul, MN/ general operating/$10,000.

Neighborhood Health Care Network/St Paul, MN/general operating/$1,000.

St Pascal Baylon School/St Paul, MN/general operating/$5,000.

Financial Information

Financial data for year ending: 12/31/2005
Foundation assets: $2,301,227
Grants paid: $96,500
Number of grants: 12
Largest/smallest: $25,000/$1,000

Application Information

Preferred form of initial contact: letter of inquiry.

Proposal deadlines: none.

Staff/Trustees

Staff: Sally Mullen.

Directors/trustees: U.S. Bank, N.A.; Terry Diebel; James P. Donner.

The Simmet Foundation

PO Box 288
Newport, MN 55055
County: Washington
Phone: (651) 735-9660
Contact: John P. Simmet
Established: 03/13/1989
Funder type: Private foundation

Program Description

Program's purpose: To promote the health and well-being of families and individuals in the south metro region of the Twin Cities, in Crow Wing County, Minnesota and in central Ohio.

Funding priorities: Programs that assist single-parent families, battered women, seniors, the disabled, and families and adults living in poverty. Supports educational programs that promote the health and well-being of the citizens in the communities we serve.

Program limitations/restrictions: Grants are given for a one-year period. Subsequent year support is on a year-by-year review basis.

Geographic limitations: South Twin Cities metro area, Crow Wing County, Minnesota and central Ohio.

Areas of interest:

EDUCATION: Adult/continuing education/literacy.

EMPLOYMENT/JOBS: Employment procurement/job training, Vocational rehabilitation.

FOOD/NUTRITION/AGRICULTURE: Food service/free food distribution.

HEALTH - DISEASES/MEDICAL DISCIPLINES.

HEALTH - GENERAL/REHABILITATIVE.

HEALTH - MENTAL HEALTH/CRISIS INTERVENTION: Alcohol/drug/substance, prevention and treatment, Counseling/support groups, Hotline/crisis intervention.

HEALTH - RESEARCH.

HOUSING/SHELTER: Homeless, temporary housing.

HUMAN SERVICES: Children/youth services, Emergency assistance (food/clothing/cash), Family services, Family services for adolescent parents, Family violence shelters and services.

PUBLIC SAFETY/DISASTERS/RELIEF: Disaster preparedness and relief.

YOUTH DEVELOPMENT: Adult/child matching programs, Multipurpose youth centers/clubs, Youth development programs.

Intended beneficiaries: Adults, Aging/elderly/senior citizens, Children and youth (infants-19 years), Disabled - general or unspecified disability, Females - all ages or age unspecified, Homeless, Males - all ages or age unspecified, Physically disabled, Poor/economically disadvantaged, Single parents.

Types of support for organizations:

CAPITAL CAMPAIGNS: Building/renovation, Equipment.

EMERGENCY FUNDS.

GENERAL PURPOSE/OPERATING SUPPORT.

PROGRAM DEVELOPMENT/PROJECT SUPPORT: Curriculum development, Faculty/staff development.

RESEARCH.

Types of support for individuals: none.

Exclusions: Capital & endowment campaigns, Individuals, Political organizations, Religious organizations, Arts, Criminal justice, Economic development.

Sample grants:

Asian Women United of MN - St Paul/MN/general operating/$1,000.

Children's Hospital Association - St Paul/MN/general operating/$2,500.

Dakota Woodlands/MN/general operating/$2,500.

Little Brothers - Friends of the Elderly - MN/MN/general operating/$2,000.

Resources for Child Caring/MN/general operating/$1,000.

Theresa Living Center/MN/general operating/$2,500.

Tubman Family Alliance - MN/MN/general operating/$2,500.

Wilderness Inquiry/Minneapolis, MN/general operating/$2,500.

Financial Information

Financial data for year ending: 12/31/2005
Foundation assets: $410,359
Grants paid: $42,000
Number of grants: 15
Largest/smallest: $4,000/$1,000

Application Information

Preferred form of initial contact: request for guidelines.

Public information available by request: proposal guidelines, application form.

Accept common grant application: yes.

Accept common report form: yes.

Proposal deadlines: none.

Contribution decisions made by: board of directors/trustees.

Frequency of contributions decisions: annually.

Specific times board meets: between Oct. and Dec.

Typical time from application deadlines to notification: 3 months.

Staff/Trustees

Directors/trustees: Christine A. Lilienthal; John P. Simmet; Margaret M. Simmet; Mary C. Simmet; Mary M. Simmet; Nancy A. Simmet; Patricia M. Simmet; Robert P. Simmet.

Sioux Falls Area Community Foundation

300 North Phillips Avenue
Suite 102
Sioux Falls, SD 57104-6006
Phone: (605) 336-7055
Fax: (605) 336-0038
E-mail: chanson@sfacf.org
Website: www.sfacf.org
Contact: Patrick Gale, program officer
Funder type: Community/public foundation

Program Description

Program's purpose: The foundation unites donors, organizations and interests around a common goal: building permanent charitable endowments and using the proceeds to strengthen local communities and improve the quality of life in the Sioux Falls area.

Funding priorities: Activities that advance the community based vision and plan for the area, Sioux Falls Tomorrow II.

Program limitations/restrictions: No grants to individuals, other than scholarships or indigents via established award processes.

Geographic limitations: The foundation attracts, manages and distributes charitable gifts for Sioux Falls and neighboring cities and towns. This area includes Minnehaha, Lincoln, Turner and McCook counties and communities within a 25-mile radius of Sioux Falls.

Areas of interest:

ANIMAL RELATED: Animal protection/welfare, Wildlife preservation/protection, Zoo/zoological societies.

ARTS, CULTURE, HUMANITIES: Arts services, Arts/cultural multipurpose, Historical societies, Humanities, Media/communications, Museums, Performing arts, Visual arts.

COMMUNITY IMPROVEMENT: Community/neighborhood development/improvement, Economic development, Nonprofit management.

EDUCATION: Adult/continuing education/literacy, Educational services, Graduate education/professional schools, Higher education, Libraries/library science, Pre-school/elementary, Secondary, Vocational/technical.

ENVIRONMENTAL QUALITY/PROTECTION/BEAUTIFICATION: Botanical/horticultural/landscape, Environmental beautification/open spaces, Natural resources conservation/protection, Pollution abatement and control.

FOOD/NUTRITION/AGRICULTURE: Food service/free food distribution, Nutrition promotion.

HEALTH - DISEASES/MEDICAL DISCIPLINES: Diseases of specific organs.

HEALTH - GENERAL/REHABILITATIVE: Childhood obesity project, "Growing Healthy Initiative."

HEALTH - MENTAL HEALTH/CRISIS INTERVENTION: Alcohol/drug/substance, prevention and treatment, Mental health associations, Mental health treatment and services.

HEALTH - RESEARCH.

HOUSING/SHELTER: Homeless, temporary housing, Housing development/construction/management.

HUMAN SERVICES: Children/youth services, Emergency assistance (food/clothing/cash), Family services, Family services for adolescent parents, Family violence shelters and services, Multipurpose human service organizations, Senior centers and services, Victims services.

PHILANTHROPY/VOLUNTARISM: Philanthropy - general, Public foundations and community foundations.

PUBLIC AFFAIRS/SOCIETY BENEFIT: Government/public administration, Military/veterans' organizations.

PUBLIC PROTECTION - CRIME/COURTS/LEGAL SERVICES: Administration of justice/courts, Protection/prevention - neglect/abuse/exploitation.

PUBLIC SAFETY/DISASTERS/RELIEF: Safety education.

RECREATION: Amateur sports clubs/leagues, Recreation and sporting camps, Recreational/pleasure/social clubs, Sports training facilities/agencies.

RELIGION/SPIRITUAL DEVELOPMENT: Specific denomination.

YOUTH DEVELOPMENT: Adult/child matching programs, Multipurpose youth centers/clubs, Scouting organizations, Youth development programs.

Intended beneficiaries: Adults, Aging/elderly/senior citizens, Blind/vision impaired, Children and youth (infants-19 years), Deaf/hearing impaired, Disabled - general or unspecified disability, Ethnic/racial populations - general, Females - all ages or age unspecified, Gay/lesbian/bisexual/transgender, Homeless, Immigrants/newcomers/refugees, Infants/babies (under age 5), Mentally/emotionally disabled, Native American/American Indians, Physically disabled, Poor/economically disadvantaged, Substance abusers, Youth/adolescents (ages 14-19).

Types of support for organizations:

CAPITAL CAMPAIGNS: Building/renovation, Endowment funds.

EMERGENCY FUNDS.

GENERAL PURPOSE/OPERATING SUPPORT.

GRANTS TO INDIVIDUALS.

MANAGEMENT/TECHNICAL ASSISTANCE.

PROGRAM DEVELOPMENT/PROJECT SUPPORT: Conferences/seminars, Curriculum development, Performance/production costs, Public awareness, Seed money/start-up funds, Leadership programs.

RESEARCH.

STUDENT AID (GRANTS TO INSTITUTIONS): Scholarship funds.

Types of support for individuals: aid to needy persons, scholarships.

Sample grants:

4-H Foundation - SD/SD/Multicultural CHARACTER COUNTS program/$8,000.

Brush Up Sioux Falls Paint-A-Thon/SD/Organize volunteers who paint homes for elderly disadvantaged/$10,000.

Health Connect of South Dakota/SD/Health House of Sioux Falls/$6,000.

PTA - SD/SD/Presentation of "Parenting with Love and Logic"/$1,000.

Schools - SD/SD/Support for Minority Youth project/$12,216.

Sioux Empire Arts Council/SD/Installation of the CommUnity Youth Mosaic/$2,000.

South Eastern Development Foundation - SD/SD/Support for 502 Home Loan Partnership program/$10,000.

Washington Pavilion of Arts and Sciences/Sioux Falls, SD/Performance of "Grandchildren of the Buffalo Soldiers"/$10,000.

Financial Information

Financial data for year ending: 06/30/2006
Foundation assets: $53,734,058
Grants paid: $5,760,199
Number of grants: 1459
Largest/smallest: $400,000/$50

Application Information

Preferred form of initial contact: telephone inquiry.

Public information available by request: proposal guidelines, application form, annual report, newsletter, website, financial statements.

Will view video: yes.

Proposal deadlines: See website for grants deadlines. Scholarship deadlines are generally March 15.

Contribution decisions made by: staff, board of directors/trustees, grants committee, community-based membership.

Frequency of contributions decisions: Every 2 months.

Typical time from application deadlines to notification: 6 weeks.

Staff/Trustees

Staff: Patrick Gale, program officer; Candy Hanson, president/CEO; Andy Patterson, vice president; Sara Patterson, communication officer; Paul W. Peterson, chief financial officer; Jennifer Sanderson, development officer; Vicki Swanson, gift and grant administrator; Myra Wulf, executive assistant.

Directors/trustees: David Austad; Miles Beacom; Larry Bierman; Jack Carmody; Dick Corcoran, Caroline Deinema; Vance Goldammer; Greg Heineman; Arlene Kirby; Kristi Niechwiadowicz; Sandra Pay; Paul Schiller; Mary Pat Sweetman, board chair; Mary Tidwell; Richard Van Denmark.

SKB Environmental Rosemount Community Trust

PO Box 392
Rosemount, MN 55068
County: Dakota
Phone: (651) 428-1549
Contact: Donald Chapdelaine
Established: 11/23/1992
Funder type: Corporate foundation

Program Description

Program's purpose: The trust is created and shall be operated exclusively for the benefit of the citizens of Rosemount and the City of Rosemount.

Funding priorities: The purposes of the trust include, but are not limited to, the following: 1) Provide for construction and maintenance of facilities for public recreation; 2) Further community, industrial, governmental and physical planning in the City of Rosemount; 3) Improve working and living conditions within the City of Rosemount for the general welfare of its citizens; 4) Further public educational opportunities, whether by establishing programs or facilities devoted to education purposes, or the furnishing of educational scholarships; 5) Provide for the charitable needs of the citizens of Rosemount and the City of Rosemount within the meaning of section 501(c)(3) of the Internal Revenue Code.

Geographic limitations: Rosemount, Minnesota area.

Areas of interest:
COMMUNITY IMPROVEMENT.
EDUCATION.
ENVIRONMENTAL QUALITY/PROTECTION/BEAUTIFICATION.
HUMAN SERVICES.
PUBLIC AFFAIRS/SOCIETY BENEFIT.
PUBLIC PROTECTION - CRIME/COURTS/LEGAL SERVICES.
RECREATION.
YOUTH DEVELOPMENT.

Intended beneficiaries: General public/unspecified.

Types of support for organizations:
CAPITAL CAMPAIGNS.
GENERAL PURPOSE/OPERATING SUPPORT.
PROGRAM DEVELOPMENT/PROJECT SUPPORT.
STUDENT AID (GRANTS TO INSTITUTIONS): Scholarship funds.

Sample grants:
American Legion - MN (Rosemount)/MN/assist in repairs of facility/$20,000.

DARTS Inc/MN/operating expenses serving Rosemount residents/$10,000.

Inver Hills Community College/MN/educational scholarships/$6,000.

Kids N Kinship - MN/MN/defray costs of establishing mentors for Rosemount youth/$5,000.

Police Department - Rosemount, MN/neighborhood watch signs/$1,000.

Rosemount Area Athletic Association/MN/$7,000.

Trust for Public Land/MN/natural area preservation/$500.

YMCA - MN (Eagan)/MN/capital fund drive/$5,000.

Financial Information

Financial data for year ending: 12/31/2005
Foundation assets: $1,033,660
Grants paid: $717,803
Number of grants: 23
Largest/smallest: $10,000/$400

Application Information

Public information available by request: application form.
Proposal deadlines: none.

Staff/Trustees

Directors/trustees: Steve Casey; Donald Chapdelaine; John Domke; Matthew Kearney; John Tapper.

William Wood Skinner Foundation

U.S. Bank
800 Nicollet Mall
Minneapolis, MN 55402
County: Hennepin
Phone: (612) 303-3813
Contact: Jotham Blodgett
Established: 11/01/1965
Funder type: Private foundation

Program Description

Geographic limitations: Preference given to organizations in the cities of St Paul, Minnesota; Chicago, Illinois; and northern Door County, Wisconsin.

Intended beneficiaries: General public/unspecified.

Sample grants:
Albany Park Community Center/IL/$2,250.

Family Service - MN (St Paul)/MN/$1,100.

Gillette Children's Hospital Foundation/MN/$1,100.

Ordway Music Theatre/MN/$1,100.

Peninsula Music Festival/WI/$2,200.

St Paul Academy & Summit School/MN/$3,300.

Steppenwolf Theatre Company/IL/$1,650.

Window to the World Communications Inc/IL/$5,500.

Financial Information

Financial data for year ending: 09/30/2006
Foundation assets: $1,933,774
Grants paid: $90,000
Number of grants: 46
Largest/smallest: $7,000/$1,000

Application Information

Preferred form of initial contact: letter of inquiry.
Proposal deadlines: none.

Staff/Trustees

Directors/trustees: U.S. Bank, N.A.; Elizabeth S. Guenzel.

R. C. Skoe Foundation

8500 Franlo Road
Suite 303
Eden Prairie, MN 55344
County: Hennepin
Phone: (952) 946-1956
Contact: Mary E. Oberle, executive director
Established: 11/09/1993
Funder type: Private foundation

Program Description

Program's purpose: To promote the educational and motivational needs of pre-school children at risk.

Funding priorities: Youth music education programs.

Geographic focus: Twin Cities Metropolitan Area.

Areas of interest:
EDUCATION: Pre-school/elementary.

Intended beneficiaries: Infants/babies (under age 5), Poor/economically disadvantaged.

Types of support for organizations:
PROGRAM DEVELOPMENT/
PROJECT SUPPORT.

Types of support for individuals: none.

Sample grants:

Catholic Charities - MN (Minneapolis)/MN/youth music education program/$16,500.

Central Care for Children/Minneapolis, MN/youth music education program/$7,100.

La Creche Early Childhood Centers Inc/MN/youth music education program/$37,200.

Phyllis Wheatley Community Center Inc/MN/youth music education program/$26,250.

Financial Information

Financial data for year ending: 12/31/2005
Foundation assets: $1,436
Grants paid: $95,650

Application Information

Preferred form of initial contact: letter of inquiry.
Accept common grant application: yes.
Proposal deadlines: ongoing.
Contribution decisions made by: board of directors/trustees.
Specific times board meets: as needed.

Staff/Trustees

Staff: Mary E. Oberle, executive director.
Directors/trustees: Jeff R. Oberle; Mary E. Oberle, executive director; Richard R. Oberle.

Slaggie Family Foundation

1870 Ralph Scharmer Drive
Winona, MN 55987
County: Winona
Phone: (507) 452-2321
Contact: Steve Slaggie, president
Funder type: Private foundation

Program Description

Geographic focus: Greater Minnesota, Winona.

Areas of interest:
EDUCATION.
HEALTH - GENERAL/
REHABILITATIVE.
YOUTH DEVELOPMENT.

Sample grants:

Church, Catholic - MN/MN/San Marko Church/$10,000.

Cotter High School - Winona/MN/$37,600.

Rock Solid Youth Center/MN/$25,000.

St Anne's Hospice/MN/$2,525.

St John's University - MN/MN/$105,000.

Winona Health Foundation/MN/$76,440.

Financial Information

Financial data for year ending: 12/31/2005
Foundation assets: $10,222,713
Grants paid: $398,909
Number of grants: 19
Largest/smallest: $105,000/$1,000

Application Information

Preferred form of initial contact: Letter stating request and purpose of organization.
Proposal deadlines: None.

Staff/Trustees

Directors/trustees: Steve Slaggie, president.

Slawik Family Foundation

1880 Livingston Avenue
Suite 100
West St Paul, MN 55118
County: Ramsey
Phone: (651) 645-8111
Fax: (651) 646-5633
Contact: Sharon Slawik, executive director
Established: 11/10/1952
Funder type: Private foundation

Program Description

Program's purpose: To support family, youth and young adult organizations in the local community that address the effects of poverty and enhance the quality of life through education.

Program limitations/restrictions: Scholarships limited to Ramsey County residents going to private high school.

Geographic focus: Twin Cities Metropolitan Area.

Areas of interest:
EDUCATION: Higher education, Pre-school/elementary, Secondary, Student services/organizations of students.
HUMAN SERVICES.
RELIGION/SPIRITUAL
DEVELOPMENT.
YOUTH DEVELOPMENT.

Intended beneficiaries: Youth/adolescents (ages 14-19).

Types of support for organizations:
CAPITAL CAMPAIGNS: Building/renovation, Endowment funds.
GENERAL PURPOSE/OPERATING SUPPORT: Annual campaigns.
PROGRAM DEVELOPMENT/
PROJECT SUPPORT.

STUDENT AID (GRANTS TO INSTITUTIONS): Scholarship funds.

Sample grants:

Breakthrough Saint Paul/MN/general operating/$5,000.

Caring Tree Foundation/MN/Campaign 2006/$1,000.

Catholic Community Foundation/St Paul, MN/Skipper Slawik scholarships/ $80,000.

Dunwoody Institute/MN/Awareness program/$4,000.

Merrick Community Center/MN/general operating/$10,000.

Salvation Army - MN/MN/Christmas campaign/$4,000.

Visitation Monastery - Minneapolis/MN/ youth camp/$6,000.

YMCA - MN (St Paul, South Family)/ MN/annual campaign/$5,000.

Financial Information

Financial data for year ending: 12/31/2005
Foundation assets: $2,633,464
Grants paid: $152,000
Number of grants: 18
Largest/smallest: $50,000/$350

Application Information

Preferred form of initial contact: letter of inquiry.

Public information available by request: application form.

Accept common grant application: yes.

Proposal deadlines: none.

Preferred time for receiving proposals: January - May.

Contribution decisions made by: board of directors/trustees.

Special application procedures: requests may be in letter form.

Staff/Trustees

Staff: Sharon Slawik, executive director.

Directors/trustees: D. Slawik; H. Slawik; J. O. Slawik Jr.; J.O. Slawik Sr., chair; M. S. Slawik; E. J. Tichenor.

Smikis Foundation

1660 South Highway 100
Parkdale Plaza
Suite 426
St Louis Park, MN 55416-1533
County: Hennepin
Phone: (952) 512-1165
Fax: (952) 512-1684
Contact: Linda Rees-Christianson
Established: 03/01/1993
Donor: Lucy B. Hartwell
Funder type: Private foundation

Program Description

Program's purpose: The main purpose of the Smikis Foundation is to support programs in Minneapolis that improve the quality of education for pre-school and K-12 grade children. The foundation also funds programs that lead to self-sufficiency and an improved quality of life for residents of the Minneapolis area.

Funding priorities: Education: Preschool through 12th grade; and Human Service Needs: Programs leading to self-sufficiency.

Program limitations/restrictions: No grants are made to individuals, political organizations or units of government.

Geographic focus: Twin Cities Metropolitan Area.

Areas of interest:

EDUCATION: Adult/continuing education/literacy, Pre-school/elementary, Secondary, Vocational/technical.

HUMAN SERVICES: Children/youth services, Family services, Multipurpose human service organizations, Services to specific groups.

Intended beneficiaries: General public/unspecified.

Types of support for individuals: none.

Sample grants:

Admission Possible/St Paul, MN/ $15,000.

Center for Victims of Torture/MN/ $15,000.

MD Anderson Cancer Center - TX/TX/ $25,000.

New Visions School/MN/$5,000.

Project for Pride in Living/MN/$25,000.

Tree Trust - Twin Cities/MN/$2,000.

Youth Farm & Market Project/ Minneapolis, MN/$7,000.

Financial Information

Financial data for year ending: 12/31/2005
Foundation assets: $15,131,406
Grants paid: $612,375
Number of grants: 53
Largest/smallest: $50,000/$500
Largest multi-year grant approved: $100,000

Staff/Trustees

Staff: Linda Rees-Christianson.

Directors/trustees: Lucy B. Hartwell.

Southern Minnesota Initiative Foundation

525 Florence Avenue
PO Box 695
Owatonna, MN 55060-4701
County: Steele
Phone: (507) 455-3215
Fax: (507) 455-2098
E-mail: inquiry@smifoundation.org
Website: www.smifoundation.org
Established: 07/01/1986
Paid Staff: Yes
Funder type: Community/public foundation

Program Description

Program's purpose: Provide programming, technical and financial resources to build stronger communities and businesses in 20 southern Minnesota counties. Our objectives include stronger businesses with quality jobs, vibrant communities that build on social and economic assets, and people working together to foster policies and practices that support positive community and economic development.

Funding priorities: Community Success Program: asset-based community development, town meeting initiative, early childhood initiative. Business Success Program: assessment/planning, customized action plans, and financing. Voices for Southern Minnesota: regional dialogues, demonstration projects related to five key business development areas: workforce, transportation, early childhood, government effectiveness and health care costs.

Program limitations/restrictions: Limited to our 20-county region in southeast/south central Minnesota: Blue Earth, Brown, Dodge, Faribault, Fillmore,

Freeborn, Goodhue, Houston, LeSueur, Martin, Mower, Nicollet, Olmsted, Rice, Sibley, Steele, Wabasha, Waseca, Watonwan and Winona counties.

Areas of interest:
COMMUNITY IMPROVEMENT: Economic development, Community asset-building, Nonprofit capacity-building & collaboration.

PHILANTHROPY/VOLUNTARISM: Public foundations and community foundations.

PUBLIC AFFAIRS/SOCIETY BENEFIT: Citizen participation, Public policy research and analysis.

YOUTH DEVELOPMENT: Early childhood care & education.

Intended beneficiaries: General public/unspecified.

Sample grants:

Albert Lea Arts Center/MN/To create a musical and artistic experience for preschool children/$7,500.

Austin Main Street Project/MN/To lead the community in revitalizing its downtown district/$7,500.

Latino Economic Development Center/MN/To support regional economic development through the training for local Latino entrepreneurs/$6,000.

Welcome Center, Inc./MN/To support efforts to build upon the assets of newcomers and connect them to resources and information to help them become part of the community/$3,000.

Working Together Group/MN/To create awareness and reduce the effects of violence in Zumbrota, Pine Island, Mazeppa, Goodhue, Kenyon and Wanamingo/$3,000.

Financial Information

Financial data for year ending: 06/30/2006
Foundation assets: $30,460,077
Grants paid: $668,100
Number of grants: 97
Largest/smallest: $28,500/$100

Application Information

Preferred form of initial contact: letter of inquiry, telephone inquiry.

Public information available by request: proposal guidelines, application form, annual report, newsletter, website, program e-journals.

Accept common grant application: yes.

Proposal deadlines: varies, open application and RFP grant process.

Preferred time for receiving proposals: no less than one month prior to project start.

Contribution decisions made by: staff.

Typical time from application deadlines to notification: 2 months.

Staff/Trustees

Staff: Pam Bishop, Business Success program officer; Heidi Brown, donor services and outreach associate; Carol Cerney, vice president & COO; Brian Conzemius, vice president & CFO; Elise Davis, Community Success director; Reuven Doron, donor services & outreach officer; Sue Draayer, Voices for Southern Minnesota program officer; Tom Gebur, technology coordinator; Barbara Gunderson, READS/AmeriCorps program director; Marcia Haley, business lending coordinator; Rae Jean Hanson, Community Success program officer; Jennifer Heien, Voices program associate; Melissa Langer, operations coordinator; Diane Lewis, business lending director; Janet Lundstrom, Community Success coordinator; Suzy Meneguzzo, administrative director; Jennifer Nelson, donor services coordinator; Anni O'Neill, Community Success director; Tim Penny, president & CEO; Tom Shea, business development coordinator; Bonita Sommers, finance coordinator; Teri Steckelberg, Community Success associate; Kathi Svoboda, operations associate.

Directors/trustees: Sandra Allaire; Dan Bonneur; Mimi Carlson; Dan Christianson; Bill Davis; Neil Eckles; Jody Feragen; Don Hayden; Carol Kamper; Michael Tuohy Jr.; Dianne Twedell; Steve Underdahl; Sherry Valley; Steve Waldhoff; Bob Wallace; David K. Williams.

Southways Foundation

601 Carlson Parkway
Suite 800
Minnetonka, MN 55305
County: Hennepin
Fax: (952) 835-8283
E-mail: southways@smcinv.com
Website: www.southwaysfoundation.org
Contact: Jon K. Crow, vice president/treasurer
Established: 12/27/1950
Funder type: Private foundation

Program Description

Program's purpose: The Southways Foundation is a general foundation interested principally in education, culture, health and welfare, environment and the disadvantaged.

Program limitations/restrictions: Annual grants are given only to arts, educational and social service organizations that have a historical connection to the John S. Pillsbury family. Capital and one-time gifts are considered for organizations in the Minneapolis area. The foundation generally does not make grants to agencies of the United Way for annual operating expenses.

Geographic focus: Twin Cities Metropolitan Area, Areas outside Minnesota.

Geographic limitations: The foundation accepts grants that are regional in nature relating primarily to the Minneapolis and St Paul metropolitan area. Grants made outside Minnesota generally are matching grants to grants given by family members.

Areas of interest:
ARTS, CULTURE, HUMANITIES.
EDUCATION.
HEALTH - GENERAL/REHABILITATIVE.
HUMAN SERVICES.

Intended beneficiaries: General public/unspecified, Poor/economically disadvantaged.

Types of support for organizations:
CAPITAL CAMPAIGNS: Building/renovation, Endowment funds, Equipment.
GENERAL PURPOSE/OPERATING SUPPORT.
PROGRAM DEVELOPMENT/PROJECT SUPPORT.

Types of support for individuals: none.

Exclusions: Individuals, Political organizations.

Sample grants:

Chrysalis Center/MN/$5,000.

Interfaith Outreach & Community Partners/MN/general operating/$1,500.

International Women's Health Coalition - NY/NY/special grant/$7,500.

Minneapolis College of Art & Design/MN/$3,750.

Minneapolis Institute of Arts/MN/general operating/$23,250.

MN Landscape Arboretum/MN/$10,000.

MN Orchestral Association/MN/general operating/$16,000.

Pillsbury Neighborhood Services Inc/MN/capital/$25,000.

Financial Information

Financial data for year ending: 12/31/2005
Foundation assets: $10,317,873
Grants paid: $636,587
Number of grants: 208
Largest/smallest: $50,000/$100

Application Information

Preferred form of initial contact: complete proposal.

Public information available by request: proposal guidelines, website.

Accept common grant application: yes.

Proposal deadlines: April 1 for a June decision and October 1 for a December decision.

Contribution decisions made by: board of directors/trustees.

Frequency of contributions decisions: semiannually.

Specific times board meets: June and December.

Typical time from application deadlines to notification: 2-3 months.

Staff/Trustees

Staff: Jon K. Crow, vice president/treasurer; Tracy D. Jackson.

Directors/trustees: Ella P. Crosby; Jon K. Crow, vice president/treasurer; Priscilla P. Gaines; Katharine P. Jose; Lucy C. Mitchell, president; John S. Pillsbury III; George S. Pillsbury Jr.; Eleanor C. Winston.

Southwest Initiative Foundation (fka Southwest Minnesota Foundation)

PO Box 428
15 Third Avenue NW
Hutchinson, MN 55350
County: McLeod
Phone: (320) 587-4848
Alt. Phone: (800) 594-9480
Fax: (320) 587-3838
E-mail: info@swifoundation.org
Website: www.swifoundation.org
Contact: Sherry Ristau, president
Established: 04/16/1986
Paid Staff: Yes
fka: Southwest Minnesota Foundation
Funder type: Community/public foundation

Program Description

Program's purpose: To be a catalyst, facilitating opportunities for economic and social growth by developing and challenging leaders to build on the region's assets.

Funding priorities: Currently under review, but in the past have included: Promote productive aging, promote inclusive communities, connect youth and communities, promote economic advancement, and promote philanthropy.

Program limitations/restrictions: No capital expenditures, religious purposes/activities, lobbying or political activities, for-profit businesses, education/curriculum development, debt retirement, ongoing grants, administrative budgets, arts, mandated programs, fundraising campaigns.

Geographic limitations: 18 counties of southwest Minnesota.

Areas of interest:

COMMUNITY IMPROVEMENT: Community coalitions, Economic development, Nonprofit management.

EDUCATION: Related to our priorities.

HUMAN SERVICES: Children/youth services, Multipurpose human service organizations, Senior centers and services, Immigrant programs.

PHILANTHROPY/VOLUNTARISM: Community foundations, Donor-advised funds, Component funds.

YOUTH DEVELOPMENT: Youth leadership programs, Children from birth to age five.

Intended beneficiaries: Aging/elderly/senior citizens, Children only (5-14 years), Ethnic/racial populations - general, Immigrants/newcomers/refugees, Infants/babies (under age 5), Youth/adolescents (ages 14-19).

Types of support for individuals: none.

Sample grants:

City of Montevideo/MN/Survival Spanish for Emergency Services Personnel: Training in basic Spanish language communications in Montevideo for law enforcement, emergency medical service and emergency dispatch workers/$1,060.

Heartland Community Action Agency Inc/MN/Circles of Support: Support for a community-based approach to move people out of poverty by building intentional personal relationships across class and race lines that increase cultural competency/$20,000.

Land Stewardship Project/MN/Montevideo, Farm Beginnings-Year 3: An intergenerational project that builds mutually beneficial relationships between a new generation of farmers and those with decades of farming experience/$15,000.

Parish Nurse Program/MN/Clarkfield Lutheran Church: Parish nurse program that promotes health and wellness through education, counsel and advocacy services/$10,000.

United Way - MN (Kandiyohi County)/MN/Youth as Resources: A youth leadership program that brings youth and adults together to allocate funds to youth-initiated, youth-led community projects/$15,000.

Willmar Municipal Utilities/MN/GENCO Feasibility Study: Study of the economic feasibility of integrating wind-generated electricity, a renewable resource, into the power mix of a municipal utility/$23,950.

Financial Information

Financial data for year ending: 06/30/2005
Foundation assets: $42,533,825
Grants paid: $1,050,946
Number of grants: 175
Largest/smallest: $50,000/$100

Application Information

Preferred form of initial contact: letter of inquiry, telephone inquiry, request for guidelines.

Public information available by request: proposal guidelines, annual report, newsletter, website.
Accept common grant application: yes.
Accept common report form: yes.
Will view video: yes.
Proposal deadlines: ongoing.
Contribution decisions made by: CEO, staff, board of directors/trustees.
Frequency of contributions decisions: monthly.
Typical time from application deadlines to notification: 2-4 months.

Staff/Trustees

Staff: Diana Anderson, chief operating officer; Berny Berger, micro enterprise program officer; Sara Carlson, program officer; Nancy Fasching, grants officer; Liz Maiers, development specialist; Cheryl Glaeser, program specialist; Dawn Hartwig, development assistant; Nancy Kaping, executive assistant; Judy Larson, program director; Sarah Libbon, communications officer; Janet Menton, assistant to accounting & administration; Margie Nelsen, accounting specialist; David Paskach, vice president; Brian Pederson, accounting & administration director; Sherry Ristau, president; Patti Rutledge, program assistant; Jackie Turner-Lovsness, program specialist; Marc Vaillancourt, development director.

Directors/trustees: Joyce Dass; Rick Ellingworth; Dr. Wayne Freese; Gary Geiger; Sander Ludeman; William McCormack; Connie VanDerBill Medin; Becky Parker, chair; Cris Remucal; Vince Robinson; Tim Ulrich.

The Spell Family Foundation

222 South Ninth Street
Suite 2880
Minneapolis, MN 55402
County: Hennepin
Phone: (612) 371-9650
Contact: William Spell, president
Established: 01/01/1994
Funder type: Private foundation

Program Description

Program's purpose: General charitable purposes.
Program limitations/restrictions: None identified.
Geographic focus: Twin Cities Metropolitan Area, Areas outside Minnesota.
Areas of interest:
HEALTH - DISEASES/MEDICAL DISCIPLINES.
HUMAN SERVICES: Children/youth services.
RELIGION/SPIRITUAL DEVELOPMENT.
Intended beneficiaries: General public/unspecified.
Types of support for organizations:
GENERAL PURPOSE/OPERATING SUPPORT: Annual campaigns.
PROGRAM DEVELOPMENT/PROJECT SUPPORT.
Sample grants:
Center of the American Experiment/MN/$10,000.
Children's Cancer Research Fund - MN/MN/$5,000.
Friends of the Minneapolis Public Library/ MN/$3,000.
Juvenile Diabetes Foundation - MN/MN/$750.
Minneapolis Heart Institute/MN/$25,000.
St Mary's Greek Orthodox Church/Minneapolis, MN/$13,000.

Financial Information

Financial data for year ending: 12/31/2006
Foundation assets: $3,500,000
Grants paid: $165,000
Number of grants: 49
Largest/smallest: $25,000/$50

Application Information

Preferred form of initial contact: letter of inquiry.
Proposal deadlines: none.

Staff/Trustees

Directors/trustees: Angeline Spell; Diane Spell; Harry Spell; William Spell, president.

Daniel J. Spiegel Family Foundation

222 South Ninth Street
Suite 1700
Minneapolis, MN 55402
County: Hennepin
Phone: (612) 379-7811
Contact: Robert Karon
Established: 06/22/2000
Funder type: Private foundation

Program Description

Program's purpose: General charitable purposes.
Geographic focus: Twin Cities Metropolitan Area, Areas outside Minnesota.
Types of support for organizations:
GENERAL PURPOSE/OPERATING SUPPORT.
Sample grants:
American Jewish Committee - NY/New York, NY/general operating/$7,500.
Beth El Synagogue/MN/general operating/$8,270.
Torah Academy - St Louis Park/MN/general operating/$1,000.

Financial Information

Financial data for year ending: 12/31/2005
Foundation assets: $556,746
Grants paid: $24,018
Typical grant amount: $1,500

Application Information

Preferred form of initial contact: complete proposal, written proposal stating charitable purpose and proposed use of requested funds.
Proposal deadlines: none.

Staff/Trustees

Directors/trustees: Marilyn J. Robinson; Benjamin S. Spiegel; Daniel J. Spiegel; Dorie M. Spiegel; Emily I. Spiegel.

St Anthony Park Community Foundation

2183 Commonwealth Avenue
St Paul, MN 55108
County: Ramsey
Phone: (651) 641-1455
Fax: (651) 641-1484
E-mail: jon@sapfoundation.org
Website: www.sapfoundation.org
Contact: Jon Schumacher, executive director
Established: 01/01/1998
Paid Staff: Yes
Funder type: Community/public foundation

Program Description

Program's purpose: To nurture the unique community assets of St Anthony Park to secure a strong and vibrant neighborhood for future generations.

Funding priorities: The foundation will provide grants to support the development of the following community assets: arts and humanities, community economic development, education, environment, health and housing. Projects that foster volunteerism and collaboration among organizations are strongly encouraged.

Geographic limitations: The St Anthony Park community, which includes St Paul's District 12 boundaries, the University Grove area, 1666 Coffman, the St Paul Campus of the University of Minnesota and the Fulham block of Lauderdale.

Areas of interest:
ARTS, CULTURE, HUMANITIES.
COMMUNITY IMPROVEMENT: Community/neighborhood development/improvement.
EDUCATION.
ENVIRONMENTAL QUALITY/PROTECTION/BEAUTIFICATION.
HEALTH - GENERAL/REHABILITATIVE.
HOUSING/SHELTER.
HUMAN SERVICES: Children/youth services, Senior centers and services.

Exclusions: Individuals, Non-501(c)(3), Political organizations, Religious organizations.

Sample grants:
District 12 Community Council/MN/$4,000.
Murray Junior High School/MN/$1,500.
Music in the Park Series/MN/$2,000.
St Anthony Park Block Nurse Program/MN/$2,000.
St Anthony Park Branch Library Association/ MN/$1,750.
St Anthony Park School Association/MN/$5,000.

Financial Information

Financial data for year ending: 01/01/2007
Foundation assets: $353,444
Grants paid: $26,000
Number of grants: 10
Largest/smallest: $5,000/$500

Application Information

Preferred form of initial contact: telephone inquiry, e-mail.

Public information available by request: proposal guidelines, application form, website.

Accept common grant application: yes.

Proposal deadlines: The large grants ($1,000-$5,000) deadline was March 16, 2007. Small grants (less than $1,000): anytime.

Contribution decisions made by: board of directors/trustees.

Frequency of contributions decisions: Large grants: annually, small grants: as received.

Typical time from application deadlines to notification: 2 months.

Staff/Trustees

Staff: Jon Schumacher, executive director.

St Croix Valley Community Foundation

516 Second Street
Suite #214
PO Box 39
Hudson, WI 54016
Phone: (715) 386-9490
Fax: (715) 386-1250
E-mail: info@scvcf.org
Website: www.scvcf.org
Contact: David H. Griffith, president
Established: 01/01/1995
Paid Staff: Yes
Funder type: Community/public foundation

Program Description

Program's purpose: To enhance the quality of life in the St Croix River Valley.

Program limitations/restrictions: While proposals from nonprofit organizations in our five-county area are welcome, currently most grants are awarded from donor-advised funds at the foundation. Exceptions are the Valley Arts Initiative, the Music Education in the Schools program, and Nonprofit Management Assistance Grants.

Geographic focus: East Metropolitan Area/St Paul only; Chisago and Washington counties in Minnesota; Pierce, St Croix and Polk counties in Wisconsin.

Areas of interest:
ANIMAL RELATED.
ARTS, CULTURE, HUMANITIES: Arts services, Arts/cultural multipurpose, Historical societies, Humanities, Museums, Performing arts, Visual arts, Music Education in the Schools.
CIVIL RIGHTS.
COMMUNITY IMPROVEMENT.
EDUCATION.
ENVIRONMENTAL QUALITY/PROTECTION/BEAUTIFICATION.
FOOD/NUTRITION/AGRICULTURE.
HEALTH - DISEASES/MEDICAL DISCIPLINES.
HEALTH - GENERAL/REHABILITATIVE.
HEALTH - MENTAL HEALTH/CRISIS INTERVENTION.
HEALTH - RESEARCH.
HOUSING/SHELTER.
HUMAN SERVICES.

PHILANTHROPY/VOLUNTARISM.
PUBLIC AFFAIRS/SOCIETY BENEFIT.
YOUTH DEVELOPMENT.

Intended beneficiaries: General public/unspecified.

Types of support for organizations:
CAPITAL CAMPAIGNS.
EMERGENCY FUNDS.
GENERAL PURPOSE/OPERATING SUPPORT.
MANAGEMENT/TECHNICAL ASSISTANCE.
PROGRAM DEVELOPMENT/PROJECT SUPPORT.
RESEARCH.
STUDENT AID (GRANTS TO INSTITUTIONS).

Types of support for individuals: scholarships.

Exclusions: Political organizations.

Sample grants:

American Refugee Committee/MN/$500.

Carpenter St Croix Valley Nature Center/MN/$2,400.

Courage St Croix/MN/general operating/$1,000.

Family Resource Center - WI (St Croix)/WI/$2,500.

Habitat for Humanity - WI (St Croix)/WI/$4,620.

River Falls Community Arts Base, Inc/MN/$1,250.

St Croix ArtBarn/WI/$2,000.

YMCA - WI (St Croix)/WI/$2,500.

Financial Information

Financial data for year ending: 06/30/2006
Foundation assets: $8,937,191
Grants paid: $1,287,917
Number of grants: 316
Largest/smallest: $156,000/$100

Application Information

Preferred form of initial contact: letter of inquiry, telephone inquiry, e-mail.

Public information available by request: annual report, website.

Accept common grant application: yes.

Contribution decisions made by: board of directors/trustees.

Frequency of contributions decisions: monthly.

Typical time from application deadlines to notification: 60 days.

Proposal deadlines: Music Education in the Schools: proposal deadline October 1. Check the website for deadlines and applications for the Valley Arts Initiative and other programs.

Staff/Trustees

Staff: David H. Griffith, president; Sally Hermann, administrative assistant; Peg Leutele, executive assistant; Jill A. Shannon, director, community partnerships initiatives.

Directors/trustees: Charles Arnason; Ann Brookman; William E. Campbell; Patty Draxler; Chris Galvin; Jim Gillespie; Karen Hansen; Martha Harding; Nate Jackson; Michael Johnson; Erv Neff; David Palmer; Gretchen Stein, chair; Kathy Tunheim; Mark Vanasse; David Wettergren; Steve Wilcox.

St Francis Regional Medical Center Foundation

1455 St Francis Avenue
Shakopee, MN 55379
County: Scott
Phone: (952) 403-2070
Fax: (952) 403-3003
E-mail: joan.fawcett@allina.com
Website: www.stfrancis-shakopee.com/foundation_overview.htm
Contact: Joan Fawcett, development officer
Paid Staff: Yes
Funder type: Private foundation

Program Description

Program's purpose: The St Francis Foundation exists to support St Francis Regional Medical Center and to enhance the healing experience in the communities we serve.

Funding priorities: The St Francis Foundation gives priority consideration to grants for programs that demonstrate and strengthen the strategic initiatives of the St Francis Regional Medical Center. The 2007 Healthy Communities Grant Program's funding priority areas 1) Behavioral health funding to support and provide community education and awareness of mental health needs in our community; 2) Healthcare access funding to provide appropriate healthcare for the uninsured and underinsured; 3) Cultural competency funding to decrease barriers to healthcare for diverse populations due to cultural or linguistic differences; 4) Heart Healthy Living funding to decrease death and disability from cardiovascular disease by promoting heart healthy living, increase screening and intervention, and improve early and effective response to cardiac events in our community; 5) Childhood obesity funding to improve nutrition and increase physical activity among children in our community; 6) Health insurance access funding to increase access to health insurance for the underinsured. In addition, St Francis Foundation looks to support organizations that promote the hospital's mission and alignment with its values: respect, hospitality, joy, partnership, justice and stewardship.

Program limitations/restrictions: Nonprofit organizations that meet the St Francis Foundation's guidelines may request support for program development/program support, direct program support, specific curriculum development. A given program may be funded a maximum of three times in a five-year period. We will not be able to fund all eligible grant applications received.

Geographic limitations: Scott, Carver and Western Dakota counties.

Areas of interest:
HEALTH - GENERAL/REHABILITATIVE: Public health programs/wellness education, Healthcare access, Cultural competency, Heart healthy living, Health insurance access, Childhood obesity.
HEALTH - MENTAL HEALTH/CRISIS INTERVENTION: Behavioral health, Community education and awareness.

Intended beneficiaries: Disabled - general or unspecified disability, Ethnic/racial populations - general, Females - all ages or age unspecified, Males - all ages or age unspecified, Poor/economically disadvantaged.

Types of support for organizations:
PROGRAM DEVELOPMENT/PROJECT SUPPORT: Curriculum development.

Exclusions: Capital & endowment campaigns, Individuals, Political organizations, Scholarships/loans, General operating funds, Campaign or lobbying activities, Religious organizations for direct religious activities, Multi-year requests.

Sample grants:

District 112 Foundation/MN/$2,000.

River Valley Nursing Center/MN/$10,000.

St Mary's Health Clinics - MN/MN/$12,000.

WellFit - MN (Prior Lake/Savage)/MN/$500.

Financial Information

Financial data for year ending: 06/30/2006
Foundation assets: $1,928,330
Grants paid: $30,446
Number of grants: 13
Largest/smallest: $500/$12,000
Typical grant amount: $5,000

Application Information

Preferred form of initial contact: letter of inquiry, telephone inquiry, request for guidelines, complete proposal.

Public information available by request: proposal guidelines, application form, annual report, newsletter, website.

Proposal deadlines: Grant applications are accepted on an ongoing basis. Grant requests over $500 are reviewed quarterly in March, June, September and December.

Preferred time for receiving proposals: March, June, September, December.

Contribution decisions made by: CEO, staff, board of directors/trustees, grant review committee.

Frequency of contributions decisions: quarterly.

Typical time from application deadlines to notification: 60 days.

Special application procedures: Grant requests are reviewed by the grant review committee with funding recommendations forwarded to the foundation board of directors. The foundation board of directors makes final approval. Unfunded grants must be resubmitted for future consideration.

Staff/Trustees

Staff: Mary J. Anderson, donor relations coordinator; Joan Fawcett, development officer; Carley Stuber, executive director.

Directors/trustees: Paul (Wally) Danielson, chair; Robert Fox; Gary Lee; Duane Marschall; Bonnie McLaughlin; Beth Schneider; Joshua Storms.

Alex Stern Family Foundation

4152 30th Ave S
Suite 102
Fargo, ND 58104
Phone: (701) 237-0170
Contact: Donald L. Scott, executive director
Funder type: Private foundation

Program Description

Geographic focus: Fargo-Moorhead area only.

Areas of interest:
ARTS, CULTURE, HUMANITIES.
EDUCATION.
HOUSING/SHELTER.
HUMAN SERVICES.
PUBLIC AFFAIRS/SOCIETY BENEFIT.
RECREATION.
YOUTH DEVELOPMENT.

Types of support for organizations:
CAPITAL CAMPAIGNS.
GENERAL PURPOSE/OPERATING SUPPORT.
PROGRAM DEVELOPMENT/PROJECT SUPPORT.

Exclusions: Individuals, Non-501(c)(3), Endowments.

Sample grants:

American Red Cross - MN/MN/local disaster relief/$5,000.

CHARISM, Inc./MN/youth enrichment center/$5,000.

Jamestown College/ND/$7,500.

Learning Bank/MN/elementary fine arts series/$3,500.

Moorhead Technical College Foundation/MN/scholarships for Fargo-Moorhead area students/$7,500.

Nokomis Child Care Center/ND/general operating/$20,000.

Red River Boy Choir/MN/$5,000.

YMCA - MN (Fargo/Moorhead)/MN/shelter operating support/$15,000.

Financial Information

Financial data for year ending: 12/31/2005
Foundation assets: $9,496,191
Grants paid: $553,230
Number of grants: 47
Largest/smallest: $100,000/$1,000

Application Information

Preferred form of initial contact: letter of inquiry.

Public information available by request: proposal guidelines, application form.

Proposal deadlines: March 31 and August 31.

Contribution decisions made by: board of directors/trustees.

Frequency of contributions decisions: semiannually.

Typical time from application deadlines to notification: 2.5-3 months.

Staff/Trustees

Staff: H. Michael Hardy; Donald L. Scott, executive director.

Directors/trustees: Dan Carey; H. Michael Hardy; Donald L. Scott, executive director.

Stevens Square Foundation

800 IDS Tower
80 South Eighth Street
Minneapolis, MN 55402
County: Hennepin
Phone: (612) 672-8669
Fax: (612) 672-3846
E-mail: info@stevenssquarefoundation.org
Website: www.stevenssquarefoundation.org
Funder type: Private foundation

Program Description

Program's purpose: The Stevens Square Foundation is dedicated to inspiring and enabling people to live with dignity, with particular emphasis on the needs of the elderly and children. We strive to improve the lives of individuals in the greater Twin Cities metropolitan area by providing support to organizations that are responsive, innovative and effective in meeting these needs.

Funding priorities: For 2007 and 2008, our funding priorities will focus on programs for seniors. We are interested in programs that are innovative and effective in advancing the welfare of the elderly, serving to promote independence by providing affordable housing and community accessibility for seniors; to meet the unique and complex needs of low-income seniors; to address the diverse and growing needs of elders and their families in different cultural and ethnic communities; to increase public awareness of services available to seniors; to offer intergenerational opportunities linking children and youth with elders in their communities; to address the unique needs of seniors with disabilities; to provide elders with opportunities for learning and social interaction; to promote volunteerism encouraging the use of the talents, time and experience of retired persons as volunteers; to provide end of life care to elders and their families.

Program limitations/restrictions: We do not make grants to individuals, political organizations or candidate, fraternal societies or orders, religious organizations for religious purposes, or umbrella organizations, such as federated fund drives.

Geographic focus: Twin Cities Metropolitan Area.

Areas of interest:

COMMUNITY IMPROVEMENT: Volunteer bureaus.

HOUSING/SHELTER: Affordable housing for seniors.

HUMAN SERVICES: Senior centers and services.

Intended beneficiaries: Aging/elderly/senior citizens.

Types of support for organizations:

GENERAL PURPOSE/OPERATING SUPPORT.

PROGRAM DEVELOPMENT/PROJECT SUPPORT.

Types of support for individuals: none.

Exclusions: Individuals, Non-501(c)(3), Political organizations.

Financial Information

Financial data for year ending: 12/31/2005
Foundation assets: $10,396,501
Largest/smallest: $50,000/$5,000

Application Information

Preferred form of initial contact: complete proposal.

Public information available by request: proposal guidelines, website.

Accept common grant application: yes.

Accept common report form: yes.

Proposal deadlines: March 1.

Preferred time for receiving proposals: From February 1 to March 1.

Contribution decisions made by: board of directors/trustees.

Frequency of contributions decisions: annually.

Typical time from application deadlines to notification: 6 months.

Staff/Trustees

Directors/trustees: Elizabeth Hawn, president; Emily Johnson.

Sundance Family Foundation and Sundance Pay It Forward Foundation

PO Box 129
3109 West 50th Street
Minneapolis, MN 55410
County: Hennepin
Phone: (612) 822-8580
Alt. Phone: (612) 822-8587
E-mail: sundancefamilyfoundation@earthlink.net
Website: www.sundancefamilyfoundation.org
Contact: Mary Karen Lynn-Klimenko
Established: 10/01/2003
Funder type: Private foundation

Program Description

Program's purpose: Sundance Family Foundation nurtures family stability worldwide. Sundance Family Foundation will make small- to medium-sized grants to support 501(c)(3) projects that address the needs of the community in one or more of the following areas: Supportive Housing – Innovative services that help families prevent homelessness, especially programs that nurture families to move toward self-sufficiency. Human Services – Healing and preventative work in the areas of Mental Health, Wellness and Addiction. The foundation is especially interested in supporting programs in which two or more family members (including children) participate, or programs that are focused on parent education. International – Social Entrepreneurship Programs directed toward empowering families in one or preferably more of the following areas: Economic Stability – especially microfinance programs; Mental Health, Wellness and Addiction; Housing; Education; Family and Community Health.

Funding priorities: The Sundance Family Foundation will give priority to proposals that contain some or all of the following characteristics: Efficient projects where Sundance Family Foundation grants would leverage additional funding or volunteers; collaborative projects, as well as organizational partnerships that encourage growth and build the capacity of young organizations; projects that stress inclusivity, that promote leadership from within, and that work in partnership with their beneficiaries to improve and empower their lives; projects that intend to impact family stability directly, and serve families for whom other resources are unsubstantial or are unavailable.

Program limitations/restrictions: In the Areas of Human Services and Supportive Housing: Proposals are only accepted on an invitation basis. Sundance Family Foundation does NOT fund the following types of projects: Individuals Scholarships or Fellowships, Endowments, Capital Funding in the Human Services and Supportive Housing areas (except by invitation), Capital support for International projects should not make up more than one-half of the project budget, General operating support (except by invitation).

Geographic limitations: Except for international grants to developing countries, Sundance Family Foundation will focus their giving to organizations whose programming benefits the residents of the following Minnesota and Wisconsin counties: Hennepin, Ramsey, Washington, Chisago, Polk and St Croix. Proposals for international support must be presented by 501(c)(3) organizations based in the United States that work in Latin America, Africa, or Russia.

Areas of interest:

HOUSING/SHELTER: Supportive Housing.

HUMAN SERVICES: Children/youth services, Family services, Family services for adolescent parents, Family violence shelters and services.

INTERNATIONAL AFFAIRS: International development/relief, International human rights.

Intended beneficiaries: Adults, Children and youth (infants-19 years), Poor/economically disadvantaged, Families.

Exclusions: Capital & endowment campaigns, Individuals, Scholarships/loans, Individual Scholarships or Fellowships; General Arts Programs; Capital Funding (except in the area of Affordable Housing); Endowments; General Operating Expenses and On-Going Programs.

Financial Information

Financial data for year ending: 12/31/2005
Foundation assets: $2,901,446
Grants paid: $546,962

Application Information

Preferred form of initial contact: complete proposal.

Public information available by request: application form, website.

Proposal deadlines: The 2007 deadline was July 18. See website for most current deadlines.

Special application procedures: See website for additional guidelines and procedures.

Staff/Trustees

Staff: Mary Karen Lynn-Klimenko.

SUPERVALU Foundation

PO Box 990
Minneapolis, MN 55440
County: Hennepin
Phone: (952) 828-4430
Fax: (952) 828-4403
Website: www.supervalu.com/sv-webapp/community/community.jsp
Funder type: Corporate foundation

Program Description

Program's purpose: SUPERVALU believes in good corporate citizenship. As a member of the community, we believe that we have a responsibility to enhance the quality of life for our customers and employees. The SUPERVALU Foundation provides support to local programs that address community needs, are measurable and are serving communities where SUPERVALU or one of our companies has a significant presence.

Funding priorities: Education, workforce development, hunger relief, fine arts education, social services through the United Way.

Program limitations/restrictions: Contributions are restricted to organizations with 501(c)(3) status, and requests for specific program support are preferred to those for general operating funds.

Geographic focus: Twin Cities Metropolitan Area.

Geographic limitations: Giving decisions for organizations located in the Minneapolis/St Paul area are made at the corporate headquarters office. Organizations located outside Minnesota should contact the management of the local SUPERVALU operation with grant requests.

Areas of interest:

ARTS, CULTURE, HUMANITIES: Arts/cultural multipurpose, Support for a limited number of arts education programs in the corporate headquarters communities.

EDUCATION: Adult/continuing education/literacy, Graduate education/professional schools, Vocational/technical, Focused on K-12 and post-secondary educational programs that include leadership development and/or school-to-work readiness programs.

EMPLOYMENT/JOBS: Employment procurement/job training, Vocational rehabilitation, Focused on programs that provide job training and self-sufficiency programs for minority, disabled, physically challenged, and disadvantaged persons.

FOOD/NUTRITION/AGRICULTURE: Food service/free food distribution, Hunger relief: generally addressed through product and financial donations to comprehensive hunger relief organizations and nonprofit food distribution centers.

HUMAN SERVICES: Generally addressed through significant grants to the United Way in the corporate headquarters communities. Additional grants may be provided to organizations that do not receive United Way funding and provide social services to at-risk populations.

YOUTH DEVELOPMENT: Multipurpose youth centers/clubs, Scouting organizations, Youth development programs.

Intended beneficiaries: Adults, Disabled - general or unspecified disability, Ethnic/racial populations - general, Poor/economically disadvantaged, Youth/adolescents (ages 14-19).

Types of support for organizations:
GENERAL PURPOSE/OPERATING SUPPORT.
STUDENT AID (GRANTS TO INSTITUTIONS): Scholarship funds.
IN-KIND PRODUCTS.

Exclusions: Capital & endowment campaigns, Individuals, Non-501(c)(3), Political organizations.

Sample grants:

Arthritis Foundation - MO/MO/$8,000.
Boys & Girls Club - MN (Twin Cities)/MN/$20,000.
Community Harvest Food Bank - IA/IA/$2,000.
Dunwoody Institute/MN/$6,000.
Goodwill Industries - MN (St Paul)/MN/$5,000.
Hopkins Center for the Arts/MN/$20,000.
MN Public Radio - St Paul/MN/$5,000.
St Croix Valley Sports Facility/MN/$5,000.

Financial Information

Financial data for year ending: 02/28/2006
Foundation assets: $659,428
Grants paid: $1,186,128
Number of grants: 273
Largest/smallest: $151,594/$100

Application Information

Preferred form of initial contact: letter of inquiry if unsure if meet guidelines; otherwise, complete proposal.

Public information available by request: proposal guidelines, application form, website.

Accept common grant application: yes.

Proposal deadlines: February 15, May 15, August 15, November 15.

Contribution decisions made by: staff, employee committee.

Typical time from application deadlines to notification: less than 90 days.

Staff/Trustees

Staff: Terry A. Polk.

Directors/trustees: David Boehnen; Karen Borman; John Breedlove; Sheila Hagen; Warren Simpson; Sherry Smith; James Stoffel.

Swan Family Foundation

c/o Lowry Hill
90 South Seventh Street
Suite 5300
Minneapolis, MN 55402
County: Hennepin
Phone: (612) 667-1764
Established: 01/01/1998
Funder type: Private foundation

Program Description

Geographic focus: Twin Cities Metropolitan Area, Greater Minnesota, Areas outside Minnesota.

Areas of interest:
EDUCATION: Higher education, Pre-school/elementary.
HUMAN SERVICES.

Types of support for organizations:
GENERAL PURPOSE/OPERATING SUPPORT: Annual campaigns.

Sample grants:
Allied Arts Fund Drive - SD/SD/general operating/$1,000.
Blake School/MN/annual campaign/$500.
Crazy Horse Memorial/Crazy Horse, SD/general operating/$1,500.
Macalester College - MN/MN/annual alumni campaign/$200.
Princeton University/NJ/annual alumni campaign/$10,000.
Princeton University/NJ/annual campaign/$250.
St Olaf College/MN/annual alumni campaign/S750.
United Way - SD/SD/general operating/$800.

Financial Information

Financial data for year ending: 12/31/2005
Foundation assets: $1,209,354
Grants paid: $57,950
Number of grants: 18
Largest/smallest: $25,000/$500

Staff/Trustees

Directors/trustees: Nancy Swan Ihle; Alan J. Swan; Esther L. Swan; James W. Swan, president.

Sweitzer Foundation

U.S. Bank
101 East Fifth Street
EP MN S14
St Paul, MN 55101
County: Ramsey
Phone: (651) 466-8735
Alt. Phone: (651) 466-8707
Contact: Jeffrey T. Peterson
Established: 01/17/1969
Funder type: Private foundation

Program Description

Intended beneficiaries: General public/unspecified.

Types of support for organizations:
GENERAL PURPOSE/OPERATING SUPPORT.

Sample grants:
American Red Cross - MN (St Paul)/MN/$3,000.
Asian Women United of MN - St Paul/MN/$1,000.
Goodwill Industries - MN/MN/capital campaign/$3,000.
Hamline University/MN/Blanche Sweitzer Scholarship Fund/$10,000.
Hearing and Service Dog Program of MN/MN/$1,000.
Junior Achievement - MN/MN/$3,000.
Project for Pride in Living/MN/$3,000.
Science Museum of MN, The/MN/$2,500.

Financial Information

Financial data for year ending: 12/31/2005
Foundation assets: $1,509,373
Grants paid: $61,000
Number of grants: 23
Largest/smallest: $10,000/$1,000

Application Information

Preferred form of initial contact: letter of inquiry, complete proposal.

Proposal deadlines: March 1 for April notification.

Frequency of contributions decisions: annually.

Specific times board meets: April.

Typical time from application deadlines to notification: notification in April.

Staff/Trustees

Directors/trustees: Jeffrey T. Peterson; James A. Sweitzer, president; Joan T. Sweitzer.

Tapemark Charity Pro-Am Golf Tournament

1685 Marthaler Lane
West St Paul, MN 55118-3517
County: Dakota
E-mail: info@proam.mn
Website: www.tapemarkproam.org
Contact: Philip Callen, president
Paid Staff: Yes
Funder type: Private foundation

Program Description

Program's purpose: Annual PGA-affiliated competitive golf event and fundraiser supported by corporate sponsorships and individual contributions. Makes annual contributions to nonprofit agencies supporting people with developmental and learning disabilities and their families.

Intended beneficiaries: Disabled - general or unspecified disability.

Sample grants:
ARC - MN/MN/$22,212.
ARC - MN (Anoka & Ramsey Counties Inc)/MN/$93,735.
Dakota Communities/MN/$4,700.
Family Service - MN (St Paul)/ MN/$41,717.

Financial Information

Financial data for year ending: 12/31/2005
Foundation assets: $46,364
Grants paid: $196,185
Number of grants: 5
Largest/smallest: $41,717/$2,800

Staff/Trustees

Staff: Philip Callen, president.

Target

33 South Sixth Street
CC-3600
Minneapolis, MN 55402
County: Hennepin
Phone: (612) 696-6098
Fax: (612) 696-4706
E-mail: community.relations@target.com
Website: www.target.com/community
Funder type: Corporate foundation and corporate giving program

Program Description

Funding priorities: Target's corporate giving programs support programs that have national scope with local impact. The core of Target's corporate giving efforts is our local store grants program. Store grants focus on three key areas: Arts, Early Childhood Reading and Family Violence Prevention. In the Arts, we fund programs that provide affordable arts and cultural experiences for the entire family such as art exhibits, classes and performances. Programs that bring arts to schools or school children to the arts are of particular interest to us. In Early Childhood Reading, we recognize that reading is an essential element of each child's educational process. Target supports programs that promote a love of reading or that encourage children to read together with their families. We have a particular focus on programs that inspire young readers, from birth through third grade. In addition, through our in-store Take Charge of Education program, we contribute to nearly 110,000 schools nationwide. In Family Violence Prevention, Target funds programs such as parenting classes and family counseling that help prevent family violence. We also provide assistance for support groups and abuse shelters. The Target Foundation focuses its community giving efforts in two key areas: Arts and Social Services. In the Arts, we support programs and organizations that promote visibility and accessibility at a community level. In Social Services, we support programs and organizations that directly provide food, clothing and shelter to individuals or families at risk.

Program limitations/restrictions: Target does not provide grants to individuals, programs outside Target communities, foundations, capital campaigns or endowment fund drives, religious organizations for religious purposes, treatment programs (such as substance or alcohol abuse), athletic teams or events, fundraiser or gala events, advocacy or research groups, or education institutions for regular instructional programs. Target's corporate giving program does not give general purpose/operating support grants. Additionally, the Target Foundation does not fund national ceremonies, memorials, conferences, testimonials or other similar events, health, recreation, or therapeutic programs, or living subsidies.

Geographic limitations: Target's corporate giving efforts are limited to areas in which we do business. The Target Foundation welcomes applications from organizations in the 7-county Minneapolis/St Paul metropolitan area that are IRS-classified 501(c)(3).

Areas of interest:
ARTS, CULTURE, HUMANITIES: (Target Corporate Giving Program and Target Foundation).
EDUCATION: Early childhood reading (Target Corporate Giving Program only).
HUMAN SERVICES: Family violence prevention programs (Target Corporate Giving Program only), Food, clothing and shelters (Target Foundation only).

Intended beneficiaries: General public/unspecified.

Types of support for organizations:
GENERAL PURPOSE/OPERATING SUPPORT.
PROGRAM DEVELOPMENT/PROJECT SUPPORT.

Types of support for individuals: none.

Exclusions: Individuals, Non-501(c)(3), Scholarships/loans.

Sample grants:
ART Station Inc - GA/GA/Support of the 2005 Tour of Southern Ghosts/$10,000.
Circus of the Star/MN/Support of general operations/$30,000.
Dakota Woodlands/MN/Support of general operations/$45,000.
Episcopal Community Services - MD/MD/Support of Ready for Success/$25,000.
Hands on Children's Museum - WA/WA/Support of Presenting Sponsor of Sand in the City event/$10,000.
ISD Chaska #112/MN/Support of Read to Me programming/$3,000.
James Sewell Dance/MN/Support of general operations/$35,000.
Neighborhood House - MN/MN/Support of the Basic Needs program/$35,000.

Financial Information

Financial data for year ending: 01/28/2006
Foundation assets: $16,900,000
Grants paid: $147,853,100
Largest/smallest: $1,225,000/$100

Application Information

Preferred form of initial contact: To be considered for a corporate giving program grant, complete an application available at your local Target store. To be considered for a foundation grant, complete a proposal.

Public information available by request: proposal guidelines, application form, website.

Accept common grant application: yes.

Proposal deadlines: none.

Preferred time for receiving proposals: Corporate Giving program: March 1 - May 31. Foundation: February 1 - October 1.

Contribution decisions made by: Corporate giving program grant decisions are made by store team leaders. Foundation grant decisions are made by foundation staff and/or the board of directors/trustees.

Typical time from application deadlines to notification: Corporate giving program: by September 30. Foundation: within 90 days.

Special application procedures: Corporate giving program: contact your local store manager (store team leader) for further information.

Staff/Trustees

Staff: Michael Dominowski, senior manager, community relations; Jennifer Higgins, manager, community relations & Target Foundation; Kris Kewitsch, senior specialist; Briana Little, associate specialist; Melinde Scott, senior manager, community relations; Laysha Ward, vice president, community relations & Target Foundation.

Directors/trustees: Tim Baer; Bart Butzer; Gail Dorn; Michael Francis; John Griffith; Jodee Kozlak; Sara Ross; Janet Schalk; Doug Scovanner; Terry Scully; Gregg Steinhafel; Bob Ulrich; Laysha Ward.

TCF Foundation

200 East Lake Street
Mail Code EX0-02-C
Wayzata, MN 55391-1693
County: Hennepin
Phone: (952) 745-2757
Fax: (952) 745-2775
Website: www.tcfbank.com
Contact: Denise Peterson, community affairs - Minnesota
Established: 10/01/1989
Paid Staff: Yes
Funder type: Corporate foundation

Program Description

Program's purpose: TCF Foundation, the philanthropic arm of TCF National Bank, extends charitable contributions to tax-exempt organizations in education, human services, community development and the arts. The foundation allocates grants to local and regional organizations engaged in nonprofit activities that are designed to improve the economic and social well being of the community.

Funding priorities: To provide assistance to organizations supported by TCF employee volunteers in the areas of community development, education, human services and arts and culture.

Program limitations/restrictions: TCF Foundation does not support social or fraternal organizations, political candidates or religious institutions.

Geographic limitations: Twin Cities Metropolitan Area, Greater Minnesota, Minnesota statewide, Communities where TCF Bank has branches (including Michigan, Illinois, Wisconsin, Indiana, and Colorado).

Areas of interest:
ARTS, CULTURE, HUMANITIES.
COMMUNITY IMPROVEMENT.
EDUCATION.
HUMAN SERVICES.

Intended beneficiaries: Adults, Children and youth (infants-19 years), Disabled - general or unspecified disability, Homeless, Infants/babies (under age 5), Physically disabled, Poor/economically disadvantaged, Youth/adolescents (ages 14-19).

Types of support for organizations:
CAPITAL CAMPAIGNS.
GENERAL PURPOSE/OPERATING SUPPORT.
PROGRAM DEVELOPMENT/PROJECT SUPPORT: Curriculum development, Fundraising.
STUDENT AID (GRANTS TO INSTITUTIONS): Scholarship funds.

Types of support for individuals: none.

Matching grants: any 501(c)(3) non-profit organization.

Exclusions: Individuals, Non-501(c)(3), Political organizations, Religious organizations, Research.

Sample grants:
Boy Scouts of America - MN (Viking Council)/MN/$10,000.
Community Neighborhood Housing Services - MN (St Paul)/MN/$5,000.
Junior Achievement - MN/MN/$15,000.
Memorial Blood Centers of MN/MN/$10,000.
Pulmonary Hypertension Association/MD/$15,000.
Special Olympics - MN/MN/$3,000.
Stages Theatre Company/MN/$5,000.
University of MN Foundation/MN/$100,000.

Financial Information

Financial data for year ending: 12/31/2006
Grants paid: $3,000,000
Number of grants: 300
Largest/smallest: $200,000/$500
Typical grant amount: $3,000
Matching gifts: $270,000
Largest multi-year grant approved: $200,000

Application Information

Preferred form of initial contact: letter of inquiry, request for guidelines.
Public information available by request: proposal guidelines, application form.
Accept common grant application: yes.
Accept common report form: yes.
Proposal deadlines: Ongoing.
Preferred time for receiving proposals: Quarterly.
Contribution decisions made by: board of directors/trustees, employee committees.
Frequency of contributions decisions: quarterly.
Typical time from application deadlines to notification: 3 months.

Staff/Trustees

Staff: Renee Capune, community affairs - Colorado; Donald Hawkins, community affairs - Michigan; Timothy Herwig, community affairs - IL, IN, WI; Denise Peterson, community affairs - Minnesota.

Directors/trustees: William A. Cooper, chairman of the board, TCF Financial Corporation; Mark Jeter, president, TCF National Bank Minnesota; Jason Korstange, SVP, TCF Foundation; Greg Pulles, EVP & general council, TCF Financial Corporation.

TEAM Foundation

105 Park Avenue NW
Bagley, MN 56621-9558
County: Clearwater
Phone: (218) 694-3550
Fax: (218) 694-3552
E-mail: TEAMFoundation@TEAM-IND.com
Website: www.TEAM-foundation.org
Established: 05/07/2003
Paid Staff: Yes
Funder type: Private foundation

Program Description

Program's purpose: We are committed to enhancing the quality of life through charitable funding within rural Minnesota by the promotion of education, healthcare and community.

Funding priorities: TEAM Foundation wants communities to not just survive, but thrive. TEAM Foundation is committed to ensuring a better quality of healthcare for rural Minnesotans. From pediatrics to geriatrics, our goal is to support programs and projects that do the most good for the most people. We also support many community and human services programs. These programs feed the hungry, care for our elderly, nurture our young and strengthen our communities. TEAM Foundation believes in investing in our future. That is why we support and promote quality education starting at the pre-K level. Due to continued state and local budget constraints, schools have been forced to reduce or cut programs and activities and are left with limited budgets to invest in improvements and technology. TEAM Foundation strives to fill the gap.

Program limitations/restrictions: Grantee must be a 501(c)(3) nonprofit organization or school (documentation must be provided), provide services to rural Minnesotans (preference is given to the rural areas surrounding TEAM Industries facilities), services must be related to education (pre-K through grade 12), healthcare, human services or community.

Geographic focus: Greater Minnesota; priority given to Bagley, Park Rapids, Audubon, Detroit Lakes, Baxter and Cambridge, MN, and surrounding areas.

Areas of interest:

EDUCATION: Accelerated reading and math programs, Technology, Pre-school programs.

HEALTH - GENERAL/REHABILITATIVE: Technology, Palliative care/hospice.

HUMAN SERVICES: Senior centers and services, Food shelves, Senior nutrition, Crisis centers.

YOUTH DEVELOPMENT: Youth development programs.

Types of support for individuals: none.

Exclusions: Non-501(c)(3).

Financial Information

Financial data for year ending: 12/31/2005
Foundation assets: $29,723
Grants paid: $301,446
Number of grants: 32
Largest/smallest: $35,500/$50

Application Information

Preferred form of initial contact: complete proposal.

Public information available by request: proposal guidelines, application form, annual report, website.

Staff/Trustees

Staff: Sara Gordon, assistant director and secretary; Debra Matthews, executive director and president; Tricia Young, assistant director and treasurer.

Directors/trustees: Sara Gordon, assistant director and secretary; Steve Kast, vice president; Debra Matthews, executive director and president; Beatrice Ricke; Nan Vobr; Tricia Young, assistant director and treasurer.

Tennant Foundation

701 North Lilac Drive
PO Box 1452
Minneapolis, MN 55440-1452
County: Hennepin
Phone: (763) 540-1209
Fax: (763) 513-1811
Contact: Cheryl Timm, administrator
Established: 12/01/1973
Funder type: Corporate foundation

Program Description

Program's purpose: Tennant believes that corporate responsibility involves the corporation's involvement in the total life of the communities in which it operates. It has focused its contribution efforts in four major areas: Social Services, Health/Safety, Cultural Activities, and Education and Workforce Readiness Programs. It is also a major supporter of the Greater Twin Cities United Way and has a policy of matching its employees' contributions to United Way agencies where Tennant has offices.

Funding priorities: Priorities to organizations in which Tennant employees are involved, applicants in Tennant geographical areas, and organizations that have previously been funded by Tennant. Most contributions are in the form of modest general operating grants.

Program limitations/restrictions: Does not normally fund agencies also funded through umbrella organizations, organizations also funded by United Way, organizations designed to influence legislation/politics, national organizations without active local chapters, religious organizations, individuals, elementary and secondary school, trips or tours, tickets, tables or advertising for benefit purposes.

Geographic focus: West Metropolitan Area/Minneapolis only.

Geographic limitations: Does not normally fund organizations located outside the Minneapolis or western suburbs area, except for a limited number of organizations located outside Minnesota in areas where Tennant has a concentration of employees.

Areas of interest:

ANIMAL RELATED: Animal protection/welfare, Zoo/zoological societies.

ARTS, CULTURE, HUMANITIES: Arts/cultural multipurpose, Historical societies, Humanities, Media/communications, Museums, Performing arts, Visual arts.

COMMUNITY IMPROVEMENT: Community/neighborhood development/improvement.

EDUCATION: Higher education, Libraries/library science, Vocational/technical.

EMPLOYMENT/JOBS: Employment procurement/job training.

ENVIRONMENTAL QUALITY/PROTECTION/BEAUTIFICATION: Botanical/horticultural/landscape, Natural resources conservation/protection.

FOOD/NUTRITION/AGRICULTURE: Soil and water conservation/farm land preservation.

HEALTH - DISEASES/MEDICAL DISCIPLINES: Birth defects/genetic disorders, Cancer, Digestive diseases/disorders.

HEALTH - GENERAL/REHABILITATIVE: Public health programs/wellness education, Rehabilitative medical services.

HEALTH - MENTAL HEALTH/CRISIS INTERVENTION: Addiction disorders, Alcohol/drug/substance, prevention and treatment, Mental health treatment and services.

HOUSING/SHELTER: Homeless, temporary housing, Housing development/construction/management, Housing owners/renter organizations, Housing support services.

HUMAN SERVICES: Children/youth services, Emergency assistance (food/clothing/cash), Family services, Multipurpose human service organizations.

PUBLIC PROTECTION - CRIME/COURTS/LEGAL SERVICES.

YOUTH DEVELOPMENT: Multipurpose youth centers/clubs, Scouting organizations, Youth development programs.

Intended beneficiaries: General public/unspecified.

Types of support for individuals: none.

Matching grants: employee matching, public broadcasting, scholarships.

Exclusions: Individuals, Non-501(c)(3), Political organizations, Religious organizations, Scholarships/loans.

Sample grants:

Blind, Inc/MN/$2,500.

Fraser Community Services/MN/$2,000.

Guthrie Theater/Minneapolis, MN/$4,500.

MN Institute for Talented Youth/MN/ $5,000.

Science Museum of MN, The/MN/ $2,000.

Financial Information

Financial data for year ending: 12/31/2006
Grants paid: $499,729
Number of grants: 32
Largest/smallest: $150,000/$1,000

Application Information

Preferred form of initial contact: letter of inquiry, telephone inquiry, request for guidelines, complete proposal, (Minnesota Common Grant is accepted.)

Public information available by request: annual report.

Accept common grant application: yes.

Proposal deadlines: 4 weeks prior to board meeting.

Contribution decisions made by: board of directors/trustees.

Specific times board meets: June and December.

Typical time from application deadlines to notification: 4-5 weeks.

Staff/Trustees

Staff: Jane Stamstad, consultant; Cheryl Timm, administrator.

Directors/trustees: Richard M. Adams, president; Thomas J. Dybsky; Vicki Haugen, treasurer; Heidi Hoard; Chris Killingstad; Kathryn Lovik.

Think Community Foundation

Think Mutual Bank
PO Box 5949
Rochester, MN 55903
County: Olmsted
Phone: (507) 536-5702
Fax: (507) 536-5730
Website: www.thinkcu.com
Funder type: Corporate giving program

Program Description

Program's purpose: Think Community Foundation has been established to oversee the distribution of charitable donations from Think Credit Union of Rochester, Minnesota. The foundation focuses on reinvesting in the communities it serves by supporting the many non-profit organizations that are working to improve those communities.

Funding priorities: 1) Nonprofit organizations providing for the physical and social well-being of people, especially children and young adults, and including initiatives to promote general education and economic well-being. 2) Organizations that alleviate suffering, provide comfort or have programs that are intended to combat physical or social problems before they occur. 3) Local organizations, or local chapters of organizations, that focus donations most directly on the health and well being of those in the community.

Geographic focus: Twin Cities Metropolitan Area, Southeast Minnesota.

Areas of interest:

COMMUNITY IMPROVEMENT: Community/neighborhood development/improvement.
EDUCATION: Adult/continuing education/literacy, Pre-school/elementary.
ENVIRONMENTAL QUALITY/ PROTECTION/BEAUTIFICATION: Environmental education.
HEALTH - GENERAL/REHABILITATIVE: Health support services, Public health programs/wellness education.
HEALTH - MENTAL HEALTH/CRISIS INTERVENTION.
HUMAN SERVICES: Children/youth services, Emergency assistance (food/clothing/cash), Family services, Family services for adolescent parents, Family violence shelters and services, Multipurpose human service organizations, Personal social services, Residential/custodial care, Senior centers and services, Services to specific groups, Victims services.
YOUTH DEVELOPMENT: Adult/child matching programs, Multipurpose youth centers/clubs, Scouting organizations, Youth development programs.

Intended beneficiaries: General public/unspecified.

Types of support for organizations:

CAPITAL CAMPAIGNS: Building/ renovation, Computer systems/technology, Equipment, Land acquisitions.
EMERGENCY FUNDS.
GENERAL PURPOSE/OPERATING SUPPORT: Annual campaigns.
PROGRAM DEVELOPMENT/ PROJECT SUPPORT: Fundraising, Mentoring programs, Publications, Leadership programs.

Financial Information

Financial data for year ending: 12/31/2006
Grants paid: $405,000

Application Information

Preferred form of initial contact: letter of inquiry, e-mail.

Accept common grant application: yes.

Accept common report form: yes.

Will view video: yes.

Proposal deadlines: March 1, June 1, September 1, December 1.

Contribution decisions made by: board of directors/trustees.

Frequency of contributions decisions: quarterly.

Typical time from application deadlines to notification: 6-8 weeks.

Staff/Trustees

Staff: Kari Jo Pugh, executive director.

Directors/trustees: Paul Dorn, vice president; Tom Floyd, secretary/treasurer; Paul Horgen, president.

Thomson West

610 Opperman Drive
Eagan, MN 55123
County: Dakota
Phone: (651) 848-5926
Alt. Phone: (651) 848-5665
Fax: (651) 687-6078
Website: west.thomson.com/about community
Contact: Martha Field, manager of corporate and employee giving
Paid Staff: Yes
Funder type: Corporate giving program

Program Description

Program's purpose: The Thomson West Community Partnership Program considers grant proposals for funding from organizations that focus on one or more of the following three areas: 1) Educating the Future Workforce - Support programs that provide skills training and mentoring for youth and adults of diverse backgrounds; 2) Providing Arts and Cultural Experiences to the Community - Support programs that are accessible, incorporate respect for diversity, offer innovation in programming and activities, and assist schools and organizations that serve disadvantaged youth; 3) Developing and Strengthening Youth, Families and Communities - Support programs that build communities, keep young children engaged in school and family, teach good citizenship, and provide access to affordable housing and health-based support services.

Areas of interest:
ARTS, CULTURE, HUMANITIES.
EDUCATION.
EMPLOYMENT/JOBS.
HOUSING/SHELTER.
HUMAN SERVICES: Children/youth services.
PUBLIC AFFAIRS/SOCIETY BENEFIT.
YOUTH DEVELOPMENT.

Types of support for organizations:
GENERAL PURPOSE/OPERATING SUPPORT.
PROGRAM DEVELOPMENT/PROJECT SUPPORT: Seed money/start-up funds.
IN-KIND PRODUCTS.
IN-KIND SERVICES.

Types of support for individuals: none.

Matching grants: employee matching. Thomson West matches employee donations to qualifying 501(c)(3) organizations and accredited educational institutions that are aligned with its three focus areas.

Exclusions: Capital & endowment campaigns, Individuals, Non-501(c)(3), Political organizations, Religious organizations, Research.

Financial Information

Financial data for year ending: 12/31/2005
Grants paid: $1,164,000
Number of grants: 171
In-kind gifts: $110,000
Matching gifts: $323,000

Application Information

Preferred form of initial contact: complete proposal.

Public information available by request: proposal guidelines, application form, annual report, website.

Proposal deadlines: Educating the Future Workforce - March 15; Arts and Culture - June 15; Developing and Strengthening Youth, Families and Communities - September 15.

Contribution decisions made by: staff, employee committee.

Frequency of contributions decisions: 3 times a year.

Typical time from application deadlines to notification: 8-12 weeks.

Staff/Trustees

Staff: Martha Field, manager of corporate and employee giving; Sheila Snapp, corporate giving specialist.

James R. Thorpe Foundation

120 Broadway Avenue South
Suite 100
Wayzata, MN 55391
County: Hennepin
Phone: (952) 476-0808
E-mail: application@jamesrthorpefoundation.org
Website: www.jamesrthorpefoundation.org
Contact: Edith D. Thorpe, president
Established: 10/01/1974
Paid Staff: Yes
Funder type: Private foundation

Program Description

Program's purpose: To provide financial assistance to a variety of educational, arts and social service nonprofit organizations that serve populations primarily within the city of Minneapolis and, to a lesser extent, the western suburbs.

Funding priorities: Grant requests in the areas of arts, education and social services are considered, with special consideration given to agencies that promote the positive development of young people.

Program limitations/restrictions: No funding to organizations with annual operating budgets exceeding $2 million. Must have at least one full-time, paid employee. No grants to individuals; no funding for conferences or seminars, tours or fundraising events; no multi-year commitments; no national organizations.

Geographic limitations: Program's geographical focus must be Minneapolis. No grants to the East Metro area, Greater Minnesota or outside the state of Minnesota.

Areas of interest:
ARTS, CULTURE, HUMANITIES: Arts/cultural multipurpose, Performing arts, Support for high-quality small and medium-sized arts organizations that primarily serve the following disciplines: dance, music, theatre and literature.
EDUCATION: A focus on private K-12 educational and scholarship programs, especially those serving special needs/disadvantaged groups and middle school-aged children, and talented youth. Programs that promote character and civility.
HOUSING/SHELTER: Homeless, temporary housing, Housing support services, Transitional housing.

HUMAN SERVICES: Children/youth services, Multipurpose human service organizations, Services to specific groups, Programs working with children and youth, the elderly, refugees, the mentally ill and other disadvantaged populations. Agencies that address child abuse, emergency needs and transitional housing will also receive priority consideration.

YOUTH DEVELOPMENT: Multipurpose youth centers/clubs, Youth development programs.

Intended beneficiaries: Adults, Aging/elderly/senior citizens, Children and youth (infants-19 years), Homeless, Immigrants/newcomers/refugees, Mentally/emotionally disabled, Poor/economically disadvantaged.

Types of support for individuals: none.

Sample grants:

Center School (NA-WAY-EE)/MN/$5,000.

Coffee House Press/MN/$5,000.

Confederation of Somali Community in MN/MN/$7,500.

Metropolitan Federation of Alternative Schools Inc/MN/$30,000.

MIGIZI Communications Inc/MN/$10,000.

MN African Women's Association/MN/$3,000.

MU Performing Arts - MN/MN/$5,000.

PRISM- MN/MN/$5,000.

Financial Information

Financial data for year ending: 11/30/2006
Foundation assets: $8,006,129
Grants paid: $462,850
Number of grants: 71

Application Information

Preferred form of initial contact: telephone inquiry, request for guidelines.

Public information available by request: proposal guidelines, annual report.

Accept common grant application: yes.

Proposal deadlines: March 1 (arts and education) for May meeting, September 1 (social services and capital) for November meeting.

Contribution decisions made by: board of directors/trustees.

Frequency of contributions decisions: semiannually.

Specific times board meets: mid-May and mid-November.

Typical time from application deadlines to notification: 2-3 months.

Special application procedures: Funding requests must be postmarked on or before the respective funding area proposal deadline. Requests postmarked after March 1 or September 1 will not be considered. Hand-delivered proposals or e-mailed proposals must arrive in our office by 4:30 p.m. on March 1 or September 1.

Staff/Trustees

Staff: Jane Stamstad, executive director.

Directors/trustees: Mary C. Boos; Robert C. Cote; Samuel D. Cote; Margaret T. Richards; Edith D. Thorpe, president; Laura A. Thorpe; Samuel S. Thorpe; Timothy D. Thorpe.

Thrivent Financial for Lutherans Foundation

625 Fourth Avenue South
Minneapolis, MN 55415
County: Hennepin
Phone: (612) 340-8281
Fax: (612) 340-4070
E-mail: david.e.jones@thrivent.com
Website: www.thriventfoundation.com
Contact: Karen Coonen, executive director
Funder type: Corporate foundation

Program Description

Program's purpose: The purpose of the Thrivent Financial for Lutherans Foundation is to enhance the health and vitality of three key communities: the Twin Cities, home of the Thrivent Financial for Lutherans corporate office; the Fox Cities in Wisconsin, location of Thrivent Financial's operations center; and the Lutheran community.

Funding priorities: For the Twin Cities and Fox Cities: Homelessness and poverty supports (housing), financial education, early childhood education. For the Lutheran Community: life needs of the working poor; church worker wellness; and leadership development, stewardship, volunteerism, and charitable fundraising.

Program limitations/restrictions: Contributions are generally not made to support of individuals, loans, investments, capital, single disease, political parties and special events.

Geographic focus: Twin Cities Metropolitan Area; preference for inner city of Minneapolis. Also Fox Cities in Wisconsin and Lutheran Community, which has a national focus.

Areas of interest:

EDUCATION: Adult/continuing education/literacy, Financial literacy, Early childhood.

EMPLOYMENT/JOBS: Employment procurement/job training, Vocational rehabilitation.

HUMAN SERVICES: Children/youth services.

PHILANTHROPY/VOLUNTARISM: Nonprofit sector assistance, Volunteerism promotion.

RELIGION/SPIRITUAL DEVELOPMENT: Lutheran community capacity building.

YOUTH DEVELOPMENT: Financial education.

Intended beneficiaries: General public/unspecified.

Types of support for organizations:
GENERAL PURPOSE/OPERATING SUPPORT.
PROGRAM DEVELOPMENT/PROJECT SUPPORT.

Types of support for individuals: none.

Exclusions: Individuals, Non-501(c)(3), Political organizations, Single disease.

Sample grants:

Bridging, Inc/MN/$50,000.

Children's Home Society - MN/MN/Op Supp/$10,000.

Church, Protestant - MN/MN/Spirit of Joy Lutheran Church, Minneapolis/$42,000.

Church, Protestant - MN/MN/St Paul Lutheran Church, Minneapolis/$48,000.

Evangelical Lutheran Church in America - MN (Mpls)/MN/$20,000.

House of Charity Inc/MN/Scholarships and general operating/$50,000.

Junior Achievement - MN/MN/Op Supp/Whole School/$25,000.

Lutheran Women's Mission League - WI/WI/$100,000.

Financial Information

Financial data for year ending: 12/31/2006
Foundation assets: $82,300,000
Grants paid: $20,700,000
Largest/smallest: $1,875,000/$100

Application Information

Preferred form of initial contact: letter of inquiry, request for guidelines.

Public information available by request: proposal guidelines.

Accept common grant application: yes.

Proposal deadlines: please see website.

Preferred time for receiving proposals: Rolling deadlines based on meeting schedule.

Contribution decisions made by: staff, employee committee, board of directors/trustees, depending on the size of the grant request.

Frequency of contributions decisions: varies by grant program.

Typical time from application deadlines to notification: 120-150 days.

Staff/Trustees

Staff: Elizabeth Anderson, community grants officer; Karen Coonen, executive director; Jenni Eickelberg, community grant program manager, Appleton, WI; Debbie Fox, community grant program manager, Appleton, WI; Tina Hanson, foundation administrative support; Yan Huss, assistant treasurer; Jody Jonas, community grant program manager, Minneapolis; David E. Jones, community grant program manager, Minneapolis; Kathy Larson, Lutheran grant program manager; Julie Pritzl, foundation administrator; Mark Simenstad, investment officer; Laurie Wilkinson, Lutheran grant program manager; John Wollner, assistant community grants officer; Jim Yagow, Lutheran community grants officer.

Directors/trustees: Randall Boushek, treasurer; Dave Hayman, secretary; Brad Hewitt, president and chair of the board; Jennifer Martin; Tim Schwan, vice president; Marie Uhrich.

Todd-Wadena Electric Cooperative Community Trust

PO Box 431
Wadena, MN 56482
County: Wadena
Phone: (218) 631-3120
Alt. Phone: (800) 321-8932
E-mail: pjohnson@toddwadena.coop
Website: www.toddwadena.com/community/op_round_up
Contact: Patricia Johnson, public relations manager
Funder type: Community/public foundation

Program Description

Program's purpose: Disbursement of funds from the Operation Round Up voluntary contribution program for charitable and educational purposes primarily in the Todd-Wadena Electric Cooperative service area.

Funding priorities: Community service, economic development, education and youth, environment, and disaster relief.

Program limitations/restrictions: Lobbying, political and religious organizations; veteran, fraternal and labor organizations; fundraising dinners, raffles and other events; individuals; capital fund campaigns; national fund drives; advertising, ongoing operational expenses.

Geographic focus: Todd-Wadena Electric Cooperative service area.

Areas of interest:

COMMUNITY IMPROVEMENT: Community service clubs, Economic development.

EDUCATION.

ENVIRONMENTAL QUALITY/PROTECTION/BEAUTIFICATION.

PUBLIC SAFETY/DISASTERS/RELIEF: Disaster preparedness and relief.

YOUTH DEVELOPMENT.

Sample grants:

Boy Scouts of America - MN/MN/Wadena/$500.

City of Menahga/MN/Long Prairie/$1,000.

Fire Department - MN/MN/Staples/$750.

Food Shelf - MN/MN/$500.

Freshwater Education District - MN (Staples 6004)/MN/$1,000.

Hands of Hope Resource Center, Inc/MN/$1,000.

Financial Information

Financial data for year ending: 12/31/2005
Foundation assets: $10,083
Grants paid: $29,400
Number of grants: 48
Largest/smallest: $1,500/$250

Application Information

Preferred form of initial contact: telephone inquiry, complete proposal, e-mail.

Public information available by request: proposal guidelines, application form, website.

Proposal deadlines: April 15 and September 15.

Contribution decisions made by: board of directors/trustees.

Frequency of contributions decisions: semiannually.

Specific times board meets: May and October.

Staff/Trustees

Staff: Patricia Johnson, public relations manager.

Directors/trustees: Linda Allebach, secretary/treasurer; Don Drouble; Peter Fink, president; Linda Gjerstad; Mike Heino; Luann Holt; Roger Houselog; Joyce LaVoie; Marci Olson.

The Toro Company Giving Program

8111 Lyndale Avenue South
Bloomington, MN 55420-1196
County: Hennepin
Phone: (952) 887-8870
Fax: (952) 887-7291
Website: www.thetorocompany.com/community/involvement.html
Established: 01/01/1978
Donor: The Toro Company
Paid Staff: Yes
Funder type: Corporate foundation and corporate giving program

Program Description

Program's purpose: Serve as an extension of the company's culture to enhance the health and well-being of all Toro communities and the turf industry through active outreach and involvement. The Giving Program is committed to beautifying and preserving outdoor environments, enhancing communities and improving people's lives.

Funding priorities: Environment, education are the primary focus areas. Support to health and human services organizations are made through the annual match of employee donations to the United Way. Arts and culture are supported on a very limited basis.

Program limitations/restrictions: No churches, individuals, athletic programs, geographic restrictions, travel programs, capital and endowment campaigns.

Geographic focus: Twin Cities Metropolitan Area, National Areas, International Areas, Communities with Toro facilities.

Geographic limitations: Windom, MN; Tomah, WI; Beatrice, NE; El Paso, TX; Abilene, TX; Riverside, CA; El Cajon, CA- communities where Toro has a major facility and a large number of employees reside.

Areas of interest:

ANIMAL RELATED: Wildlife preservation/protection, Zoo/zoological societies.

EDUCATION: Graduate education/professional schools, Higher education, Secondary, Vocational/technical, Specific interest in environmental education, water conservation, science, and turf management.

ENVIRONMENTAL QUALITY/PROTECTION/BEAUTIFICATION: Botanical/horticultural/landscape, Environmental beautification/open spaces, Environmental education/outdoor survival, Natural resources conservation/protection, Water conservation, Environmental education.

PHILANTHROPY/VOLUNTARISM: Federated Funds, Nonprofit sector assistance, Voluntarism promotion.

PUBLIC AFFAIRS/SOCIETY BENEFIT: Consumer protection/safety.

PUBLIC SAFETY/DISASTERS/RELIEF: Safety education.

RECREATION: Youth development of life skills through participation golf and activities held on sports fields.

SCIENCE/TECHNOLOGY: Physical sciences/earth sciences, Emphasis on turf and agronomic areas, engineering, and welding.

YOUTH DEVELOPMENT: Youth development of life skills through golf and sports played on fields.

Intended beneficiaries: General public/unspecified.

Types of support for organizations:

GENERAL PURPOSE/OPERATING SUPPORT.

PROGRAM DEVELOPMENT/PROJECT SUPPORT: Curriculum development, Exhibitions, Faculty/staff development, Film/video/radio production, Public awareness, Publications.

STUDENT AID (GRANTS TO INSTITUTIONS): Scholarship funds.

IN-KIND PRODUCTS: Annually, Toro provides extensive product donations using the same guidelines as the cash grant program. Donations fall in three categories: fundraising events, facility maintenance and education. Please contact Toro for more details.

Types of support for individuals: scholarships. Scholarship program is managed by an outside organization. No direct grants to individuals.

Sample grants:

Eco Education/St Paul, MN/$10,000.

Environmental Institute for Golf/KS/$50,000.

First Tee/Minnesota Chapters/$19,500.

Irrigation Association Education Foundation/VA/$50,000.

MN Landscape Arboretum/MN/$20,000.

MN Twins Community Fund/MN/$10,000.

MN Zoo/MN/$10,000.

National Amputee Golf Association/NH/$10,000.

Financial Information

Financial data for year ending: 12/31/2006
Foundation assets: $2,119,769
Grants paid: $1,501,831
Largest/smallest: $140,000/$25
In-kind gifts: $700,000

Application Information

Preferred form of initial contact: telephone inquiry, visit website.

Public information available by request: application form, annual report, website.

Accept common grant application: yes.

Accept common report form: yes.

Proposal deadlines: January 15, April 15, July 15, and October 15.

Contribution decisions made by: staff, employee committee, board of directors/trustees. Requests over $5000 require approval by the grant review committee; requests over $25,000 require approval by the board.

Frequency of contributions decisions: quarterly.

Typical time from application deadlines to notification: 90 days from deadline.

Staff/Trustees

Staff: Stacy Bogart, president; Kathy Manson, volunteer coordinator; Judson Tharin, senior community relations specialist.

Directors/trustees: Stacy Bogart, president; Tim Dordell; Dennis Himan; Mike Hoffman, CEO; Lawrence McIntyre; Sandra Meurlot; Karen Meyer; Steve Wolfe.

Tozer Foundation, Inc.

101 East Fifth Street
EP MN S14
St Paul, MN 55101
County: Ramsey
Phone: (651) 466-8744
Fax: (651) 466-8915
Contact: Ted O. Olsen, U.S. Bank
Established: 06/01/1946
Funder type: Private foundation

Program Description

Program's purpose: Scholarships for college students and for charitable purposes.

Funding priorities: Scholarships for educational and charitable purposes.

Program limitations/restrictions: Scholarships are limited to high school students who reside in Washington, Pine and Kanabec counties in Minnesota.

Geographic focus: Stillwater plus Pine, Kanebec and Washington counties.

Geographic limitations: Stillwater-St Croix Valley.

Areas of interest:

ARTS, CULTURE, HUMANITIES: Arts/cultural multipurpose, Historical societies, Performing arts.

COMMUNITY IMPROVEMENT: Economic development, Nonprofit management, Volunteer bureaus.

EDUCATION: Graduate education/professional schools, Higher education, Libraries/library science.

HEALTH - GENERAL/REHABILITATIVE: Hospitals and related primary medical care facilities, Rehabilitative medical services.

HUMAN SERVICES: Children/youth services, Family services.

YOUTH DEVELOPMENT: Scouting organizations, Junior achievement.

Intended beneficiaries: General public/unspecified.

Types of support for organizations:

CAPITAL CAMPAIGNS: Building/renovation.

PROGRAM DEVELOPMENT/PROJECT SUPPORT.

Types of support for individuals: scholarships.

Sample grants:

Croixdale Residence & apartments/MN/$12,000.

Family Means/MN/$25,000.

Girl Scout Council - MN (St Croix Valley)/ MN/$6,600.

Macalester College - MN/MN/$10,800.

Phipps Center for the Arts - WI/WI/$4,000.

St Cloud State University/MN/$31,250.

United Negro College Fund - DC/DC/$5,000.

Washington County Historical Society/MN/ $5,000.

Financial Information

Financial data for year ending: 10/31/2005
Foundation assets: $27,119,000
Grants paid: $1,587,000
Largest/smallest: $28,000/$500

Application Information

Preferred form of initial contact: letter of inquiry.

Accept common grant application: yes.

Preferred time for receiving proposals: March - April, August - September.

Contribution decisions made by: board of directors/trustees.

Typical time from application deadlines to notification: 3 months.

Staff/Trustees

Directors/trustees: Greg Benson; Allen E. Bernick; Tracey Galowitz; Orville Johnson; Gretchen M. Stein; Jon Theobald; John F. Thoreen; David Wettergren.

Travelers Corporation and Travelers Foundation

385 Washington Street
514-D
St Paul, MN 55102-1396
County: Ramsey
Phone: (651) 310-7757
Fax: (651) 310-2327
E-mail: mnewman@travelers.com
Website: www.travelers.com (select Community Support)
Established: 01/01/1998
Funder type: Corporate foundation

Program Description

Program's purpose: Partner with employees, communities and businesses to help build a civil society by investing in people and institutions for long-term success.

Funding priorities: Arts and culture; community development; education.

Program limitations/restrictions: Generally no funding for events, individuals, religious purposes, veteran or fraternal groups, benefits or fundraisers, advertising, hospital or other services generally supported by third-party reimbursement mechanisms, government services.

Geographic focus: Twin Cities Metropolitan Area, Minnesota statewide, National Areas, Limited National and International Areas.

Geographic limitations: Priority for communities, U.S. and non-U.S., where Travelers has offices.

Areas of interest:

ARTS, CULTURE, HUMANITIES: Arts services, Arts/cultural multipurpose, Historical societies, Humanities, Media/communications, Museums, Performing arts, Visual arts.

COMMUNITY IMPROVEMENT: Community/neighborhood development/improvement, Economic development, Nonprofit management.

EDUCATION: Adult/continuing education/literacy, Educational reform, Educational services, Graduate education/professional schools, Higher education, Pre-school/elementary, Secondary, Adult.

HOUSING/SHELTER: Housing development/construction/management, Housing owners/renter organizations, Housing search assistance, Low-cost temporary housing, Other.

PHILANTHROPY/VOLUNTARISM: Federated Funds, Nonprofit sector assistance, Philanthropy associations, Voluntarism promotion.

PUBLIC AFFAIRS/SOCIETY BENEFIT: Leadership development/awards programs (other than youth).

PUBLIC SAFETY/DISASTERS/RELIEF: Disaster preparedness and relief, Safety education.

YOUTH DEVELOPMENT: Youth development programs.

Intended beneficiaries: Adults, African Americans/Blacks, Asian/Pacific Islanders, Children and youth (infants-19 years), Disabled - general or unspecified disability, Ethnic/racial populations - general, Females - all ages or age unspecified, Gay/lesbian/bisexual/transgender, Hispanics/Latinos, Homeless, Immigrants/newcomers/refugees, Infants/babies (under age 5), Males - all ages or age unspecified, Native American/American Indians, Poor/economically disadvantaged, Youth/adolescents (ages 14-19).

Types of support for organizations:

GENERAL PURPOSE/OPERATING SUPPORT.

PROGRAM DEVELOPMENT/PROJECT SUPPORT.

STUDENT AID (GRANTS TO INSTITUTIONS): Scholarship funds.

CORPORATE SPONSORSHIP: Very limited basis, events in headquarters community. Priorities: consistent with guidelines. Restrictions: downtown St Paul, Minnesota. Contact: Mary Pickard, Community Affairs, (651) 310-7359, mpickard@travelers.com.

Types of support for individuals: none.

Matching grants: employee matching.

Dollars for Doers: yes.

Sample grants:

Admission Possible/St Paul, MN/$20,000.

African Development Center/MN/ Operating support to help African immigrants understand the legal system for business as well as homeownership/ $25,000.

Center for Hmong Arts & Talent/MN/ Operating support for this arts organization, which creates, presents and teaches Hmong arts, and nurtures and develops Hmong artists/$15,000.

La Escuelita/MN/Operating support for this organization, which helps Latino youth achieve greater success in school by providing cultural and language-based academic skill enhancement/$15,000.

MAP for Nonprofits/MN/Operating support to provide management assistance to Twin Cities nonprofit organizations that address Travelers' funding objectives in education, community development, and arts and culture; and one-time capital support to move the offices/$70,000.

Page Educational Foundation/MN/ Scholarship support for Minnesota low-income students of color attending Minnesota post-secondary institutions and performing community service to youth as a component of their scholarship and education/$20,000.

Pangea World Theater Company/ Minneapolis, MN/Operating support for this arts organization, which produces plays, provides workshops and offers a speaker series that promotes public understanding of internationally diverse cultures/$10,000.

Women's Campaign School - CT/CT/ Operating support to pursue increasing the number of women in political office and leadership positions within their communities/$25,000.

Financial Information

Financial data for year ending: 12/31/2005
Foundation assets: $520,717
Grants paid: $10,705,310
Number of grants: 386
Largest/smallest: $1,000,000/$2,500
In-kind gifts: $45,270
Matching gifts: $632,836

Application Information

Preferred form of initial contact: letter of inquiry, telephone inquiry, complete proposal, e-mail.
Public information available by request: proposal guidelines, application form, annual report, website. All information is available on our website. Please note: we no longer accept paper applications; everything must be submitted online.
Proposal deadlines: Ongoing. However, the final deadline for consideration for 2007 funding is August 30, 2007.
Preferred time for receiving proposals: none.
Contribution decisions made by: staff, employee committee, board of directors/trustees.
Frequency of contributions decisions: quarterly.
Typical time from application deadlines to notification: 90-120 days
Special application procedures: All applications must be submitted online.

Staff/Trustees

Staff: Athena Adkins, field operations manager; Shary Hughes-Kempainen, grants administrator; Mike Newman, vice president; Mary Pickard, president and executive director.

Directors/trustees: John Albano; Jay Benet; Andy Bessette, chairman; John Clifford; Marlene Ibsen; Ron James; Michael Klein; Mike Newman, vice president; Mary Pickard, president and executive director; Sara Radjenovic; Bill Rohde; Kurt Schwarzkopf; Ken Spence.

Trust for the Meditation Process

3010 Hennepin Avenue South
Suite 259
Minneapolis, MN 55408
County: Hennepin
Phone: (612) 824-7270
E-mail: trustmed@bitstream.net
Contact: Martha Bolinger, director
Established: 12/31/1986
Paid Staff: Yes
Funder type: Private foundation

Program Description

Program's purpose: The Trust for the Meditation Process supports the rediscovery and practice of meditation in the Christian contemplative traditions. We fund nonprofit organizations that teach, expand and enrich Christian contemplative practice and further dialogue and cooperation among contemplative traditions in all religions. We believe that contemplative practice transforms the way we see ourselves and our world, guides us in the process of becoming fully human, and develops our capacity for compassionate action in society.

Funding priorities: Teaching or enriching meditation practice through the work of a recognized, high-quality teacher. Reaching new audiences where the need is especially great and the potential for impact significant. For example: people in prison, AA or other change programs; clergy or meditation teachers; people curious about meditation; audiences that cross religious boundaries. Projects where a small grant can make a significant impact and a specific set of activities/results.

Program limitations/restrictions: We generally do not consider grants that do not focus on meditation practice but that address prayer or spiritual development more broadly.

Geographic focus: Minnesota statewide, Areas outside Minnesota, International Areas.

Geographic limitations: Because Christian contemplative practice is a worldwide movement, we do not limit grants to the United States.

Areas of interest:

RELIGION/SPIRITUAL DEVELOPMENT: Contemplative practice, Interfaith dialogue, Meditation, Spiritual development.

Intended beneficiaries: Adults, Youth/adolescents (ages 14-19).

Types of support for organizations:

CAPITAL CAMPAIGNS: Building/ renovation, Equipment.

PROGRAM DEVELOPMENT/ PROJECT SUPPORT: Conferences/seminars, Curriculum development, Faculty/ staff development, Program evaluation, Public awareness, Publications, Seed money/start-up funds.

RESEARCH.

Exclusions: Capital & endowment campaigns, Individuals, General operating.

Sample grants:

Christos Center for Spiritual Formation/St Paul, MN/meditation and contemplative prayer instruction/$6,000.

Dwelling in the Woods/McGrath, MN/administrative consultation to streamline operations/$2,419.

House of Prayer/Collegeville, MN/year-long internship in Christian meditation/$3,300.

House of Prayer/Collegeville, MN/meditation center furnishings/$4,000.

Servite Center for Life/Ladysmith, WI/half-day program on contemplative responses to tragedy/$2,305.

St Paul's Monastery - MN/MN/Contemplative Outreach Minnesota and Benedictine Center/$8,000.

University of MN - Center Spirituality & Healing/MN/meditation room furnishings and library/$2,680.

Financial Information

Financial data for year ending: 12/31/2005
Foundation assets: $2,606,525
Grants paid: $101,925
Number of grants: 13
Largest/smallest: $22,000/$1,300

Application Information

Preferred form of initial contact: request for guidelines, e-mail.

Public information available by request: proposal guidelines.

Will view video: yes.

Proposal deadlines: April 16.

Contribution decisions made by: board of directors/trustees.

Frequency of contributions decisions: annually.

Typical time from application deadlines to notification: 2-3 months.

Staff/Trustees

Staff: Martha Bolinger, director.

Directors/trustees: Carol Baker, chair; Ward Bauman; Stephen Taylor; Helen Welter; Mary White; Dr. Charles Wright.

Turner Family Foundation

301 Kenwood Parkway #502
Minneapolis, MN 55403
County: Hennepin
Phone: (612) 920-4629
Alt. Phone: (860) 651-1951
E-mail: marciesullivan@comcast.net
Contact: Marcie Turner Sullivan, president
Established: 01/01/2000
Funder type: Private foundation

Program Description

Program's purpose: The mission of the Turner Family Foundation is primarily to strengthen our communities of Minneapolis/St Paul, MN; Houston, TX; and Hartford, CT. The foundation works in partnership with other agencies, organizations and public entities.

Funding priorities: Other areas of funding are education, at-risk children and their families, health-related issues, housing, youth involvement in sports and athletics, and animal welfare.

Program limitations/restrictions: Grants are generally not made to individuals, government agencies or political or religious organizations.

Geographic limitations: Twin Cities metropolitan area, Hartford, CT and Houston, TX.

Areas of interest:
EDUCATION: Higher education.
HEALTH - DISEASES/MEDICAL DISCIPLINES: Specific named diseases.
HEALTH - RESEARCH.
HOUSING/SHELTER.
HUMAN SERVICES: Children/youth services.
RECREATION: youth sports/recreation.
YOUTH DEVELOPMENT: Adult/child matching programs, Multipurpose youth centers/clubs, Youth development programs.

Intended beneficiaries: General public/unspecified.

Sample grants:
Admission Possible/St Paul, MN/$6,000.
Children's Assessment Center Foundation - TX/TX/$10,000.
HOPE Community - MN/Minneapolis, MN/$7,500.
Prevent Child Abuse - MN (Twin Cities)/MN/$10,000.
Twin Cities RISE!/MN/$5,000.

Financial Information

Financial data for year ending: 12/31/2005
Foundation assets: $943,492
Grants paid: $120,500
Number of grants: 14
Largest/smallest: $40,000/$1,500

Application Information

Preferred form of initial contact: letter of inquiry.

Public information available by request: proposal guidelines.

Accept common grant application: yes.

Accept common report form: yes.

Will view video: yes.

Preferred time for receiving proposals: January, April, July, October.

Contribution decisions made by: board of directors/trustees.

Specific times board meets: March, June, Sept., Dec.

Typical time from application deadlines to notification: 6-8 weeks.

Staff/Trustees

Directors/trustees: Marcie Turner Sullivan, president; Andrew W. Turner; James G. Turner; John F. Turner; John G. Turner; Leslie C. Turner, vice president.

U.S. Bancorp Foundation

800 Nicollet Mall
BC-MN-H21B
Minneapolis, MN 55402-4302
County: Hennepin
Phone: (612) 303-0742
Fax: (612) 303-0787
Website: www.usbank.com/ (select "About U.S. Bancorp," then "Community Relations")
Contact: Kate Waters, foundation manager
Established: 01/11/1979
Funder type: Corporate foundation

Program Description

Program's purpose: To connect to our communities by providing support to organizations that improve the educational and economic opportunities of targeted individuals and families; and enhance the cultural and artistic life of the communities in which we live and work.

Funding priorities: Economic opportunity, affordable housing, cultural and artistic enrichment, K-12 education and United Way. U.S. Bancorp offers support to strengthen community organizations and higher education institutions through its Community and Higher Education Matching Gift Program for employees.

Program limitations/restrictions: U.S. Bank will not provide corporate giving grants for organizations that are not tax-exempt under 501(c)(3) or organizations outside U.S. Bancorp communities, individuals, travel and related expenses, endowment campaigns, deficit reduction, religious organizations designed for religious purposes, organizations designed primarily to lobby, fundraising events or sponsorships, medically oriented charities, or political campaigns.

Geographic focus: Twin Cities Metropolitan Area, Greater Minnesota, areas outside Minnesota, national areas.

Geographic limitations: U.S. Bank supports organizations in communities in which we operate.

Areas of interest:
ARTS, CULTURE, HUMANITIES: Organizations and programs that build audiences of arts organizations; bring the arts to underserved populations; bring select and limited civic amenities to underserved, rural communities; promote the arts in education.
COMMUNITY IMPROVEMENT: Community/neighborhood development/improvement, Economic development.
EDUCATION: organizations that work in collaboration with K-12 schools (public or private) that develop and/or deliver innovative programs addressing dropout prevention, economic education, mentoring and curriculum innovation.
EMPLOYMENT/JOBS: Employment procurement/job training.
HOUSING/SHELTER: Housing development/construction/management, Home buyer counseling.
PHILANTHROPY/VOLUNTARISM: United Way.

Intended beneficiaries: General public/unspecified.

Types of support for organizations:
CAPITAL CAMPAIGNS.
GENERAL PURPOSE/OPERATING SUPPORT.
PROGRAM DEVELOPMENT/PROJECT SUPPORT.

Types of support for individuals: none.

Matching grants: elementary/secondary education, employee matching, higher education.

Financial Information

Financial data for year ending: 12/31/2005
Foundation assets: $52,189,007
Grants paid: $19,900,000

Application Information

Preferred form of initial contact: visit www.usbank.com to obtain state contacts and deadlines, grant application and guidelines.

Public information available by request: proposal guidelines, application form, annual report, website.

Proposal deadlines: February 1 (Arts and Culture), April 1 (Economic Opportunity), July 1 (Education). 2008 application deadlines will be available on www.usbank.com in November 2007.

Contribution decisions made by: employee committee, board of directors/trustees.

Frequency of contributions decisions: quarterly.

Typical time from application deadlines to notification: 90 days.

Staff/Trustees

Staff: Katie Brandt, grants coordinator; Deborah Burke, foundation director; Liz Deziel, community relations specialist; Jodi Piazza, matching gifts coordinator; Kate Waters, foundation manager.

United Health Foundation

9900 Bren Road East
MN008-T800
Minnetonka, MN 55343
County: Hennepin
Phone: (952) 936-6800
Alt. Phone: (800) 985-6869
Fax: (952) 936-1675
E-mail: info@unitedhealthfoundation.org
Website: www.unitedhealthfoundation.org
Established: 01/01/1999
Funder type: Corporate foundation and corporate giving program

Program Description

Program's purpose: United Health Foundation's mission is to improve health outcomes for all Americans. To advance this mission, we provide scientifically-based information to support health and medical decisions that lead to better quality and more cost-effective medical outcomes, and support activities that expand access to health care services for individuals and families who live in challenging circumstances.

Funding priorities: Priorities are twofold: 1) To enhance the quality of health and medical care services by providing reliable, scientifically-based information to support decisions made by health professionals, communities and individuals. 2) To expand access to medical care and health-related services for individuals and families who live in challenging circumstances. Funding can be requested at any time by eligible 501(c)(3) organizations that serve people and communities in the U.S. Because we receive many more requests than we can support, only projects that closely align with our priorities will be considered. We favor projects that create sustainable improvements in communities.

Program limitations/restrictions: Organizations without 501(c)(3) status; private foundations, fiscal agents or individuals; general operating support; capital projects (buildings, remodeling or furnishings); equipment, except as related to a request for project support; endowments, fundraising events or development campaigns; political causes, candidates or legislative lobbying efforts; recreational, sporting events or athletic associations; religious organizations for religious purposes; basic or biomedical research; travel for groups or individuals; scholarships, other than through the United Health Foundation Diverse Scholars Initiative.

Geographic limitations: The United Health Foundation prefers to fund projects that have a national or regional impact. Sponsorships and community relation requests should be directed to the UnitedHealth Group business unit that operates in the requesting organization's geographic area.

Types of support for organizations:
PROGRAM DEVELOPMENT/PROJECT SUPPORT.

Types of support for individuals: none.

Sample grants:

American Public Health Association/ DC/Health Disparities Database/$15,000.

Institute of Medicine - DC/DC/Forum on Drug Discovery/$25,000.

National Patient Safety Foundation/IL/ Advocacy for safety in care delivery/ $5,000.

Research America/VA/Distribution of research on consumers' opinions of health/$50,000.

Financial Information

Financial data for year ending: 12/31/2005
Foundation assets: $20,184,977
Grants paid: $24,233,458

Application Information

Preferred form of initial contact: letter of inquiry. Those seeking support should review guidelines and priorities on the website in advance. E-mail requests are not accepted at the present time.

Public information available by request: The following information is available at www.unitedhealth foundation.org: Foundation priorities, guidelines and funding process; American Health Ranking ™ and Clinical Evidence, both produced by the foundation.

Accept common grant application: yes.

Proposal deadlines: No deadlines, inquiries are regularly accepted and reviewed; our goal is to respond to all written inquiries within 60 days.

Contribution decisions made by: staff, board of directors/trustees.

Frequency of contributions decisions: ongoing.

Special application procedures: Common grant application accepted once grantseeker has been invited to submit a proposal.

Staff/Trustees

Staff: Daniel Johnson, vice president and foundation president/executive director; Cathy Sever, contributions manager.

Directors/trustees: Walter F. Mondale; William Munsell; Reed V. Tuckson M.D.; Anthony Welters.

Unity Avenue Foundation

c/o SRI
White Pine Building
342 Fifth Avenue North
Bayport, MN 55003
County: Washington
Phone: (651) 439-1557
Fax: (651) 439-9480
E-mail: unityavefdn@srinc.biz
Website: www.srinc.biz/ua/
Contact: Bradley E. Kruse, program director
Established: 06/26/1985
Funder type: Private foundation

Program Description

Program's purpose: The mission of Unity Avenue Foundation is to foster responsible, long-term human interaction with the natural environment.

Funding priorities: The foundation prefers to fund specific projects rather than general operations, projects that can be replicated or adapted for broad adoption, and proposals for $5,000 and up.

Geographic focus: Twin Cities Metropolitan Area, Minnesota statewide, National areas, international areas, Western Hemisphere.

Geographic limitations: The foundation prefers to limit funding to projects in the Western Hemisphere.

Areas of interest:

ANIMAL RELATED: Wildlife preservation/protection.

ENVIRONMENTAL QUALITY/ PROTECTION/BEAUTIFICATION: Environmental education/outdoor survival Natural resources conservation/protection, Pollution abatement and control.

Intended beneficiaries: General public/unspecified.

Types of support for individuals: none.

Exclusions: Capital & endowment campaigns, Individuals, Non-501(c)(3), Political organizations, Religious organizations, Scholarships/loans, Tax-supported institutions.

Sample grants:

Compatible Technology International, Inc/MN/FOTECAPIII - safe water in Guatemala/$4,500.

Friends of the Mississippi River/MN/ "State of the Watershed" broadcast/ $10,000.

Great River Greening/MN/"Natural Treasures of the St Croix Valley" publication/$12,000.

Minnesotans for Responsible Recreation/MN/Distributing MRR's CD "protecting Quiet Places and Trails and Waterways from the Motorized Recreation: A Resource Library and Toolkit"/$15,000.

Twin Cities Green Guide/MN/The Twin Cities Green Guide guidebook and website/$10,000.

Women's Environmental Institute/MN/ From Home to the Summit/$5,000.

Financial Information

Financial data for year ending: 06/30/2006
Foundation assets: $1,841,262
Grants paid: $110,000
Number of grants: 12
Largest/smallest: $15,000/$2,500

Application Information

Preferred form of initial contact: letter of inquiry, one-page proposal summary.

Public information available by request: proposal guidelines, application form, website.

Accept common report form: yes.

Proposal deadlines: February 15.

Preferred time for receiving proposals: The Unity Avenue Foundation accepts one-page proposal summaries throughout the year. For a more up-to-date proposal, it is suggested that summaries be sent closer to the proposal submission deadline.

Contribution decisions made by: board of directors/trustees.

Frequency of contributions decisions: annually.

Specific times board meets: May and November.

Typical time from application deadlines to notification: 7 months.

Special application procedures: Submit only the one-page proposal summary, the Proposal Summary Cover Sheet (available on our website), and your 501(c)(3) federal tax determination letter. No other materials should be sent until requested.

Staff/Trustees

Staff: Bradley E. Kruse, program director.

Directors/trustees: Charles F. Cowles, vice president; Constance M. Cowles; Jane S. Cowles, president; John Cowles III; John Cowles Jr.; Sage Fuller Cowles; Ira S. Goldstein; Weston Hoard; Page Knudsen Cowles, treasurer; Joshi Radin; Tessa Sage Flores; Ann M. Stephens, vice president.

The Valspar Foundation

4900 IDS Center
80 South Eighth Street
Minneapolis, MN 55402
County: Hennepin
Phone: (612) 337-5903
Fax: (612) 337-5904
Website: www.valsparglobal.com/corp/about/social_responsibility.jsp
Contact: Gwen Leifeld, manager
Established: 10/22/1979
Funder type: Corporate foundation and corporate giving program

Program Description

Program's purpose: Valspar makes contributions to tax-exempt organizations in the communities in which it has major operations. Its grants are principally to: 1) Organized neighborhood restoration activities, specifically housing. Our primary relationship is with Habitat for Humanity; and 2) United Way campaigns, because of their overall community impact.

Funding priorities: Housing, United Way campaigns, educational (employee scholarship program), arts and sciences, and social service.

Program limitations/restrictions: Scholarship applications must be made by a child of a Valspar Corporation employee who is entering or attending a post secondary educational institution as a full-time student; selection based on financial need and record of achievement.

Geographic focus: Twin Cities Metropolitan Area.

Geographic limitations: Communities where Valspar has a manufacturing facility.

Areas of interest:
ARTS, CULTURE, HUMANITIES: In-kind contributions.
COMMUNITY IMPROVEMENT: Community/neighborhood development/improvement.
EDUCATION: Higher education, Scholarships to children of employees only.
HOUSING/SHELTER: In-kind contributions for existing housing, neighborhood restoration.

Intended beneficiaries: General public/unspecified.

Types of support for organizations:
GENERAL PURPOSE/OPERATING SUPPORT: Annual campaigns.
IN-KIND PRODUCTS: Architectural coatings.

Types of support for individuals: scholarships.

Exclusions: Capital & endowment campaigns, Non-501(c)(3), Political organizations, Religious organizations, Research, Ethnic, fraternal, labor or veteran organizations.

Sample grants:
Big Brothers/Big Sisters - PA/PA/$5,000.
Home Ownership Center/MN/$3,500.
Jungle Theater/MN/$2,500.
Minneapolis Neighborhood Employment Network/MN/$1,000.
MN Opera Company/MN/$3,500.
Powderhorn Community Center/MN/$7,000.

Financial Information

Financial data for year ending: 09/30/2005
Foundation assets: $728,670
Grants paid: $951,037
Number of grants: 214
Largest/smallest: $80,000/$25

Application Information

Preferred form of initial contact: request for guidelines, informal written proposal/letter.

Public information available by request: proposal guidelines, application form.

Accept common grant application: yes.

Proposal deadlines: Proposals are reviewed on an ongoing basis. Annual budgeting determined by November 1 of each year.

Contribution decisions made by: staff.

Frequency of contributions decisions: fiscal year is Nov.1 through Oct. 31.

Typical time from application deadlines to notification: 10-14 days.

Staff/Trustees

Staff: Gwen Leifeld, manager.
Directors/trustees: R. Engh; W. Mansfield; P.C. Reyelts.

DeWitt and Caroline Van Evera Foundation

431 D North Polo Drive
St Louis, MO 63105
Phone: (314) 862-2648
E-mail: grettaf@swbell.net
Contact: Margretta Forrester
Established: 12/30/1959
Funder type: Private foundation

Program Description

Program's purpose: Education serving at-risk and low-income.

Funding priorities: Funds go primarily to programs and general operations in our focus area.

Program limitations/restrictions: Grants to schools, colleges and universities. Emphasis on early education. No grants are made to individuals. Unsolicited proposals not accepted at this time.

Geographic focus: Minnesota statewide, Areas outside Minnesota.

Geographic limitations: Priorities given to Minnesota, Wisconsin and Missouri.

Areas of interest:
ARTS, CULTURE, HUMANITIES: arts education.
EDUCATION: Educational reform, Higher education, Pre-school/elementary, Secondary.

Intended beneficiaries: Infants/babies (under age 5), Poor/economically disadvantaged, Youth/adolescents (ages 14-19).

Types of support for organizations:
CAPITAL CAMPAIGNS: Building/renovation, Computer systems/technology, Equipment.
GENERAL PURPOSE/OPERATING SUPPORT.
PROGRAM DEVELOPMENT/PROJECT SUPPORT: Program evaluation.
STUDENT AID (GRANTS TO INSTITUTIONS).

Exclusions: Individuals, Political organizations.

Sample grants:

AIM High - MO (St Louis)/St Louis, MO/general operating/$7,500.

Blackburn College/IL/capital campaign/$5,000.

Center of Contemporary Arts - MO/MO/general operating/$15,000.

College of St Benedict/MN/general operating/$10,000.

College of St Scholastica - Duluth/MN/general operating/$10,000.

Logos High School/MO/$10,000.

People Serving People, Inc/MN/general operating/$25,000.

Repertory Theatre of St Louis/MO/general operating/$5,000.

Financial Information

Financial data for year ending: 12/31/2006
Foundation assets: $3,045,526
Grants paid: $201,000
Number of grants: 11
Largest/smallest: $50,000/$5,000
Largest multi-year grant approved: $100,000

Application Information

Preferred form of initial contact: Unsolicited proposals not considered at this time.
Proposal deadlines: March 15.
Preferred time for receiving proposals: After January 1.
Contribution decisions made by: board of directors/trustees.
Frequency of contributions decisions: annually.
Specific times board meets: April or May.

Staff/Trustees

Directors/trustees: U.S. Bank, N.A.; Betsy Esber; Margretta Forrester; Stephen Van Evera.

The Vos Family Foundation

32397 Nob Hill Drive
Avon, MN 56310
County: Stearns
Phone: (320) 356-7821
Fax: (320) 356-9143
E-mail: tom_vos@hotmail.com
Established: 01/01/1999
Funder type: Private foundation

Program Description

Geographic focus: Twin Cities Metropolitan Area, Greater Minnesota, Areas outside Minnesota.

Areas of interest:
HUMAN SERVICES.
YOUTH DEVELOPMENT.

Intended beneficiaries: Children and youth (infants-19 years).

Exclusions: Non-501(c)(3), Political organizations, Tax-supported institutions.

Sample grants:

Albany Area Schools/MN/$5,500.

Annual Catholic Appeal/MN/$2,000.

Birthline Inc/MN/$2,000.

Boys & Girls Club - MN (Minneapolis)/MN/$5,000.

Catholic Charities - MN (St Paul and Minneapolis)/MN/$1,000.

Jacob Wetterling Foundation/MN/$500.

Los Ninos/MN/$1,000.

Wayside House, Inc - MN/St Louis Park, MN/$10,000.

Financial Information

Financial data for year ending: 12/31/2005
Foundation assets: $743,215
Grants paid: $37,830
Number of grants: 24
Largest/smallest: $10,000/$100

Staff/Trustees

Directors/trustees: Lara Bahn, director; Kimberly Jennissen, director; Greg Lang, director; Brian Vos, director.

Archie D. and Bertha H. Walker Foundation

1121 Hennepin Avenue
Minneapolis, MN 55403-1785
County: Hennepin
Phone: (612) 332-3556
Fax: (612) 333-6615
Contact: Joan Schoepke, foundation administrator
Established: 08/31/1953
Funder type: Private foundation

Program Description

Program's purpose: The purpose of the grant program is to encourage, develop and support activity in community programs that deal with chemical dependency, the arts, and opposition to racism, prejudice and exclusivity.

Funding priorities: The foundation places primary emphasis on grants to programs dealing with the effect of chemical dependency, chiefly alcoholism, on children and their development. The trustees also consider grant proposals in areas of longstanding foundation interest. These interests include programs in the arts, and programs addressing the treatment of racism, prejudice and exclusivity. Foundation grants are made only to organizations that operate without prejudice.

Program limitations/restrictions: The foundation will ordinarily give preference to grants for programs over grants for capital needs. No grants are made either to individuals or private foundations. Grants are usually awarded for a one-year period.

Geographic focus: Twin Cities Metropolitan Area, Minnesota statewide, National Areas.

Geographic limitations: The foundation customarily limits its grantmaking activities to the state of Minnesota.

Areas of interest:

ANIMAL RELATED: Wildlife preservation/protection.

ARTS, CULTURE, HUMANITIES: Arts services, Arts/cultural multipurpose, Historical societies, Humanities, Media/communications, Museums, Performing arts, Visual arts.

CIVIL RIGHTS: Civil liberties advocacy, Equal opportunity and access, Intergroup relations/race relations, Voter education/registration.

COMMUNITY IMPROVEMENT: Community/neighborhood development/improvement, Economic development.

EDUCATION: Educational services, Libraries/library science.

ENVIRONMENTAL QUALITY/PROTECTION/BEAUTIFICATION: Natural resources conservation/protection, Pollution abatement and control.

FOOD/NUTRITION/AGRICULTURE: Soil and water conservation/farm land preservation.

HEALTH - DISEASES/MEDICAL DISCIPLINES: ALS.

HEALTH - GENERAL/REHABILITATIVE: Reproductive health care.

HEALTH - MENTAL HEALTH/CRISIS INTERVENTION: Addiction disorders, Alcohol/drug/substance, prevention and treatment, Counseling/support groups, Hotline/crisis intervention, Mental health treatment and services.

HUMAN SERVICES: Family services, Family services for adolescent parents, Family violence shelters and services.

PUBLIC PROTECTION - CRIME/COURTS/LEGAL SERVICES: Legal services.

Intended beneficiaries: Adults, African Americans/Blacks, Aging/elderly/senior citizens, Asian/Pacific Islanders, Children and youth (infants-19 years), Ethnic/racial minorities - other specified group(s), Ethnic/racial populations - general, Females - all ages or age unspecified, Gay/lesbian/bisexual/transgender, Hispanics/Latinos, Immigrants/newcomers/refugees, Males - all ages or age unspecified, Native American/American Indians, Poor/economically disadvantaged, Single parents, Substance abusers.

Types of support for organizations:
GENERAL PURPOSE/OPERATING SUPPORT.

PROGRAM DEVELOPMENT/PROJECT SUPPORT: Conferences/seminars, Curriculum development, Exhibitions, Faculty/staff development, Film/video/ radio production, Mentoring programs, Public awareness, Publications, Seed money/start-up funds, Leadership programs.

RESEARCH.

Sample grants:

Center for Victims of Torture/MN/$7,500.

Friends of the Minneapolis Public Library/MN/$10,000.

Friends of the MN Sinfonia/MN/$5,000.

Midwest Art Conservation Center/MN/$2,500.

Ramsey County Historical Society/MN/$5,000.

Retreat, The/MN/$5,000.

Southside Family School/MN/$7,500.

Financial Information

Financial data for year ending: 12/31/2006
Foundation assets: $7,265,737
Grants paid: $382,910
Number of grants: 178
Largest/smallest: $20,000/$25
Matching gifts: $40,710

Application Information

Preferred form of initial contact: letter of inquiry, telephone inquiry.

Public information available by request: proposal guidelines, application form, annual report.

Accept common grant application: yes.

Proposal deadlines: December 1 and July 1.

Contribution decisions made by: board of directors/trustees.

Frequency of contributions decisions: semiannually.

Specific times board meets: March and October.

Typical time from application deadlines to notification: 4 months.

Staff/Trustees

Staff: Joan Schoepke, foundation administrator.

Directors/trustees: Susannah B. Dunlap; Harriet W. Fitts; William S. Fitts; Bronwyn A. E. Griffith; James H. Heron, president; Catherine L. Lamb, treasurer; Julia M. Lamb, secretary; Dana D. McCannel; Teri M. Motley; Amy C. Walker; Berta B. Walker; Colin M. Walker; Elaine B. Walker; Sally L. Walker, vice president; Alexa Griffith Winton.

Warren Foundation

U.S. Bank, N.A.
101 East Fifth Street
St Paul, MN 55101
County: Ramsey
Phone: (651) 466-8718
Contact: Nancy H. Frankenberry
Established: 12/01/1958
Funder type: Private foundation

Program Description

Funding priorities: Primarily to educational, cultural, youth and community support organizations located in Minnesota.

Program limitations/restrictions: No grants to individuals or organizations that require expenditure responsibility.

Geographic focus: Twin Cities Metropolitan Area, Minnesota statewide.

Areas of interest:

ARTS, CULTURE, HUMANITIES: Historical societies, Media/communications, Museums, Performing arts.

COMMUNITY IMPROVEMENT.

EDUCATION.

ENVIRONMENTAL QUALITY/PROTECTION/BEAUTIFICATION.

HEALTH - DISEASES/MEDICAL DISCIPLINES.

HUMAN SERVICES: Children/youth services, Family services, Multipurpose human service organizations, Personal social services, Services to specific groups, Victims services.

YOUTH DEVELOPMENT: Multipurpose youth centers/clubs, Scouting organizations, Youth development programs.

Intended beneficiaries: General public/unspecified.

Types of support for organizations:
GENERAL PURPOSE/OPERATING SUPPORT.

PROGRAM DEVELOPMENT/PROJECT SUPPORT.

Types of support for individuals: none.

Sample grants:

Archdiocesan AIDS Ministry Program/MN/general operating/$5,000.

Big Brothers/Big Sisters - MN (Minneapolis)/MN/general operating/$1,500.

Center for Victims of Torture/MN/general operating/$4,000.

Children's Chance Inc/MN/general operating/$1,500.

MN Literacy Council/MN/general operating/$2,000.

Ordway Music Theatre/MN/general operating/$2,000.

Parkinson Association of MN/MN/general operating/$5,000.

St Paul Chamber Orchestra/MN/general operating/$2,000.

Financial Information

Financial data for year ending: 12/31/2005
Foundation assets: $3,799,112
Grants paid: $196,000
Number of grants: 88
Largest/smallest: $7,000/$500

Application Information

Preferred form of initial contact: letter of inquiry.
Proposal deadlines: none.

Staff/Trustees

Directors/trustees: U.S. Bank Trust, N.A.; Theodore J. Collins; John E. King.

The Wasie Foundation

4999 France Avenue South
Suite 250
Minneapolis, MN 55410-1711
County: Hennepin
Phone: (612) 455-6880
Fax: (612) 455-6888
Contact: Jan Preble, director of programs
Established: 10/18/1966
Donor: Stanley L. and Marie F. Wasie
Funder type: Private foundation

Program Description

Program's purpose: The Wasie Foundation honors donor intent and provides grants to support the charitable interests of the Wasie family.

Funding priorities: The foundation provides grants in the following areas, which were of interest to the Wasie family: 1) Education of Polish students: to support scholarship programs at specific institutions for students of Polish ancestry; 2) Schizophrenia: to support organizations providing care and treatment of individuals diagnosed with schizophrenia, as well as education and research associated with the illness; 3) Arthritis: to support organizations providing care and treatment of children and adults with arthritis, as well as associated research; 4) Cancer: to support organizations providing care and treatment of people living with cancer; 5) Children's medical problems: to support research of childhood diseases, as well as to support organizations providing care and treatment of children with severe childhood medical conditions and physical disabilities, as well as to support research of childhood diseases.

Program limitations/restrictions: The Wasie Foundation does not typically fund public policy, advocacy, or public awareness programs.

Geographic focus: Twin Cities Metropolitan Area, Areas outside Minnesota.

Geographic limitations: Preference to organizations in Minneapolis/St Paul metropolitan area and South Florida (Broward, Palm Beach and Miami-Dade counties), with occasional exceptions.

Areas of interest:
EDUCATION: Graduate education/professional schools, Higher education.
HEALTH - DISEASES/MEDICAL DISCIPLINES: Birth defects/genetic disorders, Cancer, Specific named diseases, Arthritis, Schizophrenia, and childhood diseases.
HEALTH - GENERAL/REHABILITATIVE.
HEALTH - MENTAL HEALTH/CRISIS INTERVENTION: Mental health associations, Mental health disorders, Mental health treatment and services. Mental health funding is limited to programs helping people with schizophrenia/schizo-affective disorders.
HEALTH - RESEARCH: Birth defects and genetic diseases research, Specific named disease research. Limited research funding for arthritis, schizophrenia and disabling childhood diseases.
HUMAN SERVICES: Services to specific groups.
PHILANTHROPY/VOLUNTARISM: Philanthropy associations.

Intended beneficiaries: Adults, Aging/elderly/senior citizens, Blind/vision impaired, Children and youth (infants-19 years), Mentally/emotionally disabled, Physically disabled, Physically disabled children.

Types of support for organizations:
CAPITAL CAMPAIGNS: Building/renovation, Equipment.
GENERAL PURPOSE/OPERATING SUPPORT.
PROGRAM DEVELOPMENT/PROJECT SUPPORT: Conferences/seminars, Program materials, Participant support/ programs services.
RESEARCH.
STUDENT AID (GRANTS TO INSTITUTIONS): Scholarship funds.

Types of support for individuals: none.

Exclusions: Individuals, Non-501(c)(3), Political organizations.

Sample grants:

Children's Hospital - FL/FL/Children's Diagnostic & Treatment Center/$30,000.

College of St Scholastica - Duluth/MN/$54,793.

Confidence Learning Center Inc/MN/$39,700.

Cystic Fibrosis Foundation - MD (National)/MD/$100,000.

Gillette Children's Hospital Foundation/MN/$114,926.

Hospital - FL/FL/Holy Cross Hospital/$100,000.

Kids in Distress - FL/FL/$5,000.

Stanford University/CA/$25,000.

Financial Information

Financial data for year ending: 12/31/2005
Foundation assets: $47,912,476
Grants paid: $1,583,855
Number of grants: 35
Largest/smallest: $150,000/$5,000

Application Information

Preferred form of initial contact: telephone inquiry.

Public information available by request: proposal guidelines, inquire at foundation.

Proposal deadlines: Ongoing.

Preferred time for receiving proposals: varies; grant proposals may be submitted by invitation only, but inquiry calls are taken at all times and may lead to an invitation to submit a proposal.

Contribution decisions made by: board of directors/trustees.

Frequency of contributions decisions: 3-4 times per year.

Specific times board meets: Quarterly.

Typical time from application deadlines to notification: 90 days.

Staff/Trustees

Staff: Danille B. Levenson, director of operations; Jan Preble, director of programs; Gregg D. Sjoquist, president & CEO.

Directors/trustees: Andrew J. Leemhuis M.D., medical director; Laurie Sallarulo, secretary; David Sherman, director; Gregg D. Sjoquist, president & CEO; Martin H. Wojcik, treasurer.

Frederick O. Watson Foundation

3100 West Lake Street
Suite 420
Minneapolis, MN 55416-4599
County: Hennepin
Phone: (612) 920-4077
Fax: (612) 920-5438
Contact: Douglas F. Watson
Established: 09/15/1988
Funder type: Private foundation

Program Description

Program's purpose: General contributions to charitable, religious and educational institutions.

Geographic focus: Twin Cities Metropolitan Area, Areas outside Minnesota.

Areas of interest:
ARTS, CULTURE, HUMANITIES.
EDUCATION.
ENVIRONMENTAL QUALITY/ PROTECTION/BEAUTIFICATION.
HEALTH - DISEASES/MEDICAL DISCIPLINES.
HEALTH - GENERAL/ REHABILITATIVE.
HUMAN SERVICES.
YOUTH DEVELOPMENT.

Intended beneficiaries: General public/unspecified.

Types of support for organizations:
GENERAL PURPOSE/OPERATING SUPPORT.

Sample grants:

American Refugee Committee/MN/ general operating/$1,000.

Children's Home Society - MN/MN/ general operating/$2,000.

Headwaters Fund/MN/general operating/ $2,000.

Pilot City Neighborhood Services/MN/ general operating/$1,500.

Project for Pride in Living/MN/general operating/$2,000.

Second Harvest Food Bank - MN/MN/ general operating/$3,000.

Summit Academy OIC/MN/general operating/$5,000.

Youth & Farm Project/MN/general operating/$2,000.

Financial Information

Financial data for year ending: 12/31/2005
Foundation assets: $1,940,534
Grants paid: $581,500
Number of grants: 70
Largest/smallest: $140,000/$1,000

Application Information

Preferred form of initial contact: letter of inquiry, complete proposal.

Accept common grant application: yes.

Proposal deadlines: ongoing.

Staff/Trustees

Staff: Patti Clark, secretary; Douglas F. Watson, president.

Directors/trustees: Douglas F. Watson, president; Stephen M. Watson.

WCA Foundation

10249 Yellow Circle Drive
Suite 101
Minnetonka, MN 55343-9139
County: Hennepin
Phone: (952) 932-9032
Fax: (952) 932-9036
Contact: Karen Reamer, executive director
Paid Staff: Yes
Funder type: Private foundation

Program Description

Program's purpose: Agencies/programs that help women achieve or sustain their independence and general human service programs.

Funding priorities: General human service programs that help economically disadvantaged persons (battered women, scholarships, chemical dependency treatment, vocational training, day care, programs for immigrants, etc.).

Program limitations/restrictions: Two-thirds of grants are limited to programs that help women achieve or sustain their independence.

Geographic focus: Twin Cities Metropolitan Area, Minnesota statewide.

Geographic limitations: Emphasis on Twin Cities metropolitan area.

Areas of interest:

EDUCATION: Adult/continuing education/literacy, Higher education, Preschool/elementary, Secondary, Vocational/technical, Other.

EMPLOYMENT/JOBS: Employment procurement/job training, Vocational rehabilitation.

HEALTH - MENTAL HEALTH/CRISIS INTERVENTION: Addiction disorders, Alcohol/drug/substance, prevention and treatment, Counseling/support groups, Hotline/crisis intervention, Mental health treatment and services.

HOUSING/SHELTER: Homeless, temporary housing, Housing development/construction/management, Housing support services, Low-cost temporary housing.

HUMAN SERVICES: Family violence shelters and services.

YOUTH DEVELOPMENT: Youth development programs.

Intended beneficiaries: Female adults, General public/unspecified.

Types of support for organizations:
CAPITAL CAMPAIGNS.
EMERGENCY FUNDS.
GENERAL PURPOSE/OPERATING SUPPORT.
PROGRAM DEVELOPMENT/ PROJECT SUPPORT.
STUDENT AID (GRANTS TO INSTITUTIONS): Scholarship funds.

Types of support for individuals: none.

Sample grants:

AccessAbility Inc - MN/MN/$15,000.

Breaking Free, Inc (MN)/St Paul, MN/ $10,000.

The Bridge for Runaway Youth,/MN/ $15,000.

Community University Health Care Center/MN/$15,000.

Free to Be, Inc/MN/$15,000.

Groves Academy - St Louis Park/MN/$15,000.

La Escuelita/MN/$15,000.

Page Educational Foundation/MN/$5,000.

Financial Information

Financial data for year ending: 12/31/2006
Foundation assets: $15,939,300
Grants paid: $485,500
Number of grants: 42
Largest/smallest: $15,000/$5,000

Application Information

Preferred form of initial contact: telephone inquiry, request for guidelines.

Public information available by request: proposal guidelines, application form.

Proposal deadlines: May 15 and November 15.

Preferred time for receiving proposals: late April to early May for May 15 deadline; late October to early November for November 15 deadline.

Contribution decisions made by: board of directors/trustees.

Frequency of contributions decisions: monthly.

Specific times board meets: first Friday of each month.

Typical time from application deadlines to notification: 4-6 months.

Special application procedures: Explained in application.

Staff/Trustees

Staff: Karen Reamer, executive director; Kathy Wagner, administrative & accounting manager.

Directors/trustees: Dale Crawford, third vice president; Dorothy Flynn, president; Carol Freeburg, treasurer; Mary Galbraith, second vice president; Shirley Holt, secretary; Barbara Rose, first vice president.

J. A. Wedum Foundation

2615 University Avenue SE
Minneapolis, MN 55414
County: Hennepin
Phone: (612) 789-3363
Fax: (612) 789-4044
E-mail: kathleenhansen@wedum.org
Website: www.wedum.org
Established: 01/01/1959
Paid Staff: Yes
Funder type: Private foundation

Program Description

Program's purpose: Foundation's principal charitable activity relates to education: scholarships and grants to educational institutions benefiting many scholars. Small grants to social assistance and health agencies to further their programs. Small grants to organizations dealing with the preservation of the environment.

Funding priorities: Education has a high priority.

Geographic focus: Twin Cities Metropolitan Area, Greater Minnesota.

Areas of interest:

EDUCATION: Higher education, Secondary.

ENVIRONMENTAL QUALITY/PROTECTION/BEAUTIFICATION.

HEALTH - DISEASES/MEDICAL DISCIPLINES.

HEALTH - GENERAL/REHABILITATIVE.

HEALTH - MENTAL HEALTH/CRISIS INTERVENTION.

HOUSING/SHELTER.

HUMAN SERVICES.

YOUTH DEVELOPMENT.

Intended beneficiaries: General public/unspecified.

Types of support for organizations:

PROGRAM DEVELOPMENT/PROJECT SUPPORT.

STUDENT AID (GRANTS TO INSTITUTIONS): Scholarship funds.

Financial Information

Financial data for year ending: 12/31/2005
Foundation assets: $106,714,020
Grants paid: $494,278
Number of grants: 28
Largest/smallest: $150,000/$25

Application Information

Preferred form of initial contact: complete proposal, e-mail.

Public information available by request: application form, annual report, website.

Will view video: yes.

Preferred time for receiving proposals: 30 days prior to each bi-annual board meeting.

Contribution decisions made by: staff, board of directors/trustees.

Frequency of contributions decisions: semiannually.

Specific times board meets: Typically April and August.

Typical time from application deadlines to notification: 30 days.

Staff/Trustees

Staff: Kathleen Hansen, president; Dale Vesledahl, co-chairman/vice president.

Directors/trustees: Gary Slette, board member; Dayton Soby, board member; Frank Starke, board member/secretary; Dale Vesledahl, co-chairman/vice president; Mary Beth Wedum, co-chairman; John Wosepka, board member.

Mae and Sylvester Weiss Foundation

c/o Global Advisors
4025 Orleans Lane North
Plymouth, MN 55441
County: Hennepin
Phone: (763) 545-1700
Contact: Robert Hansen
Established: 01/01/1992
Funder type: Private foundation

Program Description

Funding priorities: Preference is given to individuals and organizations benefiting Christian education and developing skills of young people.

Geographic limitations: Central Minnesota.

Areas of interest:

EDUCATION.

YOUTH DEVELOPMENT.

Sample grants:

Courage Center - MN (Golden Valley)/MN/$1,000.

Crosier Fathers & Brothers/MN/$1,000.

Holy Trinity School - MN/MN/$1,000.

MN Medical Foundation/MN/$1,000.

MN Orchestral Association/MN/$5,000.

Salvation Army - MN (Brooklyn Center)/MN/$2,000.

We Can Ride Inc/MN/$3,000.

Financial Information

Financial data for year ending: 12/31/2005
Foundation assets: $574,696
Grants paid: $5,500
Number of grants: 8
Largest/smallest: $5,000/$1,000

Application Information

Preferred form of initial contact: letter of inquiry.

Proposal deadlines: applications are accepted at any time.

Typical time from application deadlines to notification: 2 months.

Staff/Trustees

Directors/trustees: Robert Hansen; Georgina M. Wehlage; Mae Weiss, president.

Wells Fargo Foundation Minnesota

90 South Seventh Street
N9305-192
Minneapolis, MN 55479
County: Hennepin
Phone: (612) 667-7860
Fax: (612) 667-8283
Website: www.wellsfargo.com/donations
Established: 11/29/1979
Funder type: Corporate foundation and corporate giving program

Program Description

Program's purpose: Improve the quality of life in the communities where Wells Fargo does business.

Funding priorities: Organizations that serve a specific neighborhood should contact their local Wells Fargo Bank for neighborhood specific funding priorities and guidelines. Organizations serving the entire Twin Cities or cities of Minneapolis or St Paul may address their request to the Metropolitan Contributions Committee (MCC), whose priorities are employment and economic development for low-income families and neighborhoods, affordable housing and economic education.

Program limitations/restrictions: No grants for sponsorships, travel, tours, conferences, individuals, tickets, benefits, religious purposes, political campaigns, marketing, and organizations that do not comply with the foundation's non-discrimination policy. Organization must also be 501(c)(3) nonprofit, government agency or school institution. In addition, organization must have a three-year minimum track record.

Geographic focus: Twin Cities Metropolitan Area, Greater Minnesota.

Geographic limitations: Wells Fargo communities.

Areas of interest:

ARTS, CULTURE, HUMANITIES: In the Twin Cities, major arts organizations are supported directly through grants made by the MCC; small- and mid-sized organizations are supported through a grant made by the MCC to the Minnesota State Arts Board.

COMMUNITY IMPROVEMENT: Community/neighborhood development/improvement, Economic development, Nonprofit management.

EDUCATION: Wells Fargo supports education through its Employee Matching Gift Program, which matches employee donations 1:1 up to $6,500.

EMPLOYMENT/JOBS: Employment procurement/job training, Vocational rehabilitation.

HOUSING/SHELTER: Housing development/construction/management.

HUMAN SERVICES: Multipurpose human service organizations, Personal social services, supported through Wells Fargo's contribution to the United Way. Occasionally, one-time support to United Way agencies for capital campaigns may be considered. Support to non-United Way agencies is focused on one-time non-recurring expenses for employment programs.

YOUTH DEVELOPMENT: School-to-career and work readiness programs.

Intended beneficiaries: Adults, African Americans/Blacks, Asian/Pacific Islanders, Blind/vision impaired, Crime/abuse victims, Deaf/hearing impaired, Disabled - general or unspecified disability, Ethnic/racial populations - general, Females - all ages or age unspecified, Hispanics/Latinos, Homeless, Immigrants/newcomers/refugees, Males - all ages or age unspecified, Mentally/ emotionally disabled, Migrant workers, Native American/American Indians, Physically disabled, Poor/economically disadvantaged.

Types of support for organizations:

CAPITAL CAMPAIGNS: Building/renovation, Computer systems/technology, Land acquisitions.

MANAGEMENT/TECHNICAL ASSISTANCE.

PROGRAM DEVELOPMENT/PROJECT SUPPORT: Curriculum development, Faculty/staff development, Publications. Wells Fargo prefers to fund one-time non-recurring expenses versus general operating or program support.

Types of support for individuals: none.

Matching grants: Employee contributions to elementary/secondary education and higher education are matched 1:1 up to $6,500 though the Wells Fargo Education Matching Gift Program.

Sample grants:

AccountAbility MN/MN/Client & Volunteer Education Materials for 2006 Tax Season/$15,000.

African American Mutual Assistance Network - MN/MN/2006 MLK Celebration Jan. 14-16/$500.

Bridging, Inc/MN/Technology System upgrade/$40,000.

City of Northfield - MN/MN/Veterans Memorial/$2,700.

Community & Cultural Center - MN (Detroit Lakes)/MN/Financial Support/$3,000.

Dollars for Scholars - MN/MN/Scholarships/$1,050.

Itasca Development Corporation/MN/Jobs 2020/$4,000.

MN Community Foundation/MN/Warroad Library Endowment Fund/$5,000.

Financial Information

Financial data for year ending: 12/31/2005
Foundation assets: $400,000,000
Grants paid: $10,100,000
Number of grants: 2500
Largest/smallest: $1,240,000/$25

Application Information

Preferred form of initial contact: letter of inquiry, telephone inquiry, request for guidelines, complete proposal.

Public information available by request: proposal guidelines, annual report, website. Proposals must include all items listed on the Wells Fargo proposal checklist. Contact staff for checklist or download from website.

Accept common grant application: yes.

Proposal deadlines: Deadlines for the Metropolitan Contributions Committee (MCC) are February 1, April 1, July 1 and October 1. Capital campaigns are reviewed once a year in September. Capital Campaign requests should be received no later than July 1.

Contribution decisions made by: employee committee.

Frequency of contributions decisions: quarterly.

Typical time from application deadlines to notification: 2-3 months.

Special application procedures: Organizations that serve a specific neighborhood should address applications to their local Wells Fargo Bank. Organizations serving the entire Twin Cities or cities of Minneapolis or St Paul should direct their request to Carolyn Roby, 90 South 7th St, N9305-192, Minneapolis, MN 55479.

Staff/Trustees

Staff: MayKao Fredericks, program associate; Rebecca Jacobson, foundation assistant; Carolyn H. Roby, vice president.

Directors/trustees: Jon Campbell; Marilyn Dahl; Susan Davis; Jerry Gray; Jim Heinz; Neel Johnson; Diane Lilly; John McQueen; Bill Meyer; Laurie Nordquist; Debra Paterson; Paula Rak; Paul Schmidt; Jim Steiner; Gerry Stenson; Tom Tosney.

Wenger Foundation

PO Box 142
Navarre, MN 55392
County: Hennepin
Phone: (952) 471-3667
Contact: Wendy Wenger, executive director
Established: 12/20/1982
Funder type: Private foundation

Program Description

Program's purpose: Grants made to qualified nonprofit, tax-exempt organizations in the arts, business education, and public information areas at the discretion of the board of directors.

Funding priorities: 1) Local; 2) Regional; 3) National.

Geographic focus: Twin Cities Metropolitan Area, Greater Minnesota, Minnesota statewide, National Areas.

Areas of interest:

ARTS, CULTURE, HUMANITIES: Arts services, Arts/cultural multipurpose, Historical societies, Humanities, Media/communications, Museums, Performing arts, Visual arts.

COMMUNITY IMPROVEMENT: Community/neighborhood development/improvement, Owatonna only.

EDUCATION: Higher education, Vocational/technical, Business.

Types of support for organizations:
GENERAL PURPOSE/OPERATING SUPPORT.
PROGRAM DEVELOPMENT/PROJECT SUPPORT.

Sample grants:

Acoustical Society of America/MN/TCAA Design Award/$3,000.

BestPrep/MN/general operating/$4,800.

Minneapolis Institute of Arts/MN/general operating/$3,000.

MN Alliance for Arts in Education/MN/general operating/$1,250.

MN Private College Fund/MN/general operating/$3,000.

Owatonna Arts Center/MN/general operating/$3,200.

Owatonna Hospice/MN/general operating/$25,000.

St Paul Chamber Orchestra/MN/general operating/$4,500.

Financial Information

Financial data for year ending: 12/31/2005
Foundation assets: $4,773,859
Grants paid: $218,809
Number of grants: 23
Largest/smallest: $25,000/$50

Application Information

Preferred form of initial contact: letter of inquiry, complete proposal, any form.

Proposal deadlines: none.

Contribution decisions made by: board of directors/trustees.

Frequency of contributions decisions: semiannually.

Staff/Trustees

Directors/trustees: Nancy Benjamin; Kari Hoffmeister; Kirsten Johnson; Jerry A. Wenger, president; Sonja Wenger; Wendy Wenger, executive director.

West Central Initiative

1000 Western Avenue
Fergus Falls, MN 56537
County: Otter Tail
Phone: (218) 739-2239
Alt. Phone: (800) 735-2239
Fax: (218) 739-5381
E-mail: grants@wcif.org
Website: www.wcif.org
Contact: Sandra King, vice president - operations
Established: 04/01/1986
Paid Staff: Yes
Funder type: Community/public foundation

Program Description

Program's purpose: Mission: West Central Initiative is a foundation that unites people and resources to improve the quality of life in west central Minnesota.

Funding priorities: Focus on priority areas within nine counties in west central Minnesota: quality employment, workforce development, community development, early childhood, cultural diversity, strengthening communities for families.

Program limitations/restrictions: No grants for arts, cultural activities, historic facilities, museums, religious activities, sports, recreation, endowments, lobbying or political activities.

Geographic focus: Becker, Clay, Douglas, Grant, Otter Tail, Stevens, Pope, Traverse and Wilkin counties in Minnesota only.

Areas of interest:

CIVIL RIGHTS: Intergroup relations/race relations.

COMMUNITY IMPROVEMENT: Community coalitions, Economic development, Nonprofit management.

EDUCATION: Vocational/technical, Education programs addressing skilled labor shortages, Early childhood.

EMPLOYMENT/JOBS: Employment procurement/job training, Incumbent worker retraining.

HUMAN SERVICES: Regional organizing on behalf of workers and their families.

PUBLIC AFFAIRS/SOCIETY BENEFIT: Citizen participation, Leadership development/awards programs (other than youth).

Intended beneficiaries: General public/unspecified.

Exclusions: Political organizations.

Sample grants:

Alexandria Technical College/MN/SBM Fiscal Year 2005/2006 Small Business Management Tuition Scholarships/ $10,000.

Chamber of Commerce - MN (Alexandria)/MN/Leadership Alexandria/ $2,000.

ISD Pelican Rapids #548/MN/Early Childhood Initiative/$25,000.

ISD Pine Point #25/MN/Hoops and Homework project/$20,000.

MN Technology Inc/MN/Alexandria Extrusion: Multi-Company CNC Lathe & Mill Training/$10,000.

MN Technology Inc/MN/AbbeyMoore Medical Inc: Medical Device Mfg. Training/$3,200.

Financial Information

Financial data for year ending: 06/30/2006
Foundation assets: $40,401,137
Grants paid: $1,108,869
Number of grants: 457
Largest/smallest: $25,000/$250
Typical grant amount: $5,000

Application Information

Preferred form of initial contact: telephone inquiry.

Public information available by request: proposal guidelines, application form, annual report, newsletter, website.

Accept common grant application: yes.

Accept common report form: yes.

Proposal deadlines: vary by type of grant and amount sought. See website for details.

Preferred time for receiving proposals: three-week lead time for grants of up to $5,000; six weeks for larger proposals.

Contribution decisions made by: CEO, staff, board of directors/trustees.

Frequency of contributions decisions: monthly, continuously for grants up to $5,000.

Typical time from application deadlines to notification: 2-6 weeks.

Special application procedures: potential applicants should discuss projects with foundation staff before submitting applications.

Staff/Trustees

Staff: Wes Binner, development consultant; Kim Embretson, vice president - development; Sheri Booms Holm, communications director; Wayne T. Hurley, transportation planning director; Nancy Jost, early childhood initiative coordinator; Sandra King, vice president - operations; Wendy Merrick, program coordinator; Nancy Straw, president; Roberto Tapiz, community development director; Randy Wanek, healthcare workforce project coordinator.

Directors/trustees: Jana Berndt; Larry Doss; Dianna Hatfield; Ron Kirscht; Ralph Lang, chair; Don Martodam; Jenny Nellis; Mike Paulson; Chere Rikimoto, secretary; Linda Roles; Nancy Straw, president; Paul Sukke; Dave Weaklend, treasurer; Sue Weber.

Mark and Muriel Wexler Foundation

8085 Wayzata Boulevard
Suite 100C
Minneapolis, MN 55426
County: Hennepin
Phone: (952) 591-0919
Contact: Muriel Wexler, president
Established: 12/30/1985
Funder type: Private foundation

Program Description

Geographic focus: Twin Cities Metropolitan Area, Areas outside Minnesota.

Intended beneficiaries: General public/unspecified.

Sample grants:

American Diabetes Association - MN (Minneapolis)/MN/$400.

Catholic Charities - MN (Minneapolis)/ MN/$1,500.

Crohns & Colitis Foundation of America Inc - MN/MN/$1,000.

Doctors Without Borders USA/PA/ $5,000.

Freedom from Hunger Foundation/CA/ $350.

Little Brothers - Friends of the Elderly - MN/MN/$200.

Second Harvest Food Bank - MN/MN/ $300.

Temple Israel/Minneapolis, MN/$27,957.

Financial Information

Financial data for year ending: 06/30/2005
Foundation assets: $3,165,925
Grants paid: $175,762
Number of grants: 108
Largest/smallest: $50,000/$100

Application Information

Preferred form of initial contact: letter of inquiry, complete proposal.

Proposal deadlines: none.

Staff/Trustees

Directors/trustees: David Wexler; Muriel Wexler, president; Steven Wexler.

Weyerhaeuser Family Foundation, Inc.

2000 Wells Fargo Place
30 East Seventh Street
St Paul, MN 55101
County: Ramsey
Phone: (651) 215-4408
Fax: (651) 228-0935
E-mail: gmr@fidcouns.com
Website: www.wfamilyfoundation.org
Contact: Kathleen McGoldrick, president
Established: 01/24/1950
Funder type: Private foundation

Program Description

Program's purpose: The Weyerhaeuser Family Foundation supports programs of national and international significance that promote the welfare of human and natural resources. These efforts will enhance the creativity, strengths and skills already possessed by those in need and reinforce the sustaining processes inherent in nature.

Funding priorities: The foundation currently has initiatives in the environment and in the area of children's needs. Those interested in guidelines for the Children's Initiative, which focuses on programs serving children from birth to age six, or the Sustainable Forests and Communities Initiative, are invited to visit the foundation's website.

Program limitations/restrictions: The foundation prefers proposals for new projects rather than continuing projects, unless previously funded by the foundation. Normally no grants for projects with local or regional emphasis (except under its Initiative programs), operating budgets, annual campaigns of any organization, capital projects. No grants to individuals, scholarships or fellowships; or to organizations located outside the continental United States.

Geographic focus: Minnesota statewide, Areas outside Minnesota, National Areas, International Areas.

Geographic limitations: No local or regional grants except under Initiative programs.

Areas of interest:
ENVIRONMENTAL QUALITY/PROTECTION/BEAUTIFICATION: Natural resources conservation/protection, Sustainable Forests and Communities Initiative.
HUMAN SERVICES: Children/youth services, Children's Initiative - serves needs of at-risk children aged 0-6.
INTERNATIONAL AFFAIRS: International development/relief, International peace/security.

Intended beneficiaries: General public/unspecified, Infants/babies (under age 5).

Types of support for organizations:
PROGRAM DEVELOPMENT/PROJECT SUPPORT: Seed money/start-up funds.

Types of support for individuals: none.

Exclusions: Capital & endowment campaigns, Individuals, Non-501(c)(3), Political organizations, Research, Scholarships/loans.

Sample grants:

Center for Victims of Torture/MN/address mental health needs of refugees from Sierra Leone/$25,000.

Crittenton Center/MN/Project Children First/$14,904.

Framing Our Community/MN/small-diameter timber business incubator/$25,000.

House of the Children/Los Angeles, CA/health and environmental education in the village of Huacaria, Peru/$31,700.

Northwest Natural Resources Institute - WA/WA/Non-Timber Forest Products Stewardship Market Label Program/$15,000.

Opportunity Fund for Developing Countries/Salt Lake City, UT/women's microcredit project in two Kenyan communities/$13,000.

Washburn Child Guidance Center/MN/pre-school day treatment program/$25,000.

Financial Information

Financial data for year ending: 12/31/2005
Foundation assets: $19,289,611
Grants paid: $665,175
Number of grants: 31
Largest/smallest: $30,000/$5,000
Typical grant amount: $15,000

Application Information

Preferred form of initial contact: letter of intent.

Public information available by request: proposal guidelines, application form, annual report, all of which are available on the foundation's website.

Proposal deadlines: Letters of intent accepted Jan. 1-April 1.

Contribution decisions made by: board of directors/trustees.

Frequency of contributions decisions: annually.

Specific times board meets: November.

Special application procedures: Will ask for full proposals after June meeting. Final decision made in the November meeting.

Staff/Trustees

Staff: Peter A. Konrad, program consultant; Gayle Roth, grants administrator.

Directors/trustees: Susan Bonsall; Melissa B. Davis; John B. Driscoll; Lisa M. Fremont; Lucie C. Greer; Peter E. Heymann, treasurer; Brenca C. Jewett; Lucy R. Jones; Nathaniel J. W. Maher; Jane W. McFee; Kathleen McGoldrick, president; Jay Neverud; Samuel J. Pascoe; Thomas F. Rasmussen; Amy W. Stried; Frederick W. Titcomb, vice president/secretary; Megan L. Titcomb; Robert Titcomb; Justin H. Weyerhaeuser.

The Charles A. Weyerhaeuser Memorial Foundation

2000 Wells Fargo Place
30 East Seventh Street
St Paul, MN 55101
County: Ramsey
Contact: Lucy R. Jones, president
Established: 03/01/1959
Funder type: Private foundation

Program Description

Program's purpose: General charitable purposes.

Sample grants:

MN Public Radio/MN/capital campaign opera underwriting/$135,400.

Nature Conservancy - MN/MN/Lake Alexander endowment/$50,000.

Planned Parenthood - MN/MN/$25,000.

Financial Information

Financial data for year ending: 02/28/2006
Foundation assets: $8,821,450
Grants paid: $366,400

Application Information

Preferred form of initial contact: complete proposal. Applications need not be submitted in any particular form.

Proposal deadlines: Proposals are considered throughout the year, and a letter advising of the decision of the directors will be sent to the applicant as promptly as possible.

Staff/Trustees

Directors/trustees: Elise R. Donohue; Lucy R. Jones, president; J.S. Micallef; Charles W. Rosenberry II; Robert J. Silvertsen.

Frederick and Margaret L. Weyerhaeuser Foundation

30 East Seventh Street
Suite 2000
St Paul, MN 55101-4930
County: Ramsey
Phone: (651) 215-4408
Fax: (651) 228-0776
E-mail: gmr@fidcouns.com
Website: www.fmwfoundation.org
Contact: Gayle Roth, grants administrator
Established: 07/01/1963
Funder type: Private foundation

Program Description

Program's purpose: The foundation is looking to change lives through innovative programs that affect today's adolescents. We are interested in creative programs aimed at adolescent education and healing.

Funding priorities: Adolescent mental health, youth conservation education, service learning, and innovative teaching techniques.

Program limitations/restrictions: No capital funding including equipment, general operating support, endowments, travel, individuals, fellowships, scholarship, internships, public schools, research, organizations local outside of the US.

Areas of interest:
EDUCATION: Innovative, nontraditional teaching techniques.
ENVIRONMENTAL QUALITY/PROTECTION/BEAUTIFICATION: Environmental education/outdoor survival, specifically for youth.
HEALTH - MENTAL HEALTH/CRISIS INTERVENTION: Adolescent depression.
PHILANTHROPY/VOLUNTARISM: Philanthropy - general, Voluntarism promotion, specifically for youth.
YOUTH DEVELOPMENT: Youth development programs.

Intended beneficiaries: Youth/adolescents (ages 14-19).

Types of support for individuals: none.

Exclusions: Capital & endowment campaigns, Individuals, Non-501(c)(3), Research, Scholarships/loans.

Sample grants:

Center for Theological Inquiry/Princeton, NJ/publication to prepare Christian students for a racially and diverse world/ $30,000.

Fire Island Wildlife Foundation/New York, NY/operating support/$1,000.

India Rural Evangelical Fellowship/Park Ridge, IL/support of pastors/$20,000.

International Committee of the Red Cross/New York, NY/operating support/ $10,000.

Multiple Myeloma Research Foundation/ New Canaan, CT/operating support/ $3,000.

Project READ - CA/Redwood City, CA/ student materials and computer laboratory materials/$2,000.

World Association of Children & Parents - WA/Seattle, WA/child assistance program/$2,500.

Yale University/New Haven, CT/Mica Creek Intellectual Laboratory for Teaching and Research/$20,000.

Financial Information

Financial data for year ending: 06/30/2005
Foundation assets: $15,419,592
Grants paid: $170,000
Number of grants: 49
Largest/smallest: $30,000/$1,000

Application Information

Preferred form of initial contact: letter of inquiry.

Public information available by request: proposal guidelines, application form, website.

Proposal deadlines: Letter of intent, September 1.

Contribution decisions made by: board of directors/trustees.

Frequency of contributions decisions: annually.

Typical time from application deadlines to notification: 2-3 months.

Staff/Trustees

Staff: Gayle Roth, grants administrator.

Directors/trustees: Carol Caruthers; Julia L. W. Heidmann; Richard T. Holm; Margaret King; Catherine W. Morley; Thomas F. Rasmussen; Amy W. Stried; Daniel J. Weyerhaeuser.

Whitney ARCEE Foundation

c/o Lowry Hill
90 South Seventh Street
Suite 5300
Minneapolis, MN 55402
County: Hennepin
Phone: (612) 343-6561
Contact: Thomas Wright
Established: 01/01/1994
Funder type: Private foundation

Program Description

Funding priorities: Education, social service, humanities and the arts.

Program limitations/restrictions: Generally will not support capital and operating grants.

Geographic focus: Minnesota statewide.

Geographic limitations: Minnesota organizations or individuals.

Areas of interest:
ARTS, CULTURE, HUMANITIES.
EDUCATION.
HUMAN SERVICES.

Intended beneficiaries: General public/unspecified.

Sample grants:

Abbott Northwestern Hospital Foundation/MN/$250,000.

ARC - MN (Greater Twin Cities)/MN/ $25,000.

Hamline University/MN/$100,000.

MN Medical Foundation/MN/gold classic fundraiser/$29,611.

University of St Thomas - MN/MN/ $50,000.

Financial Information

Financial data for year ending: 12/31/2006
Foundation assets: $9,652,241
Grants paid: $759,611
Number of grants: 12
Largest/smallest: $250,000/$5,000

Application Information

Preferred form of initial contact: request for guidelines.

Public information available by request: proposal guidelines.

Specific times board meets: April, August and November.

Staff/Trustees

Directors/trustees: Bradley Bakken; Constance L. Bakken; Jeffrey Bakken; Pamela C. Petersmeyer; Wendy K. Watson.

Whitney Foundation

730 Second Avenue South
Suite 425
Minneapolis, MN 55402-2462
County: Hennepin
Phone: (612) 904-2302
Fax: (612) 204-0912
Contact: Carol VanOrnum, grant administrator
Established: 01/29/1959
Funder type: Private foundation

Program Description

Program's purpose: To participate with the community to provide for the human needs of its citizens.

Funding priorities: Social services, chemical dependency, civic affairs, AIDS, education, arts and economic development in the Minneapolis/St Paul area.

Program limitations/restrictions: Does not fund conference or travel expenses, publications, video or film production, medical research, fundraising expenses or financing deficits. Does not fund 509(a)(2) organizations.

Geographic focus: Twin Cities Metropolitan Area.

Areas of interest:
ARTS, CULTURE, HUMANITIES.
EDUCATION.
EMPLOYMENT/JOBS.
HUMAN SERVICES.
PUBLIC AFFAIRS/SOCIETY BENEFIT.

Intended beneficiaries: Adults, Aging/elderly/senior citizens, Infants/babies (under age 5), People with HIV/AIDS, Youth/adolescents (ages 14-19).

Types of support for organizations:
GENERAL PURPOSE/OPERATING SUPPORT: Annual campaigns.

Types of support for individuals: none.

Sample grants:

Animal Humane Society - MN (Minneapolis)/MN/$750.

Breck School/MN/$2,000.

MacPhail Center for the Arts/MN/$500.

Opportunity Housing Investment/MN/$2,500.

Union Gospel Mission/MN/$1,000.

Wilderness Inquiry/Minneapolis, MN/$1,500.

WomenVenture/MN/$1,000.

Financial Information

Financial data for year ending: 12/31/2005
Foundation assets: $2,022,613
Grants paid: $546,768
Number of grants: 282
Largest/smallest: $30,000/$25

Application Information

Preferred form of initial contact: letter of inquiry, complete proposal with Minnesota Common Grant application.

Accept common grant application: yes.

Proposal deadlines: none.

Frequency of contributions decisions: semi annually.

Staff/Trustees

Staff: Carol VanOrnum, grant administrator.

Directors/trustees: Joseph Whitney; Pennell Whitney; Wheelock Whitney, president; Wheelock Whitney III.

Winona Community Foundation

Exchange Building
51 East Fourth Street
Suite 314
Winona, MN 55987-3509
County: Winona
Phone: (507) 454-6511
Fax: (507) 454-0441
E-mail: wincomf@hbci.com
Website: www.winonacommunity foundation.com
Contact: Lisa Fakler, president
Established: 01/26/1987
Funder type: Community/public foundation

Program Description

Program's purpose: To award grants for programs or projects that meet cultural, civic, educational, environmental, medical, social and other charitable needs within the Winona area.

Funding priorities: Grants to tax-exempt organizations that have demonstrated actual or potential operating success.

Geographic focus: Greater Minnesota, Greater Winona area.

Geographic limitations: From the General Fund, grant only to Greater Winona Area. From donor-advised funds, grant more broadly.

Areas of interest:
ANIMAL RELATED.
ARTS, CULTURE, HUMANITIES.
CIVIL RIGHTS.
COMMUNITY IMPROVEMENT.
EDUCATION.
EMPLOYMENT/JOBS.
ENVIRONMENTAL QUALITY/ PROTECTION/BEAUTIFICATION.
FOOD/NUTRITION/AGRICULTURE.
HEALTH - DISEASES/MEDICAL DISCIPLINES.
HEALTH - GENERAL/ REHABILITATIVE.
HEALTH - MENTAL HEALTH/CRISIS INTERVENTION.
HEALTH - RESEARCH.
HOUSING/SHELTER.
HUMAN SERVICES.
INTERNATIONAL AFFAIRS.
PHILANTHROPY/VOLUNTARISM.
PUBLIC AFFAIRS/SOCIETY BENEFIT.

PUBLIC PROTECTION - CRIME/COURTS/LEGAL SERVICES.
PUBLIC SAFETY/DISASTERS/RELIEF.
RECREATION.
RELIGION/SPIRITUAL DEVELOPMENT.
SCIENCE/TECHNOLOGY.
SOCIAL SCIENCES.
YOUTH DEVELOPMENT.

Intended beneficiaries: General public/unspecified.

Types of support for organizations:
CAPITAL CAMPAIGNS.
EMERGENCY FUNDS.
GENERAL PURPOSE/OPERATING SUPPORT.
MANAGEMENT/TECHNICAL ASSISTANCE.
PROGRAM DEVELOPMENT/PROJECT SUPPORT: Conferences/seminars, Curriculum development, Exhibitions, Faculty/staff development, Film/video/ radio production, Fundraising, Mentoring programs, Performance/production costs, Professorships, Program evaluation, Public awareness, Public policy research/analysis, Publications, Seed money/start-up funds, Other.
PROGRAM-RELATED INVESTMENTS.
RESEARCH.
STUDENT AID (GRANTS TO INSTITUTIONS): Fellowships, Internships, Scholarship funds.

Types of support for individuals: none.

Sample grants:

American Red Cross - MN (Winona)/MN/Altura action team/$2,115.

ISD Winona #861/MN/Jefferson playground/$500.

Project FINE/MN/$10,000.

St Mary's University - MN/MN/Music Access for All/$1,000.

Volunteer Services - MN (Winona)/MN/Food Shelf Renovation/$10,000.

Winona State University/MN/Garvin Heights Park/$10,000.

Women's Resource Center of Winona/MN/Beyond Tough Guise/ $10,000.

Financial Information

Financial data for year ending: 12/31/2005
Foundation assets: $8,592,699
Grants paid: $2,555,061
Number of grants: 31
Largest/smallest: $69,650/$1,067

Application Information

Preferred form of initial contact: letter of inquiry, request for guidelines.

Public information available by request: proposal guidelines, application form, annual report.

Accept common grant application: yes.

Proposal deadlines: See website.

Contribution decisions made by: board of directors/trustees.

Specific times board meets: monthly, fourth Tuesday.

Typical time from application deadlines to notification: 6 weeks.

Staff/Trustees

Staff: Lisa Fakler, president; Deb Leaf, executive assistant; JC Pfeiffer, director of finance.

Directors/trustees: Mike Allen; Bob Bartz; Mike Bernatz; Steve Blue; Jan Brosnahan; Tim Burchill; Sandra Burke; Laura Eddy; Gary Hayes; Donna Helble; Gabe Manrique; Leone Mauszycki; Rod Nelson, chairman; Judy Shepard; Todd Thompson.

Winona Foundation

801 Second Avenue
Suite 1300
Seattle, WA 98104
Phone: (206) 464-5093
Fax: (206) 464-5250
E-mail: berger.m@lairdnorton.com
Contact: Margaret Berger, administrative assistant
Established: 08/23/1982
Funder type: Private foundation

Program Description

Program's purpose: Contributes to the cultural, historical and educational heritage of Winona, Minnesota.

Funding priorities: Arts, culture, humanities, community improvements, historical societies.

Program limitations/restrictions: Grants must be made to 501(c)(3) organizations. No grants for religious or political organizations, individuals or research.

Geographic focus: Within the Winona, MN, area only.

Areas of interest:
ARTS, CULTURE, HUMANITIES: Arts services, Arts/cultural multipurpose, Historical societies, Humanities, Media/communications, Museums, Performing arts, Visual arts, Other.
COMMUNITY IMPROVEMENT: Community service clubs, Community/neighborhood development/improvement.
EDUCATION: Libraries/library science.
ENVIRONMENTAL QUALITY/PROTECTION/BEAUTIFICATION: Botanical/horticultural/landscape.

Intended beneficiaries: General public/unspecified.

Types of support for organizations:
CAPITAL CAMPAIGNS: Building/renovation, Collections acquisitions, Equipment.
PROGRAM DEVELOPMENT/PROJECT SUPPORT: Exhibitions, Film/video/radio production, Performance/production costs, Publications.

Sample grants:

Historical Society - Winona County/MN/republish book/$6,000.

Pickwick Mill/Winona, MN/renovation and berm construction/$8,000.

Polish Cultural Institute Museum/MN/kitchenette and ethnic study center annex/$3,000.

Public Library - MN (Winona)/MN/old settlers photo collection/$4,300.

Theatre du Mississippi - MN/MN/new play/$2,000.

Winona Arts Center/MN/building repairs/$4,000.

Winona Dakota Unity Alliance/MN/The Dakota Gathering/$5,000.

Winona State University Foundation/MN/renovation of Garvin Heights overlook/$3,000.

Financial Information

Financial data for year ending: 12/31/2005
Foundation assets: $852,669
Grants paid: $29,700
Number of grants: 7
Largest/smallest: $5,900/$3,000

Application Information

Preferred form of initial contact: letter of inquiry, request for guidelines, e-mail.

Public information available by request: proposal guidelines, application form.

Proposal deadlines: February 15.

Contribution decisions made by: board of directors/trustees.

Frequency of contributions decisions: annually.

Specific times board meets: mid-April.

Typical time from application deadlines to notification: 2 months.

Staff/Trustees

Directors/trustees: Tamsin Clapp; Adam Kuhlmann; Joan Lompart, president/chair; Edith Roth; April Ueland; Todd Vorhies, vice president/treasurer; Erika Walsh.

Women's Foundation of Minnesota

155 Fifth Avenue South
Suite 500
Minneapolis, MN 55401
County: Hennepin
Phone: (612) 337-5010
Fax: (612) 337-0404
E-mail: contactus@wfmn.org
Website: www.wfmn.org
Established: 01/01/1983
Paid Staff: Yes
Funder type: Community/public foundation

Program Description

Program's purpose: The Women's Foundation of Minnesota champions economic, political and social equality for women and girls through fundraising, grantmaking, research and public advocacy. WFM makes grants to 501(c)(3) organizations or informal groups operating for charitable purposes.

Funding priorities: WFM operates two competitive grantmaking programs to build gender equality: 1) the Social Change Fund; and 2) girlsBEST. For a complete set of guidelines and grant due dates, please visit www.wfmn.org.

Program limitations/restrictions: Women's Foundation of Minnesota does not fund individuals, capital or endowment campaigns political campaigns or programs promoting religious activities.

Geographic focus: Twin Cities Metropolitan Area, Greater Minnesota, Minnesota statewide.

Geographic limitations: Women's Foundation of Minnesota will not fund programs outside Minnesota.

Intended beneficiaries: Ethnic/racial minorities - other specified group(s), Females - all ages or age unspecified, Gay/lesbian/bisexual/transgender, Immigrants/newcomers/refugees, Poor/economically disadvantaged.

Types of support for organizations:
GENERAL PURPOSE/OPERATING SUPPORT.
PROGRAM DEVELOPMENT/PROJECT SUPPORT.
RESEARCH.

Exclusions: Capital & endowment campaigns, Individuals, Religious organizations, Scholarships/loans.

Sample grants:

Aishah Center for Women/MN/To empower immigrant and refugee women by developing models to achieve collective economic power through the integration of Western business practices/$15,000.

Breaking Free, Inc (MN)/St Paul, MN/To help bring African American women and girls out of prostitution and to reframe the issue of prostitution as an act of violence against women/$15,000.

Midwest Health Center for Women/MN/For public policy advocacy to drive legislative initiatives to protect and promote women's health and reproductive freedoms at all levels of state government/ $15,000.

Mujeres Unidas of the Red River Valley/MN/To end race, class and gender bias against Latina women and girls through the organization's Circles program/$12,000.

Pangea World Theater Company/Minneapolis, MN/For its "Journey to Safety" theater program that uses the state to artistically and emotionally explore the obstacles battered immigrant women and women of color encounter when seeking help from government agencies and their communities/$14,000.

Tri-College NEW Leadership Development Institute/MN/To engage women of all ages in developing leadership skills in community organizing and running for office/$7,000.

Woodland Hills/MN/For development of a national model for a gender-based treatment program for girls who struggle with chemical dependency, grief counseling, mental health, and eating disorders/$10,000.

YWCA - MN (Minneapolis)/MN/For the Leadership Registry Project to provide women and people of color with opportunities to have a voice on the boards of nonprofit organizations within their communities/$12,000.

Financial Information

Financial data for year ending: 03/31/2007
Foundation assets: $15,770,203
Grants paid: $910,383
Number of grants: 115
Largest/smallest: $50,000/$250

Application Information

Preferred form of initial contact: telephone inquiry, request for guidelines, e-mail.

Public information available by request: proposal guidelines, application form, annual report, newsletter, website.

Proposal deadlines: Social Change Fund deadline: July 2. Check website for latest deadlines.

Frequency of contributions decisions: annually.

Typical time from application deadlines to notification: 4 months.

Staff/Trustees

Staff: Heidi Braun, receptionist and bookkeeper; Erin Ceynar, assistant development director; Charlotte Flowers, program officer; Sheila Gothmann, finance and operations director; Mary Beth Hanson, communications director; Amy Cram Helwich, director of development; Carol McGee Johnson, vice president of community philanthropy and programs; Prisca Lupambo, campaign coordinator; Sida Ly-Xiong, associate director of research and evaluation; April Oertwig, executive assistant; Lee Roper-Batker, president/CEO; Romaine Scharlemann, senior gift planner; Shunu Shrestha, development fellow; Dorothy Skobba, development associate.

Directors/trustees: Grayce Belvedere Young; Kim Borton; Sheba Coffey; Gloria Contreras Edin; Barbara Forster; Joanne Green; Nancy Gruver; Kao Ly Ilean Her, secretary; Saanii Hernandez-Mohr; Joan Higinbotham; Qamar Ibrahim; Sharon James Wade; Jan Malcolm, vice chair; Tara Mason; Catherine McBride; Teresa Richardson; Nancy Slaughter; Valerie Spencer; Terry Williams, chair; Mary Wong, treasurer.

Xcel Energy Foundation/ Corporate Citizenship

414 Nicollet Mall
Minneapolis, MN 55401
County: Hennepin
Phone: (612) 215-5304
Fax: (612) 215-4522
Website: www.xcelenergy.com/foundation
Paid Staff: Yes
Funder type: Corporate foundation

Program Description

Program's purpose: We know our company's success is directly related to the vitality of the communities we serve. Our goal is to use our collective knowledge, resources and skills to meet the needs of our communities and ensure that the service area of Xcel Energy is a highly desirable place for all citizens to live, work or own a business.

Funding priorities: We are interested in projects that empower youth, families, neighborhoods and communities to maximize skills and resources for addressing commonly held challenges and that continue building on current capabilities. Areas include education, arts and culture, environment and community development.

Program limitations/restrictions: Applicants must be nonprofit, tax-exempt 501(c)(3) organizations that are involved in enhancing the quality of life for citizens within Xcel Energy's service area.

Geographic focus: Twin Cities Metropolitan Area, Greater Minnesota, within the Xcel Energy service area. Service area includes North Dakota, South Dakota, Minnesota, Wisconsin, Michigan, Colorado, New Mexico, and Texas.

Areas of interest:
ARTS, CULTURE, HUMANITIES.
COMMUNITY IMPROVEMENT.
EDUCATION.
ENVIRONMENTAL QUALITY/ PROTECTION/BEAUTIFICATION.

Intended beneficiaries: General public/unspecified.

Types of support for individuals: none.

Matching grants: any nonprofit organization, employee matching, higher education. Higher Education: $25 or more matched up to $2,000. Nonprofit: $25 or more matched up to $500. Dollars for Doing: dollar donations for each employee volunteer hour, up to 100 hours or $500. Each program limit is per employee, per year.

Dollars for Doers: yes.

Exclusions: Capital & endowment campaigns, Individuals, Non-501(c)(3), Political organizations, Religious organizations, Scholarships/loans, Pledges, In-kind gifts, Financial aid, Sports and athletic programs.

Sample grants:

Alliance for Sustainability - MN/MN/To support volunteers in 20 Minneapolis neighborhoods/$10,000.

Boys & Girls Club - MN (St Cloud)/MN/ Support of Project Learn an after-school and summer educational enrichment initiative/$10,000.

Bridging, Inc/MN/Provide household items to individuals in need who are identified by social services agencies/ $7,500.

Chrysalis, A Center for Women - MN/ MN/$15,000.

Eco Education/St Paul, MN/Program to train teachers in the areas of environmental sciences and energy related issues/ $10,000.

Friends of the MN Sinfonia/MN/To support Free to the public, easily accessible, summer/holiday family concerts/$8,000.

Guthrie Theater/Minneapolis, MN/Support for Access programs/ $15,000.

MN Private College Fund/MN/Student Scholarships in the areas of science, technology, engineering and mathematics/ $80,000.

Financial Information

Financial data for year ending: 12/31/2006
Foundation assets: $1,784,572
Grants paid: $3,917,050
Number of grants: 551
Largest/smallest: $125,000/$1,500
In-kind gifts: $293,923
Matching gifts: $482,938

Application Information

Preferred form of initial contact: online letter of intent.

Public information available by request: proposal guidelines, website, online application.

Proposal deadlines: letter of inquiry deadlines: Environment, February 7 and August 1, 2007; Education, February 7, 2007; Community Development, May 2, 2007; Arts and Culture, August 1, 2007. Dates change from year to year; check website for current dates.

Contribution decisions made by: staff, employee committee, board of directors/trustees.

Frequency of contributions decisions: quarterly.

Typical time from application deadlines to notification: 3 weeks after deadline.

Staff/Trustees

Staff: Jim Garness, senior foundation representative, Minnesota; John Pacheco, director, Xcel Energy Foundation; Terry Price, senior foundation representative, Texas; Jim Rhodes, grant manager, Colorado.

Youthworks! Foundation, Inc.

3530 East 28th Street
Minneapolis, MN 55406-1765
County: Hennepin
Phone: (612) 729-5444
Fax: (612) 729-4113
E-mail: info@youthworksfoundation.org
Website: www.youthworksfoundation.org
Contact: Mark Wilkening, COO
Established: 09/30/2000
Funder type: Supporting organization

Program Description

Program's purpose: To support enterprising Christian ministry in communities that are served by Youthworks!, Inc.

Geographic focus: Communities served by Youthworks!, Inc.

Areas of interest:
COMMUNITY IMPROVEMENT: Community/neighborhood development/improvement, Economic development.
HUMAN SERVICES.
RELIGION/SPIRITUAL DEVELOPMENT: Specific denomination: Christian.
YOUTH DEVELOPMENT.

Intended beneficiaries: Children and youth (infants-19 years), Poor/economically disadvantaged.

Types of support for organizations:
PROGRAM DEVELOPMENT/PROJECT SUPPORT: Seed money/start-up funds.
PROGRAM-RELATED INVESTMENTS.

Sample grants:

GreaterWorks/MN/start-up funds/$75,000.

SportsLife Camps/MN/start-up funds/$120,000.

Two Rivers Community Development Center/IL/start-up funds/$75,000.

Urban Homeworks/Minneapolis, MN/program related investments/$100,000.

Youth Center - PA/PA/Schooner Youth Center/building & renovation/$100,000.

Youth Enterprise Fund/Minneapolis, MN/building renovation/$25,000.

Financial Information

Financial data for year ending: 09/30/2006
Foundation assets: $6,921,867
Grants paid: $1,171,355
Number of grants: 13
Largest/smallest: $169,428/$4,127

Application Information

Preferred form of initial contact: letter of inquiry.

Public information available by request: proposal guidelines, application form, website.

Proposal deadlines: none.

Contribution decisions made by: board of directors/trustees.

Frequency of contributions decisions: monthly.

Typical time from application deadlines to notification: 3-4 months.

Staff/Trustees

Staff: Jody Richards, administrative associate; Mark Wilkening, COO.

Directors/trustees: Ted Bailey; Paul Bertelson, president; Ed Lounsberry; John Potts; Jody Warden.

A. H. Zeppa Family Foundation

394 South Lake Avenue
Suite 303
Duluth, MN 55802
County: St Louis
Phone: (218) 726-5430
Fax: (218) 726-5431
E-mail: ahzeppa@calltel.com
Website: www.zeppa.org
Contact: Keir R. Johnson, executive director
Funder type: Private foundation

Program Description

Program's purpose: The foundation was created to support the advancement of progressive principles in environmental protection and human affairs; support the utilization of sustainable approaches to alleviate or end hunger and poverty globally; support performing and fine arts organizations on a local and regional basis; and support the creation of educational opportunities in the arts and social sciences.

Geographic focus: Greater Minnesota, National Areas, International Areas, Duluth area.

Areas of interest:
ARTS, CULTURE, HUMANITIES.
EDUCATION: In the arts and social sciences.
ENVIRONMENTAL QUALITY/PROTECTION/BEAUTIFICATION.
INTERNATIONAL AFFAIRS: International development/relief.

Financial Information

Financial data for year ending: 11/30/2005
Foundation assets: $954,332
Grants paid: $40,000

Application Information

Preferred form of initial contact: No unsolicited grant applications are being accepted at this time.

Public information available by request: application form.

Proposal deadlines: none.

Staff/Trustees

Staff: Keir R. Johnson, executive director.

Directors/trustees: Alan H. Zeppa.

Abbreviated Listings

Small Foundations/Foundations Not Accepting Unsolicited Proposals

The following foundations either do not accept unsolicited proposals or they are small (assets of less than $500,000 and/or annual grants of less than $25,000).

10-25 Tomorrow Foundation
Wayzata, MN 55391-2399
Assets: $351,635
Grants: $15,590
Fiscal Year End: 12/31/2005
EIN: 41-1894487

4481 Club, Inc.
Cannon Falls, MN 55009
Assets: $65,475
Grants: $1,789
Fiscal Year End: 12/31/2005
EIN: 41-1438372

A Better Place Inc
Minneapolis, MN 55408
Assets: $15,055,520
Grants: $694,500
Fiscal Year End: 12/31/2005
EIN: 41-1955000

The Aba Family Foundation
St Paul, MN 55116-2412
Assets: $18,721
Grants: $201
Fiscal Year End: 12/31/2005
EIN: 41-1991833

Adams Family Foundation
Fergus Falls, MN 56537-2614
Assets: $105,532
Grants: $4,500
Fiscal Year End: 12/31/2005
EIN: 41-1974483

Robert M. Adams Foundation
White Bear Lake, MN 55110-1334
Assets: $458,151
Grants: $2,200
Fiscal Year End: 12/31/2005
EIN: 41-1874410

The Adducci Family Foundation
Woodbury, MN 55125-5025
Assets: $277,719
Grants: $10,000
Fiscal Year End: 12/31/2005
EIN: 41-1418303

Adela Rindal Foundation
Mankato, MN 56001
Assets: $194,046
Grants: $7,451
Fiscal Year End: 9/30/2005
EIN: 41-1990332

Affinity Plus Federal Credit Union Foundation
St Paul, MN 55107
Assets: $153,647
Grants: $33,979
Fiscal Year End: 12/31/2005
EIN: 41-1974262

Agape Foundation
Maple Grove, MN 55311
Assets: $103,143
Grants: $6,000
Fiscal Year End: 12/31/2005
EIN: 41-1954468

Agarwala Foundation
New Brighton, MN 55112-3148
Assets: $87,400
Grants: $4,451
Fiscal Year End: 12/31/2005
EIN: 41-1896931

Leo Agranoff Perpetual Charitable Trust
St Paul, MN 55164-0713
Assets: $202,051
Grants: $6,845
Fiscal Year End: 12/31/2005
EIN: 41-6285959

Albert Lea-Freeborn County Chamber Foundation
Albert Lea, MN 56007-2961
Assets: $246,793
Grants: $2,528
Fiscal Year End: 9/30/2005
EIN: 41-1651705

Albright Foundation
Minnetonka, MN 55305
Assets: $581,474
Grants: $3,750
Fiscal Year End: 12/31/2005
EIN: 20-3911328

Alexandra Foundation
St Paul, MN 55101
Assets: $1,069,751
Grants: $47,425
Fiscal Year End: 12/31/2005
EIN: 41-6022837

Alkire Family Foundation
St Paul, MN 55164-0713
Assets: $1,699,602
Grants: $79,100
Fiscal Year End: 12/31/2005
EIN: 41-1762448

All for the Earth Foundation
Eagan, MN 55122-3141
Assets: $501,900
Grants: $59,000
Fiscal Year End: 12/31/2005
EIN: 41-1958381

Alliss Educational Foundation
Minneapolis, MN 55402
Assets: $104,489,840
Grants: $4,960,000
Fiscal Year End: 12/31/2005
EIN: 41-6011054

Alton Foundation
St Cloud, MN 56302-0848
Assets: $412,175
Grants: $46,550
Fiscal Year End: 12/31/2005
EIN: 41-1917226

Anchor Bank Family Foundation
Wayzata, MN 55391
Assets: $458,884
Grants: $10,000
Fiscal Year End: 12/31/2005
EIN: 75-3175735

Andersen Family Foundation
Excelsior, MN 55331-8211
Assets: $942,993
Grants: $55,600
Fiscal Year End: 12/31/2005
EIN: 20-2898462

Edward L. Anderson Charitable Trust
St Paul, MN 55164-0713
Assets: $457,098
Grants: $22,000
Fiscal Year End: 12/31/2005
EIN: 41-6479924

Andreas Foundation
Mankato, MN 56002-3584
Assets: $70,193,104
Grants: $2,256,996
Fiscal Year End: 11/30/2005
EIN: 41-6017057

L. and N. Andreas Foundation
Mankato, MN 56002-3584
Assets: $1,479,861
Grants: $3,010,000
Fiscal Year End: 12/31/2005
EIN: 36-3382956

William and Betty Andres Foundation
Minneapolis, MN 55402
Assets: $1,943,764
Grants: $245,770
Fiscal Year End: 12/31/2005
EIN: 41-1833413

The Ankeny Foundation
Minneapolis, MN 55402
Assets: $2,000,000
Grants: $350,000
Fiscal Year End: 3/31/2006
EIN: 41-6024188

Annexstad Family Foundation
Shorewood, MN 55331
Assets: $2,267,312
Grants: $145,650
Fiscal Year End: 12/31/2005
EIN: 41-1975043

Arden Foundation
Shoreview, MN 55126
Assets: $2,366
Fiscal Year End: 12/31/2005
EIN: 41-1773545

Argall/Hibbs Foundation
Prior Lake, MN 55372
Assets: $611,900
Grants: $30,750
Fiscal Year End: 12/31/2005
EIN: 41-1875159

ARK Foundation
St Paul, MN 55113
Assets: $412,059
Grants: $17,000
Fiscal Year End: 12/31/2005
EIN: 36-3487112

Arts and Humanities Foundation
Minnetonka, MN 55305
Assets: $474,174
Grants: $49,704
Fiscal Year End: 12/31/2005
EIN: 41-1881654

Ashmore Family Foundation
Ulen, MN 56585
Assets: $1,308,887
Fiscal Year End: 12/31/2005
EIN: 90-6036865

The Aslan Foundation
Chanhassen, MN 55317-9509
Assets: $61,502
Grants: $194,650
Fiscal Year End: 12/31/2005
EIN: 41-1907847

Astleford Foundation
Minneapolis, MN 55406-1864
Assets: $760,868
Grants: $41,913
Fiscal Year End: 12/31/2005
EIN: 41-1893317

The ATK (Alliant Techsystems) Foundation
Edina, MN 55436-1097
Assets: $237,640
Grants: $1,325,819
Fiscal Year End: 3/31/2006
EIN: 41-1683475

Avocet Foundation
St Louis Park, MN 55416-1533
Assets: $2,542,758
Grants: $79,500
Fiscal Year End: 12/31/2005
EIN: 41-1859473

B & H Way Foundation
Wayzata, MN 55391
Assets: $3,410,135
Grants: $153,200
Fiscal Year End: 12/31/2005
EIN: 41-1955405

Carl E. Bachman and Doris M. Bachman Family Foundation
Edina, MN 55435-1736
Assets: $23,060
Grants: $500
Fiscal Year End: 12/31/2005
EIN: 34-2004580

Bailey Nursery Foundation
Newport, MN 55055
Assets: $837,693
Grants: $392,663
Fiscal Year End: 12/31/2005
EIN: 41-1890034

Baillon Family Foundation, Incorporated
St Paul, MN 55101
Assets: $1,776,013
Grants: $90,977
Fiscal Year End: 1/31/2006
EIN: 36-3480741

Baillon Foundation, Incorporated
St Paul, MN 55101
Assets: $315,729
Grants: $14,735
Fiscal Year End: 1/31/2006
EIN: 36-3348159

Theresa A. and Vincent J. Baker Charitable Trust
St Paul, MN 55101
Assets: $55,912
Grants: $450,000
Fiscal Year End: 12/31/2005
EIN: 41-6543679

Jeffrey Bakken Foundation
Orono, MN 55356
Assets: $473,326
Grants: $148,850
Fiscal Year End: 12/31/2004
EIN: 41-1854501

Pamela Bakken Foundation
Minneapolis, MN 55402
Assets: $867,355
Grants: $99,400
Fiscal Year End: 12/31/2005
EIN: 41-1850599

Bank Street Foundation
Minneapolis, MN 55402
Assets: $2,107
Grants: $140,000
Fiscal Year End: 12/31/2005
EIN: 41-1858115

Bardwell Foundation
Edina, MN 55424-1554
Assets: $253,250
Grants: $12,325
Fiscal Year End: 12/31/2005
EIN: 41-1361483

Barrett Family Foundation
Woodbury, MN 55129
Assets: $518,317
Grants: $22,900
Fiscal Year End: 12/31/2005
EIN: 41-2008398

The Barry Foundation
Newport, MN 55055
Assets: $48,590,664
Grants: $1,208,525
Fiscal Year End: 12/31/2005
EIN: 41-1571983

The Baszucki Family Foundation
Carmel, CA 93923
Assets: $427,370
Grants: $5,200
Fiscal Year End: 12/31/2005
EIN: 41-1856664

Battenkill Foundation
Eden Prairie, MN 55347
Assets: $158,859
Grants: $1,600
Fiscal Year End: 12/31/2005
EIN: 36-4297877

Baxter Family Foundation
Plymouth, MN 55447
Assets: $30,272
Grants: $7,320
Fiscal Year End: 12/31/2005
EIN: 41-1893836

Edward R. Bazinet Foundation
Minneapolis, MN 55409
Assets: $7,615,651
Grants: $174,100
Fiscal Year End: 12/31/2005
EIN: 41-1737425

Javon and Vita Bea Family Foundation
Oronoco, MN 55960
Assets: $472,624
Fiscal Year End: 12/31/2005
EIN: 52-2388208

Beauty for Ashes Foundation, Inc.
Mahtomedi, MN 55115
Assets: $809,595
Grants: $42,800
Fiscal Year End: 12/31/2005
EIN: 41-1911820

Becker Furniture World Foundation
Becker, MN 55308
Assets: $120,573
Grants: $74,933
Fiscal Year End: 8/31/2005
EIN: 41-1887801

Beito Foundation
Thief River Falls, MN 56701
Assets: $2,322,600
Grants: $109,500
Fiscal Year End: 5/31/2006
EIN: 41-1911994

Belford Foundation
Minneapolis, MN 55402
Assets: $32,432
Fiscal Year End: 12/31/2005
EIN: 41-6030712

Charles P. and Mary E. Belgarde Foundation
St Louis Park, MN 55426-1400
Assets: $2,551,192
Grants: $126,313
Fiscal Year End: 6/30/2006
EIN: 06-1667326

David Winton Bell Foundation
St Louis Park, MN 55416-1533
Assets: $5,763,542
Grants: $241,000
Fiscal Year End: 12/31/2005
EIN: 41-6023104

Ginger and Martin Bell Foundation
St Louis Park, MN 55426
Assets: $20,271
Grants: $8,950
Fiscal Year End: 11/30/2005
EIN: 41-1389418

James Ford Bell Foundation
Minneapolis, MN 55405
Assets: $14,123,532
Grants: $653,063
Fiscal Year End: 12/31/2005
EIN: 41-6023099

Bemis Company Foundation
Neenah, WI 54957
Assets: $23,133
Grants: $2,434,518
Fiscal Year End: 12/31/2005
EIN: 41-6038616

Agnes M. Bendorf Charitable Trust
St Paul, MN 55164-0713
Assets: $753,010
Grants: $36,000
Fiscal Year End: 12/31/2005
EIN: 41-6490149

William J. Benfield Testamentary Trust
Buffalo, MN 55313
Assets: $92,022
Grants: $9,000
Fiscal Year End: 12/31/2005
EIN: 51-0155655

Bennett Family Foundation
White Bear Lake, MN 55110
Assets: $609,356
Grants: $25,000
Fiscal Year End: 1/31/2006
EIN: 41-1876704

Martha MacMillan Bennett Family Foundation
Minneapolis, MN 55440-5628
Assets: $3,082,069
Grants: $112,500
Fiscal Year End: 12/31/2005
EIN: 41-1924729

Donald E. Benson Foundation
Wayzata, MN 55391-3010
Assets: $19,521
Grants: $119,500
Fiscal Year End: 12/31/2005
EIN: 20-1148208

Berg Memorial Fund Trust
New Ulm, MN 556073
Assets: $678,365
Grants: $20,580
Fiscal Year End: 12/31/2005
EIN: 68-6242758

R.R.W. and Florence Berglund Family Foundation
St Paul, MN 55104
Assets: $8,887,951
Grants: $2,600
Fiscal Year End: 12/31/2005
EIN: 20-6126546

The Frank and Toby Berman Family Foundation
Edina, MN 55436
Assets: $475,446
Grants: $24,300
Fiscal Year End: 12/31/2005
EIN: 41-1857933

The Lyle and Janis Berman Family Foundation
Minneapolis, MN 55402
Assets: $49,665
Grants: $58,425
Fiscal Year End: 12/31/2005
EIN: 41-1809328

Better Way Foundation
Minnetonka, MN 55343
Assets: $29,365,027
Grants: $758,491
Fiscal Year End: 12/31/2005
EIN: 41-1795984

Claude P. Bias Charitable Foundation
Albert Lea, MN 56007
Assets: $186,391
Grants: $24,000
Fiscal Year End: 12/31/2005
EIN: 41-1807713

The Bieber Family Foundation
Plymouth, MN 55447-4718
Assets: $8,794,981
Grants: $431,040
Fiscal Year End: 12/31/2005
EIN: 41-1679484

Warren L. Bielke Charitable Foundation
Eden Prairie, MN 55347
Assets: $5,560
Grants: $21,420
Fiscal Year End: 12/31/2005
EIN: 41-1989341

Birmingham-Dorsey Charitable Trust
St Paul, MN 55101
Assets: $3,242,415
Grants: $170,000
Fiscal Year End: 12/31/2005
EIN: 41-6419645

Archie C. and Jane McDonald Black Charitable Trust
Golden Valley, MN 55422
Assets: $151,191
Grants: $3,508
Fiscal Year End: 12/31/2005
EIN: 41-6426986

Bloomington Community Foundation
Bloomington, MN 55438
Assets: $274,816
Grants: $15,116
Fiscal Year End: 6/30/2005
EIN: 41-1654627

Hilda Blowers Scholarship Foundation
Ogilvie, MN 56358
Assets: $1,983,093
Fiscal Year End: 12/31/2005
EIN: 41-1876372

The Bois Family Foundation
Edina, MN 55439
Assets: $442,840
Grants: $14,875
Fiscal Year End: 12/31/2005
EIN: 41-1628233

The Fred and Mary Boos Family Foundation
Wayzata, MN 55391
Assets: $310,656
Grants: $21,400
Fiscal Year End: 12/31/2005
EIN: 41-1875739

Marvin and Betty Borman Foundation
Minneapolis, MN 55402
Assets: $3,365,213
Grants: $137,992
Fiscal Year End: 7/31/2006
EIN: 41-1506784

Harlan Boss Foundation for the Arts
St Paul, MN 55101
Assets: $3,153,300
Grants: $161,000
Fiscal Year End: 12/31/2005
EIN: 41-1758708

John and Joyce Boss Family Foundation
Roseville, MN 55113
Assets: $115,787
Grants: $6,000
Fiscal Year End: 12/31/2005
EIN: 41-2002333

Will Bracken Family Foundation
Minneapolis, MN 55401
Assets: $1,099,763
Grants: $171,200
Fiscal Year End: 12/31/2005
EIN: 41-2022611

Branches Foundation
Sioux Falls, SD 57103
Assets: $10,548,626
Grants: $473,700
Fiscal Year End: 12/31/2005
EIN: 41-6463939

Douglass Brandenborg Family Foundation
Wayzata, MN 55391
Assets: $36,344,484
Grants: $905,000
Fiscal Year End: 12/31/2005
EIN: 41-1958170

The Braun Foundation
Golden Valley, MN 55422-4281
Assets: $1,067,784
Grants: $30,300
Fiscal Year End: 12/31/2005
EIN: 41-1731107

Breckenridge Charitable Trust
Richfield, MN 55423-2586
Assets: $534,020
Grants: $25,731
Fiscal Year End: 12/31/2005
EIN: 39-6770958

E.W. Brehm Family Foundation
Minneapolis, MN 55402
Assets: $676,614
Grants: $80,145
Fiscal Year End: 12/31/2005
EIN: 41-1924281

Kenneth W. Brimmer and Jaye Marisa Snyder Foundation
Minnetonka, MN 55305
Assets: $31,843
Grants: $2,478
Fiscal Year End: 12/31/2005
EIN: 41-6496639

Briggs and Morgan Foundation
St Paul, MN 55101
Assets: $58,121
Grants: $238,850
Fiscal Year End: 12/31/2005
EIN: 41-6009924

Broadwaters Foundation
Wayzata, MN 55391
Assets: $846,655
Grants: $40,800
Fiscal Year End: 11/30/2005
EIN: 41-1890876

Broms Family Foundation
Eden Prairie, MN 55344
Assets: $1,934,691
Grants: $140,220
Fiscal Year End: 12/31/2005
EIN: 23-7015484

Sheldon V. and Carroll C. Brooks Foundation, Inc.
Minneapolis, MN 55402
Assets: $537,877
Grants: $27,450
Fiscal Year End: 12/31/2005
EIN: 58-1763716

Brown Family Foundation, Inc.
Hopkins, MN 55343-9203
Assets: $1,410,608
Grants: $2,605
Fiscal Year End: 12/31/2005
EIN: 41-1979864

The Bumgarner Family Foundation
Richfield, MN 55423-2117
Assets: $1,437,906
Grants: $40,000
Fiscal Year End: 12/31/2005
EIN: 74-3035482

Robert and Dolores Buril Foundation
Bloomington, MN 55435
Assets: $3,297,584
Grants: $207,000
Fiscal Year End: 12/31/2005
EIN: 36-3499980

Burntside Charitable Foundation
Duluth, MN 55801-0488
Assets: $1,001,778
Grants: $137,278
Fiscal Year End: 12/31/2005
EIN: 41-1737393

Rodney and Barbara Burwell Family Foundation
Minneapolis, MN 55431
Assets: $594,447
Grants: $114,574
Fiscal Year End: 12/31/2005
EIN: 41-1939337

Buscher Foundation
Minnetonka, MN 55125
Assets: $1,049,371
Grants: $45,500
Fiscal Year End: 12/31/2005
EIN: 74-2443546

Charles and Norma Buxton Family Foundation
Lawrence, KS 66046
Assets: $39,818
Grants: $80,000
Fiscal Year End: 12/31/2005
EIN: 42-1624260

Cadahemark Foundation
Wayzata, MN 55391
Assets: $442,821
Grants: $25,500
Fiscal Year End: 12/31/2005
EIN: 41-1950636

Cadeau Foundation
Minneapolis, MN 55402
Assets: $1,218,046
Grants: $35,000
Fiscal Year End: 12/31/2005
EIN: 41-1957209

Campbell Foundation
Minneapolis, MN 55402
Assets: $9,389,697
Grants: $618,386
Fiscal Year End: 12/31/2005
EIN: 41-1988560

The Rachel Liba Cardoza Children's Foundation
Stillwater, MN 55082-5918
Assets: $524,775
Grants: $23,600
Fiscal Year End: 12/31/2005
EIN: 41-1740746

Cargill Family Fund
Minneapolis, MN 55440-9300
Assets: $119,389
Grants: $10,000
Fiscal Year End: 12/31/2005
EIN: 41-6059258

Caribou Coffee Charitable Foundation
Minneapolis, MN 55429
Assets: $60,703
Grants: $53,000
Fiscal Year End: 12/31/2005
EIN: 75-3047181

Caridad Corporation
Excelsior, MN 55331-3016
Assets: $2,917,683
Grants: $873,799
Fiscal Year End: 12/31/2005
EIN: 36-3505813

Carlock Family Foundation
Minneapolis, MN 55402
Assets: $97,198
Grants: $250
Fiscal Year End: 6/30/2005
EIN: 41-1796059

Barbara J. Carson Family Foundation
Minneapolis, MN 55402
Assets: $106,778
Grants: $4,950
Fiscal Year End: 12/31/2005
EIN: 41-6491135

Cecilian Society
St Paul, MN 55164-0713
Assets: $102,213
Grants: $3,450
Fiscal Year End: 12/31/2005
EIN: 41-1670365

Ceridian
Bloomington, MN 55425
Grants: $656,600
Fiscal Year End: 12/31/2006

Chadwick-Loher Foundation
Minneapolis, MN 55402-4523
Assets: $9,927,720
Grants: $468,344
Fiscal Year End: 12/31/2005
EIN: 52-2390635

Charisma Foundation
Minneapolis, MN 55431
Assets: $109,559
Fiscal Year End: 9/30/2005
EIN: 41-1908677

Chase Family Foundation
Prior Lake, MN 55372
Assets: $639,865
Grants: $31,875
Fiscal Year End: 12/31/2005
EIN: 37-1452120

Chelgren-Haviland Foundation
Minneapolis, MN 55435-4470
Assets: $76,326
Fiscal Year End: 12/31/2005
EIN: 41-6039237

Cherbec Advancement Foundation
St Paul, MN 55101-1394
Assets: $768,727
Grants: $646,725
Fiscal Year End: 12/31/2005
EIN: 41-1906601

B.H. Chesley Foundation
Dellwod, MN 55110
Assets: $230,294
Grants: $12,000
Fiscal Year End: 12/31/2005
EIN: 41-1674753

Chizek Family Foundation
Excelsior, MN 55331
Assets: $1,549,112
Grants: $45,000
Fiscal Year End: 12/31/2005
EIN: 41-1989004

Stanley and Marvel Chong Foundation
Bloomington, MN 55435
Assets: $451,934
Grants: $51,586
Fiscal Year End: 12/31/2005
EIN: 36-3411371

Chorzempa Family Foundation
Bloomington, MN 55437-2028
Assets: $2,171,855
Grants: $85,650
Fiscal Year End: 12/31/2005
EIN: 41-1875585

Christian Cornerstone Foundation
Eden Prairie, MN 55347-5009
Assets: $763
Fiscal Year End: 12/31/2005
EIN: 41-1907140

W. G. Christianson Foundation
St Louis Park, MN 55426
Assets: $10,357,917
Grants: $394,900
Fiscal Year End: 12/31/2005
EIN: 41-1743109

Cill Dara Foundation
Woodland, MN 55391
Assets: $263,187
Grants: $37,910
Fiscal Year End: 12/31/2005
EIN: 36-4225328

Michael V. and Ann C. Ciresi Foundation
Minneapolis, MN 55402
Assets: $188,823
Grants: $251,900
Fiscal Year End: 12/31/2005
EIN: 41-1926735

Citizens Independent Bank Community Foundation
St Louis Park, MN 55416
Assets: $7,627
Grants: $56,300
Fiscal Year End: 11/30/2005
EIN: 41-2022565

The Clara Foundation
Avon, MN 56310
Assets: $78,980
Grants: $66,950
Fiscal Year End: 12/31/2005
EIN: 20-1054729

F.B. Clements Foundation
Mankato, MN 56002
Assets: $35,928
Grants: $20,487
Fiscal Year End: 12/31/2005
EIN: 41-6081844

Cleveland Family Foundation
Sarona, WI 54870
Assets: $234,244
Grants: $15,600
Fiscal Year End: 12/31/2005
EIN: 42-1600506

Clouser Family Foundation
Orono, MN 55391
Assets: $205,731
Grants: $11,200
Fiscal Year End: 12/31/2005
EIN: 20-3742393

Cloverfields Foundation
Minneapolis, MN 55402-1498
Assets: $8,888,053
Grants: $1,656,000
Fiscal Year End: 12/31/2005
EIN: 20-1919362

The Richard and Diane Cohen Family Foundation
Minneapolis, MN 55426
Assets: $992,290
Grants: $82,308
Fiscal Year End: 12/31/2005
EIN: 41-1793403

Cokem Foundation
Eden Prairie, MN 55347-5252
Assets: $2,381
Fiscal Year End: 12/31/2005
EIN: 41-1954861

Cold Spring Community Fund
Cold Spring, MN 56320
Assets: $46,542
Grants: $1,000
Fiscal Year End: 12/31/2005
EIN: 41-1928125

Collins Family Foundation
Minneapolis, MN 55403-1148
Assets: $2,290,496
Grants: $272,625
Fiscal Year End: 12/31/2005
EIN: 41-1792606

Coon Rapids Lions Foundation
Coon Rapids, MN 55433
Assets: $201,835
Grants: $17,500
Fiscal Year End: 12/31/2005
EIN: 41-1766363

Cooper Family Foundation
Chanhassen, MN 55317
Assets: $275,649
Grants: $13,835
Fiscal Year End: 12/31/2005
EIN: 36-3616632

Patrice D. Cooper Foundation
Edina, MN 55439
Assets: $856,292
Grants: $17,600
Fiscal Year End: 12/31/2005
EIN: 41-1982224

The Coracle Foundation
Minneapolis, MN 55406-2348
Assets: $265,427
Grants: $39,452
Fiscal Year End: 12/31/2005
EIN: 41-1920761

Cornwall Foundation
Minneapolis, MN 55402
Assets: $443,529
Grants: $37,500
Fiscal Year End: 12/31/2005
EIN: 41-1956489

Coss Foundation
River Falls, WI 54022
Assets: $528
Grants: $5,000
Fiscal Year End: 12/31/2005
EIN: 41-1726797

Charles Piper Cost Foundation
San Francisco, CA 94131
Assets: $367,666
Grants: $17,800
Fiscal Year End: 12/31/2005
EIN: 41-1635764

The Covenant Foundation
Stillwater, MN 55082
Assets: $173,800
Grants: $123,000
Fiscal Year End: 11/30/2005
EIN: 36-3566128

Constance Mayeron Cowles and Charles Fuller Cowles Foundation
Minneapolis, MN 55415-1145
Assets: $371,624
Grants: $21,299
Fiscal Year End: 12/31/2005
EIN: 41-1913341

Cox Family Foundation
Minneapolis, MN 55454
Assets: $4,887,797
Grants: $385,212
Fiscal Year End: 12/31/2005
EIN: 41-1570849

Creative Foundation
Chanhassen, MN 55317-0326
Assets: $83,516
Grants: $6,500
Fiscal Year End: 12/31/2005
EIN: 23-7456793

The Culp Family Foundation
Tonka Bay, MN 55331-8576
Assets: $504,323
Grants: $102,410
Fiscal Year End: 12/31/2005
EIN: 13-4204919

Albert B. Cuppage Charitable Foundation
Albert Lea, MN 56007
Assets: $617,898
Grants: $19,500
Fiscal Year End: 12/31/2005
EIN: 41-1363927

The Paul and Patricia Curran Foundation
Edina, MN 55424-1129
Assets: $813,068
Grants: $29,885
Fiscal Year End: 12/31/2005
EIN: 41-1701319

Cutshall Foundation
Edina, MN 55439-1910
Assets: $205,114
Grants: $5,250
Fiscal Year End: 12/31/2005
EIN: 41-1939234

Stephen and Teresa Dalsin Family Foundation
Bloomington, MN 55431
Assets: $230,309
Grants: $12,100
Fiscal Year End: 12/31/2005
EIN: 41-1902153

Danbury Foundation
Prior Lake, MN 55372
Assets: $79,530
Grants: $1,500
Fiscal Year End: 12/31/2005
EIN: 47-0930671

Tom and Ruth Danielson Foundation
Atwater, MN 56209
Assets: $130,397
Grants: $5,232
Fiscal Year End: 12/31/2005
EIN: 36-3616638

Meredyth Anne Dasburg Foundation
Woodland, MN 55391
Assets: $444,776
Grants: $688,622
Fiscal Year End: 12/31/2005
EIN: 52-1608565

Data Recognition Corporation
Maple Grove, MN 55311
Grants: $105,275
Fiscal Year End: 12/31/2005

Dauwalter Family Foundation
Chaska, MN 55318
Assets: $582,193
Grants: $30,097
Fiscal Year End: 12/31/2005
EIN: 41-1988120

Edward Dayton Family Fund
Minneapolis, MN 55402-4523
Assets: $9,492,350
Grants: $673,713
Fiscal Year End: 12/31/2005
EIN: 52-2390636

Kathleen B. Dayton Foundation for Type 1 Diabetes
Minneapolis, MN 55402
Assets: $445,012
Grants: $4,500
Fiscal Year End: 12/31/2005
EIN: 41-6531012

Dellwood Foundation, Inc.
Vadnais Heights, MN 55110-4467
Assets: $3,996,426
Grants: $213,500
Fiscal Year End: 12/31/2005
EIN: 41-6019244

The DeLonais Foundation
Dellwood, MN 55110-1425
Assets: $2,009,946
Grants: $255,473
Fiscal Year End: 12/31/2005
EIN: 41-1646504

Vance C. DeMong Charitable Trust
Minneapolis, MN 55402
Assets: $217,714
Grants: $5,350
Fiscal Year End: 12/31/2005
EIN: 41-6483066

John R. and Maryanne Dennis Foundation
Edina, MN 55439-1658
Assets: $35,573
Grants: $320,087
Fiscal Year End: 12/31/2005
EIN: 36-3644050

Deziel Family Foundation, Inc.
Hamel, MN 55340
Assets: $602,190
Grants: $7,000
Fiscal Year End: 12/31/2005
EIN: 41-2000257

Robert and Susan Diamond Foundation
Hopkins, MN 55305
Assets: $947,071
Grants: $75,915
Fiscal Year End: 12/31/2005
EIN: 41-1890047

Dickman Family Foundation
Willmar, MN 56201
Assets: $114,619
Fiscal Year End: 12/31/2005
EIN: 06-6327908

George H. and Marjorie F. Dixon Charitable Foundation
Minneapolis, MN 55401
Assets: $90,691
Grants: $28,250
Fiscal Year End: 11/30/2005
EIN: 36-3490542

Doerr Family Fund
Minneapolis, MN 55402
Assets: $56,979
Grants: $1,500
Fiscal Year End: 12/31/2005
EIN: 41-6038603

Dolan Media Foundation
Minneapolis, MN 55402
Assets: $12,865
Grants: $71,875
Fiscal Year End: 12/31/2005
EIN: 20-4000022

John and Clara Dolan Foundation
Shorewood, MN 55331-7023
Assets: $608,244
Grants: $156,938
Fiscal Year End: 12/31/2005
EIN: 36-3321532

Dolbec-Vergin Foundation
Loretto, MN 55357-9706
Assets: $1,067
Grants: $500
Fiscal Year End: 12/31/2005
EIN: 91-2132809

Dorea Foundation
Minneapolis, MN 55440-9300
Assets: $11,794,484
Grants: $1,270,000
Fiscal Year End: 12/31/2005
EIN: 41-1703735

Double Eagle Foundation
Plymouth, MN 55447
Assets: $1,129,025
Grants: $23,000
Fiscal Year End: 12/31/2005
EIN: 41-1977975

Dougherty Family Foundation
Minneapolis, MN 55402-4114
Assets: $665,349
Grants: $115,220
Fiscal Year End: 12/31/2005
EIN: 41-1883370

Joseph Durda Foundation
Chaska, MN 55318
Assets: $6,224
Grants: $7,125
Fiscal Year End: 12/31/2005
EIN: 41-1672558

The Jaye F. and Betty F. Dyer Foundation
Minneapolis, MN 55402-4117
Assets: $3,454,137
Grants: $182,000
Fiscal Year End: 12/31/2005
EIN: 41-1390020

Ecotrust Foundation
Minneapolis, MN 55402
Assets: $2,132,281
Grants: $407,149
Fiscal Year End: 12/31/2005
EIN: 41-1735062

Eddy Family Foundation
Big Lake, MN 55309-0362
Assets: $2,543,986
Grants: $137,372
Fiscal Year End: 12/31/2005
EIN: 41-1931416

Eden Prairie Foundation
Eden Prairie, MN 55344
Assets: $225,037
Grants: $50,373
Fiscal Year End: 6/30/2005
EIN 41-1409203

el Jay Foundation
Minnetonka, MN 55345
Assets: $237,131
Grants: $27,300
Fiscal Year End: 12/31/2005
EIN: 41-2023125

El Shaddai Foundation
Minneapolis, MN 55402-2049
Assets: $261,900
Grants: $61,000
Fiscal Year End: 11/30/2005
EIN: 41-1654454

Ellis Foundation
Naples, FL 24102
Assets: $371,759
Grants: $62,250
Fiscal Year End: 12/31/2005
EIN: 41-1958314

Robert K. Else Family Charitable Foundation
North Mankato, MN 56003
Assets: $92,481
Grants: $5,880
Fiscal Year End: 12/31/2005
EIN: 20-1765162

Emfield Family Foundation
Wayzata, MN 55391
Assets: $262,682
Grants: $10,100
Fiscal Year End: 12/31/2005
EIN: 20-3576317

Emmerich Foundation Charitable Trust
Edina, MN 55439
Assets: $4,326,025
Grants: $325,750
Fiscal Year End: 12/31/2005
EIN: 41-1712553

Engelsma Family Foundation
Minneapolis, MN 55404
Assets: $5,134,122
Grants: $259,083
Fiscal Year End: 12/31/2005
EIN: 71-0924087

George and Phyllis Engh Charitable Trust
St Paul, MN 55164-0713
Assets: $301,352
Grants: $9,337
Fiscal Year End: 10/31/2005
EIN: 41-6216846

Enkel Foundation
Minnetonka, MN 55343
Assets: $347,050
Grants: $1,000
Fiscal Year End: 12/31/2005
EIN: 20-2040284

Alfred W. Erickson Foundation
Minneapolis, MN 55440
Assets: $108,168
Grants: $87,950
Fiscal Year End: 12/31/2005
EIN: 41-6050856

Arthur T. Erickson Foundation
Minneapolis, MN 55440
Assets: $111,016
Grants: $109,564
Fiscal Year End: 12/31/2005
EIN: 41-6050855

Dean and Jean Erickson Family Foundation
Eagan, MN 55121
Assets: $2
Grants: $2,120
Fiscal Year End: 12/31/2005
EIN: 41-1850215

Eugene E. and Grace M. Erickson Foundation
Minnetonka, MN 55305-3989
Assets: $260,282
Grants: $1,000
Fiscal Year End: 12/31/2005
EIN: 36-3416414

Ess Family Foundation
Mound, MN 55364
Assets: $92,207
Grants: $29,404
Fiscal Year End: 12/31/2005
EIN: 41-1975420

Evenstad Family Foundation
Maple Grove, MN 55369-6026
Assets: $1,132,885
Grants: $274,500
Fiscal Year End: 12/31/2005
EIN: 41-1990118

Evergreen Foundation
Mendota Heights, MN 55118
Assets: $74,802
Grants: $300
Fiscal Year End: 12/31/2005
EIN: 20-1267594

Evert Foundation
Minneapolis, MN 55402
Assets: $5,077,582
Grants: $230,000
Fiscal Year End: 12/31/2005
EIN: 41-6543299

Excel Bank Minnesota Foundation
Minneapolis, MN 55402
Assets: $66,875
Grants: $77,000
Fiscal Year End: 12/31/2005
EIN: 20-1255989

Ron and Diane Fagen Family Foundation
Granite Falls, MN 56241
Assets: $350,094
Grants: $17,075
Fiscal Year End: 12/31/2005
EIN: 20-2019581

Faith, Hope and Love Foundation
St Louis Park, MN 55416-1533
Assets: $2,286,332
Grants: $131,876
Fiscal Year End: 12/31/2005
EIN: 41-1852802

Farfellow Foundation
Edina, MN 55436
Assets: $4,323
Grants: $35,093
Fiscal Year End: 12/31/2005
EIN: 41-1781090

Ferber Family Foundation
Minneapolis, MN 55437
Assets: $2,876,531
Grants: $105,157
Fiscal Year End: 12/31/2005
EIN: 20-0228634

Mildred and Adolph Fine Family Foundation
Minneapolis, MN 55405
Assets: $103,695
Grants: $4,650
Fiscal Year End: 12/31/2005
EIN: 41-6038607

William I. and Bianca M. Fine Charitable Trust
Minneapolis, MN 55402
Assets: $297,935
Grants: $37,500
Fiscal Year End: 12/31/2005
EIN: 36-3481742

Ronald Fingerhut Family Foundation
Minneapolis, MN 55416-1607
Assets: $11,023
Grants: $88,260
Fiscal Year End: 12/31/2005
EIN: 41-1925838

Richard and Beverly Fink Family Foundation
Minneapolis, MN 55402
Assets: $291,863
Grants: $102,713
Fiscal Year End: 12/31/2005
EIN: 41-1859799

First Minnesota Foundation, Inc.
Milaca, MN 56353-1106
Assets: $10,684
Grants: $9,589
Fiscal Year End: 10/31/2005
EIN: 41-6028525

I. George Fischbein Foundation
Minneapolis, MN 55402
Assets: $63,428
Grants: $11,725
Fiscal Year End: 4/30/2006
EIN: 41-1330564

James S. Fish Family Foundation
Minneapolis, MN 55402-1498
Assets: $1,290,027
Grants: $106,150
Fiscal Year End: 12/31/2005
EIN: 41-1796666

S.S. Fisher Foundation, Inc.
Minneapolis, MN 55402
Assets: $436,050
Grants: $40,691
Fiscal Year End: 11/30/2005
EIN: 41-6024302

Steven C. and Susan L. Fiterman Charitable Foundation
Golden Valley, MN 55427
Assets: $1,834,806
Grants: $50,155
Fiscal Year End: 12/31/2005
EIN: 41-1582108

Flaherty Family Foundation
Eden Prairie, MN 55344-7636
Assets: $12,287
Grants: $313,237
Fiscal Year End: 12/31/2005
EIN: 41-1622611

Fletcher Family Foundation
Maple Grove, MN 55331
Assets: $4,519,211
Grants: $177,711
Fiscal Year End: 12/31/2005
EIN: 56-2393836

Foldcraft Foundation
Kenyon, MN 55946
Assets: $68,587
Fiscal Year End: 12/31/2005
EIN: 41-1872480

Forstrom Family Foundation
Howard Lake, MN 55349-0280
Assets: $114,701
Grants: $56,636
Fiscal Year End: 12/31/2005
EIN: 35-2191686

Foster Family Foundation
St Paul, MN 55102
Assets: $232,441
Grants: $19,500
Fiscal Year End: 12/31/2005
EIN: 41-1991254

Foundation for Classical Studies in Statecraft & Jurisprudence
Minneapolis, MN 55402
Assets: $161,977
Grants: $17,525
Fiscal Year End: 12/31/2005
EIN: 41-1970028

Foundation for Educational Research and Development
Wayzata, MN 55391
Assets: $1,278,270
Grants: $127,000
Fiscal Year End: 12/31/2005
EIN: 41-1876141

Foundation for the Development of Human Potential
St Paul, MN 55101-4930
Assets: $256,500
Grants: $40,000
Fiscal Year End: 12/31/2005
EIN: 23-7368600

Foundation for the Development of People
Minneapolis, MN 55419-1252
Assets: $381,300
Grants: $25,000
Fiscal Year End: 12/31/2005
EIN: 41-1341223

Foundation of the Law Firm of Fabyanske, Westra & Hart, P.A.
Minneapolis, MN 55402
Assets: $1,373
Grants: $3,970
Fiscal Year End: 12/31/2005
EIN: 41-1696953

Bill and Katherine Fox Foundation
Minneapolis, MN 55422
Assets: $35,735
Grants: $59,850
Fiscal Year End: 12/31/2005
EIN: 41-1954162

Frankard Foundation
Winona, MN 55987-5310
Assets: $399,829
Grants: $14,700
Fiscal Year End: 5/31/2006
EIN: 41-1563443

The Freier Family Foundation, Inc.
Roseville, MN 55113-1957
Assets: $669,799
Grants: $17,600
Fiscal Year End: 12/31/2005
EIN: 41-1990257

Frenzel Foundation
St Paul, MN 55164-0713
Assets: $708,044
Grants: $91,500
Fiscal Year End: 12/31/2005
EIN: 41-6018060

Michael J. and Karen B. Frey Foundation
Wayzata, MN 55391
Assets: $5,123,407
Grants: $211,000
Fiscal Year End: 12/31/2005
EIN: 75-3140739

Stuart and Nancy Friedell Family Foundation
Hopkins, MN 55305
Assets: $127,931
Grants: $62,250
Fiscal Year End: 12/31/2005
EIN: 41-1976795

James and Karen Frisell Family Foundation
St Paul, MN 55105-1240
Assets: $42,070
Grants: $1,000
Fiscal Year End: 12/31/2005
EIN: 41-2012284

Fudge Family Foundation
Andover, MN 55304-2236
Assets: $404,803
Grants: $99,600
Fiscal Year End: 12/31/2005
EIN: 41-6344485

The Furst Foundation
Wayzata, MN 55391
Assets: $181,205
Grants: $42,123
Fiscal Year End: 12/31/2005
EIN: 41-1926419

Gabriel Foundation
St Paul, MN 55105
Assets: $361,367
Grants: $20,144
Fiscal Year End: 6/30/2005
EIN: 41-1417537

The Galinson Foundation
Golden Valley, MN 55416-1144
Assets: $201,443
Grants: $10,280
Fiscal Year End: 5/31/2006
EIN: 41-6019941

The Gallagher Foundation
Minneapolis, MN 55402
Assets: $3,525,883
Grants: $291,470
Fiscal Year End: 12/31/2005
EIN: 41-2019884

Gandrud Foundation
Owatonna, MN 55060-0528
Assets: $341,912
Grants: $16,598
Fiscal Year End: 12/31/2005
EIN: 41-6038629

Garelick Family Foundation
St Paul Park, MN 55071-1852
Assets: $38,603
Grants: $37,300
Fiscal Year End: 10/31/2005
EIN: 41-1400379

Garmar Foundation
Dodge Center, MN 55927
Assets: $2,132,696
Grants: $482,504
Fiscal Year End: 6/30/2006
EIN: 41-1914753

Gegax Family Foundation
Minneapolis, MN 55416
Assets: $946,636
Grants: $108,057
Fiscal Year End: 12/31/2005
EIN: 41-1989478

Generations Health Care Initiatives, Inc.
Duluth, MN 55802
Assets: $13,298,465
Grants: $368,075
Fiscal Year End: 8/31/2005
EIN: 41-2000473

George Family Foundation
Minneapolis, MN 55405
Assets: $52,622,501
Grants: $2,102,666
Fiscal Year End: 12/31/2005
EIN: 41-1730855

The Geyer Family Foundation
Edina, MN 55424
Assets: $497,520
Grants: $38,529
Fiscal Year End: 12/31/2005
EIN: 41-1988121

Gilligan Foundation
Edina, MN 55435
Assets: $3,479,937
Grants: $167,500
Fiscal Year End: 11/30/2005
EIN: 36-3418218

Gise Family Foundation
Minnetonka, MN 55345
Assets: $537,745
Grants: $10,000
Fiscal Year End: 12/31/2005
EIN: 41-1926247

Give a Knit Foundation (fka The Webber Family Foundation)
Bloomington, MN 55431
Assets: $6,705
Fiscal Year End: 12/31/2005
EIN: 41-1792216

Glassman Family Foundation
White Bear Lake, MN 55110-5229
Assets: $224,761
Grants: $11,700
Fiscal Year End: 1/31/2006
EIN: 41-1876705

Global Promise Foundation
Chaska, MN 55318
Assets: $1,416,546
Grants: $63,500
Fiscal Year End: 12/31/2005
EIN: 20-1584233

GMAC ResCap
Minneapolis, MN 55437
Grants: $2,468,736
Fiscal Year End: 12/31/2006

Marvin E. and Miriam R. Goldberg Foundation
Minneapolis, MN 55410-2142
Assets: $483,634
Grants: $23,034
Fiscal Year End: 12/31/2005
EIN: 41-1858705

Stanley M. and Luella G. Goldberg Family Foundation
Minneapolis, MN 55439
Assets: $575,249
Grants: $42,456
Fiscal Year End: 12/31/2005
EIN: 41-1875783

Jacob E. Goldenberg Foundation
Bloomington, MN 55420
Assets: $938,901
Grants: $105,000
Fiscal Year End: 12/31/2005
EIN: 41-6019275

Amy R. and Philip S. Goldman Foundation
Minnetonka, MN 55343-9014
Assets: $2,694,380
Grants: $115,000
Fiscal Year End: 12/31/2005
EIN: 41-1925897

Goldstein Family Foundation
Edina, MN 55439
Assets: $131,026
Grants: $6,118
Fiscal Year End: 6/30/2006
EIN: 41-1654002

Sydney Goldstein Foundation
Minneapolis, MN 55402
Assets: $59,015
Grants: $4,857
Fiscal Year End: 6/30/2006
EIN: 41-1694014

Albert and Ruth Gomez Irrevocable Charitable Trust
Minneapolis, MN 55402
Assets: $201,667
Grants: $7,196
Fiscal Year End: 12/31/2005
EIN: 41-6510712

Good Helps, Inc.
North St Paul, MN 55109
Assets: $914,496
Grants: $77,202
Fiscal Year End: 12/31/2005
EIN: 41-1302643

Arthur and Constance Goodman Family Foundation
Mahtomedi, MN 55115-1653
Assets: $383,385
Grants: $12,797
Fiscal Year End: 12/31/2005
EIN: 41-6058730

Gossman Family Foundation
Woodbury, MN 55129
Assets: $411,236
Grants: $157,203
Fiscal Year End: 12/31/2005
EIN: 41-1858368

Gostomski Family Foundation
Winona, MN 55987
Assets: $2,513,670
Grants: $132,000
Fiscal Year End: 5/31/2006
EIN: 20-6075013

Gottstein Family Foundation
St Louis Park, MN 55416-1518
Assets: $542,040
Grants: $12,596
Fiscal Year End: 6/30/2006
EIN: 41-6054835

Ransford Ray and Clara J. Gould Foundation
St Paul, MN 55101
Assets: $800,798
Grants: $38,027
Fiscal Year End: 12/31/2005
EIN: 41-6056658

The Margot and Paul Grangaard Foundation
Edina, MN 55439
Assets: $72,122
Grants: $150,000
Fiscal Year End: 12/31/2005
EIN: 41-2022549

Granite Foundation
Roseville, MN 55113-3851
Assets: $5,810,457
Grants: $178,937
Fiscal Year End: 12/31/2005
EIN: 26-0010320

Henry K. and Mildred M. Grawe Charitable Foundation
Winona, MN 55987-3042
Assets: $30,141
Grants: $9,980
Fiscal Year End: 12/31/2005
EIN: 41-6446187

Graybrier Foundation
Excelsior, MN 55331-8790
Assets: $225,845
Grants: $7,350
Fiscal Year End: 12/31/2005
EIN: 23-7047878

Greater Wayzata Community Foundation
Wayzata, MN 55391
Assets: $87,255
Grants: $9,062
Fiscal Year End: 3/31/2006
EIN: 36-3844389

Greycoach Foundation
Plymouth, MN 55441
Assets: $10,790,621
Grants: $1,118,000
Fiscal Year End: 12/31/2005
EIN: 23-7417559

Greystone Foundation
Minneapolis, MN 55402
Assets: $12,689,091
Grants: $1,803,052
Fiscal Year End: 12/31/2005
EIN: 41-6027765

Griffiths Foundation
Minneapolis, MN 55447
Assets: $2,115,652
Grants: $75,206
Fiscal Year End: 12/31/2005
EIN: 41-1628889

Owen J. Gromme Foundation
Minneapolis, MN 55435-2025
Assets: $303,124
Grants: $3,000
Fiscal Year End: 12/31/2005
EIN: 41-1733396

Joseph C. Grossman Foundation
Minneapolis, MN 55402
Assets: $186,838
Grants: $10,600
Fiscal Year End: 6/30/2005
EIN: 36-3432434

Grouse Mountain Foundation
Minneapolis, MN 55402
Assets: $11,588
Grants: $8,300
Fiscal Year End: 12/31/2005
EIN: 41-1952289

John P. and Beverly G. Grundhofer Charitable Foundation
Minneapolis, MN 55402
Assets: $6,555,490
Grants: $449,337
Fiscal Year End: 12/31/2005
EIN: 41-1805287

Gudorf Family Foundation
Edina, MN 55436
Assets: $756,823
Grants: $31,800
Fiscal Year End: 12/31/2005
EIN: 41-1987765

The Edward and Hannah Gustafson Foundation
St Paul, MN 55112-6277
Assets: $397,842
Grants: $26,000
Fiscal Year End: 12/31/2005
EIN: 86-1052101

Haag Family Foundation
St Paul, MN 55118-3670
Assets: $1,764,123
Grants: $55,361
Fiscal Year End: 12/31/2005
EIN: 41-1885356

Hageman Foundation of Hope
Buffalo, MN 55313
Assets: $73,298
Grants: $239,663
Fiscal Year End: 12/31/2005
EIN: 20-1700412

Russell and Luaina Hagen Family Foundation
Minneapolis, MN 55414
Assets: $42,164
Grants: $2,000
Fiscal Year End: 12/31/2005
EIN: 41-1941194

Hallberg Family Foundation
Forest Lake, MN 55025
Assets: $450,279
Grants: $21,790
Fiscal Year End: 12/31/2005
EIN: 41-1989115

Jerome M. Halper Family Foundation
Golden Valley, MN 55416
Assets: $353,252
Grants: $25,497
Fiscal Year End: 12/31/2005
EIN: 41-6035524

Hansen Family Foundation
Edina, MN 55436
Assets: $4,650,598
Grants: $209,250
Fiscal Year End: 12/31/2005
EIN: 41-1740710

The Hanser Family Foundation
Sanibel, FL 33957-3648
Assets: $26,359
Grants: $31,275
Fiscal Year End: 12/31/2005
EIN: 41-1321832

Gregg W. Hanson Charitable Foundation
Spicer, MN 56288-9346
Assets: $72,889
Grants: $31,217
Fiscal Year End: 11/30/2004
EIN: 41-1766551

John O. and Barbara N. Hanson Family Foundation
Red Wing, MN 55066
Assets $1,477,870
Grants $63,369
Fiscal Year End: 12/31/2005
EIN: 41-1957108

Happy Dancing Turtle Foundation
Pine River, MN 56474
Assets: $22,436
Grants: $2,500
Fiscal Year End: 12/31/2005
EIN: 41-1908150

Dr. Daniel C. Hartnett Family Foundation
Long Lake, MN 55356
Assets: $293,624
Grants: $4,450
Fiscal Year End: 12/31/2005
EIN: 20-0500365

Harvard Club of Minnesota
Burnsville, MN 55337
Assets: $464,790
Grants: $27,340
Fiscal Year End: 6/30/2005
EIN: 41-6083667

The Hawkins Family Foundation
St Paul, MN 55101-2358
Assets: $461,414
Grants: $158,975
Fiscal Year End: 12/31/2005
EIN: 41-1925282

The Hays Foundation
Minneapolis, MN 55402
Assets: $6,785
Grants: $8,000
Fiscal Year End: 12/31/2005
EIN: 41-2021251

Hayward Foundation
Long Lake, MN 55356
Assets: $46,821
Grants: $1,180
Fiscal Year End: 12/31/2005
EIN: 41-1926010

Head Family Foundation
Minneapolis, MN 55405
Assets: $973,430
Grants: $16,850
Fiscal Year End: 6/30/2005
EIN: 20-2032551

Heaven Sent Foundation
Bloomington, MN 55431-3965
Assets: $117,146
Grants: $38,630
Fiscal Year End: 12/31/2005
EIN: 41-1919143

Hedberg Family Charitable Foundation
St Paul, MN 55164-0713
Assets: $902,446
Grants: $13,000
Fiscal Year End: 12/31/2005
EIN: 41-1543653

The Heenan Foundation
Woodbury, MN 55125
Assets: $165,604
Grants: $17,091
Fiscal Year End: 5/31/2006
EIN: 41-1718396

The Hegman Family Foundation
Edina, MN 55424
Assets: $63,150
Grants: $77,799
Fiscal Year End: 12/31/2005
EIN: 41-1751492

Menahem Heilicher Foundation
Minneapolis, MN 55427
Assets: $2,851,213
Grants: $136,213
Fiscal Year End: 12/31/2005
EIN: 41-6043457

Willis C. Helm Charitable Trust
Minneapolis, MN 55402
Assets: $1,487,155
Grants: $63,760
Fiscal Year End: 12/31/2005
EIN: 41-6385896

Hendry Family Foundation
Bloomington, MN 55431-3955
Assets: $6,387,542
Grants: $264,361
Fiscal Year End: 12/31/2005
EIN: 41-1698350

Thomas R. Hennessy Family Charitable Trust
La Crosse, WI 54602-0489
Assets: $282,492
Grants: $12,300
Fiscal Year End: 8/31/2005
EIN: 23-7417558

The Victoria Velie Henry Family Foundation
Wayzata, MN 55391
Assets: $653,646
Grants: $23,800
Fiscal Year End: 3/31/2006
EIN: 41-1967188

Hersey Foundation
St Paul, MN 55102-1119
Assets: $9,878,474
Grants: $468,604
Fiscal Year End: 12/31/2005
EIN: 23-7001771

Hertogs Family Education Foundation, Inc.
Hastings, MN 55033-2426
Assets: $521,351
Grants: $50,545
Fiscal Year End: 12/31/2005
EIN: 41-1984473

Hetland Family Foundation
Minneapolis, MN 55402
Assets: $1,658,379
Grants: $79,000
Fiscal Year End: 12/31/2005
EIN: 41-1637573

Hillswood Foundation
Eden Prairie, MN 55344
Assets: $3,692,349
Grants: $566,130
Fiscal Year End: 12/31/2005
EIN: 41-1948564

Hinz Foundation, Inc.
Woodbury, MN 55129-2517
Assets: $822,513
Grants: $42,000
Fiscal Year End: 12/31/2005
EIN: 41-1944627

The Hirsh Family Foundation
Austin, MN 55912
Assets: $3,176,643
Grants: $40,677
Fiscal Year End: 12/31/2005
EIN: 41-1749842

Timothy and Todd A. Hitchcock Foundation
Sioux Falls, SD 57103
Assets: $38,977
Grants: $3,850
Fiscal Year End: 12/31/2005
EIN: 31-1583124

The Leo A. and Doris C. Hodroff Foundation
Minneapolis, MN 55403
Assets: $743,674
Grants: $302,500
Fiscal Year End: 12/31/2005
EIN: 41-1926121

The Hoeft Family Foundation
Minneapolis, MN 55431
Assets: $1,729,671
Grants: $79,000
Fiscal Year End: 12/31/2005
EIN: 41-1926546

D. A. Hoff Charitable Foundation
Cottonwood, MN 56229
Assets: $1,908,323
Grants: $90,057
Fiscal Year End: 12/31/2005
EIN: 76-0728892

The Hognander Foundation
Edina, MN 55436-1357
Assets: $4,863,982
Grants: $152,580
Fiscal Year End: 12/31/2005
EIN: 41-1953881

Holden Family Foundation
Excelsior, MN 55331
Assets: $507,963
Grants: $15,500
Fiscal Year End: 12/31/2005
EIN: 41-1774925

Holmes/CSM Family Foundation
Minneapolis, MN 55415-1151
Assets: $1,350,324
Grants: $26,420
Fiscal Year End: 12/31/2005
EIN: 93-1220868

Holzhueter Foundation
Mankato, MN 56001-3553
Assets: $815,255
Grants: $43,000
Fiscal Year End: 12/31/2005
EIN: 41-1925651

Homecrest Foundation
Wadena, MN 56482
Assets: $107,046
Grants: $8,150
Fiscal Year End: 7/31/2006
EIN: 41-1550750

Homedale Foundation
Edina, MN 55439
Assets: $677,071
Grants: $158,600
Fiscal Year End: 12/31/2005
EIN: 41-1942264

Janice Sarah Hope Foundation, Inc.
Minneapolis, MN 55416
Assets: $765,672
Grants: $44,000
Fiscal Year End: 12/31/2005
EIN: 65-0441315

Hormel Foods Corporation Charitable Trust
Austin, MN 55912-3673
Assets: $179,774
Grants: $1,634,931
Fiscal Year End: 12/31/2005
EIN: 01-0761416

Horton Holding, Inc.
Roseville, MN 55113
Grants: $900,000
Fiscal Year End: 12/31/2006

Robert F. Hosch Foundation
St Paul, MN 55102
Assets: $53,423
Grants: $15,000
Fiscal Year End: 12/31/2005
EIN: 41-1957363

The Huang Family Foundation
North Oaks, MN 55127
Assets: $201,988
Grants: $5,737
Fiscal Year End: 12/31/2005
EIN: 41-1948737

The Huelsmann Foundation
Stillwater, MN 55082
Assets: $68,546
Grants: $4,000
Fiscal Year End: 12/31/2005
EIN: 41-1893927

The Theodore G. Huisinga Charitable Foundation
Willmar, MN 56201
Assets: $190,766
Grants: $72,500
Fiscal Year End: 12/31/2005
EIN: 41-1639703

Human Life Foundation
Maple Plain, MN 55359
Assets: $163,598
Grants: $8,000
Fiscal Year End: 12/31/2005
EIN: 41-1893619

Humboldt Family Foundation, Inc.
Minneapolis, MN 55402-4425
Assets: $699,327
Grants: $27,500
Fiscal Year End: 12/31/2005
EIN: 41-1852021

Hubert H. Humphrey Foundation, Inc.
Eden Prairie, MN 55347
Assets: $81,235
Grants: $3,200
Fiscal Year End: 12/31/2005
EIN: 52-6080469

Huntley-Dickinson Foundation
Orono, MN 55391-9349
Assets: $123,782
Grants: $5,000
Fiscal Year End: 6/30/2006
EIN: 41-2023283

Huss Foundation
St Paul, MN 55102
Assets: $12,677,330
Grants: $792,000
Fiscal Year End: 12/31/2005
EIN: 39-1474563

Hutter Family Foundation
Minneapolis, MN 55402
Assets: $427,491
Grants: $24,250
Fiscal Year End: 12/31/2005
EIN: 41-1787817

I.V. Foundation
Shorewood, MN 55331
Assets: $518,267
Grants: $40,000
Fiscal Year End: 12/31/2005
EIN: 41-1796849

IBM Corporation - Minnesota
Rochester, MN 55901
Grants: $300,000
Fiscal Year End: 12/31/2005

Impact Foundation
Lakeville, MN 55044
Assets: $111,565
Grants: $10,090
Fiscal Year End: 12/31/2005
EIN: 41-1905957

IWJ Charitable Foundation
Minnetonka, MN 55305
Assets: $134,806
Grants: $10,700
Fiscal Year End: 12/31/2005
EIN: 41-1658447

The Jackley Foundation
Wayzata, MN 55391
Assets: $316,016
Grants: $17,350
Fiscal Year End: 12/31/2005
EIN: 41-0916721

C. Charles Jackson Foundation
Minneapolis, MN 55402
Assets: $7,911,332
Grants: $242,873
Fiscal Year End: 12/31/2005
EIN: 41-1996905

Jacobsen Family Foundation
Rancho Santa Fe, CA 92067-6127
Assets: $2,519,976
Grants: $226,075
Fiscal Year End: 12/31/2005
EIN: 41-1886672

Jones P. Jacobson Family Foundation
St Paul, MN 55164-0713
Assets: $1,303,143
Grants: $58,500
Fiscal Year End: 12/31/2005
EIN: 41-1910923

Duane and Lynda Jergenson Family Foundation
Minneapolis, MN 55403-1956
Assets: $168,999
Grants: $5,100
Fiscal Year End: 12/31/2005
EIN: 41-1974230

The Jilek Family Foundation
Lester Prairie, MN 55354
Assets: $99,133
Grants: $6,600
Fiscal Year End: 12/31/2005
EIN: 41-6472023

T. H. Johansen Family Foundation
Minneapolis, MN 55402
Assets: $930,436
Grants: $23,847
Fiscal Year End: 12/31/2005
EIN: 41-6014249

Charles E. and Andriene M. Johnson Foundation
Eden Prairie, MN 55344
Assets: $107,977
Fiscal Year End: 12/31/2005
EIN: 41-1736857

Chester Johnson Charitable Trust
Balaton, MN 56115-3160
Assets: $1,796,196
Grants: $20,449
Fiscal Year End: 6/30/2006
EIN 41-1754292

David B. Johnson Family Foundation
Minneapolis, MN 55402
Assets: $1,328,146
Grants: $91,000
Fiscal Year End: 12/31/2005
EIN: 41-1859513

Elmer M. Johnson Conservation Trust
Glenville, MN 56036
Assets: $210,511
Fiscal Year End: 12/31/2005
EIN: 41-6418164

John Warren and Marion Louise Johnson Family Foundation
Minneapolis, MN 55419
Assets: $103,593
Grants: $45,600
Fiscal Year End: 12/31/2005
EIN: 41-1915363

Mark and Laura Johnson Family Foundation
Excelsior, MN 55331-8352
Assets: $902,210
Grants: $87,444
Fiscal Year End: 12/31/2005
EIN: 41-1889300

Douglas and Mary Staughton Jones Foundation
Nerstrand, MN 55053-0026
Assets: $739,326
Grants: $79,100
Fiscal Year End: 6/30/2006
EIN: 41-1891820

The Jonty Foundation for Research in Immuno Endocrine Neurological Disorders
St Paul, MN 55101
Assets: $138,043
Grants: $206,185
Fiscal Year End: 12/31/2005
EIN: 41-2001420

Joyce Family Foundation
Plymouth, MN 55446
Assets: $230,958
Grants: $31,648
Fiscal Year End: 12/31/2005
EIN: 41-1797421

Jsman Family Foundation
Hopkins, MN 55343-4818
Assets: $9,624
Grants: $27,025
Fiscal Year End: 12/31/2005
EIN: 41-1964197

Kairos Foundation
Minneapolis, MN 55406
Assets: $196,191
Grants: $9,605
Fiscal Year End: 12/31/2005
EIN: 41-1680791

Kaplan Family Foundation
Edina, MN 55435-1714
Assets: $3,652,223
Grants: $188,250
Fiscal Year End: 12/31/2005
EIN: 41-1794327

Harold F. and Muriel Kappler Foundation
St Paul, MN 55101
Assets: $456,627
Grants: $15,000
Fiscal Year End: 12/31/2005
EIN: 31-1663492

Conrad I. and Ruth V. Karleen Charitable Trust
Minneapolis, MN 55402
Assets: $1,954,577
Grants: $85,877
Fiscal Year End: 12/31/2005
EIN: 41-6455455

The Karon Family Foundation, Inc.
Minneapolis, MN 55409-5999
Assets: $703,807
Grants: $112,500
Fiscal Year End: 12/31/2005
EIN: 41-2015586

Wynn and Pamela Kearney Foundation
Mankato, MN 56001
Assets: $518,103
Fiscal Year End: 12/31/2005
EIN: 41-1877213

Hamilton H. Kellogg and Mildred Haley Kellogg Charitable Trust
St Paul, MN 55164-0713
Assets: $6,304,567
Grants: $286,000
Fiscal Year End: 12/31/2005
EIN: 31-1713052

Kelm Foundation
Minneapolis, MN 55416-4649
Assets: $216,597
Grants: $15,600
Fiscal Year End: 12/31/2005
EIN: 41-6023477

William R. Kennedy Family Foundation
St Paul, MN 55101-1002
Assets: $226,315
Grants: $2,300
Fiscal Year End: 12/31/2005
EIN: 41-1926334

Kent Family Charitable Trust
Minneapolis, MN 55402
Assets: $2,456,812
Grants: $305,500
Fiscal Year End: 12/31/2005
EIN: 36-3582818

Keymer Foundation
St Cloud, MN 56303-1249
Assets: $258,446
Grants: $19,000
Fiscal Year End: 12/31/2005
EIN: 41-1953583

King Family Foundation
Bloomington, MN 55437
Assets: $87,442
Grants: $5,700
Fiscal Year End: 11/30/2005
EIN: 41-6485350

King Family Foundation
Hastings, MN 55033
Assets: $472,980
Grants: $7,350
Fiscal Year End: 11/30/2005
EIN: 41-1951860

Kinney Family Foundation
Roseville, MN 55113
Assets: $8,401,192
Grants: $285,450
Fiscal Year End: 12/31/2005
EIN: 65-1205543

The Steven L. and Jan L. Kirchner Family Foundation
Bloomington, MN 55438-1471
Assets: $1,461,461
Grants: $33,960
Fiscal Year End: 12/31/2005
EIN: 75-3043620

Harry L. and Janet M. Kitselman Foundation
Minneapolis, MN 55479
Assets: $3,541,451
Grants: $166,000
Fiscal Year End: 12/31/2005
EIN: 41-6491134

Kiwanis Club of Edina Golden K Foundation
Edina, MN 55436
Assets: $53,458
Grants: $2,067
Fiscal Year End: 12/31/2005
EIN: 41-1948060

KKE Architects Charitable Foundation
Minneapolis, MN 55401
Assets: $3,249
Grants: $84,502
Fiscal Year End: 5/31/2006
EIN: 41-1873629

Klas Family Foundation
Minneapolis, MN 55402
Assets: $982,374
Grants: $43,500
Fiscal Year End: 12/31/2005
EIN: 20-1492415

Klein Family Foundation
Minneapolis, MN 55403
Assets: $27,546
Grants: $21,771
Fiscal Year End: 12/31/2005
EIN: 41-1779821

E. Milton Kleven Family Foundation
Minneapolis, MN 55424
Assets: $708,185
Grants: $31,265
Fiscal Year End: 12/31/2005
EIN: 41-6027419

KLM Fund
Bonita Springs, FL 34134
Assets: $390,379
Grants: $267,703
Fiscal Year End: 12/31/2005
EIN: 36-3499979

Knights of Columbus 4381
Fridley, MN 55432
Assets: $88,387
Grants: $6,771
Fiscal Year End: 6/30/2005
EIN: 23-7209031

The Knowlton Foundation
Austin, MN 55912
Assets: $2,120,786
Grants: $434,650
Fiscal Year End: 12/31/2005
EIN: 41-1877113

Ida C. Koran Trust
St Paul, MN 55164-0713
Assets: $39,196,713
Grants: $1,783,158
Fiscal Year End: 12/31/2005
EIN: 41-6124022

Jerome and Marlyce Koskovich Foundation
Rochester, MN 55920
Assets: $3,640,908
Grants: $449,500
Fiscal Year End: 6/30/2006
EIN: 20-2051209

Joel and Laurie Kramer Foundation
Minneapolis, MN 55414-1145
Assets: $834,015
Grants: $53,100
Fiscal Year End: 12/31/2005
EIN: 31-1627721

Krinkie Family Foundation
Lino Lakes, MN 55038
Assets: $75,664
Grants: $10,000
Fiscal Year End: 6/30/2005
EIN: 20-0091499

The Krisbin Foundation
Wayzata, MN 55391
Assets: $1,024,598
Grants: $132,199
Fiscal Year End: 12/31/2005
EIN: 41-6419749

Hanna R. Kristianson Testamentary Charitable Trust
Clarks Grove, MN 56016
Assets: $116,683
Grants: $1,153
Fiscal Year End: 12/31/2005
EIN: 41-6209010

Mark and Lori Kroll Family Foundation
Crystal Bay, MN 55323
Assets: $324,838
Grants: $40,000
Fiscal Year End: 12/31/2005
EIN: 37-0731913

Faye and Mayer Krupp Family Foundation
Minneapolis, MN 55416
Assets: $923,227
Grants: $73,146
Fiscal Year End: 12/31/2005
EIN: 41-1856606

Sharon and Joel Labovitz Foundation
Duluth, MN 55804
Assets: $405,235
Grants: $408,520
Fiscal Year End: 12/31/2005
EIN: 36-3460105

The Labrador Foundation
St Paul, MN 55102
Assets: $2,196,953
Grants: $106,500
Fiscal Year End: 12/31/2005
EIN: 41-1975373

LaFrenz Family Foundation
Eden Prairie, MN 55347-2440
Assets: $194,705
Grants: $20,649
Fiscal Year End: 12/31/2005
EIN: 41-1858415

Laird Norton Family Fund
Seattle, WA 98104
Assets: $313,453
Grants: $900,656
Fiscal Year End: 12/31/2005
EIN: 91-6048373

The Lakeland Group Foundation, Inc.
Minneapolis, MN 55422
Assets: $239,900
Fiscal Year End: 1/31/2006
EIN: 41-1738234

Lamarche Creek Foundation
Finlayson, MN 55735
Assets: $105,381
Grants: $23,750
Fiscal Year End: 12/31/2005
EIN: 41-2007580

The Lamm Family Foundation
Burnsville, MN 55337
Assets: $1,535,034
Grants: $86,356
Fiscal Year End: 12/31/2005
EIN: 41-1862729

Theodora H. Lang Charitable Trust
St Paul, MN 55164-0713
Assets: $750,863
Grants: $33,779
Fiscal Year End: 12/31/2005
EIN: 87-6269455

Langwater Foundation
Minneapolis, MN 55402-4523
Assets: $496,302
Grants: $22,500
Fiscal Year End: 12/31/2005
EIN: 41-1979036

Peter and Dorothy Lapp Foundation
Bloomington, MN 55435
Assets: $2,499,445
Grants: $171,000
Fiscal Year End: 12/31/2005
EIN: 41-1645557

Larkin Hoffman Daly and Lindgren, Ltd. Foundation
Bloomington, MN 55431-1128
Assets: $4,617
Grants: $34,290
Fiscal Year End: 5/31/2006
EIN: 36-3463116

John Larsen Foundation
Minneapolis, MN 55405
Assets: $6,127,370
Grants: $238,750
Fiscal Year End: 12/31/2005
EIN: 41-1715465

Larson Foundation
Little Canada, MN 55117
Assets: $1,301,655
Grants: $418,000
Fiscal Year End: 12/31/2005
EIN: 41-1605601

David and Janis Larson Foundation
Wayzata, MN 55391
Assets: $1,886,767
Grants: $23,000
Fiscal Year End: 12/31/2005
EIN: 41-1957525

Lavine Family Foundation
Naples, FL 34103-2229
Assets: $54,895
Grants: $4,005
Fiscal Year End: 12/31/2005
EIN: 41-1673350

The Lawrence Family Foundation
Minneapolis, MN 55409-1746
Assets: $940,594
Grants: $57,000
Fiscal Year End: 12/31/2005
EIN: 13-3935895

Lee Family Foundation
St Paul, MN 55118-4481
Assets: $545,152
Grants: $32,000
Fiscal Year End: 12/31/2005
EIN: 41-1766875

Leek Charitable Foundation
Duluth, MN 55802
Assets: $100,526
Grants: $19,950
Fiscal Year End: 12/31/2005
EIN: 41-1637980

Leggott Foundation
Edina, MN 55436-1356
Assets: $243,618
Grants: $9,000
Fiscal Year End: 12/31/2005
EIN: 41-2022912

Edith, Samuel and Elizabeth Leinbach Foundation
Minneapolis, MN 55440-0747
Assets: $120,389
Grants: $6,000
Fiscal Year End: 8/31/2005
EIN: 41-1543086

LeJeune Family Foundation
Long Lake, MN 55356
Assets: $87,125
Grants: $187,550
Fiscal Year End: 12/31/2005
EIN: 20-2039710

Lenzmeier Family Foundation
Minneapolis, MN 55402
Assets: $8,081,779
Grants: $99,097
Fiscal Year End: 12/31/2005
EIN: 20-0472176

Vivita and Paul Leonard Foundation
Rochester, MN 55902
Assets: $187
Fiscal Year End: 12/31/2005
EIN: 41-1981005

James D. Leslie Family Foundation
Maple Plain, MN 55359-9786
Assets: $334,052
Grants: $18,800
Fiscal Year End: 12/31/2005
EIN: 41-1918212

Bruce A. Levahn and Noreen J. Levahn Family Foundation
Bloomington, MN 55438
Assets: $86,569
Grants: $6,000
Fiscal Year End: 6/30/2006
EIN: 90-0136589

George and Marion Levine Foundation
St Louis Park, MN 55416-1621
Assets: $182,567
Grants: $12,000
Fiscal Year End: 12/31/2005
EIN: 41-6035577

Lieberman-Okinow Foundation
Minneapolis, MN 55431
Assets: $612
Grants: $32,475
Fiscal Year End: 9/30/2006
EIN: 41-6036200

The Liemandt Foundation
Cottage Grove, MN 55016
Assets: $507,904
Grants: $54,310
Fiscal Year End: 12/30/2006
EIN: 71-0899401

The Lillehei Family Charitable Foundation
St Paul, MN 55101
Assets: $1,864,139
Grants: $22,400
Fiscal Year End: 12/31/2005
EIN: 41-2009840

Richard and Jaci Lindstrom Foundation
Wayzata, MN 55391
Assets: $237,907
Grants: $8,288
Fiscal Year End: 12/31/2005
EIN: 41-1924685

The Hannah Lips Foundation
Faribault, MN 55021
Assets: $350,325
Grants: $15,491
Fiscal Year End: 10/31/2005
EIN: 41-1344355

The Liszt Family Foundation
Wayzata, MN 55391
Assets: $13,335
Grants: $11,000
Fiscal Year End: 12/31/2005
EIN: 41-1988167

Living Legacy
Waconia, MN 55387
Assets: $135,370
Grants: $6,502
Fiscal Year End: 12/31/2005
EIN: 71-0895373

Adolph and Emily Lokensgard Scholarship Trust Fund
Nicollet, MN 56074
Assets: $22,010
Grants: $750
Fiscal Year End: 6/30/2005
EIN: 31-1561754

Lommen, Nelson, Cole & Stageberg Foundation
Minneapolis, MN 55402
Assets: $519
Grants: $24,926
Fiscal Year End: 12/31/2005
EIN: 41-1692979

Lored Foundation
Minneapolis, MN 55402
Assets: $3,098,616
Grants: $166,864
Fiscal Year End: 12/31/2005
EIN: 41-1924853

The Lownade Foundation
Mankato, MN 56002-3584
Assets: $71,747
Grants: $228,200
Fiscal Year End: 11/30/2005
EIN: 41-1989647

The Don J. Lucker Foundation
Plymouth, MN 55447
Assets: $507,712
Grants: $25,000
Fiscal Year End: 11/30/2005
EIN: 41-1389230

Robert and Patricia Ludlow Family Foundation
Worthington, MN 56187
Assets: $980,954
Grants: $48,118
Fiscal Year End: 12/31/2005
EIN: 41-1632656

Lund Family Foundation
Minneapolis, MN 55402
Assets: $129,029
Grants: $5,100
Fiscal Year End: 12/31/2005
EIN: 41-6014341

Lois and Allan W. Lund Foundation
Plymouth, MN 55446
Assets: $508,294
Grants: $98,750
Fiscal Year End: 6/30/2006
EIN: 41-1808103

Lundborg Foundation
Hopkins, MN 55343-7756
Assets: $444,720
Grants: $5,800
Fiscal Year End: 12/31/2005
EIN: 41-1708796

Lundeen Foundation
Fergus Falls, MN 56537-2106
Assets: $1,779,471
Grants: $55,100
Fiscal Year End: 12/31/2005
EIN: 41-1321858

Lupient Foundation
Minneapolis, MN 55426-1629
Assets: $29,955
Grants: $72,095
Fiscal Year End: 12/31/2005
EIN: 1-0547931

H. William Lurton Foundation
Long Lake, MN 55356
Assets: $641,146
Grants: $119,760
Fiscal Year End: 12/31/2005
EIN: 36-3492652

Lutheran Community Foundation
Minneapolis, MN 55415
Assets: $162,282,256
Grants: $7,986,049
Fiscal Year End: 12/31/2005
EIN: 41-1802412

The Lyman Lumber Company Foundation
Excelsior, MN 55331-3016
Assets: $1,525,890
Grants: $547,596
Fiscal Year End: 12/31/2005
EIN: 41-1889416

The Lytwyn Foundation
Minnetonka, MN 55305-5219
Assets: $191,126
Grants: $3,070
Fiscal Year End: 6/30/2006
EIN: 41-2023484

M-O-M Cares Employee Foundation
Northfield, MN 55057
Assets: $23,117
Grants: $64,178
Fiscal Year End: 12/31/2005
EIN: 41-1843367

Cargill MacMillan Jr. Family Foundation
Minneapolis, MN 55440
Assets: $1,505,218
Grants: $100,000
Fiscal Year End: 12/31/2005
EIN: 41-1706249

Sarah Stevens MacMillan Foundation
Minneapolis, MN 55440-9300
Assets: $6,676,983
Grants: $275,114
Fiscal Year End: 12/31/2005
EIN: 41-1830212

Ruth Spies Macrostie Irrevocable Trust
Duluth, MN 55802
Assets: $1,071,037
Grants: $54,592
Fiscal Year End: 9/30/2006
EIN: 41-6438110

Mahon Foundation
Minneapolis, MN 55431
Assets: $1,713,841
Grants: $634,800
Fiscal Year End: 12/31/2005
EIN: 41-6542523

Thomas and Judith Mahoney Family Foundation
Minnetonka, MN 55343-9014
Assets: $2,701,773
Grants: $104,100
Fiscal Year End: 12/31/2005
EIN: 41-1925964

Maleska Family Foundation
Melrose, MN 56352-1210
Assets: $67,293
Grants: $2,610
Fiscal Year End: 6/30/2006
EIN: 36-3432465

Malm Family Foundation
Hallock, MN 56728
Assets: $418,665
Grants: $19,600
Fiscal Year End: 12/31/2005
EIN: 41-1875424

David C. Malmberg Family Foundation
Burnsville, MN 55337
Assets: $146,850
Grants: $5,200
Fiscal Year End: 12/31/2005
EIN: 41-1952369

Mark and Roberta Mandel Family Charitable Trust
St Louis Park, MN 55416-4027
Assets: $2,842
Grants: $22,016
Fiscal Year End: 12/31/2005
EIN: 41-6391992

Manitou Fund
St Paul, MN 55113-2717
Assets: $12,509,025
Grants: $1,061,035
Fiscal Year End: 12/31/2005
EIN: 41-6055113

The Samuel S. and Joyce C. Marfield Charitable Foundation
Wayzata, MN 55391
Assets: $496,126
Grants: $5,072
Fiscal Year End: 6/30/2005
EIN: 41-1957654

Marlu Foundation
Minneapolis, MN 55440
Assets: $2,207,511
Grants: $71,012
Fiscal Year End: 12/31/2005
EIN: 41-1850047

Marquit-Grieser Fund
Minneapolis, MN 55416
Assets: $18,341
Grants: $2,940
Fiscal Year End: 12/31/2005
EIN: 41-1827841

David R. Marshall Foundation
Rice, MN 556367
Assets: $22,733
Grants: $107,469
Fiscal Year End: 12/31/2005
EIN: 41-1850600

Martin & Brown Foundation
Plymouth, MN 55446-0286
Assets: $11,767,752
Grants: $404,500
Fiscal Year End: 6/30/2006
EIN: 41-1997225

Lillian Marvin Trust
St Paul, MN 55164-0713
Assets: $735,922
Grants: $38,132
Fiscal Year End: 6/30/2006
EIN: 41-6249065

The Jack and Sarah Matasosky Foundation
Lakeville, MN 55044-4654
Assets: $6,712
Grants: $45,751
Fiscal Year End: 12/31/2005
EIN: 41-1973635

Richard J. and Mary Lou Mathiowetz Foundation
Sleepy Eye, MN 56085
Assets: $320,002
Grants: $6,500
Fiscal Year End: 6/30/2005
EIN: 41-1766191

Matrix Foundation
Rosemount, MN 55068
Assets: $534,600
Grants: $24,000
Fiscal Year End: 12/31/2005
EIN: 41-1906360

The D. and J. Maurer Foundation
Marine On St Croix, MN 55047-0315
Assets: $213,980
Grants: $39,000
Fiscal Year End: 12/31/2005
EIN: 41-1877112

John J. and Maryanne T. Mauriel Family Foundation
Edina, MN 55435-1723
Assets: $391,353
Grants: $21,000
Fiscal Year End: 12/31/2005
EIN: 75-3160255

May Family Foundation
St Louis Park, MN 55426
Assets: $27,992
Grants: $14,000
Fiscal Year End: 12/31/2005
EIN: 41-6364995

Roger and Nancy McCabe Foundation
Edina, MN 55424
Assets: $8,187,626
Grants: $124,020
Fiscal Year End: 12/31/2005
EIN: 20-2990948

Jim and Diane McCarthy Foundation
Excelsior, MN 55331-9351
Assets: $349,051
Grants: $19,045
Fiscal Year End: 12/31/2005
EIN: 41-1957943

McCarthy-Bjorklund Foundation
St Paul, MN 55101
Assets: $15,721,859
Grants: $789,275
Fiscal Year End: 12/31/2005
EIN: 41-1794941

The Thomas and Mary McCary Family Foundation
St Paul, MN 55164-0713
Assets: $3,919
Grants: $42,600
Fiscal Year End: 12/31/2005
EIN: 75-3074681

Marcus McCoy Foundation
Plymouth, MN 55447
Assets: $4,899,336
Grants: $258,000
Fiscal Year End: 12/31/2005
EIN: 41-1989867

McDowell Foundation
Minneapolis, MN 55402
Assets: $388,594
Grants: $35,500
Fiscal Year End: 12/31/2005
EIN: 41-1684151

McElrath Foundation
Edina, MN 55424
Assets: $205,369
Grants: $6,750
Fiscal Year End: 12/31/2005
EIN: 41-1481173

McGlynn Family Foundation
St Paul, MN 55105
Assets: $1,237,534
Grants: $100,000
Fiscal Year End: 12/31/2005
EIN: 41-1784157

William W. and Nadine M. McGuire Family Foundation
Minneapolis, MN 55402
Assets: $6,760,320
Grants: $3,860,000
Fiscal Year End: 12/31/2005
EIN: 41-1861103

John and Esther McLaughlin Foundation
Marshall, MN 56258
Assets: $74,559
Grants: $52,280
Fiscal Year End: 12/31/2005
EIN: 41-1712035

Richard F. McNamara Family Foundation
Minneapolis, MN 55439
Assets: $4,019,276
Grants: $870,110
Fiscal Year End: 12/31/2005
EIN: 41-1725127

McVay Foundation
Minnetonka, MN 55345-4576
Assets: $11,917,742
Grants: $558,062
Fiscal Year End: 12/31/2005
EIN: 36-3311833

Meadowood Foundation
Minneapolis, MN 55402-4523
Assets: $12,014,123
Grants: $558,935
Fiscal Year End: 12/31/2005
EIN: 41-0943749

Kendrick B. Melrose Family Foundation
Minneapolis, MN 55420
Assets: $6,244,547
Grants: $281,073
Fiscal Year End: 12/31/2005
EIN: 41-1894134

Mercedes Foundation
Mahtomedi, MN 55155
Assets: $1,547,643
Grants: $80,000
Fiscal Year End: 12/31/2005
EIN: 41-6041352

Mersky Family Foundation
Minneapolis, MN 55401
Assets: $547,926
Grants: $5,500
Fiscal Year End: 12/31/2005
EIN: 41-1869152

Walter S. and Margaret L. Meyers Charitable Foundation
Minneapolis, MN 55402-3395
Assets: $150,054
Grants: $14,233
Fiscal Year End: 12/31/2005
EIN: 41-1867239

MGR Foundation
Minnetonka, MN 55343-9014
Assets: $2,733,399
Grants: $106,500
Fiscal Year End: 12/31/2005
EIN: 41-1939826

Ernest S. and Sally A. Micek Family Foundation
Minneapolis, MN 55402
Assets: $959,636
Grants: $39,100
Fiscal Year End: 12/31/2005
EIN: 31-1723426

Mickelson Media Foundation
St Paul, MN 55108
Assets: $584,334
Grants: $35,000
Fiscal Year End: 12/31/2005
EIN: 74-2530419

Midcontinent Media Foundation
Minneapolis, MN 55435-7979
Assets: $110,139
Grants: $168,299
Fiscal Year End: 8/31/2005
EIN: 36-3556764

The Millennium Foundation
Wayzata, MN 55391
Assets: $28,416
Grants: $5,660
Fiscal Year End: 12/31/2005
EIN: 41-1867813

Alan and Diane Miller Family Foundation
Wayzata, MN 55391
Assets: $5,309
Grants: $21,725
Fiscal Year End: 12/31/2005
EIN: 41-1867756

Ben Miller Foundation
Minneapolis, MN 55416-4446
Assets: $1,279,610
Grants: $55,000
Fiscal Year End: 12/31/2005
EIN: 41-1775239

Craig and Beverley Miller Family Foundation
Edina, MN 55435
Assets: $989,200
Grants: $27,730
Fiscal Year End: 12/31/2005
EIN: 20-3181426

The Doug and Martha Miller Foundation
Edina, MN 55435-5872
Assets: $1,550,057
Grants: $54,950
Fiscal Year End: 12/31/2005
EIN: 20-1909215

The Kathy and Tom Miller Family Foundation
Edina, MN 55435
Assets: $1,419,993
Grants: $156,050
Fiscal Year End: 12/31/2005
EIN: 20-0117082

The Rudolph W. and Gladys Miller Medical Research Foundation
Excelsior, MN 55331-3306
Assets: $979,802
Grants: $114,720
Fiscal Year End: 11/30/2005
EIN: 41-1388774

Sam Miller Foundation
Minneapolis, MN 55458-1398
Assets: $835,845
Grants: $53,915
Fiscal Year End: 12/31/2005
EIN: 41-6035570

Minnesota Center for Philanthropy
Northfield, MN 55057
Assets: $12,052,988
Grants: $1,066,954
Fiscal Year End: 12/31/2005
EIN: 41-2010078

Minnesota Chamber Foundation
St Paul, MN 55101-4901
Assets: $158,091
Fiscal Year End: 9/30/2005
EIN: 41-1453093

Minnesota Community Foundation
St Paul, MN 55101-1797
Assets: $148,301,161
Grants: $6,881,799
Fiscal Year End: 12/31/2005
EIN: 41-0832480

Minnesota Dental Foundation
St Paul, MN 55104
Assets: $255,605
Grants: $8,000
Fiscal Year End: 12/31/2005
EIN: 41-1927049

Minnesota Music Teachers Association Foundation
Edina, MN 55435
Assets: $307,684
Grants: $8,340
Fiscal Year End: 7/31/2005
EIN: 81-0635967

Miracle - Ear Children's Foundation
Plymouth, MN 55446
Assets: $36,781
Grants: $71,747
Fiscal Year End: 12/31/2005
EIN: 41-1677967

Wildey H. Mitchell Family Foundation
Duluth, MN 55802
Assets: $7,919,642
Grants: $450,000
Fiscal Year End: 12/31/2005
EIN: 41-6222997

Mithun Family Foundation
Minneapolis, MN 55402
Assets: $53,411,182
Grants: $450,000
Fiscal Year End: 12/31/2005
EIN: 36-3495071

Molitor Family Foundation
Minneapolis, MN 55402
Assets: $161,191
Fiscal Year End: 12/31/2005
EIN: 41-1876568

The Lourdes and John Moore Foundation
Minneapolis, MN 55402
Assets: $27,629
Grants: $9,000
Fiscal Year End: 12/31/2005
EIN: 41-1826109

The Morning Foundation
St Paul, MN 55108
Assets: $7,578,354
Grants: $452,246
Fiscal Year End: 12/31/2005
EIN: 74-2803921

Ralph K. Morris Foundation
Minneapolis, MN 55402
Grants: $12,214
Fiscal Year End: 12/31/2005

Morrow Foundation
Minneapolis, MN 55405
Assets: $47,286
Grants: $1,088
Fiscal Year End: 12/31/2005
EIN: 41-1859316

The Morsman Family Foundation
Deephaven, MN 55391
Assets: $484,933
Grants: $22,500
Fiscal Year End: 12/31/2005
EIN: 41-2008689

The Mortenson Family Foundation
Minneapolis, MN 55422-4899
Assets: $5,790,329
Grants: $190,000
Fiscal Year End: 12/31/2005
EIN: 41-1958621

Kevin J. Mossier Foundation
Edina, MN 55439-2148
Assets: $6,635,789
Grants: $538,550
Fiscal Year End: 12/31/2005
EIN: 41-1863691

Thomas Ryan Mulcahy Foundation
Arden Hills, MN 55112-3671
Assets: $211,170
Grants: $2,500
Fiscal Year End: 9/30/2005
EIN: 41-1765500

The Mullen Flynn Foundation
St Paul, MN 55118-4146
Assets: $339,918
Grants: $451
Fiscal Year End: 12/31/2005
EIN: 36-4171920

The Ina and Harry Murphy Foundation
Bloomington, MN 55431-1115
Assets: $273,331
Grants: $325
Fiscal Year End: 12/31/2005
EIN: 23-7047042

Ali Murtaza Foundation
Eden Prairie, MN 55347-1120
Assets: $44,942
Grants: $2,000
Fiscal Year End: 10/31/2005
EIN: 41-1766988

Myers Foundation, Inc.
St Paul, MN 55116
Assets: $1,412,374
Grants: $58,500
Fiscal Year End: 12/31/2005
EIN: 41-6022295

Charles and Candice Nadler Family Foundation
Excelsior, MN 55331-9574
Assets: $539,980
Grants: $50,550
Fiscal Year End: 12/31/2005
EIN: 41-1856259

Nandale Foundation
Marine On St Croix, MN 55047
Assets: $75,293
Grants: $9,050
Fiscal Year End: 12/31/2005
EIN: 41-1814184

NBC Foundation
Wayzata, MN 55391-4305
Assets: $2,279,511
Grants: $104,000
Fiscal Year End: 12/31/2005
EIN: 31-1727616

Curtis and Marjorie Nelson Family Foundation
Minnetonka, MN 55305
Assets: $7,643
Grants: $61,569
Fiscal Year End: 12/31/2005
EIN: 41-1861482

Gordon Nelson Memorial Foundation
Hugo, MN 55038
Assets: $66,501
Grants: $4,000
Fiscal Year End: 12/31/2005
EIN: 41-1783820

New Life Christian Foundation
Edina, MN 55436-1616
Assets: $1,541
Grants: $58,100
Fiscal Year End: 12/31/2005
EIN: 41-1654964

Harriet and Nathan Newman Foundation
Minnetonka, MN 55305
Assets: $122,642
Grants: $21,590
Fiscal Year End: 12/31/2005
EIN: 41-1907379

Jane R. Newman Charitable Trust
St Louis Park, MN 55409
Assets: $413,466
Grants: $64,950
Fiscal Year End: 12/31/2005
EIN: 41-6417159

Louis E. Newman Charitable Trust
Mendota Heights, MN 55118
Assets: $432,624
Grants: $52,462
Fiscal Year End: 12/31/2005
EIN: 41-1850021

Nicholson Family Foundation
St Paul, MN 55102
Assets: $11,159,508
Grants: $414,600
Fiscal Year End: 6/30/2006
EIN: 41-1572346

The Charles E. and Nancy E. Nolan Foundation
Wayzata, MN 55391-1350
Assets: $2,689,554
Grants: $125,000
Fiscal Year End: 12/31/2005
EIN: 54-6507800

R. B. Nordick Foundation
West Fargo, ND 58078-3500
Assets: $25,627,664
Grants: $1,071,000
Fiscal Year End: 12/31/2005
EIN: 45-0442920

Norling Brothers Foundation
St Paul, MN 55101
Assets: $953,303
Grants: $109,500
Fiscal Year End: 12/31/2005
EIN: 41-6100113

North Country Health Services Foundation
Bemidji, MN 56601
Assets: $4,556,584
Grants: $40,000
Fiscal Year End: 9/30/2005
EIN: 41-1389317

North End Community Foundation
St Paul, MN 55117-4426
Assets: $292,760
Grants: $126,697
Fiscal Year End: 12/31/2005
EIN: 41-1972134

North Star Foundation
Duluth, MN 55802
Assets: $3,962,654
Grants: $109,650
Fiscal Year End: 12/31/2005
EIN: 41-1894264

Northern Coop Foundation
Wadena, MN 56482-0052
Assets: $193,367
Grants: $6,900
Fiscal Year End: 9/30/2005
EIN: 36-3258840

Northern Star Foundation
St Paul, MN 55102
Assets: $5,823,054
Grants: $279,592
Fiscal Year End: 10/31/2005
EIN: 41-6030832

Northwest Area Foundation
St Paul, MN 55107
Assets: $483,303,560
Grants: $16,933,789
Fiscal Year End: 3/31/2006
EIN: 41-0719221

Northwest Title Foundation
St Paul, MN 55101
Assets: $70,085
Grants: $6,554
Fiscal Year End: 12/31/2005
EIN: 41-2021032

James B. and Catherine L. O'Meara Charitable Trust
Burnsville, MN 55337-1602
Assets: $63,428
Grants: $10,000
Fiscal Year End: 12/31/2005
EIN: 41-6384929

Oak Grove Foundation
Minneapolis, MN 55402
Assets: $1,111,556
Grants: $95,720
Fiscal Year End: 12/31/2005
EIN: 41-1913047

Oakleaf Foundation
Minneapolis, MN 55402-4523
Assets: $1,745,012
Fiscal Year End: 12/31/2005
EIN: 41-6080485

The John K. and Margaret A. Ogren Foundation
Stillwater, MN 55082
Assets: $862,651
Grants: $48,681
Fiscal Year End: 12/31/2005
EIN: 41-1819638

The Olseth Foundation
Hopkins, MN 55343-8520
Assets: $3,602,121
Fiscal Year End: 12/31/2005
EIN: 41-1875950

Olson Foundation
Bloomington, MN 55437-1927
Assets: $215,021
Grants: $8,000
Fiscal Year End: 12/31/2005
EIN: 23-7152509

Earl B. Olson Foundation
Willmar, MN 56201
Assets: $3,262,350
Grants: $98,500
Fiscal Year End: 12/31/2005
EIN: 41-6315927

Onan Family Foundation
Minneapolis, MN 55426-4911
Assets: $7,488,769
Grants: $280,000
Fiscal Year End: 12/31/2005
EIN: 41-6033631

Open Door Foundation
St Louis Park, MN 55416-1684
Assets: $2,747,950
Grants: $126,000
Fiscal Year End: 12/31/2005
EIN: 41-1859476

Oppegaard Family Foundation, Inc.
Walker, MN 56484
Assets: $32,324
Grants: $67,859
Fiscal Year End: 12/31/2005
EIN: 41-2021741

Opus Foundation
Minnetonka, MN 55343-9002
Assets: $46,882,690
Grants: $1,450,096
Fiscal Year End: 12/31/2005
EIN: 41-1983284

Opus Prize Foundation
Minnetonka, MN 55343
Assets: $28,187,774
Grants: $1,260,000
Fiscal Year End: 12/31/2005
EIN: 46-0434399

Muriel Orcutt Charitable Trust
Minneapolis, MN 55402
Assets: $1,011,867
Grants: $52,772
Fiscal Year End: 12/31/2005
EIN: 41-6502349

The Oswald Family Foundation
Minnetonka, MN 55305-5219
Assets: $17,705,510
Grants: $589,600
Fiscal Year End: 12/31/2005
EIN: 36-3486546

Paul M. Otteson Foundation
Owatonna, MN 55060
Assets: $765,683
Grants: $42,000
Fiscal Year End: 12/31/2005
EIN: 41-6079412

Ouellette Foundation
St Paul, MN 55101
Assets: $439,106
Grants: $24,459
Fiscal Year End: 12/31/2005
EIN: 41-6038366

The Owasso Foundation
St Paul, MN 55113
Assets: $9,578
Grants: $44,400
Fiscal Year End: 12/31/2005
EIN: 41-1797115

Owens-Pesavento Family Foundation
Hibbing, MN 55746
Assets: $229,778
Grants: $10,479
Fiscal Year End: 12/31/2005
EIN: 41-1812134

Pacific Foundation
Hibbing, MN 55746-0408
Assets: $47,555
Grants: $950
Fiscal Year End: 3/31/2006
EIN: 41-6033767

Palm Foundation
Wayzata, MN 55391-3219
Assets: $134
Fiscal Year End: 12/31/2005
EIN: 31-1802684

Panamerican Foundation
St Paul, MN 55116
Assets: $122,712
Grants: $35,670
Fiscal Year End: 12/31/2005
EIN: 41-1579854

Paparella Family Foundation
Minneapolis, MN 55405
Assets: $225,111
Grants: $8,258
Fiscal Year End: 12/31/2005
EIN: 41-1930076

J. Paper Foundation
St Paul, MN 55101-4901
Assets: $106,746
Fiscal Year End: 12/31/2005
EIN: 36-3290829

L. and A. F. Paper Foundation
St Paul, MN 55101-4901
Assets: $165,287
Grants: $7,000
Fiscal Year End: 12/31/2005
EIN: 36-3290827

Paradigm Foundation, Inc.
Burnsville, MN 55337
Assets: $20,450
Grants: $8,000
Fiscal Year End: 12/31/2005
EIN: 73-1627902

The Patch Foundation
St Anthony, MN 55418
Assets: $1,526,488
Grants: $134,800
Fiscal Year End: 12/31/2005
EIN: 41-1873951

Paulson Family Foundation
Excelsior, MN 55331
Assets: $447,134
Grants: $69,000
Fiscal Year End: 12/31/2005
EIN: 20-0483376

Pax Christi Foundation
Minneapolis, MN 55431
Assets: $7,116,125
Grants: $2,317,250
Fiscal Year End: 6/30/2006
EIN: 36-3550495

Charles D. Gilfillan Paxton Memorial
Redwood Falls, MN 56283
Assets: $101,275
Grants: $5,395
Fiscal Year End: 12/31/2005
EIN: 41-6023986

Peace Maker Foundation
Roseville, MN 55113
Assets: $130,403
Grants: $21,750
Fiscal Year End: 12/31/2005
EIN: 41-1913867

Peace Shalom Foundation
St Paul, MN 55118-3918
Assets: $2,512,748
Grants: $105,000
Fiscal Year End: 11/30/2005
EIN: 41-1654125

Penstemon Foundation
Edina, MN 55439
Assets: $465,684
Grants: $157,260
Fiscal Year End: 12/31/2005
EIN: 41-1797004

Norman Perl Foundation
Palm Beach, FL 33480
Assets: $256,529
Grants: $12,517
Fiscal Year End: 12/31/2005
EIN: 41-6080064

Frieda Perschau Irrevocable Trust
Glencoe, MN 55336
Assets: $252,443
Grants: $10,000
Fiscal Year End: 12/31/2005
EIN: 41-6486621

Marvin J. Pertzik Foundation
St Paul, MN 55101-1792
Assets: $856,993
Grants: $46,250
Fiscal Year End: 12/31/2005
EIN: 41-1364755

John and Sara Peterman Foundation
Minneapolis, MN 55403
Assets: $66,599
Grants: $15,110
Fiscal Year End: 12/31/2005
EIN: 41-1925526

G. and D. Peterson Foundation
Minneapolis, MN 55402
Assets: $1,003,872
Grants: $44,500
Fiscal Year End: 12/31/2005
EIN: 41-1866420

Thomas J. Petters Family Foundation
Minnetonka, MN 55343
Assets: $5,136
Grants: $1,384,175
Fiscal Year End: 12/31/2005
EIN: 41-2010037

The Phileona Foundation
Minneapolis, MN 55416
Assets: $42,083,749
Grants: $1,045,790
Fiscal Year End: 9/30/2005
EIN: 41-1763225

Edward and Leslye Phillips Family Foundation
Minneapolis, MN 55414
Assets: $30,471,615
Grants: $251,994
Fiscal Year End: 12/31/2005
EIN: 20-2041201

Phynque Phamily Phoundation
Minneapolis, MN 55402
Assets: $3,279,812
Grants: $0
Fiscal Year End: 12/31/2005
EIN: 32-0022811

Raymond B. Pinson Family Foundation
Rosemount, MN 55068
Assets: $1,851,201
Grants: $131,261
Fiscal Year End: 12/31/2005
EIN: 41-1922232

Pipestone Adventist Church Foundation
Pipestone, MN 56164
Assets: $34,906
Grants: $7,600
Fiscal Year End: 12/31/2005
EIN: 41-1627368

John Joseph Plank Charitable Trust
Minneapolis, MN 55402
Assets: $574,815
Grants: $12,885
Fiscal Year End: 5/31/2006
EIN: 20-2610711

Poehler/Stremel Charitable Trust
St Paul, MN 55164-9912
Assets: $2,113,019
Grants: $114,529
Fiscal Year End: 6/30/2006
EIN: 41-6494501

Poepl Family Foundation
Vermillion, MN 55085
Assets: $294,937
Grants: $261,000
Fiscal Year End: 12/31/2005
EIN: 41-1894854

The Pomegranate Philanthropic Foundation
Minneapolis, MN 55416-4691
Assets: $25,207
Grants: $5,975
Fiscal Year End: 12/31/2005
EIN: 02-0608376

Arthur J. Popehn Foundation
Minneapolis, MN 55402
Assets: $936,541
Grants: $40,000
Fiscal Year End: 12/31/2005
EIN: 41-6014558

The Portland Trust
St Paul, MN 55164-0713
Assets: $8,512
Grants: $173
Fiscal Year End: 12/31/2005
EIN: 36-7396158

The Powell Family Foundation
Edina, MN 55424
Assets: $14,395
Grants: $1,500
Fiscal Year End: 12/31/2005
EIN: 41-1859266

Power Charitable Foundation
Alexandria, MN 56308
Assets: $130,141
Grants: $8,000
Fiscal Year End: 12/31/2005
EIN: 41-1654470

Pritschet Foundation
Minneapolis, MN 55409
Assets: $273,138
Grants: $14,554
Fiscal Year End: 12/31/2005
EIN: 41-1972432

David C. and Margaret F. Prosser Foundation
Shorewood, MN 55331
Assets: $217,012
Grants: $26,204
Fiscal Year End: 12/31/2005
EIN: 41-1875877

Pump Foundation
Minneapolis, MN 55402-3395
Assets: $1,634,547
Grants: $77,000
Fiscal Year End: 12/31/2005
EIN: 41-1653992

Mark A. Pursley Memorial Foundation
St Paul, MN 55107-2507
Assets: $118,719
Grants: $6,700
Fiscal Year End: 12/31/2005
EIN: 36-3557150

Quadion Foundation
Plymouth, MN 55441
Assets: $551,159
Grants: $62,931
Fiscal Year End: 12/31/2005
EIN: 41-1377918

Quiet Waters Foundation
Minneapolis, MN 55403
Assets: $1,231
Grants: $21,472
Fiscal Year End: 12/31/2005
EIN: 41-1733673

William D. Radichel Foundation
Mankato, MN 56002-0880
Assets: $169,750
Grants: $456,000
Fiscal Year End: 6/30/2006
EIN: 41-1944317

Raft Charitable Foundation
Minneapolis, MN 55402
Assets: $8,835,467
Grants: $245,500
Fiscal Year End: 12/31/2005
EIN: 41-6463940

Raleigh Foundation
Lake Elmo, MN 55042
Assets: $801,560
Grants: $1,500
Fiscal Year End: 12/31/2005
EIN: 20-1054002

Ramy Foundation
Mankato, MN 56001
Assets: $355,168
Grants: $5,175
Fiscal Year End: 12/31/2005
EIN: 41-6053741

The Randall Family Foundation
Edina, MN 55439
Assets: $155,372
Grants: $35,750
Fiscal Year End: 12/31/2005
EIN: 72-1544179

R. and S. Rappaport Family Foundation
Hopkins, MN 55343
Assets: $412,382
Grants: $16,942
Fiscal Year End: 12/31/2005
EIN: 20-1948425

Walter C. Rasmussen - Northeast Bank Foundation
Minneapolis, MN 55413
Assets: $12,199
Grants: $72,900
Fiscal Year End: 12/31/2005
EIN: 41-6373302

Herman and Therese Ratelle Foundation
Edina, MN 55436
Assets: $297,598
Grants: $17,000
Fiscal Year End: 12/31/2005
EIN: 41-1870709

Mark and Karen Rauenhorst Family Foundation
Minnetonka, MN 55343
Assets: $3,873,323
Grants: $19,600
Fiscal Year End: 12/31/2005
EIN: 41-1925821

RCS Foundation
South St Paul, MN 55075-5918
Assets: $9,889
Grants: $6,000
Fiscal Year End: 12/31/2005
EIN: 38-3654688

Frank and Evelyn Rechtzigel Family Foundation
Lakeville, MN 55044
Assets: $546,473
Fiscal Year End: 12/31/2005
EIN: 41-1889747

Regis Foundation for Breast Cancer Research
Minneapolis, MN 55439-2103
Assets: $243,579
Grants: $491,805
Fiscal Year End: 6/30/2005
EIN: 41-1729911

R. William and Mary Ann Reilly Family Foundation
Lilydale, MN 55118-4481
Assets: $54,570
Grants: $16,316
Fiscal Year End: 12/31/2005
EIN: 36-3311965

Reimer Foundation
Bloomington, MN 55437
Assets: $5,226,531
Grants: $621,600
Fiscal Year End: 11/30/2005
EIN: 41-1557662

Bernard D. Reisberg and Joan B. Reisberg Family Foundation
Robbinsdale, MN 55422
Assets: $47,785
Grants: $4,750
Fiscal Year End: 12/31/2005
EIN: 75-3159170

James L. Reissner Family Foundation
Minneapolis, MN 55439
Assets: $6,167
Grants: $11,235
Fiscal Year End: 12/31/2005
EIN: 41-1989610

The Robert and Helen Remick Charitable Foundation
Lakefield, MN 56150
Assets: $7,927,596
Grants: $194,890
Fiscal Year End: 12/31/2005
EIN: 41-1950527

The Retel Foundation
Waconia, MN 55387-9691
Assets: $145,402
Grants: $5,375
Fiscal Year End: 12/31/2005
EIN: 41-6443943

The Kurt and Rali Retzler Family Foundation
Orono, MN 55391-9133
Assets: $164,221
Grants: $8,000
Fiscal Year End: 12/31/2005
EIN: 41-1925650

Robert and Anne Reznick Family Foundation
Minneapolis, MN 55416-3840
Assets: $947,743
Grants: $64,943
Fiscal Year End: 12/31/2005
EIN: 41-1341420

The Rhm Foundation
Bloomington, MN 55431
Assets: $204,541
Grants: $35,500
Fiscal Year End: 12/31/2005
EIN: 41-1988494

Page Jones Richards Family Foundation
St Paul, MN 55164-0713
Assets: $1,357,160
Grants: $46,000
Fiscal Year End: 12/31/2005
EIN: 41-1910977

Autumn Rieks Foundation
Woodbury, MN 55125-2921
Assets: $214,930
Grants: $43,850
Fiscal Year End: 12/31/2005
EIN: 41-1832517

Rikkers Foundation
Minneapolis, MN 55405-2456
Assets: $78,073
Grants: $16,000
Fiscal Year End: 12/31/2005
EIN: 41-1892869

Ring Foundation
Minneapolis, MN 55416
Assets: $225,255
Grants: $19,287
Fiscal Year End: 12/31/2005
EIN: 41-6024430

RJW Foundation
Excelsior, MN 55331
Assets: $2,190,065
Grants: $90,750
Fiscal Year End: 12/31/2005
EIN: 41-1858383

RMCGK Wood Family Foundation
Plymouth, MN 55446
Assets: $99,054
Grants: $14,500
Fiscal Year End: 12/31/2005
EIN: 41-1994414

Donald and Marie Roberts Charitable Foundation
White Bear Lake, MN 55110
Assets: $3,103,242
Grants: $163,042
Fiscal Year End: 12/31/2005
EIN: 41-1765517

Robina Foundation
Minneapolis, MN 55402
Assets: $9,837,990
Grants: $150,000
Fiscal Year End: 12/31/2005
EIN: 20-1163610

Robins Family Foundation
Gem Lake, MN 55110
Assets: $746,572
Grants: $40,000
Fiscal Year End: 12/31/2005
EIN: 41-6033422

Robins, Kaplan, Miller & Ciresi, L.L.P. Private Foundation
Minneapolis, MN 55402
Assets: $1,498,334
Grants: $1,692,874
Fiscal Year End: 8/31/2005
EIN: 41-1735325

Robinson Trust
Coon Rapids, MN 55433-5402
Assets: $97,750
Grants: $14,205
Fiscal Year End: 12/31/2005
EIN: 41-6337797

C. H. Robinson Worldwide Foundation
Eden Prairie, MN 55344
Assets: $3,728,232
Grants: $329,360
Fiscal Year End: 12/31/2005
EIN: 68-0599299

D. B. Robinson Foundation
Winona, MN 55987-5548
Assets: $519,246
Grants: $43,400
Fiscal Year End: 12/31/2005
EIN: 41-6022097

Rockler Jackson Family Foundation
Orono, MN 55356-9730
Assets: $556,564
Grants: $123,794
Fiscal Year End: 12/31/2005
EIN: 41-2023713

The Rodman Foundation
St Paul, MN 55101
Assets: $4,979,658
Grants: $220,250
Fiscal Year End: 12/31/2005
EIN: 23-7025570

Rogers Plastics Foundation
Rogers, MN 55374
Assets: $160,239
Grants: $9,000
Fiscal Year End: 6/30/2005
EIN: 41-1680724

John F. Rooney Family Charitable Foundation
Afton, MN 55001-9773
Assets: $2,329,928
Grants: $124,100
Fiscal Year End: 12/31/2005
EIN: 41-1925764

Laura Rose Irrevocable Trust
St Paul, MN 55164-0713
Assets: $127,398
Grants: $2,439
Fiscal Year End: 12/31/2005
EIN: 41-6178176

The Rosen Family Foundation
Fairmont, MN 56031
Assets: $670,643
Grants: $40,000
Fiscal Year End: 11/30/2005
EIN: 41-2054672

Guenther Roth Foundation
Edina, MN 55439
Assets: $818,049
Grants: $47,000
Fiscal Year End: 12/31/2005
EIN: 36-3545401

Rothfork Family Foundation
Melrose, MN 56352-1375
Assets: $560,508
Grants: $24,600
Fiscal Year End: 8/31/2006
EIN: 41-1339508

Roycraft Foundation
Minneapolis, MN 55403
Assets: $965,169
Grants: $44,774
Fiscal Year End: 12/31/2005
EIN: 41-6019643

Genevieve J. Rudbeck Irrevocable Trust
St Cloud, MN 56302
Assets: $669,916
Grants: $50,338
Fiscal Year End: 12/31/2005
EIN: 41-6334577

Max and Linda Rutman Family Foundation
Scottsdale, AZ 85258
Assets: $215,998
Grants: $210,665
Fiscal Year End: 12/31/2005
EIN: 91-2139114

Rutstrum Wilderness Trust
St Paul Park, MN 55071-0310
Assets: $303,531
Grants: $10,000
Fiscal Year End: 12/31/2005
EIN: 41-6339414

S. J. Electro Systems Foundation
Detroit Lakes, MN 56502-1708
Assets: $579,327
Grants: $15,909
Fiscal Year End: 12/31/2005
EIN: 36-3556774

The Sabes Family Foundation
Minneapolis, MN 55402
Assets: $46,174,815
Grants: $1,796,215
Fiscal Year End: 12/31/2005
EIN: 41-1699714

Sabeti Carretta Foundation
North Oaks, MN 55127
Assets: $70,428
Grants: $5,000
Fiscal Year End: 6/30/2004
EIN: 52-2388455

Sam Foundation
Minneapolis, MN 55402
Assets: $5,000
Grants: $330
Fiscal Year End: 12/31/2005
EIN: 20-0353925

Sampson Family Charitable Foundation
Eden Prairie, MN 55344
Assets: $1,154,313
Grants: $51,113
Fiscal Year End: 9/30/2005
EIN: 41-1986354

Sampson Family Foundation
Hector, MN 55342
Assets: $19,073
Grants: $50,372
Fiscal Year End: 12/31/2005
EIN: 41-1681957

Sampson Foundation, Inc.
Edina, MN 55439
Assets: $22,673
Grants: $7,781
Fiscal Year End: 12/31/2005
EIN: 41-1886805

Katharine Moore Sanderson Trust
St Paul, MN 55164-0713
Assets: $865,327
Grants: $41,954
Fiscal Year End: 12/31/2005
EIN: 41-6203801

Thomas C. and Lois L. Sando Foundation
Minneapolis, MN 55402-1498
Assets: $1,306,333
Grants: $110,000
Fiscal Year End: 12/31/2005
EIN: 41-1676820

Sanger Family Foundation
Wayzata, MN 55391-2915
Assets: $2,974,308
Grants: $755,136
Fiscal Year End: 12/31/2005
EIN: 41-1859638

Sayer Charitable Foundation
Long Lake, MN 55356
Assets: $3,240,214
Grants: $275,950
Fiscal Year End: 12/31/2005
EIN: 41-1793832

Scherber Family Foundation
Plymouth, MN 55447
Assets: $129,959
Grants: $7,146
Fiscal Year End: 12/31/2005
EIN: 41-1731032

Clement W. and Anastasia M. Scheurer Family Catholic Church Fund
Mankato, MN 56001
Assets: $72,095
Grants: $1,289
Fiscal Year End: 12/31/2005
EIN: 41-6151959

Schoeneckers Foundation
Minneapolis, MN 55440
Assets: $100,912
Grants: $561,561
Fiscal Year End: 9/30/2005
EIN: 41-1369001

Arlan A. Schonberg Foundation
St Paul, MN 55101
Grants: $25,000
Fiscal Year End: 6/30/2005

Richard M. Schulze Family Foundation
Minneapolis, MN 55437
Assets: $15,291,119
Grants: $700,000
Fiscal Year End: 12/31/2005
EIN: 20-0752440

Mendon F. Schutt Foundation
Minneapolis, MN
Assets: $584,937
Grants: $100,000
Fiscal Year End: 12/31/2005
EIN: 41-6028059

Arvid W. and Judy R. Schwartz Family Foundation
Green Isle, MN 55338
Assets: $175,217
Grants: $16,300
Fiscal Year End: 12/31/2005
EIN: 41-2013422

Scottish Rite Foundation of Minneapolis
Minneapolis, MN 55405
Assets: $939,060
Grants: $70,000
Fiscal Year End: 6/30/2006
EIN: 41-6024265

The Scrooby Foundation
St Paul, MN 55101-1792
Assets: $14,406,753
Grants: $283,078
Fiscal Year End: 6/30/2006
EIN: 41-1795397

Seba Foundation
Maple Plain, MN 55359-9716
Assets: $1,650,548
Grants: $15,000
Fiscal Year End: 12/31/2005
EIN: 55-0789357

Second Wind Charitable Trust
Stillwater, MN 55082
Assets: $75,078
Grants: $11,152
Fiscal Year End: 12/31/2005
EIN: 41-1748812

Security State Bank Foundation
Hibbing, MN 55746
Assets: $255,148
Grants: $32,052
Fiscal Year End: 12/31/2005
EIN: 41-1830282

The Sedona Foundation
Minneapolis, MN 55405
Assets: $39,363
Grants: $5,000
Fiscal Year End: 12/31/2005
EIN: 41-2005511

Fred M. Seed Foundation
Minneapolis, MN 55403
Assets: $915,961
Grants: $48,988
Fiscal Year End: 12/31/2005
EIN: 41-6029620

The Thomas W. and Janice A. Segar Charitable Trust
Bloomington, MN 55431-2841
Assets: $42,720
Grants: $2,478
Fiscal Year End: 12/31/2005
EIN: 41-6451322

Andrew John Sellner Memorial Foundation
Montevideo, MN 56265-1311
Assets: $42,079
Grants: $2,515
Fiscal Year End: 12/31/2005
EIN: 41-1892710

The Richard and Rossy Shaller Family Foundation
West St Paul, MN 55118
Assets: $505,533
Grants: $24,053
Fiscal Year End: 12/31/2005
EIN: 41-2009631

The Hy and Myra Shapiro Family Foundation
Minneapolis, MN 55402-1415
Assets: $211,366
Grants: $3,409
Fiscal Year End: 12/31/2005
EIN: 38-3671618

Carl Sharpe Foundation, Inc.
Minneapolis, MN 55416-4755
Assets: $1,990
Grants: $1,254
Fiscal Year End: 12/31/2005
EIN: 41-6038714

The Shaw Family Foundation
Stillwater, MN 55082
Assets: $127,032
Grants: $6,980
Fiscal Year End: 12/31/2005
EIN: 41-1896465

Shezada Begum Cancer Foundation
Hopkins, MN 55343-7756
Assets: $11,697
Grants: $0
Fiscal Year End: 12/31/2005
EIN: 41-1706875

Shimek Family Foundation
Minneapolis, MN 55401
Assets: $2,720
Grants: $202,331
Fiscal Year End: 12/31/2005
EIN: 41-1859984

Dan and Kay Shimek Family Foundation
Minneapolis, MN 55401
Assets: $31,855
Grants: $358,354
Fiscal Year End: 12/31/2005
EIN: 27-0035772

Sieben Foundation, Inc.
Minnetonka, MN 55343-9014
Assets: $16,322,951
Grants: $652,390
Fiscal Year End: 12/31/2005
EIN: 36-3608625

Sieff Family Foundation
St Louis Park, MN 55416
Assets: $291,771
Grants: $20,970
Fiscal Year End: 12/31/2005
EIN: 23-7011890

Dennis K. and Vivian D. Siemer Foundation, Inc.
Mankato, MN 56001
Assets: $95,490
Grants: $4,500
Fiscal Year End: 12/31/2005
EIN: 41-1957558

Sime Foundation
Brooklyn Park, MN 55445
Assets: $41,599
Grants: $82,500
Fiscal Year End: 12/31/2005
EIN: 41-1908908

The Simons Family Foundation
Edina, MN 55439
Assets: $363,429
Grants: $34,900
Fiscal Year End: 12/31/2005
EIN: 41-1957458

The Singer Family Foundation
Minneapolis, MN 55405
Assets: $59,792
Grants: $1,750
Fiscal Year End: 6/30/2006
EIN: 41-1988452

Sit Investment Associates Foundation
Minneapolis, MN 55402
Assets: $19,229,127
Grants: $860,657
Fiscal Year End: 12/31/2005
EIN: 41-1468021

Andrew David Sit Foundation
Golden Valley, MN 55422
Assets: $266,765
Grants: $20,000
Fiscal Year End: 12/31/2005
EIN: 41-1890289

Eugene C. and Gail V. Sit Foundation
Minneapolis, MN 55402
Assets: $7,048,411
Grants: $395,175
Fiscal Year End: 11/30/2005
EIN: 41-1572465

The Paul and Dawn Sjolund Foundation
Minneapolis, MN 55402
Assets: $216,486
Grants: $720,750
Fiscal Year End: 12/31/2005
EIN: 41-6421780

Slye Family Foundation
St Anthony, MN 55418
Assets: $104,192
Fiscal Year End: 12/31/2005
EIN: 41-6392077

The Smaby Family Foundation
Bloomington, MN 55438
Assets: $1,667,554
Grants: $85,000
Fiscal Year End: 12/31/2005
EIN: 41-1876913

Smith Foundation, Inc.
Minneapolis, MN 55441
Assets: $557,808
Grants: $22,295
Fiscal Year End: 3/31/2006
EIN: 41-6021792

Harold and Mickey Smith Charitable Fund, Inc.
St Paul, MN 55116
Assets: $1,652,720
Grants: $98,351
Fiscal Year End: 6/30/2006
EIN: 41-1437160

Soar Foundation
Minneapolis, MN 55401
Assets: $610,654
Grants: $95,315
Fiscal Year End: 12/31/2005
EIN: 41-1880574

Sorlie Family Foundation
Fergus Falls, MN 56537-3949
Assets: $27,472
Grants: $3,300
Fiscal Year End: 12/31/2005
EIN: 41-1958210

South Washington County Scholarship Committee
St Paul Park, MN 55071
Assets: $67,264
Grants: $26,000
Fiscal Year End: 12/31/2005
EIN: 41-1433314

Spicola Family Foundation
Edina, MN 55439
Assets: $192,012
Grants: $9,677
Fiscal Year End: 12/31/2005
EIN: 41-1696272

Spiller L'Chaim Fund
Minneapolis, MN 55410
Assets: $79,509
Grants: $2,400
Fiscal Year End: 12/31/2005
EIN: 20-1261369

Raymond H. and Florence L. Sponberg Foundation
North Mankato, MN 56003
Assets: $1,471,819
Grants: $51,100
Fiscal Year End: 12/31/2005
EIN: 41-6363938

The Springsteen Foundation for the Humane Treatment of Animals, Inc.
Thief River Falls, MN 56701
Assets: $90,012
Grants: $4,300
Fiscal Year End: 6/30/2005
EIN: 46-0511441

The Spruce Grove Charitable Foundation
Roseville, MN 55113
Assets: $69,632
Grants: $6,300
Fiscal Year End: 12/31/2005
EIN: 41-1990256

Squam Lake Foundation
Minneapolis, MN 55402-1805
Assets: $2,719,627
Grants: $98,000
Fiscal Year End: 11/30/2005
EIN: 35-3492677

St Jude Medical Foundation
St Paul, MN 55117
Assets: $6,566,246
Grants: $6,036,364
Fiscal Year End: 12/31/2005
EIN: 41-1868372

The Jack and Marie St Martin Family Foundation
Bemidji, MN 56619-1069
Assets: $107,937
Grants: $1
Fiscal Year End: 12/31/2005
EIN: 41-1989822

Robert S. Starr Foundation
Bloomington, MN 55431
Assets: $850,278
Grants: $30,000
Fiscal Year End: 12/31/2005
EIN: 41-1974767

Stassen Family Foundation
Edina, MN 55436
Assets: $1,000,824
Grants: $35,000
Fiscal Year End: 12/31/2005
EIN: 41-1924702

Stearns Foundation, Inc.
Hutchinson, MN 55350-0050
Assets: $303,901
Grants: $16,820
Fiscal Year End: 3/31/2006
EIN: 41-1609446

Stenson Charitable Foundation
Marshall, MN 56258
Assets: $149,061
Grants: $34,435
Fiscal Year End: 12/31/2005
EIN: 20-1954452

The June Stern Family Foundation
Wayzata, MN 55391
Assets: $471,115
Grants: $20,540
Fiscal Year End: 12/31/2005
EIN: 41-2019896

Ruth M. Stewart Family Foundation
Alexandria, MN 56308
Assets: $127,692
Grants: $7,000
Fiscal Year End: 12/31/2005
EIN: 36-3432026

Stiles Foundation
Bloomington, MN 55438-2428
Assets: $329,909
Grants: $44,205
Fiscal Year End: 12/31/2005
EIN: 41-1976588

Still Ain't Satisfied - A Foundation with Attitude (SAS)
Minneapolis, MN 55407-3147
Assets: $2,353,118
Grants: $140,500
Fiscal Year End: 12/31/2005
EIN: 41-1906698

Howie Stillman Foundation
Minnetonka, MN 55305
Assets: $224,734
Grants: $7,500
Fiscal Year End: 12/31/2005
EIN: 4-3660599

Norton Stillman Foundation
Minneapolis, MN 55416
Assets: $47,103
Grants: $11,147
Fiscal Year End: 12/31/2005
EIN: 41-1689100

Robert and Estelle Stillman Family Foundation
Plymouth, MN 55446-3818
Assets: $521
Grants: $30,000
Fiscal Year End: 12/31/2005
EIN: 41-1914624

Stone Pier Foundation
Minneapolis, MN 55402-4523
Assets: $9,478,802
Grants: $616,899
Fiscal Year End: 12/31/2005
EIN: 52-2390637

Stronge Family Foundation
North Oaks, MN 55127
Assets: $859,666
Grants: $50,500
Fiscal Year End: 12/31/2005
EIN: 41-2023746

Stanley S. and Sylvia D. Stroup Family Foundation
Minneapolis, MN 55402-4120
Assets: $1,221,490
Grants: $20,000
Fiscal Year End: 6/30/2006
EIN: 02-0700309

Stull Family Foundation
St Paul, MN 55108-1434
Assets: $442,916
Grants: $19,850
Fiscal Year End: 12/31/2005
EIN: 04-6047391

Summer Fund
St Paul, MN 55101-2435
Assets: $3,061,835
Grants: $138,450
Fiscal Year End: 12/31/2005
EIN: 41-6054048

Sundet Foundation
Eden Prairie, MN 55344
Assets: $11,359,313
Grants: $634,204
Fiscal Year End: 12/31/2005
EIN: 41-1378654

R. E. Swager Family Foundation
Minneapolis, MN 55416-4319
Assets: $333,230
Grants: $15,000
Fiscal Year End: 12/31/2005
EIN: 41-1766356

Charles B. Sweatt Foundation
Minneapolis, MN 55402
Assets: $2,215,236
Grants: $90,750
Fiscal Year End: 2/28/2006
EIN: 41-6075853

Harold W. Sweatt Foundation
Minneapolis, MN 55429
Assets: $3,439,110
Grants: $191,200
Fiscal Year End: 2/28/2006
EIN: 41-6075860

The Sweeney Family Foundation
Medina, MN 55340
Assets: $24,922
Grants: $5,500
Fiscal Year End: 12/31/2005
EIN: 41-1859472

Sweere Family Foundation
Minneapolis, MN 55417-2667
Assets: $100,468
Grants: $28,900
Fiscal Year End: 12/31/2005
EIN: 71-6187304

Bernard and Betty Sweet Family Foundation
Minneapolis, MN 55402-4140
Assets: $388,636
Grants: $17,847
Fiscal Year End: 12/31/2005
EIN: 41-1965931

David Swenson Foundation
Arden Hills, MN 55112
Assets: $574,033
Grants: $17,000
Fiscal Year End: 6/30/2006
EIN: 41-1706682

Otto Swoboda Foundation, Inc.
Woodbury, MN 55125-1670
Assets: $25,380
Grants: $909
Fiscal Year End: 12/31/2005
EIN: 41-6035016

Syal Foundation
Vadnais Heights, MN 55127
Assets: $187,551
Grants: $10,000
Fiscal Year End: 12/31/2005
EIN: 41-1892773

Alan R. and Eleanor A. Syverson Scholarship Foundation
Barnum, MN 55707-9789
Assets: $116,196
Grants: $1,000
Fiscal Year End: 12/31/2005
EIN: 47-0878828

T.I.H. Foundation
Bloomington, MN 55438
Assets: $343,205
Grants: $70,500
Fiscal Year End: 12/31/2005
EIN: 41-6038711

Norman H. Tallakson Charitable Trust
Willmar, MN 56201
Assets: $190,910
Grants: $3,100
Fiscal Year End: 12/31/2005
EIN: 41-6054010

Tamarack Foundation
Minneapolis, MN 55402-4523
Assets: $4,108,071
Grants: $157,825
Fiscal Year End: 12/31/2005
EIN: 41-1796504

Tanji-Furzer Foundation
Eagan, MN 55122
Assets: $75,543
Grants: $12,625
Fiscal Year End: 12/31/2005
EIN: 41-1989793

Tankenoff Families Foundation
Minneapolis, MN 55413
Assets: $6,043,491
Grants: $335,134
Fiscal Year End: 12/31/2005
EIN: 41-1905115

Alex G. and Mollie Tankenoff Family Foundation
Edina, MN 55436
Assets: $942,156
Grants: $67,980
Fiscal Year End: 12/31/2005
EIN: 41-6032235

James and Paula Tankenoff Foundation
Minnetonka, MN 55305
Assets: $330,159
Grants: $49,608
Fiscal Year End: 12/31/2005
EIN: 41-1961022

Glen A. Taylor Foundation
North Mankato, MN 56003
Assets: $2,785,619
Grants: $523,764
Fiscal Year End: 12/31/2005
EIN: 41-1737411

TCMK Foundation
Minneapolis, MN 55402-3395
Assets: $737,759
Grants: $39,000
Fiscal Year End: 12/31/2005
EIN: 41-6427792

Tebben Foundation
Marshall, MN 56258
Assets: $56,845
Grants: $23,945
Fiscal Year End: 12/31/2005
EIN: 41-1314020

Ten Times Ten Foundation
St Louis Park, MN 55416-1533
Assets: $2,171,007
Grants: $93,608
Fiscal Year End: 12/31/2005
EIN: 41-1856926

Terhuly Foundation
Roseville, MN 55113
Assets: $4,254,447
Grants: $246,000
Fiscal Year End: 12/31/2005
EIN: 41-1818562

Terra Et Educare Foundation
Jordan, MN 55352-9308
Assets: $152,729
Grants: $11,000
Fiscal Year End: 8/31/2006
EIN: 41-1815690

Therese Foundation
St Paul, MN 55101-1792
Assets: $1,730,786
Grants: $110,000
Fiscal Year End: 12/31/2005
EIN: 41-1364261

Thief River Falls Foundation
Thief River Falls, MN 56701
Assets: $141,581
Grants: $300
Fiscal Year End: 11/30/2005
EIN: 41-6038686

Thom Charitable Foundation
Milwaukee, WI 53224
Assets: $684,259
Fiscal Year End: 12/31/2005
EIN: 41-6363881

Thom Family Foundation
Milwaukee, WI 53201-2980
Assets: $384,355
Grants: $18,000
Fiscal Year End: 12/31/2005
EIN: 20-0374684

Thomson Family Foundation
Edina, MN 55435
Assets: $1,479,076
Grants: $72,000
Fiscal Year End: 12/31/2005
EIN: 95-6189522

Towhee-Rainbow Foundation
Prior Lake, MN 55372
Assets: $15,522
Grants: $5,000
Fiscal Year End: 12/31/2005
EIN: 43-2037958

Tradition Family Foundation
Edina, MN 55435
Assets: $562,847
Grants: $80,293
Fiscal Year End: 12/31/2005
EIN: 41-1958548

The Traverse Foundation
Minneapolis, MN 55402
Assets: $1,518,528
Grants: $75,000
Fiscal Year End: 12/31/2005
EIN: 41-1734297

Tri-Lakes Sportsmans Club, Inc.
Lonsdale, MN 55046
Assets: $109,323
Grants: $7,926
Fiscal Year End: 12/31/2005
EIN: 41-1579650

Trillium Family Foundation
St Paul, MN 55114-1506
Assets: $971,851
Grants: $46,000
Fiscal Year End: 12/31/2005
EIN: 41-2009698

Trillium, A Charitable Corporation
Edina, MN 55436
Assets: $763,728
Grants: $17,500
Fiscal Year End: 12/31/2005
EIN: 41-1783174

J. S. Turner Family Foundation (fka SMR Foundation)
Minnetonka, MN 55343-9014
Assets: $2,612,300
Grants: $103,400
Fiscal Year End: 12/31/2005
EIN: 41-1957680

Turnquist Foundation
Hamel, MN 55340
Assets: $470,657
Grants: $37,500
Fiscal Year End: 12/31/2005
EIN: 41-1525407

Tursso Foundation
St Paul, MN 55107
Assets: $191,172
Grants: $26,485
Fiscal Year End: 7/31/2006
EIN: 41-1759643

Turtle Trust
New Brighton, MN 55112-1723
Assets: $174,028
Grants: $218,518
Fiscal Year End: 12/31/2005
EIN: 41-1850596

Upland & Marsh
Mahtomedi, MN 55115-1950
Assets: $246,333
Grants: $2,010
Fiscal Year End: 12/31/2005
EIN: 41-1956790

Joseph Urdahl Memorial Foundation
Twin Valley, MN 56584
Assets: $64,254
Grants: $1,250
Fiscal Year End: 2/28/2006
EIN: 41-1563189

The UTI Foundation, Inc.
Brooklyn Center, MN 55430-2123
Assets: $386,013
Grants: $49,800
Fiscal Year End: 5/31/2006
EIN: 41-1859780

Valley News Charity Fund
Mankato, MN 56001
Assets: $917,618
Grants: $40,347
Fiscal Year End: 12/31/2005
EIN: 36-3339339

Sande Van Charitable Trust
Duluth, MN 55802
Assets: $144,294
Grants: $2,037
Fiscal Year End: 12/31/2005
EIN: 41-6375516

Vandalia Foundation
St Paul, MN 55164
Assets: $296,378
Grants: $30,000
Fiscal Year End: 12/31/2005
EIN: 41-1627134

The VCJ Family Foundation
Bloomington, MN 55437-3856
Assets: $569,639
Grants: $27,000
Fiscal Year End: 12/31/2005
EIN: 41-1876872

Frank W. Veden Charitable Trust
St Paul, MN 55164-0713
Assets: $10,392,112
Grants: $475,178
Fiscal Year End: 12/31/2005
EIN: 41-6432193

Vaughn Arthur Veit Foundation
Rogers, MN 55374-9583
Assets: $347,217
Grants: $15,500
Fiscal Year End: 12/31/2005
EIN: 41-1824636

C. Paul and Irene G. Venables Foundation
Winona, MN 55987-0248
Assets: $1,606,360
Grants: $100,000
Fiscal Year End: 12/31/2005
EIN: 41-1596060

Sid and Carol Verdoorn Family Foundation
Eden Prairie, MN 55347
Assets: $1,943,777
Grants: $60,450
Fiscal Year End: 12/31/2005
EIN: 41-1926065

Veritas Foundation
Maple Plain, MN 55359
Assets: $4,617,226
Grants: $56,000
Fiscal Year End: 12/31/2005
EIN: 20-2522960

The Armin F. Vetter Foundation
St Paul, MN 55119-5063
Assets: $229,546
Grants: $8,198
Fiscal Year End: 4/30/2006
EIN: 41-6021324

Vinaya Foundation
St Louis Park, MN 55416-1533
Assets: $272,696
Grants: $12,000
Fiscal Year End: 12/31/2005
EIN: 41-1912241

Vintage Foundation
Edina, MN 55435
Assets: $503,233
Grants: $351,714
Fiscal Year End: 6/30/2005
EIN: 41-1925672

Virginia Foundation
Virginia, MN 55792
Assets: $1,872,979
Grants: $29,392
Fiscal Year End: 12/31/2005
EIN: 31-1739538

Jeanne M. Voigt Foundation
St Paul, MN 55405-2345
Assets: $699,288
Grants: $26,855
Fiscal Year End: 12/31/2005
EIN: 20-0512213

Von Blon Family Charitable Foundation
Minneapolis, MN 55402
Assets: $660,412
Grants: $314,100
Fiscal Year End: 12/31/2005
EIN: 41-6362685

W M Foundation
Minneapolis, MN 55402-4523
Assets: $22,888,802
Grants: $1,308,500
Fiscal Year End: 12/31/2005
EIN: 41-6080486

Lyman E. Wakefield Charitable Foundation
Minneapolis, MN 55402-2458
Assets: $792,628
Grants: $24,350
Fiscal Year End: 12/31/2005
EIN: 41-6494372

Lillian F. Wallace Charitable Trust
St Paul, MN 55164-0713
Assets: $1,603,643
Grants: $76,600
Fiscal Year End: 12/31/2005
EIN: 41-6314876

Wallestad Foundation
Minneapolis, MN 55415
Assets: $9,957,277
Grants: $1,050,369
Fiscal Year End: 12/31/2005
EIN: 36-3485265

Phadoris Wallestad Foundation
Minneapolis, MN 55415
Assets: $144,475
Grants: $245,711
Fiscal Year End: 12/31/2005
EIN: 41-1723942

Wallin Foundation
Minneapolis, MN 55402
Assets: $24,204,893
Grants: $1,744,212
Fiscal Year End: 12/31/2005
EIN: 41-6283068

R. J. Walser Foundation
Burnsville, MN 55306
Assets: $620,660
Grants: $145,740
Fiscal Year End: 12/31/2005
EIN: 41-1855415

Ward Charitable Trust
Grand Forks, MN 58206-6001
Assets: $930,397
Grants: $148,000
Fiscal Year End: 11/30/2005
EIN: 91-6515936

The Watlov Family Charitable Foundation
Brainerd, MN 56401-7980
Assets: $100,712
Grants: $10,000
Fiscal Year End: 12/31/2005
EIN: 76-0715258

Watts Family Foundation
Rochester, MN 55901
Assets: $640,729
Grants: $85,270
Fiscal Year End: 12/31/2005
EIN: 71-0882769

WBC Foundation
Minneapolis, MN 55413
Assets: $62,608
Grants: $15,000
Fiscal Year End: 9/30/2005
EIN: 36-7087061

Warren F. Weck, Jr. Charitable Trust
Minneapolis, MN 55402
Assets: $5,734,240
Grants: $300,000
Fiscal Year End: 12/31/2005
EIN: 41-6486803

Donald Weesner Charitable Trust
St Paul, MN 55164-0713
Assets: $13,484,649
Grants: $600,350
Fiscal Year End: 12/31/2005
EIN: 41-6463406

David J. Weiner Foundation
Minneapolis, MN 55401
Assets: $592,695
Grants: $7,200
Fiscal Year End: 12/31/2005
EIN: 41-1639059

Weiser Family Foundation
Minneapolis, MN 55401
Assets: $5,338,299
Grants: $259,634
Fiscal Year End: 12/31/2005
EIN: 41-1987618

Jody Harris Weisman Family Foundation
Minnetonka, MN 55305
Assets: $211,060
Grants: $10,500
Fiscal Year End: 12/31/2005
EIN: 41-1878197

Wells Family Foundation Trust
St Paul, MN 55111
Assets: $6,368,948
Grants: $377,000
Fiscal Year End: 12/31/2005
EIN: 41-1732561

Wells Family Foundation, Incorporated
St Paul, MN 55111
Assets: $5,990,681
Grants: $286,000
Fiscal Year End: 12/31/2005
EIN: 41-1732563

The Welsh Charitable Foundation
Minneapolis, MN 55439
Assets: $14,101
Grants: $8,000
Fiscal Year End: 12/31/2005
EIN: 41-2009309

Elmer M. Weltz Irrevocable Trust
Minneapolis, MN 55402
Assets: $31,651
Fiscal Year End: 9/30/2005
EIN: 41-6059265

WEM Foundation
Minneapolis, MN 55440-9300
Assets: $128,194,446
Grants: $5,900,596
Fiscal Year End: 12/31/2005
EIN: 41-1604640

Hall and Deborah Wendel Foundation
Loretto, MN 55357-0173
Assets: $6,405,447
Grants: $30,000
Fiscal Year End: 12/31/2005
EIN: 41-1584487

The Werner Foundation
Minnetonka, MN 55305
Assets: $1,676,899
Grants: $214,221
Fiscal Year End: 12/31/2005
EIN: 41-0645531

Wert Family Foundation
Greenwood, MN 55331
Assets: $1,206,575
Grants: $120,500
Fiscal Year End: 12/31/2005
EIN: 41-1956034

Wessner Foundation
Shorewood, MN 55331
Assets: $14,018,207
Grants: $667,450
Fiscal Year End: 12/31/2005
EIN: 36-3480120

The West Fork Foundation
Minneapolis, MN 55403
Assets: $1,077,762
Grants: $91,500
Fiscal Year End: 12/31/2005
EIN: 52-2436208

Westcliff Foundation
Minneapolis, MN 55402
Assets: $9,937
Grants: $326,500
Fiscal Year End: 12/31/2005
EIN: 41-1999931

William N. and Ruth M. Westhoff Family Foundation
Plymouth, MN 55446
Assets: $412,873
Grants: $24,463
Fiscal Year End: 12/31/2005
EIN: 41-1987869

Whaley Foundation
St Paul, MN 55105
Assets: $924,515
Grants: $53,000
Fiscal Year End: 12/31/2005
EIN: 41-1988112

Dare Lamberton White and William F. White Foundation
Winona, MN 55987-3416
Assets: $992,532
Grants: $50,200
Fiscal Year End: 12/31/2005
EIN: 27-0021886

Muriel Whiteside Charitable Trust
St Paul, MN 55164-0713
Assets: $12,872,637
Grants: $806,036
Fiscal Year End: 12/31/2005
EIN: 41-6370669

B. K. Whitney Fund
Minneapolis, MN 55402
Assets: $516,315
Grants: $24,300
Fiscal Year End: 12/31/2005
EIN: 41-1465414

Wicker Family Foundation
Grant, MN 55110
Assets: $1,677,327
Grants: $103,008
Fiscal Year End: 12/31/2005
EIN: 41-1990788

Widow's Mite Foundation
Grey Eagle, MN 56336-0129
Assets: $169,102
Grants: $13,800
Fiscal Year End: 11/30/2005
EIN: 41-1550301

George F. Wikstrom, Sr. and Delores M. Wikstrom Foundation
St Paul, MN 55164-0713
Assets: $61,324
Grants: $27,494
Fiscal Year End: 9/30/2006
EIN: 41-6481110

Phillip and Sara Wilensky Family Foundation
New Hope, MN 55427-1727
Assets: $193,581
Grants: $5,200
Fiscal Year End: 12/31/2005
EIN: 41-6027291

Frances and Frank Wilkinson Foundation
Minneapolis, MN 55401
Assets: $1,775,696
Grants: $134,950
Fiscal Year End: 12/31/2005
EIN: 41-1911630

Williams Family Foundation
Excelsior, MN 55331
Assets: $291,786
Grants: $22,400
Fiscal Year End: 12/31/2005
EIN: 41-6363480

Wilmac Foundation
Minneapolis, MN 55440-5638
Assets: $1,294,552
Grants: $80,000
Fiscal Year End: 12/31/2005
EIN: 41-1949369

Willmar Blue Line Club, Inc.
Willmar, MN 56201
Assets: $20,371
Grants: $3,016
Fiscal Year End: 3/31/2006
EIN: 41-1726452

Edward Willmus Family Charitable Trust
Roseville, MN 55113
Assets: $219,896
Grants: $15,625
Fiscal Year End: 12/31/2005
EIN: 41-6051861

Elizabeth Adams Wilson Family Foundation
Wayzata, MN 55391
Assets: $5,083
Grants: $31,000
Fiscal Year End: 12/31/2005
EIN: 20-3324360

J. Morgan and Myrna B. Wilson Charitable Trust
Minneapolis, MN 55479-0053
Assets: $1,436,602
Grants: $43,788
Fiscal Year End: 12/31/2005
EIN: 41-6343023

Virginia Wimmer Charitable Trust
Minneapolis, MN 55402
Assets: $2,413,155
Grants: $120,000
Fiscal Year End: 6/30/2006
EIN: 41-6465189

WIN Foundation
Bloomington, MN 55437-1019
Assets: $122,821
Fiscal Year End: 12/31/2005
EIN: 36-3363424

Windibrow Foundation
Orono, MN 55356-4508
Assets: $922,277
Grants: $37,730
Fiscal Year End: 12/31/2005
EIN: 41-1856843

Winds of Peace Foundation
Kenyon, MN 55946
Assets: $7,332,065
Grants: $269,751
Fiscal Year End: 12/31/2005
EIN: 41-1343012

Windsor Community Foundation
Minneapolis, MN 55402
Assets: $253,390
Grants: $22,000
Fiscal Year End: 12/31/2005
EIN: 41-1890127

Winslow Family Foundation
Minneapolis, MN 55402
Assets: $42,866
Grants: $8,833
Fiscal Year End: 12/31/2005
EIN: 41-1925882

Winsted Foundation
Minneapolis, MN 55402-4523
Assets: $549,183
Grants: $19,810
Fiscal Year End: 12/31/2005
EIN: 41-2017445

Saul Winton Fund
Wayzata, MN 55391
Assets: $556,091
Grants: $111,680
Fiscal Year End: 12/31/2005
EIN: 41-1451143

Winton-Whitney Fund
Minneapolis, MN 55402-2921
Assets: $427,417
Grants: $91,310
Fiscal Year End: 12/31/2005
EIN: 41-1727264

Stephan Larsen Wolf Foundation
Minnetonka, MN 55305-2962
Assets: $21,924
Grants: $6,360
Fiscal Year End: 12/31/2005
EIN: 41-1740331

Womack Family Foundation
New Brighton, MN 55112
Assets: $1,012,540
Grants: $45,000
Fiscal Year End: 12/31/2005
EIN: 41-1796480

Wood Family Foundation
Minneapolis, MN 55405
Assets: $20,579
Grants: $5,650
Fiscal Year End: 12/31/2005
EIN: 41-6045822

Wood-Rill Foundation
Minneapolis, MN 55402-4523
Assets: $1,364,167
Grants: $3,776,235
Fiscal Year End: 12/31/2005
EIN: 41-6080487

D. Donald and Angela W. Wozniak Family Foundation
St Paul, MN 55101
Assets: $209,084
Grants: $40,000
Fiscal Year End: 12/31/2005
EIN: 41-1892808

WPC Mission Investment Fund
Wahkon, MN 56386
Assets: $46,511
Grants: $2,800
Fiscal Year End: 12/31/2005
EIN: 01-0756452

John P. and Eleanor R. Yackel Foundation
Circle Pines, MN 55014
Assets: $1,734,847
Grants: $87,000
Fiscal Year End: 10/31/2005
EIN: 41-1703210

Leo and Catherine Yaggie Family
Breckenridge, MN 56520
Assets: $127,004
Grants: $5,300
Fiscal Year End: 12/31/2005
EIN: 41-1899264

Yanish Family Foundation
Rochester, MN 55901
Assets: $244,754
Grants: $10,600
Fiscal Year End: 12/31/2005
EIN: 41-2011111

Frank J. Zaher Charitable Trust
Lakefield, MN 56150
Assets: $761,367
Grants: $45,813
Fiscal Year End: 12/31/2005
EIN: 41-1824504

Zeller Family Charitable Foundation
Apple Valley, MN 55424
Assets: $361,943
Grants: $35,000
Fiscal Year End: 12/31/2005
EIN: 41-1958310

Donald and Luella Zibell Family Foundation
Shoreview, MN 55126-3914
Assets: $78,460
Grants: $22,724
Fiscal Year End: 12/31/2005
EIN: 41-1945987

Foundations Giving to Designated Recipients

The following foundations give only to specific organizations named in their articles of incorporation or trust document.

Alexandria Technical College Foundation
S.P. Andersch Charitable Remainder Unitrust
A.H. Anderson Charitable Trust
Gerrit Beckering Trust
James F. Bell Trust FBO University of Minnesota
Bethel University - Pooled Common Fund
Charles K. Blandin Residuary Trust
Mary Briggs Charitable Trust
Harry Rowatt Brown Trust
Cammack Marshall Fund for Children
Conley Family Foundation
Elbridge C. Cooke Trust
John C. and Nettie V. David Memorial Trust
DeForce Foundation for Protestant Home
Detroit Country Club Improvement Trust
Dhein Foundation
James E. Doherty Medical Assistance Fund
Edelstein Family Foundation
Effress-Hymanson Family Foundation
Effress-Miller Family Foundation
Evansville Historical Foundation
Lawrence T. Fallander Trust
Charlotte Ferguson Memorial
Friends of the Iron Range Interpretative Center
Friends of the Lewisville Library, Inc.
Anthony L. and Ann B. Gaughan Charitable Trust
E.W. Hallett Charitable Trust
Jessie F. Hallett Charitable Trust

Helen Harrington Charitable Trust
The Hormel Foundation
Henry C. Hornby Trust d/b/a Cloquet Cemeteries Trust
Robert J. Hughes, Jr. Trust
Clive T. Jaffray Employees Trust
Addie M. Jones Trust
Kappa Chapter/Gamma Phi Beta Foundation
The Harry Kay Charitable Foundation
Augustus H. Kennedy Memorial Fund Trust
Joseph Kitrick Charitable Trust
James B. Ladd Trust
Emil and Mildred Larson Minneapolis Public Library Trust
Edith H. Lynum Trust
Marcel K. Lynum Trust
Cargill Macmillan, Jr. Charitable Trust
W. Duncan MacMillan Foundation (Wayzata)
Charles W. Mayo Trust - Olmsted Historical Society
Walter S. and Margaret L. Meyers Charitable Foundation II
Minnesota American Legion and Auxiliary Heart Research Foundation
Edwin W. Norberg Charitable Trust
Ella and Kaare Nygaard Foundation
Edward M. Ozias Charitable Trust
Vivian Fraser Schuh Residuary Trust
C. Mildred Speranza Scholarship Trust
F. W. Veden Endowment for St James Episcopal Church
Lee and Rose Warner Foundation

Foundations Giving to Designated Scholarships

The following foundations give scholarships to specific organizations named in their articles of incorporation or trust document.

3-H Farms Charitable Foundation
Ada Scholarship Foundation
Adams Educational Fund, Inc.
Marshall H. and Nellie Alworth Memorial Fund
American Finnish Workers Educational Trust
American Legion/VFW Onamia Scholarship Foundation, Inc.
Everett L. Amis Foundation
L.A. Amundson Scholarships, Inc.
Royle B. Arvig Memorial Scholarship Fund
Automotive Recyclers of Minnesota Foundation
S. Eugene Bailey Scholarship Trust
Joseph, Gretel, and Victor Blaha Foundation
Sister Thea Bowman Black Catholic Education Foundation
John and Zola Boylan Scholarship Trust
Ben and Verna Carson Scholarship Fund
Jean Covington Foundation
Crosslake Ideal Scholarship Fund, Inc.
Daggett Scholarship Fund, Inc.
James Wakefield Dickson Scholarship Fund
James E. Doherty Scholarship Fund
James Doherty Seminary Training Fund
Doughty Family Foundation
Berenice M. Eiswirth Scholarship Foundation
Ely-Winton Hospital Scholarship Fund Trust
Feipel Scholarship Trust
E. David Fischman Scholarship Trust
Francis H. Fitzgerald Trust
Harry Foley Scholarship Foundation
Joe Francis Haircare Scholarship Foundation
Catherine A. Friedrich Memorial Fund
Garden Valley Education Foundation
The Grand Lodge of Minnesota IOOF Foundation
Grannis-Martin Memorial Foundation
Harrington Foundation
Hoffman & McNamara Foundation
W.R. Hotchkiss Foundation
Cedric L. Hughes Scholarship Trust
Hull Educational Foundation
James W. Hunt Scholarship Fund
Hutchinson Technology
L. A. Isermann Scholarship Foundation Trust
Clem Jaunich Educational Trust
Gladys L. Johnson Scholarship Trust
Mae L. Johnson Scholarship Trust
Henry A. and Gladys F. Just Scholarship Fund
Killen Scholarship Trust
Ellen Korpy Foundation, Inc.
Anna M. Kuhl Scholarship Trust
Lake Region Electric Cooperative Scholarship Fund
Geraldine N. Lemieux Charitable Testamentary Trust
Gladys and Arnold Lueck Scholarship Fund
Carol MacPherson Memorial Scholarship Fund
Madeline Applauds Great Goals in Education, Inc.
Masonic Benevolence
Ethel Melum Trust
Roy E. and Merle Meyer Foundation
Minneapolis Admirals Foundation
Minnesota Masonic Foundation, Inc.
Minnesota State College - Southeast Technical Foundation
Minnesota Veterinary Medical Association Foundation
Oscar Mitchell, Jr. Trust U/A Scholarship Fund
Jack Moon Scholarship Foundation
National Distillers Distributors Foundation
Joyce L. Osborn Scholarship Trust
George W. and Mary B. Patton Scholarship Fund
Hans and Thora Petraborg Education Trust Fund
Vernon J. Pick Foundation
Charles E. Proshek Foundation
Mark R. Pryor Foundation, Inc.
Rainy River Community College Foundation
Remmele Foundation
Louis A. Roberg Endowment Trust
Arvid and Anna R. Sandberg Irrevocable Scholarship Trust
Floy Gilman Scheidler Scholarship Foundation, Inc.
John J. Schneider Memorial Scholarship Fundicers, Inc.
Scott Scholarship Trust
Walter and Anna Soneson Scholarship Fund Trust
Spencer Scholarship Foundation
Santo J. Speranza Scholarship Trust
St Paul College Club - AAUW Scholarship Trust
Albert L. Steinke Trust
Dr. W.C. Stillwell Foundation
Taylor Scholarship Trust
Dave Templeton Memorial Scholarship Fund, Inc.
Oliver W. Tews Trust
Thorbeck Foundation
Harlan R. Thurston Foundation
Trinity Lutheran Scholarship Fund
Two Harbors High School Senior Scholarship Fund
United Church of Christ Christian Fellowship of the Peace
Vallely Will Fund
Minnie Velo Memorial Charitable Trust
Charles E. Voige Trust
Voiture Locale No. 45 of Societe Des 40 Hommes et 8 Chevaux
Welshons Family Scholarship Trust
Whiteside Scholarship Fund Trust
Winslow Foundation
A.R. Wood Educational Trust
Thomas C. Wright Educational Trust

Foundations Giving Grants Only Outside Minnesota

The following foundations are registered in Minnesota but
give grants primarily to organizations outside the state.

Adams-Mastrovich Family Foundation
Beaverdale Foundation
Bend Foundation
Hazel Briggs Bradford Scholarship Fund, Inc.
1988 Irrevocable Cochrane Memorial Trust
Community Foundation of Grand Forks, East Grand Forks & Region
James N. Cost Foundation
Dennis and Nancy Ditlove Family Foundation
Gesner-Johnson Foundation
Sabra M. Hamilton Foundation
The Hankes Foundation
Alfred A. Iversen and Family Foundation
David B. Jones Foundation
Lion's Pride Foundation
Living Springs Foundation
Louis Foundation
The M & L Foundation, Inc.
The Jonathan Madding Foundation
NJR Foundation
North Dakota Community Foundation
Omaha Community Foundation
Piasecki Family Foundation
Joyce Swan Foundation
Weyand Charitable Trust
Louis F. and Florence H. Weyand 1977 Charitable Trust
Weyerhaeuser/Day Foundation

Foundations Currently Inactive/No Recent Information

The following foundations are not currently making grants or have no recent information available.

The Alliance for Youth Foundation
Dean R. Anderson Family Foundation
Bakken Galbraith Foundation
The BMC Foundation
Cardiac Rhythm Management Research Foundation
Carter Family Foundation
Colonial Craft, Inc.
Common Ground Foundation
Cummins Family Foundation
Edward and Karayn Cunnington Family Foundation
Diamond Builder Foundation
Diercks Foundation
Doherty Foundation
Norm and Val Duininck Family Foundation
The Ross Dunham Memorial Foundation
Donald and Elaine Erickson Family Foundation
Karen and Richard Evans Foundation
Flagship Foundation
Robert E. Fraser Foundation
Galatians 5:22 Foundation
Gannett Foundation
Gesme Foundation
Johnny B. Good Foundation
Reynolds and Mary Guyer Family Foundation
India Association of Minnesota, Inc.
Intertech Foundation
Jerge Foundation for Quality Improvement in Dentistry
Harry A. Johnson Foundation
Kaminski Family Foundation
Knife Lake Sportsmen Club, Inc.
Leroy R. and Shalmerdean A. Knuths Family Foundation
The Lacek Foundation
Lakeside Capital Foundation

David D. MacMillan Family Foundation
Katherine Wells MacMillan Foundation
Marso Foundation
Minneapolis Parks Legacy Society
Minnesota Valley Bancshares Foundation
Thomas Moore Memorial Fire Fighter Education, Health and Safety Foundation
MWVE Fund
Northwest Airlines, Incorporated
James T. Nystrom Foundation
Thomas W. and Helen K. O'Kane Family Foundation
Park Region Telephone Charitable Trust, Inc.
Pearson Assessments
John Pritchard Memorial Fund
Harold and Kate Reed Family Foundation
Harold Roitenberg Family Foundation
Ruand Foundation
Scottish Rite Foundation of St Paul
Seibold Foundation
Berel and Chana Silverberg Charitable Foundation
Spring Rock Foundation
Gregg W. and Denise E. Steinhafel Family Foundation
The Ralph P. and Faye R. Stillman Family Foundation Charitable Trust
Vadnais Heights Community Foundation
Roger A. Vasko Family Foundation
Alice and Fred Wall Family Foundation
Weeres Foundation, Inc.
Wensmann Family Foundation
Williams Steel & Hardware Company
Winter Wheat Foundation
Wilfred R. Yetzer Charitable Trust

Foundations Recently Terminated

The following foundations have recently been terminated.

Elizabeth Amis Foundation
The Jonathan D. and Catherine L. Anderson Foundation
The Apostle Foundation
Aquinas Foundation
The Lloyd A. and Marion E. Bachman Foundation
The Sidney and June H. Barrows Foundation
Benn-Crosby Family Foundation
Berdass Family Foundation
Blitzer Golden Family Foundation
Boehnen Foundation
Bonaria Foundation
Borochoff Family Foundation
Braun Family Foundation
The Buyse Foundation
Carl and Yetta Chalfen Foundation
Albert W. Cherne Foundation
Children Helping Children Foundation
Lavinia R. Clark Trust
Duluth Improvement Trust
East West Design Center
Ehrhardt Family Foundation
Fallon McElligott Scholarship Fund
Harold and Florence Fischbein Foundation
Foundation for the Prevention of Human & Animal Violence
Getsch Family Foundation Trust
Charles D. Gilfillan Memorial Foundation
Golle Family Foundation
Meyer (Mickey) Gordon Family Foundation
David and Miriam Hanson Charitable Foundation
James Hartzell Family Foundation
Robert and Clyde Haugan Foundation
Heath Foundation
Hoeschler Family Foundation
Ruth S. Hoffert Charitable Trust
Holden Foundation
Emma B. Howe Memorial Foundation
Laura and Walter Hudson Foundation
Humphries Foundation
Leif K. and Joen Jacobsen Foundation
Maynard B. Johnson Family Foundation
R. L. Roz Johnson Family Foundation
Norman and Eunice Jones Family Foundation
Jordan Foundation
Andrew S. and Grace Y. Juang Foundation

Alan and Beverly Kasdan Foundation, Inc.
Clayton Kaufman Family Foundation
Ella Knees Trust
Hertha Knees Trust
Don and Jean Lein Family Foundation
Loomer-Mortenson Scholarship Foundation
W. Duncan MacMillan Family Foundation (Minneapolis)
Malinski Family Foundation
Markman Capital Foundation
Master Brewers Association of The Americas Scholarship Foundation, Inc.
Len Mattson Scholarship Fund, Inc.
Mediclinics Educational Fund
Melrose Community Improvement Association
Metris Companies Foundation
Benjamin A. Miller Foundation
Joseph T. Morton Family Foundation
Murray County Health Alliance Foundation
Elizabeth W. Musser Charitable Trust
Charles and Elynor Nelson Family Foundation
Numero-Steinfeldt Foundation
T.J. O'Gara Family Charitable Foundation
Wayne and Mary Packard Foundation
E.M. Pearson Foundation
Paul and Doris Prestegaard Memorial Foundation
The Ritz Foundation
John and Beverly Rollwagen Family Foundation
William A. Ross Foundation
Sand Dollar Foundation
William Sawyer and Betty S. Eisenstadt Foundation
Schmitt Biomimetic Charitable Foundation
Sam and Lorraine Shark Foundation
Spanner Foundation
Star Tribune Foundation
Strauss Family Foundation
Sumasil Foundation
Tew Foundation
Then Family Charitable Foundation
Travis-Mcilroy Foundation
Ben J. Trebesch Trust
Loretta A. Treml Charitable Trust
U.S. Medical Aid Foundation
Urban Tree Research Foundation
The Van Dam Foundation
Velie Charitable Trust

The Vincent S. Velie, Jr. Family Foundation
Villafana Family Foundation
James D. Watkins Charitable Trust
Edith G. Weyerhaeuser Charitable Trust
Constance Bultman Wilson Foundation for Education and Psychiatry
Charles J. and Henrietta McDonald Winton Fund
The Father Paul Wolf Foundation
Donald D. Yablonsky Scholarship Foundation
Ziff-Hymanson Family Foundation
Zona Charitable Foundation

Information for Grantseekers

Grantmaking Basics

Grantmakers play a critical role in funding the important work of nonprofit organizations in Minnesota and around the country. Although more than 75 percent of private charitable contributions come from individuals, foundations and corporate giving programs can be important funding partners for nonprofits.

In 2004, Minnesota's more than 1,300 active foundations and corporate giving programs gave a total of more than $1 billion in grants and program-related investments to nonprofit organizations. Minnesota ranks eighth in foundation giving per capita out of all 50 states, according to The Foundation Center. (For more facts and figures on Minnesota grantmaking, visit the Minnesota Council on Foundations website at www.mcf.org (select "Trends & Analysis").

What Is a Foundation?

Foundations are nonprofit, tax-exempt 501(c)(3) organizations, just like the charities they support with their grants. Like charities, foundations are governed by boards of directors or trustees; some also have paid staff who help manage the grantmaking process. Decisions about grants are usually made by the board.

Private foundations are governed by stricter IRS regulations than public charities. Most foundations have an endowment (their "principal" or "assets") that is invested in financial securities (stocks, bonds, etc.) that earn interest and dividends. The IRS requires private foundations to pay out at least 5 percent of the year-end fair market value of their assets. This payout may be a combination of grants and administrative expenses. Private foundations must also pay an excise tax of 1 or 2 percent on earnings.

Foundations generally are required by federal law to give money only to tax-exempt, charitable 501(c)(3) organizations. Under some circumstances, foundations may give money to individuals or organizations that do not have tax-exempt status. But since doing so requires them to comply with even more IRS rules, most foundations choose not to do so.

If your organization is not tax-exempt and you wish to apply for a grant, you may need to work through what is called a "fiscal agent" or "fiscal sponsor," which is a tax-exempt organization that can work with you and the funder to make a grant possible.

Note: Some organizations bear the name "foundation" but are not included in the Guide because their primary purpose is not grantmaking. This category includes organizations raising funds from the general public for specific, narrowly defined purposes or for specific institutions, such as universities or hospitals.

Types of Grantmakers

The Guide has listings for the three main types of grantmakers: private foundations, corporate foundations and giving programs, and community/public foundations.

PRIVATE FOUNDATIONS

The vast majority of grantmakers in Minnesota — more than 80 percent — are private foundations. Private foundations are generally founded by an individual, a group of individuals or a family. A family foundation is a private foundation in which the donor and/or the donor's family are actively involved in the management of the foundation. An independent foundation is a private foundation in which no or few family members are actively involved in the foundation's operations. There is no legal distinction between a family foundation and an independent foundation.

Many private foundations, especially in their early years, are run by a board consisting of members of the founder's family. As the years go by, family members may disperse around the country or may lose interest in the foundation, and may be partly or entirely replaced on the board by "outsiders" unrelated to the family.

Some private foundations focus their giving in areas dear to the heart of the founder. Others are led by the interests and activities of the board or staff, or by their interpretation of the donor's interests or assessment of community needs.

Because private foundation earnings do not depend on direct commercial activity, they tend to be more insulated from public pressures, such as consumer boycotts or shareholder demands that may affect corporate donors.

CORPORATE FOUNDATIONS AND CORPORATE GIVING PROGRAMS

As their name suggests, corporate foundations and giving programs are connected to business corporations, and the money they give as contributions and grants comes from the corporation's profits. Corporations are allowed by law to receive a tax deduction for giving up to 10 percent of their pre-tax earnings to charity.

Minnesota is fortunate to have a strong tradition of corporate giving. The Keystone Recognition Program, initiated in 1976 by the Greater Minneapolis Chamber of Commerce, annually recognizes companies that commit 2 to 5 percent of their pre-tax earnings for charitable purposes. In 2003, the program recognized more than 250 Minnesota companies for giving at these levels. For a list of these companies, call the Chamber at 612.370.9100, or visit www.minneapolis chamber.org.

Some corporate foundations have endowments, just like private foundations, and make grants from the investment earnings of these assets. Other corporate foundations simply operate as a flow-through vehicle, where the full amount the corporation donates to its foundation each year is contributed to nonprofit organizations. Some companies choose not to establish a separate legal entity, and instead make their charitable contributions through a corporate giving program. In many cases, corporations operate both a foundation and a corporate giving program. There are legal distinctions between corporate foundations and corporate giving programs, but in general these distinctions are not important to grantseekers.

Like other foundations, the giving decisions at corporate foundations tend to be made by a board of directors, which usually consists of representatives from the company's senior management. Some corporations assign some or all of the giving decisions to various employee committees. Some larger corporate foundations have staff assigned to the foundation. In other corporations, the foundation may be operated by the corporate communications department, the human resources department or the chief executive officer's staff.

Corporations generally focus their giving in the geographic communities where they have operations and where their employees live. Many corporate donors are particularly interested in supporting charities in which their employees are personally involved. Some corporate donors will match their employees' gifts to charitable organizations; the corporation decides which kinds of charities and which employees qualify for the match (see the "matching grants" entry in some corporate grantmakers' profiles for information on the types of employee gifts that qualify for a match at those companies).

Corporations often focus their giving in subject areas related to the corporation's business. Other companies simply want to encourage a healthy community in which to do business. Because corporations depend on sales revenue for their income (and eventually for any charitable gifts they make), they may be more sensitive than other types of grantmakers to non-profit activities that are considered controversial.

Some corporations support charities through their marketing budgets. Such support is often in the form of "corporate sponsorships," and tends to be given to charitable activities with high public visibility, such as major art exhibits or public television shows.

Corporations sometimes give in-kind gifts of goods or services in addition to, or instead of, cash donations. For example, a law firm may provide free legal services, a newspaper may donate printing, or a paint company may supply free paint. Sometimes it may be easier for some companies to give this way. A growing number of companies are exploring ways to better integrate their grantmaking activities with their in-kind donations and/or their employees' volunteer efforts, in order to strengthen their overall commitment to the community.

Because corporations that don't have a foundation are not required by law to make their contributions public, there is no easy way to track this information. So it is likely that there are many businesses making charitable gifts that are not listed in this Guide.

COMMUNITY/PUBLIC FOUNDATIONS

Community foundations are publicly supported foundations operated by, and for the benefit of, a specific community, population, area of interest or geographic area. These foundations are sometimes referred to as public foundations or public charity foundations. A community/public foundation is governed by a board of private citizens chosen to be representative of the public interest and for their knowledge of the community being served by the foundation.

A community/public foundation administers individual funds contributed or bequeathed to it by individuals, other foundations, governments, corporations and other sources. A community/public foundation serves three publics: its donors, the nonprofit sector and the community as a whole. A community/public foundation may focus to some extent on one of these publics over the other two, but by structure and by regulation it must always serve all three.

Community/public foundations have different categories of funds for a donor's consideration. Unrestricted funds are those that are not restricted by the donor to any one purpose or activity. Field of interest funds are used to support particular fields or activities of interest to the donor. These two types of funds are typically the primary sources of community/public foundation grant dollars that are available to nonprofits through a grant application process.

Donors can also contribute to community/public foundations through designated funds, which are used to benefit one or more specific organizations. When the donor wants to be actively involved in recommending which organizations receive grants, donor-advised funds can be established. In Minnesota, community foundations have been the fastest-growing segment of the grantmaking field, according to the Minnesota Council on Foundations' *Giving in Minnesota* research, and much of that growth has been attributed to the rising popularity of donor-advised funds.

In addition to these various funds, community/public foundations may also manage supporting organizations. A supporting organization is a foundation that supports the goals of another organization. A supporting organization has its own board of directors and giving policies, and makes grants compatible with the goals and objectives of the community/public foundation that it supports.

Historically, the focal point of most community/public foundation missions has been tied to a geographic area, with the foundation giving to a wide range of causes and charities within a specific city, state or region. But for a growing number of new community/public foundations in Minnesota, the primary focus of their giving is a community of donors and grantees defined not so much by geography but by a common interest or affinity. This might

be religious (such as the Catholic Community Foundation or the Lutheran Community Foundation), philosophical (such as Headwaters Foundation for Justice) or focused on a specific population group (such as the Women's Foundation of Minnesota). These types of community/public foundations are sometimes referred to as issues-oriented foundations or affinity foundations.

PRIVATE OPERATING FOUNDATIONS

Operating foundations are private foundations with one big difference. Like private foundations, operating foundations have an endowment that is invested and that earns interest. But instead of distributing the earnings to other charities, the operating foundation uses the earnings to hire its own staff and run its own programs. Since operating foundations generally do not make grants, they are not listed in the Guide.

Types of Grants

Grantmakers in Minnesota, as in the rest of the country, provide a number of different types of support for nonprofits. Here are some of the most common types of grants that funders make:

GENERAL PURPOSE OR OPERATING SUPPORT GRANTS

When a grantmaker gives provides an operating grant, you can use it to support the general expenses of operating your organization, from running a specific program to paying the heating bill. An operating grant means the funder supports your organization's overall mission and lets you decide how to use the money.

PROGRAM OR PROJECT SUPPORT GRANTS

In general, a project grant supports a specific, connected set of activities having a defined beginning and end, explicit objectives and a predetermined cost. When a funder gives a grant for a specific project, it is generally a restricted grant and must be used for that purpose.

In general, project grants are given to support projects related to the mission of the charity receiving the money. There are dozens of types of project grants, and you will find many of them named specifically in grantmaker entries in this Guide. Here are some of the most common:

Planning Grants

If your organization is planning a major new program, you may need to spend a good deal of time and money just figuring out what the program will look like. Before you can even write a proposal to fund the new effort, you may want to research the needs of your constituents, consult with experts in the field, or conduct other planning activities. A planning grant supports such initial project development work.

Seed Money or Start-up Grants

A start-up grant helps a new organization or program in its first few years. The idea is to give the new effort a strong push forward, so it can devote its energy to setting up programs without worrying constantly about raising money. Such grants are often for more than one year, and frequently decrease in amount each year. The funder assumes that the new organization will begin to raise other funds to replace the decreasing start-up grant.

MANAGEMENT OR TECHNICAL ASSISTANCE GRANTS

A management or technical assistance grant does not directly support the mission-related activities of the charity. Instead, it supports the charity's management or administration — its fundraising, marketing, financial management and so on. Such a grant might help hire a marketing consultant or pay the salary of a new fundraiser position.

CAPITAL GRANTS

Sometimes called "bricks-and-mortar" grants, capital grants help an organization buy some long-lasting physical asset — a building, computer or van, for example. The applicant must make the case that the new acquisition will help the organization serve its clients better. Funders considering a request like this will not only be interested in the applicant's current activities and financial health, but will also ask about financial and program plans for the next several years. They want to be sure that if they help an organization move into a permanent space, for example, the organization will have the resources to manage and maintain it. No funder wants to help pay for a new building only to have it close in four years because it is too expensive for the charity to maintain.

ENDOWMENT GRANTS

Some nonprofits set aside money that is invested and earns interest. The charity spends only the interest and keeps the original sum (the principal) untouched. Such a fund is called an endowment and is commonly found at charities with large physical plants, such as hospitals and colleges. Periodically, charities launch fundraising efforts to start, or add to, an endowment. Like capital grant proposals, endowment requests will prompt funders to ask hard questions about the long-term financial outlook of the applicant. The funder wants to be sure that its gift to an endowment will stay in the endowment earning interest, and not be taken out to meet annual operating costs.

PROGRAM-RELATED INVESTMENTS

In addition to grants, the IRS allows foundations to make loans — called program-related investments (PRIs) — to nonprofits. PRIs must be for projects that would be eligible for grant support and are usually made at low interest, or even no interest. Unlike grants, PRIs must be paid back to the grantmaker. PRIs often involve building projects.

Grantseeking Basics

To be successful in seeking funds from grantmakers, nonprofits need to make the best possible use of their time and resources in seeking the right kinds of grants from the most appropriate funding sources. To help, the Minnesota Council on Foundations offers the following step-by-step grantseeking primer, culled from its popular and time-tested grantseeking courses and materials.

Step 1: Research

The single most important success factor in seeking funds from foundations and corporate grantmakers is doing the necessary research and preparation. Grantmaking organizations have distinct personalities and histories, with unique requirements and interests. A major element in successful grantseeking is finding the appropriate match between a program's needs and a donor's interests.

There are several resources available to help you find potential funders, including this Guide. A good place to start is with the indexes, which begin on page 281. Use these indexes to find grantmakers that fund in your geographic area, your area of interest and/or the populations you serve, and those that provide the type or support that you're seeking:

Geographic focus: Does your group serve the same geographic area as the funder? Some grantmakers will only fund organizations in a specific city or region, while others will fund organizations statewide.

Areas of interest: Do you and the funder share an interest in the arts, education or the environment? Remember that your project may touch on more than one subject area. A theater wanting to develop a play about AIDS and tour it to schools might consider funders interested in theater, health care or youth education.

Intended beneficiaries: Are you and the funder both trying to help the same people? Perhaps you are both interested in children, or Asian Americans/Pacific Islanders.

Types of support: Does the funder provide the type of grant that you are seeking? (See the "Types of Grants" section on page 270 for more information.)

In addition to the Guide, MCF offers the Minnesota Grantmakers Online subscription database service (MGO), which allows you to search the web's largest and most up-to-date database of Minnesota foundations and corporate grantmakers, and their grants, for an annual subscription fee. You can search for funders on up to nine different criteria — including areas of interest, geographic focus, type of support and beneficiary — to find grantmakers that provide the type of funding that you're seeking. For more information, go to www.mcf.org/mngrants.

Another good grantseeking resource is the Foundation Center Cooperating Collection nearest you. These collections were established by Foundation Center, a nonprofit research and publishing organization in New York City. The collections provide a core collection of Foundation Center publications, including print and electronic directories of national funders, and a variety of supplementary materials and services useful to grantseekers. There is a specially trained librarian assigned to each collection. All six collections provide free access to Minnesota Grantmakers Online.

In Minnesota, there are six Cooperating Collection locations:

- Brainerd Public Library (218.829.5574)
- Duluth Public Library (218.723.3802)
- Minneapolis Public Library, Sociology Department (612.630.6000)
- Rochester Public Library (507.285.8002)
- St. Paul Public Library (651.266.7000)
- Southwest State University Library in Marshall (507.537.6176)

Once you have used these resources to find some potential matches, you will need to gather more information about the funders' grant application policies and guidelines to see if they are still a good fit for your organization. Read the "application information" section of a funder's Guide entry. If the funder indicates under "public information available" that it has written guidelines or an annual report, your next step should be to call and get those publications. A funder's guidelines and policies will likely provide more detailed information about the types of organizations and projects they do and don't fund.

A growing number of grantmakers now post their funding policies and guidelines on the web. You can find an up-to-date list of websites for Minnesota grantmakers at MCF's website; go to www.mcf.org/grantsource (select "Grantmaker Links").

If you have difficulty finding information about a foundation's funding guidelines, you can try reading its federal informational tax return, called a Form 990-PF, which all private foundations are required to file with the IRS each year. The 990-PF is typically not the best source of information on a foundation, but sometimes it can help you learn more about a foundation's grants, programs and mission. You can search for a foundation's 990-PF online at the GuideStar website (www.guidestar.org).

Note: If you send out mass mailings of your grant proposal to funders without paying attention to their funding guidelines, you significantly reduce your chances of getting funded. Even worse, by wasting a grantmaker's time reviewing a proposal that is clearly outside its guidelines, you risk damaging your long-term reputation with that funder.

Step 2: Applying for a Grant

If you have done thorough research on a grantmaker and believe that your organization or project is a good fit with the funder's guidelines, it's time to apply for the grant. Read the grantmaker's application guidelines carefully to determine how to apply to the organization for funding.

Be sure to note the grantmaker's application deadlines, if any, and submit your proposal on time. Some funders list deadlines in the Guide entry. MCF also maintains an up-to-date calendar of grantmaker deadlines at www.mcf.org/grantsource (select "Grantmaker Deadlines").

A few local funders allow and/or require you to apply for a grant online. Other funders may ask that the first step you take in applying for a grant is to write a "letter of inquiry," which is a one- or two-page letter in which you describe your organization and the proposed project and ask for guidance on whether a full proposal is appropriate. Other funders will ask that you submit a full grant proposal from the start.

A written grant proposal is the primary tool that most funders use for making grant decisions. In a nutshell, the grant proposal is your opportunity to communicate to the funder who you are, why you are seeking a grant, what you plan to do with the money, and why you are a good fit with the funder's priorities.

When preparing a grant proposal, some funders prefer that you fill out their own grant application forms or cover sheets. Many grantmakers will also accept proposals that use the Minnesota Common Grant Application Form in place of all or part of their own forms. Introduced by MCF in 1996, the Common Grant Application can reduce the amount of time nonprofits must spend rearranging basic information from one grant proposal to the next to fit grantmakers' varying application requirements. A funder's Guide entry will indicate if it accepts the Minnesota Common Grant Application Form (look under "Application Information").

The Minnesota Common Grant Application Form is not a substitute for good research. Grant applicants must still seek and adhere to each foundation's guidelines. The form simply provides a base of information that foundations will require in a grant application. Many foundations, especially smaller foundations with little or no staff, have found that all the information they want and need to make their grant decisions is on the form. Other funders have indicated that the form asks all the basics, but require a few additional pieces of information. You will find a copy of the Minnesota Common Grant Application Form starting on page 355. You can also find the form at www.mcf.org/grantsource, or by contacting MCF at 612.338.1989, info@mcf.org.

Once you have obtained the necessary forms and other application guidelines and materials for a particular funder, it's time to write the grant proposal. If you have never written a grant proposal before, don't feel intimidated. Grantwriting is a skill that can be learned, and there are a number of grantwriting resources that are available to help, including the popular "Writing a Successful Grant Proposal" tutorial on page 276.

For additional assistance, MCF offers beginning grantseeking seminars (for more information, go to www.mcf.org/seminars or contact MCF at 612.338.1989, info@mcf.org). Many other organizations in Minnesota also provide grantwriting and fundraising workshops and programs. Find a list of upcoming dates at www.mcf.org/grantsource (select "Nonprofit Calendar").

Step 3: Grant Review

After you have submitted your grant proposal to a funder, you must wait while the grantmaker reviews your proposal and makes a decision. The time it will take to hear back from a funder can vary greatly from organization to organization. Funders have different review processes and schedules. Some organizations review grant proposals just once a year, while others review them on an ongoing basis. Many funders list their typical turnaround time for a grant application in their application materials and/or in their Guide entry.

In some foundations, staff screens out proposals that are ineligible or poorly planned or simply not within the funder's focus. The staff then researches the remaining proposals and writes recommendations for the board. The research may include meeting with the applicants and conducting site visits, where the funder meets you at your office and/or program site to learn more about your organization and your needs. Site visits provide funders with a feel and understanding of an agency or programs that rarely come across completely in a written grant proposal.

Grant recommendations may go to the foundation's board with or without the original proposals, and the board makes the final decisions. In some foundations, staff members make grant decisions on smaller requests. In still other foundations, the board sees every grant proposal unscreened by staff.

Step 4: Grant Decision & Follow-Up

If a funder turns down your grant request, the letter giving you the unhappy news will probably be a form letter. But if you wish, and the funder has staff, you may phone and ask, "Can you tell me anything that will help us another time?" Perhaps they liked your proposal but just ran out of money; perhaps there was some tiny point of confusion that could be easily resolved. But don't make such a call if you are feeling angry or combative. You are trying to get information, not argue a case in court.

If your grant request is turned down, but after an objective review of the funder's guidelines you still feel there is a good match, apply again in about a year. Many applicants are only successful on the second or third try. You can also ask the funder's staff person if she thinks it would be worth your time to apply again.

If your proposal is funded, you may receive the check in the mail with a cover letter. Or you may get a full-blown contract stipulating, among other things, that you must submit a report when the project is done.

In all cases, write immediately to acknowledge the gift. If you sign a contract, be sure to read it first and note when and what kinds of reports are due. Then turn in the report on time. If you realize you can't do so, send a note, or call to say it will be late. Even if the funder doesn't ask for a report, send one anyway.

A funder may provide its own reporting forms and procedures. Many of the state's grantmakers will also accept grant reports that use the Minnesota Common Report Form. Unveiled by MCF in 2001, the Minnesota Common Report Form provides a standardized format for a nonprofit grantee to use in reporting to different grantmakers about work it has accomplished with their grants, helping to make the reporting process more efficient and effective for nonprofits and funders alike.

A funder's Guide entry will indicate if it accepts the Minnesota Common Report Form (look under "Application Information"). You will find a copy of the Minnesota Common Report Form starting on page 361. Access the form at www.mcf.org/grantsource or by contacting MCF at 612.338.1989, info@mcf.org.

What if you get some funding, but not all that you wanted for the project? For example, you budgeted $50,000 for the project but could raise just $35,000. You will then have to decide whether you can do the project in a meaningful way with the money you have. If you can, you must write all those who funded the project and explain how you will adapt to the lower budget. If you can't, write the donors to ask if you can transfer their money to another project (which you describe fully). They might say yes. If not, then you must return the money.

Grantseekers Toolbox

Free Resources

The Minnesota Council on Foundations provides a number of free resources for grantseekers in Minnesota. Listed below are a few of the major offerings:

MCF.ORG

The Council's website offers many useful resources free of charge, including the latest news on Minnesota grantmaking, information and resources on grantseeking and upcoming grantseeking seminars, links to funders and much more. For further information, select "Grantseeking Resources."

GIVING MEMO E-NEWSLETTER

The Council's free bi-weekly e-mail newsletter delivers the latest Minnesota grantmaking news right to your desktop, including recent grants of note, upcoming grant deadlines, new resources and tools, new job openings and more. There is no better way to stay on top of new grant opportunities and in touch with the field. To sign up for your free subscription to *Giving Memo,* go to www.mcf.org/enews.

GIVING FORUM NEWSPAPER

The Council's quarterly *Giving Forum* newspaper publishes a wide range of news and information on Minnesota grantmaking, with original, in-depth articles that explore current giving issues, offer insights into the grantmaking field and report on giving trends. To sign up for your free subscription to *Giving Forum,* go to www.mcf.org/givingforum or contact MCF at 612.338.1989, info@mcf.org.

Fee-Based Services

The Minnesota Council on Foundations also offers three major grantseeking tools as fee-based services:

MINNESOTA GRANTMAKERS ONLINE

The MGO subscription service allows you to search the web's largest and most up-to-date database of Minnesota foundations and corporate grantmakers and their grants for an annual subscription fee. You can search for funders using up to nine different criteria, including areas of interest, geographic focus, type of support and beneficiary. For more information, go to www.mcf.org/mngrants.

GUIDE TO MINNESOTA GRANTMAKERS

The *Guide* is the most comprehensive print directory of Minnesota foundations and corporate giving programs, providing information on Minnesota's largest foundations and difficult-to-find information on small and mid-sized foundations and corporate giving programs. The current 15th edition lists more than 1,400 active Minnesota grantmakers and profiles 370 of these funding organizations in detail. To order a copy, go to www.mcf.org/guide.

GRANTSEEKING FOR BEGINNERS SEMINARS

Minnesota Council on Foundations' popular, long-running Grantseeking for Beginners Seminar provides beginning grantseekers with a solid, comprehensive introduction to the basics of grantwriting — featuring a panel session with Minnesota grantmakers.

The Grantseeking for Beginners Seminar will help you:

- Identify potential funding sources in an informed, well-researched manner, using the leading print and electronic research tools.
- Learn the key elements of an effective grant proposal — including budget development.
- Understand the grant proposal review and decision-making process from a grantmaker's point of view through an interactive panel discussion with some of Minnesota's leading foundations and corporate giving programs.

For more information, go to www.mcf.org/seminars.

Publications

Stay informed on Minnesota grantmaking trends and new grant opportunities.

MCF is the leading provider of Minnesota grantmaking news, information and research, which can greatly enhance and inform your grantseeking efforts.

REPRINTS — MCF offers reprints of its most popular articles and essays:

- *Writing a Successful Grant Proposal*
- *The Truth About Site Visits*
- *A Day in the Life of a Program Officer*

These articles can be accessed at www.mcf.org/grantsource. Print copies are available for $1 each.

RESEARCH REPORTS — MCF publishes regular in-depth research on Minnesota's grantmaking field, giving you comprehensive grantmaking data you'll find nowhere else and offering valuable insights on the state's grantmaking trends. Recent research reports include:

Minnesota Grantmaking 2007 Outlook Report (Jan. 2007)

This report summarizes the results of a survey of MCF members to assess the outlook for grantmaking activity in Minnesota in 2007. The report can be downloaded at www.mcf.org/outlook.

Giving in Minnesota Report, 2006 Edition

MCF's definitive research on charitable giving in Minnesota. The report includes analysis and breakdowns of grantmaking by subject area, geographic area, beneficiary populations and types of support; rankings of Minnesota's top grantmakers in several categories; and more. The report can be downloaded at www.mcf.org/gim.

Other Web Resources

MINNESOTA COMMON GRANT APPLICATION FORM

The Minnesota Common Grant Application Form is designed to help make the grantseeking process simpler and more efficient for nonprofits. The Minnesota Council on Foundations introduced the Common Grant Application Form in 1996 and revised it in December 2000. The form was developed based on input from MCF members and representatives from the state's nonprofit community. To access the form, go to www.mcf.org/grantsource.

MINNESOTA COMMON REPORT FORM

The Minnesota Common Report Form provides a standardized format for a nonprofit grantee to use in reporting to grantmakers about work it has accomplished with their grants. The Minnesota Council on Foundations introduced the Common Report Form in March 2001. The form was developed based on input from Council members and representatives from the state's nonprofit community. To access the form, go to www.mcf.org/grantsource.

Helpful Links

www.ag.state.mn.us/charities — The Minnesota Attorney General's Charities Database allows quick public access to registration data filed by organizations that solicit and grant funds in the state of Minnesota. These organizations are required to register with the Charities Division of the Minnesota Attorney General's Office, and registration data in the searchable database is taken directly from each organization's financial statement and tax return.

www.guidestar.org — GuideStar is a leader in providing comprehensive data on more than 1.5 million nonprofit organizations, connecting them with donors, grantees, foundations, businesses and governing agencies in a nationwide community of giving. The searchable database offers IRS Forms 990 and the IRS Business Master File, including comprehensive facts on employee compensation and grant activity. Basic searches are offered for free, but registration is required.

www.foundationcenter.org — The Foundation Center is a leading national authority and information provider on philanthropy, serving a wide audience that includes grantseekers, grantmakers, researchers, policymakers, the media and the general public. The center's website provides public access to a comprehensive menu of information and services, as well as a large collection of print and electronic publications and resources.

Other Resources for Nonprofits

CENTER FOR NONPROFIT MANAGEMENT
CNM, part of the University of St Thomas Opus College of Business, offers seminars, workshops and courses on such topics as board governance, strategic planning, program evaluation, budgeting and accounting, and organizational and personal development.
www.stthomas.edu/cnm

CHARITIES REVIEW COUNCIL
The Charities Review Council empowers the public to make informed decisions about charitable giving by providing information, tools and resources to the giving public, encouraging greater confidence in giving and fostering public trust in charitable organizations.
www.smartgivers.org

FIELDSTONE ALLIANCE
Wilder Publishing Center and Wilder National Consulting Services joined to create Fieldstone Alliance, an independent nonprofit dedicated to strengthening the nonprofit sector through consulting, publishing, training, network development, demonstration projects and capacity-building for nonprofits and their communities.
www.fieldstonealliance.org

HAMLINE UNIVERSITY GRADUATE SCHOOL OF MANAGEMENT
Hamline offers degree programs in public administration, business management and nonprofit management.
www.hamline.edu/gsm

HANDS ON TWIN CITIES
Hands On Twin Cities links volunteers with volunteer opportunities, builds partnerships with local agencies and companies, and cultivates community citizenship and civic participation.
www.handsontwincities.org

MAP FOR NONPROFITS
MAP (Management Assistance Program) promotes effective nonprofits by providing management consulting services and board recruitment services.
www.mapfornonprofits.org

METROPOLITAN REGIONAL ARTS COUNCIL
MRAC promotes incorporation of the arts into the daily lives of all communities by providing leadership, advocacy, grants and services.
www.mrac.org

MINNESOTA COUNCIL OF NONPROFITS
MCN meets the increasing information needs of nonprofits and convenes nonprofits to address issues facing the sector. MCN is the statewide association of more than 1,750 member nonprofit organizations.
www.mncn.org

NONPROFITS ASSISTANCE FUND
NAF helps foster community development and vitality by building financially healthy nonprofit organizations, providing loans, financial management workshops and financial management assistance.
www.nonprofitsassistancefund.org

PUBLIC AND NONPROFIT LEADERSHIP CENTER
Located in the Hubert H. Humphrey School of Public Affairs at the University of Minnesota, the Public and Nonprofit Leadership Center works to enhance the leadership of nonprofits, philanthropy and the public sector to work together and with the private sector to advance the common good and serve the public interest.
www.hhh.umn.edu/centers/pnlc

SPRINGBOARD FOR THE ARTS
Springboard strives to cultivate a vibrant arts community by connecting artists with the skills, contacts, information and services they need, supporting the arts community (artists, arts organizations and arts administrators) with management and consulting services.
www.springboardforthearts.org

TWIN CITIES LISC
Twin Cities LISC combines corporate, government and philanthropic support to provide Community Development Corporations (CDCs) with financial tools, technical assistance and policy support to build strong, durable organizations.
www.lisc.org/twin_cities

Writing a Successful Grant Proposal
by Barbara Davis

A funder's guidelines will tell you what to include in a grant proposal for its organization. Most funders want the same information, even if they use different words or ask questions in a different order.

Some funders prefer that you fill out their own application forms or cover sheets. If the funder uses an application form, be sure to get a copy and follow the instructions. You may also use the Minnesota Common Grant Application Form if the funder you are approaching accepts it. To download the form and view a list of funders that accept it, visit the Council's website at www.mcf.org/grantsource. Copies of the form are also available from the Foundation Center Cooperating Collections in Brainerd (218.829.5574), Duluth (218.723.3802), Marshall (507.537.6176), Minneapolis (612.630.6000), Rochester (507.285.8002) and St. Paul (651.266.7000).

Proposal Outline

The following outline should meet the needs of most funders, or guide you when approaching a funder with no written guidelines. The outline is for a project proposal, and is most appropriate for a project that is trying to correct a problem, such as water pollution, school truancy or ignorance about how HIV/AIDS is transmitted. (See Variations on the Standard Outline on page 279 for guidance on other types of proposals.) The grant proposal as a whole, not including supplementary materials, should usually be five pages or less.

Note: Consider using subheads for each section, such as "Organization Information," to help you, and your reader, keep track of what you're trying to say.

SUMMARY
At the beginning of your proposal, or on a cover sheet, write a two- or three-sentence summary of the proposal. This summary helps the reader follow your argument in the proposal itself. For example:

"Annunciation Shelter requests $5,000 for a two-year, $50,000 job training program for homeless women in southwestern Minnesota. Training will be offered at four rural shelters and will include basic clerical skills, interview techniques and job seeker support groups."

ORGANIZATION INFORMATION
In two or three paragraphs, tell the funder about your organization and why it can be trusted to use funds effectively. Briefly summarize your organization's history. State your mission, whom you serve and your track record of achievement. Clearly describe, or at least list, your programs. If your programs are many or complex, consider adding an organization chart or other attachments that explain them. Describe your budget size, where you are located and who runs the organization and does the work. Add other details that build the credibility of your group. If other groups in your region work on the same issues, explain how they are different and how you collaborate with them, if you do.

Even if you have received funds from this grantmaker before, your introduction should be complete. Funders sometimes hire outside reviewers who may not be familiar with your organization.

PROBLEM/NEED/SITUATION DESCRIPTION
This is where you convince the funder that the issue you want to tackle is important and show that your organization is an expert on the issue. Here are some tips:

- **Don't assume the funder knows much about your subject area.** Most grantmaking staff people are generalists. They will probably know something about topics like Shakespeare, water pollution and HIV/AIDS, but you should not assume that they are familiar with *Troilus and Cressida*, taconite disposal methods or Kaposi's sarcoma. If your topic is complex, you might add an informative article or suggest some background reading.

- **Why is this situation important?** To whom did your organization talk, or what research did you do, to learn about the issue and decide how to tackle it?

- **Describe the situation in both factual and human interest terms,** if possible. Providing good data demonstrates that your organization is expert in the field. If there are no good data on your issue, consider doing your own research study, even if it is simple.

- **Describe your issue in as local a context as possible.** If you want to educate people in your county about HIV/AIDS, tell the funder about the epidemic in your county — not in the United States as a whole.

- **Describe a problem that is about the same size as your solution.** Don't draw a dark picture of nuclear war, teen suicide and lethal air pollution if you are planning a modest neighborhood arts program for children.

- **Don't describe the problem as the absence of your project.** "We don't have enough beds in our battered women's shelter" is not the problem. The *problem* is increased levels of domestic violence. More shelter beds is a *solution*.

WORK PLAN/SPECIFIC ACTIVITIES
Explain what your organization plans to do about the problem. What are your overall goals? You might say:

"The goals of this project are to increase the understanding among Minneapolis middle school students about the impact of smoking on their health, and to reduce the number of students who smoke."

Then go on to give details, including:

- **Who is the target audience, and how will you involve them in the activity? How many people do you intend to serve?** Some projects have two audiences: the *direct participants* (the musicians in the community band, the kids doing summer clean-up in the parks) and the *indirect beneficiaries* (the music lovers in the audience, the people who use the parks). If so, describe both. How will you ensure that people actually participate in the program?

- **What are you going to do?** Describe the activities. Tell the funder about the project's "output," or how many "units of service" you intend to deliver over a specific time period: how many hours of nutrition counseling to how many pregnant women; how many HIV/AIDS hotline calls answered by how many volunteers. Be sure you don't promise an unrealistic level of service.

- **What project planning has already taken place?** If you have already done research, secured the commitment of participants or done other initial work, describe it so the funder can see that you are well-prepared.

- **Who is going to do the work and what are their credentials?** Some funders ask for the name of a *project director*: the person most responsible for the project, whether volunteer or paid. Demonstrate that the staff or volunteers have the expertise to do a good job. Attach résumés of key people.

- **When will the project take place?** Some funders ask for the *project start date* and *project end date*. In general, a project can be said to start when you start spending money on it. If the project is long, consider including a timeline.
- **Where will the project take place?**

You may not know the answers to all these questions when you submit your proposal. But the more you know, the better the proposal will look. Apply the "mind's eye test" to your description. After reading it, could the reader close his eyes and imagine what he would see if he came into the room where your project is happening? Many project descriptions are too vague.

Remember: You can continue to submit updated information to foundation staff almost until the date the board actually reviews the proposal.

OUTCOMES/IMPACT OF ACTIVITIES

Tell the funder what impact your project will have — what will change about the situation as a result of your project. For example, your pregnancy nutrition counseling program intends to increase the birth weights of your clients' babies.

The impact of a project is sometimes hard to define. What is the intended impact of a performance of Beethoven's *Ninth Symphony*, for example?

Impact can be difficult to measure. The desired impact of a smoking cessation program is clear, but the desired impact of a leadership program for teenagers may be ambiguous and difficult to quantify.

To add to the difficulty, few nonprofits can prove conclusively that a given impact was caused directly by their project. Your clients' babies may weigh more, but the cause may not be your nutrition program. Nevertheless, you must do the best job you can to define your intended impacts.

OTHER FUNDING

Here the funder wants to know if other organizations have committed funds to the project or been asked to do so. Few funders want to be the sole support of a project. (This may not be true if the project cost is very small — less than $5,000, for instance — or if a corporation is seeking public visibility by sponsoring the project.) Funders generally expect you to ask for support from more than one source. In this section, you can also describe the in-kind contributions (goods or services instead of cash) that people are giving to the project.

FUTURE FUNDING

If you continue this project in the future, how will it be supported? Most funders don't want to support the same set of projects forever. Many funders see their niche as funding innovation: supporting new approaches to old problems or finding solutions to new problems.

What the funder really wants to see is that you have a long-term vision and funding plan for the project, that the project is "sustainable," especially if it is a new activity. If you don't have such a plan, start thinking about it — if not for your funders then for the success of your project or organization.

EVALUATION

How will you know whether you achieved the desired impacts? If you have done a good job of defining them (see above), all you need to do here is describe the information you will gather to tell you how close you came. Will you keep records of incoming hotline calls? Will you call your counseling clients six months after they leave the program to ask how they are doing? Explain who will gather the evaluation information and how you will use it. Be sure your evaluation plan is achievable given your resources. If the evaluation will cost money, be sure to put that cost in the project budget.

BUDGET

How much will the project cost? Attach a one- or two-page budget showing expected expenses and income for the project. Or you can use the budget format in the Minnesota Common Grant Application Form.

Expenses

Divide the expense side into three sections:

- Personnel Expenses
- Direct Project Expenses
- Administrative or Overhead Expenses

Personnel Expenses include the expenses for all the people who will work on the project. They may be employees of your organization or independent contractors. If they are employees, list the title, the annual pay rate and, if the person will be working less than full-time or less than 12 months on the project, the portion of time to be dedicated to the project. For example, if an employee will work half-time on the project from October through May:

Counseling director ($35,000 x 50% x 8 months) = $11,667

Also consider the time that may be contributed by other staff who are not directly involved. For instance, the executive director must supervise the counseling director:

Executive director ($40,000 x 5% x 8 months) = $1,333

If you are using employees for the project, don't forget to add payroll taxes (FICA, Medicare, unemployment and workers' compensation) and fringe benefits such as health insurance. You can include a portion of these costs equal to the portion of the person's time dedicated to the project.

For independent contractors, list either the flat fee you will pay ($1,500 to design costumes for a play) or the hourly rate ($40/hour x 40 hours).

Direct Project Expenses are non-personnel expenses you would not incur if you did not do the project. They can be almost anything: travel costs, printing, space or equipment rental, supplies, insurance, or meeting expenses such as food.

Remember that you will have to live with this budget; you can't go back to the funder and ask for more money because you forgot something. Think carefully about all the expenses you will have. If you will be hiring new people, for example, don't forget that you may have to pay for classified ads. Also take the time to get accurate estimates. If you will be printing a brochure, don't guess at the cost. Call your printer and ask for a rough estimate.

Administrative or Overhead Expenses are non-personnel expenses you will incur whether or not you do the project. But if you do the project, these resources can't be used for anything else. For example, if you pay $500 a month for an office with space for four employees, you will continue to rent the office even if the project doesn't happen. But if the project does happen, one-quarter of the office space will be occupied by the project director. So you can charge for one-quarter of your office rent, utilities and administrative costs, such as phone, copying, postage and office supplies.

Be sure to read the funder's fine print on administrative or overhead expenses (sometimes called *indirect expenses*). Some funders don't cover administrative expenses. Some instruct you to charge a flat percentage of your direct expenses. Others will allow you to itemize. If the funder has rules about overhead, remember that some of your personnel costs may in fact be "overhead" and should be moved to this section. An example is an executive director supervising a project director. You will pay the executive director whether or not you do the project, so she could be considered an administrative expense.

Note: Be sure to add up all your expenses carefully. Incorrect addition on budgets is one of the most common errors in a grant proposal.

Income
All income for a project fits into two categories:
- Earned Income
- Contributed Income

Earned Income is what people give you in exchange for the service or product your project generates. Not all projects generate income, but many do. A play generates ticket income and maybe concession income. An education project may have income from publication sales or tuition. Show how you calculated the estimated earned income:

Ticket sales ($10/ticket x 3 performances x 200 seats x 50% of house) = $3,000

Contributed Income comes in two categories: *cash* and *in-kind*. Show cash contributions first and indicate whether each item is *received, committed, pending* (you've made the request but no decision has been made) or *to be submitted*. This section should correspond to the Other Funding section (see page 277). For instance:

Ardendale Community Fnd (received) $5,000

City of Ardendale (committed) $2,500

Acme Widget Corporation (pending) $3,300

Jones Family Foundation (to be submitted) $4,000

Other funders (to be submitted) $5,400

If you plan to seek funds from a number of other funders but don't know which ones will say yes, an "other funders" line is an easy way to indicate how much *total* money you need to receive from all other sources to balance the budget.

In-kind contributions are gifts of goods or services instead of cash. They can include donated space, materials or time. If you list in-kind contributions as income in your budget, you must also show the corresponding expenses. If someone gives you something at a major discount, you would show the whole expense and then list the portion being donated under in-kind contributions. Here are some examples:

Expenses:

Classroom rental $1,500

Curriculum consultant $2,000

Teacher aides (4 x 40 hours each x $5/hour) $800

In-kind contributions:

Ardendale Community Ed. (classroom rental) $1,500

Jane Doe (curriculum consultant) $1,000

Parents of students (teacher aides) $800

In this example, Jane Doe, the curriculum consultant, is doing the work for half-price while the parents are volunteering as teacher aides.

In-kind contributions can be important for three reasons:

1. It shows all the ways in which the community is supporting your project, even though not everyone is giving cash.
2. It shows the true cost of the project — what you would have to spend without the community support. If you want to show in-kind for these reasons, you can either show it in the budget, as above, or simply add a footnote to the bottom of the budget, like this:

"This project will also receive more than $3,000 of in-kind support from the school district, participating parents and various education professionals."

3. If you are applying for a matching grant, the in-kind income may sometimes be used as part of the match. If you want to use in-kind contributions as part of your match, then you must put a dollar value on them and put them in the budget. Funders who provide matching grants may have policies on how much in-kind you can use in your match and how it must be documented.

SUPPLEMENTARY MATERIALS
Funders may ask for a variety of materials along with the proposal itself. Almost all funders want at least the following:

- **A copy of your IRS letter declaring your organization tax-exempt.** If your group is not tax-exempt, you may need to apply through a fiscal agent, or fiscal sponsor. In that case, send a copy of your fiscal agent's IRS letter. If you are part of a government agency, usually a cover letter on your letterhead will be sufficient to show that your group is eligible for grants.

- **A list of your board of directors and their affiliations,** such as "CPA," "marketing director, Acme Widget" or "parent volunteer."

- **A financial statement from your last complete fiscal year,** including a statement of income and expenses and a balance sheet showing assets and liabilities at the end of the year. Some funders ask for an audited statement. If you are too small to be audited, call to ask whether an audited statement is mandatory or just preferred.

- **A budget for your current fiscal year.** If you are well along in the fiscal year, also show actual year-to-date income and expenses next to the budget projections.

- **A budget for the next fiscal year** if you are within three or four months of the new year.

Some applicants are small parts of very large institutions, such as a department at the University of Minnesota or an after-school program in the Minneapolis Public Schools. In such cases, you may be better off submitting supplementary materials only for your program, not for the whole institution. Ask the funder what you should do.

Grantmakers may ask for other materials, such as a copy of your most recent IRS Form 990. If you don't understand what a funder is requesting from you, ask. If you don't have some of the requested materials, attach a note explaining why.

You can also attach résumés of your key personnel as well as general information about your organization, such as newsletters, brochures or annual reports. If you have a lot of supplementary materials, consider adding a sheet that lists them in the order in which they are attached.

PUTTING IT ALL TOGETHER

Now put the whole thing together: the cover sheet (if appropriate), the proposal itself, the budget and the supplementary materials. Add a cover letter if you wish. Don't put the proposal in a fancy binder; a paper clip is fine. Be sure to note if the funder wants multiple copies of anything, or if a cover sheet needs to be signed by a staff or board member.

VARIATIONS ON THE STANDARD OUTLINE

The proposal format described above is most appropriate for a problem-based project costing $5,000 or more. At times you will need to alter this format to suit other circumstances:

- Small request
- Non-problem-based project
- General operating proposal
- Capital or endowment proposal

Small request

If you are asking for a small amount of money ($1,000 or less), you can put the entire proposal in a two- or three-page letter with required attachments. Use the same outline, but keep it short.

Non-problem-based project

Many arts and humanities projects are not trying to solve a problem. A performance of Beethoven's *Ninth Symphony* is not a response to some societal ill. If that is your situation, you can alter this outline by deleting the situation description. After you have described your project, insert a new section in which you discuss the benefits of the project.

General operating proposal

Often you are asking for money not just for a specific project but to support all your activities for one fiscal year. In this case, adapt the standard proposal as follows:

- **Organization information:** No change.
- **Situation description:** What issues was your organization founded to address? Why is your organization needed? (If yours is not a "problem-based" organization, you can skip this part.)
- **Work plan/specific activities:** Use this section to explain what your organization plans to accomplish during the year for which you seek operating funding.
- **Impact of activities:** What are the intended impacts for that year's activities?
- **Other funding:** Who are the other funders providing operating support for this year?
- **Future funding:** What is your long-term funding plan for the organization, especially if your operating budget is growing?
- **Evaluation:** In general, how do you evaluate your work?
- **Budget:** You don't need a special project budget, just the financial information described under Supplementary Materials on the previous page.

Capital or endowment proposal

Include the same information as for a project proposal. Explain how this building project, or the creation or expansion of your endowment, will help you do a better job of serving your community. But also write about your long-term plans for financial health, especially if you want money for a building. The funder doesn't want to help you buy a building if you can't afford to maintain and operate it.

Other Common Questions about Grantwriting

1. Should I apply to more than one grantmaker at a time? Should I ask each one for the project's entire cost or just a portion?
As noted in the Other Funding section, few funders want to be the sole support for a project. You should usually apply to multiple funders, asking each for partial support. Ideally, the total of all your funding requests will add up to about 200 percent of the money you actually need. This allows for the likelihood that some funders will turn you down or give you less than you requested.

2. Should I use a professional grantwriter?
There are plenty of freelance grantwriters in most communities who write proposals for a fee. (Most experienced writers will not work on commission, however.) There are both good and bad reasons to hire a freelancer.

Good reasons to hire a freelance grantwriter:

- To write a good, basic proposal — the "mother proposal" — that your group can then adapt to suit different circumstances. After a year or so, however, you should be able to write this on your own.
- To search grantmaker directories and databases and identify likely funding sources. Again, your organization should soon develop these skills internally.
- Because you have five proposals due in one week.

Bad reasons to hire a freelance grantwriter:

- Because your group wants grant money but neither your volunteers nor your staff want to "dirty their hands" by asking for money. Seeking money is a core activity for most nonprofits. Learn to live with it.
- Because a freelance fundraiser promises he can get you a lot of money through his "connections." Particularly with major funders, projects are generally funded because of their worth, not due to connections.
- Because your organization has never tried to raise money before and suddenly wants a large amount of money for a big capital project. Alas, big money tends to go to groups with a long track record and solid funding base. There are exceptions, but don't count on being one of them.

If you decide to hire a freelance grantwriter, be sure to look at some writing samples. And ask for the names and phone numbers of past clients who work in your field.

3. What happens to my proposal after it reaches the grantmaker?
In some foundations, the staff screen out proposals that are ineligible or poorly planned or simply not within the organization's current focus. Staff then research the remaining proposals and write recommendations for the board. The research may include meeting with the applicants. Recommendations may go to the board with or without the original proposals. The board makes the final decisions.

In other foundations, staff members make decisions on smaller requests. In still other foundations, the board sees every proposal unscreened by staff.

Grantmakers with no paid staff typically do not have the resources to do a thorough review of each applicant. They therefore tend to fund projects and proposals that are already familiar to their boards, perhaps through personal involvement or because an applicant has been recommended by someone they know and trust.

4. What should I do if my proposal is rejected?

The letter giving you the unhappy news will probably be a form letter. But if you wish and the funder has staff, you may phone and ask, "Can you tell me anything that will help us another time?" Perhaps they liked your proposal but just ran out of money; perhaps there was some tiny point of confusion that could be resolved easily. But don't make such a call if you are feeling angry or combative. You are trying to get information, not argue a case in court.

If you are rejected, but after an objective review of the funder's guidelines you still believe there is a match, apply again in about a year. Many applicants are only successful on the second or third try.

5. What should I do if my proposal is funded?

If your proposal is funded, you may receive the check with a cover letter. Or you may get a full-blown contract stipulating, among other things, that you must submit a report when the project is done.

In all cases, write immediately to acknowledge the gift. If you sign a contract, be sure to read it first and note when and what kinds of reports are due. Then turn the report in on time. If you realize you can't do so, send a note or call to say it will be late.

Before preparing a report for a funder, check to see if the funder has specific reporting forms and guidelines. You may also use the Minnesota Common Report Form if the funder accepts it. Introduced by the Minnesota Council on Foundations in March 2001, the Minnesota Common Report Form provides a standardized format for a nonprofit grantee to use in reporting to different grantmakers about work it has accomplished with their grants, reducing the amount of time the grantee must spend rearranging basic information to fit funders' varying reporting requirements. To download the form and view a list of funders that accept it, visit the Council's website at www.mcf.org/grantsource.

Even if the funder doesn't ask for a report, send one anyway. Show the funder how well you are using the money. If your project generates a newspaper article or other publication, send a copy. If it includes a public event, invite the funder to attend. If you get heartfelt letters of thanks from participants, send a sampling to the funder. Don't be like the stereotypical college student who only writes home when he needs money.

6. What should I do if I raise some money, but not all I need?

For example, you had budgeted $50,000 for the project but you could only raise $35,000. You could submit another round of proposals to different funders. Or you could decide to do the project in a smaller way with the money you have. If you do so, you must write all those who funded the project and explain how you will adapt to the lower budget. If you can't do the project and can't raise additional funds, explain the situation and ask if you can transfer their money to another project (which you describe fully). They might say yes. If not, you must return the money.

Conclusion

Seeking grant money can be time-consuming and sometimes frustrating. Among Minnesota's largest grantmakers, about one proposal in three is funded. You may find that you can get project money but not the operating money you need to keep your basic activities going. You may be surprised by funders' generosity, but you may also be surprised by their periodic changes in focus, especially if those changes leave you on the outside looking in.

But remember that Minnesota has an extraordinary fundraising climate. People from other states envy the major corporations and large family foundations that form the backbone of many of our innovative social and cultural programs. Most funders have board and staff people who are thoughtful, careful, curious, well-educated about community issues and willing to help you. If you have a good project that has been carefully planned to meet some real needs, you will find people willing to talk with you and advise you. Good luck!

Indexes

Geographic Focus Index

This geographic focus index lists those grantmakers that identified specific areas of geographic focus. The index lists nine geographic areas.

1 - Twin Cities Metropolitan Area
(focus on Minneapolis, St Paul and their suburbs)
2 - East Metropolitan Area/St Paul only
(focus on St Paul and the eastern metropolitan area)
3 - West Metropolitan Area/Minneapolis only
(focus on Minneapolis and the western metropolitan area)
4 - Greater Minnesota other than the Twin Cities
(focus on locations within the state of Minnesota excluding the metropolitan area)
5 - Minnesota Statewide
(focus on the entire state, the Twin Cities metropolitan area and Greater Minnesota)

6 - Areas outside Minnesota
(focus on specific states or other geographic regions outside Minnesota)
7 - National Areas
(focus on the nation as a whole)
8 - International Areas
(focus on specific countries or other geographic regions outside the United States)
9 - Other
(other specific areas listed in a grantmaker's profile)

3M/3M Foundation 2, 9
Acorn Foundation 1, 4, 7
ADC Foundation 1, 9
Affiliated Community Health Foundation 9
AgStar Fund for Rural America 4, 6
AHS Foundation 1, 7, 9
Airport Foundation MSP 1
Allianz Life Insurance Company of North America 1
Ameriprise Financial, Inc. 1, 5, 7, 9
Lloyd and Barbara Amundson Charity Foundation, Inc. 1, 4, 5, 6
Andersen Corporate Foundation 1, 6, 7, 8, 9
Andersen Corporation 2, 7, 9
Fred C. and Katherine B. Andersen Foundation 9
Hugh J. Andersen Foundation 1, 4, 6, 9
Arsher Charitable Trust U/A 4
Athwin Foundation 1, 5, 9
Bernard and Fern Badzin Foundation 3
Bahl Foundation 1, 4, 6, 7, 8
Marjorie and V.M. Baich Foundation 4
Gordon and Margaret Bailey Foundation 5, 8
Baker Foundation 1
Ann Bancroft Foundation 5
Baratz Family Foundation 1, 6
Beim Foundation 1, 4, 5, 6
The Bentson Foundation 1, 6
Lillian Wright and C. Emil Berglund Foundation, Inc. 2
Best Buy Children's Foundation 1, 6, 7
The Beverly Foundation 5, 6
F.R. Bigelow Foundation 2, 9
Blandin Foundation 4
Blue Cross and Blue Shield of Minnesota Foundation/Blue Cross and Blue Shield of Minnesota 5
The Boss Foundation 1
W. Glen Boyd Charitable Foundation 5, 6, 9
Otto Bremer Foundation 1, 4, 5, 6
Bromelkamp Foundation 1, 9
Burdick-Craddick Family Foundation 1
Bush Foundation 5, 9
Patrick and Aimee Butler Family Foundation 1, 5

Buuck Family Foundation 1, 4, 5, 7, 9
Cade Foundation 1, 6
Caliber Foundation 1
Martin and Esther Capp Foundation 1, 7
Cargill Citizenship Fund 7, 8, 9
Cargill Foundation 3
The Curtis L. Carlson Family Foundation 1, 9
Catholic Aid Association Foundation 5, 6, 9
Catholic Community Foundation in the Archdiocese of Saint Paul and Minneapolis 1, 4
The CCP Foundation 1, 2
CDF Foundation 1
CenterPoint Energy 1, 4, 9
Central Minnesota Community Foundation 9
Charity, Inc. 1, 4, 6
Charlson Foundation 1
CHS Foundation 7
ClearWay Minnesota 5
Cloquet Educational Foundation 4
Comcast Cable Company 1, 6, 9
The Cooperative Foundation 1, 4, 5, 6, 9
Arthur and David Cosgrove Memorial Fund 4, 9
Cote Foundation 9
Cottonwood Foundation 1, 4, 5, 6, 7, 8
Coughlan Companies 4, 5
Charles and Kathryn Cunningham Family Foundation 1
Frances Curran Foundation, Inc. 1, 4, 5
Dakota Medical Foundation/Dakota Medical Charities 4, 6, 9
Edwin W. and Catherine M. Davis Foundation 1, 6
The Deikel Family Foundation 1
Roger L. and Agnes C. Dell Charitable (Trust 1) 4
Roger L. and Agnes C. Dell Charitable (Trust 2) 4
Delta Dental of Minnesota 5
Deluxe Corporation Foundation/Deluxe Corporation 1, 6
The Donaldson Foundation 5, 6, 9
The Dorsey & Whitney Foundation 1, 6, 9
Driscoll Foundation 1, 6

Joseph C. and Lillian A. Duke Foundation 2
Duluth Superior Area Community Foundation 9
Eagan Foundation, Incorporated 1, 2
Ecolab Foundation and Corporation 2, 9
Eddy (Edwin H.) Foundation 4
Edina Community Foundation 9
Edina Realty Foundation 1, 4, 5, 6, 9
Edwards Memorial Trust 9
ELEOS Foundation 7, 8
Charles Engasser Memorial Foundation, Inc. 5, 6
Otto C. and Elsie Ewert Charitable Trust 4
Extendicare Foundation 5, 6
Faegre & Benson Foundation 1, 6
Arlin Falck Foundation 4, 6
Fargo-Moorhead Area Foundation 4, 9
Farmers Union Marketing and Processing Foundation 5, 6
Federated Insurance Foundation, Inc. 1, 4, 6, 9
Fingerhut Family Foundation 3, 8
First National Bank of Bemidji Foundation 4
The Jack and Bessie Fiterman Foundation 5, 6
Fredrikson & Byron Foundation 1
Fremont Foundation 5
Frey Foundation 1
H.B. Fuller Company Foundation 1, 5, 6, 7, 9
G&K Services Foundation 1, 9
Donald G. Gardner Humanities Trust 4, 9
The Janice Gardner Foundation 1, 6
General Mills Community Action 1, 9
Getsch Charitable Trust 1, 6, 8
Fanny S. Gilfillan Memorial, Incorporated 4
The Graco Foundation 1, 6
Grand Rapids Area Community Foundation 9
Gray Plant Mooty Foundation 1, 4
Mary Livingston Griggs and Mary Griggs Burke Foundation 1, 6, 9
Virginia A. Groot Foundation 5, 7
N. Bud and Beverly Grossman Foundation 5, 6
Grotto Foundation, Inc. 5
Haggerty Family Foundation 1, 5, 6
Hardenbergh Foundation 2
Olga B. Hart Education Foundation 1, 5
Hartz Foundation 4, 5, 6
Hatlen Foundation 1, 4, 6

283
Indexes

Geographic Focus

Headwaters Foundation for Justice 1, 5
Healthier Minnesota Community Clinic Fund 5
HealthPartners 1
Anna M. Heilmaier Charitable Foundation 2
Hennepin County Bar Foundation 1, 9
The Hermundslie Foundation 1, 6, 9
Hiawatha Education Foundation 4
Hickory Tech Corporation Foundation 9
Honeywell Hometown Solutions 1, 7
George A. Hormel Testamentary Trust 9
HRK Foundation 1
The Hubbard Broadcasting Foundation 1, 4, 6
Nevin Huested Foundation for Handicapped Children, Inc. 5
Imation 1, 6
Impact Foundation, Inc. 1, 4, 6
Indian Land Tenure Foundation 5, 6
ING Foundation 1, 6, 7
Initiative Foundation 9
Italian American Club Foundation, Inc. 1
Jennings Family Foundation 1, 4, 5, 6
Jerome Foundation 5, 9
JNM 1966 Gift Trust U/A 4
Lewis H. Johnson Family Foundation 1, 6
Lloyd K. Johnson Foundation 4, 9
The Lynn Johnson Family Foundation 1, 7
Mitchell and Lois Johnson Charitable Foundation 1, 6
The Jostens Foundation 1, 4, 6, 9
Jundt Family Foundation 1
George Kaplan Memorial Foundation, Incorporated 1
Margaret H. and James E. Kelley Foundation, Inc. 1, 7, 8
W.K. Kellogg Foundation 5, 6, 7, 8
Elizabeth Callender King Foundation 4, 5, 9
Hess Kline Foundation, Inc. 1, 6
John S. and James L. Knight Foundation 2, 9
Knitcraft - St Croix Foundation, Inc. 4, 5
Knox Foundation 5
Kopp Family Foundation 1, 4
Ethel Mae Kreutz Private Foundation 4, 6, 9
Lahti Family Foundation 1, 4, 9
Land O'Lakes Foundation 1, 4, 5, 6, 7
Leonette M. and Fred T. Lanners Foundation 1, 4, 6
Lawson 1
Helen Sperry Lea Foundation 1, 6
Leonard, Street and Deinard Foundation 5, 6
Lerner Foundation 1, 6
Steven C. Leuthold Family Foundation 1, 4, 5, 6
Liebhaber Family Foundation 1, 6
R. C. Lilly Foundation 5
Carl and Aune Lind Family Foundation 1, 4, 5, 6, 9
The Charles A. and Anne Morrow Lindbergh Foundation 7, 8
James G. Lindell Irrevocable Charitable Trust 1, 6
Longview Foundation 1, 6
Russell T. Lund Charitable Trust 1, 4, 5, 6
Luverne Area Community Foundation 9
The M.B. Foundation 1, 4, 6
Mall of America Foundation for Youth 1
Mankato Area Foundation 4, 9
Ted and Roberta Mann Foundation 1, 9
Marbrook Foundation 1
Mardag Foundation 9

Marquette Financial Companies Community Support Program 1, 9
Martinson Clinic Foundation 6, 9
The Martinson Foundation 4, 9
McGough Foundation 5, 9
The McKnight Foundation 1, 4, 5, 8
McNeely Foundation 2, 9
Medica Foundation 5, 6, 9
The Medtronic Foundation 1, 6, 7, 8
Donald and Marjorie Meredith Foundation 5, 6
Martin and Esther Miller Foundation 1
Minneapolis Area Association of Realtors Foundation, Inc. 3, 4
The Minneapolis Foundation 1, 4, 5
Minneapolis Kiwanis Foundation 3
Minneapolis Rotary Community Service Foundation 3
Minnesota Power Foundation 4, 9
Minnesota State Bar Foundation 1, 4, 5
The Minnesota Timberwolves FastBreak Foundation 5
Minnesota Twins Community Fund 1, 4, 5, 6, 7
Marjorie Weil and Marvin Edward Mitchell Foundation 1
Jane N. Mooty Foundation Trust 1, 4, 5, 6
John W. Mooty Foundation Trust 1
Moscoe Family Foundation 1, 6
Kingsley H. Murphy Family Foundation 1, 6
The Laura Jane Musser Fund 5, 6, 7
The Nash Foundation 1, 5
George W. Neilson Foundation 4
The Nelson Family Foundation 1, 6
Richard A. Newman Foundation 1
NFC Foundation 1, 6
Noel Foundation 1, 4, 6
Roger and Violet Noreen Charitable Trust 1
North Suburban Community Foundation 9
North Suburban Youth Foundation 2
Northland Foundation 9
Northwest Minnesota Foundation 4
Alice M. O'Brien Foundation 1, 4, 5, 6
Casey Albert T. O'Neil Foundation 1, 4, 5, 6
O'Shaughnessy Foundation 5, 6
I. A. O'Shaughnessy Foundation, Incorporated 7
E.O. Olson Trust U/A Water Resources 4, 9
Ordean Foundation 9
OSilas Foundation 1, 4, 6
Osterud-Winter Foundation 4
Otter Tail Power Company 4, 6, 9
Ben and Jeanne Overman Charitable Trust 4, 9
Owatonna Foundation 4, 9
P.G.N. Foundation 1, 5, 6, 9
Pagel Foundation 1, 4, 6
Pajor Family Foundation 1, 4, 6
Lewis and Annie F. Paper Foundation, Inc. 1
Park Nicollet Foundation 3, 9
Patterson Foundation 7
The Pentair Foundation 1, 2, 3
People in Business Care, Inc. 1, 4, 5, 6, 7, 8
Perkins Foundation 1, 4, 5
The Lawrence and Linda Perlman Family Foundation 1
John T. Petters Foundation 1, 5, 6
Philanthrofund Foundation (PFund) 1, 4, 5, 6
The Jay and Rose Phillips Family Foundation 1
Piper Jaffray 1, 6
Carl and Eloise Pohlad Family Foundation 1, 5, 9

The Polaris Foundation 1, 4, 6
The Irwin Andrew Porter Foundation 5, 6, 8
Prospect Creek Foundation 1, 6
Quetico Superior Foundation 9
The Elizabeth C. Quinlan Foundation, Inc. 1, 4, 5
Rahr Foundation 1
Rappaport Family Foundation 4, 7, 8
RBC Dain Rauscher Foundation 1, 9
Horst M. Rechelbacher Foundation 1, 7, 8
Red Wing Shoe Company Foundation 4, 6, 9
Redwood Area Communities Foundation, Inc. 4, 9
Regis Foundation 1, 4, 6
Luther I. Replogle Foundation 3, 9
Richfield Community Foundation 1, 9
Ripley Memorial Foundation, Inc. 1, 9
Margaret Rivers Fund 1, 6
The Riverway Foundation 1
Robins, Kaplan, Miller & Ciresi, L.L.P. Foundation for Education, Public Health & Social Justice 1, 4
Rochester Area Foundation 9
Rochester Post Bulletin Charities 4
Runestone Electric Association Community Trust 4, 9
Sacred Portion Foundation 1, 4, 6
The Saint Paul Foundation 2, 9
Salem Foundation, Inc. 1, 6
Samsara Foundation 1, 6
Sauer Children's Renew Foundation 5
Saunders Family Foundation 1, 9
Carl and Verna Schmidt Foundation 4
Schmoker Family Foundation 1, 6
Arlan Schonberg Irrevocable Trust 1
Securian Foundation/Securian Financial Group 1
Sexton Foundation 1, 4, 6, 9
Shakopee Mdewakanton Sioux Community 1, 9
Shapiro Family Philanthropic Foundation 1, 6
The Shared Fund 1, 6
The Sheltering Arms Foundation 5
The Shiebler Family Foundation 1, 6
Gertrude R. Shiely Charitable Trust 2
The Simmet Foundation 1, 4, 6
Sioux Falls Area Community Foundation 6
SKB Environmental Rosemount Community Trust 2
William Wood Skinner Foundation 1, 6
R. C. Skoe Foundation 1
Slaggie Family Foundation 4, 9
Slawik Family Foundation 1
Smikis Foundation 1
Southern Minnesota Initiative Foundation 4
Southways Foundation 1, 6
Southwest Initiative Foundation 4, 9
The Spell Family Foundation 1, 6
Daniel J. Spiegel Family Foundation 1, 6
St Anthony Park Community Foundation 2, 9
St Croix Valley Community Foundation 2, 6, 9
St Francis Regional Medical Center Foundation 9
Alex Stern Family Foundation 9
Stevens Square Foundation 1
Sundance Family Foundation and Sundance Pay It Forward Foundation 1, 8
SUPERVALU Foundation 1
Swan Family Foundation 1, 4, 6
Target 9

Geographic Focus

TCF Foundation 1, 4, 5, 9
TEAM Foundation 4
Tennant Foundation 3
Think Community Foundation 1, 9
James R. Thorpe Foundation 3
Thrivent Financial for Lutherans Foundation 1, 9
Todd-Wadena Electric Cooperative Community Trust 4, 9
The Toro Company Giving Program 1, 7, 8, 9
Tozer Foundation, Inc. 9
Travelers Corporation and Travelers Foundation 1, 5, 7, 9
Trust for the Meditation Process 5, 6, 8

Turner Family Foundation 1, 6
U.S. Bancorp Foundation 1, 4, 6, 7
United Health Foundation 9
Unity Avenue Foundation 1, 5, 7, 8, 9
The Valspar Foundation 1
DeWitt and Caroline Van Evera Foundation 5, 6
The Vos Family Foundation 1, 4, 6
Archie D. and Bertha H. Walker Foundation 1, 5, 7
Warren Foundation 1, 5
The Wasie Foundation 1, 6
Frederick O. Watson Foundation 1, 6
WCA Foundation 1, 5
J. A. Wedum Foundation 1, 4

Wells Fargo Foundation Minnesota 1, 4
Wenger Foundation 1, 4, 5, 7
West Central Initiative 9
Mark and Muriel Wexler Foundation 1, 6
Weyerhaeuser Family Foundation, Inc. 5, 6, 7, 8
Whitney ARCEE Foundation 5
Whitney Foundation 1
Winona Community Foundation 4, 9
Winona Foundation 9
Women's Foundation of Minnesota 1, 4, 5
Xcel Energy Foundation/Corporate Citizenship 1, 4, 9
Youthworks! Foundation, Inc. 9
A. H. Zeppa Family Foundation 4, 7, 8, 9

Areas of Interest Index

This index includes grantmakers that identified specific program areas that they support. The index is divided into 24 major field areas of the National Taxonomy of Exempt Entities (NTEE).

Animal Related	.287
Arts, Culture, Humanities	.287
Civil Rights, Social Action, Advocacy	.288
Community Improvement/Capacity Building	.289
Education	.290
Employment/Jobs	.292
Environmental Quality/Protection/Beautification	.292
Food/Nutrition/Agriculture	.293
Health - Diseases/Medical Disciplines	.294
Health - General/Rehabilitative	.295
Health - Mental Health/Crisis Intervention	.296
Health - Research	.296
Housing/Shelter	.297
Human Services	.298
International Affairs	.299
Philanthropy/Voluntarism	.300
Public Affairs/Society Benefit	.300
Public Protection: Crime/Courts/Legal Services	.301
Public Safety, Disaster Preparedness and Relief	.301
Recreation, Leisure, Sports and Athletics	.302
Religion/Spiritual Development	.302
Science/Technology	.303
Social Science Organizations	.303
Youth Development	.303

Areas of Interest

Animal Related
1 - Animal protection/welfare
2 - Veterinary services
3 - Wildlife preservation/protection
4 - Zoo/zoological societies
5 - Other

Ameriprise Financial, Inc. 4, 5
Lloyd and Barbara Amundson Charity Foundation, Inc.
Andersen Corporation
Fred C. and Katherine B. Andersen Foundation 1
Hugh J. Andersen Foundation 1
Athwin Foundation 1, 3, 4
Gordon and Margaret Bailey Foundation 4
The Bentson Foundation
Martin and Esther Capp Foundation 3
Central Minnesota Community Foundation 1, 3
Cottonwood Foundation 3
Frances Curran Foundation, Inc. 5
The Deikel Family Foundation 3
Duluth Superior Area Community Foundation 1, 3, 4

Fargo-Moorhead Area Foundation
Farmers Union Marketing and Processing Foundation
H.B. Fuller Company Foundation 3, 4
The Janice Gardner Foundation 1
George A. Hormel Testamentary Trust 1
HRK Foundation 1
The Hubbard Broadcasting Foundation 4
Kopp Family Foundation
Steven C. Leuthold Family Foundation 1, 3
The Charles A. and Anne Morrow Lindbergh Foundation 3, 5
Richard A. Newman Foundation 1
Otter Tail Power Company 3, 4
Patterson Foundation 2
The Irwin Andrew Porter Foundation 3
The Elizabeth C. Quinlan Foundation, Inc. 3, 4

Rahr Foundation 1, 3
Margaret Rivers Fund
Rochester Area Foundation 1
Saunders Family Foundation 1, 3
Carl and Verna Schmidt Foundation 1, 3
Sioux Falls Area Community Foundation 1, 3, 4
St Croix Valley Community Foundation
Tennant Foundation 1, 4
The Toro Company Giving Program 3, 4
Unity Avenue Foundation 3
Archie D. and Bertha H. Walker Foundation 3
Winona Community Foundation

Arts, Culture, Humanities
1 - Arts/cultural multipurpose
2 - Arts services
3 - Historical societies
4 - Humanities
5 - Media/communications
6 - Museums
7 - Performing arts
8 - Visual arts
9 - Other

3M/3M Foundation 1, 6, 7, 8, 9
AHS Foundation
Airport Foundation MSP 2, 9
Allianz Life Insurance Company of North America 1
Ameriprise Financial, Inc. 1, 9
Lloyd and Barbara Amundson Charity Foundation, Inc.
Andersen Corporate Foundation 1, 6, 7, 8
Elmer L. and Eleanor J. Andersen Foundation
Fred C. and Katherine B. Andersen Foundation 1
Hugh J. Andersen Foundation 1, 4, 7, 9
Athwin Foundation 1, 3, 4, 2, 6, 7, 8
Bernard and Fern Badzin Foundation
Bahl Foundation 6
Gordon and Margaret Bailey Foundation 5, 6
Baker Foundation 3, 7, 8
Baratz Family Foundation
Beim Foundation 1, 2, 4, 5, 7, 8, 9
The Bentson Foundation
Lillian Wright and C. Emil Berglund Foundation, Inc. 1, 2, 3, 6, 7, 8
F.R. Bigelow Foundation
Blandin Foundation 9
The Boss Foundation 1, 3, 4, 5, 6, 7, 8
Burdick-Craddick Family Foundation 9
Bush Foundation 1, 4, 5, 6, 7, 8

Patrick and Aimee Butler Family Foundation 3, 4, 6, 9
Buuck Family Foundation 1, 6, 7, 8, 9
Carolyn Foundation
CDF Foundation
Central Minnesota Community Foundation 1, 3, 4, 6, 7, 8
Arthur and David Cosgrove Memorial Fund
Cote Foundation
Charles and Kathryn Cunningham Family Foundation
Edwin W. and Catherine M. Davis Foundation 3, 6, 7
Roger L. and Agnes C. Dell Charitable (Trust 1)
Roger L. and Agnes C. Dell Charitable (Trust 2)
Deluxe Corporation Foundation/Deluxe Corporation 1, 3, 6, 7
The Dorsey & Whitney Foundation
Driscoll Foundation
Duluth Superior Area Community Foundation 1, 2, 3, 4, 5, 6, 7, 8
Ecolab Foundation and Corporation 1, 2, 6, 7
Edina Community Foundation 1, 2, 3, 4, 5, 6, 7, 8
Otto C. and Elsie Ewert Charitable Trust
Faegre & Benson Foundation
Arlin Falck Foundation
Fargo-Moorhead Area Foundation

Federated Insurance Foundation, Inc. 1, 3, 6, 7, 8
First National Bank of Bemidji Foundation 1
The Jack and Bessie Fiterman Foundation
Fredrikson & Byron Foundation
Fremont Foundation
Frey Foundation 3, 6
H.B. Fuller Company Foundation 1, 2, 3, 4, 5, 6, 7, 8
Donald G. Gardner Humanities Trust 7, 8
The Janice Gardner Foundation
General Mills Community Action 1, 6, 7, 8, 9
Grand Rapids Area Community Foundation 1, 2, 3, 4, 5, 6, 7, 8
Gray Plant Mooty Foundation
Mary Livingston Griggs and Mary Griggs Burke Foundation 3, 4, 6, 7, 8
Virginia A. Groot Foundation 8, 9
N. Bud and Beverly Grossman Foundation 6, 7, 8
Grotto Foundation, Inc.
Hartz Foundation 3, 5, 6
Hatlen Foundation
Anna M. Heilmaier Charitable Foundation 7, 9
Hickory Tech Corporation Foundation 7
George A. Hormel Testamentary Trust 1, 7
HRK Foundation 1, 2, 3, 4, 6, 7, 8, 9

Areas of Interest

The Hubbard Broadcasting Foundation 3, 6, 7, 8
Imation
ING Foundation
Jerome Foundation 1, 2, 5, 6, 7, 8
JNM 1966 Gift Trust U/A
Lewis H. Johnson Family Foundation 5
Lloyd K. Johnson Foundation 1, 3, 6, 7
The Lynn Johnson Family Foundation
The Jostens Foundation 9
Jundt Family Foundation 6, 7
Margaret H. and James E. Kelley Foundation, Inc.
Elizabeth Callender King Foundation 3, 7
Hess Kline Foundation, Inc. 6
Kopp Family Foundation
Land O'Lakes Foundation 1, 2, 3, 4, 6, 7, 8
Leonette M. and Fred T. Lanners Foundation 3
Helen Sperry Lea Foundation
Lerner Foundation 3, 4, 5, 6, 7
Steven C. Leuthold Family Foundation 3, 5
Liebhaber Family Foundation
R. C. Lilly Foundation
Carl and Aune Lind Family Foundation 3, 5
The Charles A. and Anne Morrow Lindbergh Foundation 4
Russell T. Lund Charitable Trust 5, 6, 7
The Luther Family Foundation
Luverne Area Community Foundation
Macy's North
Mankato Area Foundation
Ted and Roberta Mann Foundation 1, 8, 9
Marbrook Foundation 1, 2 6, 7, 8
Mardag Foundation
The Martinson Foundation 3, 5
Mayo Clinic 1, 4, 6, 7, 8
The McKnight Foundation 1, 2, 5, 6, 7, 8
McNeely Foundation 1
The Medtronic Foundation 1, 9
Martin and Esther Miller Foundation 5

Minnesota Power Foundation 1, 7
Minnesota Twins Community Fund
Marjorie Weil and Marvin Edward Mitchell Foundation 4, 5, 7
Jane N. Mooty Foundation Trust 3, 5
Moscoe Family Foundation
The Laura Jane Musser Fund
The Nash Foundation 1, 7, 8
The Nelson Family Foundation 6, 7, 8
Roger and Violet Noreen Charitable Trust
North Suburban Community Foundation 3, 7
Alice M. O'Brien Foundation 3, 6, 7, 8
Casey Albert T. O'Neil Foundation 3, 5, 6, 7
OSi as Foundation
Otter Tail Power Company 1, 3, 6, 7
Owatonna Foundation 1, 2, 3, 4, 5, 6, 7, 8
P.G.N. Foundation
Lewis and Annie F. Paper Foundation, Inc.
The Pentair Foundation 2, 6, 7, 8, 9
The Lawrence and Linda Perlman Family Foundation
The Jay and Rose Phillips Family Foundation 1, 2, 6, 7, 8, 9
Piper Jaffray 1
Carl and Eloise Pohlad Family Foundation
The Irwin Andrew Porter Foundation
Prospect Creek Foundation
The Elizabeth C. Quinlan Foundation, Inc. 1, 2, 3, 4, 5, 6, 7, 8
Rahr Foundation 7
RBC Dain Rauscher Foundation 1, 2, 4, 6, 7, 8
Horst M. Rechelbacher Foundation
Red Wing Shoe Company Foundation
Regis Foundation 5, 6, 7, 8
Margaret Rivers Fund 1, 2, 3, 5, 6, 7, 8
Rochester Area Foundation 1, 2, 3, 6, 7, 8
The Saint Paul Foundation 1, 2, 3, 4, 5, 6, 7, 8
Salem Foundation, Inc.
Saunders Family Foundation 3, 7, 8
Carl and Verna Schmidt Foundation 1, 3, 7

Schmoker Family Foundation 6, 7, 8, 9
Securian Foundation/Securian Financial Group 1, 3, 6, 7, 8
Sexton Foundation
Shapiro Family Philanthropic Foundation 5, 6, 7, 8
The Shared Fund 6, 7
The Shiebler Family Foundation
Sioux Falls Area Community Foundation 1, 2, 3, 4, 5, 6, 7, 8
Southways Foundation
St Anthony Park Community Foundation
St Croix Valley Community Foundation 1, 2, 3, 4, 6, 7, 8, 9
Alex Stern Family Foundation
SUPERVALU Foundation 1, 9
Target 9
TCF Foundation
Tennant Foundation 1, 3, 4, 5, 6, 7, 8
Thomson West
James R. Thorpe Foundation 1, 7, 9
Tozer Foundation, Inc. 1, 3, 7
Travelers Corporation and Travelers Foundation 1, 2, 3, 4, 5, 6, 7, 8
U.S. Bancorp Foundation 9
The Valspar Foundation 9
DeWitt and Caroline Van Evera Foundation 9
Archie D. and Bertha H. Walker Foundation 1, 2, 3, 4, 5, 6, 7, 8
Warren Foundation 3, 5, 6, 7
Frederick O. Watson Foundation
Wells Fargo Foundation Minnesota 9
Wenger Foundation 1, 2, 3, 4, 5, 6, 7, 8
Whitney ARCEE Foundation
Whitney Foundation
Winona Community Foundation
Winona Foundation 1, 2, 3, 4, 5, 6, 7, 8, 9
Xcel Energy Foundation/Corporate Citizenship
A. H. Zeppa Family Foundation

Civil Rights, Social Action, Advocacy

1 - Civil liberties advocacy
2 - Civil rights/advocacy for specific groups
3 - Equal opportunity and access
4 - Intergroup relations/race relations
5 - Voter education/registration
6 - Other

Blue Cross and Blue Shield of Minnesota Foundation/Blue Cross and Blue Shield of Minnesota 4
Otto Bremer Foundation 1, 2, 3, 4, 5
Bush Foundation 2, 3
Central Minnesota Community Foundation 1, 2, 3, 4
Cottonwood Foundation 4
The Deikel Family Foundation 2
Deluxe Corporation Foundation/Deluxe Corporation 5
Duluth Superior Area Community Foundation 2, 4, 5
Edina Community Foundation 3, 4
Fargo-Moorhead Area Foundation 2

General Mills Community Action 6
Grotto Foundation, Inc. 2, 4
Headwaters Foundation for Justice 1, 2, 3, 4, 5
George A. Hormel Testamentary Trust 3
HRK Foundation 2, 5
Indian Land Tenure Foundation 2
Mitchell and Lois Johnson Charitable Foundation
Margaret H. and James E. Kelley Foundation, Inc. 2
The Minneapolis Foundation 1, 2, 3, 4, 5
Marjorie Weil and Marvin Edward Mitchell Foundation 3
The Laura Jane Musser Fund 4
Northland Foundation 2, 3, 4

Philanthrofund Foundation (PFund) 1, 2, 3, 4, 6
The Jay and Rose Phillips Family Foundation 1, 2, 3, 4, 6
The Irwin Andrew Porter Foundation 4
The Elizabeth C. Quinlan Foundation, Inc. 1, 3, 5
Rochester Area Foundation 1, 2, 3, 4
The Saint Paul Foundation 2, 3, 4, 5, 6
Samsara Foundation
St Croix Valley Community Foundation
Archie D. and Bertha H. Walker Foundation 1, 3, 4, 5
West Central Initiative 4
Winona Community Foundation

Areas of Interest

Community Improvement/Capacity Building

1 - Business services
2 - Community coalitions
3 - Community funds/federated giving programs
4 - Community service clubs
5 - Community/neighborhood development/improvement
6 - Economic development
7 - Nonprofit management
8 - Volunteer bureaus
9 - Other

3M/3M Foundation 7, 8
AgStar Fund for Rural America 9
AHS Foundation
Allianz Life Insurance Company of North America 2, 5
Ameriprise Financial, Inc. 6
Lloyd and Barbara Amundson Charity Foundation, Inc.
Andersen Corporate Foundation 9
Hugh J. Andersen Foundation 5, 7
Athwin Foundation 2, 5, 7
Baratz Family Foundation
F.R. Bigelow Foundation 5, 6
Blandin Foundation 9
Blue Cross and Blue Shield of Minnesota Foundation/Blue Cross and Blue Shield of Minnesota 5, 7
The Boss Foundation 5
W. Glen Boyd Charitable Foundation 6
Otto Bremer Foundation 2, 5, 7
Bush Foundation 6, 7, 9
Carolyn Foundation 9
Central Minnesota Community Foundation 2, 5, 7
ClearWay Minnesota 2, 9
Comcast Cable Company
The Cooperative Foundation 6, 9
Cote Foundation
Cottonwood Foundation 6
The Deikel Family Foundation 5, 7
Roger L. and Agnes C. Dell Charitable (Trust 1)
Delta Dental of Minnesota 2, 9
Deluxe Corporation Foundation/Deluxe Corporation 7, 8
The Dorsey & Whitney Foundation
Duluth Superior Area Community Foundation 2, 5, 6, 7, 8
Ecolab Foundation and Corporation 5, 6
Edina Community Foundation 2, 4, 5, 7
Edina Realty Foundation 5
Fargo-Moorhead Area Foundation 6
Federated Insurance Foundation, Inc. 9
First National Bank of Bemidji Foundation 6
Frey Foundation 5
General Mills Community Action 5
The Graco Foundation 5
Grand Rapids Area Community Foundation 2, 6, 7

N. Bud and Beverly Grossman Foundation
Grotto Foundation, Inc. 5, 7, 9
Hickory Tech Corporation Foundation 5
Honeywell Hometown Solutions
George A. Hormel Testamentary Trust 5, 6
HRK Foundation 2, 5, 6, 9
The Hubbard Broadcasting Foundation
Indian Land Tenure Foundation 5
Initiative Foundation 2, 5, 6, 7, 8
Jennings Family Foundation
JNM 1966 Gift Trust U/A
Lloyd K. Johnson Foundation 5, 6
The Lynn Johnson Family Foundation
John S. and James L. Knight Foundation 6
Kopp Family Foundation 5
Land O'Lakes Foundation 2, 3, 5
Leonette M. and Fred T. Lanners Foundation 5
R. C. Lilly Foundation
Luverne Area Community Foundation
Mankato Area Foundation
Marbrook Foundation 5, 6, 7
Mardag Foundation 5
Marquette Financial Companies Community Support Program 6, 9
The Martinson Foundation 2, 5
Mayo Clinic 5, 6, 7, 8
The McKnight Foundation 2, 5, 6
McNeely Foundation 5, 6
Martin and Esther Miller Foundation
The Minneapolis Foundation 5, 6, 9
Minneapolis Rotary Community Service Foundation 8
Minnesota Business and Professional Women's Foundation 9
Minnesota Power Foundation 2, 5, 6, 8
Minnesota Twins Community Fund 5
Marjorie Weil and Marvin Edward Mitchell Foundation 2
John W. Mooty Foundation Trust 2, 3, 4
The Laura Jane Musser Fund 9
North Suburban Youth Foundation
Northland Foundation 6, 7, 8
Northwest Minnesota Foundation 1, 5, 6, 7, 9
Otter Tail Power Company 5, 6
Owatonna Foundation 2, 4, 5, 6
P.G.N. Foundation
Park Nicollet Foundation 5
The Pentair Foundation 5

People in Business Care, Inc.
The Lawrence and Linda Perlman Family Foundation
Philanthrofund Foundation (PFund) 2, 9
Piper Jaffray 5, 6
The Polaris Foundation 5
Prospect Creek Foundation
The Elizabeth C. Quinlan Foundation, Inc. 5
Rahr Foundation 5
Red Wing Shoe Company Foundation
Margaret Rivers Fund
Rochester Area Foundation 2, 5, 6, 7, 8
Runestone Electric Association Community Trust
The Saint Paul Foundation 2, 5, 6, 7
Saunders Family Foundation 5
Carl and Verna Schmidt Foundation
Schmoker Family Foundation 9
Shakopee Mdewakanton Sioux Community 2, 5, 6, 7
Sioux Falls Area Community Foundation 5, 6, 7
SKB Environmental Rosemount Community Trust
Southern Minnesota Initiative Foundation 6, 9
Southwest Initiative Foundation 2, 6, 7
St Anthony Park Community Foundation 5
St Croix Valley Community Foundation
Stevens Square Foundation 8
TCF Foundation
Tennant Foundation 5
Think Community Foundation 5
Todd-Wadena Electric Cooperative Community Trust 4, 6
Tozer Foundation, Inc. 6, 7, 8
Travelers Corporation and Travelers Foundation 5, 6, 7
U.S. Bancorp Foundation 5, 6
The Valspar Foundation 5
Archie D. and Bertha H. Walker Foundation 5, 6
Warren Foundation
Wells Fargo Foundation Minnesota 5, 6, 7
Wenger Foundation 5, 9
West Central Initiative 2, 6, 7
Winona Community Foundation
Winona Foundation 4, 5
Xcel Energy Foundation/Corporate Citizenship
Youthworks! Foundation, Inc. 5, 6

Areas of Interest

Education
1 - Adult/continuing education/literacy
2 - Educational reform
3 - Educational services
4 - Graduate education/professional schools
5 - Higher education
6 - Libraries/library science
7 - Pre-school/elementary
8 - Secondary
9 - Student services/organizations of students
10 - Vocational/technical
11 - Other

3M/3M Foundation 11
ACA International Foundation
Acorn Foundation
ADC Foundation 11
AgStar Fund for Rural America 11
AHS Foundation
Ameriprise Financial, Inc. 1, 3, 5, 6, 7, 8, 10
Lloyd and Barbara Amundson Charity Foundation, Inc.
Andersen Corporate Foundation 1, 7, 8, 11
Andersen Corporation
Elmer L. and Eleanor J. Andersen Foundation 6
Fred C. and Katherine B. Andersen Foundation 5
Hugh J. Andersen Foundation 1, 6, 8, 11
Athwin Foundation
Bahl Foundation 5
Marjorie and V.M. Baich Foundation
Gordon and Margaret Bailey Foundation 7, 8, 11
Baker Foundation 5
Baratz Family Foundation
Beim Foundation 7, 11
The Bentson Foundation
Lillian Wright and C. Emil Berglund Foundation, Inc. 3, 6, 7, 8, 9, 10
Best Buy Children's Foundation 11
F.R. Bigelow Foundation
Blandin Foundation 11
Blue Cross and Blue Shield of Minnesota Foundation/Blue Cross and Blue Shield of Minnesota 11
The Boss Foundation 6
W. Glen Boyd Charitable Foundation 1, 3, 4, 5, 7, 8, 9, 10, 11
Otto Bremer Foundation 1, 4, 5, 11
Bromelkamp Foundation 1
Bush Foundation 5, 7, 8
Buuck Family Foundation 4, 5, 7, 11
Cade Foundation 5, 7, 8
Caliber Foundation
Cargill Citizenship Fund 11
Cargill Foundation 11
The Curtis L. Carlson Family Foundation
Catholic Aid Association Foundation 8
Catholic Community Foundation in the Archdiocese of Saint Paul and Minneapolis 3, 5, 7, 8
CenterPoint Energy 11
Central Minnesota Community Foundation 1, 3, 5, 7, 8, 9, 10, 11
Charity, Inc.
CHS Foundation 5, 10, 11
Cloquet Educational Foundation 7, 8

Comcast Cable Company 6, 11
The Cooperative Foundation 1, 4, 5, 6, 8, 10, 11
Arthur and David Cosgrove Memorial Fund
Cote Foundation 6
Coughlan Companies 6
Charles and Kathryn Cunningham Family Foundation 5
Edwin W. and Catherine M. Davis Foundation
Roger L. and Agnes C. Dell Charitable (Trust 1)
Roger L. and Agnes C. Dell Charitable (Trust 2)
Delta Dental of Minnesota 11
Deluxe Corporation Foundation/Deluxe Corporation 11
The Donaldson Foundation
The Dorsey & Whitney Foundation
Driscoll Foundation 5, 7, 8
Duluth Superior Area Community Foundation 1, 3, 4, 5, 6, 7, 8, 9, 10
Ecolab Foundation and Corporation 3, 7, 8
Edina Community Foundation 5, 7, 11
Charles Engasser Memorial Foundation, Inc.
Otto C. and Elsie Ewert Charitable Trust
Extendicare Foundation 11
Faegre & Benson Foundation
Arlin Falck Foundation
Fargo-Moorhead Area Foundation
Federated Insurance Foundation, Inc. 5, 8, 10
First National Bank of Bemidji Foundation 5
Fremont Foundation
Frey Foundation 2, 3, 7, 8
H.B. Fuller Company Foundation 1, 3, 4, 5, 6, 7, 8, 10, 11
G&K Services Foundation
Donald G. Gardner Humanities Trust 6
General Mills Community Action 5, 7, 8, 10
The Graco Foundation 1, 3, 4, 5, 6, 8, 10
Grand Rapids Area Community Foundation 6, 7, 8, 10
Gray Plant Mooty Foundation
Mary Livingston Griggs and Mary Griggs Burke Foundation 5, 6
N. Bud and Beverly Grossman Foundation
Grotto Foundation, Inc. 11
Olga B. Hart Education Foundation
Hartz Foundation 1, 4, 5, 6, 7, 8, 10
Hatlen Foundation 5, 8
Headwaters Foundation for Justice 2, 11
The Hermundslie Foundation
Hiawatha Education Foundation 7, 8
Hickory Tech Corporation Foundation 5, 6, 8
Honeywell Hometown Solutions
George A. Hormel Testamentary Trust 1, 6, 7
HRK Foundation 5, 6, 7, 11
The Hubbard Broadcasting Foundation 1, 5, 6

Imation
Indian Land Tenure Foundation 11
ING Foundation 1, 2, 3, 4, 5, 7, 8, 10
Initiative Foundation 11
Italian American Club Foundation, Inc. 5, 8
JNM 1966 Gift Trust U/A
Lewis H. Johnson Family Foundation 5, 8
Lloyd K. Johnson Foundation 1, 7, 8, 10
The Lynn Johnson Family Foundation
Mitchell and Lois Johnson Charitable Foundation
The Jostens Foundation 3, 9, 11
Jundt Family Foundation 5, 7, 8
George Kaplan Memorial Foundation, Incorporated
Margaret H. and James E. Kelley Foundation, Inc.
W.K. Kellogg Foundation
Elizabeth Callender King Foundation 5, 7, 8
Hess Kline Foundation, Inc.
Knitcraft - St Croix Foundation, Inc.
Kopp Family Foundation 1, 5, 6, 7, 11
Land O'Lakes Foundation 11
Lang Family Charitable Trust 8
Leonette M. and Fred T. Lanners Foundation 2, 5, 7, 8
Lawson 11
Helen Sperry Lea Foundation
Lerner Foundation 5, 6
Liebhaber Family Foundation
R. C. Lilly Foundation
The Charles A. and Anne Morrow Lindbergh Foundation 11
James G. Lindell Irrevocable Charitable Trust
Russell T. Lund Charitable Trust
The Luther Family Foundation
The M.B. Foundation
Macy's North 11
Mall of America Foundation for Youth 5
Mankato Area Foundation
Ted and Roberta Mann Foundation 5, 11
Marbrook Foundation 5, 7, 8, 10
Mardag Foundation 7, 8, 10
The Martinson Foundation 6, 7, 8
Mayo Clinic 3, 5, 6, 7, 8
McNeely Foundation 3, 7, 8
The Medtronic Foundation 4, 5, 7, 8, 10, 11
Martin and Esther Miller Foundation
The Minneapolis Foundation 1, 2, 7, 8, 10, 11
Minneapolis Kiwanis Foundation
Minneapolis Rotary Community Service Foundation 1, 3, 5, 7, 8, 10
Minnesota Business and Professional Women's Foundation 4, 5, 11

Areas of Interest

Minnesota Early Learning Foundation 11
Minnesota Power Foundation 5, 7, 8, 11
Minnesota State Bar Foundation 11
Minnesota Twins Community Fund 3, 5, 6, 7, 8
Marjorie Weil and Marvin Edward Mitchell Foundation 2, 7, 8, 11
MoneyGram International 1, 11
Jane N. Mooty Foundation Trust 5
John W. Mooty Foundation Trust 4, 5
The Nelson Family Foundation 4, 5, 6, 7, 8
Richard A. Newman Foundation 9, 10
NFC Foundation
North Suburban Community Foundation 6, 7, 8
North Suburban Youth Foundation
Northwest Minnesota Foundation 11
Alice M. O'Brien Foundation
Casey Albert T. O'Neil Foundation
Ordean Foundation 5, 10, 11
I. A. O'Shaughnessy Foundation, Incorporated 4, 5, 7, 8
OSilas Foundation 5, 6, 7, 8
Otter Tail Power Company 4, 5, 6, 10
Ben and Jeanne Overman Charitable Trust 5
Owatonna Foundation 1, 3, 5, 6, 7, 8, 9, 10
P.G.N. Foundation
Pagel Foundation
Pajor Family Foundation
Lewis and Annie F. Paper Foundation, Inc.
The Pentair Foundation 1, 3, 5, 7, 8, 10
People in Business Care, Inc.
The Lawrence and Linda Perlman Family Foundation
John T. Petters Foundation 5, 11
Philanthrofund Foundation (PFund) 9, 11
The Jay and Rose Phillips Family Foundation 1, 3, 5, 7, 8, 9, 11
Piper Jaffray 11
The Irwin Andrew Porter Foundation 7, 8
Prospect Creek Foundation
The Elizabeth C. Quinlan Foundation, Inc. 1, 5, 6
Rahr Foundation 5
RBC Dain Rauscher Foundation 3, 8, 11
Red Wing Shoe Company Foundation 7, 8

Redwood Area Communities Foundation, Inc. 11
Regis Foundation 5, 7, 8
Luther I. Replogle Foundation 7, 8, 9, 11
Richfield Community Foundation 7, 8
Ripley Memorial Foundation, Inc. 11
Margaret Rivers Fund
Rochester Area Foundation 1, 2, 3, 5, 6, 7, 8, 10
Rukavina Family Foundation
Runestone Electric Association Community Trust
The Saint Paul Foundation 1, 3, 6, 7, 8, 10
Salem Foundation, Inc. 5, 7, 8
Samsara Foundation
Sauer Children's Renew Foundation
Saunders Family Foundation 5, 7, 8, 10
Carl and Verna Schmidt Foundation 6
Schmoker Family Foundation 5, 6, 7, 8
Arlan Schonberg Irrevocable Trust
Schott Foundation
Securian Foundation/Securian Financial Group 4, 5, 11
Sexton Foundation 5, 7, 8
Shakopee Mdewakanton Sioux Community 7, 8, 11
Shamrock Foundation
The Shared Fund 5, 7, 8
The Sheltering Arms Foundation 7, 11
Gertrude R. Shiely Charitable Trust
The Simmet Foundation 1
Sioux Falls Area Community Foundation 1, 3, 4, 5, 6, 7, 8, 10
SKB Environmental Rosemount Community Trust
R. C. Skoe Foundation 7
Slaggie Family Foundation
Slawik Family Foundation 5, 7, 8, 9
Smikis Foundation 1, 7, 8, 10
Southways Foundation
Southwest Initiative Foundation 11
St Anthony Park Community Foundation
St Croix Valley Community Foundation
Alex Stern Family Foundation
SUPERVALU Foundation 1, 4, 10, 11

Swan Family Foundation 5, 7
Target 11
TCF Foundation
TEAM Foundation 11
Tennant Foundation 5, 6, 10
Think Community Foundation 1, 7
Thomson West
James R. Thorpe Foundation 11
Thrivent Financial for Lutherans Foundation 1, 11
Todd-Wadena Electric Cooperative Community Trust
The Toro Company Giving Program 4, 5, 8, 10, 11
Tozer Foundation, Inc. 4, 5, 6
Travelers Corporation and Travelers Foundation 1, 2, 3, 4, 5, 7, 8, 11
Turner Family Foundation 5
U.S. Bancorp Foundation 11
The Valspar Foundation 5, 11
DeWitt and Caroline Van Evera Foundation 2, 5, 7, 8
Archie D. and Bertha H. Walker Foundation 3, 6
Warren Foundation
The Wasie Foundation 4, 5
Frederick O. Watson Foundation
WCA Foundation 1, 5, 7, 8, 10, 11
J. A. Wedum Foundation 5, 8
Mae and Sylvester Weiss Foundation
Wells Fargo Foundation Minnesota 11
Wenger Foundation 5, 10, 11
West Central Initiative 10, 11
Frederick and Margaret L. Weyerhaeuser Foundation 11
Whitney ARCEE Foundation
Whitney Foundation
Winona Community Foundation
Winona Foundation 6
Xcel Energy Foundation/Corporate Citizenship
A. H. Zeppa Family Foundation 11

Areas of Interest

Employment/Jobs

1 - Employment procurement/job training
2 - Labor unions/organizations
3 - Vocational rehabilitation
4 - Other

3M/3M Foundation 1
ACA International Foundation 1
Allianz Life Insurance Company of North America 1, 4
Ameriprise Financial, Inc. 1
Andersen Corporate Foundation 3
Hugh J. Andersen Foundation 1
Athwin Foundation
Blandin Foundation 4
W. Glen Boyd Charitable Foundation 1, 3, 4
Otto Bremer Foundation 1, 2, 3
Bromelkamp Foundation 1
Bush Foundation 1
Buuck Family Foundation 1, 3
Cote Foundation
Deluxe Corporation Foundation/Deluxe Corporation 3
Duluth Superior Area Community Foundation 1, 3
Ecolab Foundation and Corporation 1, 3
Edina Realty Foundation 1
Fargo-Moorhead Area Foundation
Frey Foundation 1
The Graco Foundation 1, 3
Grotto Foundation, Inc. 1, 2
Headwaters Foundation for Justice 2
ING Foundation 1, 3
Initiative Foundation 4
Luverne Area Community Foundation
Marbrook Foundation 1
McNeely Foundation 1
The Minneapolis Foundation 1, 4
Minnesota Business and Professional Women's Foundation 1
Ordean Foundation 4
Owatonna Foundation 1, 3
The Pentair Foundation 1, 3
The Jay and Rose Phillips Family Foundation 1, 3
The Elizabeth C. Quinlan Foundation, Inc. 1
RBC Dain Rauscher Foundation 1
The Saint Paul Foundation 1
Securian Foundation/Securian Financial Group 1, 3
The Simmet Foundation 1, 3
SUPERVALU Foundation 1, 3, 4
Tennant Foundation 1
Thomson West
Thrivent Financial for Lutherans Foundation 1, 3
U.S. Bancorp Foundation 1
WCA Foundation 1, 3
Wells Fargo Foundation Minnesota 1, 3
West Central Initiative 1, 4
Whitney Foundation
Winona Community Foundation

Environmental Quality/Protection/Beautification

1 - Botanical/horticultural/landscape
2 - Environmental beautification/open spaces
3 - Environmental education/outdoor survival
4 - Natural resources conservation/protection
5 - Pollution abatement and control
6 - Other

3M/3M Foundation 4, 6
AgStar Fund for Rural America 6
Ameriprise Financial, Inc. 6
Andersen Corporation
Elmer L. and Eleanor J. Andersen Foundation
Hugh J. Andersen Foundation 6
Athwin Foundation
Gordon and Margaret Bailey Foundation 1, 2, 4
Baker Foundation 3
Beim Foundation 4, 6
Lillian Wright and C. Emil Berglund Foundation, Inc. 1, 2, 3
Blue Cross and Blue Shield of Minnesota Foundation/Blue Cross and Blue Shield of Minnesota 5
Bush Foundation 4, 5
Patrick and Aimee Butler Family Foundation 3, 4, 6
Buuck Family Foundation 2, 4, 6
Martin and Esther Capp Foundation
Cargill Citizenship Fund 6
Carolyn Foundation 6
CenterPoint Energy 2, 4
Central Minnesota Community Foundation 1, 2, 3, 4
Cote Foundation
Cottonwood Foundation 4
Coughlan Companies
Edwin W. and Catherine M. Davis Foundation
The Deikel Family Foundation 2, 4
Driscoll Foundation 4
Duluth Superior Area Community Foundation 2, 3, 4, 5
Ecolab Foundation and Corporation 4
Edina Community Foundation 1, 2, 3, 4, 5
Faegre & Benson Foundation
Fargo-Moorhead Area Foundation 2
Federated Insurance Foundation, Inc. 4
First National Bank of Bemidji Foundation 4
Fremont Foundation
H.B. Fuller Company Foundation 4
Grand Rapids Area Community Foundation 3, 4, 5
Mary Livingston Griggs and Mary Griggs Burke Foundation
Grotto Foundation, Inc. 6
Hartz Foundation 1, 2, 3, 4
Headwaters Foundation for Justice 5, 6
HRK Foundation 2, 3, 4, 6
Initiative Foundation 4
Lloyd K. Johnson Foundation 4
Margaret H. and James E. Kelley Foundation, Inc.
Kopp Family Foundation 2
Land O'Lakes Foundation 6
Lang Family Charitable Trust 1, 4
Helen Sperry Lea Foundation
Steven C. Leuthold Family Foundation 3, 4, 5
R. C. Lilly Foundation
The Charles A. and Anne Morrow Lindbergh Foundation 4, 6
Luverne Area Community Foundation
Marbrook Foundation 2, 3, 4
The McKnight Foundation 2, 4, 5, 6
McNeely Foundation 3, 4
The Minneapolis Foundation
Minnesota Power Foundation 1, 2, 4
Minnesota Research Fund 5
Minnesota Twins Community Fund 2
Marjorie Weil and Marvin Edward Mitchell Foundation
The Laura Jane Musser Fund 6
The Nash Foundation 4
Noel Foundation
Northwest Minnesota Foundation 2, 4, 6
E.O. Olson Trust U/A Water Resources 4
Casey Albert T. O'Neil Foundation
OSilas Foundation
Otter Tail Power Company 4, 6
Owatonna Foundation
P.G.N. Foundation
The Polaris Foundation
The Irwin Andrew Porter Foundation 3, 4
Prospect Creek Foundation
Quetico Superior Foundation 4
The Elizabeth C. Quinlan Foundation, Inc. 1, 4
Rahr Foundation 1, 3, 4
Horst M. Rechelbacher Foundation 4
Rochester Area Foundation 3, 4

The Saint Paul Foundation 3, 4
Salem Foundation, Inc.
Carl and Verna Schmidt Foundation 1, 2, 4
Sexton Foundation
Shapiro Family Philanthropic Foundation
Gertrude R. Shiely Charitable Trust
Sioux Falls Area Community Foundation 1, 2, 4, 5
SKB Environmental Rosemount Community Trust
St Anthony Park Community Foundation
St Croix Valley Community Foundation
Tennant Foundation 1, 4
Think Community Foundation 6
Todd-Wadena Electric Cooperative Community Trust
The Toro Company Giving Program 1, 2, 3, 4, 6
Unity Avenue Foundation 3, 4, 5
Archie D. and Bertha H. Walker Foundation 4, 5
Warren Foundation
Frederick O. Watson Foundation
J. A. Wedum Foundation
Weyerhaeuser Family Foundation, Inc. 4, 6
Frederick and Margaret L. Weyerhaeuser Foundation 3, 6
Winona Community Foundation
Winona Foundation 1
Xcel Energy Foundation/Corporate Citizenship
A. H. Zeppa Family Foundation

Food/Nutrition/Agriculture

1 - Agricultural programs
2 - Food service/free food distribution
3 - Home economics
4 - Nutrition promotion
5 - Soil and water conservation/farm land preservation
6 - Other

AgStar Fund for Rural America 1, 5, 6
Hugh J. Andersen Foundation 1
Gordon and Margaret Bailey Foundation 2
Otto Bremer Foundation 1, 4, 5
Bush Foundation 1, 5
Cargill Citizenship Fund 6
Catholic Community Foundation in the Archdiocese of Saint Paul and Minneapolis 1, 5
CHS Foundation 1, 6
The Cooperative Foundation 1, 6
Cote Foundation 2
Cottonwood Foundation 5
The Deikel Family Foundation 2
Deluxe Corporation Foundation/Deluxe Corporation 2
Duluth Superior Area Community Foundation 1, 2, 4, 5
Edina Realty Foundation 2
Fargo-Moorhead Area Foundation
Farmers Union Marketing and Processing Foundation
Federated Insurance Foundation, Inc. 6
First National Bank of Bemidji Foundation 5
Frey Foundation 2
H.B. Fuller Company Foundation 5
General Mills Community Action 2
Hartz Foundation 2
Headwaters Foundation for Justice 6
HealthPartners 4
HRK Foundation 2, 5
W.K. Kellogg Foundation 6
Land O'Lakes Foundation 1, 2, 4, 5, 6
The Charles A. and Anne Morrow Lindbergh Foundation 1
The McKnight Foundation 5, 6
Medica Foundation 4
Minnesota Power Foundation 2
Minnesota Research Fund 1
NFC Foundation 2
Northwest Minnesota Foundation 1
Ordean Foundation 2, 4
Owatonna Foundation
Rahr Foundation
Rochester Area Foundation 2
Runestone Electric Association Community Trust 2
The Saint Paul Foundation 2, 4, 5
Samsara Foundation 2
The Simmet Foundation 2
Sioux Falls Area Community Foundation 2, 4
St Croix Valley Community Foundation
SUPERVALU Foundation 2, 6
Tennant Foundation 5
Archie D. and Bertha H. Walker Foundation 5
Winona Community Foundation

Areas of Interest

Health - Diseases/Medical Disciplines

1 - AIDS/HIV
2 - Allergy related diseases
3 - Birth defects/genetic disorders
4 - Cancer
5 - Digestive diseases/disorders
6 - Diseases of specific organs
7 - Medical disciplines
8 - Nerve/muscle/bone diseases
9 - Specific named diseases
10 - Other

Affiliated Community Health Foundation
Lloyd and Barbara Amundson Charity Foundation, Inc.
Andersen Corporate Foundation 10
Fred C. and Katherine B. Andersen Foundation 4
Hugh J. Andersen Foundation 1, 10
Arsher Charitable Trust U/A 4
Baratz Family Foundation 4, 10
The Bentson Foundation
Buuck Family Foundation 8, 9
Cade Foundation 4
CDF Foundation
Cote Foundation
Dakota Medical Foundation/Dakota Medical Charities 10
The Deikel Family Foundation 1, 2, 10
Roger L. and Agnes C. Dell Charitable (Trust 1)
Delta Dental of Minnesota
Deluxe Corporation Foundation/Deluxe Corporation 1, 10
Dovenberg Family Foundation 4
Duluth Superior Area Community Foundation 1
Edina Realty Foundation 10
Edwards Memorial Trust
Extendicare Foundation 9, 10
Fargo-Moorhead Area Foundation
The Jack and Bessie Fiterman Foundation
Gray Plant Mooty Foundation
Grotto Foundation, Inc. 1, 10
Headwaters Foundation for Justice 10
HealthPartners 4, 10
Anna M. Heilmaier Charitable Foundation 4, 10

HRK Foundation 1, 10
The Hubbard Broadcasting Foundation
ING Foundation
Jennings Family Foundation
The Lynn Johnson Family Foundation
Mitchell and Lois Johnson Charitable Foundation
Hess Kline Foundation, Inc. 10
Lang Family Charitable Trust 4
Leorette M. and Fred T. Lanners Foundation 3
Lerner Foundation
Steven C. Leuthold Family Foundation
Carl and Aune Lind Family Foundation
The Charles A. and Anne Morrow Lindbergh Foundation 10
James G. Lindell Irrevocable Charitable Trust
Russell T. Lund Charitable Trust 4
Luverne Area Community Foundation
The M.B. Foundation
Ted and Roberta Mann Foundation 10
Martinson Clinic Foundation
Mayo Clinic 4
Medica Foundation 10
The Medtronic Foundation 1, 4, 6, 8, 9
Martin and Esther Miller Foundation 4
Minnesota Power Foundation 10
Minnesota Research Fund 5
The Minnesota Timberwolves FastBreak Foundation
John W. Mooty Foundation Trust
Moscoe Family Foundation 4
NFC Foundation
North Star Charitable Foundation 10

Casey Albert T. O'Neil Foundation
Owatonna Foundation
P.G.N. Foundation
Pajor Family Foundation
Park Nicollet Foundation 10
Patterson Foundation 10
People in Business Care, Inc.
The Jay and Rose Phillips Family Foundation 1, 7, 10
Prospect Creek Foundation
The Elizabeth C. Quinlan Foundation, Inc. 1, 10
Margaret Rivers Fund
The Riverway Foundation 4, 10
Rochester Area Foundation 1
Saunders Family Foundation 1, 4
Carl and Verna Schmidt Foundation
Shakopee Mdewakanton Sioux Community 4, 10
Shamrock Foundation
Shapiro Family Philanthropic Foundation
The Shiebler Family Foundation
The Simmet Foundation
Sioux Falls Area Community Foundation 6
The Spell Family Foundation
St Croix Valley Community Foundation
Tennant Foundation 3, 4, 5
Turner Family Foundation 9
Archie D. and Bertha H. Walker Foundation 10
Warren Foundation
The Wasie Foundation 3, 4, 9, 10
Frederick O. Watson Foundation
J. A. Wedum Foundation
Winona Community Foundation

Areas of Interest

Health - General/Rehabilitative
1 - Emergency medical services
2 - Health care financing activities
3 - Health support services
4 - Health treatment facilities - primarily outpatient
5 - Hospitals and related primary medical care facilities
6 - Nursing care/services
7 - Public health programs/wellness education
8 - Rehabilitative medical services
9 - Reproductive health care
10 - Other

Affiliated Community Health Foundation 10
Lloyd and Barbara Amundson Charity Foundation, Inc.
Andersen Corporate Foundation 3, 5, 7, 10
Andersen Corporation
Fred C. and Katherine B. Andersen Foundation 5
Hugh J. Andersen Foundation 3, 7, 9
Baker Foundation 5
Blue Cross and Blue Shield of Minnesota Foundation/Blue Cross and Blue Shield of Minnesota 7, 10
Otto Bremer Foundation 1, 7
Buuck Family Foundation 8
Catholic Aid Association Foundation 3, 8
Central Minnesota Community Foundation 3, 7
Cote Foundation
Dakota Medical Foundation/Dakota Medical Charities 10
The Deikel Family Foundation 3, 7
Delta Dental of Minnesota 7, 10
Deluxe Corporation Foundation/Deluxe Corporation 10
The Dorsey & Whitney Foundation
Duluth Superior Area Community Foundation 4, 7, 9
Eddy (Edwin H.) Foundation 8, 10
Edina Realty Foundation 1
Edwards Memorial Trust 10
Extendicare Foundation 6, 10
Fargo-Moorhead Area Foundation 8
Federated Insurance Foundation, Inc. 7
Frey Foundation 3, 4, 8
Fanny S. Gilfillan Memorial, Incorporated
Gray Plant Mooty Foundation
N. Bud and Beverly Grossman Foundation
Grotto Foundation, Inc. 3, 4, 7
Healthier Minnesota Community Clinic Fund 2, 3, 5, 6, 7, 9, 10
HealthPartners 7, 10
Anna M. Heilmaier Charitable Foundation
George A. Hormel Testamentary Trust 5, 7
HRK Foundation 7, 9

The Hubbard Broadcasting Foundation
Nevin Huested Foundation for Handicapped Children, Inc. 8
ING Foundation
JNM 1966 Gift Trust U/A
Lewis H. Johnson Family Foundation
Mitchell and Lois Johnson Charitable Foundation
Margaret H. and James E. Kelley Foundation, Inc. 9
W.K. Kellogg Foundation
Knitcraft - St Croix Foundation, Inc.
Kopp Family Foundation 3, 7
The Charles A. and Anne Morrow Lindbergh Foundation 10
The Luther Family Foundation
Luverne Area Community Foundation
Macy's North 10
Ted and Roberta Mann Foundation 10
Marbrook Foundation 3, 10
Martinson Clinic Foundation 10
The Martinson Foundation
Mayo Clinic 3
Medica Foundation 10
The Medtronic Foundation 3, 6, 7, 8
Martin and Esther Miller Foundation
The Minneapolis Foundation 7, 9, 10
Minneapolis Kiwanis Foundation
Minneapolis Rotary Community Service Foundation 2, 3, 5, 6, 7, 8
Minnesota Power Foundation 7
Minnesota Twins Community Fund 7
Marjorie Weil and Marvin Edward Mitchell Foundation 10
MoneyGram International 10
Jane N. Mooty Foundation Trust
John W. Mooty Foundation Trust
Moscoe Family Foundation
Noel Foundation 9
Casey Albert T. O'Neil Foundation
Ordean Foundation 1, 3, 7, 8
Otter Tail Power Company 2, 5, 7
Owatonna Foundation

P.G.N. Foundation
Lewis and Annie F. Paper Foundation, Inc.
Park Nicollet Foundation 3, 4, 7, 10
Patterson Foundation 8
The Pentair Foundation 1, 2, 3, 7, 8, 9
People in Business Care, Inc.
The Lawrence and Linda Perlman Family Foundation
The Jay and Rose Phillips Family Foundation 3, 7, 9, 10
The Elizabeth C. Quinlan Foundation, Inc. 6
Rahr Foundation 5
Rappaport Family Foundation 5
Ripley Memorial Foundation, Inc. 9, 10
Margaret Rivers Fund
Rochester Area Foundation 3, 4, 6, 7
The Saint Paul Foundation 3, 4, 7
Salem Foundation, Inc.
Carl and Verna Schmidt Foundation
Securian Foundation/Securian Financial Group 7, 10
Shakopee Mdewakanton Sioux Community 5, 7
The Shiebler Family Foundation
The Simmet Foundation
Sioux Falls Area Community Foundation 10
Slaggie Family Foundation
Southways Foundation
St Anthony Park Community Foundation
St Croix Valley Community Foundation
St Francis Regional Medical Center Foundation 7, 10
TEAM Foundation 10
Tennant Foundation 7, 8
Think Community Foundation 3, 7
Tozer Foundation, Inc. 5, 8
Archie D. and Bertha B. Walker Foundation 9
The Wasie Foundation
Frederick O. Watson Foundation
J. A. Wedum Foundation
Winona Community Foundation

Areas of Interest

Health - Mental Health/Crisis Intervention
1 - Addiction disorders
2 - Alcohol/drug/substance, prevention and treatment
3 - Counseling/support groups
4 - Hotline/crisis intervention
5 - Mental health associations
6 - Mental health disorders
7 - Mental health treatment and services
8 - Other

Acorn Foundation
Andersen Corporate Foundation 8
Fred C. and Katherine B. Andersen Foundation 2
Hugh J. Andersen Foundation 1, 2, 4, 5, 7
Athwin Foundation
Gordon and Margaret Bailey Foundation 1, 2, 3, 7, 8
Blue Cross and Blue Shield of Minnesota Foundation/Blue Cross and Blue Shield of Minnesota 8
The Boss Foundation 2
W. Glen Boyd Charitable Foundation 1, 3, 4
Otto Bremer Foundation 3, 5, 7
Burdick-Craddick Family Foundation
Bush Foundation 2, 7
Central Minnesota Community Foundation 3, 4
ClearWay Minnesota 3, 4, 8
Cote Foundation
Dakota Medical Foundation/Dakota Medical Charities 8
Edwin W. and Catherine M. Davis Foundation
The Deikel Family Foundation 2, 4, 7
Deluxe Corporation Foundation/Deluxe Corporation 2, 3, 4, 5, 6, 7
Duluth Superior Area Community Foundation 1, 2, 3, 4, 5, 6, 7

Fargo-Moorhead Area Foundation 5
First National Bank of Bemidji Foundation 2
Grotto Foundation, Inc. 2, 7, 8
Haggerty Family Foundation
George A. Hormel Testamentary Trust 3, 4, 7
The Hubbard Broadcasting Foundation
John S. and James L. Knight Foundation 8
Kopp Family Foundation 3, 4, 7
Lang Family Charitable Trust 7
Luverne Area Community Foundation
Ted and Roberta Mann Foundation
Medica Foundation 8
Minneapolis Rotary Community Service Foundation 2, 3, 5, 7
Minnesota Power Foundation
Marjorie Weil and Marvin Edward Mitchell Foundation 8
Northland Foundation 3, 4
Ordean Foundation 1, 2, 3, 4, 5, 6, 7
O'Shaughnessy Foundation 6, 7
Owatonna Foundation
Park Nicollet Foundation 3, 4, 7, 8
The Pentair Foundation 1, 2, 3, 4, 7
People in Business Care, Inc.
Perkins Foundation 2
The Jay and Rose Phillips Family Foundation 7, 8

The Elizabeth C. Quinlan Foundation, Inc. 7
Rappaport Family Foundation 7, 8
Ripley Memorial Foundation, Inc. 3, 8
Rochester Area Foundation 1, 2, 3, 7
The Saint Paul Foundation 2, 3, 4, 6, 7
Saunders Family Foundation 2
Securian Foundation/Securian Financial Group 2
Shakopee Mdewakanton Sioux Community 2
Shamrock Foundation
The Simmet Foundation 2, 3, 4
Sioux Falls Area Community Foundation 2, 5, 7
St Croix Valley Community Foundation
St Francis Regional Medical Center Foundation 8
Tennant Foundation 1, 2, 7
Think Community Foundation
Archie D. and Bertha H. Walker Foundation 1, 2, 3, 4, 7
The Wasie Foundation 5, 6, 7, 8
WCA Foundation 1, 2, 3, 4, 7
J. A. Wedum Foundation
Frederick and Margaret L. Weyerhaeuser Foundation 8
Winona Community Foundation

Health - Research
1 - Allergy related research
2 - Birth defects & genetic diseases research
3 - Cancer research
4 - Digestive disease/disorder research
5 - Medical specialty research
6 - Nerve, muscle and bone research
7 - Specific named disease research
8 - Specific organ research
9 - Other

Baratz Family Foundation 3, 9
The Bentson Foundation
Blue Cross and Blue Shield of Minnesota Foundation/Blue Cross and Blue Shield of Minnesota 9
Buuck Family Foundation 6, 7, 9
Cade Foundation 3
ClearWay Minnesota 9
Duluth Superior Area Community Foundation 7
Eddy (Edwin H.) Foundation 7, 9
Extendicare Foundation 7, 9
Fargo-Moorhead Area Foundation
Anna M. Heilmaier Charitable Foundation 3, 9
The Hermundslie Foundation

The Hubbard Broadcasting Foundation
Hess Kline Foundation, Inc.
Lerner Foundation
Steven C. Leuthold Family Foundation
The Charles A. and Anne Morrow Lindbergh Foundation
Luverne Area Community Foundation
Mayo Clinic 9
Medica Foundation 9
Minnesota Research Fund 2, 4, 7
John W. Mooty Foundation Trust
North Star Charitable Foundation 9
Alice M. O'Brien Foundation
O'Shaughnessy Foundation 9

Otter Tail Power Company 3
Owatonna Foundation
Park Nicollet Foundation 9
Rahr Foundation 2
The Riverway Foundation 3
Samsara Foundation
Saunders Family Foundation 3, 7
The Simmet Foundation
Sioux Falls Area Community Foundation
St Croix Valley Community Foundation
Turner Family Foundation
The Wasie Foundation 2, 7, 9
Winona Community Foundation

Housing/Shelter

1 - Homeless, temporary housing
2 - Housing development/construction/management
3 - Housing owners/renter organizations
4 - Housing search assistance
5 - Housing support services
6 - Low-cost temporary housing
7 - Other

3M/3M Foundation 1, 5
Andersen Corporate Foundation 2, 5, 7
Andersen Corporation 2, 7
Fred C. and Katherine B. Andersen Foundation 1
Hugh J. Andersen Foundation 1, 2, 5, 7
Athwin Foundation
Gordon and Margaret Bailey Foundation 1
Baker Foundation 2
Blue Cross and Blue Shield of Minnesota Foundation/Blue Cross and Blue Shield of Minnesota
Otto Bremer Foundation 1, 2, 3, 4, 5, 6
Bromelkamp Foundation 1
Burdick-Craddick Family Foundation
Bush Foundation 5
Patrick and Aimee Butler Family Foundation 1, 2, 5
Buuck Family Foundation 1, 3, 5, 7
CenterPoint Energy 2, 7
Central Minnesota Community Foundation 2, 5
Charlson Foundation 7
The Cooperative Foundation 7
Cote Foundation
The Deikel Family Foundation 1, 2
Deluxe Corporation Foundation/Deluxe Corporation 1, 6
Duluth Superior Area Community Foundation 1, 3, 4, 5, 6
Ecolab Foundation and Corporation 1, 2, 5
Edina Realty Foundation 1, 5, 6
Fargo-Moorhead Area Foundation
First National Bank of Bemidji Foundation 1, 2
Frey Foundation 2, 5, 7

Grand Rapids Area Community Foundation 1, 2, 5, 6
Grotto Foundation, Inc. 5, 6
Headwaters Foundation for Justice 3, 4
Honeywell Hometown Solutions
HRK Foundation 1, 5, 7
John S. and James L. Knight Foundation
Kopp Family Foundation
Leonette M. and Fred T. Lanners Foundation 1
Marbrook Foundation 2, 5
Marquette Financial Companies Community Support Program 7
Mayo Clinic 2
The McKnight Foundation 7
McNeely Foundation 5
Minneapolis Area Association of Realtors Foundation, Inc.
The Minneapolis Foundation 7
Minnesota Power Foundation 1, 6
Marjorie Weil and Marvin Edward Mitchell Foundation 1, 7
MoneyGram International 1, 2, 7
Richard A. Newman Foundation 5
Northland Foundation 5, 7
Northwest Minnesota Foundation 5, 7
Ordean Foundation 1, 2, 4, 5, 6
Otter Tail Power Company 7
Owatonna Foundation
Park Nicollet Foundation 5
The Pentair Foundation 1, 3, 5
People in Business Care, Inc.
The Jay and Rose Phillips Family Foundation 5, 6, 7
The Irwin Andrew Porter Foundation

The Elizabeth C. Quinlan Foundation, Inc.
Rahr Foundation 1
RBC Dain Rauscher Foundation 1
Luther I. Replogle Foundation
Rochester Area Foundation 1, 2
The Saint Paul Foundation 1, 2, 5, 6
Samsara Foundation 1
Saunders Family Foundation 1
Carl and Verna Schmidt Foundation
Securian Foundation/Securian Financial Group 2, 6
Sexton Foundation
The Sheltering Arms Foundation 5
The Simmet Foundation 1
Sioux Falls Area Community Foundation 1, 2
St Anthony Park Community Foundation
St Croix Valley Community Foundation
Alex Stern Family Foundation
Stevens Square Foundation 7
Sundance Family Foundation and Sundance Pay It Forward Foundation 7
Tennant Foundation 1, 2, 3, 5
Thomson West
James R. Thorpe Foundation 1, 5, 7
Travelers Corporation and Travelers Foundation 2, 3, 4, 6, 7
Turner Family Foundation
U.S. Bancorp Foundation 2, 7
The Valspar Foundation 7
WCA Foundation 1, 2, 5, 6
J. A. Wedum Foundation
Wells Fargo Foundation Minnesota 2
Winona Community Foundation

Areas of Interest

Human Services
1 - Children/youth services
2 - Emergency assistance (food/clothing/cash)
3 - Family services
4 - Family services for adolescent parents
5 - Family violence shelters and services
6 - Multipurpose human service organizations
7 - Personal social services
8 - Residential/custodial care
9 - Senior centers and services
10 - Services to specific groups
11 - Victims services
12 - Other

3M/3M Foundation 1, 3, 4, 5, 6
Acorn Foundation
AHS Foundation
Allianz Life Insurance Company of North America 1, 3, 4, 6, 7, 8, 9
Ameriprise Financial, Inc. 1, 2, 3, 5, 6, 10, 12
Lloyd and Barbara Amundson Charity Foundation, Inc.
Andersen Corporate Foundation 1, 2, 3, 5, 6, 7, 9, 12
Andersen Corporation
Elmer L. and Eleanor J. Andersen Foundation
Fred C. and Katherine B. Andersen Foundation 1, 5, 6, 9
Hugh J. Andersen Foundation 1, 2, 3, 4, 5, 6, 7, 9, 11
Athwin Foundation 1, 2, 3, 4, 5, 6, 8, 11
Bernard and Fern Badzin Foundation
Gordon and Margaret Bailey Foundation 1, 2, 3, 5, 6
Baker Foundation 3, 6
Baratz Family Foundation
Beim Foundation 1, 3, 12
The Bentson Foundation
Lillian Wright and C. Emil Berglund Foundation, Inc. 1, 3, 10
Best Buy Children's Foundation 1, 2, 6, 12
The Beverly Foundation
F.R. Bigelow Foundation
Blandin Foundation 12
Blue Cross and Blue Shield of Minnesota Foundation/Blue Cross and Blue Shield of Minnesota 1, 3, 4, 6, 10, 12
W. Glen Boyd Charitable Foundation 1, 2, 3, 4, 5, 6, 7, 10, 11, 12
Otto Bremer Foundation 1, 2, 3, 4, 5, 6, 10, 11
Bromelkamp Foundation 2
Burdick-Craddick Family Foundation 12
Bush Foundation 1, 3, 5, 6, 10
Patrick and Aimee Butler Family Foundation 3, 4, 5, 6
Buuck Family Foundation 2, 5, 12
Caliber Foundation
The Curtis L. Carlson Family Foundation 1
Catholic Aid Association Foundation 3
Catholic Community Foundation in the Archdiocese of Saint Paul and Minneapolis 1, 6, 8
CDF Foundation
Central Minnesota Community Foundation 1, 2, 3, 4, 5, 6, 9, 10, 11
Charlson Foundation 1, 3, 4, 6

ClearWay Minnesota 10
Arthur and David Cosgrove Memorial Fund
Cote Foundation
Cottonwood Foundation
Charles and Kathryn Cunningham Family Foundation
Edwin W. and Catherine M. Davis Foundation
The Deikel Family Foundation 1, 2, 3, 6, 7
Roger L. and Agnes C. Dell Charitable (Trust 2)
Delta Dental of Minnesota 1, 12
Deluxe Corporation Foundation/Deluxe Corporation 1, 2, 3, 5, 6, 10, 11
The Donaldson Foundation 12
The Dorsey & Whitney Foundation
Doverberg Family Foundation
Driscoll Foundation
Duluth Superior Area Community Foundation 1, 2, 3, 4, 5, 6, 7, 8, 9, 10, 11
Ecolab Foundation and Corporation 1, 2, 3, 6
Edina Community Foundation 1, 2, 3, 6, 7
Edina Realty Foundation 2, 5
Charles Engasser Memorial Foundation, Inc.
Otto C. and Elsie Ewert Charitable Trust
Faegre & Benson Foundation
Arlin Falck Foundation
Fargo-Moorhead Area Foundation 1, 8
Federated Insurance Foundation, Inc. 1, 2, 3, 7, 12
First National Bank of Bemidji Foundation 1, 9
The Jack and Bessie Fiterman Foundation
Fremont Foundation
Frey Foundation 1, 2, 3, 6
H.B. Fuller Company Foundation 12
G&K Services Foundation
The Janice Gardner Foundation
General Mills Community Action 1, 3, 6
The Graco Foundation
Grand Rapids Area Community Foundation 1, 2, 3, 4, 5, 6, 7, 8, 9, 11
Gray Plant Mooty Foundation
Mary Livingston Griggs and Mary Griggs Burke Foundation
N. Bud and Beverly Grossman Foundation
Grotto Foundation, Inc. 1, 3, 10
Haggerty Family Foundation
Hartz Foundation 9
George A. Hormel Testamentary Trust 1, 3, 6, 9, 11
HRK Foundation 1, 3, 12
The Hubbard Broadcasting Foundation 1, 3
Nevin Huested Foundation for Handicapped Children, Inc. 1, 10, 12

Imation
ING Foundation 1, 6
Initiative Foundation 1, 6, 9, 10, 12
Italian American Club Foundation, Inc. 2, 9
Jennings Family Foundation 1, 2, 3, 6
Lewis H. Johnson Family Foundation
Lloyd K. Johnson Foundation 1, 2, 3, 4, 5, 6, 9, 11
Mitchell and Lois Johnson Charitable Foundation
The Jostens Foundation 1
Jundt Family Foundation
Margaret H. and James E. Kelley Foundation, Inc. 6
Elizabeth Callender King Foundation
Hess Kline Foundation, Inc.
John S. and James L. Knight Foundation 1
Knitcraft - St Croix Foundation, Inc.
Kopp Family Foundation
Land O'Lakes Foundation 2, 12
Leonette M. and Fred T. Lanners Foundation 1, 3
Lerner Foundation
Steven C. Leuthold Family Foundation 1, 6
Liebhaber Family Foundation
Carl and Aune Lind Family Foundation 1, 2, 3, 6
Russell T. Lund Charitable Trust 1, 2, 3, 6
The Luther Family Foundation 1, 3, 5
Luverne Area Community Foundation
Ted and Roberta Mann Foundation 12
Marbrook Foundation 1, 3, 6
Mardag Foundation 9
Marquette Financial Companies Community Support Program 12
The Martinson Foundation
Mayo Clinic 1, 2, 3, 6
The McKnight Foundation 1, 6, 12
McNeely Foundation 1, 3, 6
The Medtronic Foundation 12
The Minneapolis Foundation 1, 3, 4, 5, 6, 12
Minneapolis Kiwanis Foundation
Minneapolis Rotary Community Service Foundation 1, 3, 6, 8
Minnesota Power Foundation 1, 2, 6, 11
Minnesota State Bar Foundation 1, 3, 5, 9, 12
The Minnesota Timberwolves FastBreak Foundation 1
Minnesota Twins Community Fund 1
Marjorie Weil and Marvin Edward Mitchell Foundation 1, 2, 3, 10
MoneyGram International 1, 12

Areas of Interest

Jane N. Mooty Foundation Trust
John W. Mooty Foundation Trust 1
Moscoe Family Foundation
The Laura Jane Musser Fund 1, 12
The Nash Foundation 1, 2, 3, 6, 10
The Nelson Family Foundation
Richard A. Newman Foundation 1
NFC Foundation 1, 2, 3
Noel Foundation 1, 3, 5
Roger and Violet Noreen Charitable Trust
Northland Foundation 1, 3, 6, 7
Northwest Minnesota Foundation 1, 2, 6, 9
Alice M. O'Brien Foundation
Casey Albert T. O'Neil Foundation 1, 2, 3, 6
Ordean Foundation 1, 2, 3, 4, 5, 6, 7, 8, 11
Otter Tail Power Company 1, 2, 5, 6, 9
Ben and Jeanne Overman Charitable Trust
 1, 2, 3, 5, 6
Owatonna Foundation
P.G.N. Foundation
Pajor Family Foundation
Park Nicollet Foundation 1, 2, 3, 4, 5, 6, 10
The Pentair Foundation 1, 2, 3, 5, 6
People in Business Care, Inc.
Perkins Foundation 1
The Lawrence and Linda Perlman Family
 Foundation
The Jay and Rose Phillips Family Foundation
 1, 3, 4, 5, 6, 9, 10, 12
Carl and Eloise Pohlad Family Foundation 1, 6
The Irwin Andrew Porter Foundation 1, 3, 6, 7
Prospect Creek Foundation
The Elizabeth C. Quinlan Foundation, Inc. 6
Rahr Foundation 1, 5
Rappaport Family Foundation 1, 3, 4
RBC Dain Rauscher Foundation 1, 3, 5, 6, 7, 12

Luther I. Replogle Foundation 1
Richfield Community Foundation 1, 12
Ripley Memorial Foundation, Inc. 1, 12
Margaret Rivers Fund 1, 2, 3
The Riverway Foundation 1, 3, 4, 5, 9
Rochester Area Foundation
 1, 2, 3, 4, 5, 6, 8, 9, 10, 11
The Saint Paul Foundation
 1, 2, 3, 4, 5, 6, 7, 8, 9, 10, 11
Salem Foundation, Inc.
Samsara Foundation 1, 2, 3
Sauer Children's Renew Foundation 1
Saunders Family Foundation 1, 3, 10
Schmoker Family Foundation
Securian Foundation/Securian Financial Group
 1, 3, 6, 10
Sexton Foundation 1, 2, 3
Shakopee Mdewakanton Sioux Community
 1, 2, 3, 6, 7, 10
Shamrock Foundation
Shapiro Family Philanthropic Foundation
The Shared Fund
The Sheltering Arms Foundation
 1, 3, 4, 5, 6, 12
The Shiebler Family Foundation
Gertrude R. Shiely Charitable Trust
The Simmet Foundation 1, 2, 3, 4, 5
Sioux Falls Area Community Foundation
 1, 2, 3, 4, 5, 6, 9, 11
SKB Environmental Rosemount Community
 Trust
Slawik Family Foundation
Smikis Foundation 1, 3, 6, 10
Southways Foundation
Southwest Initiative Foundation 1, 6, 9, 12
The Spell Family Foundation 1

St Anthony Park Community Foundation 1, 9
St Croix Valley Community Foundation
Alex Stern Family Foundation
Stevens Square Foundation 9
Sundance Family Foundation and Sundance Pay
 It Forward Foundation 1, 3, 4, 5
SUPERVALU Foundation 12
Swan Family Foundation
Target 12
TCF Foundation
TEAM Foundation 9, 12
Tennant Foundation 1, 2, 3, 6
Think Community Foundation
 1, 2, 3, 4, 5, 6, 7, 8, 9, 10, 11
Thomson West 1
James R. Thorpe Foundation 1, 6, 10, 12
Thrivent Financial for Lutherans Foundation 1
Tozer Foundation, Inc. 1, 3
Turner Family Foundation 1
The Vos Family Foundation
Archie D. and Bertha H. Walker
 Foundation 3, 4, 5
Warren Foundation 1, 3, 6, 7, 10, 11
The Wasie Foundation 10
Frederick O. Watson Foundation
WCA Foundation 5
J. A. Wedum Foundation
Wells Fargo Foundation Minnesota 6, 7, 12
West Central Initiative 12
Weyerhaeuser Family Foundation, Inc. 1, 12
Whitney ARCEE Foundation
Whitney Foundation
Winona Community Foundation
Youthworks! Foundation, Inc.

International Affairs

1 - Foreign policy research/analysis
2 - International development/relief
3 - International human rights
4 - International peace/security
5 - Promotion of international understanding
6 - Other

Otto Bremer Foundation 3, 5
Cottonwood Foundation 5
The Deikel Family Foundation 2
Duluth Superior Area Community
 Foundation 3, 4, 5
Fargo-Moorhead Area Foundation
Margaret H. and James E. Kelley Foundation,
 Inc. 3

The McKnight Foundation 6
Minneapolis Rotary Community Service
 Foundation 5
MoneyGram International 6
The Laura Jane Musser Fund 4, 5
The Irwin Andrew Porter Foundation 2, 4, 5
Rappaport Family Foundation 2
Horst M. Rechelbacher Foundation

Sundance Family Foundation and Sundance Pay
 It Forward Foundation 2, 3
Weyerhaeuser Family Foundation, Inc. 2, 4
Winona Community Foundation
A. H. Zeppa Family Foundation 2

Areas of Interest

Philanthropy/Voluntarism
1 - Federated funds
2 - Nonprofit sector assistance
3 - Philanthropy associations
4 - Philanthropy - general
5 - Public foundations and community foundations
6 - Voluntarism promotion
7 - Other

3M/3M Foundation 2, 7
Airport Foundation MSP 4, 6
Lloyd and Barbara Amundson Charity Foundation, Inc.
Hugh J. Andersen Foundation 2, 3
Athwin Foundation 2
Best Buy Children's Foundation 7
Otto Bremer Foundation 1, 3, 5, 6
Bush Foundation 2, 3, 4
Patrick and Aimee Butler Family Foundation 2, 5
Cargill Citizenship Fund 7
Central Minnesota Community Foundation 2, 3, 4, 5, 6
The Deikel Family Foundation 1
Deluxe Corporation Foundation/Deluxe Corporation 3
Duluth Superior Area Community Foundation 6
Edina Community Foundation 2, 4, 5, 6
Fargo-Moorhead Area Foundation

Federated Insurance Foundation, Inc. 6
The Jack and Bessie Fiterman Foundation
Grand Rapids Area Community Foundation 6
HealthPartners 1
HRK Foundation 4
ING Foundation 3, 6, 7
Initiative Foundation 6
Jerome Foundation 3
The Jostens Foundation 6
W.K. Kellogg Foundation
Carl and Aune Lind Family Foundation
Luverne Area Community Foundation
The Minneapolis Foundation 2, 3
Minnesota Power Foundation 6
Minnesota Twins Community Fund 5
Northwest Minnesota Foundation 4, 5, 7
Otter Tail Power Company 2, 6
Philanthrofund Foundation (PFund) 6, 7
Piper Jaffray 4
The Irwin Andrew Porter Foundation 7

The Elizabeth C. Quinlan Foundation, Inc. 3
Rappaport Family Foundation 5
Rochester Area Foundation 2, 6
The Saint Paul Foundation 2
Saunders Family Foundation 3
Sioux Falls Area Community Foundation 4, 5
Southern Minnesota Initiative Foundation 5
Southwest Initiative Foundation 7
St Croix Valley Community Foundation
Thrivent Financial for Lutherans Foundation 2, 7
The Toro Company Giving Program 1, 2, 6
Travelers Corporation and Travelers Foundation 1, 2, 3, 6
U.S. Bancorp Foundation 7
The Wasie Foundation 3
Frederick and Margaret L. Weyerhaeuser Foundation 4, 6, 7
Winona Community Foundation

Public Affairs/Society Benefit
1 - Citizen participation
2 - Consumer protection/safety
3 - Government/public administration
4 - Leadership development/awards programs (other than youth)
5 - Military/veterans' organizations
6 - Public policy research and analysis
7 - Public transportation services
8 - Telecommunications services
9 - Welfare policy and reform
10 - Other

Airport Foundation MSP 5, 7
Allianz Life Insurance Company of North America 1
Lloyd and Barbara Amundson Charity Foundation, Inc.
Ann Bancroft Foundation 4, 10
Blandin Foundation 6
Blue Cross and Blue Shield of Minnesota Foundation/Blue Cross and Blue Shield of Minnesota 1, 4, 6
W. Glen Boyd Charitable Foundation 4, 10
Otto Bremer Foundation 1, 3, 6, 7
Central Minnesota Community Foundation 1, 4
The Cooperative Foundation 3, 4, 6, 10
Roger L. and Agnes C. Dell Charitable (Trust 1)
Roger L. and Agnes C. Dell Charitable (Trust 2)
Duluth Superior Area Community Foundation 1, 5, 9
Edina Community Foundation 1
Fargo-Moorhead Area Foundation 6

Grand Rapids Area Community Foundation 4
Grotto Foundation, Inc. 4
Headwaters Foundation for Justice 1, 9
George A. Hormel Testamentary Trust 4, 7
Initiative Foundation 1, 3, 4, 7
W.K. Kellogg Foundation 10
Luverne Area Community Foundation
Mankato Area Foundation
The Martinson Foundation
Mayo Clinic 1, 4, 6, 8
The Minneapolis Foundation
The Laura Jane Musser Fund 10
Northwest Minnesota Foundation 4
Owatonna Foundation
The Lawrence and Linda Perlman Family Foundation
Philanthrofund Foundation (PFund) 1, 4, 10
The Jay and Rose Phillips Family Foundation 1, 4, 6, 9, 10
The Irwin Andrew Porter Foundation 1

Rochester Area Foundation 1
The Saint Paul Foundation 1
Securian Foundation/Securian Financial Group 10
Shakopee Mdewakanton Sioux Community 4
The Sheltering Arms Foundation 6
Sioux Falls Area Community Foundation 3, 5
SKB Environmental Rosemount Community Trust
Southern Minnesota Initiative Foundation 1, 6
St Croix Valley Community Foundation
Alex Stern Family Foundation
Thomson West
The Toro Company Giving Program 2
Travelers Corporation and Travelers Foundation 4
West Central Initiative 1, 4
Whitney Foundation
Winona Community Foundation

Areas of Interest

Public Protection: Crime/Courts/Legal Services
1 - Crime prevention
2 - Correctional facilities and prisoner services
3 - Courts and administration of justice
4 - Dispute/conflict resolution
5 - Law enforcement agencies
6 - Legal services
7 - Protection/prevention - neglect/abuse/exploitation
8 - Rehabilitation of offenders
9 - Other

Andersen Corporate Foundation 6, 7
W. Glen Boyd Charitable Foundation 6, 7
Otto Bremer Foundation 4, 6, 7
Bush Foundation 1, 4, 6, 7, 8
Central Minnesota Community Foundation 1, 4, 6, 7
Cote Foundation
Deluxe Corporation Foundation/Deluxe Corporation 1, 9
Duluth Superior Area Community Foundation 1, 2, 4, 6, 7, 8
Edina Community Foundation 5
Faegre & Benson Foundation 6
Fargo-Moorhead Area Foundation 6
Fredrikson & Byron Foundation

Grand Rapids Area Community Foundation 1
Gray Plant Mooty Foundation 6
Grotto Foundation, Inc. 7
Hartz Foundation 5
Headwaters Foundation for Justice 9
Hennepin County Bar Foundation 3, 6, 9
George A. Hormel Testamentary Trust 4, 5
The Minneapolis Foundation 4, 6, 7, 8
Minneapolis Rotary Community Service Foundation 7
Minnesota Power Foundation 1
Minnesota State Bar Foundation 1, 3, 6, 7
Northland Foundation 1, 4, 7
Ordean Foundation 6, 7, 8
Otter Tail Power Company 1, 5

Owatonna Foundation
Park Nicollet Foundation 1
People in Business Care, Inc.
The Jay and Rose Phillips Family Foundation 1
Rochester Area Foundation 1, 4, 7, 8
The Saint Paul Foundation 1, 6, 7
Saunders Family Foundation 2, 8
Securian Foundation/Securian Financial Group 1, 7
Sioux Falls Area Community Foundation 3, 7
SKB Environmental Rosemount Community Trust
Tennant Foundation
Archie D. and Bertha H. Walker Foundation 6
Winona Community Foundation

Public Safety, Disaster Preparedness and Relief
1 - Disaster preparedness and relief
2 - Safety education
3 - Other

3M/3M Foundation 1
Ameriprise Financial, Inc. 1, 3
Lloyd and Barbara Amundson Charity Foundation, Inc.
Andersen Corporate Foundation 1
Andersen Corporation
Hugh J. Andersen Foundation 1
Best Buy Children's Foundation 1, 3
Otto Bremer Foundation 1
Cargill Citizenship Fund 3
CenterPoint Energy 1, 2, 3
Central Minnesota Community Foundation 1, 2
Deluxe Corporation Foundation/Deluxe Corporation 1
Duluth Superior Area Community Foundation 1

Ecolab Foundation and Corporation 1
Edina Community Foundation 1
Fargo-Moorhead Area Foundation 1
Federated Insurance Foundation, Inc. 1, 2
General Mills Community Action 3
Honeywell Hometown Solutions 3
The Hubbard Broadcasting Foundation 1
Initiative Foundation 3
Luverne Area Community Foundation
Minnesota Power Foundation 1, 2
MoneyGram International 1
NFC Foundation 1, 2
Otter Tail Power Company 1, 2
Owatonna Foundation
The Pentair Foundation 1, 2

People in Business Care, Inc.
The Riverway Foundation 1
Carl and Verna Schmidt Foundation
Securian Foundation/Securian Financial Group 1, 2
The Simmet Foundation 1
Sioux Falls Area Community Foundation 2
Todd-Wadena Electric Cooperative Community Trust 1
The Toro Company Giving Program 2
Travelers Corporation and Travelers Foundation 1, 2
Winona Community Foundation

Areas of Interest

Recreation, Leisure, Sports and Athletics
1 - Amateur sports clubs/leagues
2 - Amateur sports competitions
3 - Physical fitness/recreational facilities
4 - Professional athletic leagues
5 - Recreational/pleasure/social clubs
6 - Recreation and sporting camps
7 - Sports training facilities/agencies
8 - Other

Andersen Corporate Foundation 3, 8
Andersen Corporation
Athwin Foundation
The Bentson Foundation
W. Glen Boyd Charitable Foundation 8
Central Minnesota Community Foundation 3, 6
Cloquet Educational Foundation
Duluth Superior Area Community Foundation 6, 8
Edina Community Foundation 1, 2, 3, 5, 7
Fargo-Moorhead Area Foundation
First National Bank of Bemidji Foundation 1, 3
The Graco Foundation 8
Grand Rapids Area Community Foundation 1, 3
Hartz Foundation 3, 6, 7

George A. Hormel Testamentary Trust 1, 3
Italian American Club Foundation, Inc. 1, 2
The Luther Family Foundation 2
Luverne Area Community Foundation
Mankato Area Foundation
Minneapolis Rotary Community Service Foundation 3
Minnesota Power Foundation 8
The Minnesota Timberwolves FastBreak Foundation 8
Minnesota Twins Community Fund 1, 2, 3, 4, 5, 6, 7, 8
North Suburban Community Foundation 8
North Suburban Youth Foundation 1, 2
Owatonna Foundation

The Elizabeth C. Quinlan Foundation, Inc. 6
RBC Dain Rauscher Foundation 8
Rochester Area Foundation 1, 3
Rochester Area Foundation
The Shiebler Family Foundation
Sioux Falls Area Community Foundation 1, 5, 6, 7
SKB Environmental Rosemount Community Trust
Alex Stern Family Foundation
The Toro Company Giving Program 8
Turner Family Foundation 8
Winona Community Foundation

Religion/Spiritual Development
1 - Interfaith issues
2 - Specific denomination
3 - Other

Acorn Foundation
AHS Foundation
Lloyd and Barbara Amundson Charity Foundation, Inc.
Arsher Charitable Trust U/A
Bernard and Fern Badzin Foundation
Baratz Family Foundation
The Bentson Foundation
Otto Bremer Foundation 1
Martin and Esther Capp Foundation 2
Catholic Aid Association Foundation 2
Catholic Community Foundation in the Archdiocese of Saint Paul and Minneapolis 2, 3
CDF Foundation
Central Minnesota Community Foundation 1
Charity, Inc.
Roger L. and Agnes C. Dell Charitable (Trust 2)
Duluth Superior Area Community Foundation 1
ELEOS Foundation
Otto C. and Elsie Ewert Charitable Trust
Arlin Falck Foundation
Fidelis Foundation
Frey Foundation 2
The Janice Gardner Foundation
Getsch Charitable Trust

Hatler Foundation
Headwaters Foundation for Justice 3
The Hermundslie Foundation
HRK Foundation 1
Impact Foundation, Inc.
Initiative Foundation 1, 3
Jennings Family Foundation
Lewis H. Johnson Family Foundation
The Lynn Johnson Family Foundation
Mitchell and Lois Johnson Charitable Foundation
George Kaplan Memorial Foundation, Incorporated
Hess Kline Foundation, Inc. 2
Kopp Family Foundation
Lerner Foundation
Liebhaber Family Foundation
James G. Lindell Irrevocable Charitable Trust
Ted and Roberta Mann Foundation 3
Marbrook Foundation 3
The Martinson Foundation
Mayo Clinic 1
Jane N. Mooty Foundation Trust
Moscoe Family Foundation
The Laura Jane Musser Fund 3
Roger and Violet Noreen Charitable Trust

Ben and Jeanne Overman Charitable Trust
P.G.N. Foundation
Pagel Foundation
Pajor Family Foundation
People in Business Care, Inc.
The Jay and Rose Phillips Family Foundation 1, 3
The Elizabeth C. Quinlan Foundation, Inc. 2, 3
Rappaport Family Foundation
Rukavina Family Foundation
Sacred Portion Foundation
Salem Foundation, Inc.
Carl and Verna Schmidt Foundation
Sexton Foundation
Shamrock Foundation
Shapiro Family Philanthropic Foundation
The Shared Fund
Gertrude R. Shiely Charitable Trust
Sioux Falls Area Community Foundation 2
Slawik Family Foundation
The Spell Family Foundation
Thrivent Financial for Lutherans Foundation 3
Trust for the Meditation Process 3
Winona Community Foundation
Youthworks! Foundation, Inc. 2, 3

Areas of Interest

Science/Technology
1 - Biological/life science
2 - Engineering/technology research
3 - Physical sciences/earth sciences
4 - Science - general
5 - Other

3M/3M Foundation 2
ADC Foundation 5
AgStar Fund for Rural America 5
Andersen Corporate Foundation 5
Best Buy Children's Foundation 5
Bromelkamp Foundation
Ecolab Foundation and Corporation 2
Fargo-Moorhead Area Foundation 4, 5
George A. Hormel Testamentary Trust 4
The Hubbard Broadcasting Foundation
Lawson 5
The Charles A. and Anne Morrow Lindbergh Foundation 1, 3
Luverne Area Community Foundation
The Medtronic Foundation 5
Minnesota Research Fund 1, 2, 3, 4
Otter Tail Power Company 2
Owatonna Foundation
The Pentair Foundation 4
Piper Jaffray
Schott Foundation
The Toro Company Giving Program 3, 5
Winona Community Foundation

Social Science Organizations
1 - Interdisciplinary research/studies to improve understanding of particular populations
2 - Mystic/paranormal studies
3 - Social science research institutes/services
4 - Other

The Cooperative Foundation 1, 4
Duluth Superior Area Community Foundation 1
Fargo-Moorhead Area Foundation
Grotto Foundation, Inc.
HRK Foundation 1
Leonette M. and Fred T. Lanners Foundation 3
Luverne Area Community Foundation
Owatonna Foundation
Park Nicollet Foundation 1
Winona Community Foundation

Youth Development
1 - Adult/child matching programs
2 - Multipurpose youth centers/clubs
3 - Scouting organizations
4 - Youth development programs
5 - Other

3M/3M Foundation 1, 2, 3, 4
Allianz Life Insurance Company of North America 1, 2, 3, 4
Ameriprise Financial, Inc. 4
Lloyd and Barbara Amundson Charity Foundation, Inc.
Andersen Corporate Foundation 1, 2, 3
Fred C. and Katherine B. Andersen Foundation 3, 4
Hugh J. Andersen Foundation 1, 2, 3, 4, 5
Athwin Foundation 2, 4
Bahl Foundation
Baker Foundation 2, 3
Ann Bancroft Foundation 5
Baratz Family Foundation
Beim Foundation 4
Lillian Wright and C. Emil Berglund Foundation, Inc. 2, 4
Best Buy Children's Foundation 2, 4, 5
Blandin Foundation 4, 5
W. Glen Boyd Charitable Foundation 1, 2, 3, 4, 5
Bush Foundation 4
The Curtis L. Carlson Family Foundation 1, 2, 4
Carolyn Foundation 4, 5
Central Minnesota Community Foundation 1, 2, 3, 4
Charlson Foundation 1, 4
CHS Foundation 5
Cloquet Educational Foundation
Comcast Cable Company 5
Cote Foundation
The Deikel Family Foundation 2
Roger L. and Agnes C. Dell Charitable (Trust 2)
Delta Dental of Minnesota 2, 4
Deluxe Corporation Foundation/Deluxe Corporation 1, 2, 3, 4, 5
The Dorsey & Whitney Foundation
Joseph C. and Lillian A. Duke Foundation
Duluth Superior Area Community Foundation 1, 2, 3, 4
Ecolab Foundation and Corporation 2, 4, 5
Edina Community Foundation 1, 2, 4
Fargo-Moorhead Area Foundation
Federated Insurance Foundation, Inc. 1, 4
First National Bank of Bemidji Foundation 1, 2, 4
Fremont Foundation
Frey Foundation 1, 3, 4
General Mills Community Action 5
The Graco Foundation
Grand Rapids Area Community Foundation 1, 2, 4
Grotto Foundation, Inc. 4
Hartz Foundation 3
George A. Hormel Testamentary Trust 2, 3, 4
The Hubbard Broadcasting Foundation
ING Foundation 2, 4
Initiative Foundation 1, 4
Italian American Club Foundation, Inc. 4
Jennings Family Foundation
Lloyd K. Johnson Foundation 1, 2, 3, 4
The Jostens Foundation 1, 2, 4
W.K. Kellogg Foundation 5
Kopp Family Foundation
Lahti Family Foundation
Land O'Lakes Foundation 4, 5
Lawson
R. C. Lilly Foundation
Russell T. Lund Charitable Trust 2
The Luther Family Foundation
Luverne Area Community Foundation
The M.B. Foundation
Mall of America Foundation for Youth
Ted and Roberta Mann Foundation
Mardag Foundation
The Martinson Foundation 2, 3, 4
Mayo Clinic 1, 2, 3, 4
The McKnight Foundation 4
McNeely Foundation 4
The Minneapolis Foundation 4, 5
Minneapolis Rotary Community Service Foundation 1, 2, 3, 4

Areas of Interest

Minnesota Power Foundation 2, 3, 4
The Minnesota Timberwolves FastBreak Foundation 2, 4
Minnesota Twins Community Fund 4
Marjorie Weil and Marvin Edward Mitchell Foundation 4
Jane N. Mooty Foundation Trust
John W. Mooty Foundation Trust 2, 3, 4
The Nash Foundation 2, 4
Richard A. Newman Foundation 4
North Suburban Community Foundation
North Suburban Youth Foundation 2, 3, 4
Northland Foundation 1, 2, 4
Northwest Minnesota Foundation 4
Ordean Foundation 1, 2, 4
Otter Tail Power Company 2, 3
Ben and Jeanne Overman Charitable Trust 2, 4
Owatonna Foundation
P.G.N. Foundation
Pajor Family Foundation
Park Nicollet Foundation 2, 4
The Pentair Foundation 2, 3, 4
People in Business Care, Inc.
Perkins Foundation 4
Philanthrofund Foundation (PFund) 4, 5
The Jay and Rose Phillips Family Foundation 1, 2, 4
Piper Jaffray
Carl and Eloise Pohlad Family Foundation
The Polaris Foundation 2, 3, 4

The Irwin Andrew Porter Foundation 4
Rahr Foundation 3, 4
Rappaport Family Foundation 4
RBC Dain Rauscher Foundation 1, 5
Red Wing Shoe Company Foundation
Redwood Area Communities Foundation, Inc.
Richfield Community Foundation 1
Ripley Memorial Foundation, Inc. 4, 5
Margaret Rivers Fund 2, 3, 4
The Riverway Foundation 1, 2, 3, 4
Rochester Area Foundation 1, 2, 3, 4
Runestone Electric Association Community Trust
The Saint Paul Foundation 1, 2, 3, 4
Salem Foundation, Inc.
Sauer Children's Renew Foundation
Saunders Family Foundation 2, 4
Securian Foundation/Securian Financial Group 2
Sexton Foundation
Shakopee Mdewakanton Sioux Community 2, 4
The Simmet Foundation 1, 2, 4
Sioux Falls Area Community Foundation 1, 2, 3, 4
SKB Environmental Rosemount Community Trust
Slagge Family Foundation
Slawik Family Foundation
Southern Minnesota Initiative Foundation 5
Southwest Initiative Foundation 5

St Croix Valley Community Foundation
Alex Stern Family Foundation
SUPERVALU Foundation 2, 3, 4
TEAM Foundation 4
Tennant Foundation 2, 3, 4
Think Community Foundation 1, 2, 3, 4
Thomson West
James R. Thorpe Foundation 2, 4
Thrivent Financial for Lutherans Foundation 5
Todd-Wadena Electric Cooperative Community Trust
The Toro Company Giving Program 5
Tozer Foundation, Inc. 3, 5
Travelers Corporation and Travelers Foundation 4
Turner Family Foundation 1, 2, 4
The Vos Family Foundation
Warren Foundation 2, 3, 4
Frederick O. Watson Foundation
WCA Foundation 4
J. A. Wedum Foundation
Mae and Sylvester Weiss Foundation
Wells Fargo Foundation Minnesota 5
Frederick and Margaret L. Weyerhaeuser Foundation 4
Winona Community Foundation
Youthworks! Foundation, Inc.

Types of Support Index

This index includes those grantmakers that identified specific types of support that they consider funding. The index includes ten categories.

Capital Campaigns	306
Corporate Sponsorships	306
Emergency Funds	306
General Purpose/Operating Support	307
In-Kind	308
Management/Technical Assistance	308
Program-Related Investments	308
Program Development/Project Support	308
Research	309
Student Aid	310

Types of Support

Capital Campaigns

1 - Building/renovation
2 - Collection acquisitions
3 - Computer sytstems/technology development
4 - Debt reduction
5 - Endowment funds
6 - Equipment
7 - Land acquisitions

3M/3M Foundation 1
AgStar Fund for Rural America 3, 6
Allianz Life Insurance Company of North America 1, 3, 6
Andersen Corporate Foundation 1, 6, 7
Fred C. and Katherine B. Andersen Foundation 1
Hugh J. Andersen Foundation 1, 6
Athwin Foundation
The Beverly Foundation
F.R. Bigelow Foundation
The Boss Foundation
Burdick-Craddick Family Foundation
Bush Foundation 1
Buuck Family Foundation 7
Charity, Inc. 1
Cote Foundation 1, 6
Cottonwood Foundation 1, 3, 6, 7
Roger L. and Agnes C. Dell Charitable Trust 2 1
Deluxe Corporation Foundation/Deluxe Corporation 1, 3, 6
Driscoll Foundation 1, 5
Ecolab Foundation and Corporation 1
Edina Community Foundation 2, 6
Edina Realty Foundation 6
Faegre & Benson Foundation
Federated Insurance Foundation, Inc. 1
First National Bank of Bemidji Foundation 1, 3, 6, 7
H.B. Fuller Company Foundation 1, 6
General Mills Community Action
The Graco Foundation 1, 3
Grand Rapids Area Community Foundation 5, 6
Hardenbergh Foundation

Hartz Foundation 1, 3, 6
Healthier Minnesota Community Clinic Fund 1, 3, 6
Anna M. Heilmaier Charitable Foundation
George A. Hormel Testamentary Trust 3, 6
HRK Foundation
The Hubbard Broadcasting Foundation
Lewis H. Johnson Family Foundation
Lloyd K. Johnson Foundation
Jundt Family Foundation
Kopp Family Foundation
Land O'Lakes Foundation
Marbrook Foundation
Mardag Foundation
Martinson Clinic Foundation 6
Mayo Clinic 1
The McKnight Foundation 1, 6
The Minneapolis Foundation 1, 3, 6, 7
Minneapolis Rotary Community Service Foundation 1, 3, 6
Minnesota State Bar Foundation 6
Minnesota Twins Community Fund 1
The Nelson Family Foundation
Roger and Violet Noreen Charitable Trust
Alice M. O'Brien Foundation 1
OSilas Foundation 5
Otter Tail Power Company 1
Ben and Jeanne Overman Charitable Trust
Owatonna Foundation 1
Lewis and Annie F. Paper Foundation, Inc.
Patterson Foundation 1, 5
Philanthrofund Foundation (PFund) 1, 3, 6
The Jay and Rose Phillips Family Foundation 1, 3, 6, 7

The Elizabeth C. Quinlan Foundation, Inc. 1, 3, 4, 5, 6, 7
Rahr Foundation 1
Rappaport Family Foundation
Red Wing Shoe Company Foundation
Regis Foundation
The Riverway Foundation 1, 5, 6
Rochester Area Foundation 1, 6
The Saint Paul Foundation 1, 3, 5, 6
Saunders Family Foundation 1, 6
Securian Foundation/Securian Financial Group 1, 3, 6
Shakopee Mdewakanton Sioux Community 1
Shamrock Foundation
The Shared Fund
The Simmet Foundation 1, 6
Sioux Falls Area Community Foundation 1, 5
SKB Environmental Rosemount Community Trust
Slawik Family Foundation 1, 5
Southways Foundation 1, 5, 6
St Croix Valley Community Foundation
Alex Stern Family Foundation
TCF Foundation
Think Community Foundation 1, 3, 6, 7
Tozer Foundation, Inc. 1
Trust for the Meditation Process 1, 6
U.S. Bancorp Foundation
DeWitt and Caroline Van Evera Foundation 1, 3, 6
The Wasie Foundation 1, 6
WCA Foundation
Wells Fargo Foundation Minnesota 1, 3, 7
Winona Community Foundation
Winona Foundation 1, 2, 6

Corporate Sponsorships

CenterPoint Energy
Delta Dental of Minnesota
Edina Realty Foundation
HealthPartners
Imation
The Medtronic Foundation
Minnesota Power Foundation
RBC Dain Rauscher Foundation
Travelers Corporation and Travelers Foundation

Emergency Funds

Cote Foundation
Deluxe Corporation Foundation/Deluxe Corporation
Edina Realty Foundation
Federated Insurance Foundation, Inc.
Grand Rapids Area Community Foundation
Lloyd K. Johnson Foundation
Kopp Family Foundation
Northwest Minnesota Foundation
People in Business Care, Inc.
Rahr Foundation
The Riverway Foundation
The Simmet Foundation
Sioux Falls Area Community Foundation
St Croix Valley Community Foundation
Think Community Foundation
WCA Foundation
Winona Community Foundation

General Purpose/Operating Support

1 - Annual campaigns
2 - General purpose/operating support

3M/3M Foundation 2
AgStar Fund for Rural America 2
AHS Foundation 2
Airport Foundation MSP 2
Ameriprise Financial, Inc. 2
Lloyd and Barbara Amundson Charity Foundation, Inc. 2
Andersen Corporate Foundation 1, 2
Fred C. and Katherine B. Andersen Foundation 1, 2
Hugh J. Andersen Foundation 1, 2
Athwin Foundation 2
Baker Foundation 1, 2
The Beverly Foundation 2
The Boss Foundation 1, 2
W. Glen Boyd Charitable Foundation 2
Burdick-Craddick Family Foundation 2
Patrick and Aimee Butler Family Foundation 2
Buuck Family Foundation 1, 2
Cade Foundation 2
Caliber Foundation 2
Carolyn Foundation 2
CenterPoint Energy 2
Central Minnesota Community Foundation 2
Charity, Inc. 2
Charlson Foundation 1, 2
Cote Foundation 2
Cottonwood Foundation 2
Charles and Kathryn Cunningham Family Foundation 1, 2
Edwin W. and Catherine M. Davis Foundation 2
The Deikel Family Foundation 2
Roger L. and Agnes C. Dell Charitable Trust 1 2
Roger L. and Agnes C. Dell Charitable Trust 2 2
Deluxe Corporation Foundation/Deluxe Corporation 1, 2
The Dorsey & Whitney Foundation 1, 2
Driscoll Foundation 1, 2
Joseph C. and Lillian A. Duke Foundation 2
Ecolab Foundation and Corporation 2
Edina Realty Foundation 1, 2
Charles Engasser Memorial Foundation, Inc. 2
Otto C. and Elsie Ewert Charitable Trust 2
Faegre & Benson Foundation 2
Arlin Falck Foundation 2
Federated Insurance Foundation, Inc. 2
First National Bank of Bemidji Foundation 2
Fremont Foundation 2
Frey Foundation 2
H.B. Fuller Company Foundation 2
G&K Services Foundation 2
Donald G. Gardner Humanities Trust 2
The Janice Gardner Foundation 2
General Mills Community Action 2
Mary Livingston Griggs and Mary Griggs Burke Foundation 2
N. Bud and Beverly Grossman Foundation 2

Grotto Foundation, Inc. 2
Haggerty Family Foundation 2
Hardenbergh Foundation 1, 2
Hatlen Foundation 1, 2
HealthPartners 2
Anna M. Heilmaier Charitable Foundation 2
Hennepin County Bar Foundation 2
The Hubbard Broadcasting Foundation 2
ING Foundation 2
Italian American Club Foundation, Inc. 2
JNM 1966 Gift Trust U/A 2
Lewis H. Johnson Family Foundation 2
Lloyd K. Johnson Foundation 2
Mitchell and Lois Johnson Charitable Foundation 2
The Jostens Foundation 2
Jundt Family Foundation 2
George Kaplan Memorial Foundation, Incorporated 2
Margaret H. and James E. Kelley Foundation, Inc. 2
Hess Kline Foundation, Inc. 2
Kopp Family Foundation 2
Land O'Lakes Foundation 2
Leonette M. and Fred T. Lanners Foundation 2
Leonard, Street and Deinard Foundation 1, 2
Lerner Foundation 2
Steven C. Leuthold Family Foundation 2
James G. Lindell Irrevocable Charitable Trust 2
Russell T. Lund Charitable Trust 2
The Luther Family Foundation 2
The M.B. Foundation 1, 2
Marbrook Foundation 2
Marquette Financial Companies Community Support Program 2
Martinson Clinic Foundation 2
The Martinson Foundation 1, 2
Mayo Clinic 2
McGough Foundation 2
The McKnight Foundation 2
Minneapolis Area Association of Realtors Foundation, Inc. 2
The Minneapolis Foundation 2
Minneapolis Kiwanis Foundation 2
Minnesota Power Foundation 2
Minnesota State Bar Foundation 2
Moscoe Family Foundation 2
The Nash Foundation 1, 2
The Nelson Family Foundation 1, 2
Richard A. Newman Foundation 2
Roger and Violet Noreen Charitable Trust 2
North Suburban Community Foundation 2
Northland Foundation 2
Alice M. O'Brien Foundation 2
Casey Albert T. O'Neil Foundation 2
Ordean Foundation 2
OSilas Foundation 1, 2
Otter Tail Power Company 1, 2
Ben and Jeanne Overman Charitable Trust 2

Pajor Family Foundation 2
Lewis and Annie F. Paper Foundation, Inc. 1, 2
The Pentair Foundation 2
People in Business Care, Inc. 2
Perkins Foundation 2
Philanthrofund Foundation (PFund) 1, 2
Piper Jaffray 2
Prospect Creek Foundation 2
The Elizabeth C. Quinlan Foundation, Inc. 1, 2
Rahr Foundation 1, 2
Rappaport Family Foundation 2
RBC Dain Rauscher Foundation 2
Red Wing Shoe Company Foundation 2
Regis Foundation 1, 2
Luther I. Replogle Foundation 2
Richfield Community Foundation 2
The Riverway Foundation 1, 2
Saunders Family Foundation 2
Securian Foundation/Securian Financial Group 1, 2
Sexton Foundation 2
Shamrock Foundation 2
The Shared Fund 1, 2
Gertrude R. Shiely Charitable Trust 2
The Simmet Foundation 2
Sioux Falls Area Community Foundation 2
SKB Environmental Rosemount Community Trust 2
Slawik Family Foundation 1, 2
Southways Foundation 2
The Spell Family Foundation 1, 2
Daniel J. Spiegel Family Foundation 2
St Croix Valley Community Foundation 2
Alex Stern Family Foundation 2
Stevens Square Foundation 2
SUPERVALU Foundation 2
Swan Family Foundation 1, 2
Sweitzer Foundation 2
Target 2
TCF Foundation 2
Think Community Foundation 1, 2
Thomson West 2
Thrivent Financial for Lutherans Foundation 2
The Toro Company Giving Program 2
Travelers Corporation and Travelers Foundation 2
U.S. Bancorp Foundation 2
The Valspar Foundation 1, 2
DeWitt and Caroline Van Evera Foundation 2
Archie D. and Bertha H. Walker Foundation 2
Warren Foundation 2
The Wasie Foundation 2
Frederick O. Watson Foundation 2
WCA Foundation 2
Wells Fargo Foundation Minnesota 1
Wenger Foundation 2
Whitney Foundation 1, 2
Winona Community Foundation 2
Women's Foundation of Minnesota 2

Types of Support

In-Kind

1 - In-kind services
2 - In-kind products

3M/3M Foundation 2
ADC Foundation 1
Andersen Corporation 2
Bromelkamp Foundation 1
Cargill Citizenship Fund 1, 2
The Cooperative Foundation 1
Coughlan Companies 2
The Dorsey & Whitney Foundation 1
Faegre & Benson Foundation 1
Fredrikson & Byron Foundation 1
H.B. Fuller Company Foundation 2
Gray Plant Mooty Foundation 1
The Jostens Foundation 1
Otter Tail Power Company 1
The Polaris Foundation 2
SUPERVALU Foundation 2
Thomson West 1, 2
The Toro Company Giving Program 2
The Valspar Foundation 2

Management/Technical Assistance

AgStar Fund for Rural America
Bush Foundation
The CCP Foundation
Hennepin County Bar Foundation
Northland Foundation
Northwest Minnesota Foundation
Philanthrofund Foundation (PFund)
The Jay and Rose Phillips Family Foundation
Rochester Area Foundation
The Saint Paul Foundation
Sioux Falls Area Community Foundation
St Croix Valley Community Foundation
Wells Fargo Foundation Minnesota
Winona Community Foundation

Program-Related Investments

The CCP Foundation
Ecolab Foundation and Corporation
Edina Realty Foundation
HealthPartners
Winona Community Foundation
Youthworks! Foundation, Inc.

Program Development/Project Support

1 - Conferences/seminars
2 - Curriculum development
3 - Exhibitions
4 - Faculty/staff development
5 - Film/video/radio production
6 - Fundraising
7 - Mentoring programs
8 - Other
9 - Performance/production costs
10 - Professorships
11 - Program evaluation
12 - Public awareness
13 - Public policy research/analysis

3M/3M Foundation 2, 4, 7, 8
ADC Foundation
AgStar Fund for Rural America
AHS Foundation
Airport Foundation MSP
Allianz Life Insurance Company of North America
Ameriprise Financial, Inc. 8
Andersen Corporate Foundation
Fred C. and Katherine B. Andersen Foundation
Hugh J. Andersen Foundation 6
Athwin Foundation
Lillian Wright and C. Emil Berglund Foundation, Inc. 2, 7, 8, 9
Best Buy Children's Foundation 2
The Beverly Foundation
F.R. Bigelow Foundation
Blue Cross and Blue Shield of Minnesota Foundation/Blue Cross and Blue Shield of Minnesota
The Boss Foundation
W. Glen Boyd Charitable Foundation 7, 15
Bush Foundation 4, 11, 13
Patrick and Aimee Butler Family Foundation
Cargill Citizenship Fund 8
Carolyn Foundation
The CCP Foundation
CenterPoint Energy
Central Minnesota Community Foundation 1, 2, 3, 7, 8, 9, 12, 15
Charlson Foundation
Comcast Cable Company
The Cooperative Foundation 1, 2, 4, 5, 8, 13, 14, 15
Arthur and David Cosgrove Memorial Fund
Cote Foundation 7
Cottonwood Foundation 15
Charles and Kathryn Cunningham Family Foundation
Dakota Medical Foundation/Dakota Medical Charities
Edwin W. and Catherine M. Davis Foundation
The Deikel Family Foundation
Roger L. and Agnes C. Dell Charitable (Trust 2)
Delta Dental of Minnesota
Deluxe Corporation Foundation/Deluxe Corporation 2, 7, 14
Driscoll Foundation
Joseph C. and Lillian A. Duke Foundation
Duluth Superior Area Community Foundation
Eddy (Edwin H.) Foundation
Edina Community Foundation 1, 3, 5, 7, 8, 9, 15
Otto C. and Elsie Ewert Charitable Trust
Extendicare Foundation 2, 4, 15
Arlin Falck Foundation
First National Bank of Bemidji Foundation 7, 15
Frey Foundation

H.B. Fuller Company Foundation 8
G&K Services Foundation
Donald G. Gardner Humanities Trust
 1, 3, 4, 5, 9, 14
General Mills Community Action
Grand Rapids Area Community Foundation
Mary Livingston Griggs and Mary Griggs
 Burke Foundation
Grotto Foundation, Inc. 2, 4, 12, 15
Haggerty Family Foundation
Hartz Foundation
Healthier Minnesota Community Clinic Fund 8
HealthPartners
Anna M. Heilmaier Charitable Foundation
Hennepin County Bar Foundation
Hickory Tech Corporation Foundation 4, 9
George A. Hormel Testamentary Trust 9
HRK Foundation 6
Nevin Huested Foundation for Handicapped
 Children, Inc. 1, 2, 4, 7, 8, 11, 12, 14, 15
Imation
Indian Land Tenure Foundation 1, 2, 12, 13, 15
Italian American Club Foundation, Inc.
Jerome Foundation 3, 5, 7, 9, 14, 15
Lloyd K. Johnson Foundation 7, 15
Margaret H. and James E. Kelley Foundation,
 Inc.
Kopp Family Foundation
Land O'Lakes Foundation
Leonette M. and Fred T. Lanners Foundation
Steven C. Leuthold Family Foundation
James G. Lindell Irrevocable Charitable Trust
Mall of America Foundation for Youth
Marbrook Foundation
Mardag Foundation
Marquette Financial Companies Community
 Support Program 8
The Martinson Foundation
The McKnight Foundation
McNeely Foundation 2, 7
Medica Foundation
The Medtronic Foundation
The Minneapolis Foundation 12, 13
Minneapolis Rotary Community Service
 Foundation 15

Minnesota Business and Professional Women's
 Foundation 1
Minnesota Power Foundation
Minnesota State Bar Foundation
Minnesota Twins Community Fund 6
Marjorie Weil and Marvin Edward Mitchell
 Foundation 8
The Laura Jane Musser Fund 15
The Nash Foundation 7, 8, 15
The Nelson Family Foundation
NFC Foundation
North Suburban Community Foundation
North Suburban Youth Foundation
Northland Foundation 7, 15
Northwest Minnesota Foundation
Ordean Foundation 7
I. A. O'Shaughnessy Foundation, Incorporated
Otter Tail Power Company 1
Ben and Jeanne Overman Charitable Trust
Park Nicollet Foundation
Patterson Foundation 2, 4, 7, 9, 12, 13
The Pentair Foundation
People in Business Care, Inc.
Philanthrofund Foundation (PFund)
 1, 2, 3, 5, 7, 9, 11, 12, 13, 14, 15
The Jay and Rose Phillips Family Foundation
 2, 4, 6, 7, 9, 11, 12, 13, 14, 15
Piper Jaffray
The Irwin Andrew Porter Foundation
The Elizabeth C. Quinlan Foundation,
 Inc. 1, 4, 15
Rahr Foundation 6
Rappaport Family Foundation
RBC Dain Rauscher Foundation 7, 8
Red Wing Shoe Company Foundation
Regis Foundation
Luther I. Replogle Foundation
Richfield Community Foundation 7
Ripley Memorial Foundation, Inc. 2
Rochester Area Foundation 7, 8, 15
Sacred Portion Foundation
The Saint Paul Foundation 4, 7, 15
Shakopee Mdewakanton Sioux Community
The Sheltering Arms Foundation 7, 12, 13, 15
The Simmet Foundation 2, 4

Sioux Falls Area Community Foundation
 1, 2, 8, 9, 12, 15
SKB Environmental Rosemount Community
 Trust
R. C. Skoe Foundation
Slawik Family Foundation
Southways Foundation
The Spell Family Foundation
St Croix Valley Community Foundation
St Francis Regional Medical Center
 Foundation 2
Alex Stern Family Foundation
Stevens Square Foundation
Target
TCF Foundation 2, 6
Think Community Foundation 6, 7, 8, 14
Thomson West 15
Thrivent Financial for Lutherans Foundation
The Toro Company Giving Program
 2, 3, 4, 5, 12, 14
Tozer Foundation, Inc.
Travelers Corporation and Travelers Foundation
Trust for the Meditation Process
 1, 2, 4, 11, 12, 14, 15
U.S. Bancorp Foundation
United Health Foundation
DeWitt and Caroline Van Evera Foundation 11
Archie D. and Bertha H. Walker Foundation
 1, 2, 3, 4, 5, 7, 8, 12, 14, 15
Warren Foundation
The Wasie Foundation 1, 8
WCA Foundation
J. A. Wedum Foundation
Wells Fargo Foundation Minnesota 2, 4, 8, 14
Wenger Foundation
Weyerhaeuser Family Foundation, Inc. 15
Winona Community Foundation
 1, 2, 3, 4, 5, 6, 7, 8, 9, 10, 11, 12, 13, 14, 15
Winona Foundation 3, 5, 9, 14
Women's Foundation of Minnesota
Youthworks! Foundation, Inc. 15

Research

Blue Cross and Blue Shield of Minnesota
 Foundation/Blue Cross and Blue Shield of
 Minnesota
Buuck Family Foundation
The Cooperative Foundation
Eddy (Edwin H.) Foundation
Extendicare Foundation
Steven C. Leuthold Family Foundation
The Charles A. and Anne Morrow Lindbergh
 Foundation

Martinson Clinic Foundation
Minnesota Research Fund
Alice M. O'Brien Foundation
The Elizabeth C. Quinlan Foundation, Inc.
Rahr Foundation
The Riverway Foundation
The Simmet Foundation
Sioux Falls Area Community Foundation
St Croix Valley Community Foundation
Trust for the Meditation Process

Archie D. and Bertha H. Walker Foundation
The Wasie Foundation
Winona Community Foundation
Women's Foundation of Minnesota

Types of Support

Student Aid
1 - Fellowships
2 - Internships
3 - Scholarship funds
4 - Student aid (grants to institutions)

3M/3M Foundation 1, 4
Acorn Foundation 4
Lloyd and Barbara Amundson Charity Foundation, Inc. 3, 4
Marjorie and V.M. Baich Foundation 3, 4
Best Buy Children's Foundation 3, 4
W. Glen Boyd Charitable Foundation 2, 3, 4
Buuck Family Foundation 3, 4
Central Minnesota Community Foundation 3, 4
The Cooperative Foundation 1, 4
Edwin W. and Catherine M. Davis Foundation 1, 3, 4
Roger L. and Agnes C. Dell Charitable Trust 2 4
Edina Community Foundation 3, 4
Otto C. and Elsie Ewert Charitable Trust 4
Arlin Falck Foundation 3, 4
Federated Insurance Foundation, Inc. 1, 3, 4
First National Bank of Bemidji Foundation 3, 4
Donald G. Gardner Humanities Trust 3, 4
The Graco Foundation 3, 4
Virginia A. Groot Foundation 3, 4
Hartz Foundation 3, 4
Hickory Tech Corporation Foundation 3, 4
HRK Foundation 3, 4

Imation 3, 4
Italian American Club Foundation, Inc. 4
Margaret H. and James E. Kelley Foundation, Inc. 3, 4
Mall of America Foundation for Youth 3, 4
Marbrook Foundation 4
The Martinson Foundation 4
Minneapolis Rotary Community Service Foundation 3, 4
Minnesota Power Foundation 3, 4
Minnesota Twins Community Fund 3, 4
The Nelson Family Foundation 3, 4
NFC Foundation 3, 4
North Suburban Community Foundation 3, 4
Ordean Foundation 3, 4
OSilas Foundation 3, 4
Otter Tail Power Company 3, 4
Ben and Jeanne Overman Charitable Trust 3, 4
Owatonna Foundation 3, 4
Patterson Foundation 3, 4
John T. Petters Foundation 3, 4
Philanthrofund Foundation (PFund) 3, 4
The Elizabeth C. Quinlan Foundation, Inc. 1, 2, 3, 4
Rahr Foundation 3, 4

Redwood Area Communities Foundation, Inc. 3, 4
Regis Foundation 3, 4
Saunders Family Foundation 3, 4
Shakopee Mdewakanton Sioux Community 3, 4
Sioux Falls Area Community Foundation 3, 4
SKB Environmental Rosemount Community Trust 3, 4
Slawik Family Foundation 3, 4
St Croix Valley Community Foundation 4
SUPERVALU Foundation 3, 4
TCF Foundation 3, 4
The Toro Company Giving Program 3, 4
Travelers Corporation and Travelers Foundation 3, 4
DeWitt and Caroline Van Evera Foundation 4
The Wasie Foundation 3, 4
WCA Foundation 3, 4
J. A. Wedum Foundation 3, 4
Winona Community Foundation 1, 2, 3, 4

Intended Beneficiary Index

This index includes all funders that identified populations supported by their grantmaking. The index includes five major categories.

Age	.312
Disabled	.313
Gender	.313
Other	.314
Race/Ethnicity	.315

Intended Beneficiary

Age

1 - Infants/babies (under age 5)
2 - Infants/children (ages 0-14)
3 - Children only (5-14 years)
4 - Children and youth (infants-19 years)
5 - Youth/adolescents (ages 14-19)
6 - Adults
7 - Aging/elderly/senior citizens

3M/3M Foundation 6
Allianz Life Insurance Company of North America 4, 6, 7
Ameriprise Financial, Inc. 4, 7
Andersen Corporate Foundation 4, 5, 6, 7
Fred C. and Katherine B. Andersen Foundation 4, 7
Hugh J. Andersen Foundation 4, 5, 6, 7
Arsher Charitable Trust U/A 4
Lillian Wright and C. Emil Berglund Foundation, Inc. 2, 4, 5
W. Glen Boyd Charitable Foundation 4, 5
Bromelkamp Foundation 4
Patrick and Aimee Butler Family Foundation 4
Buuck Family Foundation 1, 5, 6
Cargill Foundation 3
Carolyn Foundation 2, 4, 5
Catholic Community Foundation in the Archdiocese of Saint Paul and Minneapolis 4, 6, 7
Charlson Foundation 5
ClearWay Minnesota 6
Cloquet Educational Foundation 4
Charles and Kathryn Cunningham Family Foundation 4
Dakota Medical Foundation/Dakota Medical Charities 4
The Daulton Foundation 4
Deluxe Corporation Foundation/Deluxe Corporation 1, 2, 3, 4, 5, 6, 7
Joseph C. and Lillian A. Duke Foundation 5
Duluth Superior Area Community Foundation 1, 2, 3, 4, 5, 6, 7
Ecolab Foundation and Corporation 1, 4, 5, 6
Edina Realty Foundation 3, 4, 6
Extendicare Foundation 7
First National Bank of Bemidji Foundation 1, 5
The Jack and Bessie Fiterman Foundation 4
H.B. Fuller Company Foundation 1
Virginia A. Groot Foundation 6

Hartz Foundation 6, 7
Headwaters Foundation for Justice 1, 6, 7
Nevin Huested Foundation for Handicapped Children, Inc. 4
Italian American Club Foundation, Inc. 4, 7
Jerome Foundation 6
The Jostens Foundation 1, 4, 5
John S. and James L. Knight Foundation 1
Kopp Family Foundation 4, 5, 6, 7
Lawson 4
The Charles A. and Anne Morrow Lindbergh Foundation 6
Russell T. Lund Charitable Trust 4
The Luther Family Foundation 4
Macy's North 4
Mall of America Foundation for Youth 4
The Martinson Foundation 4
Mayo Clinic 4, 6
The McKnight Foundation 4, 6
McNeely Foundation 4, 5
Minneapolis Kiwanis Foundation 4
Minneapolis Rotary Community Service Foundation 1, 3, 5, 7
Minnesota Early Learning Foundation 1
The Minnesota Timberwolves FastBreak Foundation 4
Minnesota Twins Community Fund 4
The Laura Jane Musser Fund 4
The Nash Foundation 4, 5
Richard A. Newman Foundation 5, 6
NFC Foundation 4
North Suburban Community Foundation 4
North Suburban Youth Foundation 3, 5
Ordean Foundation 6
Park Nicollet Foundation 2, 4, 5, 6, 7
Patterson Foundation 4
The Pentair Foundation 4, 6, 7
Perkins Foundation 5
Philanthrofund Foundation (PFund) 5, 6, 7

The Jay and Rose Phillips Family Foundation 1, 5, 7
Piper Jaffray 5
RBC Dain Rauscher Foundation 3, 5, 6
Redwood Area Communities Foundation, Inc. 4, 5, 6
Richfield Community Foundation 1, 4, 5, 7
Ripley Memorial Foundation, Inc. 5
The Riverway Foundation 4, 6, 7
Rochester Post Bulletin Charities 4
Sauer Children's Renew Foundation 4
Saunders Family Foundation 4, 6
The Sheltering Arms Foundation 1
The Simmet Foundation 4, 6, 7
Sioux Falls Area Community Foundation 1, 4, 5, 6, 7
R. C. Skoe Foundation 1
Slawik Family Foundation 5
Southwest Initiative Foundation 1, 3, 5, 7
Stevens Square Foundation 7
Sundance Family Foundation and Sundance Pay It Forward Foundation 4, 6
SUPERVALU Foundation 5, 6
TCF Foundation 1, 4, 5, 6
James R. Thorpe Foundation 4, 6, 7
Travelers Corporation and Travelers Foundation 1, 4, 5, 6
Trust for the Meditation Process 5, 6
DeWitt and Caroline Van Evera Foundation 1, 5
The Vos Family Foundation 4
Archie D. and Bertha H. Walker Foundation 4, 6, 7
The Wasie Foundation 4, 6, 7
Wells Fargo Foundation Minnesota 6
Weyerhaeuser Family Foundation, Inc. 1
Frederick and Margaret L. Weyerhaeuser Foundation 5
Whitney Foundation 1, 5, 6, 7
Youthworks! Foundation, Inc. 4

Intended Beneficiary

Disabled

1 - Disabled - general or unspecified disability
2 - Physically disabled
3 - Blind/vision impaired
4 - Deaf/hearing impaired
5 - Mentally/emotionally disabled

Ameriprise Financial, Inc. 1
Andersen Corporate Foundation 1, 2, 5
Fred C. and Katherine B. Andersen Foundation 2, 3, 4, 5
Hugh J. Andersen Foundation 1, 2, 5
The Bentson Foundation 1
W. Glen Boyd Charitable Foundation 1, 2, 3, 4
Patrick and Aimee Butler Family Foundation 4
Buuck Family Foundation 1, 2, 3, 4
Deluxe Corporation Foundation/Deluxe Corporation 1, 2, 3, 4, 5
Duluth Superior Area Community Foundation 1, 2, 3, 4, 5
Ecolab Foundation and Corporation 1
Eddy (Edwin H.) Foundation 4
Frey Foundation 1
Haggerty Family Foundation 2, 5

Hartz Foundation 4, 5
Headwaters Foundation for Justice 1
Anna M. Heilmaier Charitable Foundation 3
Nevin Huested Foundation for Handicapped Children, Inc. 1, 2, 3, 4, 5
Knitcraft - St Croix Foundation, Inc. 2
Kopp Family Foundation 5
Mayo Clinic 1, 2
Minneapolis Rotary Community Service Foundation 1
Minnesota Twins Community Fund 2
Ordean Foundation 2, 5
Park Nicollet Foundation 2, 3, 4, 5
The Pentair Foundation 1, 2, 3, 4, 5
The Jay and Rose Phillips Family Foundation 1, 2, 5
The Sheltering Arms Foundation 1

The Simmet Foundation 1, 2
Sioux Falls Area Community Foundation 1, 2, 3, 4, 5
St Francis Regional Medical Center Foundation 1
SUPERVALU Foundation 1
Tapemark Charity Pro-Am Golf Tournament 1
TCF Foundation 1, 2
James R. Thorpe Foundation 5
Travelers Corporation and Travelers Foundation 1
The Wasie Foundation 2, 3, 5
Wells Fargo Foundation Minnesota 1, 2, 3, 4, 5

Gender

1 - Females - all ages or age unspecified
2 - Female infants/babies (under age 5)
3 - Female children and youth (infants-19 years)
4 - Female youth/adolescents (ages 14-19)
5 - Female adults
6 - Female aging/elderly/senior citizens
7 - Males - all ages or age unspecified
8 - Male infants/babies (under age 5)
9 - Male children and youth (infants-19 years)
10 - Male youth/adolescents (ages 14-19)
11 - Male adults
12 - Male aging/elderly/senior citizens

Allianz Life Insurance Company of North America 1, 7
Ameriprise Financial, Inc. 1, 7
Andersen Corporate Foundation 1, 7
Hugh J. Andersen Foundation 1, 7
Ann Bancroft Foundation 5
W. Glen Boyd Charitable Foundation 1, 3, 5, 6, 9
Patrick and Aimee Butler Family Foundation 1
Buuck Family Foundation 1, 7
Catholic Community Foundation in the Archdiocese of Saint Paul and Minneapolis 5
The Daulton Foundation 5
Deluxe Corporation Foundation/Deluxe Corporation 1, 2, 3, 4, 5, 6, 7, 9, 10, 11, 12
Duluth Superior Area Community Foundation 1, 2, 3, 4, 5, 6, 7, 9, 10, 11, 12
Ecolab Foundation and Corporation 1, 9

First National Bank of Bemidji Foundation 1, 7
Headwaters Foundation for Justice 1, 7
Margaret H. and James E. Kelley Foundation, Inc. 5
Kopp Family Foundation 5
Macy's North 1
The McKnight Foundation 1, 7
Minnesota Business and Professional Women's Foundation 5
Richard A. Newman Foundation 1
The Pentair Foundation 1, 7
Philanthrofund Foundation (PFund) 1, 7
RBC Dain Rauscher Foundation 4, 5, 10, 11
The Simmet Foundation 1, 7
Sioux Falls Area Community Foundation 1
St Francis Regional Medical Center Foundation 1, 7

Travelers Corporation and Travelers Foundation 1, 7
Archie D. and Bertha H. Walker Foundation 1, 7
WCA Foundation 5
Wells Fargo Foundation Minnesota 1, 7
Women's Foundation of Minnesota 1

Intended Beneficiary

Other

1 - Gay/lesbian/bisexual/transgender
2 - Immigrants/newcomers/refugees
3 - Poor/economically disadvantaged
4 - Homeless
5 - Migrant workers
6 - Offenders/ex-offenders
7 - Substance abusers
8 - People with HIV/AIDS
9 - Single parents
10 - Crime/abuse victims
11 - Other

3M/3M Foundation 3, 11
ADC Foundation 11
AgStar Fund for Rural America 11
Allianz Life Insurance Company of North America 1, 2, 3
Ameriprise Financial, Inc. 1, 2, 3, 9, 11
Andersen Corporate Foundation 3, 4
Hugh J. Andersen Foundation 1, 2, 3, 4, 8
Marjorie and V.M. Baich Foundation 11
Ann Bancroft Foundation 11
The Bentson Foundation 3
Best Buy Children's Foundation 11
The Beverly Foundation 3
F.R. Bigelow Foundation 11
W. Glen Boyd Charitable Foundation 1, 2, 3, 4, 5, 8, 9, 10, 11
Bromelkamp Foundation 3, 4
Burdick-Craddick Family Foundation 3
Patrick and Aimee Butler Family Foundation 2, 3, 4, 7, 9
Buuck Family Foundation 3
Cargill Foundation 3
Carolyn Foundation 3
Charlson Foundation 3, 5, 9
ClearWay Minnesota 1, 2, 5
The Daulton Foundation 11
Edwin W. and Catherine M. Davis Foundation 3
Deluxe Corporation Foundation/Deluxe Corporation 1, 2, 3, 4, 9, 10, 11
Duluth Superior Area Community Foundation 1, 2, 3, 4, 5, 6, 7, 8, 9, 10, 11
Ecolab Foundation and Corporation 2, 3, 4, 6, 9
Eddy (Edwin H.) Foundation 11
Edina Realty Foundation 3, 4
First National Bank of Bemidji Foundation 3, 4, 7
Frey Foundation 4

H.B. Fuller Company Foundation 11
Fanny S. Gilfillan Memorial, Incorporated 3
Hardenbergh Foundation 3
Headwaters Foundation for Justice 1, 2, 3, 4, 5, 8
Healthier Minnesota Community Clinic Fund 3, 11
Hiawatha Education Foundation 11
HRK Foundation 11
Italian American Club Foundation, Inc. 3
The Jostens Foundation 3
George Kaplan Memorial Foundation, Incorporated 11
John S. and James L. Knight Foundation 2, 3
Kopp Family Foundation 2, 3, 4
Mardag Foundation 11
Mayo Clinic 1, 2, 3, 4
The McKnight Foundation 2, 3, 9
Medica Foundation 11
The Medtronic Foundation 3
Minneapolis Area Association of Realtors Foundation, Inc. 3
Minneapolis Rotary Community Service Foundation 3, 9, 10
Minnesota Research Fund 11
Minnesota State Bar Foundation 2, 3
Minnesota Twins Community Fund 3
The Laura Jane Musser Fund 11
The Nash Foundation 3, 4
NFC Foundation 3
Ordean Foundation 3, 4, 9, 11
Park Nicollet Foundation 2, 3, 10
Patterson Foundation 3, 4
The Pentair Foundation 1, 2, 3, 4, 5, 6, 7, 8, 9, 10, 11
Perkins Foundation 7
Philanthrofund Foundation (PFund) 1

The Jay and Rose Phillips Family Foundation 1, 2, 3, 4, 8, 9
Piper Jaffray 3
RBC Dain Rauscher Foundation 1, 2, 3, 4, 9
Richfield Community Foundation 2
The Riverway Foundation 3, 9
Sacred Portion Foundation 3
Samsara Foundation 3
Saunders Family Foundation 4
The Sheltering Arms Foundation 2, 3, 4, 5, 9, 11
The Simmet Foundation 3, 4, 9
Sioux Falls Area Community Foundation 1, 2, 3, 4, 7
R. C. Skoe Foundation 3
Southways Foundation 3
Southwest Initiative Foundation 2
St Francis Regional Medical Center Foundation 3
Sundance Family Foundation and Sundance Pay It Forward Foundation 3, 11
SUPERVALU Foundation 3
TCF Foundation 3, 4
James R. Thorpe Foundation 2, 3, 4
Travelers Corporation and Travelers Foundation 1, 2, 3, 4
DeWitt and Caroline Van Evera Foundation 3
Archie D. and Bertha H. Walker Foundation 1, 2, 3, 7, 9
The Wasie Foundation 11
Wells Fargo Foundation Minnesota 2, 3, 4, 5, 10
Whitney Foundation 8
Women's Foundation of Minnesota 1, 2, 3
Youthworks! Foundation, Inc. 3

Race/Ethnicity

1 - Ethnic/racial populations - general
2 - Hispanics/Latinos
3 - Native American/American Indians
4 - African Americans/Blacks
5 - Asian/Pacific Islanders
6 - Ethnic/racial minorities - other

3M/3M Foundation 1
Allianz Life Insurance Company of North America 1
Ameriprise Financial, Inc. 1, 2, 3, 4, 5, 6
Andersen Corporate Foundation 1
Hugh J. Andersen Foundation 1
W. Glen Boyd Charitable Foundation 1, 2, 3, 4, 5, 6
Patrick and Aimee Butler Family Foundation 1
Buuck Family Foundation 1
Carolyn Foundation 1
Charlson Foundation 1
ClearWay Minnesota 1, 2, 3, 4, 5, 6
Deluxe Corporation Foundation/Deluxe Corporation 1, 2, 3, 4, 5, 6
Duluth Superior Area Community Foundation 1, 2, 3, 4, 5, 6

Ecolab Foundation and Corporation 1, 2, 3, 4, 5
First National Bank of Bemidji Foundation 1, 3
Grotto Foundation, Inc. 1, 3
Headwaters Foundation for Justice 1, 2, 3, 4, 5
Healthier Minnesota Community Clinic Fund 1
Indian Land Tenure Foundation 3
John S. and James L. Knight Foundation 1, 2
Macy's North 1
Mayo Clinic 1, 2, 3, 4, 5
The McKnight Foundation 1
The Medtronic Foundation 1
Minnesota Twins Community Fund 1
The Laura Jane Musser Fund 1
Park Nicollet Foundation 1, 2, 4, 5, 6
The Pentair Foundation 1, 2, 3, 4, 5, 6
Philanthrofund Foundation (PFund) 1, 2, 3, 4, 5
The Jay and Rose Phillips Family Foundation 1

RBC Dain Rauscher Foundation 1, 2, 3, 4, 5, 6
Rochester Area Foundation 5
Saunders Family Foundation 1, 2
Shakopee Mdewakanton Sioux Community 3
The Sheltering Arms Foundation 1, 2, 3, 4, 5
Sioux Falls Area Community Foundation 1, 3
Southwest Initiative Foundation 1
St Francis Regional Medical Center Foundation 1
SUPERVALU Foundation 1
Travelers Corporation and Travelers Foundation 1, 2, 3, 4, 5
Archie D. and Bertha H. Walker Foundation 1, 2, 3, 4, 5, 6
Wells Fargo Foundation Minnesota 1, 2, 3, 4, 5
Women's Foundation of Minnesota 6

Officers and Trustees Index

Aakre, Richard; Fanny S. Gilfillan Memorial, Incorporated
Acheson, Mike; Cloquet Educational Foundation
Adams, Jean; Ripley Memorial Foundation, Inc.
Adams, Margaret M.; Ted and Roberta Mann Foundation
Adams, Richard M.; Tennant Foundation
Aho, Colleen; ClearWay Minnesota
Ajaz, Erick; Minneapolis Rotary Community Service Foundation
Albano, John; Travelers Corporation and Travelers Foundation
Alexander, Al; Edina Community Foundation
Alexander, Pamela G.; The Minneapolis Foundation
Allaire, Sandra; Southern Minnesota Initiative Foundation
Allebach, Linda; Todd-Wadena Electric Cooperative Community Trust
Allen, Mike; Winona Community Foundation
Alton, Robert D., Jr.; Hickory Tech Corporation Foundation
Amundson, Barbara; Lloyd and Barbara Amundson Charity Foundation, Inc.
Amundson, L. A.; Lloyd and Barbara Amundson Charity Foundation, Inc.
Andersen, Amy; Elmer L. and Eleanor J. Andersen Foundation
Andersen, Christine E.; Hugh J. Andersen Foundation
Andersen, Eleanor J.; Elmer L. and Eleanor J. Andersen Foundation
Andersen, Julian L.; Elmer L. and Eleanor J. Andersen Foundation
Andersen, Sarah J.; Hugh J. Andersen Foundation
Anderson, Alan C.; Arlin Falck Foundation
   Carl and Verna Schmidt Foundation
Anderson, Andrea C.; P.G.N. Foundation
Anderson, Barb; Initiative Foundation
Anderson, Brad H.; Best Buy Children's Foundation
Anderson, Bruce; CHS Foundation
Anderson, Dean; Central Minnesota Community Foundation
Anderson, Jennifer A.; Deluxe Corporation Foundation/Deluxe Corporation
Anderson, Jim; Initiative Foundation
Anderson, Jonathan; Carl and Verna Schmidt Foundation
Anderson, Keith; Shakopee Mdewakanton Sioux Community
Anderson, M. K.; George A. Hormel Testamentary Trust
Anderson, Mark J.; Impact Foundation, Inc.
Anderson, Philip; Grand Rapids Area Community Foundation
Anderson, Robin; Cloquet Educational Foundation
Anderson, Terri; Northwest Minnesota Foundation
Anding, J. D.; The Charles A. and Anne Morrow Lindbergh Foundation
Andrews, Albert, Jr.; Gray Plant Mooty Foundation
   The Minneapolis Foundation
Andrews, Stephanie; Ripley Memorial Foundation, Inc.
Andrews, Sue; Fargo-Moorhead Area Foundation
Anema, Sophia Gebhard; Luther I. Replogle Foundation
Anfinson, J. A.; George A. Hormel Testamentary Trust
Angell, Janice K.; Mardag Foundation
Anik, Ruby K.; Best Buy Children's Foundation
Annette, Kathleen, M.D.; Blue Cross and Blue Shield of Minnesota Foundation/Blue Cross and Blue Shield of Minnesota
Anthony, Don; CHS Foundation
Apter, Abbot G.; Duluth Superior Area Community Foundation
Archbold, Armar A.; McNeely Foundation
Argento, Celeste; Jundt Family Foundation
Armstrong, Kristin Richard; Carl and Aune Lind Family Foundation
Arnason, Charles; St Croix Valley Community Foundation
Arnold, Patricia; Beim Foundation
Arrigoni, Deborah F.; Lewis and Annie F. Paper Foundation, Inc.
Asta, Catherine; Ripley Memorial Foundation, Inc.
Atwater, Martha; Prospect Creek Foundation
Atwater, H. Brewster, Jr.; Prospect Creek Foundation
Atwood, Barbara; The Nash Foundation

Atwood, Nicolas; The Nash Foundation
Atwood, Thomas; The Nash Foundation
Austad, David; Sioux Falls Area Community Foundation
Aycock, Charles T.; Minneapolis Kiwanis Foundation

Badzin, Fern; Bernard and Fern Badzin Foundation
Baer, Tim; Target
Bagaason, Linda; O'Shaughnessy Foundation
Bahl, Felicia V.; Bahl Foundation
Bahl, Tracy L.; Bahl Foundation
Bahn, Lara; The Vos Family Foundation
Baich, Gregory; Marjorie and V.M. Baich Foundation
Baich, Michael; Marjorie and V.M. Baich Foundation
Bailey, Jerome; Gordon and Margaret Bailey Foundation
Bailey, Joseph; Gordon and Margaret Bailey Foundation
Bailey, Ted; Youthworks! Foundation, Inc.
Baker, Carol; Trust for the Meditation Process
Baker, Doris; Baker Foundation
Baker, Morris T.; Baker Foundation
Baker-Philbin, Mary; Baker Foundation
Bakken, Bradley; Whitney ARCEE Foundation
Bakken, Constance L.; Whitney ARCEE Foundation
Bakken, Eric; Regis Foundation
Bakken, Jeffrey; Whitney ARCEE Foundation
Balma, Frank; Italian American Club Foundation, Inc.
Bancroft, Ann; Ann Bancroft Foundation
Bang, Otto; Edina Community Foundation
Banks, Mark W., M.D.; Blue Cross and Blue Shield of Minnesota Foundation/Blue Cross and Blue Shield of Minnesota
Baratz, Stan; Baratz Family Foundation
Baratz, Zollie; Baratz Family Foundation
Barbe, Linda C.; Minnesota State Bar Foundation
Barcus, Marian; Blandin Foundation
Barone, James P.; Minnesota State Bar Foundation
Barreiro, Terri; Cargill Foundation
Barrett, Myra; The Sheltering Arms Foundation
Barrow, Justin; The Lawrence and Linda Perlman Family Foundation
Barrow, Sara Perlman; The Lawrence and Linda Perlman Family Foundation
Barry, Jean M.; Margaret Rivers Fund
Barsness, W.E.; McNeely Foundation
Bartch, Chris; Gordon and Margaret Bailey Foundation
Barten, Frances M.; Catholic Aid Association Foundation
Bartsch, Glenn; Mary S. Gray Charitable Trust
Bartz, Bob; Winona Community Foundation
Baskerville, H.M., Jr.; The M.B. Foundation
   The Riverway Foundation
Bass, Robert; CHS Foundation
Bassett, Elizabeth; Nevin Huested Foundation for Handicapped Children, Inc.
Bassingthwaite, Dwight; Farmers Union Marketing and Processing Foundation
Bastian, Bernard; Catholic Aid Association Foundation
Bather, Theodore; Minneapolis Rotary Community Service Foundation
Batulis, Ruthe; Eagan Foundation, Incorporated
Bauer, M. J.; The Jostens Foundation
Bauman, Ward; Trust for the Meditation Process
Baumgarten, Allan; George Kaplan Memorial Foundation, Incorporated
Bausch, Maureen; Mall of America Foundation for Youth
Beacom, Miles; Sioux Falls Area Community Foundation
Bean, Bruce W.; Athwin Foundation
Bean, Glen Atherton; Athwin Foundation

Officers and Trustees

Bean, Mary F.; Athwin Foundation
Beard, Brad; Edina Community Foundation
Beck, Ann; Northwest Minnesota Foundation
Becker, Arliss; Fanny S. Gilfillan Memorial, Incorporated
Becker, Laura Lee; The Riverway Foundation
Becker, Terry R.; The Riverway Foundation
Beem, John; Runestone Electric Association Community Trust
Behling, Lisa; Extendicare Foundation
Bell, Duane; Minneapolis Kiwanis Foundation
Bell, Lawrence; Ecolab Foundation and Corporation
Belland, Nancy; Donald and Marjorie Meredith Foundation
Belton, Y.M.; General Mills Community Action
Benet, Jay; Travelers Corporation and Travelers Foundation
Benjamin, Nancy; Wenger Foundation
Bennett, Daniel; The Charles A. and Anne Morrow Lindbergh Foundation
Bensen, M. James; Blandin Foundation
    Minnesota Research Fund
Benson, Donald E.; Ted and Roberta Mann Foundation
Benson, Greg; Fred C. and Katherine B. Andersen Foundation
    Tozer Foundation, Inc.
Bentson, N. Lawrence; The Bentson Foundation
Berbee, Jim; Kopp Family Foundation
Berens, William J.; Noel Foundation
Berg, David; Best Buy Children's Foundation
Berg, Norbert; H.B. Fuller Company Foundation
Bergenstol, Carol; Park Nicollet Foundation
Bergeson, Eric; Northwest Minnesota Foundation
Berggren, Trudy L.; The Graco Foundation
Bergin, Mary J.; Knitcraft - St Croix Foundation, Inc.
Bergman, David; Northwest Minnesota Foundation
Bergquist, Vivian; Cloquet Educational Foundation
Bernatz, Mike; Winona Community Foundation
Berndt, Jana; West Central Initiative
Bernhardson, Ivy S.; Bush Foundation
Bernick, Allen E.; Tozer Foundation, Inc.
Bernstein, Erik P.; The Jay and Rose Phillips Family Foundation
Bernstein, Jim; Healthier Minnesota Community Clinic Fund
Bernstein, Paula P., Ph.D.; The Jay and Rose Phillips Family Foundation
Bernstein, William E., M.D.; The Jay and Rose Phillips Family Foundation
Berquist, Alice; Alice M. O'Brien Foundation
Bertel, John; Dakota Medical Foundation/Dakota Medical Charities
Bertelson, Paul; Youthworks! Foundation, Inc.
Bertschy, Francios; OSilas Foundation
Bertschy, Nannette; OSilas Foundation
Besikof, Marshall K.; The Minneapolis Foundation
Bessette, Andy; Travelers Corporation and Travelers Foundation
Bessinger, Blanton; ClearWay Minnesota
Bettencourt, Neil; Noel Foundation
Biedron, Donna; Ann Bancroft Foundation
Bierman, Larry; Sioux Falls Area Community Foundation
Binger, Anne; The McKnight Foundation
Binger, Ben; The McKnight Foundation
Binger, Erika L.; The McKnight Foundation
Binger, James M.; The McKnight Foundation
Binger, Patricia S.; The McKnight Foundation
Birk, Peg; The McKnight Foundation
Bjorlie, M. T.; George A. Hormel Testamentary Trust
Black Bear, Ben, Jr.; Indian Land Tenure Foundation
Blackburn, Bruce; Virginia A. Groot Foundation
Blade, Christy; Rochester Post Bulletin Charities
Blomme, Edward; Minnesota State Bar Foundation
Blue, Steve; Winona Community Foundation
Blue, Suzanne; Red Wing Shoe Company Foundation
Blumer, Barb; Eagan Foundation, Incorporated
Blute, Michael L.; Mayo Clinic
Boadwine, Lynn; Land O'Lakes Foundation
Boardman, T. A.; 3M/3M Foundation
Boehnen, David; SUPERVALU Foundation
Bogart, Stacy; The Toro Company Giving Program

Bohn, Karen; Blue Cross and Blue Shield of Minnesota Foundation/Blue Cross and Blue Shield of Minnesota
Boman, Peter L.; Duluth Superior Area Community Foundation
Bonine, Bruce; North Suburban Youth Foundation
Bonner, Timothy, M.D.; Blandin Foundation
Bonneur, Dan; Southern Minnesota Initiative Foundation
Bonsall, Susan; Weyerhaeuser Family Foundation, Inc.
Boos, Mary C.; Cote Foundation
    James R. Thorpe Foundation
Borman, Karen; SUPERVALU Foundation
Borton, Kim; Women's Foundation of Minnesota
Bosacker, Lyle T.; Hickory Tech Corporation Foundation
Boss, W. Andrew; The Boss Foundation
    Jerome Foundation
Boushek, Randall; Thrivent Financial for Lutherans Foundation
Bowser, Shirley D.; W.K. Kellogg Foundation
Boynton, Cynthia Binger; The McKnight Foundation
Boyum, Kelly; Fargo-Moorhead Area Foundation
Bracke, James W.; Hickory Tech Corporation Foundation
Bradshaw, James H.; F.R. Bigelow Foundation
Bradshaw, Wilson G.; Bush Foundation
    The Saint Paul Foundation
Brady, John; Mankato Area Foundation
Brainerd, Mary K.; The Saint Paul Foundation
Brataas, Nancy; ClearWay Minnesota
Brautigam, Steven; The Nash Foundation
Bray, Laura; Cottonwood Foundation
Brazas, Joseph; Carl and Aune Lind Family Foundation
Brazas, Karen S.; Carl and Aune Lind Family Foundation
Breedlove, John; SUPERVALU Foundation
Brenden, Blythe A.; Ted and Roberta Mann Foundation
Brenden, John T.; Ted and Roberta Mann Foundation
Brennan, Gerald D.; Catholic Community Foundation in the Archdiocese of Saint Paul and Minneapolis
Brennan, Lee; Hennepin County Bar Foundation
Brenner, Bernard J.; Knitcraft - St Croix Foundation, Inc.
Brenner, Colleen; Knitcraft - St Croix Foundation, Inc.
Brenner, Richard; Cloquet Educational Foundation
Brenny, Bonita; Charity, Inc.
Brentnall, John; Philanthrofund Foundation (PFund)
Brezicka, D. R.; George A. Hormel Testamentary Trust
Bridges, Dorothy J.; The Minneapolis Foundation
Bridges, John Knox; The Charles A. and Anne Morrow Lindbergh Foundation
Briggs, Eleanor; Mary Livingston Griggs and Mary Griggs Burke Foundation
Briggs, Robert; Margaret Rivers Fund
Broback, Carol C.; Ripley Memorial Foundation, Inc.
Broderick, Mary; Catholic Community Foundation in the Archdiocese of Saint Paul and Minneapolis
Broms, Cathy; Moscoe Family Foundation
Bronson, Edgerton; Hardenbergh Foundation
Brookman, Ann; St Croix Valley Community Foundation
Brooks, Conley, Jr.; Marbrook Foundation
Brooks, Conley; Marbrook Foundation
Brooks, Markell; Marbrook Foundation
Brooks, Stephen B.; Marbrook Foundation
Brosnahan, Jan; Winona Community Foundation
Brown, David; Richfield Community Foundation
Brown, Judy Harris; Minnesota State Bar Foundation
Brown, Kevin P.; ING Foundation
Brown, Meghan Binger; The McKnight Foundation
Brown, Pamela L.; Perkins Foundation
Brown, Timothy W.; ING Foundation
Brubaker, Nancy; Rochester Area Foundation
Brusseau, Carolyn J.; F.R. Bigelow Foundation
Buckley, G. W.; 3M/3M Foundation
Buckley, Paul R.; Duluth Superior Area Community Foundation
Budge, Kathleen L.; The Elizabeth C. Quinlan Foundation, Inc.

Officers and Trustees

Bullock, Ellis; Grotto Foundation, Inc.
Burchill, Tim; Winona Community Foundation
Burdick, Allan L.; Burdick-Craddick Family Foundation
Burdick, Lou Brum; Burdick-Craddick Family Foundation
Burdick, Stephen; Burdick-Craddick Family Foundation
Burke, Mary Griggs; Mary Livingston Griggs and Mary Griggs Burke Foundation
Burke, Sandra; Winona Community Foundation
Burleson, Bill; Philanthrofund Foundation (PFund)
Burquest, Thomas; Runestone Electric Association Community Trust
Burrows, Jim; The Donaldson Foundation
Burton, B. Scott; ING Foundation
Bushman, J. L.; 3M/3M Foundation
Busta, Suzanne; Ripley Memorial Foundation, Inc.
Butler, Brigid M.; Patrick and Aimee Butler Family Foundation
Butler, Catherine C.; Patrick and Aimee Butler Family Foundation
Butler, Cecilia M.; Patrick and Aimee Butler Family Foundation
Butler, John K.; Patrick and Aimee Butler Family Foundation
    Catholic Community Foundation in the Archdiocese of Saint Paul and Minneapolis
Butler, Matt; Fargo-Moorhead Area Foundation
Butler, Patricia M.; Patrick and Aimee Butler Family Foundation
Butler, Patrick; Patrick and Aimee Butler Family Foundation
Butler, Paul S.; Patrick and Aimee Butler Family Foundation
Butler, Peter M.; Patrick and Aimee Butler Family Foundation
Butler, Sandra K.; Patrick and Aimee Butler Family Foundation
Butzer, Bart; Target
Buuck, David A.; Buuck Family Foundation
Buuck, Gail P.; Buuck Family Foundation
Buuck, John R.; Buuck Family Foundation
Buuck, Robert E.; Buuck Family Foundation
Buyse, L. John; Fidelis Foundation
Bye, Julianne; Minnesota Twins Community Fund
Byom, John; Park Nicollet Foundation

Cade, Brian; Cade Foundation
Cade, Kevin; Cade Foundation
Cahn, Becky; The Donaldson Foundation
Calabresi, Guido; Carolyn Foundation
Campbell, Jon; Wells Fargo Foundation Minnesota
Campbell, Keith; Securian Foundation/Securian Financial Group
Campbell, William E.; St Croix Valley Community Foundation
Capp, Lisa; Martin and Esther Capp Foundation
Carey, Dan; Alex Stern Family Foundation
Carey, Jennifer L.; Duluth Superior Area Community Foundation
Carlos, Laurie; Jerome Foundation
Carlson, Barbara Z.; Park Nicollet Foundation
Carlson, Carl; Sauer Children's Renew Foundation
Carlson, Dennis; CHS Foundation
Carlson, Kristin; Cade Foundation
Carlson, Mimi; Southern Minnesota Initiative Foundation
Carlson, Robert; Farmers Union Marketing and Processing Foundation
Carmody, Jack; Sioux Falls Area Community Foundation
Caruthers, Carol; Frederick and Margaret L. Weyerhaeuser Foundation
Casey, Lynn; The Minneapolis Foundation
Casey, Steve; SKB Environmental Rosemount Community Trust
Cassellius, Christine; Eagan Foundation, Incorporated
Castillo, Lupe; Philanthrofund Foundation (PFund)
Cattoor, Kevin; Minnesota Twins Community Fund
Chang, Mo; Lillian Wright and C. Emil Berglund Foundation, Inc.
Chapdelaine, Donald; SKB Environmental Rosemount Community Trust
Cheney, Arta; The Irwin Andrew Porter Foundation
Cheung Ho, Yvonne; The Minneapolis Foundation
Christensen, David; Mankato Area Foundation
Christensen, Ray, M.D.; Healthier Minnesota Community Clinic Fund
Christian, Chuck; Initiative Foundation
Christianson, Dan; Southern Minnesota Initiative Foundation
Christopherson, Mark; Edina Realty Foundation
Chronister, Mark; The Minneapolis Foundation

Ciganik, Gina; Ripley Memorial Foundation, Inc.
Cihak, Connie; The Cooperative Foundation
Ciresi, Michael V.; Robins, Kaplan, Miller & Ciresi, L.L.P. Foundation for Education, Public Health & Social Justice
Cirillo, A. C., Jr.; 3M/3M Foundation
Clapp, Tamsin; Winona Foundation
Clark, David A.; Sacred Portion Foundation
Clark, John L.; Sacred Portion Foundation
Clark, Nancy E.; Sacred Portion Foundation
Clifford, John; Travelers Corporation and Travelers Foundation
Clusiau, David; Northland Foundation
Clutter, David, M.D.; Dakota Medical Foundation/Dakota Medical Charities
Cobb, Virginia; Luther I. Replogle Foundation
Cocke, Dudley; Bush Foundation
Coffey, Sheba; Women's Foundation of Minnesota
Coleman, Kim; Philanthrofund Foundation (PFund)
Collins, Arthur D.; The Medtronic Foundation
Collins, Billy; Minnesota Twins Community Fund
Collins, Brian; Indian Land Tenure Foundation
Collins, Theodore J.; Warren Foundation
Collins, William, Jr.; Blue Cross and Blue Shield of Minnesota Foundation/Blue Cross and Blue Shield of Minnesota
Cone, Roger; CDF Foundation
Connolly, Elizabeth A.; Prospect Creek Foundation
Connors, KC; Ripley Memorial Foundation, Inc.
Conover, Margo; Beim Foundation
Constable, Donald M.; The Constable Family Foundation
Constable, Tracy B.; The Constable Family Foundation
Contreras Edin, Gloria; Initiative Foundation
    Women's Foundation of Minnesota
Conzemius, Norbert; Catholic Community Foundation in the Archdiocese of Saint Paul and Minneapolis
Coons, Darryl; Lloyd K. Johnson Foundation
Cooper, William A.; TCF Foundation
Copeland, Lisa W.; Hugh J. Andersen Foundation
Copp, Betsey; Carolyn Foundation
Corcoran, Dick; Sioux Falls Area Community Foundation
Corey, Jeff; Northland Foundation
Corness, John; The Polaris Foundation
Cornwall, Sue; Elizabeth Callender King Foundation
Cosgrove, Dodd; Arthur and David Cosgrove Memorial Fund
Cosgrove, R.C., Jr ; Arthur and David Cosgrove Memorial Fund
Cote, James Randolph; Cote Foundation
Cote, Robert C; Cote Foundation
    James R. Thorpe Foundation
Cote, Samual Ruggles; Cote Foundation
Cote, Samuel D.; James R. Thorpe Foundation
Covington, Alec; NFC Foundation
Cowles, Charles F.; Unity Avenue Foundation
Cowles, Constance M.; Unity Avenue Foundation
Cowles, Jane S.; Unity Avenue Foundation
Cowles, John, III; The Saint Paul Foundation
    Unity Avenue Foundation
Cowles, John, Jr.; Unity Avenue Foundation
Cowles, Michael A.; Duluth Superior Area Community Foundation
Cowles, Page Knudsen; Unity Avenue Foundation
Cowles, Sage Fuller ; Unity Avenue Foundation
Coyte, Julia D.; The Hubbard Broadcasting Foundation
Crabtree, Sam; Fidelis Foundation
Craddick, Helen S ; Burdick-Craddick Family Foundation
Craig, Myrita P.; Hickory Tech Corporation Foundation
Crane, Lucia L.; The Elizabeth C. Quinlan Foundation, Inc.
Craven, Julie; Minnesota Twins Community Fund
Crawford, Dale; WCA Foundation
Crawford, Ed; Northland Foundation
Crispin, Robert; ING Foundation
Croft, D. L.; Fred C. and Katherine B. Andersen Foundation
Crooks, Glynn A.; Shakopee Mdewakanton Sioux Community

Officers and Trustees

Crooks, Stanley R.; Shakopee Mdewakanton Sioux Community
Crosby, Andrew; Carolyn Foundation
Crosby, David P.; Longview Foundation
Crosby, Ella P.; Longview Foundation
    Southways Foundation
Crosby, Harriett; Carolyn Foundation
Crosby, Stewart F.; Carolyn Foundation
Crosby, Thomas M., Jr.; Carolyn Foundation
    Faegre & Benson Foundation
    Longview Foundation
    Ted and Roberta Mann Foundation
Crosby, Timothy B.; Carolyn Foundation
Crosby, Sumner McKnight, III; Carolyn Foundation
Crow, Jon K.; Southways Foundation
Crownhart, Stacy; Red Wing Shoe Company Foundation
Cuddyer, Michael; Minnesota Twins Community Fund
Cullen, Melissa; Gordon and Margaret Bailey Foundation
Cunningham, Charles G.; Charles and Kathryn Cunningham Family Foundation
Cunningham, Greg C.; Charles and Kathryn Cunningham Family Foundation
Cunningham, Kathryn M.; Charles and Kathryn Cunningham Family Foundation
Cuperus, Ron; First National Bank of Bemidji Foundation
Curb, B. Scott; First National Bank of Bemidji Foundation
Curlee, John; Eagan Foundation, Incorporated
Curme, June; Arthur and David Cosgrove Memorial Fund
Curtin, John D.; P.G.N. Foundation
Curtin, John S.; P.G.N. Foundation
Curtin, Paula S.; P.G.N. Foundation

Dabbs, Dwayne; Extendicare Foundation
Dahl, Marilyn; Wells Fargo Foundation Minnesota
Dallas, Terri; The Cooperative Foundation
Dally, Linda; Donald G. Gardner Humanities Trust
Daniels, Carol; Noel Foundation
Danielson, Paul (Wally); St Francis Regional Medical Center Foundation
Darcy, R.G.; General Mills Community Action
Dass, Joyce; Southwest Initiative Foundation
Dathe, Mary Jo; Osterud-Winter Foundation
Daugherty, Kelly; Extendicare Foundation
Daulton, Patrick J.; The Daulton Foundation
Daulton, Renee T.; The Daulton Foundation
Daulton-Saad, Julie; The Daulton Foundation
Davidson, Gretchen D.; Mardag Foundation
Davis, Bill; Southern Minnesota Initiative Foundation
Davis, Debra; Philanthrofund Foundation (PFund)
Davis, Gale Lansing; Mary Livingston Griggs and Mary Griggs Burke Foundation
Davis, John L..; Edwin W. and Catherine M. Davis Foundation
Davis, Mary E.; Edwin W. and Catherine M. Davis Foundation
Davis, Melissa B.; Weyerhaeuser Family Foundation, Inc.
Davis, Mitchell, Jr.; ClearWay Minnesota
Davis, Robert S.; Hardenbergh Foundation
Davis, Susan; Wells Fargo Foundation Minnesota
Dayton, Charles; Elmer L. and Eleanor J. Andersen Foundation
Debele, Gary; Hennepin County Bar Foundation
Decker, Laura Sherman; Baker Foundation
Decker, Michael L.; Baker Foundation
Deeney, Gerald D.; The Hubbard Broadcasting Foundation
DeGrio, Lynn; Grand Rapids Area Community Foundation
Deikel, Beverly; The Beverly Foundation
    Fingerhut Family Foundation
Deikel, Theodore; The Deikel Family Foundation
Deinema, Caroline; Sioux Falls Area Community Foundation
Delkoski, M. P.; 3M/3M Foundation
Dempsey, Jack; The Pentair Foundation
Dena Torres, Luis Mario; ADC Foundation
Dethomasis, Brother Louis; The Minneapolis Foundation

Deuth, Roger; Affiliated Community Health Foundation
Devlin, Barbara; Richfield Community Foundation
Dewitt, Gregory; Lillian Wright and C. Emil Berglund Foundation, Inc.
Dickie, Elizabeth; Luther I. Replogle Foundation
Didier, Alex; Central Minnesota Community Foundation
Diebel, Terry; Gertrude R. Shiely Charitable Trust
Diedrich, Judith; Salem Foundation, Inc.
Dienhart, Mark; Minnesota Twins Community Fund
Dieringer, Stephen; Minneapolis Area Association of Realtors Foundation, Inc.
Dietz, William; The Nash Foundation
Dille, Roland; Fargo-Moorhead Area Foundation
Dillon, Grethe Langeland; Edina Community Foundation
Dimond, Bob; NFC Foundation
Diver, Karen; Blandin Foundation
Dobson, Charles C.; Carolyn Foundation
Doidge, Vera; Fanny S. Gilfillan Memorial, Incorporated
Domaille, Nancy; Rochester Area Foundation
Domke, John; SKB Environmental Rosemount Community Trust
Domm, Bruce, M.D.; Dakota Medical Foundation/Dakota Medical Charities
Donaldson, Phil; Andersen Corporate Foundation
Donerkiel, Linda Leuthold; Steven C. Leuthold Family Foundation
Dong, Z.; George A. Hormel Testamentary Trust
Donner, James P.; Gertrude R. Shiely Charitable Trust
Donohue, Elise R.; The Charles A. Weyerhaeuser Memorial Foundation
Dordell, Tim; The Toro Company Giving Program
Dorn, Gail; Target
Dorn, Paul; Think Community Foundation
Dorry, Barbara; Northland Foundation
Dorsey, Jacqueline A.; The Saint Paul Foundation
Doss, Larry; West Central Initiative
Doucette, Lee; Minneapolis Area Association of Realtors Foundation, Inc.
Dougherty, Bonnie S.; Frances Curran Foundation, Inc.
Dovenberg, Dave; Dovenberg Family Foundation
Dovenberg, Jean Marie; Dovenberg Family Foundation
Dovenberg, Kirsten; Dovenberg Family Foundation
Dovenberg, Robert; Dovenberg Family Foundation
Dowd, Bill; Extendicare Foundation
Draxler, Patty; St Croix Valley Community Foundation
Dreier, Jeffrey; Runestone Electric Association Community Trust
Driscoll, Elizabeth S.; Driscoll Foundation
Driscoll, John B.; Weyerhaeuser Family Foundation, Inc.
Driscoll, W. John; Driscoll Foundation
Drouble, Don; Todd-Wadena Electric Cooperative Community Trust
Duea, Steve; The Pentair Foundation
Duffy, Joe; Rochester Area Foundation
Dufresne-Harden, Raphael; Richfield Community Foundation
Duggan, Teresa O'Shaughnessy; I. A. O'Shaughnessy Foundation, Incorporated
Dumas, Gina; Minneapolis Area Association of Realtors Foundation, Inc.
Duniway, Sarah; Gray Plant Mooty Foundation
Dunlap, Susannah B.; Archie D. and Bertha H. Walker Foundation
Dupuis, Virgil; Indian Land Tenure Foundation
Dusek, Ivan; ClearWay Minnesota
Dwight, Thomas; Casey Albert T. O'Neil Foundation
Dwyer, Joe; Eagan Foundation, Incorporated
Dwyer, Timothy J.; Margaret H. and James E. Kelley Foundation, Inc.
Dybsky, Thomas J.; Tennant Foundation
Dybvig, Mary; Nevin Huested Foundation for Handicapped Children, Inc.
Dyke, Pete; The Pentair Foundation

Eberhage, Mark; Extendicare Foundation
Eberhart, Cornelia Ober; Mardag Foundation
Eckenberg, Gary; ClearWay Minnesota
Eckles, Neil; Southern Minnesota Initiative Foundation
Eddy, Laura; Winona Community Foundation
Edwards, Rodney E.; Eddy (Edwin H.) Foundation

Officers and Trustees

Edwards, Trace; Minneapolis Area Association of Realtors Foundation, Inc.
Eggum, Mari Oyanagi; Ripley Memorial Foundation, Inc.
Ehman, Richard; Mayo Clinic
Eilers, Ronald E.; Deluxe Corporation Foundation/Deluxe Corporation
Eisberg, John F.; The Minneapolis Foundation
Eisberg, John F.; Robins, Kaplan, Miller & Ciresi, L.L.P. Foundation for Education, Public Health & Social Justice
Eischens, Curt; CHS Foundation
Eisenbeis, Jay; Dakota Medical Foundation/Dakota Medical Charities
Elder, Alfred O.; Catholic Community Foundation in the Archdiocese of Saint Paul and Minneapolis
Elkins, Scott; The Irwin Andrew Porter Foundation
Ellingworth, Rick; Southwest Initiative Foundation
Ellis, Gary; The Medtronic Foundation
Elwell, Joanne; Charity, Inc.
Engasser, Mark; Charles Engasser Memorial Foundation, Inc.
Engebretsen, Robert A.; The Saint Paul Foundation
Engel, Susan S.; First National Bank of Bemidji Foundation
Enger, Robert; Minnesota State Bar Foundation
Engh, R.; The Valspar Foundation
Engholm, Kerri; North Suburban Youth Foundation
Erickson, Kirby; ClearWay Minnesota
Erickson, Nancy; Park Nicollet Foundation
Erickson, Sandy; Eagan Foundation, Incorporated
Erlandson, Romy P. Jundt ; Jundt Family Foundation
Esber, Betsy; DeWitt and Caroline Van Evera Foundation
Ettinger, J. M.; George A. Hormel Testamentary Trust
Evans, Christine B.; The Nash Foundation
Evavold, Dale; Arlin Falck Foundation
Evert, Diana; ELEOS Foundation
Evert, Harry; ELEOS Foundation

Fandrei, Phil; Acorn Foundation
Farrell, Cathy; Dwight D. Opperman Foundation
Farrish, John R.; Headwaters Foundation for Justice
Fasteland, Tom; Grand Rapids Area Community Foundation
Faulkner, Heather; Ann Bancroft Foundation
Federighi, Christine; Virginia A. Groot Foundation
Feragen, Jody; Southern Minnesota Initiative Foundation
Ferrara, Ted; Minneapolis Kiwanis Foundation
Ferraro, Kris; Blandin Foundation
   Grand Rapids Area Community Foundation
Ferrell, Charles S.; Faegre & Benson Foundation
Ferris, Bruce; Runestone Electric Association Community Trust
Fife, Jim; Land O'Lakes Foundation
Filipovitch, Tony; Mankato Area Foundation
Finch, Mike; Healthier Minnesota Community Clinic Fund
Fingerhut, Ronald; The Beverly Foundation
   Fingerhut Family Foundation
Fingerhut, Rose; Fingerhut Family Foundation
Fink, Bruce; George Kaplan Memorial Foundation, Incorporated
Fink, Peter; Todd-Wadena Electric Cooperative Community Trust
Finkelstein, Paul; Regis Foundation
Finley, Joseph M.; Leonard, Street and Deinard Foundation
Finstad, Keith; Central Minnesota Community Foundation
Fisher, Curt; Mankato Area Foundation
Fisher, David; ClearWay Minnesota
   G&K Services Foundation
Fiterman, Ben; The Jack and Bessie Fiterman Foundation
Fiterman, Carolyn D.; CDF Foundation
Fiterman, Linda; The Jack and Bessie Fiterman Foundation
Fiterman, Michael; The Jack and Bessie Fiterman Foundation
Fitts, Harriet W.; Archie D. and Bertha H. Walker Foundation
Fitts, William S.; Archie D. and Bertha H. Walker Foundation
Fitzgerald, Gloria; The Hermundslie Foundation
Fitzgibbons, Betty; Lloyd K. Johnson Foundation
Flores, Tessa Sage ; Unity Avenue Foundation
Floyd, Paul; Hennepin County Bar Foundation

Floyd, Tom; Think Community Foundation
Flynn, Archbishop Harry; Catholic Community Foundation in the Archdiocese of Saint Paul and Minneapolis
Flynn, Dorothy; WCA Foundation
Foot, Silas B., III; Red Wing Shoe Company Foundation
Forbes, Glenn S.; Mayo Clinic
Ford, Christopher; OSilas Foundation
Ford, Corri; Minnesota Twins Community Fund
Ford, David C.; OSilas Foundation
Ford, Durand G.; OSilas Foundation
Ford, Jamie; Cottonwood Foundation
Ford, Margaret; OSilas Foundation
Ford, Olivia C.; OSilas Foundation
Ford, Silas M., III; OSilas Foundation
Ford-Werling, Kimberly; OSilas Foundation
Forman, Brenda; The Cooperative Foundation
Forman, Carolyn D.; Lewis and Annie F. Paper Foundation, Inc.
Forman, James D.; Lewis and Annie F. Paper Foundation, Inc.
Forman, Willis M.; Lewis and Annie F. Paper Foundation, Inc.
Forrester, Margretta; DeWitt and Caroline Van Evera Foundation
Forro, David; Hennepin County Bar Foundation
Forster, Barbara; Women's Foundation of Minnesota
Fortner, Larry; Ordean Foundation
Foster, Andrew; Mankato Area Foundation
Fox, Donald Whipple; Philanthrofund Foundation (PFund)
Fox, Robert; St Francis Regional Medical Center Foundation
Francis, Michael; Target
Frank, Steven J.; Park Nicollet Foundation
Franklin, Jim; Ecolab Foundation and Corporation
Fratzke, Katherine Buuck; Buuck Family Foundation
Frederick, Phil; Otto C. and Elsie Ewert Charitable Trust
Freeburg, Carol; WCA Foundation
Freese, Dr. Wayne; Southwest Initiative Foundation
Fremming, Michele; Edina Realty Foundation
Fremont, Lisa M.; Edwin W. and Catherine M. Davis Foundation
   Weyerhaeuser Family Foundation, Inc.
French, Janel W.; The Graco Foundation
Frey, Eugene U.; Frey Foundation
Frey, James R.; Frey Foundation
   The Saint Paul Foundation
Frey, John J.; Frey Foundation
Frey, Mary F.; Frey Foundation
Frey, Mary W.; Frey Foundation
Frias, Luz Maria; Blue Cross and Blue Shield of Minnesota Foundation/Blue Cross and Blue Shield of Minnesota
Friswold, Fred; Minneapolis Rotary Community Service Foundation
Fritel, Steve; CHS Foundation
Frommelt, Julie A.; Gray Plant Mooty Foundation

Gaalswyk, Kathy; Blue Cross and Blue Shield of Minnesota Foundation/Blue Cross and Blue Shield of Minnesota
Gabriel, Sherine E.; Mayo Clinic
Gackle, George D.; Rahr Foundation
Gage, Barbara C.; The Curtis L. Carlson Family Foundation
Gage, Geoffrey C.; The Curtis L. Carlson Family Foundation
Gage, Gina M.; The Curtis L. Carlson Family Foundation
Gage, Richard C.; The Curtis L. Carlson Family Foundation
Gaines, Priscilla P.; Southways Foundation
Galbraith, Mary; WCA Foundation
Gallagher, Ellen Mitchell; Marjorie Weil and Marvin Edward Mitchell Foundation
Gallivan, Carol J.; Sauer Children's Renew Foundation
Gallivan, Karen P.; The Graco Foundation
Gallmon, Rev. Albert, Jr.; Robins, Kaplan, Miller & Ciresi, L.L.P. Foundation for Education, Public Health & Social Justice
Galowitz, Tracey; Tozer Foundation, Inc.
Galvin, Chris; St Croix Valley Community Foundation
Ganey, Anne; Mankato Area Foundation
Gardner, George W.; The Janice Gardner Foundation

Officers and Trustees

Gardner, Jacqui Catherine; The Janice Gardner Foundation
    Ripley Memorial Foundation, Inc.
Garvis, Marlene; Hennepin County Bar Foundation
Gebhard, Paul R.S.; Luther I. Replogle Foundation
Geiger, Gary; Southwest Initiative Foundation
Geis, Mari; The Elizabeth C. Quinlan Foundation, Inc.
Genereaux, Bruce; OSilas Foundation
Genereaux, Olivia J.; OSilas Foundation
Gerdes, Tom; Extendicare Foundation
Gernander, Kent A.; Elizabeth Callender King Foundation
Geronime, Karen; The Donaldson Foundation
Gertz, Morrie A.; Mayo Clinic
Getsch, David D.; Getsch Charitable Trust
Getsch, Dianne H.; Getsch Charitable Trust
Getsch, Edward W.; Getsch Charitable Trust
Getsch, John H.; Getsch Charitable Trust
Getsch, Marilyn; Getsch Charitable Trust
Getsch, Marjorie D.; Getsch Charitable Trust
Giefer, Michael J.; Driscoll Foundation
Giles, Eric; Indian Land Tenure Foundation
Gillespie, Jim; St Croix Valley Community Foundation
Gillett, Lowell; George W. Neilson Foundation
Gillstrom, M. F.; Fred C. and Katherine B. Andersen Foundation
Gillum, Roderick D.; W.K. Kellogg Foundation
Gilmore, Kent; The Jostens Foundation
Gish, Brent; Minnesota Twins Community Fund
Givens, Archie, Jr.; H.B. Fuller Company Foundation
Givens Copeland, Roxanne; Bush Foundation
Gjerstad, Linda; Todd-Wadena Electric Cooperative Community Trust
Glaeser, Elizabeth; The Janice Gardner Foundation
Glaser, Barbara L.; Jane N. Mooty Foundation Trust
Glaser, Kenneth C.; Jane N. Mooty Foundation Trust
Glover, Gleason E.; The Irwin Andrew Porter Foundation
Godfrey, Sarah; The Laura Jane Musser Fund
Goettel, Debbie; Richfield Community Foundation
Goetz, Julie; The Jostens Foundation
Goff, Cindy; Healthier Minnesota Community Clinic Fund
Goff, Janel M.; Ripley Memorial Foundation, Inc.
Goff, Phyllis Rawls; Mardag Foundation
Goldammer, Vance; Sioux Falls Area Community Foundation
Goldberg, Jay; The Irwin Andrew Porter Foundation
Goldfine, Beverly; Ben and Jeanne Overman Charitable Trust
Goldfine, Manley; Ben and Jeanne Overman Charitable Trust
Goldfine, Steve; Ben and Jeanne Overman Charitable Trust
Goldstein, Ira S.; Unity Avenue Foundation
Goldstein, Steve; Bush Foundation
Gomez, Jesse Bethke; The Minneapolis Foundation
Goodwin, Morris, Jr.; The Minneapolis Foundation
Gordon, Marc; Best Buy Children's Foundation
Gordon, Sara; TEAM Foundation
Goss, Marguerite; Carolyn Foundation
Gothberg, Bridget; Park Nicollet Foundation
Gould, Cara; The Sheltering Arms Foundation
Gould, Holly; Extendicare Foundation
Gourneau, Dwight; Bush Foundation
Grabarski, Robert; CHS Foundation
Graham, Edmund C.; Carolyn Foundation
Graham, Gail; The Cooperative Foundation
Graham, Tom; Elizabeth Callender King Foundation
Grant, Lori; Gordon and Margaret Bailey Foundation
Gray, Jerry; Wells Fargo Foundation Minnesota
Green, Joanne; Women's Foundation of Minnesota
Green-Rupert, Aretha; Ripley Memorial Foundation, Inc.
Greenside, Peg; Grand Rapids Area Community Foundation
Greer, Lucie C.; Weyerhaeuser Family Foundation, Inc.
Gregory, Dennis; Central Minnesota Community Foundation
Greupner, James R.; Hess Kline Foundation, Inc.
    Horst M. Rechelbacher Foundation

Griffith, Bronwyn A. E.; Archie D. and Bertha H. Walker Foundation
Griffith, John; Target
Griffith, Roger; The Minnesota Timberwolves FastBreak Foundation
Griffith, Sima; The Minneapolis Foundation
Grigal, Dennis; The Donaldson Foundation
Griggs, C. E. Bayliss; Mary Livingston Griggs and Mary Griggs Burke Foundation
Grindberg, Tony; Dakota Medical Foundation/Dakota Medical Charities
Groff, Keralyn; H.B. Fuller Company Foundation
Groot, Candice B.; Virginia A. Groot Foundation
Grossman, Beverly N.; N. Bud and Beverly Grossman Foundation
Grossman, N. Bud; N. Bud and Beverly Grossman Foundation
Growe, Joan Anderson; The Minneapolis Foundation
Gruenes, Dave; Initiative Foundation
Grundman, Vincent; The Elizabeth C. Quinlan Foundation, Inc.
Gruver, Nancy; Women's Foundation of Minnesota
Grzywinski, Joan A.; The Saint Paul Foundation
Guenzel, Elizabeth S.; William Wood Skinner Foundation
Guerrero-Anderson, Esperanza; Bush Foundation
Gustafson, Michael; The Cooperative Foundation
Gutierrez, Carrie; Ann Bancroft Foundation
Guy, William; Fargo-Moorhead Area Foundation
Guyer, Cricket; Grand Rapids Area Community Foundation

Haberer, Wyman; Martinson Clinic Foundation
Haddad, Anne; Headwaters Foundation for Justice
Hadley, Katherine; The Minneapolis Foundation
Hagedorn, Jessica; Jerome Foundation
Hagen, Jerome; Runestone Electric Association Community Trust
Hagen, Sheila; SUPERVALU Foundation
Hager, Robert; Northwest Minnesota Foundation
Haggerty, Daniel J.; Haggerty Family Foundation
Haggerty, John; Haggerty Family Foundation
Haggerty, Ruth; Haggerty Family Foundation
Hahn, Wilfried J.; Knitcraft - St Croix Foundation, Inc.
Hain, Kelly; Grand Rapids Area Community Foundation
Hale, Arvel; Indian Land Tenure Foundation
Hall, Debra J.; The Graco Foundation
Hall, Loran; Central Minnesota Community Foundation
Hallin, Gayle; Healthier Minnesota Community Clinic Fund
Hallward, Clare; The Charles A. and Anne Morrow Lindbergh Foundation
Hamilton, R. J.; Fredrikson & Byron Foundation
Hancock, James; Minneapolis Rotary Community Service Foundation
Hanley, Joshua; Richfield Community Foundation
Hansen, Cindy; Northland Foundation
Hansen, Karen; St Croix Valley Community Foundation
Hansen, Robert; Mae and Sylvester Weiss Foundation
Hanson, Carl; Minneapolis Kiwanis Foundation
Hanson, Gordon; Richfield Community Foundation
Hanson, Jonathon R.; Federated Insurance Foundation, Inc.
Hanson, Lee; Initiative Foundation
Hanson, Mark; Acorn Foundation
Hanson, Shirly; Acorn Foundation
Harberts, Jane; Lloyd and Barbara Amundson Charity Foundation, Inc.
Harding, Martha; St Croix Valley Community Foundation
Hardy, H. Michael; Alex Stern Family Foundation
Harkess, Paul; Rochester Area Foundation
Harmon, Robin; Park Nicollet Foundation
Harris, Barney W.; Lewis and Annie F. Paper Foundation, Inc.
Harris, Lewis R.; Lewis and Annie F. Paper Foundation, Inc.
Harrison, Susan; The Pentair Foundation
Hartert, Rita; Osterud-Winter Foundation
Hartman, Elaine; Nevin Huested Foundation for Handicapped Children, Inc.
Hartmann, Tracy; Fargo-Moorhead Area Foundation
Hartwell, Lucy B.; Smikis Foundation
Hartz, Onealee; Hartz Foundation
Harwood, Nevin R.; Gray Plant Mooty Foundation
Hasbargen, Vernae; ClearWay Minnesota

Officers and Trustees

Haselow, Robert E.; Park Nicollet Foundation
Hasnedl, Jerry; CHS Foundation
Hatch, Robert W.; Minnesota Research Fund
Hatfield, Dianna; West Central Initiative
Hatlen, Beverly J.; Hatlen Foundation
Hatlen, Kari; Hatlen Foundation
Hatlen, Roe; Hatlen Foundation
Haugen, Joel, M.D.; Dakota Medical Foundation/Dakota Medical Charities
Haugen, Ronalee; Fredrikson & Byron Foundation
Haugen, Vicki; Tennant Foundation
Hausman, Alice; Lillian Wright and C. Emil Berglund Foundation, Inc.
Hawkins, Daniel; Headwaters Foundation for Justice
Hawn, Elizabeth; Stevens Square Foundation
Hawtin, Michael; ADC Foundation
Hayden, Don; Southern Minnesota Initiative Foundation
Hayden, Henry; Minneapolis Kiwanis Foundation
Hayes, Gary; Winona Community Foundation
Hayes, Jim; HRK Foundation
Hayes, Katherine D. R.; HRK Foundation
Hayman, Dave; Thrivent Financial for Lutherans Foundation
Hedges, Tom; Eagan Foundation, Incorporated
Hefte, Richard C.; Roger L. and Agnes C. Dell Charitable (Trust 1)
   Roger L. and Agnes C. Dell Charitable (Trust 2)
Hegelund, Barbara; Lloyd and Barbara Amundson Charity Foundation, Inc.
Heidmann, Julia L. W.; Frederick and Margaret L. Weyerhaeuser Foundation
Heiling, Duane; Redwood Area Communities Foundation, Inc.
Heimerman, Quentin O.; Hardenbergh Foundation
Heineman, Greg; Sioux Falls Area Community Foundation
Heino, Mike; Todd-Wadena Electric Cooperative Community Trust
Heinz, Jim; Wells Fargo Foundation Minnesota
Helble, Donna; Winona Community Foundation
Helmberger, Joan; Richfield Community Foundation
Heltzer, James R.; Mardag Foundation
Hemmady, Gokul; ADC Foundation
Hemmelgarn, Kathy; Catholic Aid Association Foundation
Hendrickson, Richard; Minnesota State Bar Foundation
Hendrixson, Peter; The Dorsey & Whitney Foundation
Her, Kao Ly Ilean; Women's Foundation of Minnesota
Herman, David C.; Mayo Clinic
Hermundslie, Carol; The Hermundslie Foundation
Hermundslie, Gerold; The Hermundslie Foundation
Hernandez-Mohr, Saanii; Women's Foundation of Minnesota
Heron, James H.; Archie D. and Bertha H. Walker Foundation
Herrick, Greg; The Charles A. and Anne Morrow Lindbergh Foundation
Hertzberg, Edwina; Northland Foundation
Herzog, Kim; Charlson Foundation
Hesdorffer, Lisa Schmoker; Schmoker Family Foundation
Hewitt, Brad; Thrivent Financial for Lutherans Foundation
Hewitt, Mark; Northwest Minnesota Foundation
Heydinger, Dr. Richard B.; F.R. Bigelow Foundation
Heymann, Peter E.; Weyerhaeuser Family Foundation, Inc.
Hibbard, John; The Hermundslie Foundation
Higinbotham, Joan; Ann Bancroft Foundation
   Women's Foundation of Minnesota
Hilger, Andy; Central Minnesota Community Foundation
Hill, Kathrine E.; Grotto Foundation, Inc.
Hill, Louis Fors; Grotto Foundation, Inc.
Hill, Louis Shea; Grotto Foundation, Inc.
Hill, Pete; Central Minnesota Community Foundation
Hill, Robert L.; Rochester Area Foundation
   Rochester Post Bulletin Charities
Hill, Scott; Grotto Foundation, Inc.
Himan, Dennis; The Toro Company Giving Program
Hoag, JoAnn; Ordean Foundation
Hoard, Heidi; Tennant Foundation
Hoard, Weston; Unity Avenue Foundation
Hockert, Carol T.; Leonette M. and Fred T. Lanners Foundation

Hoel, G. O.; Fred C. and Katherine B. Andersen Foundation
Hoff, Susan S.; Best Buy Children's Foundation
Hoffman, Mike; The Toro Company Giving Program
Hoffman, Terry D.; F.R. Bigelow Foundation
Hoffmeister, Kari; Wenger Foundation
Hogan, Audrey; Ripley Memorial Foundation, Inc.
Hogan, Randall J.; The Pentair Foundation
Holdrege, James H.; Hickory Tech Corporation Foundation
Holland, Bryce; The Dorsey & Whitney Foundation
Holm, Richard T.; Frederick and Margaret L. Weyerhaeuser Foundation
Holmberg, Lisa; The Sheltering Arms Foundation
Holmgren, Ronald L., M.D.; Affiliated Community Health Foundation
Holt, Luann; Todd-Wadena Electric Cooperative Community Trust
Holt, Shirley; WCA Foundation
Hooks, Lawrence; Land O'Lakes Foundation
Hopkins, Jane; The Sheltering Arms Foundation
Horgen, Paul; Think Community Foundation
Horowitz, Leonard; Martin and Esther Capp Foundation
Houselog, Roger; Todd-Wadena Electric Cooperative Community Trust
Hoven, Patricia; ClearWay Minnesota
Hoversten, K. F.; George A. Hormel Testamentary Trust
Hovland, James B.; Edina Community Foundation
Howse, G. Craig; Fidelis Foundation
Hoyos, Juan; Minnesota State Bar Foundation
Hubbard, Amy L.; The Irwin Andrew Porter Foundation
Hubbard, Karen H.; The Hubbard Broadcasting Foundation
Hubbard, Robert W.; The Hubbard Broadcasting Foundation
Hubbard, Stanley S.; The Hubbard Broadcasting Foundation
Hubbard, Stanley E.; The Hubbard Broadcasting Foundation
Huber, Patricia; Catholic Community Foundation in the Archdiocese of Saint Paul and Minneapolis
Hubler, Thomas; Minneapolis Rotary Community Service Foundation
Hughes, Kevin; Central Minnesota Community Foundation
Hull, Sandy; The Sheltering Arms Foundation
Humphrey, Jim; Andersen Corporate Foundation
Hunnewell, Catherine S.; Schmoker Family Foundation
Huntington, Karissa; Cottonwood Foundation
Huntley, Larke; Grand Rapids Area Community Foundation
Huntrods, Ann; The Saint Paul Foundation
Hutcheson, Susanne L.; Knox Foundation
   R. C. Lilly Foundation
Hutcheson, Zenas W.; Knox Foundation
Hutchinson, Margie; Indian Land Tenure Foundation
Hynnek, Eric M.; HRK Foundation
Hynnek, Julia L.; HRK Foundation

Iaquinto, Sam; Italian American Club Foundation, Inc.
Ibrahim, Qamar; Women's Foundation of Minnesota
Ibsen, Marlene; Travelers Corporation and Travelers Foundation
Ihle, Nancy Swan; Swan Family Foundation
Ihlenfeld, J. W.; 3M/3M Foundation
Iles, Randy; Andersen Corporate Foundation
Ingber, Jerry; George Kaplan Memorial Foundation, Incorporated

Jacker, Richard E.; Noel Foundation
Jackson, Helena E.; Duluth Superior Area Community Foundation
Jackson, Nate; St Croix Valley Community Foundation
Jackson, Peter F.; F.R. Bigelow Foundation
Jacobs, Michael; Mankato Area Foundation
Jacobson, Lyle G.; Hickory Tech Corporation Foundation
James, Ron; Travelers Corporation and Travelers Foundation
Jasper, Kelly Cote; Cote Foundation
Jelinek, Diane F.; Mayo Clinic
Jennings, Joel C.; Jennings Family Foundation
Jennings, Mary Lee; Jennings Family Foundation
Jennissen, Kimberly; The Vos Family Foundation
Jensen, Tami; Ann Bancroft Foundation
Jenson, Marlys; Park Nicollet Foundation
Jeter, Mark; TCF Foundation

Officers and Trustees

Jewett, Brenca C.; Weyerhaeuser Family Foundation, Inc.
Johnson, A. H.; Fred C. and Katherine B. Andersen Foundation
Johnson, Amy; Philanthrofund Foundation (PFund)
Johnson, Carol McGee; Headwaters Foundation for Justice
Johnson, Charlotte; Otto Bremer Foundation
Johnson, Chris, M.D.; Park Nicollet Foundation
Johnson, Dean; Northwest Minnesota Foundation
Johnson, Dorothy A.; W.K. Kellogg Foundation
Johnson, Emily; Stevens Square Foundation
Johnson, Gerald; Runestone Electric Association Community Trust
Johnson, Gloria; The Lynn Johnson Family Foundation
Johnson, Harold M.; Frances Curran Foundation, Inc.
    Ritt Family Foundation
Johnson, J. W.; George A. Hormel Testamentary Trust
Johnson, Jeff; North Suburban Youth Foundation
Johnson, Josie; Catholic Community Foundation in the Archdiocese of Saint Paul and Minneapolis
Johnson, Kenneth A.; Northland Foundation
Johnson, Kirsten; Wenger Foundation
Johnson, Leigh; Rochester Area Foundation
Johnson, Lois; Mitchell and Lois Johnson Charitable Foundation
Johnson, Lynn; The Lynn Johnson Family Foundation
Johnson, Michael; The Lynn Johnson Family Foundation
    St Croix Valley Community Foundation
Johnson, Michael J.; Park Nicollet Foundation
Johnson, Mike; Blandin Foundation
Johnson, Mitchell; Mitchell and Lois Johnson Charitable Foundation
Johnson, Neel; Wells Fargo Foundation Minnesota
Johnson, Orville; Tozer Foundation, Inc.
Johnson, Paula; The Jostens Foundation
Johnson, Rhonda; Cloquet Educational Foundation
Johnson, Robbin; Cargill Foundation
Johnson, Sally; Ann Bancroft Foundation
Johnson, Salome Z.; Lewis H. Johnson Family Foundation
Johnson, Scott W.; Lewis H. Johnson Family Foundation
Johnson, Timothy A.; Impact Foundation, Inc.
Johnson, Todd; Edina Realty Foundation
Johnson, Tom; Hennepin County Bar Foundation
    Lloyd K. Johnson Foundation
Johnson, Walter, M.D.; Dakota Medical Foundation/Dakota Medical Charities
Jolly, Eric J., Ph.D.; The Minneapolis Foundation
Jones, Carolyn; Cote Foundation
Jones, Louise G.; F.R. Bigelow Foundation
Jones, Lucy R.; Weyerhaeuser Family Foundation, Inc.
    The Charles A. Weyerhaeuser Memorial Foundation
Jones, R. Scott; The Saint Paul Foundation
Jones, Robert J.; Bush Foundation
Jordan, Catherine; Jerome Foundation
Jordheim, Neil; Fargo-Moorhead Area Foundation
Jose, Katharine P.; Southways Foundation
Josephson, Kim; Cloquet Educational Foundation
Joul, Steven R.; Central Minnesota Community Foundation
Jundt, James R.; Jundt Family Foundation
Jundt, Marcus E.; Jundt Family Foundation
Jundt, Mary; Jundt Family Foundation

Kabat, Tom; Knitcraft - St Croix Foundation, Inc.
Kaemmer, Arthur W.; HRK Foundation
Kaemmer, Frederick C.; HRK Foundation
Kaemmer, Martha H.; HRK Foundation
Kahler, Maggie; North Suburban Youth Foundation
Kahler, Mike; Park Nicollet Foundation
Kaiser, Cindy; Philanthrofund Foundation (PFund)
Kaiser, Robert, M.D.; Affiliated Community Health Foundation
Kamper, Carol; Rochester Area Foundation
    Southern Minnesota Initiative Foundation

Kaplan, Elliot S.; Robins, Kaplan, Miller & Ciresi, L.L.P. Foundation for Education, Public Health & Social Justice
Kaplan, Sylvia; ClearWay Minnesota
Kappenman, Elizabeth Wons ; Hennepin County Bar Foundation
Karri, Prabhakar; Cottonwood Foundation
Kast, Steve; TEAM Foundation
Kastner, Rich; H.B. Fuller Company Foundation
Kaufmann, B. W.; 3M/3M Foundation
Kauth, Kimberly; The Bentson Foundation
Kauth, Laurie Bentson; The Bentson Foundation
Kayser, David; CHS Foundation
Kearney, Matthew; SKB Environmental Rosemount Community Trust
Kearney, R. Wynn, Jr.; Hickory Tech Corporation Foundation
Kehoe, Geoffrey James; The Irwin Andrew Porter Foundation
Keller, Fred P.; W.K. Kellogg Foundation
Keller, Michael N.; Federated Insurance Foundation, Inc.
Kelley, John; Casey Albert T. O'Neil Foundation
Kelly, Beth; Ordean Foundation
Kennelly, Chris; Dakota Medical Foundation/Dakota Medical Charities
Kenney, William O.; Park Nicollet Foundation
Keough-Wilson, Patricia; The Cooperative Foundation
Kerwin, Diana; Extendicare Foundation
Khaury, Susan M.; The Janice Gardner Foundation
Kiefer, Markell; Marbrook Foundation
Kierlin, Lara; Hiawatha Education Foundation
Kierlin, Monique; Hiawatha Education Foundation
Kierlin, Robert; Hiawatha Education Foundation
Kile, James; CHS Foundation
Kill, David; North Suburban Youth Foundation
Killingstad, Chris; Tennant Foundation
Kincade, Rachel; Northland Foundation
King, John; The Charles A. and Anne Morrow Lindbergh Foundation
King, John E.; Warren Foundation
King, Margaret; Frederick and Margaret L. Weyerhaeuser Foundation
King, Martha; The Charles A. and Anne Morrow Lindbergh Foundation
Kingston, Thomas W.; The Saint Paul Foundation
Kinzig, Kathy; Cottonwood Foundation
Kirby, Arlene; Sioux Falls Area Community Foundation
Kirby, Barbara; The Sheltering Arms Foundation
Kirk, Judy; Minneapolis Rotary Community Service Foundation
Kirklin, Starr J.; Hickory Tech Corporation Foundation
Kirsch, Martin; Richfield Community Foundation
Kirschner, Mike; North Suburban Youth Foundation
Kirscht, Ron; West Central Initiative
Kishel, Judith; F.R. Bigelow Foundation
Kiskis, Nancy; Minnesota State Bar Foundation
Kitchenmaster, Bob; Mankato Area Foundation
Klatzky, Howard T.; Duluth Superior Area Community Foundation
Klaus, Claire; The Jostens Foundation
Klein, Michael; Travelers Corporation and Travelers Foundation
Klein, Richard A.; The Elizabeth C. Quinlan Foundation, Inc.
Kleinkramer, Jane; Land O'Lakes Foundation
Kleinschmidt, Amy; Edina Realty Foundation
Kleven, Cindy; 3M/3M Foundation
Kline, Hess; Hess Kline Foundation, Inc.
Kline, Renee; Hess Kline Foundation, Inc.
Klus, George; Edina Community Foundation
Knabel, Tom; Philanthrofund Foundation (PFund)
Knecht, Randy; CHS Foundation
Knight, Pauline; Elizabeth Callender King Foundation
Knoblach, Janet; Central Minnesota Community Foundation
Knowlton, R. L.; George A. Hormel Testamentary Trust
Kobel, Sandy; Fargo-Moorhead Area Foundation
Koblas, George; Minneapolis Rotary Community Service Foundation
Koch, Cindy; Park Nicollet Foundation
Kochevar, Jason; The Nash Foundation
Koepp, Marcia; Mankato Area Foundation
Kolars, Maura; Minneapolis Area Association of Realtors Foundation, Inc.
Koosman, Chuck; Headwaters Foundation for Justice

Officers and Trustees

Kopel, Shelly Bauerly; Central Minnesota Community Foundation
Kopp, Barbara; Kopp Family Foundation
Kopp, Brian; Kopp Family Foundation
Kopp, Debbie; Kopp Family Foundation
Kopp, Debra; Kopp Family Foundation
Kopp, Kristin; Kopp Family Foundation
Kopp, Leroy C.; Kopp Family Foundation
Kopp, Missy; Kopp Family Foundation
Kopp, Terry; Kopp Family Foundation
Korsmo, Jeffrey O.; Mayo Clinic
Korstange, Jason; TCF Foundation
Koury, Fred; The Pentair Foundation
Kozlak, Jodee; Target
Kremeier, Lawrence; Otto C. and Elsie Ewert Charitable Trust
Kreutz, Marilyn; Park Nicollet Foundation
Krienke, George H.; North Suburban Community Foundation
Kruger, Al; Grand Rapids Area Community Foundation
Kueppers, Joseph F.; Catholic Aid Association Foundation
Kuhlmann, Adam; Winona Foundation
Kuhnley, Marc; Edina Realty Foundation
Kunin, Constance B.; F.R. Bigelow Foundation
Kunin, David B.; Regis Foundation
Kunin, Myron; Regis Foundation
Kurth, Tineka; Samsara Foundation
Kurtz, Harold; Lillian Wright and C. Emil Berglund Foundation, Inc.

Lacy-Campos, Brandon; Headwaters Foundation for Justice
LaFortune, Richard; Philanthrofund Foundation (PFund)
Laird, Stewart; Catholic Community Foundation in the Archdiocese of Saint Paul and Minneapolis
Lais, Greg; Ann Bancroft Foundation
Lamb, Catherine L.; Archie D. and Bertha H. Walker Foundation
Lamb, Julia M.; Archie D. and Bertha H. Walker Foundation
Lang, Greg; The Vos Family Foundation
Lang, Jeremy T.; Lang Family Charitable Trust
Lang, Phoebe Hamm; Lang Family Charitable Trust
Lang, Ralph; West Central Initiative
Lang, William Scheffer; Lang Family Charitable Trust
Lange, Chad S.; Owatonna Foundation
Lannan, Maureen; Catholic Community Foundation in the Archdiocese of Saint Paul and Minneapolis
Lanners, Alan; Leonette M. and Fred T. Lanners Foundation
Lanners, F. Thomas; Leonette M. and Fred T. Lanners Foundation
Lanners, John J.; Leonette M. and Fred T. Lanners Foundation
Lanners, Leonette; Leonette M. and Fred T. Lanners Foundation
Larkin, Susan; Eagan Foundation, Incorporated
LaRogue, Dennis; Nevin Huested Foundation for Handicapped Children, Inc.
Larsen, Lauren; Ordean Foundation
Larsen, Libby; Jerome Foundation
Larson, Tim; The Jostens Foundation
Laskey, Bob; Minneapolis Rotary Community Service Foundation
Lau, Barry; Philanthrofund Foundation (PFund)
Lavander, John M.; Caliber Foundation
  The Minneapolis Foundation
Lavin, Jerry; George Kaplan Memorial Foundation, Incorporated
LaVoie, Joyce; Todd-Wadena Electric Cooperative Community Trust
Lawien, John P.; Duluth Superior Area Community Foundation
Lawrence, J.A.; General Mills Community Action
Lea, Anna L.; Helen Sperry Lea Foundation
Lea, Brooke; Helen Sperry Lea Foundation
Lea, Helena A.; Helen Sperry Lea Foundation
Lea, Sperry; Helen Sperry Lea Foundation
Leagjeld, Erik; Mankato Area Foundation
LeClaire, William; Minnesota Twins Community Fund
Lee, Andrea; Catholic Community Foundation in the Archdiocese of Saint Paul and Minneapolis
Lee, Gary; St Francis Regional Medical Center Foundation
Leedom, Kathy; Affiliated Community Health Foundation

Leemhuis, Andrew J.M.D.; The Wasie Foundation
LeFevour, Suzanne A.; Patrick and Aimee Butler Family Foundation
Leiferman, Troy; Mankato Area Foundation
Leighton, Katherine M.; Marbrook Foundation
Lenzen, David; The Jack and Bessie Fiterman Foundation
Lerner, Harry J.; Lerner Foundation
Lesher, Cynthia; The Saint Paul Foundation
Leslie, David R.; The Elizabeth C. Quinlan Foundation, Inc.
Leslie, Kathleen; The Elizabeth C. Quinlan Foundation, Inc.
Letourneau, Jane E.; Frey Foundation
Leuthold, Kurt A.; Steven C. Leuthold Family Foundation
Leuthold, Michael S.; Steven C. Leuthold Family Foundation
Leuthold, Russell C.; Steven C. Leuthold Family Foundation
Leuthold, Steven C.; Steven C. Leuthold Family Foundation
Levin, Ilene F.; Duluth Superior Area Community Foundation
Levin, John P.; The Jay and Rose Phillips Family Foundation
Levin, Suzan; The Jay and Rose Phillips Family Foundation
Levin, Terryl A.; The Jay and Rose Phillips Family Foundation
Levonowich, Wally; Extendicare Foundation
Lewis, Diana; Ecolab Foundation and Corporation
Lewis, Katherine; The Sheltering Arms Foundation
Lichty, Marshall; Hennepin County Bar Foundation
Liebe, Carolyn; Grand Rapids Area Community Foundation
Liebhaber, Henia; Liebhaber Family Foundation
Liebhaber, Marc; Liebhaber Family Foundation
Liebhaber, Sharon F.; Liebhaber Family Foundation
Liemandt-Reimann, Diane; Catholic Community Foundation in the Archdiocese of Saint Paul and Minneapolis
Lietha, Tom; Mankato Area Foundation
Lighthizer-Schmidt, M. D.; George A. Hormel Testamentary Trust
Lilienthal, Christine A.; The Simmet Foundation
Lilly, Bruce A.; Fremont Foundation
  R. C. Lilly Foundation
Lilly, David M., Jr.; R. C. Lilly Foundation
  Peravid Foundation
Lilly, David M.; Fremont Foundation
  Knox Foundation
  R. C. Lilly Foundation
  Peravid Foundation
Lilly, Diane P.; Peravid Foundation
  Wells Fargo Foundation Minnesota
Lilly, Mary P.; Fremont Foundation
Lind, Aune E.; Carl and Aune Lind Family Foundation
Lind, Carl V.; Carl and Aune Lind Family Foundation
Lind, Dennis A.; Carl and Aune Lind Family Foundation
Lind, Jeanne M.; Carl and Aune Lind Family Foundation
Lindahl, Nancy E.; The Saint Paul Foundation
Lindbergh, Erik R.; The Charles A. and Anne Morrow Lindbergh Foundation
Lindbergh, Kristina; The Charles A. and Anne Morrow Lindbergh Foundation
Lindbergh, Lars; The Charles A. and Anne Morrow Lindbergh Foundation
Lindbergh, Reeve; The Charles A. and Anne Morrow Lindbergh Foundation
Lindbergh, Wendy R.; The Charles A. and Anne Morrow Lindbergh Foundation
Linde, Ron; Philanthrofund Foundation (PFund)
Lindholm, Paul; Otto C. and Elsie Ewert Charitable Trust
Lipschultz, William H.; Otto Bremer Foundation
Liu, Hanmin; W.K. Kellogg Foundation
Livingston, James; Italian American Club Foundation, Inc.
Lizarde, Rosa; Carolyn Foundation
Locke, Jean; Rochester Area Foundation
Lofquist, Perry; North Suburban Youth Foundation
Lokken, Mary; Fargo-Moorhead Area Foundation
Lompart, Joan; Winona Foundation
Longstreet, Al; H.B. Fuller Company Foundation
Loosbrock, Todd; Mankato Area Foundation
Lopez, Manuel Mariano; The Saint Paul Foundation

Officers and Trustees

Lott, Ralph, III; Burdick-Craddick Family Foundation
Lott, Susan C.; Burdick-Craddick Family Foundation
Lounsberry, Ed; Youthworks! Foundation, Inc.
Love-Mickelson, Anne; The Sheltering Arms Foundation
Lovik, Kathryn; Tennant Foundation
Lowe, David; The Graco Foundation
Lu, Weiming; The Minneapolis Foundation
Ludeman, Sander; Southwest Initiative Foundation
Lund, Jay; Andersen Corporate Foundation
Lund, Russell T., III; Russell T. Lund Charitable Trust
Lund, Sharon; Nevin Huested Foundation for Handicapped Children, Inc.
Lundgren, Kenneth; Blandin Foundation
Luther, Charles D.; The Luther Family Foundation
Luther, Rudy D.; The Luther Family Foundation
Lutz, Fred; Mankato Area Foundation
Lyman, Charles; I. A. O'Shaughnessy Foundation, Incorporated
Lyon, Marina Muñoz; Carl and Eloise Pohlad Family Foundation

Maas, Kathy; Minneapolis Area Association of Realtors Foundation, Inc.
MacDonald, R. D.; 3M/3M Foundation
MacDonell, Jean; Grand Rapids Area Community Foundation
Maciel, Jr., Manuel; Land O'Lakes Foundation
MacKinnon, Kate; Hennepin County Bar Foundation
Madson, Deborah B.; Blue Cross and Blue Shield of Minnesota Foundation/Blue Cross and Blue Shield of Minnesota Healthier Minnesota Community Clinic Fund
Maetzold, Dennis; Edina Community Foundation
Mager, William; Marjorie and V.M. Baich Foundation
Magnuson, Deb; Dakota Medical Foundation/Dakota Medical Charities
Maher, Nathaniel J. W.; Weyerhaeuser Family Foundation, Inc.
Mahle, Steve; The Medtronic Foundation
Mahoney, Kathleen; NFC Foundation
Malcolm, Jan K.; Ann Bancroft Foundation
  Bush Foundation
  Women's Foundation of Minnesota
Mallon, Laurel; Rahr Foundation
Malm, Roger; Northwest Minnesota Foundation
Malmberg, Ann, M.S., R.N.; Dakota Medical Foundation/Dakota Medical Charities
Malone, Kathleen; Haggerty Family Foundation
Mamdani, Arif; Headwaters Foundation for Justice
Mangan, Lorna; Cloquet Educational Foundation
Mann, Dave; Headwaters Foundation for Justice
Mann, Roberta L.; Ted and Roberta Mann Foundation
Manrique, Gabe; Winona Community Foundation
Mansfield, W.; The Valspar Foundation
Manuel, Mary; Grotto Foundation, Inc.
Marcantonio, Richard; G&K Services Foundation
Marino, James; Italian American Club Foundation, Inc.
Maristuen, Dale; North Suburban Youth Foundation
Markland, Kyle; Minnesota Twins Community Fund
Marley, Bob; Land O'Lakes Foundation
Marschall, Duane; St Francis Regional Medical Center Foundation
Marsden, Gary; Central Minnesota Community Foundation
Marshall, S.S.; General Mills Community Action
Martin, James; Minneapolis Rotary Community Service Foundation
Martin, Jennifer; Thrivent Financial for Lutherans Foundation
Martinez, Cecilia; Headwaters Foundation for Justice
Martinson, Bruce; Martinson Clinic Foundation
Martinson, Elmer; Martinson Clinic Foundation
Martinson, Tom; Martinson Clinic Foundation
Martodam, Don; West Central Initiative
Maryniak, Gregg; The Charles A. and Anne Morrow Lindbergh Foundation
Mason, Tara; Women's Foundation of Minnesota
Massee, Leonard; The Martinson Foundation
Mastel, Barb; North Suburban Youth Foundation
Mathern, Tim; Bush Foundation

Mathison, Susan, M.D.; Dakota Medical Foundation/Dakota Medical Charities
Matson, Betty; North Suburban Youth Foundation
Matson, Robert; North Suburban Youth Foundation
Matthees, Donald, M.D.; Dakota Medical Foundation/Dakota Medical Charities
Matthews, Debra; TEAM Foundation
Mattson, Lucy; Minneapolis Rotary Community Service Foundation
Mauszycki, Leone; Winona Community Foundation
May, Jeff; The Donaldson Foundation
Mayeda, Cynthia; Jerome Foundation
May-Machunda, Phyllis; Fargo-Moorhead Area Foundation
McBride, Catherine; Women's Foundation of Minnesota
McCabe, James; Osterud-Winter Foundation
McCannel, Dana D.; Archie D. and Bertha H. Walker Foundation
McClure, Elizabeth; Park Nicollet Foundation
McCluskey, Glen; Hennepin County Bar Foundation
McCormack, William; Southwest Initiative Foundation
McCrary, Kelly; Minneapolis Kiwanis Foundation
McDonald, Malcolm W.; Grotto Foundation, Inc.
McDonough, Fr. Kevin; Catholic Community Foundation in the Archdiocese of Saint Paul and Minneapolis
McDonough, Maureen; Andersen Corporate Foundation
McElrath, Karen K.; Charlson Foundation
McElveen, Darnell; The Donaldson Foundation
McFarland, Richard D.; The McKnight Foundation
McFee, Jane W.; Weyerhaeuser Family Foundation, Inc.
McGoldrick, Kathleen; Weyerhaeuser Family Foundation, Inc.
McGough, L.B.; McGough Foundation
McGough, Lawrence; Catholic Community Foundation in the Archdiocese of Saint Paul and Minneapolis
  McGough Foundation
McGough, T.J.; McGough Foundation
McGovern, Michael F.; Catholic Aid Association Foundation
McGrath, Bonnie; Edina Community Foundation
McInerney, Thomas J.; ING Foundation
McIntyre, Lawrence; The Toro Company Giving Program
McKasy, Bert J.; F.R. Bigelow Foundation
McKay, Glen; Redwood Area Communities Foundation, Inc.
McKellip, John B.; Martinson Clinic Foundation
McKeown, Daniel W.; The Boss Foundation
McKeown, Heidi S.; The Boss Foundation
McKeown, Thomas; Catholic Community Foundation in the Archdiocese of Saint Paul and Minneapolis
McKinley, Ron; Headwaters Foundation for Justice
McLaughlan, Bonnie; St Francis Regional Medical Center Foundation
McMahon, Mary-Megan; Sauer Children's Renew Foundation
McManimon, Timothy; Owatonna Foundation
McManus, Hugh; Extendicare Foundation
McNaughton, Russell J.; Minnesota Research Fund
McNeely, Gregory; McNeely Foundation
McNeely, Kevin; McNeely Foundation
McNeely, Paddy; McNeely Foundation
McNeil, Michael; Rochester Area Foundation
McQueen, John; Wells Fargo Foundation Minnesota
McReavy, William W.; Park Nicollet Foundation
Medin, Connie VanDerBill; Southwest Initiative Foundation
Medure, Pat; Grand Rapids Area Community Foundation
Meersman, Tom; Cottonwood Foundation
Meghjee, Munir; Headwaters Foundation for Justice
Meissner, Edie; The Sheltering Arms Foundation
Melhus, Mark; Ordean Foundation
Melicher, Kevin, O.D.; Dakota Medical Foundation/Dakota Medical Charities
Mellema, Burnell J., M.D.; Affiliated Community Health Foundation
Meredith, Bruce; Donald and Marjorie Meredith Foundation
Meredith, Donald C., II; Donald and Marjorie Meredith Foundation
Meredith, Donald C.; Donald and Marjorie Meredith Foundation
Meredith, Marjorie; Donald and Marjorie Meredith Foundation

Officers and Trustees

Meshke, Sheryl Doering ; The Cooperative Foundation
Meslow, John A.; Minnesota Research Fund
Messinger, Kera; Samsara Foundation
Messinger, William; Samsara Foundation
Meurlot, Sandra; The Toro Company Giving Program
Meyer, Bill; Wells Fargo Foundation Minnesota
Meyer, Karen; The Toro Company Giving Program
Meyer, Michael G.; The Pentair Foundation
Meyers, Lisa; Ritt Family Foundation
Micallef, Joseph S.; The Laura Jane Musser Fund
    The Charles A. Weyerhaeuser Memorial Foundation
Mielke, Paula; Lillian Wright and C. Emil Berglund Foundation, Inc.
Miller, Craig R.; Cottonwood Foundation
Miller, Esther; Martin and Esther Miller Foundation
Miller, Katherine L.; Deluxe Corporation Foundation/Deluxe Corporation
Miller, Michael; Martin and Esther Miller Foundation
Miller, R. M.; 3M/3M Foundation
Miller, Teresa; Martin and Esther Miller Foundation
Miller, Vicki M.; Lillian Wright and C. Emil Berglund Foundation, Inc.
Miller-Van Oort, Sonia; Hennepin County Bar Foundation
Milligan, Cynthia H.; W.K. Kellogg Foundation
Minkkinen, David; Cloquet Educational Foundation
Minsberg, Sol; George Kaplan Memorial Foundation, Incorporated
Minsker, Barry; Eagan Foundation, Incorporated
Mischinski, Maureen L.; Haggerty Family Foundation
Mischke, Herbert; North Suburban Community Foundation
Mitau, Lee; The Minneapolis Foundation
Mitchell, Daisy; The Curtis L. Carlson Family Foundation
Mitchell, Jan; Frances Curran Foundation, Inc.
Mitchell, Lucy C.; Longview Foundation
    Southways Foundation
Mitchell, Steve; ADC Foundation
Mixner, A.R.; Lloyd and Barbara Amundson Charity Foundation, Inc.
Mock, Kathleen; Blue Cross and Blue Shield of Minnesota Foundation/Blue Cross and Blue Shield of Minnesota
Modec, Denny; Cloquet Educational Foundation
Moe, Paul; The Polaris Foundation
Moe, Roger; Minnesota Twins Community Fund
Moe, Thomas; Cargill Foundation
Mohring, Andrew; Hennepin County Bar Foundation
Monahan, Michael; Ecolab Foundation and Corporation
Mondale, Walter F.; United Health Foundation
Monson, Jodie; H.B. Fuller Company Foundation
Montury, James; Italian American Club Foundation, Inc.
Moor, Robert K.; The Minnesota Timberwolves FastBreak Foundation
Moore, John; Catholic Community Foundation in the Archdiocese of Saint Paul and Minneapolis
Moore, Wenda Weekes; W.K. Kellogg Foundation
Moorhead, Tracey; Fargo-Moorhead Area Foundation
Moorman, Bette D.; Edwin W. and Catherine M. Davis Foundation
Mooty, Bruce W.; John W. Mooty Foundation Trust
Mooty, Charles W.; John W. Mooty Foundation Trust
Mooty, David N.; John W. Mooty Foundation Trust
Mootz, Anne; Ripley Memorial Foundation, Inc.
Moran, Asha Morgan; Central Minnesota Community Foundation
Moran, Janet; Initiative Foundation
Morem, Neil R.; Arthur and David Cosgrove Memorial Fund
Morgan, LeRoy; People in Business Care, Inc.
Morgan, Thomas G.; Faegre & Benson Foundation
Morley, Catherine W.; Frederick and Margaret L. Weyerhaeuser Foundation
Morris, Michael; Richfield Community Foundation
Morris, Virginia Hubbard; The Hubbard Broadcasting Foundation
    Minnesota Twins Community Fund
Morrison, Susan; Catholic Community Foundation in the Archdiocese of Saint Paul and Minneapolis
Morrissey, Stephanie A.; Sauer Children's Renew Foundation
Moscoe, Thomas; Moscoe Family Foundation
Mosner, Lawrence J.; Deluxe Corporation Foundation/Deluxe Corporation
Moss, Paul; Cottonwood Foundation
Motley, Teri M.; Archie D. and Bertha H. Walker Foundation
Moyer, Cynthia Jokela; Minnesota State Bar Foundation
Mueller, J. R.; George A. Hormel Testamentary Trust
Mukherjee, Dipankar; The Irwin Andrew Porter Foundation
Mulcahey, Michael; CHS Foundation
Mulder, Richard; ClearWay Minnesota
Mumma, Marty; Ann Bancroft Foundation
Munsell, William; United Health Foundation
Murphy, Katherine B.; Kingsley H. Murphy Family Foundation
Murphy, Kathleen; ING Foundation
Murphy, Kingsley H., Jr.; Kingsley H. Murphy Family Foundation
Murray, Brian C.; Catholic Community Foundation in the Archdiocese of Saint Paul and Minneapolis
Muscoplat, Charles C.; Minnesota Research Fund
Musicant, Gretchen; Healthier Minnesota Community Clinic Fund
Mutter, Pat; Elizabeth Callender King Foundation
Myers, J. D.; George A. Hormel Testamentary Trust
Myres, Brian; Central Minnesota Community Foundation

Nakamoto, Mindy; Philanthrofund Foundation (PFund)
Napgezek, Marvin; Affiliated Community Health Foundation
Napper, Diane; Philanthrofund Foundation (PFund)
Nash, Rebecca; The Nash Foundation
Naylor, Charles; George W. Neilson Foundation
Neff, Erv; St Croix Valley Community Foundation
Nellis, Jenny; West Central Initiative
Nelson, C. David; The Nelson Family Foundation
Nelson, Charley; The Jostens Foundation
Nelson, Diana L.; The Curtis L. Carlson Family Foundation
Nelson, Erik; Cottonwood Foundation
Nelson, Glen D.; The Nelson Family Foundation
Nelson, Julie; Cade Foundation
Nelson, Kathleen V.; Arlin Falck Foundation
Nelson, Kathy; Runestone Electric Association Community Trust
Nelson, LaRae; Extendicare Foundation
Nelson, Marilyn C.; The Nelson Family Foundation
    The Curtis L. Carlson Family Foundation
Nelson, Nancy; Blue Cross and Blue Shield of Minnesota Foundation/Blue Cross and Blue Shield of Minnesota
Nelson, Rob; Cloquet Educational Foundation
Nelson, Rod; Winona Community Foundation
Nelson, Ron; Minnesota Twins Community Fund
Nelson, Russell C.; The Minneapolis Foundation
Nelson, Wendy M.; The Curtis L. Carlson Family Foundation
Nestegard, Susan; Ecolab Foundation and Corporation
Neverud, Jay; Weyerhaeuser Family Foundation, Inc.
Newman, Mike; Travelers Corporation and Travelers Foundation
Newman, Robert; Richard A. Newman Foundation
Newman, Sarah C.; Richard A. Newman Foundation
Newman, Trixie; Eagan Foundation, Incorporated
Niblick, Mark S.; The Bentson Foundation
Nickelson, Jessica; Sauer Children's Renew Foundation
Nicklason, Brian R.; Blandin Foundation
Niechwiadowicz, Kristi; Sioux Falls Area Community Foundation
Nielsen, D. James; Schott Foundation
Nielsen, Jeff; The Cooperative Foundation
Nobrega, Fred; ClearWay Minnesota
Nolan, Eleanor; Athwin Foundation
Nollenberger, Todd; Richfield Community Foundation
Nordquist, Laurie; Wells Fargo Foundation Minnesota
Norr, Nancy; Northland Foundation
Northey, Lyle W.; Duluth Superior Area Community Foundation
Norton, Jon; ADC Foundation
Noseworthy, John H.; Mayo Clinic
Novak, Lance; The Jostens Foundation
Noyes, Curt; Dakota Medical Foundation/Dakota Medical Charities
Nulsen, Carol; Beim Foundation
Numainville, Brian; NFC Foundation

Officers and Trustees

Nuness, Al; The Jostens Foundation
Nyman, Connie; Philanthrofund Foundation (PFund)

Ober, Gayle M.; Mardag Foundation
Ober, Richard B.; Mardag Foundation
Ober, Timothy M.; Mardag Foundation
Oberle, Jeff R.; R. C. Skoe Foundation
Oberle, Mary E.; R. C. Skoe Foundation
Oberle, Richard R.; R. C. Skoe Foundation
O'Brien, Alvina; Alice M. O'Brien Foundation
O'Brien, Eleanor; Alice M. O'Brien Foundation
O'Brien, Miles; The Charles A. and Anne Morrow Lindbergh Foundation
O'Brien, Pat; ADC Foundation
O'Brien, Terrence, Jr.; Alice M. O'Brien Foundation
O'Brien, Thomond R.; Alice M. O'Brien Foundation
O'Connell, Father Michael; Robins, Kaplan, Miller & Ciresi, L.L.P.
   Foundation for Education, Public Health & Social Justice
Oesterle, Stephen N., M.D.; The Medtronic Foundation
Ogg, Leslie; Minneapolis Rotary Community Service Foundation
Okerman, Gerald (Jerry) A.; Minnesota Research Fund
Olsen, Lea B.; Minnesota Twins Community Fund
Olson, Dennis; Catholic Aid Association Foundation
Olson, Jim; Cote Foundation
Olson, Keith; Andersen Corporate Foundation
Olson, Larry; Richfield Community Foundation
Olson, Marci; Todd-Wadena Electric Cooperative Community Trust
Olson, Sue; Cloquet Educational Foundation
Omann, Pam; Carl and Eloise Pohlad Family Foundation
O'Neil, Casey Albert; Casey Albert T. O'Neil Foundation
O'Neill, James C.; Margaret H. and James E. Kelley Foundation, Inc.
O'Neill, Mr. & Mrs. Hampton K.; Margaret H. and James E. Kelley Foundation, Inc.
O'Neill, Mr. & Mrs. James W.; Margaret H. and James E. Kelley Foundation, Inc.
O'Neill, Mr. & Mrs. Kelley McC.; Margaret H. and James E. Kelley Foundation, Inc.
Opitz, Richard E.; McGough Foundation
Opperman, Dwight D.; Dwight D. Opperman Foundation
Opperman, Fane W.; Dwight D. Opperman Foundation
Opperman, Vance K.; Dwight D. Opperman Foundation
O'Rourke, J. E.; George A. Hormel Testamentary Trust
Orth, Ginny; Ripley Memorial Foundation, Inc.
Ortland, Warren; Minnesota State Bar Foundation
Osborn, Tom; Grand Rapids Area Community Foundation
O'Shaughnessy, Betty; O'Shaughnessy Foundation
O'Shaughnessy, Eileen A.; I. A. O'Shaughnessy Foundation, Incorporated
O'Shaughnessy, John F., Jr.; I. A. O'Shaughnessy Foundation, Incorporated
O'Shaughnessy, Kathleen E.; I. A. O'Shaughnessy Foundation, Incorporated
O'Shaughnessy, Michael W.; I. A. O'Shaughnessy Foundation, Incorporated
O'Shaughnessy, Susan; O'Shaughnessy Foundation
O'Shaughnessy, Terence P.; I. A. O'Shaughnessy Foundation, Incorporated
O'Shaughnessy, Timothy J.; I. A. O'Shaughnessy Foundation, Incorporated
Ostrem, Dawn; Charles and Kathryn Cunningham Family Foundation
Osvold, Karrie; Cloquet Educational Foundation
O'Toole-Tomczik, Erin; Minnesota State Bar Foundation
Otos, Claudia; Northland Foundation
Overman, Jane; Ben and Jeanne Overman Charitable Trust
Owen, Laura; ADC Foundation
Owen, Nancy F.; Caliber Foundation
Owen, Richard; CHS Foundation

Pabst, Timothy J.; Leonard, Street and Deinard Foundation
Packard, Betsy; Park Nicollet Foundation
Pagel, Jack W.; Pagel Foundation
Pajor, Michaeline D.; Pajor Family Foundation

Pajor, Robert E.; Pajor Family Foundation
Pajor, Scott R.; Pajor Family Foundation
Pajor, Steven M.; Pajor Family Foundation
Pajor, Wendy R.; Pajor Family Foundation
Palmer, David; St Croix Valley Community Foundation
Palmerhall, Juanita; The Sheltering Arms Foundation
Parish, Ivy; The Laura Jane Musser Fund
Parish, John C., Jr.; Salem Foundation, Inc.
Parish, Michael; Salem Foundation, Inc.
Parish, Robert S.; Salem Foundation, Inc.
Park, Molly Rumsey; Catholic Community Foundation in the Archdiocese of Saint Paul and Minneapolis
Parker, Becky; Southwest Initiative Foundation
Parker, Dale E.; Hickory Tech Corporation Foundation
Parker, Jan; North Suburban Community Foundation
Parker, Rick; Extendicare Foundation
Parran, Richard; ADC Foundation
Parriott, Ann; H.B. Fuller Company Foundation
Pascoe, Samuel J.; Weyerhaeuser Family Foundation, Inc.
Patel, Anita; Ripley Memorial Foundation, Inc.
Paterson, Debra; Wells Fargo Foundation Minnesota
Pates, Bishop Richard; Catholic Community Foundation in the Archdiocese of Saint Paul and Minneapolis
Patterson, Sally D.; F.R. Bigelow Foundation
Paulson, Anna; Eagan Foundation, Incorporated
Paulson, Mike; West Central Initiative
Pauly, Deb; Catholic Aid Association Foundation
Pay, Sandra; Sioux Falls Area Community Foundation
Paymar, Michael; ClearWay Minnesota
Pearce, Randy; Regis Foundation
Pearson, Bruce; Fidelis Foundation
Peck, Dawn; ING Foundation
Pederson, Gale; North Suburban Youth Foundation
Peel, M.A.; General Mills Community Action
Pegues-Smart, Elizabeth A.; Grotto Foundation, Inc.
Pemberton, Richard L., Jr.; Roger L. and Agnes C. Dell Charitable (Trust 1)
   Roger L. and Agnes C. Dell Charitable (Trust 2)
Pendergast, Edward G.; F.R. Bigelow Foundation
Pendergrass, David S.; ING Foundation
Perez Jordan, Gloria; The Irwin Andrew Porter Foundation
   Ripley Memorial Foundation, Inc.
Perkins, Daniel S.; Perkins Foundation
Perkins, Richard C.; Perkins Foundation
Perkins, Richard W.; Perkins Foundation
Perlman, David M.; The Lawrence and Linda Perlman Family Foundation
Perlman, Lawrence; The Lawrence and Linda Perlman Family Foundation
Perlman, Linda Peterson; The Lawrence and Linda Perlman Family Foundation
Perron, William; The Shiebler Family Foundation
Person, Carol; Ordean Foundation
Pertler, Jill; Cloquet Educational Foundation
Pertzik, Marvin; Mary Livingston Griggs and Mary Griggs Burke Foundation
Peter, James W.; Baker Foundation
Peters, Dr. Dan; O'Shaughnessy Foundation
Petersen, John L.; The Charles A. and Anne Morrow Lindbergh Foundation
Petersen, William O.; Luther I. Replogle Foundation
Petersmeyer, Pamela C.; Whitney ARCEE Foundation
Peterson, Doug; Farmers Union Marketing and Processing Foundation
Peterson, Jeffrey T.; Fremont Foundation
   Hardenbergh Foundation
   Knox Foundation
   R. C. Lilly Foundation
   Peravid Foundation
   Sweitzer Foundation
Peterson, Joel; Cottonwood Foundation
Peterson, Kathleen Flynn; Robins, Kaplan, Miller & Ciresi, L.L.P.

Officers and Trustees

Foundation for Education, Public Health & Social Justice
Peterson, Timothy M.; Blue Cross and Blue Shield of Minnesota Foundation/Blue Cross and Blue Shield of Minnesota
Petite, Patty; Cloquet Educational Foundation
Petracek, Doris; Fanny S. Gilfillan Memorial, Incorporated
Pflaum, Jeff; ADC Foundation
Phelps, Jennifer C.; Carolyn Foundation
Philbin, Tobias R.; Baker Foundation
Phillips, Dean; The Jay and Rose Phillips Family Foundation
Phillips, Edward J.; The Jay and Rose Phillips Family Foundation
Phillips, Jeanne; The Jay and Rose Phillips Family Foundation
Phillips, Mark; Northland Foundation
Phillips, Morton; The Jay and Rose Phillips Family Foundation
Phillips, Pauline; The Jay and Rose Phillips Family Foundation
Pickard, Mary; Travelers Corporation and Travelers Foundation
Piepel, J. D.; Fred C. and Katherine B. Andersen Foundation
Pierskalla, William P.; Bush Foundation
Piersol, Catherine V.; Bush Foundation
Pillsbury, George S., Jr.; Southways Foundation
Pillsbury, John S., III; Southways Foundation
Pincus, Steve; Hennepin County Bar Foundation
Pineo, Charles C., III; Baker Foundation
Pineo, Linda B.; Baker Foundation
Pins, Richard; Hennepin County Bar Foundation
Pohl, David; Margaret Rivers Fund
Pohlad, Carl R.; Carl and Eloise Pohlad Family Foundation
Pohlad, James O.; The Minneapolis Foundation
  Carl and Eloise Pohlad Family Foundation
Pohlad, John M.; Catholic Community Foundation in the Archdiocese of Saint Paul and Minneapolis
Pohlad, Robert C.; Carl and Eloise Pohlad Family Foundation
Pohlad, William M.; Carl and Eloise Pohlad Family Foundation
Pollock, Kathy; Eagan Foundation, Incorporated
Portnoy, Scott; Cargill Foundation
Potts, John; Youthworks! Foundation, Inc.
Powell, K.J.; General Mills Community Action
Powers, Joe; Rochester Area Foundation
Pradhan, Fiona; The Sheltering Arms Foundation
Pratt, Carolyn; Park Nicollet Foundation
Priebe, Dan; HRK Foundation
Proulx, Tom; Cloquet Educational Foundation
Pulles, Gregory J.; Catholic Community Foundation in the Archdiocese of Saint Paul and Minneapolis
  TCF Foundation
Punch, Jackie; G&K Services Foundation
Purath, Gary; Northwest Minnesota Foundation
Pust, Tammy; North Suburban Community Foundation

Quay, Mary; ADC Foundation
Quaye, Brenda; Edina Community Foundation
Quitter, Greg; North Suburban Youth Foundation

Racine, Ross; Indian Land Tenure Foundation
Radecki, Eugene; Blandin Foundation
Radel, Dwayne; Securian Foundation/Securian Financial Group
Radin, Joshi; Unity Avenue Foundation
Radjenovic, Sara; Travelers Corporation and Travelers Foundation
Rahr, Frederick W.; Rahr Foundation
Rahr, Heid; Rahr Foundation
Rahr, William; Rahr Foundation
Rajala, Pam; Grand Rapids Area Community Foundation
Rak, Paula; Wells Fargo Foundation Minnesota
Randall-Dana, Nancy; Grotto Foundation, Inc.
Rappaport, Diane S.; Rappaport Family Foundation
Rappaport, Fred J.; Rappaport Family Foundation
Rappaport, Jon D.; Rappaport Family Foundation
Rappaport, Naomi R.; Rappaport Family Foundation
Rappaport, Shira J.; Rappaport Family Foundation

Rasmussen, Thomas F.; Weyerhaeuser Family Foundation, Inc.
  Frederick and Margaret L. Weyerhaeuser Foundation
Rauenhorst, Gerald; Catholic Community Foundation in the Archdiocese of Saint Paul and Minneapolis
Ray, G. J.; George A. Hormel Testamentary Trust
Reardon, Daniel; Otto Bremer Foundation
Rechelbacher, Horst; Horst M. Rechelbacher Foundation
Rechelbacher, Peter; Horst M. Rechelbacher Foundation
Reed, K. E.; 3M/3M Foundation
Reid, Malcolm D.; Gray Plant Mooty Foundation
Reilly, Denise; The Sheltering Arms Foundation
Reilly, George; The Bentson Foundation
Reinert, Dave; Richfield Community Foundation
Remucal, Cris; Southwest Initiative Foundation
Renner, Beth; Fargo-Moorhead Area Foundation
Replogle, David; Luther I. Replogle Foundation
Reyelts, P.C.; The Valspar Foundation
Reynolds, Anne; The Cooperative Foundation
Rhodes, James; Park Nicollet Foundation
Rhude, James E.; Arsher Charitable Trust U/A
Riach, Ronald J.; North Suburban Community Foundation
Ribnick, Louise; Martin and Esther Miller Foundation
Rice, Mary H.; HRK Foundation
Rice, Molly E.; HRK Foundation
Richard, David; Carl and Aune Lind Family Foundation
Richard, Ethel A.; Carl and Aune Lind Family Foundation
Richards, Frederick S.; Edina Community Foundation
Richards, Margaret T.; James R. Thorpe Foundation
Richards, Phillip; North Star Charitable Foundation
Richards, Scott; North Star Charitable Foundation
Richards, Steven, M.D.; Blue Cross and Blue Shield of Minnesota Foundation/Blue Cross and Blue Shield of Minnesota
Richards, Susan; North Star Charitable Foundation
Richardson, Teresa; Women's Foundation of Minnesota
Ricke, Beatrice; TEAM Foundation
Riegel, Steve; CHS Foundation
Riemersma, Michele; H.B. Fuller Company Foundation
Ries, Kevin; Edina Community Foundation
Rikimoto, Chere; West Central Initiative
Rippy, Mary; Charlson Foundation
Ritt, John A.; Frances Curran Foundation, Inc.
  Ritt Family Foundation
Ritt, Steven; Ritt Family Foundation
Rivard, Laurie; Haggerty Family Foundation
Riviere, Mary Scott; Arthur and David Cosgrove Memorial Fund
Rizzi, S. T., Jr.; George A. Hormel Testamentary Trust
Roberts, David A.; The Graco Foundation
Robinson, Kathy; Philanthrofund Foundation (PFund)
Robinson, Marilyn J.; Daniel J. Spiegel Family Foundation
Robinson, Vince; Southwest Initiative Foundation
Rockwell, James W.; The Minneapolis Foundation
Rogosheske, Judy; Hennepin County Bar Foundation
Rohde, Bill; Travelers Corporation and Travelers Foundation
Roles, Linda; West Central Initiative
Rominski, Kathryn Hubbard; The Hubbard Broadcasting Foundation
Ronning, H. Rudy; The Martinson Foundation
Rose, Barbara; WCA Foundation
Rosen, Dennis; Farmers Union Marketing and Processing Foundation
Rosenberry, Charles W., II; The Charles A. Weyerhaeuser Memorial Foundation
Rosenblatt, Cynthia; Martin and Esther Capp Foundation
Ross, David; Affiliated Community Health Foundation
Ross, Sara; Target
Roszell, Stephen; The Minneapolis Foundation
Roth, Edith; Winona Foundation
Rotsch, J.J.; General Mills Community Action
Rounds, Charlie; ClearWay Minnesota
Rourke, Mike; Grand Rapids Area Community Foundation
Rousse, Sally; Sewell Family Foundation

Officers and Trustees

Routman, Brent; Hennepin County Bar Foundation
Rowell, Saundra; Ripley Memorial Foundation, Inc.
Ruben, Doris; Ethel Mae Kreutz Private Foundation
Ruben, Ralph P., Jr.; Ethel Mae Kreutz Private Foundation
Rubenstein, William H.; Hugh J. Andersen Foundation
Rubin, Wendy H.; The Saint Paul Foundation
Rufer, Stephen F.; Roger L. and Agnes C. Dell Charitable (Trust 1)
   Roger L. and Agnes C. Dell Charitable (Trust 2)
Rukavina, John; Rukavina Family Foundation
Rummans, Teresa A.; Mayo Clinic
Rumsey, Julie; The Donaldson Foundation
Russell, Judie; Ripley Memorial Foundation, Inc.
Ryan, John R., Jr.; The Saint Paul Foundation
Ryan, Peter; Catholic Aid Association Foundation
Rykken, Miriam; Hennepin County Bar Foundation

Sala, Rex; Grand Rapids Area Community Foundation
Salinas, Elaine; Headwaters Foundation for Justice
Sallarulo, Laurie; The Wasie Foundation
Salverda, Don; North Suburban Community Foundation
Sam, Mary; Initiative Foundation
Samatar, Hussein; The Minneapolis Foundation
Sand, Anne; Northwest Minnesota Foundation
Sandahl, Mike; Richfield Community Foundation
Sanger, S.W.; General Mills Community Action
Santori, Mary Beth; Ordean Foundation
Sather, Paul; Fargo-Moorhead Area Foundation
Sauer, Chad B.; Sauer Children's Renew Foundation
Sauer, Gary B.; Sauer Children's Renew Foundation
Sauer, Kay; Sauer Children's Renew Foundation
Sauer, Patricia A.; Sauer Children's Renew Foundation
Saunders, Arthur W.; Saunders Family Foundation
Saunders, John D.; Saunders Family Foundation
Saunders, W. B.; Saunders Family Foundation
Sawyer, Nan B.; Mayo Clinic
Scandrett, Michael; ClearWay Minnesota
Scanlan, John M.; F.R. Bigelow Foundation
Scanlan, Tim; Catholic Community Foundation in the Archdiocese of Saint Paul and Minneapolis
Scarbrough, Ken; Cloquet Educational Foundation
Scarfone, Anthony C.; Deluxe Corporation Foundation/Deluxe Corporation
Scavo, Mike; Italian American Club Foundation, Inc.
Schafer, Alan; Rochester Area Foundation
Schaffer, Tom; Fargo-Moorhead Area Foundation
Schalk, Janet; Target
Scherer, Roger; Catholic Community Foundation in the Archdiocese of Saint Paul and Minneapolis
Schiff, Judith A.; The Charles A. and Anne Morrow Lindbergh Foundation
Schiller, Paul; Sioux Falls Area Community Foundation
Schlagel, John; Initiative Foundation
Schlepp, Rollie; Farmers Union Marketing and Processing Foundation
Schmidt, Christie; North Suburban Youth Foundation
Schmidt, Paul; Wells Fargo Foundation Minnesota
Schmoker, Catherine S.; Schmoker Family Foundation
Schmoker, Richard C.; Schmoker Family Foundation
Schmoker, William C.; Schmoker Family Foundation
Schnack, Tom; Ecolab Foundation and Corporation
Schneeberger, David L.; Otto C. and Elsie Ewert Charitable Trust
Schneider, Beth; Park Nicollet Foundation
   St Francis Regional Medical Center Foundation
Schneider, M. C.; George A. Hormel Testamentary Trust
Schnobrich, Roger; Catholic Community Foundation in the Archdiocese of Saint Paul and Minneapolis
Schoenwetter, Robin B.; Ripley Memorial Foundation, Inc.
Schoeppner, Peter; Arthur and David Cosgrove Memorial Fund
Schooff, Dave; Mankato Area Foundation
Schoonmaker, Jon; Richfield Community Foundation
Schoonmaker, Lynn; Richfield Community Foundation
Schorr, Donna; 3M/3M Foundation

Schott, Owen W.; Schott Foundation
Schott, Wendell; Schott Foundation
Schroeder, Carolyn; Edina Community Foundation
Schubert, Gage A.; AHS Foundation
Schubert, John D.; AHS Foundation
Schubert, Leland W.; AHS Foundation
Schulkers, Joan; Hennepin County Bar Foundation
Schultz, Florence M.; Nevin Huested Foundation for Handicapped Children, Inc.
Schultz, Vernon A.; Nevin Huested Foundation for Handicapped Children, Inc.
Schulze, Arthur R., Jr.; The Schulze Family Foundation
Schulze, Joan M.; The Schulze Family Foundation
Schulze, Richard M.; Best Buy Children's Foundation
Schuman, Al; Ecolab Foundation and Corporation
Schurr, Don; CHS Foundation
Schwalm, Donald; Charity, Inc.
Schwan, Tim; Thrivent Financial for Lutherans Foundation
Schwarzkopf, Kurt; Travelers Corporation and Travelers Foundation
Score, Shawn; Best Buy Children's Foundation
Scott, Donald L.; Alex Stern Family Foundation
Scovanner, Doug; Target
Scovil, Ann; Ripley Memorial Foundation, Inc.
Scribner, Brett E.; Deluxe Corporation Foundation/Deluxe Corporation
Scully, Terry; Target
Seebold, Kenneth; Elizabeth Callender King Foundation
Seeger, Nancy Lavander; Caliber Foundation
Self, Karl; Healthier Minnesota Community Clinic Fund
Senkler, Robert L.; Securian Foundation/Securian Financial Group
Senske, Jim; Minnesota Twins Community Fund
Severson, Bonnie; The Jostens Foundation
Severson, Kim; The Dorsey & Whitney Foundation
Severson, Lawrence; Margaret Rivers Fund
Sewell, Frederick; Sewell Family Foundation
Sewell, Gloria; Sewell Family Foundation
Sewell, James; Sewell Family Foundation
Sewell, Laura; Sewell Family Foundation
Sexton, James W.; Sexton Foundation
Sexton, Thomas; Sexton Foundation
Sexton, Yvonne; Sexton Foundation
Shapiro, Jane; Shapiro Family Philanthropic Foundation
Shapiro, Peter; Shapiro Family Philanthropic Foundation
Shapiro, Richard; Shapiro Family Philanthropic Foundation
Shapiro, Sidney K.; Shapiro Family Philanthropic Foundation
Shaughnessy, Patrick; Extendicare Foundation
Shea, Samuel P.; Knitcraft - St Croix Foundation, Inc.
Sheahan, Mark; The Graco Foundation
Sheehan, Bill; The Jostens Foundation
Shelley, Steve; Initiative Foundation
Shepard, Judy; Winona Community Foundation
Sher, James; Ben and Jeanne Overman Charitable Trust
Sherman, David C.; Baker Foundation
   The Wasie Foundation
Sherman, Morris M.; N. Bud and Beverly Grossman Foundation
Sherman, Sandra B.; Baker Foundation
Sherman, William J.; Baker Foundation
Sherritt, Jill; Frances Curran Foundation, Inc.
Sherwood, Richard J.; Federated Insurance Foundation, Inc.
Shetka, Stanley; Virginia A. Groot Foundation
Shiebler, Christina; The Shiebler Family Foundation
Shiebler, Jason; The Shiebler Family Foundation
Shiebler, Joanne; The Shiebler Family Foundation
Shiebler, William; The Shiebler Family Foundation
Shields, Tim; Hennepin County Bar Foundation
Shiffman, Mark; Minnesota Twins Community Fund
Shotley, Marsha; Blue Cross and Blue Shield of Minnesota Foundation/Blue Cross and Blue Shield of Minnesota
Siegel, Marty; Park Nicollet Foundation
Silberberg, Richard; The Dorsey & Whitney Foundation

Officers and Trustees

Silvertsen, Robert J.; The Charles A. Weyerhaeuser Memorial Foundation
Simer, Lisa; Ann Bancroft Foundation
Simmet, John P.; The Simmet Foundation
Simmet, Margaret M.; The Simmet Foundation
Simmet, Mary C.; The Simmet Foundation
Simmet, Mary M.; The Simmet Foundation
Simmet, Nancy A.; The Simmet Foundation
Simmet, Patricia M.; The Simmet Foundation
Simmet, Robert P.; The Simmet Foundation
Simon, John; CDF Foundation
Simonson, Elizabeth; Eddy (Edwin H.) Foundation
Simpson, Rhonda Mims; ING Foundation
Simpson, Warren; SUPERVALU Foundation
Sims, Frank; Cargill Foundation
Sirois, John; Indian Land Tenure Foundation
Siska, Nancy; The Minneapolis Foundation
Sjoberg, Richard; Hartz Foundation
Sjoquist, Gregg D.; The Wasie Foundation
Skanse, C.A.; Douglas Foundation
Skanse, Douglas; Douglas Foundation
Skanse, Ronald D.; Douglas Foundation
Skuza, Tracy; Catholic Aid Association Foundation
Slaggie, Steve; Slaggie Family Foundation
Slattery, Joan; Shamrock Foundation
Slattery, John P.; Shamrock Foundation
Slattery, Kevin J.; Shamrock Foundation
Slattery, Linda; Shamrock Foundation
Slattery, Robert M.; Shamrock Foundation
Slattery, W. Daniel, Jr.; Shamrock Foundation
Slattery, William; Shamrock Foundation
Slaughter, Nancy; Women's Foundation of Minnesota
Slawik, D.; Slawik Family Foundation
Slawik, H.; Slawik Family Foundation
Slawik, J. O., Jr.; Slawik Family Foundation
Slawik, J. O., Sr.; Slawik Family Foundation
Slawik, M. S.; Slawik Family Foundation
Slette, Gary; J. A. Wedum Foundation
Slye, Terry L.; Elmer L. and Eleanor J. Andersen Foundation
Smidt, Stephanie; Marjorie and V.M. Baich Foundation
Smith, Eleanor W.; Carolyn Foundation
Smith, Joseph L.; Fidelis Foundation
Smith, Julie; Andersen Corporate Foundation
Smith, Russell; Cloquet Educational Foundation
Smith, Sherry; SUPERVALU Foundation
Soby, Dayton; J. A. Wedum Foundation
Somerville, Ron; The Jostens Foundation
Sorenson, Susan; Ripley Memorial Foundation, Inc.
Sorlie, Oscar J., Jr.; Otto C. and Elsie Ewert Charitable Trust
Sorrentino, Ed; Grand Rapids Area Community Foundation
Sortland, Paul; Minneapolis Kiwanis Foundation
Southall, Roderic; Philanthrofund Foundation (PFund)
Spanier, Florbert L.; Catholic Aid Association Foundation
Speirn, Sterling K.; W.K. Kellogg Foundation
Spell, Angeline; The Spell Family Foundation
Spell, Diane; The Spell Family Foundation
Spell, Harry; The Spell Family Foundation
Spell, William; The Spell Family Foundation
Spence, Ken; Travelers Corporation and Travelers Foundation
Spence, Patricia; Initiative Foundation
Spencer, Barbara A.; Eddy (Edwin H.) Foundation
Spencer, Valerie; Women's Foundation of Minnesota
Spiegel, Benjamin S.; Daniel J. Spiegel Family Foundation
Spiegel, Daniel J.; Daniel J. Spiegel Family Foundation
Spiegel, Dorie M.; Daniel J. Spiegel Family Foundation
Spiegel, Emily I.; Daniel J. Spiegel Family Foundation
Splinter, Ann; Mankato Area Foundation
Sponheim, Sarah F.; Lang Family Charitable Trust
Sprenger, Gordon M.; Bush Foundation
Spruill, Amelia; Noel Foundation
Spruill, Kevin; Noel Foundation
St Peter, David; Minnesota Twins Community Fund
   Park Nicollet Foundation
Stafford, Jan; Lillian Wright and C. Emil Berglund Foundation, Inc.
Stafsholt, Honorable Jon; Minnesota State Bar Foundation
Stainbrook, Cris E.; Grotto Foundation, Inc.
   The Saint Paul Foundation
Stake, J. B.; 3M/3M Foundation
Stampohar, Jeff; Grand Rapids Area Community Foundation
Starke, Frank; J. A. Wedum Foundation
Starns, Byron E.; Leonard, Street and Deinard Foundation
Staryk, Ted; The McKnight Foundation
Stauffer, Joe; Grand Rapids Area Community Foundation
Stawarz, Ray; Federated Insurance Foundation, Inc.
Stead, David; Minnesota Twins Community Fund
Stein, Gretchen M.; St Croix Valley Community Foundation
   Tozer Foundation, Inc.
Steiner, Jim; Wells Fargo Foundation Minnesota
Steinhafel, Gregg; Target
Stender, Bruce; Blandin Foundation
Stenerson, James; Fargo-Moorhead Area Foundation
Stenhaug, David; Rochester Area Foundation
Stenson, Gerald; The Minneapolis Foundation
   Wells Fargo Foundation Minnesota
Stenzel, Duane; CHS Foundation
Stephens, Ann M.; Unity Avenue Foundation
Stephenson, Julie; Beim Foundation
Stevens, Cheryl; Healthier Minnesota Community Clinic Fund
Stewart, Joseph M.; W.K. Kellogg Foundation
Stibbe, John; Fargo-Moorhead Area Foundation
Stiles, Leslie H.; Charlson Foundation
Stoffel, James; SUPERVALU Foundation
Stoltz, Daniel E.; The Cooperative Foundation
   The Charles A. and Anne Morrow Lindbergh Foundation
Stone, Gayne; Affiliated Community Health Foundation
Storms, Joshua; St Francis Regional Medical Center Foundation
Storms, Roger; Park Nicollet Foundation
Straka, Stacey; Mankato Area Foundation
Strand, Lindsay; The Sheltering Arms Foundation
Strasburg, Robert; The Laura Jane Musser Fund
Straw, Nancy; West Central Initiative
Stried, Amy W.; Weyerhaeuser Family Foundation, Inc.
   Frederick and Margaret L. Weyerhaeuser Foundation
Stroik, Gregory J.; Federated Insurance Foundation, Inc.
Stromborg, Janet; Donald and Marjorie Meredith Foundation
Strong, Gregory; Securian Foundation/Securian Financial Group
Struyk, Robert; The McKnight Foundation
Stuge, Oern R.; The Medtronic Foundation
Stumne, Deb; Edina Realty Foundation
Stump, MaryAnn, R.N.; Blue Cross and Blue Shield of Minnesota Foundation/Blue Cross and Blue Shield of Minnesota
Styx, Ann; Eagan Foundation, Incorporated
Suir, Steve; Mankato Area Foundation
Sukke, Paul; West Central Initiative
Sullivan, Arleen; Eagan Foundation, Incorporated
Sullivan, John; Central Minnesota Community Foundation
Sullivan, Marcie Turner; Turner Family Foundation
Sullivan, Michael F.; Ted and Roberta Mann Foundation
Sunderman, Dave; Mankato Area Foundation
Sutter, Fred A.; The Graco Foundation
Swan, Alan J.; Swan Family Foundation
Swan, Esther L.; Swan Family Foundation
Swan, James W.; Swan Family Foundation
Swanhorst, Jeffrey; The Cooperative Foundation
Swanson, Jay; The Dorsey & Whitney Foundation
Swanson, Sandy; H.B. Fuller Company Foundation
Swanson, Shane; Philanthrofund Foundation (PFund)
Swartz, Joan; The Pentair Foundation
Swartz, Lonnie; Ordean Foundation

Officers and Trustees

Sweasy, William J.; Red Wing Shoe Company Foundation
Sweetman, Mary Pat; Sioux Falls Area Community Foundation
Sweitzer, James A.; Sweitzer Foundation
Sweitzer, Joan T.; Sweitzer Foundation
Swenson, Roland; Affiliated Community Health Foundation
Switz, Robert E.; ADC Foundation
Swon, Lynn; Minneapolis Rotary Community Service Foundation
Szitta, Christina; Hennepin County Bar Foundation

Tanaka, Jodie; Minnesota Twins Community Fund
Tanquist, Dwight; Hartz Foundation
Tapani, Kevin; Minnesota Twins Community Fund
Tapper, John; SKB Environmental Rosemount Community Trust
Taylor, Glen A.; The Minnesota Timberwolves FastBreak Foundation
Taylor, Jane; The Laura Jane Musser Fund
Taylor, Stephen; Trust for the Meditation Process
Teckman, Lynne; The Sheltering Arms Foundation
Terry, Paul E.; Park Nicollet Foundation
Thatcher, R. J.; George A. Hormel Testamentary Trust
Theobald, Jon; Hardenbergh Foundation
  Tozer Foundation, Inc.
Thomas, Jack; O'Shaughnessy Foundation
Thomas, Nicole; Horst M. Rechelbacher Foundation
Thompson, George; Blandin Foundation
Thompson, John R.; Best Buy Children's Foundation
Thompson, Kris; The Jostens Foundation
Thompson, Robert F.; Minneapolis Kiwanis Foundation
Thompson, Sally A.; Lillian Wright and C. Emil Berglund Foundation, Inc.
Thompson, Todd; Winona Community Foundation
Thor, Mai; Headwaters Foundation for Justice
Thoreen, John F.; Tozer Foundation, Inc.
Thoreson, Louise K.; The Saint Paul Foundation
Thorpe, Edith D.; James R. Thorpe Foundation
Thorpe, Laura A.; James R. Thorpe Foundation
Thorpe, Samuel S.; James R. Thorpe Foundation
Thorpe, Timothy D.; James R. Thorpe Foundation
Thorpe-Mease, Mary; Minneapolis Area Association of Realtors Foundation, Inc.
Thorstad, Anntionette D.; Ordean Foundation
Tichenor, E. J.; Slawik Family Foundation
Tidwell, Mary; Sioux Falls Area Community Foundation
Tiller, Tom; The Polaris Foundation
Tilney, Katherine R.; HRK Foundation
Titcomb, Frederick W.; Weyerhaeuser Family Foundation, Inc.
Titcomb, Judith L.; The Saint Paul Foundation
Titcomb, Megan L.; Weyerhaeuser Family Foundation, Inc.
Titcomb, Robert; Weyerhaeuser Family Foundation, Inc.
Tobin, Ann; Headwaters Foundation for Justice
Tokach, S. K.; 3M/3M Foundation
Tone, Terry; Affiliated Community Health Foundation
Toombs, John P.; Noel Foundation
Toombs, Polly; Noel Foundation
Tosney, Tom; Wells Fargo Foundation Minnesota
Touchin, David; George Kaplan Memorial Foundation, Incorporated
Tovey, David; Indian Land Tenure Foundation
Traeger, Michele O'Shaughnessy; I. A. O'Shaughnessy Foundation, Incorporated
Trauger, Kathy; Mankato Area Foundation
Treff, Douglas J.; Deluxe Corporation Foundation/Deluxe Corporation
Treichel, Christa; Frances Curran Foundation, Inc.
Treinis, David E.; The Charles A. and Anne Morrow Lindbergh Foundation
Trusty, Jay; Affiliated Community Health Foundation
Tschumper, Edith; Elizabeth Callender King Foundation
Tubbs, Maureen; Minneapolis Rotary Community Service Foundation
Tuckson, Reed V., M.D.; United Health Foundation
Tunheim, Kathryn H.; Bush Foundation
  St Croix Valley Community Foundation
Tuohy, Michael, Jr.; Southern Minnesota Initiative Foundation

Turner, Andrew W.; Turner Family Foundation
Turner, James G.; Turner Family Foundation
Turner, John F.; Turner Family Foundation
Turner, John G.; Turner Family Foundation
Turner, Leslie C.; Turner Family Foundation
Turnquist, Vicki; Minneapolis Rotary Community Service Foundation
Twedell, Dianne; Southern Minnesota Initiative Foundation

Ueland, April; Winona Foundation
Uhrich, Marie; Thrivent Financial for Lutherans Foundation
Ulrich, Bob; Target
Ulrich, Doreen; Eagan Foundation, Incorporated
Ulrich, Tim; Southwest Initiative Foundation
Underdahl, Steve; Southern Minnesota Initiative Foundation

Valle, Chris; The Donaldson Foundation
Vallenga, Kathleen; H.B. Fuller Company Foundation
Valley, Sherry; Southern Minnesota Initiative Foundation
Van Denmark, Richard; Sioux Falls Area Community Foundation
Van Evera, Stephen; DeWitt and Caroline Van Evera Foundation
Van Valkenburg, James; Edina Community Foundation
Vanasse, Mark; St Croix Valley Community Foundation
Vanderpoel, Jane; Eagan Foundation, Incorporated
Vang-Johnson, Friendly; Headwaters Foundation for Justice
VanNurden, Steven P.; Minnesota Research Fund
Vasaly, Mary; Hennepin County Bar Foundation
Vasko, Roger; Catholic Community Foundation in the Archdiocese of Saint Paul and Minneapolis
Vega-Perez, Elsa; The Saint Paul Foundation
Venne, Bill; Philanthrofund Foundation (PFund)
Vesledahl, Dale; J. A. Wedum Foundation
Vetter, Richard, M.D.; Dakota Medical Foundation/Dakota Medical Charities
Villani, Allison; Beim Foundation
Villella, Harry; Italian American Club Foundation, Inc.
Villella, Jerry; Italian American Club Foundation, Inc.
Vobr, Nan; TEAM Foundation
Voegele, Gary; Minnesota State Bar Foundation
Volpi, Michele; H.B. Fuller Company Foundation
Vorhies, Todd; Winona Foundation
Vos, Brian; The Vos Family Foundation

Wade, John; Rochester Area Foundation
Wade, Sharon James; Women's Foundation of Minnesota
Waggoner, Pamela; Minnesota State Bar Foundation
Walburn, Roberta; Robins, Kaplan, Miller & Ciresi, L.L.P. Foundation for Education, Public Health & Social Justice
Waldhoff, Steve; Southern Minnesota Initiative Foundation
Waldock, Janelle; Eagan Foundation, Incorporated
Waldorf, Gene; Initiative Foundation
Walker, Amy C.; Archie D. and Bertha H. Walker Foundation
Walker, Berta B.; Archie D. and Bertha H. Walker Foundation
Walker, Colin M.; Archie D. and Bertha H. Walker Foundation
Walker, Drew; The Laura Jane Musser Fund
Walker, Elaine B.; Archie D. and Bertha H. Walker Foundation
Walker, Joyce; The Sheltering Arms Foundation
Walker, Kate; Minnesota Twins Community Fund
Walker, Meg; The Laura Jane Musser Fund
Walker, Sally L.; Archie D. and Bertha H. Walker Foundation
Wallace, Bob; Southern Minnesota Initiative Foundation
Wallgren, Donald L.; Duluth Superior Area Community Foundation
Wallin, George; Initiative Foundation
Wallman, Joyce; Fargo-Moorhead Area Foundation
Walsh, Erika; Winona Foundation
Walsh, John; Minneapolis Area Association of Realtors Foundation, Inc.
Walt, Chuck; Northland Foundation
Wangen, Gail; Cloquet Educational Foundation
Wanzek, Jon; Dakota Medical Foundation/Dakota Medical Charities
Ward, Laysha; Target

Officers and Trustees

Ward, Scott R.; The Medtronic Foundation
Warden, Jody; Youthworks! Foundation, Inc.
Ward-Reichard, Courtney; Hennepin County Bar Foundation
Warner, Ann Cosgrove; Arthur and David Cosgrove Memorial Fund
Warner, Bradley; Arthur and David Cosgrove Memorial Fund
Warner, Mark A.; Mayo Clinic
Warren, Garth; Fidelis Foundation
Washko, Leonard J.; Minneapolis Kiwanis Foundation
Wasko, Robert J.; Olga B. Hart Education Foundation
Waterbury, David; Headwaters Foundation for Justice
Watkins, Don; Central Minnesota Community Foundation
Watson, Douglas F.; Frederick O. Watson Foundation
Watson, Stephen M.; Frederick O. Watson Foundation
Watson, Wendy K.; Whitney ARCEE Foundation
Weaklend, Dave; West Central Initiative
Weber, Michael; Minneapolis Rotary Community Service Foundation
Weber, Sue; West Central Initiative
Webster, S. C.; 3M/3M Foundation
Wedum, Mary Beth; J. A. Wedum Foundation
Wehlage, Georgina M.; Mae and Sylvester Weiss Foundation
Weichmann, Marcus; George W. Neilson Foundation
Weidner, Kay; Extendicare Foundation
Weiner, Frederick; The Shared Fund
Weiner, Howard; The Shared Fund
Weismantel, Lyle; Affiliated Community Health Foundation
Weiss, Mae; Mae and Sylvester Weiss Foundation
Weiss, Robert M.; Park Nicollet Foundation
Welle, E. Joseph; First National Bank of Bemidji Foundation
Welle, Paul N.; First National Bank of Bemidji Foundation
    George W. Neilson Foundation
Welle, Robert J.; First National Bank of Bemidji Foundation
Welter, Helen; Trust for the Meditation Process
Welters, Anthony; United Health Foundation
Wendel, Kristin; The Donaldson Foundation
Wendland, Craig; Rochester Area Foundation
Wenger, Jerry A.; Wenger Foundation
Wenger, Sonja; Wenger Foundation
Wenger, Wendy; Wenger Foundation
Werling, Robert; OSilas Foundation
Werth, Caleb; Cottonwood Foundation
Wessner, David K.; Park Nicollet Foundation
Wettergren, David; St Croix Valley Community Foundation
    Tozer Foundation, Inc.
Wexler, David; Mark and Muriel Wexler Foundation
Wexler, Muriel; Mark and Muriel Wexler Foundation
Wexler, Steven; Mark and Muriel Wexler Foundation
Weyerhaeuser, Daniel J.; Frederick and Margaret L. Weyerhaeuser Foundation
Weyerhaeuser, Justin H.; Weyerhaeuser Family Foundation, Inc.
Wheeler, John; Mall of America Foundation for Youth
Wheeler, Thomas B.; Duluth Superior Area Community Foundation
Whitaker, Shannon McNeely; McNeely Foundation
White, Frank; Richfield Community Foundation
White, Mary; Trust for the Meditation Process
White Hat, Emily; Indian Land Tenure Foundation
Whitley, Steven R.; The Charles A. and Anne Morrow Lindbergh Foundation
Whitney, Joseph; Whitney Foundation
Whitney, Pennell; Whitney Foundation
Whitney, Wheelock; Whitney Foundation
Whitney, Wheelock, III; Whitney Foundation
Widener, Luann E.; Deluxe Corporation Foundation/Deluxe Corporation
Wiener, Barbra; Headwaters Foundation for Justice
Wigchers, Nancy; Richfield Community Foundation
Wilcox, Kenneth E.; Owatonna Foundation
Wilcox, Noah; Grand Rapids Area Community Foundation
Wilcox, Steve; St Croix Valley Community Foundation
Wilcox, Thomas P.; Alice M. O'Brien Foundation
Wilkinson, Catherine W.; Helen Sperry Lea Foundation

Williams, Christopher, M.D.; Park Nicollet Foundation
Williams, David K.; Southern Minnesota Initiative Foundation
Williams, Terry; Women's Foundation of Minnesota
Williams, Warren; Initiative Foundation
Wilson, C. Steven; Gray Plant Mooty Foundation
Wilson, Kim; Northwest Minnesota Foundation
Wilson, Mark L.; The Saint Paul Foundation
Wilson, Perry; Headwaters Foundation for Justice
Wilson, Tom; Hennepin County Bar Foundation
Wilson, Tracey; Minneapolis Area Association of Realtors Foundation, Inc.
Wilson, Walter R.; Mayo Clinic
Wind, Todd; Fredrikson & Byron Foundation
Winston, Eleanor C.; Southways Foundation
Winston, Frederick; Quetico Superior Foundation
Winton, Alexa Griffith; Archie D. and Bertha H. Walker Foundation
Witkowsky, Anne; Luther I. Replogle Foundation
Wittrock, Quentin R.; Gray Plant Mooty Foundation
Wixon, Renee Vanman ; Ripley Memorial Foundation, Inc.
Wojcik, Martin H.; The Wasie Foundation
Wolfe, Carol F.; Frey Foundation
Wolfe, Daniel T.; Frey Foundation
Wolfe, Steve; The Toro Company Giving Program
Wolfe, Tim; The Jostens Foundation
Wolfson, Stephen W.; Hugh J. Andersen Foundation
Wong, Mary; Women's Foundation of Minnesota
Woodford, Barbara; Donald and Marjorie Meredith Foundation
Woodworth, J. K.; 3M/3M Foundation
Wordell, Angie; The Graco Foundation
Workinger, Geof; Edina Community Foundation
Wosepka, John; J. A. Wedum Foundation
Wright, Dr. Charles; Trust for the Meditation Process
Wright, Jeff; G&K Services Foundation
Wright, Mary; Richard A. Newman Foundation
Wright, Thomas; AHS Foundation
Wright, Wilhelmina M.; Mardag Foundation
Wulf, J. W.; Fred C. and Katherine B. Andersen Foundation
Wyman, James C.; Quetico Superior Foundation
Wynne, Liz; Park Nicollet Foundation
Wysong, Kathryn; I. A. O'Shaughnessy Foundation, Incorporated

Yeomans, J. L.; 3M/3M Foundation
Yorston, James; Cloquet Educational Foundation
Young, Grayce Belvedere ; Women's Foundation of Minnesota
Young, Kyle; First National Bank of Bemidji Foundation
Young, Tricia; TEAM Foundation
Yrjo, Don; Redwood Area Communities Foundation, Inc.

Zahariades, Gust; North Suburban Community Foundation
Zelle, Julie B.; Marbrook Foundation
Zemsky, Beth; Headwaters Foundation for Justice
Zeppa, Alan H.; A. H. Zeppa Family Foundation
Zibell, Donald F.; North Suburban Community Foundation
Ziemer, Joan; Park Nicollet Foundation
Zimmerman, Honorable Lloyd B.; Minnesota State Bar Foundation
Zimmerman, Rabbi Marcia; Robins, Kaplan, Miller & Ciresi, L.L.P. Foundation for Education, Public Health & Social Justice
Zoidis, Susan Saunders; Saunders Family Foundation

Staff Index

Aaland, Karla; Fargo-Moorhead Area Foundation
Abbott, Becky; Catholic Community Foundation in the Archdiocese of Saint Paul and Minneapolis
Adams, Jean; The Minneapolis Foundation
Adkins, Athena; Travelers Corporation and Travelers Foundation
Albrecht, Lois; Duluth Superior Area Community Foundation
Aldrich, Duane; Central Minnesota Community Foundation
Allen, Gregory E.; The Minneapolis Foundation
Allen, Mark; Minneapolis Area Association of Realtors Foundation, Inc.
Allen, Marty; The Medtronic Foundation
Allen, Sean; Rochester Area Foundation
Amys, Jan; Northland Foundation
Ancheta, Jocelyn; Blue Cross and Blue Shield of Minnesota Foundation/Blue Cross and Blue Shield of Minnesota
Anderson, Allison; Rochester Area Foundation
Anderson, DeAnne; Petters Group Worldwide, LLC
Anderson, Deb; The Medtronic Foundation
Anderson, Diana; Southwest Initiative Foundation
Anderson, Duane Roger; Farmers Union Marketing and Processing Foundation
Anderson, Elizabeth; Thrivent Financial for Lutherans Foundation
Anderson, Eric L.; The Minneapolis Foundation
Anderson, Jennifer A.; Deluxe Corporation Foundation/Deluxe Corporation
Anderson, Liz; RBC Dain Rauscher Foundation
Anderson, Mary J.; St Francis Regional Medical Center Foundation
Andreasen, Anne; Minnesota Business and Professional Women's Foundation
Appelbaum, Stuart; The Minneapolis Foundation
Archabal, John; Bush Foundation
Armstrong, Steve; Patterson Foundation
Atkins-Sakry, Martha; Land O'Lakes Foundation
Atwood, Anne; Ann Bancroft Foundation
Aubinger, Jeana; The Minneapolis Foundation

Bachleitner, Paul; The Minneapolis Foundation
Bachman, Lisa; The Minneapolis Foundation
Backstrom, Lin; Northwest Minnesota Foundation
Bail, Zane; Northland Foundation
Bailey, Penny; Bahl Foundation
Baker, Susan; The McKnight Foundation
Balfour, Jeannine; The McKnight Foundation
Barlow, Ruth; General Mills Community Action
Barrow, Sara Perlman; The Lawrence and Linda Perlman Family Foundation
Bartholomay, Dan; The McKnight Foundation
Behling, Lisa; Extendicare Foundation
Benson, Duane; Minnesota Early Learning Foundation
Benson, Lee-Hoon; Bush Foundation
Benson, Vickie; The McKnight Foundation
Berg, Daniel; The Minneapolis Foundation
Berger, Berny; Southwest Initiative Foundation
Berg-Kirsch, Lori A.; The Saint Paul Foundation
Berndt, Janie; Mankato Area Foundation
Binner, Wes; West Central Initiative
Birkeland, Peter A.; Minnesota Research Fund
Birkholz, JoAnn M.; Medica Foundation
Bishop, Pam; Southern Minnesota Initiative Foundation
Bjergen, Joan; Park Nicollet Foundation
Blackburn, Frank; The Cooperative Foundation
Blair, Jammi Hansen; The CCP Foundation
Blaisdell, Patricia M.; Minnesota Research Fund

Blevins, Kerrie; Beim Foundation
Patrick and Aimee Butler Family Foundation
The Laura Jane Musser Fund
Bloemke, Jody; AgStar Fund for Rural America
Bogart, Stacy; The Toro Company Giving Program
Bolinger, Martha; Trust for the Meditation Process
Bonfert, Gretchen; The McKnight Foundation
Bonnifield, Kathy; The McKnight Foundation
Bordeaux, D'Arcy; Indian Land Tenure Foundation
Borsheim, Becky; The Minneapolis Foundation
Borth, Janet; Blandin Foundation
Borzo, Nancy; Catholic Community Foundation in the Archdiocese of Saint Paul and Minneapolis
Botham, Lydia; Land O'Lakes Foundation
Boudreau, Paul; Honeywell Hometown Solutions
Brandt, Katie; U.S. Bancorp Foundation
Braun, Heidi; Women's Foundation of Minnesota
Breems, Nora; Duluth Superior Area Community Foundation
Bridger, Pamela; Deluxe Corporation Foundation/Deluxe Corporation
Brindle, Mary; Edina Community Foundation
Brink, Jennifer; The Minneapolis Foundation
Brouse, Heather; Northland Foundation
Brown, Donnie; Minneapolis Area Association of Realtors Foundation, Inc.
Brown, Heidi; Southern Minnesota Initiative Foundation
Brunner, Jim; Owatonna Foundation
Bryand, Monica; Headwaters Foundation for Justice
Bucher, Matt; Otter Tail Power Company
Buchholz, John; Philanthrofund Foundation (PFund)
Bullock, Ellis; Grotto Foundation, Inc.
Burdick, Judy; Park Nicollet Foundation
Burke, Cecelia; Indian Land Tenure Foundation
Burke, Deborah; U.S. Bancorp Foundation
Burton, Michael; Central Minnesota Community Foundation
Buxbaum, Laurence R.; Hennepin County Bar Foundation
Byers Strand, Becky; Duluth Superior Area Community Foundation
Byrd, Robert; Jerome Foundation
Byrne, Colleen; The Minneapolis Foundation

Callen, Philip; Tapemark Charity Pro-Am Golf Tournament
Campion, Jane; Rochester Area Foundation
Capune, Renee; TCF Foundation
Carlson, Barbara; Central Minnesota Community Foundation
Carlson, Betty; Allianz Life Insurance Company of North America
Carlson, Sara; Southwest Initiative Foundation
Carlton, Bethany; Initiative Foundation
Cash, Jennifer; ClearWay Minnesota
Cerney, Carol; Southern Minnesota Initiative Foundation
Ceynar, Erin; Women's Foundation of Minnesota
Chang, Claire J.; The Saint Paul Foundation
Chapin, Barb; Duluth Superior Area Community Foundation
Chase, Patricia; Indian Land Tenure Foundation
Cheslog, Danielle; Otto Bremer Foundation
Chester, Lesley A.; Eagan Foundation, Incorporated
Chipman, Carol; Northland Foundation
Christiansen, Bernadette; The McKnight Foundation
Christiansen, Nilla; Fredrikson & Byron Foundation
Cirillo, A. C., Jr.; 3M/3M Foundation
Clark, Patti; Frederick O. Watson Foundation
Cleary, Joan; Blue Cross and Blue Shield of Minnesota Foundation/Blue Cross and Blue Shield of Minnesota
Codega, Kelly; Park Nicollet Foundation

Staff

Cogger, Susan; Philanthrofund Foundation (PFund)
Conzemius, Brian; Southern Minnesota Initiative Foundation
Coonen, Karen; Thrivent Financial for Lutherans Foundation
Copeland, Sarah; Grand Rapids Area Community Foundation
Corriston, Ann; John S. and James L. Knight Foundation
Cote, Robert; Cote Foundation
Cottington, Jean Hayes; ACA International Foundation
Couchman, John G.; F.R. Bigelow Foundation
   Mardag Foundation
   The Saint Paul Foundation
Coughlan, Robert J.; Coughlan Companies
Coughlan, T. William; Coughlan Companies
Cowsert, Susan; Edina Realty Foundation
Craig, Heather; Medica Foundation
Crandall, Peggy; Northwest Minnesota Foundation
Crawford, Amy K.; The Jay and Rose Phillips Family Foundation
Crockett, Dick; Edina Community Foundation
Crow, Jon K.; Southways Foundation
Cuthbert, Neal; The McKnight Foundation

Dahl, Jeanine; Northland Foundation
Daily, Mary; Securian Foundation/Securian Financial Group
Davis, Elise; Southern Minnesota Initiative Foundation
Davis, Katy; HRK Foundation
DeBoer, Al; Rochester Area Foundation
Delp-Cassidy, Maureen; Honeywell Hometown Solutions
DeMark, Sharon; The Saint Paul Foundation
Deters, Marigrace; The Minneapolis Foundation
Deziel, Liz; U.S. Bancorp Foundation
Dingels, Patricia; Redwood Area Communities Foundation, Inc.
Dokos, Diana; W. Glen Boyd Charitable Foundation
Dominowski, Michael; Target
Doron, Reuven; Southern Minnesota Initiative Foundation
Dostal, Nancy; Saunders Family Foundation
Draayer, Sue; Southern Minnesota Initiative Foundation
Dreher, Marietta; ClearWay Minnesota
D'Silva, Joanne; ClearWay Minnesota
Duffy, Stephanie; The McKnight Foundation
Dufner, Terri; Blandin Foundation

Eastlund, Rob; Impact Foundation, Inc.
Egge, Terry; Marquette Financial Companies Community Support Program
   Carl and Eloise Pohlad Family Foundation
Eggl, Cynthia; Dakota Medical Foundation/Dakota Medical Charities
Eggum, Mari Oyanagi; Elmer L. and Eleanor J. Andersen Foundation
Eichers, Christy; The Medtronic Foundation
Eickelberg, Jenni; Thrivent Financial for Lutherans Foundation
Ekechuku, Ilse; Carl and Eloise Pohlad Family Foundation
Elden, John; Northland Foundation
Eldred, Marilou; Catholic Community Foundation in the Archdiocese of Saint Paul and Minneapolis
Elj, Rebecca; Burdick-Craddick Family Foundation
Embretson, Kim; West Central Initiative
Epstein, Lois; Philanthrofund Foundation (PFund)
Erdahl, Becky; Carolyn Foundation
Etzwiler, David; The Medtronic Foundation
Everett, Joe E.; Ordean Foundation

Facey, Nadia; Park Nicollet Foundation
Fakler, Lisa; Winona Community Foundation
Fasching, Nancy; Southwest Initiative Foundation
Fastner, Chris; Initiative Foundation
Fauth, Wade; Blandin Foundation
Fawcett, Joan; St Francis Regional Medical Center Foundation
Feigh, Casey; Mall of America Foundation for Youth
Fetzer, Carol; Longview Foundation
Field, Martha; Thomson West
Fish, Dawn; John T. Petters Foundation
Fjorden, Karen; Jerome Foundation

Fleitman, Sandra K.; Andersen Corporate Foundation
Flood, Chris; Rochester Area Foundation
Flower, Donald; The Minneapolis Foundation
Flowers, Charlotte; Women's Foundation of Minnesota
Fluegel, Kathleen; HRK Foundation
Fox, Debbie; Thrivent Financial for Lutherans Foundation
Frank, Dan; Initiative Foundation
Fredericks, MayKao; Wells Fargo Foundation Minnesota
Friesz, Katy; ADC Foundation
Frisbie, Liz; Southwest Initiative Foundation
Fushan, Nancy; Bush Foundation

Gaalswyk, Kathy; Initiative Foundation
Gale, Patrick; Sioux Falls Area Community Foundation
Ganzlin, Christine; The McKnight Foundation
Gardner-Goodno, Joan; Lloyd K. Johnson Foundation
Garness, Jim; Xcel Energy Foundation/Corporate Citizenship
Gebhard, Gwenn; Luther I. Replogle Foundation
Gebur, Tom; Southern Minnesota Initiative Foundation
Gehrig, Cynthia A.; Jerome Foundation
Gerst, Bill; Minneapolis Area Association of Realtors Foundation, Inc.
Geving, Sarah; Bromelkamp Foundation
Giardina, Carmela F.; Faegre & Benson Foundation
Gibb, David; Dakota Medical Foundation/Dakota Medical Charities
Gibeau, Linda; Blandin Foundation
Gilbert, Linda; Jerome Foundation
Gillstrom, M. F.; Fred C. and Katherine B. Andersen Foundation
Glaeser, Cheryl; Southwest Initiative Foundation
Gloege, Kristen; Healthier Minnesota Community Clinic Fund
Glomb, Gerald; The CCP Foundation
Glomb, Mary; The CCP Foundation
Gonzalez, Jose; Bush Foundation
Gordon, Kerri; ClearWay Minnesota
Gordon, Sara; TEAM Foundation
Gothmann, Sheila; Women's Foundation of Minnesota
Gottwalt, Sharon; Initiative Foundation
Gray, John J., Jr.; George A. Hormel Testamentary Trust
Griffith, David H.; St Croix Valley Community Foundation
Grinley, Gregory; Philanthrofund Foundation (PFund)
Groff, Keralyn; H.B. Fuller Company Foundation
Grogg, Michelle; Cargill Citizenship Fund
Grossman, Diane; The Sheltering Arms Foundation
Gruesner, Jo Ann; Frey Foundation
Grundstrom, Eileen J.; Indian Land Tenure Foundation
Guglielmo, Rudy, Jr.; Bush Foundation
Gunderson, Barbara; Southern Minnesota Initiative Foundation
Guse, Carol M.; Blue Cross and Blue Shield of Minnesota Foundation/Blue Cross and Blue Shield of Minnesota
Gustad, Carol; Fargo-Moorhead Area Foundation
Gustafson, Maureen; Coughlan Companies

Hagen, Tami; Minneapolis Rotary Community Service Foundation
Hagerty, Jamie; The McKnight Foundation
Haglin, Lynn; Northland Foundation
Haider, Jessica; Best Buy Children's Foundation
Haley, Marcia; Southern Minnesota Initiative Foundation
Hall, Tracy; Ameriprise Financial, Inc.
Hang, Kaying; Otto Bremer Foundation
Hanley, Stacy; Best Buy Children's Foundation
Hannaher, Michael; Fargo-Moorhead Area Foundation
Hanrahan, Tim; The McKnight Foundation
Hansen, Kathleen; J. A. Wedum Foundation
Hansen, Lisa M.; The Saint Paul Foundation
Hanson, Candy; Sioux Falls Area Community Foundation
Hanson, Curt; Initiative Foundation
Hanson, Mary Beth; Women's Foundation of Minnesota
Hanson, Peggy; Minnesota Power Foundation
Hanson, Rae Jean; Southern Minnesota Initiative Foundation
Hanson, Tina; Thrivent Financial for Lutherans Foundation

Staff

Hara, Julie; Marbrook Foundation
Hardy, H. Michael; Alex Stern Family Foundation
Harris, Trista; The Saint Paul Foundation
Harshner, Jennifer; The McKnight Foundation
Hartle, Cathy; Initiative Foundation
Hartwig, Dawn; Southwest Initiative Foundation
Haugen, Emily; The Medtronic Foundation
Hawkins, Donald; TCF Foundation
Hayden, Brenda; The Minneapolis Foundation
Heck, Nancy; Otter Tail Power Company
Hedin, Samantha; Northwest Minnesota Foundation
Heien, Jennifer; Southern Minnesota Initiative Foundation
Helland, Mark; Otter Tail Power Company
Heller, Desiree; The Minneapolis Foundation
Helwich, Amy Cram; Women's Foundation of Minnesota
Henderson, Amy; ClearWay Minnesota
Henley, Sandra; Central Minnesota Community Foundation
Her, Lue; Otto Bremer Foundation
Hermann, Sally; St Croix Valley Community Foundation
Hernandez, Sarah; The McKnight Foundation
Herwig, Timothy; TCF Foundation
Hickman, Don; Initiative Foundation
Higgins, Jennifer; Target
Hinke, Heather; The Saint Paul Foundation
Hinkle, Jody; MoneyGram International
Hohlfeld, Louis; The McKnight Foundation
Holgin, Tina; Joseph C. and Lillian A. Duke Foundation
    Edwards Memorial Trust
    Anna M. Heilmaier Charitable Foundation
    Arlan Schonberg Irrevocable Trust
Hollenhorst, Anita; Initiative Foundation
Holm, Sheri Booms; West Central Initiative
Holton, Susan A.; Minneapolis Rotary Community Service Foundation
Hom, Peggy; Ordean Foundation
Hoolihan, James; Blandin Foundation
Hosier, Steve; The Minneapolis Foundation
Houge, Ritchie; Northwest Minnesota Foundation
Houle, Lynn; Initiative Foundation
Howard, Jolene; Initiative Foundation
Hughes-Kempainen, Shary; Travelers Corporation and Travelers Foundation
Hultman, Jim; Runestone Electric Association Community Trust
Hurley, Wayne T.; West Central Initiative
Huss, Yan; Thrivent Financial for Lutherans Foundation
Hybben, Robert; The Minneapolis Foundation
Hynes, Stephanie; HRK Foundation

Ihnen, Karin; Initiative Foundation
Iverson, Kathryn H.; The Elizabeth C. Quinlan Foundation, Inc.

Jablonske, Janet; Blue Cross and Blue Shield of Minnesota Foundation/Blue Cross and Blue Shield of Minnesota
Jackson, Juan; The Medtronic Foundation
Jackson, Tracy D.; Southways Foundation
Jacobson, Rebecca; Wells Fargo Foundation Minnesota
Janis, Terry; Indian Land Tenure Foundation
Jarosh, Rachael; The Pentair Foundation
Jensen, Dana L.; The Jay and Rose Phillips Family Foundation
Johnson, Ann; Delta Dental of Minnesota
Johnson, Carol McGee; Women's Foundation of Minnesota
Johnson, Chris; Park Nicollet Foundation
Johnson, Daniel; United Health Foundation
Johnson, Donjia; The Minneapolis Foundation
Johnson, Karen; North Star Charitable Foundation
Johnson, Keir R.; A. H. Zeppa Family Foundation
Johnson, Kurt; Northland Foundation
Johnson, Michael J.; Park Nicollet Foundation
Johnson, Patricia; Todd-Wadena Electric Cooperative Community Trust
Jonas, Jody; Thrivent Financial for Lutherans Foundation
Jones, David E.; Thrivent Financial for Lutherans Foundation
Jordan, Adrienne; General Mills Community Action
Joselyn, Bernadine; Blandin Foundation
Jost, Nancy; West Central Initiative
Joul, Steven R.; Central Minnesota Community Foundation
Juergens, Laura; Allianz Life Insurance Company of North America

Kaliszewski, John; Initiative Foundation
Kallsen, Lois; Initiative Foundation
Kamnikar, Sandra; Northwest Minnesota Foundation
Kaping, Nancy; Southwest Initiative Foundation
Kashaeva, Julia; Headwaters Foundation for Justice
Kastel, Gina; Faegre & Benson Foundation
Kaufmann, B. W.; 3M/3M Foundation
Kaufmann, Linda; Initiative Foundation
Keller, Matt; Coughlan Companies
Kelley-Ariwoola, Karen; The Minneapolis Foundation
Kennedy-Logan, David; The McKnight Foundation
Keran, Kristen; Carl and Eloise Pohlad Family Foundation
Kewitsch, Kris; Target
Kilian, Matt; Initiative Foundation
King, Sandra; West Central Initiative
Kinniry, Shawn; The McKnight Foundation
Kintopf, Adam; ClearWay Minnesota
Kiscaden, Sheila; Rochester Area Foundation
Kleven, Cindy; 3M/3M Foundation
Kling, Cris; Otter Tail Power Company
Knollenberg, Susan; Park Nicollet Foundation
Knutson, Lindsey; ClearWay Minnesota
Koenigsmark, Kathryn; The McKnight Foundation
Konrad, Peter A.; Weyerhaeuser Family Foundation, Inc.
Koperski, Joan; Dakota Medical Foundation/Dakota Medical Charities
Kopylov, Lana; ClearWay Minnesota
Kosek, Kris; Best Buy Children's Foundation
Koster, Sherry R.; RBC Dain Rauscher Foundation
Kostishack, John; Otto Bremer Foundation
Koutsky, Lori J.; Securian Foundation/Securian Financial Group
Kovacs, Patty; Imation
Kowalzek, Kris; Initiative Foundation
Kretzmann, Jane; Bush Foundation
Krile, Jim; Blandin Foundation
Kroese, Ron; The McKnight Foundation
Krotzer, Brenda; The McKnight Foundation
Kruse, Bradley E.; Hugh J. Andersen Foundation
    Unity Avenue Foundation

Lang, Lindsey R.; Kopp Family Foundation
Langer, Christelle; The Minneapolis Foundation
Langer, Melissa; Southern Minnesota Initiative Foundation
LaPlant, Becky; Blandin Foundation
Larson, Judy; Southwest Initiative Foundation
Larson, Kathy; Thrivent Financial for Lutherans Foundation
Lauer, Andrea; The Antioch Company
Leaf, Deb; Winona Community Foundation
Lease, Mark; Initiative Foundation
Lee, Julie; Blue Cross and Blue Shield of Minnesota Foundation/Blue Cross and Blue Shield of Minnesota
Lee, LaVon; Grotto Foundation, Inc.
Lee, Shannon; The McKnight Foundation
Lee, Shirley; Rochester Area Foundation
Lee, Thomas J.; Blue Cross and Blue Shield of Minnesota Foundation/Blue Cross and Blue Shield of Minnesota
Lee, Valerie; The Minneapolis Foundation
Leifeld, Gwen; The Valspar Foundation
Leining, Barb; Minnesota Business and Professional Women's Foundation
Lemke, Kristin; ClearWay Minnesota
Leonard, Theresa; ClearWay Minnesota
Leutele, Peg; St Croix Valley Community Foundation
Levenson, Danille B.; The Wasie Foundation

Staff

Lewis, Andre; RBC Dain Rauscher Foundation
Lewis, Diane; Southern Minnesota Initiative Foundation
Liapis, Suzanne; George W. Neilson Foundation
Libbon, Sarah; Southwest Initiative Foundation
Lick, Jennifer; The Minneapolis Foundation
Lindberg, Mark; Otto Bremer Foundation
Lindell, MaryAnn; Initiative Foundation
Linder-Scholer, Bill; ADC Foundation
Linnell, Norman C.; The Donaldson Foundation
Little, Briana; Target
Lloyd, Cosandra; The McKnight Foundation
Lommen, Brenda; I. A. O'Shaughnessy Foundation, Incorporated
Longaecker, Emily; Cargill Citizenship Fund
Longendyke, Robert M.; Medica Foundation
Lorenz, Susan; Central Minnesota Community Foundation
Lovan, Sarah; The McKnight Foundation
Luedtke, Joel; The Jay and Rose Phillips Family Foundation
Luger, Ellen Goldberg; General Mills Community Action
Luhning, Becky; Otter Tail Power Company
Lundquist, Claudia; Duluth Superior Area Community Foundation
Lundstrom, Janet; Southern Minnesota Initiative Foundation
Lupambo, Prisca; Women's Foundation of Minnesota
Lynn Klimenko, Mary Karen; The Laura Jane Musser Fund
    Beim Foundation
    Sundance Family Foundation and Sundance Pay It Forward Foundation
Lyon, Marina Muñoz; Carl and Eloise Pohlad Family Foundation
    Marquette Financial Companies Community Support Program
Ly-Xiong, Sida; Women's Foundation of Minnesota

Maddox, LaRae; Northwest Minnesota Foundation
Maloney-Vinz, Lisa; Ecolab Foundation and Corporation
Maly, Jodi; The Minneapolis Foundation
Mangan, Lorna; Cloquet Educational Foundation
Mangan, Stephen A.; Ordean Foundation
Manson, Kathy; The Toro Company Giving Program
March, Sallie Saunders; Saunders Family Foundation
Marquardt, Sarah; Grotto Foundation, Inc.
Mart, Chris; Rochester Area Foundation
Martinez, Jaime; ClearWay Minnesota
Masco, Jeff; HRK Foundation
Matson, Robert; North Suburban Youth Foundation
Matter, Chris; ClearWay Minnesota
Matthews, Debra; TEAM Foundation
Mattis, Katie; The Minnesota Timberwolves FastBreak Foundation
Mayotte, Denise; The Sheltering Arms Foundation
McBride, Sheila; Honeywell Hometown Solutions
McCarty, Suzanne; Cargill Citizenship Fund
McCorison, Shari; Northland Foundation
McCuskey, Connie; Piper Jaffray
McDonald, Tahasha; The Minneapolis Foundation
McDonough, Maureen; Andersen Corporation
McKinnon, Nora; Patrick and Aimee Butler Family Foundation
Mead, Leslie; The Cooperative Foundation
Melendez, Mary Jane; General Mills Community Action
Mellin, Cindy; Carolyn Foundation
Mellor, Joan; The Medtronic Foundation
Meneguzzo, Suzy; Southern Minnesota Initiative Foundation
Menton, Janet; Southwest Initiative Foundation
Merchant, Rush, III; Jerome Foundation
Merrick, Wendy; West Central Initiative
Messler, Sharon; Park Nicollet Foundation
Meyer, Christine; H.B. Fuller Company Foundation
Migely, Kristine; The Minneapolis Foundation
Miletich, Steve; The CCP Foundation
Miller, Tom; The McKnight Foundation
Miller, Vicki M.; Lillian Wright and C. Emil Berglund Foundation, Inc.
Milligan, Wendy DeLane; Fargo-Moorhead Area Foundation
Moen, Shirley A.; The Riverway Foundation
Mohamed, Mariam; The McKnight Foundation

Moilanen, Molly; ClearWay Minnesota
Mollner, Carol; Headwaters Foundation for Justice
Moore, Sonja A.; The Saint Paul Foundation
Moothart, Cynthia; Headwaters Foundation for Justice
Morey, Diane; Northwest Minnesota Foundation
Moss, Paul; Cottonwood Foundation
Moua, Sandy 'Ci; The Minneapolis Foundation
Mowery, Andrea; ClearWay Minnesota
Mozey, Sherril; Park Nicollet Foundation
Mullen, Sally; Gertrude R. Shiely Charitable Trust
Mullin, Jim; Catholic Community Foundation in the Archdiocese of Saint Paul and Minneapolis
Munger, Julie; Duluth Superior Area Community Foundation
Murphy, Mark; Cargill Citizenship Fund
    Cargill Foundation
Murphy, Michelle; The Pentair Foundation
Muschler, Eric; The McKnight Foundation

Nash, Douglas; Indian Land Tenure Foundation
Naumann, Paul; Catholic Aid Association Foundation
Nehl, Shelley; The Charles A. and Anne Morrow Lindbergh Foundation
Nelsen, Margie; Southwest Initiative Foundation
Nelson, C. David; The Curtis L. Carlson Family Foundation
Nelson, Jennifer; Southern Minnesota Initiative Foundation
Nelson, Julie R.; Dwight D. Opperman Foundation
Nelson, William J.; The Cooperative Foundation
    CHS Foundation
Newes, Diane; Piper Jaffray
Newman, Mike; Travelers Corporation and Travelers Foundation
Newton, Eric; John S. and James L. Knight Foundation
Nicholson, David; Headwaters Foundation for Justice
Noronha, June; Bush Foundation

Oberle, Mary E.; R. C. Skoe Foundation
O'Brien, Mollie; John T. Petters Foundation
O'Donnell, Kathleen; The Minneapolis Foundation
Oertwig, April; Women's Foundation of Minnesota
O'Keefe, Colleen; Sauer Children's Renew Foundation
O'Keefe, Kathleen; The Medtronic Foundation
Okerman, Gerald (Jerry) A.; Minnesota Research Fund
Olsen, Ted; E.O. Olson Trust U/A Water Resources
Olson, Beth; Northland Foundation
Olson, Jim; Cote Foundation
Olson, Nyla; Fargo-Moorhead Area Foundation
Olson, Teresa; The Jostens Foundation
Omann, Pamela E.; Carl and Eloise Pohlad Family Foundation
O'Neill, Anni; Southern Minnesota Initiative Foundation
Orman, Paul; ClearWay Minnesota
Ostrem, John; Northwest Minnesota Foundation
Oswald, Rebecca; Cargill Citizenship Fund
Overson, Kevin; The McKnight Foundation
Oyewole, Tola; Best Buy Children's Foundation

Pabon, Angelines; The Minneapolis Foundation
Pacheco, John; Xcel Energy Foundation/Corporate Citizenship
Palm, Kim; Dakota Medical Foundation/Dakota Medical Charities
Palmer, Caroline; Minnesota State Bar Foundation
Pampusch, Anita, Ph.D.; Bush Foundation
Paskach, David; Southwest Initiative Foundation
Patterson, Andy; Sioux Falls Area Community Foundation
Patterson, Sara; Sioux Falls Area Community Foundation
Patton, Karen; Boston Scientific Foundation - Cardiovascular
Paulson, Donna; The Saint Paul Foundation
Pedersen, Jeff; Catholic Community Foundation in the Archdiocese of Saint Paul and Minneapolis
Pederson, Brian; Southwest Initiative Foundation
Peinovich, Jeana; Dakota Medical Foundation/Dakota Medical Charities
Penny, Tim; Southern Minnesota Initiative Foundation
Perkins, Kelly; Headwaters Foundation for Justice

Staff

Peterson, Amy; The Medtronic Foundation
Peterson, Denise; TCF Foundation
Peterson, Janet; The McKnight Foundation
Peterson, Jeffrey; Best Buy Children's Foundation
Peterson, Lisa; Northwest Minnesota Foundation
Peterson, Mary Ellis; The Minneapolis Foundation
Peterson, Paul W.; Sioux Falls Area Community Foundation
Peterson, Rose A.; Marquette Financial Companies Community Support Program
    Carl and Eloise Pohlad Family Foundation
Pfeiffer, JC; Winona Community Foundation
Piazza, Jodi; U.S. Bancorp Foundation
Pickard, Mary; Travelers Corporation and Travelers Foundation
Pierazek, Suzanne; CenterPoint Energy
Pietsch, Brian; Ameriprise Financial, Inc.
Pohl, Jack H.; F.R. Bigelow Foundation
    Mardag Foundation
Pohlkamp, Geri; Initiative Foundation
Polk, Terry A.; SUPERVALU Foundation
Posterick, Leah; Initiative Foundation
Prahl, Paula; Best Buy Children's Foundation
Prather, Regina; Blue Cross and Blue Shield of Minnesota Foundation/Blue Cross and Blue Shield of Minnesota
Preble, Jan; The Wasie Foundation
Price, Terry; Xcel Energy Foundation/Corporate Citizenship
Pritzl, Julie; Thrivent Financial for Lutherans Foundation
Pugh, Kari Jo; Think Community Foundation

Quick, Sarah; Philanthrofund Foundation (PFund)

Rabbie, April; Central Minnesota Community Foundation
Rauvola, Suzanne; Northland Foundation
Reamer, Karen; WCA Foundation
Reed, Arlene M.; The Jay and Rose Phillips Family Foundation
Rees-Christianson, Linda; Smikis Foundation
Rein, Heather; Flint Hills Resources
Reinhardt, Jeri; ClearWay Minnesota
Renier, Thomas S.; Northland Foundation
Reynolds, Karen; McNeely Foundation
Rhodes, Carleen K.; The Saint Paul Foundation
    F.R. Bigelow Foundation
Rhodes, Jim; Xcel Energy Foundation/Corporate Citizenship
Richards, Jody; Youthworks! Foundation, Inc.
Richardson, Cheryl; Rochester Area Foundation
Richie, Renee; The McKnight Foundation
Ridley, Kristin; The Graco Foundation
Ristau, Sherry; Southwest Initiative Foundation
Roberts, Jean Vukas; The Saint Paul Foundation
Robillard, Mary; Northland Foundation
Roby, Carolyn H.; Wells Fargo Foundation Minnesota
Roeder, Susan; Andersen Corporation
Rominski, Kathryn Hubbard; The Hubbard Broadcasting Foundation
Roper-Batker, Lee; Women's Foundation of Minnesota
Ross, Melissa; Blandin Foundation
Roth, Gayle; Weyerhaeuser Family Foundation, Inc.
    Edwin W. and Catherine M. Davis Foundation
    Frederick and Margaret L. Weyerhaeuser Foundation
Roy, Wendy; Grand Rapids Area Community Foundation
Rutledge, Patti; Southwest Initiative Foundation
Ryan, Denise; The Minneapolis Foundation
Rysted, Kathleen; The McKnight Foundation

Sampson, Holly C.; Duluth Superior Area Community Foundation
Sanderson, Jennifer; Sioux Falls Area Community Foundation
Sattler, Kate; The Minneapolis Foundation
Sauder, Jim; Headwaters Foundation for Justice
Sauer, Corey D.; Sauer Children's Renew Foundation
Saul, Jessie; ClearWay Minnesota
Saylor, Carole; Northland Foundation

Scharlemann, Romaine; Women's Foundation of Minnesota
Schefers, MaryAnn; Initiative Foundation
Scheibel, Nick; The Minneapolis Foundation
Schein, Robyn; The Minneapolis Foundation
Schillo, Barbara; ClearWay Minnesota
Schmidt, Jordana; HealthPartners
Schoepke, Joan; Archie D. and Bertha H. Walker Foundation
Schubert, Mary Beth; Comcast Cable Company
Schultz, Terri S.; Blue Cross and Blue Shield of Minnesota Foundation/Blue Cross and Blue Shield of Minnesota
Schumacher, Jon; St Anthony Park Community Foundation
Sciortino, Karyn; The McKnight Foundation
Scott, Donald L.; Alex Stern Family Foundation
Scott, Melinde; Target
Scott, Richard J.; The McKnight Foundation
Seidel, James; Catholic Community Foundation in the Archdiocese of Saint Paul and Minneapolis
Sever, Cathy; United Health Foundation
Shannon, Jill A.; St Croix Valley Community Foundation
Shea, Chris; General Mills Community Action
Shea, Tom; Southern Minnesota Initiative Foundation
Sheldon, Michael; ClearWay Minnesota
Sherlock, Donna; The Beverly Foundation
    Fingerhut Family Foundation
Sherman, David C.; Baker Foundation
Short, Carrie Jo; The Saint Paul Foundation
Shotley, Marsha; Blue Cross and Blue Shield of Minnesota Foundation/Blue Cross and Blue Shield of Minnesota
Showalter-Loch, Tim; Macy's North
Shrestha, Shunu; Women's Foundation of Minnesota
Shuler, Leslie; CHS Foundation
Sieve, Marty; Northwest Minnesota Foundation
Simenstad, Mark; Thrivent Financial for Lutherans Foundation
Simer, Lisa; Blue Cross and Blue Shield of Minnesota Foundation/Blue Cross and Blue Shield of Minnesota
Simmons, Therese; The McKnight Foundation
Simpson, Colleen C.; Park Nicollet Foundation
Sjoquist, Gregg D.; The Wasie Foundation
Skobba, Dorothy; Women's Foundation of Minnesota
Slawik, Sharon; Slawik Family Foundation
Slocum, Paula; Park Nicollet Foundation
Smida, Stacey; Cargill Citizenship Fund
    Cargill Foundation
Smith, Joseph L.; Fidelis Foundation
Smith, Kevin; Minnesota Twins Community Fund
Snapp, Sheila; Thomson West
Sommers, Bonita; Southern Minnesota Initiative Foundation
Spartz, Greg; Affiliated Community Health Foundation
Spaude, Jennifer; Hickory Tech Corporation Foundation
Spotts, Linda M.; Gray Plant Mooty Foundation
Springan, Sara; Leonard, Street and Deinard Foundation
Sproat, Brenda; Duluth Superior Area Community Foundation
St Claire, Ann; ClearWay Minnesota
Stainbrook, Cris; Indian Land Tenure Foundation
Stamstad, Jane; I. A. O'Shaughnessy Foundation, Incorporated
    Tennant Foundation
    James R. Thorpe Foundation
Stark-Kraker, Greta; Central Minnesota Community Foundation
Starr, Karen; Otto Bremer Foundation
Stately, Jo-Anne E.; Indian Land Tenure Foundation
Steadman, Lillian; The Minneapolis Foundation
Steckelberg, Teri; Southern Minnesota Initiative Foundation
Steenerson, Jim; Northwest Minnesota Foundation
Steffens, Janine; The McKnight Foundation
Sternberg, William M.; The Minneapolis Foundation
Storm, Candi; Athwin Foundation
Storm, Jim; Athwin Foundation
Straw, Nancy; West Central Initiative
Stringfield, Kathleen; Lawson

Staff

Strom, Monika; Blue Cross and Blue Shield of Minnesota Foundation/Blue Cross and Blue Shield of Minnesota
Stuber, Carley; St Francis Regional Medical Center Foundation
Suzuki Bardy, Kari; Otto Bremer Foundation
Svendsen, Donna Nicholson; General Mills Community Action
Svoboda, Kathi; Southern Minnesota Initiative Foundation
Swanson, Carol A.; Catholic Community Foundation in the Archdiocese of Saint Paul and Minneapolis
Swanson, Vicki; Sioux Falls Area Community Foundation
Swintek, Al; CenterPoint Energy

Talen, Polly M.; John S. and James L. Knight Foundation
Tapiz, Roberto; West Central Initiative
Tautges, Glen; Central Minnesota Community Foundation
Taylor, Kris; Ecolab Foundation and Corporation
Tharin, Judson; The Toro Company Giving Program
Thatcher, Jennifer; CHS Foundation
The Cooperative Foundation
Theisen, Bette; The Minneapolis Foundation
Thelen, Cynthia Ann; General Mills Community Action
Theobald, Veronica; Park Nicollet Foundation
Tholkes, Christine; ClearWay Minnesota
Thompson, Jenifer; The Minneapolis Foundation
Thompson, Jennifer, J.D.; Dakota Medical Foundation/Dakota Medical Charities
Thompson, Kimberly; Grand Rapids Area Community Foundation
Thon, Jan; General Mills Community Action
Thornton, Steve; Rochester Area Foundation
Timian, Gerald C.; The Saint Paul Foundation
Timm, Cheryl; Tennant Foundation
Todd, Lori; The McKnight Foundation
Toren, Shannon; Ecolab Foundation and Corporation
Traynor, J. Patrick, J.D.; Dakota Medical Foundation/Dakota Medical Charities
Tri, Holly; Northwest Minnesota Foundation
Troska, Patrick J.; The Jay and Rose Phillips Family Foundation
Troske, Carrie; The Daulton Foundation
Turner-Lovsness, Jackie; Southwest Initiative Foundation
Turnow, Caryl; Northwest Minnesota Foundation
Tusler, Jan; The Minneapolis Foundation

Vaillancourt, Marc; Southwest Initiative Foundation
Valandra, Howard D.; Indian Land Tenure Foundation
Van Dyke, Michele; Luverne Area Community Foundation
Van Niewaal, Sarah; Rochester Area Foundation
Van Wychen, Peggie; The Nash Foundation
Vander Molen, Tom; The Dorsey & Whitney Foundation
VanOrnum, Carol; Whitney Foundation
Vargas, Sandra; The Minneapolis Foundation
Vargo, Ashley; Initiative Foundation
Vasquez, Anthony; Otto Bremer Foundation
Vaughn, Jana; Airport Foundation MSP
Vaynberg, Alla; The McKnight Foundation
Vega-Perez, Elsa; Otto Bremer Foundation
Vesledahl, Dale; J. A. Wedum Foundation
Viere, Constance M.; Central Minnesota Community Foundation
Vierling, Jules; Catholic Community Foundation in the Archdiocese of Saint Paul and Minneapolis
Voigt, Sandy; Initiative Foundation
Volcke, Connie; The Minneapolis Foundation

Wagner, Kathy; WCA Foundation
Wall, Juli; Allianz Life Insurance Company of North America
Waller, Larry; N. Bud and Beverly Grossman Foundation
Walter, Melinda; The Polaris Foundation
Walz, Joanne; The Minneapolis Foundation
Wanek, Randy; West Central Initiative
Wang, Tim; Northwest Minnesota Foundation
Ward, Laysha; Target

Waters, Kate; U.S. Bancorp Foundation
Watne, Deb; Dakota Medical Foundation/Dakota Medical Charities
Watson, Douglas F.; Frederick O. Watson Foundation
Weber, Jill; Leonard, Street and Deinard Foundation
Weigel, Karel M.; Mayo Clinic
Weir, Rebecca; Northwest Minnesota Foundation
Welf, Kelley; The Charles A. and Anne Morrow Lindbergh Foundation
Wendling, Ann; ClearWay Minnesota
West, David; Northwest Minnesota Foundation
Whittet, Megan; ClearWay Minnesota
Wilkening, Mark; Youthworks! Foundation, Inc.
Wilkinson, Laurie; Thrivent Financial for Lutherans Foundation
Williams, Keiko L.; Donald G. Gardner Humanities Trust
Williams, Rita; Best Buy Children's Foundation
Williams, Twana; Otto Bremer Foundation
Willoughby, David; ClearWay Minnesota
Wilson, Rose; The Dorsey & Whitney Foundation
Wolff, Lisa; Andersen Corporation
Wolford, Kate; The McKnight Foundation
Wollner, John; Thrivent Financial for Lutherans Foundation
Wulf, Myra; Sioux Falls Area Community Foundation

Yagow, Jim; Thrivent Financial for Lutherans Foundation
Yang, Kayla; Cargill Foundation
Yargici, Senay; Headwaters Foundation for Justice
Yates, Barbara; Minnesota Early Learning Foundation
Yorek, Tina; Initiative Foundation
Young, Jo; The Minneapolis Foundation
Young, Tricia; TEAM Foundation

Zhdanova, Gouzel; ClearWay Minnesota
Zimmerman, Donna; HealthPartners
Zimmerman, Trisha; Blandin Foundation
Zimmermann, Laura; The McKnight Foundation
Zirbes, Michelle; G&K Services Foundation

Grantmaker Name Index

Name	Page
10-25 Tomorrow Foundation	227
3-H Farms Charitable Foundation	262
3M/3M Foundation	1
4481 Club, Inc.	227
A Better Place Inc	227
The Aba Family Foundation	227
ACA International Foundation	2
Acorn Foundation	2
Ada Scholarship Foundation	262
Adams Educational Fund, Inc.	262
Adams Family Foundation	227
Robert M. Adams Foundation	227
Adams-Mastrovich Family Foundation	263
ADC Foundation	2
The Adducci Family Foundation	227
Adela Rindal Foundation	227
Affiliated Community Health Foundation	3
Affinity Plus Federal Credit Union Foundation	227
Agape Foundation	227
Agarwala Foundation	227
Leo Agranoff Perpetual Charitable Trust	227
AgStar Fund for Rural America	4
AHS Foundation	5
Airport Foundation MSP	5
Albert Lea-Freeborn County Chamber Foundation	227
Albright Foundation	227
Alexandra Foundation	227
Alexandria Technical College Foundation	261
Alkire Family Foundation	227
All for the Earth Foundation	227
The Alliance for Youth Foundation	264
Allianz Life Insurance Company of North America	6
Alliss Educational Foundation	227
Alton Foundation	227
Marshall H. and Nellie Alworth Memorial Fund	262
American Finnish Workers Educational Trust	262
American Legion/VFW Onamia Scholarship Foundation, Inc.	262
Ameriprise Financial, Inc.	6
Elizabeth Amis Foundation	265
Everett L. Amis Foundation	262
L.A. Amundson Scholarships, Inc.	262
Lloyd and Barbara Amundson Charity Foundation, Inc.	7
Anchor Bank Family Foundation	227
S.P. Andersch Charitable Remainder Unitrust	261
Andersen Corporate Foundation (fka The Bayport Foundation of Andersen Corporation)	8
Andersen Corporation	9
Andersen Family Foundation	227
Elmer L. and Eleanor J. Andersen Foundation	10
Fred C. and Katherine B. Andersen Foundation	10
Hugh J. Andersen Foundation	11
A.H. Anderson Charitable Trust	261
Dean R. Anderson Family Foundation	264
Edward L. Anderson Charitable Trust	228
The Jonathan D. and Catherine L. Anderson Foundation	265
Andreas Foundation	228
L. and N. Andreas Foundation	228
William and Betty Andres Foundation	228
The Ankeny Foundation	228
Annexstad Family Foundation	228
The Antioch Company	12
The Apostle Foundation	265
Aquinas Foundation	265
Arden Foundation	228
Argall/Hibbs Foundation	228
ARK Foundation	228
Arsher Charitable Trust U/A	12
Arts and Humanities Foundation	228
Royle B. Arvig Memorial Scholarship Fund	262
Ashmore Family Foundation	228
The Aslan Foundation	228
Astleford Foundation	228
Athwin Foundation	13
The ATK (Alliant Techsystems) Foundation	228
Automotive Recyclers of Minnesota Foundation	262
Avocet Foundation	228
B & H Way Foundation	228
Carl E. Bachman and Doris M. Bachman Family Foundation	228
The Lloyd A. and Marion E. Bachman Foundation	265
Bernard and Fern Badzin Foundation	13
Bahl Foundation	14
Marjorie and V.M. Baich Foundation	14
Bailey Nursery Foundation	228
Gordon and Margaret Bailey Foundation	15
S. Eugene Bailey Scholarship Trust	262
Baillon Family Foundation, Incorporated	228
Baillon Foundation, Incorporated	228
Baker Foundation	15
Theresa A. and Vincent J. Baker Charitable Trust	228
Bakken Galbraith Foundation	264
Jeffrey Bakken Foundation	228
Pamela Bakken Foundation	228
Ann Bancroft Foundation	16
Bank Street Foundation	228
Baratz Family Foundation	16
Bardwell Foundation	228
Barrett Family Foundation	229
The Sidney and June H. Barrows Foundation	265
The Barry Foundation	229
The Baszucki Family Foundation	229
Battenkill Foundation	229
Baxter Family Foundation	229
Edward R. Bazinet Foundation	229
Javon and Vita Bea Family Foundation	229
Beauty for Ashes Foundation, Inc.	229
Beaverdale Foundation	263
Becker Furniture World Foundation	229
Gerrit Beckering Trust	261
Beim Foundation	17
Beito Foundation	229
Belford Foundation	229
Charles P. and Mary E. Belgarde Foundation	229
David Winton Bell Foundation	229
Ginger and Martin Bell Foundation	229
James F. Bell Trust FBO University of Minnesota	261
James Ford Bell Foundation	229
Bemis Company Foundation	229
Bend Foundation	263
Agnes M. Bendorf Charitable Trust	229
William J. Benfield Testamentary Trust	229
Benn-Crosby Family Foundation	265
Bennett Family Foundation	229
Martha MacMillan Bennett Family Foundation	229
Donald E. Benson Foundation	229

Grantmaker Name

The Bentson Foundation	18
Berdass Family Foundation	265
Berg Memorial Fund Trust	229
Lillian Wright and C. Emil Berglund Foundation, Inc.	18
R.R.W. and Florence Berglund Family Foundation	229
The Frank and Toby Berman Family Foundation	229
The Lyle and Janis Berman Family Foundation	229
Best Buy Children's Foundation	19
Bethel University - Pooled Common Fund	261
Better Way Foundation	230
The Beverly Foundation	20
Claude P. Bias Charitable Foundation	230
The Bieber Family Foundation	230
Warren L. Bielke Charitable Foundation	230
F.R. Bigelow Foundation	20
Birmingham-Dorsey Charitable Trust	230
Archie C. and Jane McDonald Black Charitable Trust	230
Joseph, Gretel, and Victor Blaha Foundation	262
Blandin Foundation	21
Charles K. Blandin Residuary Trust	261
Blitzer Golden Family Foundation	265
Bloomington Community Foundation	230
Hilda Blowers Scholarship Foundation	230
Blue Cross and Blue Shield of Minnesota Foundation/ Blue Cross and Blue Shield of Minnesota	22
The BMC Foundation	264
Boehnen Foundation	265
The Bois Family Foundation	230
Bonaria Foundation	265
The Fred and Mary Boos Family Foundation	230
Marvin and Betty Borman Foundation	230
Borochoff Family Foundation	265
The Boss Foundation	24
Harlan Boss Foundation for the Arts	230
John and Joyce Boss Family Foundation	230
Boston Scientific Foundation - Cardiovascular	24
Sister Thea Bowman Black Catholic Education Foundation	262
W. Glen Boyd Charitable Foundation	25
John and Zola Boylan Scholarship Trust	262
Will Bracken Family Foundation	230
Hazel Briggs Bradford Scholarship Fund, Inc.	263
Branches Foundation	230
Douglass Brandenborg Family Foundation	230
Braun Family Foundation	265
The Braun Foundation	230
Breckenridge Charitable Trust	230
E.W. Brehm Family Foundation	230
Otto Bremer Foundation	26
Briggs and Morgan Foundation	230
Mary Briggs Charitable Trust	261
Kenneth W. Brimmer and Jaye Marisa Snyder Foundation	230
Broadwaters Foundation	230
Bromelkamp Foundation	27
Broms Family Foundation	230
Sheldon V. and Carroll C. Brooks Foundation, Inc.	230
Brown Family Foundation, Inc.	231
Harry Rowatt Brown Trust	261
The Bumgarner Family Foundation	231
Burdick-Craddick Family Foundation	27
Robert and Dolores Buril Foundation	231
Burntside Charitable Foundation	231
Rodney and Barbara Burwell Family Foundation	231
Buscher Foundation	231
Bush Foundation	28
Patrick and Aimee Butler Family Foundation	29
Buuck Family Foundation	30
Charles and Norma Buxton Family Foundation	231
The Buyse Foundation	265
Cadahemark Foundation	231
Cade Foundation	31
Cadeau Foundation	231
Caliber Foundation	31
Cammack Marshall Fund for Children	261
Campbell Foundation	231
Martin and Esther Capp Foundation	32
Cardiac Rhythm Management Research Foundation	264
The Rachel Liba Cardoza Children's Foundation	231
Cargill Citizenship Fund	32
Cargill Family Fund	231
Cargill Foundation	33
Caribou Coffee Charitable Foundation	231
Caridad Corporation	231
Carlock Family Foundation	231
The Curtis L. Carlson Family Foundation	34
Carolyn Foundation	35
Barbara J. Carson Family Foundation	231
Ben and Verna Carson Scholarship Fund	262
Carter Family Foundation	264
Catholic Aid Association Foundation	35
Catholic Community Foundation in the Archdiocese of Saint Paul and Minneapolis	36
The CCP Foundation	37
CDF Foundation	37
Cecilian Society	231
CenterPoint Energy	38
Central Minnesota Community Foundation	38
Ceridian	231
Chadwick-Loher Foundation	231
Carl and Yetta Chalfen Foundation	265
Charisma Foundation	231
Charity, Inc.	39
Charlson Foundation	40
Chase Family Foundation	231
Chelgren-Haviland Foundation	231
Cherbec Advancement Foundation	231
Albert W. Cherne Foundation	265
B.H. Chesley Foundation	231
Children Helping Children Foundation	265
Chizek Family Foundation	231
Stanley and Marvel Chong Foundation	232
Chorzempa Family Foundation	232
Christian Cornerstone Foundation	232
W. G. Christianson Foundation	232
CHS Foundation	40
Cill Dara Foundation	232
Michael V. and Ann C. Ciresi Foundation	232
Citizens Independent Bank Community Foundation	232
The Clara Foundation	232
Lavinia R. Clark Trust	265
ClearWay Minnesota (fka Minnesota Partnership for Action Against Tobacco)	41
F.B. Clements Foundation	232
Cleveland Family Foundation	232
Cloquet Educational Foundation	42
Clouser Family Foundation	232
Cloverfields Foundation	232
1988 Irrevocable Cochrane Memorial Trust	263
The Richard and Diane Cohen Family Foundation	232
Cokem Foundation	232
Cold Spring Community Fund	232
Collins Family Foundation	232
Colonial Craft, Inc.	264
Comcast Cable Company	42
Common Ground Foundation	264
Community Foundation of Grand Forks, East Grand Forks & Region	263
Conley Family Foundation	261
The Constable Family Foundation	43
Elbridge C. Cooke Trust	261

Grantmaker Name

Coon Rapids Lions Foundation ... 232
Cooper Family Foundation ... 232
Patrice D. Cooper Foundation ... 232
The Cooperative Foundation ... 43
The Coracle Foundation ... 232
Cornwall Foundation ... 232
Arthur and David Cosgrove Memorial Fund ... 44
Coss Foundation ... 232
Charles Piper Cost Foundation ... 232
James N. Cost Foundation ... 263
Cote Foundation ... 44
Cottonwood Foundation ... 45
Coughlan Companies ... 46
The Covenant Foundation ... 232
Jean Covington Foundation ... 262
Constance Mayeron Cowles and Charles Fuller Cowles Foundation ... 232
Cox Family Foundation ... 233
Creative Foundation ... 233
Crosslake Ideal Scholarship Fund, Inc. ... 262
The Culp Family Foundation ... 233
Cummins Family Foundation ... 264
Charles and Kathryn Cunningham Family Foundation ... 46
Edward and Karayn Cunnington Family Foundation ... 264
Albert B. Cuppage Charitable Foundation ... 233
Frances Curran Foundation, Inc. ... 46
The Paul and Patricia Curran Foundation ... 233
Cutshall Foundation ... 233
Daggett Scholarship Fund, Inc. ... 262
Dakota Medical Foundation/Dakota Medical Charities ... 47
Stephen and Teresa Dalsin Family Foundation ... 233
Danbury Foundation ... 233
Tom and Ruth Danielson Foundation ... 233
Meredyth Anne Dasburg Foundation ... 233
Data Recognition Corporation ... 233
The Daulton Foundation ... 48
Dauwalter Family Foundation ... 233
John C. and Nettie V. David Memorial Trust ... 261
Edwin W. and Catherine M. Davis Foundation ... 48
Edward Dayton Family Fund ... 233
Kathleen B. Dayton Foundation for Type 1 Diabetes ... 233
DeForce Foundation for Protestant Home ... 261
The Deikel Family Foundation ... 49
Roger L. and Agnes C. Dell Charitable Trust 1 ... 49
Roger L. and Agnes C. Dell Charitable Trust 2 ... 50
Dellwood Foundation, Inc. ... 233
The DeLonais Foundation ... 233
Delta Dental of Minnesota ... 50
Deluxe Corporation Foundation/Deluxe Corporation ... 51
Vance C. DeMong Charitable Trust ... 233
John R. and Maryanne Dennis Foundation ... 233
Detroit Country Club Improvement Trust ... 261
Deziel Family Foundation, Inc. ... 233
Dhein Foundation ... 261
Diamond Builder Foundation ... 264
Robert and Susan Diamond Foundation ... 233
Dickman Family Foundation ... 233
James Wakefield Dickson Scholarship Fund ... 262
Diercks Foundation ... 264
Dennis and Nancy Ditlove Family Foundation ... 263
George H. and Marjorie F. Dixon Charitable Foundation ... 233
Doerr Family Fund ... 233
Doherty Foundation ... 264
James E. Doherty Medical Assistance Fund ... 261
James E. Doherty Scholarship Fund ... 262
James Doherty Seminary Training Fund ... 262
Dolan Media Foundation ... 233
John and Clara Dolan Foundation ... 233
Dolbec-Vergin Foundation ... 234
The Donaldson Foundation ... 52

Dorea Foundation ... 234
The Dorsey & Whitney Foundation ... 53
Double Eagle Foundation ... 234
Dougherty Family Foundation ... 234
Doughty Family Foundation ... 262
Douglas Foundation ... 54
Dovenberg Family Foundation ... 54
Driscoll Foundation ... 54
Norm and Val Duininck Family Foundation ... 264
Joseph C. and Lillian A. Duke Foundation ... 55
Duluth Improvement Trust ... 265
Duluth Superior Area Community Foundation ... 55
The Ross Dunham Memorial Foundation ... 264
Joseph Durda Foundation ... 234
The Jaye F. and Betty F. Dyer Foundation ... 234
Eagan Foundation, Incorporated ... 57
East West Design Center ... 265
Ecolab Foundation and Corporation ... 57
Ecotrust Foundation ... 234
Eddy (Edwin H.) Foundation ... 58
Eddy Family Foundation ... 234
Edelstein Family Foundation ... 261
Eden Prairie Foundation ... 234
Edina Community Foundation ... 59
Edina Realty Foundation ... 59
Edwards Memorial Trust ... 60
Effress-Hymanson Family Foundation ... 261
Effress-Miller Family Foundation ... 261
Ehrhardt Family Foundation ... 265
Berenice M. Eiswirth Scholarship Foundation ... 262
el Jay Foundation ... 234
El Shaddai Foundation ... 234
ELEOS Foundation ... 61
Ellis Foundation ... 234
Robert K. Else Family Charitable Foundation ... 234
Ely-Winton Hospital Scholarship Fund Trust ... 262
Emfield Family Foundation ... 234
Emmerich Foundation Charitable Trust ... 234
Charles Engasser Memorial Foundation, Inc. ... 61
Engelsma Family Foundation ... 234
George and Phyllis Engh Charitable Trust ... 234
Enkel Foundation ... 234
Alfred W. Erickson Foundation ... 234
Arthur T. Erickson Foundation ... 234
Dean and Jean Erickson Family Foundation ... 234
Donald and Elaine Erickson Family Foundation ... 264
Eugene E. and Grace M. Erickson Foundation ... 234
Ess Family Foundation ... 234
Karen and Richard Evans Foundation ... 264
Evansville Historical Foundation ... 261
Evenstad Family Foundation ... 234
Evergreen Foundation ... 235
Evert Foundation ... 235
Otto C. and Elsie Ewert Charitable Trust ... 62
Excel Bank Minnesota Foundation ... 235
Extendicare Foundation ... 62
Faegre & Benson Foundation ... 63
Ron and Diane Fagen Family Foundation ... 235
Faith, Hope and Love Foundation ... 235
Arlin Falck Foundation ... 64
Lawrence T. Fallander Trust ... 261
Fallon McElligott Scholarship Fund ... 265
Farfellow Foundation ... 235
Fargo-Moorhead Area Foundation ... 64
Farmers Union Marketing and Processing Foundation ... 65
Federated Insurance Foundation, Inc. ... 66
Feipel Scholarship Trust ... 262
Ferber Family Foundation ... 235
Charlotte Ferguson Memorial ... 261

Grantmaker Name

Fidelis Foundation 66
Mildred and Adolph Fine Family Foundation 235
William I. and Bianca M. Fine Charitable Trust 235
Fingerhut Family Foundation 67
Ronald Fingerhut Family Foundation 235
Richard and Beverly Fink Family Foundation 235
First Minnesota Foundation, Inc. 235
First National Bank of Bemidji Foundation 67
Harold and Florence Fischbein Foundation 265
I. George Fischbein Foundation 235
E. David Fischman Scholarship Trust 262
James S. Fish Family Foundation 235
S.S. Fisher Foundation, Inc. 235
The Jack and Bessie Fiterman Foundation 68
Steven C. and Susan L. Fiterman Charitable Foundation . 235
Francis H. Fitzgerald Trust 262
Flagship Foundation 264
Flaherty Family Foundation 235
Fletcher Family Foundation 235
Flint Hills Resources 68
Foldcraft Foundation 235
Harry Foley Scholarship Foundation 262
Forstrom Family Foundation 235
Foster Family Foundation 235
Foundation for Classical Studies in Statecraft & Jurisprudence 235
Foundation for Educational Research and Development .. 235
Foundation for the Development of Human Potential 235
Foundation for the Development of People 236
Foundation for the Prevention of Human & Animal Violence ... 265
Foundation of the Law Firm of Fabyanske, Westra & Hart, P.A. ... 236
Bill and Katherine Fox Foundation 236
Joe Francis Haircare Scholarship Foundation 262
Frankard Foundation 236
Robert E. Fraser Foundation 264
Fredrikson & Byron Foundation 68
The Freier Family Foundation, Inc. 236
Fremont Foundation 68
Frenzel Foundation 236
Frey Foundation 69
Michael J. and Karen B. Frey Foundation 236
Stuart and Nancy Friedell Family Foundation 236
Catherine A. Friedrich Memorial Fund 262
Friends of the Iron Range Interpretative Center 261
Friends of the Lewisville Library, Inc. 261
James and Karen Frisell Family Foundation 236
Fudge Family Foundation 236
H.B. Fuller Company Foundation 70
The Furst Foundation 236
G&K Services Foundation 71
Gabriel Foundation 236
Galatians 5:22 Foundation 264
The Galinson Foundation 236
The Gallagher Foundation 236
Gandrud Foundation 236
Gannett Foundation 264
Garden Valley Education Foundation 262
Donald G. Gardner Humanities Trust 71
The Janice Gardner Foundation 72
Garelick Family Foundation 236
Garmar Foundation 236
Anthony L. and Ann B. Gaughan Charitable Trust 261
Gegax Family Foundation 236
General Mills Community Action 72
Generations Health Care Initiatives, Inc. 236
George Family Foundation 236
Gesme Foundation 264
Gesner-Johnson Foundation 263
Getsch Charitable Trust 73
Getsch Family Foundation Trust 265

The Geyer Family Foundation 236
Charles D. Gilfillan Memorial Foundation 265
Fanny S. Gilfillan Memorial, Incorporated 74
Gilligan Foundation 236
Gise Family Foundation 236
Give a Knit Foundation (fka The Webber Family Foundation) ... 236
Glassman Family Foundation 237
Global Promise Foundation 237
GMAC ResCap 237
Marvin E. and Miriam R. Goldberg Foundation 237
Stanley M. and Luella G. Goldberg Family Foundation . 237
Jacob E. Goldenberg Foundation 237
Amy R. and Philip S. Goldman Foundation 237
Goldstein Family Foundation 237
Sydney Goldstein Foundation 237
Golle Family Foundation 265
Albert and Ruth Gomez Irrevocable Charitable Trust ... 237
Good Helps, Inc. 237
Johnny B. Good Foundation 264
Arthur and Constance Goodman Family Foundation ... 237
Meyer (Mickey) Gordon Family Foundation 265
Gossman Family Foundation 237
Gostomski Family Foundation 237
Gottstein Family Foundation 237
Ransford Ray and Clara J. Gould Foundation 237
The Graco Foundation 74
The Grand Lodge of Minnesota IOOF Foundation 262
Grand Rapids Area Community Foundation 75
The Margot and Paul Grangaard Foundation 237
Granite Foundation 237
Grannis-Martin Memorial Foundation 262
Henry K. and Mildred M. Grawe Charitable Foundation . 237
Gray Plant Mooty Foundation 76
Mary S. Gray Charitable Trust 76
Graybrier Foundation 237
Greater Wayzata Community Foundation 237
Greycoach Foundation 237
Greystone Foundation 237
Griffiths Foundation 237
Mary Livingston Griggs and Mary Griggs Burke Foundation ... 76
Owen J. Gromme Foundation 237
Virginia A. Groot Foundation 77
Joseph C. Grossman Foundation 238
N. Bud and Beverly Grossman Foundation 77
Grotto Foundation, Inc. 78
Grouse Mountain Foundation 238
John P. and Beverly G. Grundhofer Charitable Foundation ... 238
Gudorf Family Foundation 238
The Edward and Hannah Gustafson Foundation 238
Reynolds and Mary Guyer Family Foundation 264
Haag Family Foundation 238
Hageman Foundation of Hope 238
Russell and Luaina Hagen Family Foundation 238
Haggerty Family Foundation 79
Hallberg Family Foundation 238
E.W. Hallett Charitable Trust 261
Jessie F. Hallett Charitable Trust 261
Jerome M. Halper Family Foundation 238
Sabra M. Hamilton Foundation 263
The Hankes Foundation 263
Hansen Family Foundation 238
The Hanser Family Foundation 238
David and Miriam Hanson Charitable Foundation 265
Gregg W. Hanson Charitable Foundation 238
John O. and Barbara N. Hanson Family Foundation ... 238
Happy Dancing Turtle Foundation 238
Hardenbergh Foundation (fka St Croix Foundation) 79
Harrington Foundation 262
Helen Harrington Charitable Trust 261

Grantmaker Name

Olga B. Hart Education Foundation	80
Dr. Daniel C. Hartnett Family Foundation	238
Hartz Foundation	80
James Hartzell Family Foundation	265
Harvard Club of Minnesota	238
Hatlen Foundation	81
Robert and Clyde Haugan Foundation	265
The Hawkins Family Foundation	238
The Hays Foundation	238
Hayward Foundation	238
Head Family Foundation	238
Headwaters Foundation for Justice	81
Healthier Minnesota Community Clinic Fund	82
HealthPartners	82
Heath Foundation	265
Heaven Sent Foundation	238
Hedberg Family Charitable Foundation	238
The Heenan Foundation	238
The Hegman Family Foundation	239
Menahem Heilicher Foundation	239
Anna M. Heilmaier Charitable Foundation	83
Willis C. Helm Charitable Trust	239
Hendry Family Foundation	239
Hennepin County Bar Foundation	84
Thomas R. Hennessy Family Charitable Trust	239
The Victoria Velie Henry Family Foundation	239
The Hermundslie Foundation	84
Hersey Foundation	239
Hertogs Family Education Foundation, Inc.	239
Hetland Family Foundation	239
Hiawatha Education Foundation	85
Hickory Tech Corporation Foundation	85
Hillswood Foundation	239
Hinz Foundation, Inc.	239
The Hirsh Family Foundation	239
Timothy and Todd A. Hitchcock Foundation	239
The Leo A. and Doris C. Hodroff Foundation	239
The Hoeft Family Foundation	239
Hoeschler Family Foundation	265
D. A. Hoff Charitable Foundation	239
Ruth S. Hoffert Charitable Trust	265
Hoffman & McNamara Foundation	262
The Hognander Foundation	239
Holden Family Foundation	239
Holden Foundation	265
Holmes/CSM Family Foundation	239
Holzhueter Foundation	239
Homecrest Foundation	239
Homedale Foundation	239
Honeywell Hometown Solutions	86
Janice Sarah Hope Foundation, Inc.	239
Hormel Foods Corporation Charitable Trust	239
The Hormel Foundation	261
George A. Hormel Testamentary Trust	86
Henry C. Hornby Trust d/b/a Cloquet Cemeteries Trust	261
Horton Holding, Inc.	239
Robert F. Hosch Foundation	240
W.R. Hotchkiss Foundation	262
Emma B. Howe Memorial Foundation	265
HRK Foundation	87
The Huang Family Foundation	240
The Hubbard Broadcasting Foundation	88
Laura and Walter Hudson Foundation	265
The Huelsmann Foundation	240
Nevin Huested Foundation for Handicapped Children, Inc.	89
Cedric L. Hughes Scholarship Trust	262
Robert J. Hughes, Jr. Trust	261
The Theodore G. Huisinga Charitable Foundation	240
Hull Educational Foundation	262
Human Life Foundation	240
Humboldt Family Foundation, Inc.	240
Hubert H. Humphrey Foundation, Inc.	240
Humphries Foundation	265
James W. Hunt Scholarship Fund	262
Huntley-Dickinson Foundation	240
Huss Foundation	240
Hutchinson Technology	262
Hutter Family Foundation	240
I.V. Foundation	240
IBM Corporation - Minnesota	240
Imation	89
Impact Foundation	240
Impact Foundation, Inc.	90
India Association of Minnesota, Inc.	264
Indian Land Tenure Foundation	90
ING Foundation	91
Initiative Foundation	92
Intertech Foundation	264
L. A. Isermann Scholarship Foundation Trust	262
Italian American Club Foundation, Inc.	93
Alfred A. Iversen and Family Foundation	263
IWJ Charitable Foundation	240
The Jackley Foundation	240
C. Charles Jackson Foundation	240
Jacobsen Family Foundation	240
Leif K. and Joen Jacobsen Foundation	265
Jones P. Jacobson Family Foundation	240
Clive T. Jaffray Employees Trust	261
Clem Jaunich Educational Trust	262
Jennings Family Foundation (fka Prophet Corporation Foundation)	93
Jerge Foundation for Quality Improvement in Dentistry	264
Duane and Lynda Jergenson Family Foundation	240
Jerome Foundation	94
The Jilek Family Foundation	240
JNM 1966 Gift Trust U/A	94
T. H. Johansen Family Foundation	240
Charles E. and Andriene M. Johnson Foundation	240
Chester Johnson Charitable Trust	240
David B. Johnson Family Foundation	240
Elmer M. Johnson Conservation Trust	240
Gladys L. Johnson Scholarship Trust	262
Harry A. Johnson Foundation	264
John Warren and Marion Louise Johnson Family Foundation	241
Lewis H. Johnson Family Foundation	95
Lloyd K. Johnson Foundation	95
The Lynn Johnson Family Foundation	96
Mae L. Johnson Scholarship Trust	262
Mark and Laura Johnson Family Foundation	241
Maynard B. Johnson Family Foundation	265
Mitchell and Lois Johnson Charitable Foundation	96
R. L. Roz Johnson Family Foundation	265
Addie M. Jones Trust	261
David B. Jones Foundation	263
Douglas and Mary Staughton Jones Foundation	241
Norman and Eunice Jones Family Foundation	265
The Jonty Foundation for Research in Immuno Endocrine Neurological Disorders	241
Jordan Foundation	265
The Jostens Foundation	97
Joyce Family Foundation	241
Jsman Family Foundation	241
Andrew S. and Grace Y. Juang Foundation	265
Jundt Family Foundation	98
Henry A. and Gladys F. Just Scholarship Fund	262
Kairos Foundation	241
Kaminski Family Foundation	264
Kaplan Family Foundation	241
George Kaplan Memorial Foundation, Incorporated	98

Grantmaker Name

Kappa Chapter/Gamma Phi Beta Foundation 261
Harold F. and Muriel Kappler Foundation 241
Conrad I. and Ruth V. Karleen Charitable Trust 241
The Karon Family Foundation, Inc. 241
Alan and Beverly Kasdan Foundation, Inc. 265
Clayton Kaufman Family Foundation 265
The Harry Kay Charitable Foundation 261
Wynn and Pamela Kearney Foundation 241
Margaret H. and James E. Kelley Foundation, Inc. 98
Hamilton H. Kellogg and Mildred Haley Kellogg Charitable Trust . . .241
W.K. Kellogg Foundation 99
Kelm Foundation 241
Augustus H. Kennedy Memorial Fund Trust 261
William R. Kennedy Family Foundation 241
Kent Family Charitable Trust 241
Keymer Foundation 241
Killen Scholarship Trust 262
King Family Foundation 241
King Family Foundation 241
Elizabeth Callender King Foundation 100
Kinney Family Foundation 241
The Steven L. and Jan L. Kirchner Family Foundation 241
Joseph Kitrick Charitable Trust 261
Harry L. and Janet M. Kitselman Foundation 241
Kiwanis Club of Edina Golden K Foundation 241
KKE Architects Charitable Foundation 241
Klas Family Foundation 242
Klein Family Foundation 242
E. Milton Kleven Family Foundation 242
Hess Kline Foundation, Inc. 100
KLM Fund 242
Ella Knees Trust 265
Hertha Knees Trust 265
Knife Lake Sportsmen Club, Inc. 264
John S. and James L. Knight Foundation 101
Knights of Columbus 4381 242
Knitcraft - St Croix Foundation, Inc. 101
The Knowlton Foundation 264
Knox Foundation 102
Leroy R. and Shalmerdean A. Knuths Family Foundation 264
Kopp Family Foundation 102
Ida C. Koran Trust 242
Ellen Korpy Foundation, Inc. 262
Jerome and Marlyce Koskovich Foundation 242
Joel and Laurie Kramer Foundation 242
Ethel Mae Kreutz Private Foundation 103
Krinkie Family Foundation 242
The Krisbin Foundation 242
Hanna R. Kristianson Testamentary Charitable Trust 242
Mark and Lori Kroll Family Foundation 242
Faye and Mayer Krupp Family Foundation 242
Anna M. Kuhl Scholarship Trust 262
Sharon and Joel Labovitz Foundation 242
The Labrador Foundation 242
The Lacek Foundation 264
James B. Ladd Trust 261
LaFrenz Family Foundation 242
Lahti Family Foundation 103
Laird Norton Family Fund 242
Lake Region Electric Cooperative Scholarship Fund 262
The Lakeland Group Foundation, Inc. 242
Lakeside Capital Foundation 264
Lamarche Creek Foundation 242
The Lamm Family Foundation 242
Land O'Lakes Foundation 103
Lang Family Charitable Trust 104
Theodora H. Lang Charitable Trust 242
Langwater Foundation 242
Leonette M. and Fred T. Lanners Foundation 105

Peter and Dorothy Lapp Foundation 242
Larkin Hoffman Daly and Lindgren, Ltd. Foundation 243
John Larsen Foundation 243
Larson Foundation 243
David and Janis Larson Foundation 243
Emil and Mildred Larson Minneapolis Public Library Trust 261
Lavine Family Foundation 243
The Lawrence Family Foundation 243
Lawson 105
Helen Sperry Lea Foundation 106
Lee Family Foundation 243
Leek Charitable Foundation 243
Leggott Foundation 243
Don and Jean Lein Family Foundation 265
Edith, Samuel and Elizabeth Leinbach Foundation 243
LeJeune Family Foundation 243
Geraldine N. Lemieux Charitable Testamentary Trust 262
Lenzmeier Family Foundation 243
Leonard, Street and Deinard Foundation 106
Vivita and Paul Leonard Foundation 243
Lerner Foundation 107
James D. Leslie Family Foundation 243
Steven C. Leuthold Family Foundation 107
Bruce A. Levahn and Noreen J. Levahn Family Foundation 243
George and Marion Levine Foundation 243
Lieberman-Okinow Foundation 243
Liebhaber Family Foundation 108
The Liemandt Foundation 243
The Lillehei Family Charitable Foundation 243
R. C. Lilly Foundation 108
Carl and Aune Lind Family Foundation 108
The Charles A. and Anne Morrow Lindbergh Foundation 109
James G. Lindell Irrevocable Charitable Trust 109
Richard and Jaci Lindstrom Foundation 243
Lion's Pride Foundation 263
The Hannah Lips Foundation 243
The Liszt Family Foundation 243
Living Legacy 243
Living Springs Foundation 263
Adolph and Emily Lokensgard Scholarship Trust Fund 243
Lommen, Nelson, Cole & Stageberg Foundation 244
Longview Foundation 110
Loomer-Mortenson Scholarship Foundation 265
Lored Foundation 244
Louis Foundation 263
The Lownade Foundation 244
The Don J. Lucker Foundation 244
Robert and Patricia Ludlow Family Foundation 244
Gladys and Arnold Lueck Scholarship Fund 262
Lund Family Foundation 244
Lois and Allan W. Lund Foundation 244
Russell T. Lund Charitable Trust 110
Lundborg Foundation 244
Lundeen Foundation 244
Lupient Foundation 244
H. William Lurton Foundation 244
The Luther Family Foundation 111
Lutheran Community Foundation 244
Luverne Area Community Foundation 111
The Lyman Lumber Company Foundation 244
Edith H. Lynum Trust 261
Marcel K. Lynum Trust 261
The Lytwyn Foundation 244
The M & L Foundation, Inc. 263
M-O-M Cares Employee Foundation 244
The M.B. Foundation 112
Cargill Macmillan, Jr. Charitable Trust 261
Cargill MacMillan Jr. Family Foundation 244
David D. MacMillan Family Foundation 264

Grantmaker Name

Entry	Page
Katherine Wells MacMillan Foundation	264
Sarah Stevens MacMillan Foundation	244
W. Duncan MacMillan Family Foundation (Minneapolis)	265
W. Duncan MacMillan Foundation (Wayzata)	261
Carol MacPherson Memorial Scholarship Fund	262
Ruth Spies Macrostie Irrevocable Trust	244
Macy's North	112
The Jonathan Madding Foundation	263
Madeline Applauds Great Goals in Education, Inc.	262
Mahon Foundation	244
Thomas and Judith Mahoney Family Foundation	244
Maleska Family Foundation	244
Malinski Family Foundation	265
Mall of America Foundation for Youth	113
Malm Family Foundation	244
David C. Malmberg Family Foundation	244
Mark and Roberta Mandel Family Charitable Trust	244
Manitou Fund	245
Mankato Area Foundation	113
Ted and Roberta Mann Foundation	114
Marbrook Foundation	114
Mardag Foundation	115
The Samuel S. and Joyce C. Marfield Charitable Foundation	245
Markman Capital Foundation	265
Marlu Foundation	245
Marquette Financial Companies Community Support Program	116
Marquit-Grieser Fund	245
David R. Marshall Foundation	245
Marso Foundation	264
Martin & Brown Foundation	245
Martinson Clinic Foundation	116
The Martinson Foundation	117
Lillian Marvin Trust	245
Masonic Benevolence	262
Master Brewers Association of The Americas Scholarship Foundation, Inc.	265
The Jack and Sarah Matasosky Foundation	245
Richard J. and Mary Lou Mathiowetz Foundation	245
Matrix Foundation	245
Len Mattson Scholarship Fund, Inc.	265
The D. and J. Maurer Foundation	245
John J. and Maryanne T. Mauriel Family Foundation	245
May Family Foundation	245
Mayo Clinic	117
Charles W. Mayo Trust - Olmsted Historical Society	261
Roger and Nancy McCabe Foundation	245
Jim and Diane McCarthy Foundation	245
McCarthy-Bjorklund Foundation	245
The Thomas and Mary McCary Family Foundation	245
Marcus McCoy Foundation	245
McDowell Foundation	245
McElrath Foundation	245
McGlynn Family Foundation	245
McGough Foundation	118
William W. and Nadine M. McGuire Family Foundation	245
The McKnight Foundation	118
John and Esther McLaughlin Foundation	245
Richard F. McNamara Family Foundation	245
McNeely Foundation	119
McVay Foundation	246
Meadowood Foundation	246
Medica Foundation	119
Mediclinics Educational Fund	265
The Medtronic Foundation	121
Melrose Community Improvement Association	265
Kendrick B. Melrose Family Foundation	246
Ethel Melum Trust	262
Mercedes Foundation	246
Donald and Marjorie Meredith Foundation	122
Mersky Family Foundation	246
Metris Companies Foundation	265
Roy E. and Merle Meyer Foundation	262
Walter S. and Margaret L. Meyers Charitable Foundation	246
Walter S. and Margaret L. Meyers Charitable Foundation II	261
MGR Foundation	246
Ernest S. and Sally A. Micek Family Foundation	246
Mickelson Media Foundation	246
Midcontinent Media Foundation	246
The Millennium Foundation	246
Alan and Diane Miller Family Foundation	246
Ben Miller Foundation	246
Benjamin A. Miller Foundation	265
Craig and Beverley Miller Family Foundation	246
The Doug and Martha Miller Foundation	246
The Kathy and Tom Miller Family Foundation	246
Martin and Esther Miller Foundation	123
The Rudolph W. and Gladys Miller Medical Research Foundation	246
Sam Miller Foundation	246
Minneapolis Admirals Foundation	262
Minneapolis Area Association of Realtors Foundation, Inc.	123
The Minneapolis Foundation	124
Minneapolis Kiwanis Foundation	125
Minneapolis Parks Legacy Society	264
Minneapolis Rotary Community Service Foundation	126
Minnesota American Legion and Auxiliary Heart Research Foundation	261
Minnesota Business and Professional Women's Foundation	127
Minnesota Center for Philanthropy	246
Minnesota Chamber Foundation	246
Minnesota Community Foundation	246
Minnesota Dental Foundation	246
Minnesota Early Learning Foundation	127
Minnesota Masonic Foundation, Inc.	262
Minnesota Music Teachers Association Foundation	246
Minnesota Power Foundation	128
Minnesota Research Fund (fka SOTA TEC Fund)	128
Minnesota State Bar Foundation	129
Minnesota State College - Southeast Technical Foundation	262
The Minnesota Timberwolves FastBreak Foundation	130
Minnesota Twins Community Fund	130
Minnesota Valley Bancshares Foundation	264
Minnesota Veterinary Medical Association Foundation	262
Miracle - Ear Children's Foundation	246
Marjorie Weil and Marvin Edward Mitchell Foundation	131
Oscar Mitchell, Jr. Trust U/A Scholarship Fund	262
Wildey H. Mitchell Family Foundation	247
Mithun Family Foundation	247
Molitor Family Foundation	247
MoneyGram International	132
Jack Moon Scholarship Foundation	262
The Lourdes and John Moore Foundation	247
Thomas Moore Memorial Fire Fighter Education, Health and Safety Foundation	264
Jane N. Mooty Foundation Trust	132
John W. Mooty Foundation Trust	133
The Morning Foundation	247
Ralph K. Morris Foundation	247
Morrow Foundation	247
The Morsman Family Foundation	247
The Mortenson Family Foundation	247
Joseph T. Morton Family Foundation	265
Moscoe Family Foundation	133
Kevin J. Mossier Foundation	247
Thomas Ryan Mulcahy Foundation	247
The Mullen Flynn Foundation	247
The Ina and Harry Murphy Foundation	247
Kingsley H. Murphy Family Foundation	133
Murray County Health Alliance Foundation	265

Grantmaker Name

Name	Page
Ali Murtaza Foundation	247
Elizabeth W. Musser Charitable Trust	265
The Laura Jane Musser Fund	134
MWVE Fund	264
Myers Foundation, Inc.	247
Charles and Candice Nadler Family Foundation	247
Nandale Foundation	247
The Nash Foundation	135
National Distillers Distributors Foundation	262
NBC Foundation	247
George W. Neilson Foundation	135
The Nelson Family Foundation	136
Charles and Elynor Nelson Family Foundation	265
Curtis and Marjorie Nelson Family Foundation	247
Gordon Nelson Memorial Foundation	247
New Life Christian Foundation	247
Harriet and Nathan Newman Foundation	247
Jane R. Newman Charitable Trust	247
Louis E. Newman Charitable Trust	247
Richard A. Newman Foundation	136
NFC Foundation	137
Nicholson Family Foundation	247
NJR Foundation	263
Noel Foundation	137
The Charles E. and Nancy E. Nolan Foundation	248
Edwin W. Norberg Charitable Trust	261
R. B. Nordick Foundation	248
Roger and Violet Noreen Charitable Trust	137
Norling Brothers Foundation	248
North Country Health Services Foundation	248
North Dakota Community Foundation	263
North End Community Foundation	248
North Star Charitable Foundation	138
North Star Foundation	248
North Suburban Community Foundation	138
North Suburban Youth Foundation	139
Northern Coop Foundation	248
Northern Star Foundation	248
Northland Foundation	139
Northwest Airlines, Incorporated	264
Northwest Area Foundation	248
Northwest Minnesota Foundation	140
Northwest Title Foundation	248
Numero-Steinfeldt Foundation	265
Ella and Kaare Nygaard Foundation	261
James T. Nystrom Foundation	264
Alice M. O'Brien Foundation	141
T.J. O'Gara Family Charitable Foundation	265
Thomas W. and Helen K. O'Kane Family Foundation	264
James B. and Catherine L. O'Meara Charitable Trust	248
Casey Albert T. O'Neil Foundation	142
O'Shaughnessy Foundation	143
I. A. O'Shaughnessy Foundation, Incorporated	143
Oak Grove Foundation	248
Oakleaf Foundation	248
The John K. and Margaret A. Ogren Foundation	248
The Olseth Foundation	248
Olson Foundation	248
E.O. Olson Trust U/A Water Resources	143
Earl B. Olson Foundation	248
Omaha Community Foundation	263
Onan Family Foundation	248
Open Door Foundation	248
Oppegaard Family Foundation, Inc.	248
Dwight D. Opperman Foundation	144
Opus Foundation	248
Opus Prize Foundation	248
Muriel Orcutt Charitable Trust	248
Ordean Foundation	144
Joyce L. Osborn Scholarship Trust	262
OSilas Foundation	145
Osterud-Winter Foundation	145
The Oswald Family Foundation	248
Otter Tail Power Company	146
Paul M. Otteson Foundation	248
Ouellette Foundation	249
Ben and Jeanne Overman Charitable Trust	147
The Owasso Foundation	249
Owatonna Foundation	147
Owens-Pesavento Family Foundation	249
Edward M. Ozias Charitable Trust	261
P.G.N. Foundation	148
Pacific Foundation	249
Wayne and Mary Packard Foundation	265
Pagel Foundation	148
Pajor Family Foundation	149
Palm Foundation	249
Panamerican Foundation	249
Paparella Family Foundation	249
J. Paper Foundation	249
L. and A. F. Paper Foundation	249
Lewis and Annie F. Paper Foundation, Inc.	149
Paradigm Foundation, Inc.	249
Park Nicollet Foundation	149
Park Region Telephone Charitable Trust, Inc.	264
The Patch Foundation	249
Patterson Foundation	151
George W. and Mary B. Patton Scholarship Fund	262
Paulson Family Foundation	249
Pax Christi Foundation	249
Charles D. Gilfillan Paxton Memorial	249
Peace Maker Foundation	249
Peace Shalom Foundation	249
Pearson Assessments	264
E.M. Pearson Foundation	265
Penstemon Foundation	249
The Pentair Foundation	151
People in Business Care, Inc.	152
Peravid Foundation	152
Perkins Foundation	153
Norman Perl Foundation	249
The Lawrence and Linda Perlman Family Foundation	153
Frieda Perschau Irrevocable Trust	249
Marvin J. Pertzik Foundation	249
John and Sara Peterman Foundation	249
G. and D. Peterson Foundation	249
Hans and Thora Petraborg Education Trust Fund	262
Petters Group Worldwide, LLC	154
John T. Petters Foundation	154
Thomas J. Petters Family Foundation	249
Philanthrofund Foundation (PFund)	154
The Phileona Foundation	249
Edward and Leslye Phillips Family Foundation	249
The Jay and Rose Phillips Family Foundation	155
Phynque Phamily Phoundation	249
Piasecki Family Foundation	263
Vernon J. Pick Foundation	262
Raymond B. Pinson Family Foundation	250
Piper Jaffray	156
Pipestone Adventist Church Foundation	250
John Joseph Plank Charitable Trust	250
Poehler/Stremel Charitable Trust	250
Poepl Family Foundation	250
Carl and Eloise Pohlad Family Foundation	157
The Polaris Foundation	158
The Pomegranate Philanthropic Foundation	250
Arthur J. Popehn Foundation	250
The Irwin Andrew Porter Foundation	158

Grantmaker	Page
The Portland Trust	250
The Powell Family Foundation	250
Power Charitable Foundation	250
Paul and Doris Prestegaard Memorial Foundation	265
John Pritchard Memorial Fund	264
Pritschet Foundation	250
Charles E. Proshek Foundation	262
Prospect Creek Foundation	159
David C. and Margaret F. Prosser Foundation	250
Mark R. Pryor Foundation, Inc.	262
Pump Foundation	250
Mark A. Pursley Memorial Foundation	250
Quadion Foundation	250
Quetico Superior Foundation	159
Quiet Waters Foundation	250
The Elizabeth C. Quinlan Foundation, Inc.	160
William D. Radichel Foundation	250
Raft Charitable Foundation	250
Rahr Foundation	161
Rainy River Community College Foundation	262
Raleigh Foundation	250
Ramy Foundation	250
The Randall Family Foundation	250
Rappaport Family Foundation	161
R. and S. Rappaport Family Foundation	250
Walter C. Rasmussen - Northeast Bank Foundation	250
Herman and Therese Ratelle Foundation	250
Mark and Karen Rauenhorst Family Foundation	251
RBC Dain Rauscher Foundation	162
RCS Foundation	251
Horst M. Rechelbacher Foundation	163
Frank and Evelyn Rechtzigel Family Foundation	251
Red Wing Shoe Company Foundation	163
Redwood Area Communities Foundation, Inc.	164
Harold and Kate Reed Family Foundation	264
Regis Foundation	164
Regis Foundation for Breast Cancer Research	251
R. William and Mary Ann Reilly Family Foundation	251
Reimer Foundation	251
Bernard D. Reisberg and Joan B. Reisberg Family Foundation	251
James L. Reissner Family Foundation	251
The Robert and Helen Remick Charitable Foundation	251
Remmele Foundation	262
Luther I. Replogle Foundation	164
The Retel Foundation	251
The Kurt and Rali Retzler Family Foundation	251
Robert and Anne Reznick Family Foundation	251
The Rhm Foundation	251
Page Jones Richards Family Foundation	251
Richfield Community Foundation	165
Autumn Rieks Foundation	251
Rikkers Foundation	251
Ring Foundation	251
Ripley Memorial Foundation, Inc.	166
Ritt Family Foundation	167
The Ritz Foundation	265
Margaret Rivers Fund	167
The Riverway Foundation	168
RJW Foundation	251
RMCGK Wood Family Foundation	251
Louis A. Roberg Endowment Trust	262
Donald and Marie Roberts Charitable Foundation	251
Robina Foundation	251
Robins Family Foundation	251
Robins, Kaplan, Miller & Ciresi, L.L.P. Foundation for Education, Public Health & Social Justice	168
Robins, Kaplan, Miller & Ciresi, L.L.P. Private Foundation	251
Robinson Trust	251
C. H. Robinson Worldwide Foundation	252
D. B. Robinson Foundation	252
Rochester Area Foundation	168
Rochester Post Bulletin Charities	169
Rockler Jackson Family Foundation	252
The Rodman Foundation	252
Rogers Plastics Foundation	252
Harold Roitenberg Family Foundation	264
John and Beverly Rollwagen Family Foundation	265
John F. Rooney Family Charitable Foundation	252
Laura Rose Irrevocable Trust	252
The Rosen Family Foundation	252
William A. Ross Foundation	265
Guenther Roth Foundation	252
Rothfork Family Foundation	252
Roycraft Foundation	252
Ruand Foundation	264
Genevieve J. Rudbeck Irrevocable Trust	252
Rukavina Family Foundation	170
Runestone Electric Association Community Trust	170
Max and Linda Rutman Family Foundation	252
Rutstrum Wilderness Trust	252
S. J. Electro Systems Foundation	252
The Sabes Family Foundation	252
Sabeti Carretta Foundation	252
Sacred Portion Foundation	170
The Saint Paul Foundation	171
Salem Foundation, Inc.	173
Sam Foundation	252
Sampson Family Charitable Foundation	252
Sampson Family Foundation	252
Sampson Foundation, Inc.	252
Samsara Foundation	173
Sand Dollar Foundation	265
Arvid and Anna R. Sandberg Irrevocable Scholarship Trust	262
Katharine Moore Sanderson Trust	252
Thomas C. and Lois L. Sando Foundation	252
Sanger Family Foundation	252
Sauer Children's Renew Foundation	173
Saunders Family Foundation	174
William Sawyer and Betty S. Eisenstadt Foundation	265
Sayer Charitable Foundation	253
Floy Gilman Scheidler Scholarship Foundation, Inc.	262
Scherber Family Foundation	253
Clement W. and Anastasia M. Scheurer Family Catholic Church Fund	253
Carl and Verna Schmidt Foundation	175
Schmitt Biomimetic Charitable Foundation	265
Schmoker Family Foundation	175
John J. Schneider Memorial Scholarship Fundicers, Inc.	262
Schoeneckers Foundation	253
Arlan A. Schonberg Foundation	253
Arlan Schonberg Irrevocable Trust	175
Schott Foundation	176
Vivian Fraser Schuh Residuary Trust	261
The Schulze Family Foundation	176
Richard M. Schulze Family Foundation	253
Mendon F. Schutt Foundation	253
Arvid W. and Judy R. Schwartz Family Foundation	253
Scott Scholarship Trust	262
Scottish Rite Foundation of Minneapolis	253
Scottish Rite Foundation of St Paul	264
The Scrooby Foundation	253
Seba Foundation	253
Second Wind Charitable Trust	253
Securian Foundation/Securian Financial Group	176
Security State Bank Foundation	253
The Sedona Foundation	253
Fred M. Seed Foundation	253
The Thomas W. and Janice A. Segar Charitable Trust	253
Seibold Foundation	264

Grantmaker Name

Name	Page
Andrew John Sellner Memorial Foundation	253
Sewell Family Foundation	177
Sexton Foundation	178
Shakopee Mdewakanton Sioux Community	178
The Richard and Rossy Shaller Family Foundation	253
Shamrock Foundation	179
Shapiro Family Philanthropic Foundation	179
The Hy and Myra Shapiro Family Foundation	253
The Shared Fund	180
Sam and Lorraine Shark Foundation	265
Carl Sharpe Foundation, Inc.	253
The Shaw Family Foundation	253
The Sheltering Arms Foundation	180
Shezada Begum Cancer Foundation	253
The Shiebler Family Foundation	181
Gertrude R. Shiely Charitable Trust	181
Shimek Family Foundation	253
Dan and Kay Shimek Family Foundation	253
Sieben Foundation, Inc.	254
Sieff Family Foundation	254
Dennis K. and Vivian D. Siemer Foundation, Inc.	254
Berel and Chana Silverberg Charitable Foundation	264
Sime Foundation	254
The Simmet Foundation	182
The Simons Family Foundation	254
The Singer Family Foundation	254
Sioux Falls Area Community Foundation	182
Sit Investment Associates Foundation	254
Andrew David Sit Foundation	254
Eugene C. and Gail V. Sit Foundation	254
The Paul and Dawn Sjolund Foundation	254
SKB Environmental Rosemount Community Trust	184
William Wood Skinner Foundation	184
R. C. Skoe Foundation	185
Slaggie Family Foundation	185
Slawik Family Foundation	185
Slye Family Foundation	254
The Smaby Family Foundation	254
Smikis Foundation	186
Smith Foundation, Inc.	254
Harold and Mickey Smith Charitable Fund, Inc.	254
Soar Foundation	254
Walter and Anna Soneson Scholarship Fund Trust	262
Sorlie Family Foundation	254
South Washington County Scholarship Committee	254
Southern Minnesota Initiative Foundation	186
Southways Foundation	187
Southwest Initiative Foundation (formerly Southwest Minnesota Foundation)	188
Spanner Foundation	265
The Spell Family Foundation	189
Spencer Scholarship Foundation	262
C. Mildred Speranza Scholarship Trust	261
Santo J. Speranza Scholarship Trust	262
Spicola Family Foundation	254
Daniel J. Spiegel Family Foundation	189
Spiller L'Chaim Fund	254
Raymond H. and Florence L. Sponberg Foundation	254
Spring Rock Foundation	264
The Springsteen Foundation for the Humane Treatment of Animals, Inc.	254
The Spruce Grove Charitable Foundation	254
Squam Lake Foundation	254
St Anthony Park Community Foundation	190
St Croix Valley Community Foundation	190
St Francis Regional Medical Center Foundation	191
St Jude Medical Foundation	254
The Jack and Marie St Martin Family Foundation	255
St Paul College Club - AAUW Scholarship Trust	262
Star Tribune Foundation	265
Robert S. Starr Foundation	255
Stassen Family Foundation	255
Stearns Foundation, Inc.	255
Gregg W. and Denise E. Steinhafel Family Foundation	264
Albert L. Steinke Trust	262
Stenson Charitable Foundation	255
Alex Stern Family Foundation	192
The June Stern Family Foundation	255
Stevens Square Foundation	192
Ruth M. Stewart Family Foundation	255
Stiles Foundation	255
Still Ain't Satisfied - A Foundation with Attitude (SAS)	255
Howie Stillman Foundation	255
Norton Stillman Foundation	255
The Ralph P. and Faye R. Stillman Family Foundation Charitable Trust	264
Robert and Estelle Stillman Family Foundation	255
Dr. W.C. Stillwell Foundation	262
Stone Pier Foundation	255
Strauss Family Foundation	265
Stronge Family Foundation	255
Stanley S. and Sylvia D. Stroup Family Foundation	255
Stull Family Foundation	255
Sumasil Foundation	265
Summer Fund	255
Sundance Family Foundation and Sundance Pay It Forward Foundation	193
Sundet Foundation	255
SUPERVALU Foundation	194
R. E. Swager Family Foundation	255
Swan Family Foundation	195
Joyce Swan Foundation	263
Charles B. Sweatt Foundation	255
Harold W. Sweatt Foundation	255
The Sweeney Family Foundation	255
Sweere Family Foundation	255
Bernard and Betty Sweet Family Foundation	255
Sweitzer Foundation	195
David Swenson Foundation	256
Otto Swoboda Foundation, Inc.	256
Syal Foundation	256
Alan R. and Eleanor A. Syverson Scholarship Foundation	256
T.I.H. Foundation	256
Norman H. Tallakson Charitable Trust	256
Tamarack Foundation	256
Tanji-Furzer Foundation	256
Tankenoff Families Foundation	256
Alex G. and Mollie Tankenoff Family Foundation	256
James and Paula Tankenoff Foundation	256
Tapemark Charity Pro-Am Golf Tournament	195
Target	196
Taylor Scholarship Trust	262
Glen A. Taylor Foundation	256
TCF Foundation	197
TCMK Foundation	256
TEAM Foundation	197
Tebben Foundation	256
Dave Templeton Memorial Scholarship Fund, Inc.	262
Ten Times Ten Foundation	256
Tennant Foundation	198
Terhuly Foundation	256
Terra Et Educare Foundation	256
Tew Foundation	265
Oliver W. Tews Trust	262
Then Family Charitable Foundation	265
Therese Foundation	256
Thief River Falls Foundation	256
Think Community Foundation	199

Grantmaker Name

Entry	Page
Thom Charitable Foundation	256
Thom Family Foundation	256
Thomson Family Foundation	256
Thomson West	200
Thorbeck Foundation	262
James R. Thorpe Foundation	200
Thrivent Financial for Lutherans Foundation	201
Harlan R. Thurston Foundation	202
Todd-Wadena Electric Cooperative Community Trust	202
The Toro Company Giving Program	202
Towhee-Rainbow Foundation	256
Tozer Foundation, Inc.	203
Tradition Family Foundation	256
Travelers Corporation and Travelers Foundation	204
The Traverse Foundation	256
Travis-Mcilroy Foundation	265
Ben J. Trebesch Trust	265
Loretta A. Treml Charitable Trust	265
Tri-Lakes Sportsmans Club, Inc.	257
Trillium Family Foundation	257
Trillium, A Charitable Corporation	257
Trinity Lutheran Scholarship Fund	262
Trust for the Meditation Process	205
Turner Family Foundation	206
J. S. Turner Family Foundation (fka SMR Foundation)	257
Turnquist Foundation	257
Tursso Foundation	257
Turtle Trust	257
Two Harbors High School Senior Scholarship Fund	262
U.S. Bancorp Foundation	206
U.S. Medical Aid Foundation	265
United Church of Christ Christian Fellowship of the Peace	262
United Health Foundation	207
Unity Avenue Foundation	208
Upland & Marsh	257
Urban Tree Research Foundation	265
Joseph Urdahl Memorial Foundation	257
The UTI Foundation, Inc.	257
Vadnais Heights Community Foundation	264
Vallely Will Fund	262
Valley News Charity Fund	257
The Valspar Foundation	209
The Van Dam Foundation	265
Sande Van Charitable Trust	257
Vandalia Foundation	257
DeWitt and Caroline Van Evera Foundation	209
Roger A. Vasko Family Foundation	264
The VCJ Family Foundation	257
F. W. Veden Endowment for St James Episcopal Church	261
Frank W. Veden Charitable Trust	257
Vaughn Arthur Veit Foundation	257
Velie Charitable Trust	265
The Vincent S. Velie, Jr. Family Foundation	266
Minnie Velo Memorial Charitable Trust	262
C. Paul and Irene G. Venables Foundation	257
Sid and Carol Verdoorn Family Foundation	257
Veritas Foundation	257
The Armin F. Vetter Foundation	257
Villafana Family Foundation	266
Vinaya Foundation	257
Vintage Foundation	257
Virginia Foundation	257
Charles E. Voige Trust	262
Jeanne M. Voigt Foundation	257
Voiture Locale No. 45 of Societe Des 40 Hommes et 8 Chevaux	262
Von Blon Family Charitable Foundation	258
The Vos Family Foundation	210
W M Foundation	258
Lyman E. Wakefield Charitable Foundation	258
Archie D. and Bertha H. Walker Foundation	210
Alice and Fred Wall Family Foundation	264
Lillian F. Wallace Charitable Trust	258
Wallestad Foundation	258
Phadoris Wallestad Foundation	258
Wallin Foundation	258
R. J. Walser Foundation	258
Ward Charitable Trust	258
Lee and Rose Warner Foundation	261
Warren Foundation	211
The Wasie Foundation	212
James D. Watkins Charitable Trust	266
The Watlov Family Charitable Foundation	258
Frederick O. Watson Foundation	213
Watts Family Foundation	258
WBC Foundation	258
WCA Foundation	213
Warren F. Weck, Jr. Charitable Trust	258
J. A. Wedum Foundation	214
Weeres Foundation, Inc.	264
Donald Weesner Charitable Trust	258
David J. Weiner Foundation	258
Weiser Family Foundation	258
Jody Harris Weisman Family Foundation	258
Mae and Sylvester Weiss Foundation	214
Wells Family Foundation Trust	258
Wells Family Foundation, Incorporated	258
Wells Fargo Foundation Minnesota	215
The Welsh Charitable Foundation	258
Welshons Family Scholarship Trust	262
Elmer M. Weltz Irrevocable Trust	258
WEM Foundation	258
Hall and Deborah Wendel Foundation	258
Wenger Foundation	216
Wensmann Family Foundation	264
The Werner Foundation	258
Wert Family Foundation	259
Wessner Foundation	259
West Central Initiative	216
The West Fork Foundation	259
Westcliff Foundation	259
William N. and Ruth M. Westhoff Family Foundation	259
Mark and Muriel Wexler Foundation	217
Weyand Charitable Trust	263
Louis F. and Florence H. Weyand 1977 Charitable Trust	263
Weyerhaeuser Family Foundation, Inc.	218
The Charles A. Weyerhaeuser Memorial Foundation	218
Edith G. Weyerhaeuser Charitable Trust	266
Frederick and Margaret L. Weyerhaeuser Foundation	219
Weyerhaeuser/Day Foundation	263
Whaley Foundation	259
Dare Lamberton White and William F. White Foundation	259
Whiteside Scholarship Fund Trust	262
Muriel Whiteside Charitable Trust	259
Whitney ARCEE Foundation	219
Whitney Foundation	220
B. K. Whitney Fund	259
Wicker Family Foundation	259
Widow's Mite Foundation	259
George F. Wikstrom, Sr. and Delores M. Wikstrom Foundation	259
Phillip and Sara Wilensky Family Foundation	259
Frances and Frank Wilkinson Foundation	259
Williams Family Foundation	259
Williams Steel & Hardware Company	264
Wilmac Foundation	259
Willmar Blue Line Club, Inc.	259
Edward Willmus Family Charitable Trust	259
Constance Bultman Wilson Foundation for Education and Psychiatry	266
Elizabeth Adams Wilson Family Foundation	259

Grantmaker Name

J. Morgan and Myrna B. Wilson Charitable Trust .... .259
Virginia Wimmer Charitable Trust .... .259
WIN Foundation .... .259
Windibrow Foundation .... .259
Winds of Peace Foundation .... .259
Windsor Community Foundation .... .260
Winona Community Foundation .... .220
Winona Foundation .... .221
Winslow Family Foundation .... .260
Winslow Foundation .... .262
Winsted Foundation .... .260
Winter Wheat Foundation .... .264
Charles J. and Henrietta McDonald Winton Fund .... .266
Saul Winton Fund .... .260
Winton-Whitney Fund .... .260
The Father Paul Wolf Foundation .... .266
Stephan Larsen Wolf Foundation .... .260
Womack Family Foundation .... .260
Women's Foundation of Minnesota .... .222
Wood Family Foundation .... .260
A.R. Wood Educational Trust .... .262
Wood-Rill Foundation .... .260
D. Donald and Angela W. Wozniak Family Foundation .... .260
WPC Mission Investment Fund .... .260
Thomas C. Wright Educational Trust .... .262
Xcel Energy Foundation/Corporate Citizenship .... .223
Donald D. Yablonsky Scholarship Foundation .... .266
John P. and Eleanor R. Yackel Foundation .... .260
Leo and Catherine Yaggie Family .... .260
Yanish Family Foundation .... .260
Wilfred R. Yetzer Charitable Trust .... .264
Youthworks! Foundation, Inc. .... .224
Frank J. Zaher Charitable Trust .... .260
Zeller Family Charitable Foundation .... .260
A. H. Zeppa Family Foundation .... .224
Donald and Luella Zibell Family Foundation .... .260
Ziff-Hymanson Family Foundation .... .266
Zona Charitable Foundation .... .266

Addenda

Minnesota Common Grant Application Form & Minnesota Common Report Form

Please keep in mind that every grantmaker has different guidelines and priorities, as well as different deadlines and timetables. Before submitting the Common Grant Application to a potential funder, it is very important that you check to see whether your project or program matches its published interests. Before submitting the Common Report Form to a funder, it is important that you check to see when, if at all, the grantmaker would like a report, and whether there is additional information the funder requests when reporting. Any funder that has agreed to accept these forms may request additional information as needed.

Photocopy the form as necessary to meet your needs. You can also download the form from the Council's website at mcf.org (select "Grantseeking Resources").

Minnesota Common Grant Application Form
Grant Application Cover Sheet
You may reproduce this form on your computer

Date of application: _____ Application submitted to: _____

Organization Information

_____ _____
Name of organization   *Legal name, if different*

_____ _____
Address   *City, State, Zip*   *Employer Identification Number (EIN)*

_____ _____
Phone   *Fax*   *Web site*

_____ _____
Name of top paid staff   *Title*   *Phone*   *E-mail*

_____ _____
Name of contact person regarding this application   *Title*   *Phone*   *E-mail*

Is your organization an IRS 501(c)(3) not-for-profit? _____ Yes _____ No

   If no, is your organization a public agency/unit of government? _____ Yes _____ No

   If no, check with funder for details on using fiscal agents, and list name and address of fiscal agent:

_____
_____ _____
                                                             Fiscal agent's EIN number

Proposal Information

Please give a 2-3 sentence summary of request:

Population served: _____   Geographic area served: _____

Funds are being requested for (check one) *Note: Please be sure funder provides the type of support you are requesting.*

_____ General operating support   _____ Start-up costs   _____ Capital
_____ Project/program support   _____ Technical assistance   _____ Other (list) _____

Project dates (if applicable): _____   Fiscal year end: _____

Budget

Dollar amount requested: $ _____
Total annual organization budget: $ _____
Total project budget (for support other than general operating): $ _____

Authorization

Name and title of top paid staff or board chair: _____
Signature   _____

12/2000

Minnesota Common Grant Application Form

PROPOSAL NARRATIVE

Please use the following outline as a guide to your proposal narrative. Most grantmakers prefer up to five pages, excluding attachments, but *be sure to ask each individual funder if they have page limitations or any additional requirements.* Also, include a cover letter with your application that introduces your organization and proposal and makes the link between your proposal and the mission of the grantmaker to whom you are applying. For assistance with terms, refer to MCF's Web site (www.mcf.org; select "Grantseeking in Minnesota").

I. ORGANIZATION INFORMATION

A. Brief summary of organization history, including the date your organization was established.
B. Brief summary of organization mission and goals.
C. Brief description of organization's current programs or activities, including any service statistics and strengths or accomplishments. Please highlight new or different activities, if any, for your organization.
D. Your organization's relationship with other organizations working with similar missions. What is your organization's role relative to these organizations?
E. Number of board members, full-time paid staff, part-time paid staff and volunteers.
F. Additional organization information required by each individual funder.

II. PURPOSE OF GRANT

General operating proposals: Complete Section A below and move to Part III - Evaluation.
All other proposal types: Complete Section B below and move to Part III - Evaluation.

A. General Operating Proposals

1. The opportunity, challenges, issues or need currently facing your organization.
2. Overall goal(s) of the organization for the funding period.
3. Objectives or ways in which you will meet the goal(s).
4. Activities and who will carry out these activities.
5. Time frame in which this will take place.
6. Long-term funding strategies.
7. Additional information regarding general operating proposals required by each individual funder.

B. All Other Proposal Types

1. Situation
   a. The opportunity, challenges, issues or need and the community that your proposal addresses.
   b. How that focus was determined and who was involved in that decision-making process.
2. Activities
   a. Overall goal(s) regarding the situation described above.
   b. Objectives or ways in which you will meet the goal(s).
   c. Specific activities for which you seek funding.
   d. Who will carry out those activities.
   e. Time frame in which this will take place.
   f. How the proposed activities will benefit the community in which they will occur, being as clear as you can about the impact you expect to have.
   g. Long-term funding strategies (if applicable) for sustaining this effort.

12/2000

Minnesota Common Grant Application Form

III. EVALUATION

A. Please describe your criteria for success. What do you want to happen as a result of your activities? You may find it helpful to describe both immediate and long-term effects.
B. How will you measure these changes?
C. Who will be involved in evaluating this work (staff, board, constituents, community, consultants)?
D. What will you do with your evaluation results?

ATTACHMENTS

Generally the following attachments are required:

1. Finances (*for assistance with terms, check MCF's Web site at www.mcf.org.*)
   - Most recent financial statement from most recently completed year, audited if available, showing actual expenses. This information should include a balance sheet, a statement of activities (or statement of income and expenses) and functional expenses. Some funders require your most recent Form 990 tax return.
   - Organization budget for current year, including income and expenses.
   - Project Budget, including income and expenses (if not a general operating proposal).
   - Additional funders. List names of corporations and foundations from which you are requesting funds, with dollar amounts, indicating which sources are committed or pending.

2. List of board members and their affiliations.
3. Brief description of key staff, including qualifications relevant to the specific request.
4. A copy of your current IRS determination letter (or your fiscal agent's) indicating tax-exempt 501(c)(3) status.
5. If applying to a corporate funder only: if an employee of this corporation is involved with your organization, list names and involvement.

Be sure to check each funder's guidelines, and use discretion when sending additional attachments.

PROPOSAL CHECKLIST

- ☐ Cover letter.
- ☐ Cover sheet.
- ☐ Proposal narrative.
- ☐ Organization budget.
- ☐ Project budget (if not general operating grant).
- ☐ Financial statements, preferably audited, showing actual expenses including:
  - ☐ Balance sheet.
  - ☐ Statement of activities (income and expenses).
  - ☐ Statement of functional expenses.
- ☐ List of additional funders.
- ☐ List of board members and their affiliations.
- ☐ Brief description of key staff.
- ☐ IRS determination letter.
- ☐ Confirmation letter of fiscal agent (if required).
- ☐ Additional information required by each individual funder.

Minnesota Common Grant Application Form

ORGANIZATION BUDGET

This format is optional and can serve as a guide to budgeting. If you already prepare an organization budget that contains this information, please feel free to submit it in its original form. Feel free to attach a budget narrative explaining your numbers if necessary.

INCOME

Source	Amount
Support	
Government grants	$
Foundations	$
Corporations	$
United Way or other federated campaigns	$
Individual contributions	$
Fundraising events and products	$
Membership income	$
In-kind support	$
Investment income	$
Revenue	
Government contracts	$
Earned income	$
Other (specify)	$
	$
	$
	$
Total Income	**$**

EXPENSES

Item	Amount
Salaries and wages	$
Insurance, benefits and other related taxes	$
Consultants and professional fees	$
Travel	$
Equipment	$
Supplies	$
Printing and copying	$
Telephone and fax	$
Postage and delivery	$
Rent and utilities	$
In-kind expenses	$
Depreciation	$
Other (specify)	$
	$
	$
Total Expense	**$**
Difference (Income less Expense)	**$**

12/2000

Minnesota Common Grant Application Form
PROJECT BUDGET

This format is optional and can serve as a guide to budgeting. If you already prepare project budgets that contain this information, please feel free to submit them in their original forms. Feel free to attach a budget narrative explaining your numbers if necessary.

INCOME

Source	Amount
Support	
Government grants	$
Foundations	$
Corporations	$
United Way or other federated campaigns	$
Individual contributions	$
Fundraising events and products	$
Membership income	$
In-kind support	$
Investment income	$
Revenue	
Government contracts	$
Earned income	$
Other (specify)	$
	$
Total Income	$

EXPENSES

Item	Amount	%FT/PT
Salaries and wages (breakdown by individual position and indicate full- or part-time.)	$	
	$	
	$	
	$	
	$	
SUBTOTAL	$	
Insurance, benefits and other related taxes	$	
Consultants and professional fees	$	
Travel	$	
Equipment	$	
Supplies	$	
Printing and copying	$	
Telephone and fax	$	
Postage and delivery	$	
Rent and utilities	$	
In-kind expenses	$	
Depreciation	$	
Other (specify)	$	
	$	
Total Expense	$	
Difference (Income less Expense)	$	

12/2000

Minnesota Common Report Form
Cover Sheet

Date of Report: _____

Report Submitted to: _____

Organization Information

_____   _____
Name of organization   *Legal name, if different*

_____   _____
Address   *Employer Identification Number (EIN)*

_____
City, State, Zip

_____   _____   _____
Phone   *Fax*   *Web site*

_____   _____   _____
Contact person   *Phone*   *E-mail*

Grant Information

Grant ID, if applicable: _____

Amount and support type: Date grant issued:

_____   _____

2-3 sentence description of grant:

_____

_____

_____

Check one:
Interim Report _____   Final Report _____

Minnesota Common Report Form

Please use the following format for a report to grantmakers that have agreed to use the Minnesota Common Report Form. Your report should only be 1-2 pages, but don't forget to check each individual funder's guidelines for reporting.

Report Narrative

1. Please briefly outline your original goals and objectives, as stated in your proposal.

2. What progress have you made toward your original goals and objectives? What activities led to meeting these goals and objectives?

3. If applicable, describe the population served or community reached during the grant period. Use numbers and demographics such as race/ethnicity, gender or geographic location.

4. Were there any unanticipated results, either positive or negative? What did you learn because of this grant?

5. Will you make any changes based on these results?

6. *(for program/project grants only)* What are your future plans for sustaining this program or project?

7. Are there any other important outcomes as a result of this grant?

8. Do you have any plans to share your results or findings? How?

Financials

1. Please attach an income and expense statement for this grant period. Also, include your original budget.

2. If this is an interim report, please attach a statement including income and expenses for grant period *to date*. If this is a final report, please attach a statement including *actual* income and expenses.

3. Please feel free to include a narrative for any of your expenses and income, if necessary.

4. *(for program/project grants only)* Please include a list of additional funders, including amounts received for this project or program.

Be sure to check each individual funder's guidelines for other reporting requirements.